Fiscal Federalism
in
Theory *and*
Practice

Fiscal Federalism
in
Theory *and*
Practice

Teresa Ter-Minassian
Editor

International Monetary Fund
Washington • 1997

© 1997 International Monetary Fund

Design and production: IMF Graphics Section

Cataloging-in-Publication Data

Fiscal federalism in theory and practice / Teresa Ter-Minassian, editor. — Washington : International Monetary Fund, 1997.
    p.   cm.

Papers prepared by the staff of the International Monetary Fund.

ISBN 1-55775-663-5

1. Intergovernmental fiscal relations. 2. Finance, Public. I. Ter-Minassian, Teresa. II. International Monetary Fund.
HJ197.F57   1997

Price: $35.00

Address orders to:
External Relations Department, Publication Services
International Monetary Fund, Washington D.C. 20431
Telephone: (202) 623-7430; Telefax: (202) 623-7201
E-mail: publications@imf.org
Internet: http://www.imf.org

Foreword

A few years ago, when Teresa Ter-Minassian first approached me with the idea that the staff of the Fiscal Affairs Department could produce, over the medium run, a book containing a number of country studies dealing with the prevailing fiscal arrangements between national governments and subnational governments or jurisdictions, my reaction was not enthusiastic. The department was very busy with many activities, some new ones, and its staff was greatly overworked. It did not seem wise to add to its work, especially to deal with an area that was not at the forefront of policymakers' or economists' interests. It was only her insistence that made me agree. She pointed out that while there was much information on the fiscal arrangements of a few industrial countries, little was known about most of the developing ones.

Over the following years, staff of the Fiscal Affairs Department prepared papers on a large number of countries and also on a few analytical topics on fiscal federalism. These papers were for the most part written by economists operationally engaged in the IMF's country work. These individuals had, thus, the benefit of access to current information and to the countries' experts, but, at the beginning, they did not have particular knowledge of issues related to fiscal federalism. Most studies had to be revised more than once because either the situation in some of the countries was changing rapidly or, with the passing of time, the authors acquired much greater sophistication in the subject and thus felt that they could improve the studies, or they realized that some of their earlier analyses or conclusions were wrong. Over this period, the combined knowledge that the Fiscal Affairs Department had of issues and practices related to fiscal federalism and fiscal decentralization grew significantly, owing to both the preparation of the studies and the technical assistance missions undertaken at the request of country authorities. These requests, rare in the past, have become progressively more frequent. This book thus represents the result of much collective thinking by the staff of the department on the design of intergovernmental fiscal relations. Given the IMF's basic mandate, its emphasis is on the impact of those relations on macroeconomic management.

Since the time when Teresa Ter-Minassian first proposed the project, fiscal federalism has become a hot political issue in many countries and has attracted the attention of an increasing number of economists. Developments in the European Union and in countries such as Argentina, Brazil, Canada, China, India, Italy, Russia, and others have made policymakers and experts pay close attention to the arrangements in fiscal relations between the national government and the local governments that exist not only in federal but also in unitary countries. The increased attention also reflects a recent trend that favors greater fiscal decentralization in public spending. And decentralization requires a rethinking of the roles and responsibilities of various levels of government in relation to the traditional policy objectives of allocation, stabilization, and redistribution.

The studies contained in this book show the great variety of experiences ranging from those of highly centralized countries, where most spending and taxing decisions are made at the national or central level, to those of decentralized countries (such as Brazil, Canada, and the United States) where local jurisdictions have considerable power in these decisions.

Existing intergovernmental fiscal arrangements are generally not the product of detailed analytical studies by economists or political scientists but are the result of historical developments or even of historical accidents. It is unlikely that the same arrangements would be chosen if today the countries had the freedom to start from scratch. However, changing in a substantive way arrangements that are often specified in the countries' constitutions or in their laws is very difficult, even when there are grounds to believe that some changes would be highly beneficial. In some cases, the existing arrangements have created (or have contributed to) political problems and economic difficulties. Arrangements that might have made sense in the past may be less adequate in a world in which economic conditions and technology are changing rapidly. For example, the assignment of particular tax bases (such as property, sales, and incomes) to different levels of government may create macroeconomic and allocational difficulties when some bases tend to grow faster than others and when some expenditure responsibilities have a different dynamic. These difficulties may also be connected with the impact of tax competition on tax revenues. Therefore, subnational jurisdictions may end up with spending responsibilities that exceed the available resources and may be tempted to rely excessively on borrowing.

Fiscal federalism and fiscal decentralization give rise to many difficult issues and questions. Some are related to the allocation of resources, some to stabilization, and some to income or resource redistribution. Many of these are discussed in the various papers. A few are mentioned below.

It has often been argued that a decentralized fiscal arrangement improves the allocation of resources because the decentralization of fiscal decisions implies that the package of spending and taxing tends to better reflect the wishes of the local voters. This, however, may be true only under certain circumstances. For example, voters don't normally vote with their feet as assumed in many studies done by U.S. economists.

An important question relates to the assignment of tax revenue. Should the local jurisdictions have tax bases or tax revenue assigned to them? If tax bases, which ones? And what are the implications of these decisions for tax administration and for tax competition? If tax revenue, how should the allocation be made? On the basis of sharing of total tax revenue or of the revenue of particular taxes? What about arrangements that allow differentiated sharing of different taxes rather than tax revenue? To what extent do these arrangements compromise tax policy because of the incentives they create that makes some taxes preferable to others?

If a country is large, such as Brazil, it is likely that some areas will be more developed than others. If local jurisdictions must rely on their own revenue sources, the poorer jurisdictions will have less resources than the richer ones. Therefore, they will not be able to finance services at the same level as the richer jurisdictions. Should a country accept this differentiation in the quality of services? If not, there is a need for the transfer of resources from rich to poor jurisdictions. How will this be accomplished? By what method? And how much will be transferred? Very difficult issues arise in this context. Of course, the more centralized a country, the greater can be the role of the central government in implicitly redistributing income by providing services of equal quality. Some of the papers address this question.

Finally, some literature going back a few decades deals with the implications of decentralization for stabilization. Those who wrote on these issues in earlier years maintained that stabilization was the responsibility of the national government and could be pursued better in centralized countries, because a national government would have more of an incentive, and more efficient policy tools, for pursuing a stabilizing policy. In more recent years, however, the focus in stabilization policy has changed from pursuing countercyclical, Keynesian fiscal policy to one of bringing equilibrium to the fiscal accounts that have become structurally unbalanced. In this connection, some have maintained that a decentralized fiscal arrangement makes it more difficult to correct the structural imbalance, especially when the local governments have access to borrowing and can put political pressures on the national government to bail them out when they run into difficulties. This is an aspect that attracts considerable attention in the studies.

The book is made up of 7 issue-related chapters, which deal with some of the conceptual or theoretical underpinnings, and 21 case studies. The case studies represent a wealth of information on many countries of which little was available in the literature. It is hoped that the book will not only help the staff of the IMF in its operational work but that it will also be useful to the many policymakers who are contemplating reforms or are concerned about these issues.

This project was supervised by Teresa Ter-Minassian, who spent many hours reading manuscripts, advising and encouraging authors, and writing her own chapters. Given the fact that both she and the other authors were very busy with their normal work, it was a great achievement to have taken this project to completion and to have created such a useful and interesting book. It is my hope that this book will improve in some way the policymaking in many countries. As it represents much collective thinking by the staff of the Fiscal Affairs Department, it is fair that the whole department should share in the responsibility of any remaining errors.

In conclusion, I wish to express my deep gratitude to all those who participated in this creation, and especially to Teresa Ter-Minassian for her remarkable management of a difficult enterprise.

VITO TANZI
Director
Fiscal Affairs Department

Preface

This book presents a collection of essays on the principal theoretical and institutional aspects of intergovernmental fiscal relations, prepared mainly by staff of the Fiscal Affairs Department of the IMF. The literature on intergovernmental fiscal relations has been expanding rapidly in recent years, in line with a growing worldwide trend toward fiscal decentralization. The book is intended to contribute to this evolving body of knowledge by providing an overview of the current thinking in the literature on these issues (the *theory* of fiscal federalism) and the current status of intergovernmental fiscal relations in a broad range of industrial, developing, and transition economies (the *practice* of fiscal federalism). As a reflection of the IMF's focus on macroeconomic issues, the book emphasizes the macroeconomic dimensions of intergovernmental fiscal relations, an area that until recently had been relatively neglected in the fiscal federalism literature.

Given its coverage and focus, the book should prove especially useful to policymakers and academic scholars who wish to know about best and worst practices in intergovernmental fiscal relations across a broad range of different countries and to draw relevant lessons from these experiences.

As the Director of the Fiscal Affairs Department, Vito Tanzi, observes in the Foreword, the book is very much a collective effort of the department and has benefited greatly from the dialogue on fiscal federalism issues that over the last few years the staff of the department has carried out with policymakers in many IMF member countries. It has also benefited from the contributions of a number of authors who were associated with the department when the papers were prepared, Juan Amieva-Huerta, Giorgio Brosio, Nicoletta Emiliani, Sergio Lugaresi, and Paul Bernd Spahn, and from comments by colleagues in other departments of the IMF.

Special thanks are due to Esha Ray of the External Relations Department, who provided editorial assistance and coordinated the publication process, and to Champa Nguyen and Meike Gretemann of the Fiscal Affairs Department, Lilián Martínez of the Western Hemisphere Department, and Alicia Etchebarne-Bourdin of the External Relations

Department, who provided technical support in the production of the book.

The views expressed are those of the authors and do not necessarily reflect those of the IMF.

TERESA TER-MINASSIAN

Contents

	Page
Foreword	v
Preface	ix

Part I: Theory

1. Intergovernmental Fiscal Relations in a Macroeconomic Perspective: An Overview
   Teresa Ter-Minassian 3

2. Assigning Expenditure Responsibilities
   Ehtisham Ahmad, Daniel Hewitt, and Edgardo Ruggiero 25

3. Tax Assignment
   John Norregaard 49

4. Intergovernmental Transfers
   Ehtisham Ahmad and Jon Craig 73

5. Tax Administration
   Charles L. Vehorn and Ehtisham Ahmad 108

6. Budgetary and Financial Management
   Barry Potter 135

7. Control of Subnational Govrenment Borrowing
   Teresa Ter-Minassian and Jon Craig 156

Part II: Practice—Industrial Countries

8. Australia
   Jon Craig 175

9. Canada
   Russell Krelove, Janet G. Stotsky, and Charles L. Vehorn 201

10. Germany
    Paul Bernd Spahn and Wolfgang Föttinger 226

11 Italy
    Nicoletta Emiliani, Sergio Lugaresi, and Edgardo Ruggiero 249

12 Japan
    Dubravko Mihaljek 285

13 Switzerland
    Paul Bernd Spahn 324

14 United Kingdom
    Barry Potter 342

15 United States
    Janet G. Stotsky and Emil M. Sunley 359

Part III: Practice—Developing Countries

16 Argentina
    Gerd Schwartz and Claire Liuksila 387

17 Bolivia
    G.A. Mackenzie and José-Luís Ruiz 423

18 Brazil
    Teresa Ter-Minassian 438

19 Colombia
    Ehtisham Ahmad and Katherine Baer 457

20 Ethiopia
    Giorgio Brosio and Sanjeev Gupta 504

21 India
    Richard Hemming, Neven Mates, and Barry Potter 527

22 Korea
    Ke-young Chu and John Norregaard 540

23 Mexico
    Juan Amieva-Huerta 570

24 Nigeria
    Michael Mered 598

Part IV: Practice—Economies in Transition

25 Bulgaria
    Željko Bogetić 615

26 China
    Ehtisham Ahmad 634
27 Hungary
    Mark Lutz, Edgardo Ruggiero, Paul Bernd Spahn,
    and Emil M. Sunley 660
28 Russian Federation
    Jon Craig, John Norregaard, and George Tsibouris 680

The following symbols have been used throughout this publication:

... to indicate that data are not available;

— to indicate that the figure is zero or less than half the final digit shown, or that the item does not exist;

– between years or months (e.g., 1995–96 or January–June) to indicate the years or months covered, including the beginning and ending years or months; and

/ between years (e.g., 1996/97) to indicate a fiscal (financial) year.

"Billion" means a thousand million.

Minor discrepancies between constituent figures and totals are due to rounding.

The term "country," as used in this publication, does not in all cases refer to a territorial entity that is a state as understood by international law and practice; the term also covers some territorial entities that are not states, but for which statistical data are maintained and provided internationally on a separate and independent basis.

PART I
Theory

1

Intergovernmental Fiscal Relations in a Macroeconomic Perspective: An Overview

TERESA TER-MINASSIAN

Over the past few decades a clear trend has emerged worldwide toward the devolution of spending and, to a lesser extent, revenue-raising responsibilities to subnational levels of government (state and local).[1] This trend is evident not only in federal, but also in many unitary countries, including some that have had a long tradition of centralist government. This trend is partly a reflection of the political evolution toward more democratic and participatory forms of government, seeking to improve the responsiveness and accountability of political leaders to their electorate, and to ensure a closer correspondence of the quantity, quality, and composition of publicly provided goods and services to the preferences of their beneficiaries.

The view that decentralization of spending responsibilities can entail substantial gains in terms of efficiency and welfare has long been held in the economic literature, Tiebout (1961), Musgrave (1969), and Oates (1972). Also common in the literature is, however, the view that decentralization can entail significant costs in terms of distributional equity and macroeconomic management (see, for exam-

---

The author wishes to thank in particular Ehtisham Ahmad, Isaias Coelho, G.A. Mackenzie, John Norregaard, Barry Potter, Gerd Schwartz, Emil Sunley, and Vito Tanzi for their useful comments.

[1]In this chapter state refers to the regional level (encompassing states, regions, or provinces) and local to the municipal level (including counties, towns, and villages).

ple, Prud'homme, 1995; Tanzi, 1996). This chapter examines the validity of these views, in the light not only of theoretical considerations, but also of the experience of a number of countries worldwide, which are discussed in detail in Chapter 8 through Chapter 28 of this book. A major conclusion of this analysis is that substantial decentralization is indeed likely to make it more difficult to carry out both redistribution and macroeconomic management through the budget. It does not, however, make it impossible. The specific design of intergovernmental fiscal relations, as well as of institutional arrangements within and among the various tiers of government, plays a crucial role in this respect.

This chapter briefly reviews and discusses the main issues to be faced in the design of various aspects of intergovernmental fiscal relations: expenditure assignment, revenue assignment, intergovernmental transfers, tax administration, budgeting and financial management in a multilevel government setting, and the control of subnational government borrowing. These topics are developed in greater depth in subsequent chapters (Chapter 2 through Chapter 7) of the book. In this chapter, emphasis is placed on the implications that different choices in the design of intergovernmental fiscal relations have for macroeconomic management.

Expenditure Assignment

As indicated above, there is broad consensus in the literature that decentralization of spending responsibilities can entail substantial welfare gains. According to this view, efficiency in the allocation of resources is best served by assigning responsibility for each type of public expenditure to the level of government that most closely represents the beneficiaries of these outlays. In this perspective, a clear case for centralized provision can be made—at least on allocative grounds—only for national public goods, that is, goods whose benefits extend nationwide or whose provision is subject to substantial economies of scale. Defense, foreign affairs, and infrastructures for interstate transport and telecommunications are the categories of expenditure that most closely fit these criteria.

Proponents of centralization argue, however, that allocative considerations can come into conflict with distributional and macroeconomic management objectives. Especially in large countries characterized by substantial regional disparities in the distribution of productive resources and incomes, the ability of subnational governments to provide public goods and services to their residents can vary widely, leading to undesirable internal migrations, as well as, in some cases, to unsustainable social and political pressures. To the extent that substandard levels of provision of certain public goods (for instance, primary education or basic health care) affect adversely the stock of human capital of the country (and, thereby, the prospects for long-term growth of the economy), there can be even significant efficiency costs from the decentralization of these types of expenditures.

While these are certainly valid points, they do not necessarily imply that the provision of public goods and services—other than those of a clearly national nature—should be administered centrally. The central government can influence the decentralized delivery of such goods and services through the setting of policy guidelines (or mandates) for this delivery; a transfer of resources to the subnational governments to equalize their capacity to meet these mandates; and the ex post control of the use of the transfers and of the level and quality of the services provided by the lower levels of governments.

The decentralization of a large share of public expenditure can have significant implications for macroeconomic management. Even if the overall level of expenditures of subnational governments is effectively constrained by limits on their taxation and borrowing powers, changes in the composition of their expenditures can affect aggregate demand in ways which may run counter to the stabilization objectives of the central government. This may be the case, for example, if the composition of subnational expenditures shifts in favor of items that have a relatively large impact on demand (such as transfers to individuals with a high propensity to consume). Even a balanced budget expansion by subnational governments could boost aggregate demand, and worsen the balance of payments, if the average multiplier of their expenditures exceeded significantly that of their revenues. Purely from a macroeconomic management perspective, therefore, central governments should retain responsibility for expenditures that have a particularly strong impact on demand or that are particularly sensitive to changes in the cycle, such as unemployment benefits. More broadly, it is clear that the greater the share of public expenditure that is assigned to the subnational levels of government, the greater the need to involve the latter (especially the states or provinces and large municipalities) in the pursuit of any needed fiscal adjustment. The section on Administrative Aspects of Fiscal Decentralization will discuss some possible mechanisms of such coordination, referring in particular to the experience of some large federations like Germany and Australia.

It is important to recognize that the theoretical efficiency gains from decentralization can be significantly undermined in practice by institutional constraints (Tanzi, 1996). First, the administrative capacity of subnational governments may be quite weak. Overstaffing, poor technical skills and training of employees, and the inability to formulate and implement effective spending programs to fully exploit potential financing sources characterize many regional and local jurisdictions in a number of countries worldwide. The incidence of corruption at the local level is not negligible either.[2] Second, subnational governments often have not been able to develop modern and transparent public expenditure management systems, including adequate mechanisms of financial control, reporting and accounting, and evaluation of expenditure programs. Third, the size of local jurisdictions (which is often the result of historical developments or political factors) is not always consistent with the full realization of potential efficiency gains from decentralization.

Against the background of these considerations, it is not surprising that country experiences regarding expenditure assignments vary widely. As indicated in Chapter 2, during the 1980s the shares of state (provincial) governments in total expenditures of the general government ranged from less than 8 percent (in Mexico) to over 40 percent (in Australia, Canada, and India). The corresponding shares of local governments ranged from 2 percent (in Mexico) to over 50 percent (in Denmark).

These differences reflect varying practices with respect to the choice of functions to be covered by each level of government. Most countries assign such functions as defense, foreign affairs, foreign trade, and regulation of immigration to the central (federal) level. At the other end of the spectrum, services such as local police, fire prevention, sanitation, transportation, and certain utilities are typically assigned to the municipal or county level. For the other expenditure functions, however, which account for the bulk of government noninterest spending, there is no uniform pattern of assignments. Moreover, the legal framework regulating these assignments is not always clear, allowing the persistence of ambiguities regarding the respective roles of the various levels of government in the formulation of policies, the financing, and the delivery of shared expenditures (see, for example, the cases of Italy (Chapter 11) and Brazil (Chapter 18)).

A prevalent tendency is to reserve to the central or federal level the intervention in, and regulation of, strategic sectors of industry, as well as of interstate transport and telecommunications. The central government is also generally responsible for the promotion of research and development. State or provincial governments tend to share responsibility with the central government in the areas of agriculture, forestry,

---

[2]See, however, Huther and Shah (1996) for an empirical analysis suggesting that decentralization promotes accountability and strengthens governance.

fishing, and environmental protection. They are generally responsible for regional infrastructures, notably the road network. Local governments tend to regulate locally based businesses.

Substantial diversity can be found in the assignment of responsibilities within the broad area of social spending. There is a case for the assignment to the central level of responsibilities for social insurance mechanisms against life-cycle and economic contingencies (such as old age, disability, and unemployment), since a main rationale for the setting up of such mechanisms is a pooling of risks. This case is reinforced by the desire in most societies to ensure nationwide standards for social insurance. Indeed, this is the prevailing pattern in the countries surveyed in this book, at least as far as old age and disability pensions are concerned. The provision of unemployment benefits, however, which is a federal function in most countries, is a responsibility of the states in the United States (although the federal government contributes to its financing through grants). As regards social assistance, for administrative efficiency reasons, its delivery is frequently devolved to the local level, but the federal and/or regional level generally plays a role in setting standards for, as well as in funding, local programs.

In the area of education, the most frequent pattern is the assignment of responsibility for the primary and secondary levels to local governments and for the postsecondary level to the national or regional governments. In a number of unitary states, however, education at all levels remains a central government responsibility. Even in countries that decentralize expenditures on education to the state and/or local levels, the central government generally maintains a significant role in shaping nationwide education policies and standards, and in funding various education programs.

Concurrent responsibilities are also frequent in the area of health expenditures. Local governments are often responsible for basic and preventive health care provision. The states, or, in unitary countries, the central government, are generally responsible for the prevention of communicable diseases, more advanced curative facilities, such as hospitals, and the funding of medical research. In some cases, there is overlapping and even duplication of services in this area, leading to inefficiencies and waste of resources. In some countries, particularly developing and transition economies (for example, China, Russia), the devolution of health expenditure responsibility to lower levels of government, in the absence of adequate equalization transfers, has led to increased regional discrepancies in the level and quality of public health care services, with adverse effects especially on the lower income groups in the poorer regions, which cannot substitute private health care for the deteriorating public services.

The Assignment of Revenue-Raising Responsibility

There is a degree of consensus in the public finance literature on a number of desirable criteria to guide the assignment of revenue-raising responsibilities across the various levels of government. Nevertheless, country experiences do not always conform to those criteria and exhibit a fairly wide range of variation.

It is generally recognized that both distributional and, especially, macroeconomic management considerations argue against arrangements (such as the ones in the former Yugoslavia and, until recently, in China) that would assign all or most taxing powers to subnational governments, with upward revenue sharing, especially if the sharing formulas were to be renegotiated frequently. Such arrangements deprive the central government of tax instruments for macroeconomic management. Moreover, they do not facilitate a redistributive role for the central government budget, either across regions or across income groups. Therefore, upward revenue-sharing arrangements can only be viable in countries (such as Germany) with a long-established tradition of close policy coordination among different government levels and relative homogeneity of economic conditions across regions, or in loose confederations, or common economic areas, in which the responsibility for redistribution and stabilization policies continues to rest primarily with the member states. Moreover, since substantial regional variations in the bases and/or rates of certain taxes would tend to lead, in an integrated economic space, to distortions in the flow of goods and factors of production, even in common economic areas efforts have to be made to achieve a degree of harmonization of national tax policies, to avoid such allocative distortions. This is illustrated by the experience of the European Union, especially since the beginning of the single market in 1993.

Arrangements that assign all or most taxing powers to the central government are undesirable as well. By separating spending authority from revenue-raising responsibilities, these arrangements obscure the link between the benefits of public expenditures and their price, namely, the taxes levied to finance them. Thus, they do not promote fiscal responsibility in subnational politicians and their electorate.[3]

Therefore, the alternative favored in the literature and most frequently observed in countries around the world is one that provides for

---

[3]In Italy recognition of the shortcomings of a system (enacted after the tax reform of 1973) that concentrated all the major taxes at the central government level—making both the regions and the local authorities highly dependent on transfers from the central government—has led to reforms that in the last few years have increased significantly the share of own revenues for the lower levels of government (see Chapter 11 for details).

the assignment of own sources of revenue to each level of government, in combination with various types of intergovernmental transfers, to bridge any resulting gap between revenue and expenditure assignments. There is, however, wide variation in the forms of both revenue assignments and intergovernmental transfers.

Some countries espouse a principle of complete separation of the tax bases for the different levels of government. Others allow different levels to tap the same tax base. Examples of tax separation can be found in, among others, India, Australia, and, for nonshared taxes, Germany. By contrast, there is a considerable degree of tax overlapping in the United States and Canada.

There is broad consensus in the literature that the central government should be assigned taxes that have certain characteristics (see Chapter 3):

(1) They are levied on the more mobile tax bases. This is necessary to avoid tax-induced movements of factors of production, and also to avoid tax competition driving down revenues excessively.

(2) They are more sensitive to changes in income, that is, they have higher income elasticity. This is to provide the central government with stabilization instruments, and also to shelter to the extent possible the budgets of subnational governments from cyclical fluctuations.

(3) They are levied on tax bases that are distributed unevenly across regions.

These criteria would argue for the assignment to the central government of income taxes on enterprises (criteria (1) and (2)) and of taxes on natural resources (criterion (3)). For the latter, however, a plausible case can be made for a sharing of the base between the federal and the relevant subnational governments, especially in view of the impact that the exploitation of these resources might have on the local environment. There is also general consensus that taxes on foreign trade should be assigned to the central government.

Since the mobility of individuals and households tends to be less than that of businesses, the personal income tax appears more suitable for partial assignment—through tax overlapping—to the subnational (especially state or provincial) level.[4] However, to minimize distortions and tax-induced movements of labor and capital, it is preferable that the definition of the tax base be homogeneous throughout the country and also that rate differentials among subnational jurisdictions be kept relatively small. Since this tax should be levied on the basis of the res-

---

[4]In Canada, the provinces levy a personal income tax, which is calculated as a surcharge on the federal income tax.

idence principle, including in the base income from out-of-state sources, its administration would be carried out most effectively by the central government. If it is carried out at the state level, it is crucial that there be adequate and systematic exchange of information among the states, to permit the identification of out-of-state incomes.

As regards multistage sales taxes, such as the value-added tax (VAT), the difficulties of coordinating and administering such taxes, if levied at the subnational level, are frequently pointed out in the literature, and are exemplified by the case of Brazil where the state-level VAT on interstate transactions is levied on an origin basis—at a lower rate than on transactions within the state—giving rise to significant distortions and administrative difficulties (see Chapter 18 for details). Although in principle a destination-based VAT could be levied at different rates in different regions of a common economic area (with a deferred payment mechanism) without allocative distortions (along the current model of the European Union), the requirements for its effective administration (including exchange of relevant information among the regional tax administrations) are substantial, making it a difficult option for most countries.

By contrast, single-stage sales and excise taxes are generally considered good candidates for assignment to the regional governments, provided that the rates do not differ excessively among the regions. Property taxes, business license taxes, and various types of user fees for local services are generally regarded as ideal candidates for local taxation, since their base is relatively immobile.

As indicated above, country experiences conform only partially to these recommended criteria for revenue assignment. In some countries, state-level taxation of corporate profits, in the absence of a coordinated approach, has been accompanied by strong competition (tax wars), leading to distortions in enterprises' location decisions, tax avoidance through transfer pricing by enterprises operating in multiple areas, and erosion of revenues. Compliance costs for enterprises have also been substantially increased by regionally differentiated corporate tax regimes and by having to deal with multiple tax administrations. Also, in contrast with recommended principles of tax assignment, natural resources are assigned in some federations wholly to the region in which the resources are located. This arrangement, which reflects economic and political power balances, tends to exacerbate horizontal imbalances among regions. This is, for example, the case in Canada.

The substantial variation across countries of arrangements for revenue assignment is reflected in wide disparities in the shares of own revenues in total revenues of regional and local governments. These shares provide an indication of the degree of dependence of subnational governments on financial support from the central government. Rough calculations suggest that for regional governments these shares ranged from 4 percent in Italy, prior to the 1992 reform mentioned above, to over 80 percent in the United States and Canada. Comparable data are not available for the local governments in all countries. Those available point to a variation from about 17 percent in Germany and the United Kingdom to about 70 percent in the United States and Australia.

Intergovernmental Transfers

Since most major taxes are typically assigned to the central government, while substantial and growing expenditure responsibilities are devolved to regional and local governments, sizable vertical imbalances (that is, pre-transfer fiscal deficits) frequently emerge at the subnational government level. There are also horizontal imbalances, because the capacity to raise own revenues differs across jurisdictions, depending on the distribution of their assigned tax bases, and also because different regions may face different costs and demand pressures in meeting their assigned expenditure responsibilities.

These imbalances must be addressed through intergovernmental transfers, or borrowing by deficit jurisdictions, or a combination of the two. The design of an appropriate system of intergovernmental transfers is crucial not only to promote any desirable redistribution of resources among subnational jurisdictions, but also to ensure that effective limits can be set, and enforced on a sustained basis, on the borrowing of subnational governments. The design of intergovernmental transfers is also one of the more complex aspects of fiscal federalism, as demonstrated by the wide range of country experiences in this area. Intergovernmental transfer mechanisms can be broadly grouped into two main categories, revenue-sharing arrangements and grants.

Revenue-Sharing Arrangements

Revenue-sharing arrangements of various types are quite common in the international experience, and tend to be primarily geared to correcting, to varying degrees, the vertical imbalances generated by revenue and expenditure assignments. Sharing of tax revenues can be arranged on a tax-by-tax basis, with different coefficients of distribution among levels of government for each tax or on the entire pool of central government tax revenues. Examples of tax-by-tax sharing can be found in a number of countries, including Argentina, Brazil, Germany,

Hungary, India, and Russia.[5] A disadvantage of this type of arrangement is the fact that it may provide an incentive for the tax administration at the federal level to concentrate its collection and enforcement efforts on the taxes that are not shared or are shared to a lesser degree. Moreover, the central government has also an incentive to concentrate on those taxes in any tax reforms (base broadening or rate increases) that may be needed for stabilization purposes, with possible distortive effects on the structure of the tax system. For these reasons, it would be preferable that revenue sharing be applied on the entire pool of central government revenues.

Revenue-sharing arrangements with coefficients set in law, or in the constitution (as in Brazil or Colombia), provide the subnational governments a degree of predictability of revenues, which is important for their budgetary planning. However, they impart considerable rigidity to the central government budget. In particular, they can substantially dilute the impact of a fiscal tightening by the central government, as tax increases by the latter also boost the capacity of the subnational governments to spend. This shortcoming could be avoided if the portion of revenues going to the subnational governments was determined by applying a constant rate to the shared tax base. Fixed revenue-sharing arrangements can also have pro-cyclical effects, as increases in shared revenues during periods of boom increase the capacity to spend of the subnational governments, while declines in revenues during economic downturns force them to cut back spending. To address this problem, elements of flexibility could be introduced in these sharing arrangements, for instance, by relating the transfers to a moving average over a few years of central government revenues, or by requiring subnational governments to constitute revenue stabilization funds,[6] to even out cyclical fluctuations in the shared taxes.

The distribution of shared revenues among subnational jurisdictions is often made on a derivation basis, with each jurisdiction getting the share of the revenue collected in its territory.[7] This is, for example, the principle used in Germany for the sharing of revenues from the personal and corporate income taxes (Chapter 10). Revenue-sharing arrangements based on a derivation principle cannot be used to correct hori-

---

[5]See relevant chapters for details.

[6]In the United States, most states have constituted so-called rainy day funds, which are drawn down during cyclical downturns and reconstituted during the subsequent recovery (see Chapter 15).

[7]Specific rules have to be defined for the apportionment of revenues from incomes generated by companies operating in different jurisdictions, or by individuals working and residing in different states.

zontal imbalances since, under these arrangements, the level of the transfer from the center to each subnational government is positively correlated with the taxing capacity of the latter. To promote horizontal balance, in allocating shared revenues among regions or localities, some countries utilize formulas based on redistributive criteria. For example, in Germany shared revenue from the VAT is apportioned on a per capita basis, which entails a degree of redistribution to the less affluent states. India utilizes formulas that combine population, income per capita, indicators of backwardness, and the state's own tax effort (Chapter 21). Brazil utilizes a set of coefficients agreed among the states in 1988, which are only loosely linked to relative per capita income levels of the states. Hungary distributes the local governments' share of the personal income tax partly on a derivation and partly on an equalization basis (Chapter 27).

Grants

Besides revenue sharing, the main mechanism for intergovernmental transfers are grants from higher (federal or state) to lower (state or local, respectively) levels. Grants can be grouped into the following main categories:
- *General purpose grants.* These are unconditional transfers, aimed at addressing vertical and horizontal imbalances.
- *Specific purpose grants.* These grants carry more or less tight conditions regarding the use of the funds and/or the performance achieved in the program or programs financed through them. They may be open-ended or subject to a cap. They may or may not have matching requirements for the recipient government. Specific purpose grants may be of a recurrent nature, if used to finance current expenditures, or of a once-off nature, if used to finance investment projects.

In between these two categories fall the so-called block grants, which are earmarked for the financing of broad areas of expenditure (such as education) rather than of specific programs.

The choices between conditional and unconditional transfers should be based on a number of considerations. On the one hand, the imposition of conditions clearly detracts from the autonomy of subnational governments, partly negating the welfare (efficiency) arguments for decentralization. On the other hand, the imposition of conditions may be justified by distributional considerations (for example, ensuring the observance of minimum nationwide standards for the provision of services of national concern, such as primary education and health care, or pollution control). Whether or not desirable in theory, the design and enforcement of appropriate conditions for grants is not easy in practice, and controls on the use of grants often end up being more formal than substantive. Even more difficult is to specify and enforce conditionality on the performance of the programs supported by the grants.[8]

The amounts transferred under open-ended, specific purpose grants can often be influenced by the recipient institution (for example, by unnecessarily admitting patients to hospitals, if the size of the grant is based on the number of inpatients). Moreover, these types of grants may create opportunities for corruption. Therefore, it is important that the norms regulating them be specified with care, to avoid inappropriate incentives and minimize the scope for abuse.

Within conditional grants, the choice of whether or not to impose matching requirements has also to take into account various considerations. Matching requirements may induce a redirection of resources of subnational governments to the areas of spending considered of priority by the central government, but obviously at a cost for the local provision of other services. Also, matching requirements may place poorer, resource-constrained, regions at a disadvantage vis-à-vis the richer ones in the utilization of federal grants. Finally, budgetary and, more broadly, macroeconomic management considerations clearly argue against open-ended grants.

A brief review of grant mechanisms in a number of countries indicates that combinations of different types are used in most cases, with special purpose grants generally predominating over general purpose ones. The two main federal countries that use general purpose equalization schemes are Canada and Australia. Equalization mechanisms are also used in a number of unitary countries (notably the Scandinavian countries). The Australian system can be viewed as the most comprehensive effort at equalization, but it is also very complex, and demanding in terms of information requirements. The system is aimed at ensuring equal ability of the states to provide a standard level of public services at an average level of taxation. Other countries (including Denmark, Japan, and Korea) use simpler indicators of expenditure needs, such as demographic characteristics, population density, and length of roads, information on which is more easily available.

In Canada, equalization transfers to provinces are based only on their relative taxing capacities; they do not take into account relative expenditure needs. Equalization payments are complemented by block grants for the financing of health care and postsecondary education, which ini-

---

[8]See Chapters 4 and 6, and the case study of Italy (Chapter 11), in particular, for an illustration of these difficulties.

tially were open-ended, but more recently have been capped, as part of the effort to reduce the overall government deficit (Chapter 9).

Block grants are also extensively used in the United States, in combination with a large number of special purpose grants. These latter grants currently account for almost 90 percent of total federal transfers to state and local governments in the United States. About 70 percent of such grants are project-specific. Concern over the escalating costs of some of the programs supported by these grants (for example, Medicaid and the Aid to Families with Dependent Children), and dissatisfaction with the effectiveness of the federal government control over the use of these funds, has led to proposals for reform, and to initial steps in the direction of reducing the linkage of the grants to specific projects, and allowing greater responsibility (and hopefully political accountability) to the states in their management (Chapter 15).

In Germany, central government grants to the states are essentially an instrument for the former to influence specific state programs in areas that are defined as of common interest. These transfers have acquired greater importance, especially vis-à-vis the constituent states of the former east Germany, in the aftermath of unification. Equalization objectives are pursued in Germany through direct horizontal redistribution among the states, without participation of the central government. Interstate "solidarity" came under severe stress in the years following unification, given the enormous disparities in taxing capacity and expenditure needs of the eastern states vis-à-vis the western ones (see Chapter 10 for details).

Administrative Aspects of Fiscal Decentralization

The fiscal federalism literature has focused to date much more on policy than administrative issues. There is little doubt, however, that substantial devolution of revenue raising and expenditure responsibilities poses new challenges for tax administration and for public expenditure management. These aspects are discussed in some detail at a theoretical level in Chapters 5 and 6 and, to the extent that information is available on individual countries' practices in these areas, in the case studies (Chapter 8 through Chapter 28). This section highlights some main conclusions of these analyses.

Tax Administration

The assignment of certain taxes to subnational governments need not involve a decentralized administration of these taxes. In principle, especially if the definition of the base of some taxes assigned to the states is uniform, or nearly uniform, across the nation—with the states deciding only the rate or rates—those taxes could be administered by the central government. A centralized administration would have certain advantages, notably a uniformity of procedures, which would promote consistency of treatment of taxpayers across the country and reduce compliance costs, especially for enterprises conducting business in, and individuals receiving income from, more than one subnational jurisdiction. It would also permit economies of scale, in particular in the utilization of computer hardware and systems. A decentralized administration, on the other hand, would entail greater responsibility and accountability of the subnational authorities for the performance of taxes assigned to them, as well as greater flexibility in adapting systems and procedures to local needs and conditions.

Decentralized administration is more likely to be effective for local taxes, such as property taxes, business licence fees, user fees, and other minor levies. Decentralized administration of state-level taxes, such as personal or company income taxes, or even a general sales tax, may require, to be carried out effectively, a systematic exchange of relevant information among state administrations (especially on cross-border transactions). More generally, if devolution of revenue-raising responsibilities is to be accompanied by decentralization of the tax administration, substantial efforts have to be made to ensure that subnational tax administrations are equipped—through the development of their systems and procedures, technology, and human resources—to carry out the basic functions of collection and enforcement effectively. In this effort, the central government can play an important role, by providing guidance and technical support. This support may extend, for instance, to the carrying out of joint audits for the more complex taxes, and/or to the monitoring of large taxpayers who operate in several states.

Public Expenditure Management

Substantial decentralization of expenditure responsibilities also poses new challenges for public expenditure management by the various levels of government. These challenges relate to
- The need to coordinate the budgetary policies of the central and subnational governments, to ensure their consistency with national macroeconomic objectives (for example, for growth, inflation, and the external accounts).
- The need to promote responsiveness of all levels of government to the preferences of their constituents in both the allocation of bud-

getary resources and the delivery of goods and services assigned to them, in as efficient and cost-effective a manner as possible.
- The need to ensure sound financial management of the operations of each level of government.

These objectives should be pursued through all aspects of the public expenditure management process: planning and budget preparation, budget implementation and revisions, financial planning and cash management, debt management, accounting, and audit and evaluation.

Especially in federal countries, the objective of macroeconomic coordination could be pursued through the creation of an institutional forum—such as the Premiers' Conference and the Loan Council in Australia (Chapter 8) or the Financial Planning Council in Germany (Chapter 10).[9] In such a forum, the main lines of budgetary policy would be discussed each year—preferably within the framework of medium-term rolling budget plans—in advance of the preparation of national and subnational budgets; agreement would be reached on the major budgetary aggregates for the central and state governments, and at least for the larger municipalities; and a common set of procedures and assumptions would be adopted for the preparation of those budgets. The same forum should monitor the implementation of agreed plans during the year and approve any significant modifications that may be required in the light of changing circumstances.

In unitary countries, the central government needs to provide adequate and timely guidance to the local governments for their budget preparation. The creation of institutional forums for promoting frequent dialogue between the central and local authorities can be also useful in this respect. Examples of such an approach can be found in a number of European countries, such as the United Kingdom (Chapter 14), Denmark, and Sweden.

The steps to promote sound expenditure choices and a cost-effective delivery of public goods and services, as well as to strengthen financial management, are not dissimilar at the central and the subnational government levels.
- A clear definition of respective expenditure assignments is crucial, in particular to avoid duplication and waste of public resources.
- It is important that the system of intergovernmental transfers be also clearly defined, so that each level of government can anticipate the level and timing of these transfers as much as possible. In

---

[9]A high-level forum of this type would need, of course, to be supported by a similar committee at a more technical level, to prepare relevant analysis.

this respect—as noted in the section on Intergovernmental Transfers—open-ended, matching, and conditional grants, which inherently entail significant uncertainty for both donor and recipient governments, are clearly inferior to formula-based general purpose grants.
- Effective budgeting and accounting can be greatly helped by the adoption by all levels of government of modern, comprehensive, standardized, and transparent budget classifications, and accounting rules.
- Each level of government should prepare, and update frequently, rolling financial plans, and exchange relevant information about them with other levels of government.
- The development and implementation by subnational, as well as the central, governments of modern, integrated, computerized and accounting-based information systems, allowing the monitoring and control of all phases of the public expenditure process, would greatly facilitate effective financial management and control and help prevent the accumulation of budgetary arrears.
- Finally, the improvements in audit and evaluation that have occurred, or are occurring, at the central government level in many countries (for example, the United Kingdom, New Zealand, and Australia), need to be disseminated and replicated at the subnational level.

The Control of Subnational Government Borrowing

A review of country experiences with the control of subnational government borrowing shows considerable diversity in approaches. These indicate, among other things, the legal or constitutional status of subnational governments, the degree of political and administrative controls of the central government over them, the country's overall tradition of financial discipline, the presence or absence of serious fiscal and macroeconomic imbalances, and the state of development of the country's financial market.

Country approaches to the control of subnational borrowing can be grouped into four broad categories, although most countries utilize a mix of them. The four "stylized" categories are
(1) sole or primary reliance on market discipline;
(2) cooperation by different levels of government in the design and implementation of debt controls;
(3) rules-based controls; and
(4) administrative controls.

Examples of the first model can be found in Canada, and in Brazil until recent years. Notable examples of the second model are the Scandinavian countries, Australia, and Germany, although in the latter country subnational governments have also to follow the golden rule, which prohibits borrowing to fill current budgetary deficits. Other types of rules prevailing in different countries stipulate limits to the absolute level of subnational indebtedness, or allow new borrowing up to a level of debt consistent with maximum debt service ratio, or ban or restrict certain types of borrowing that involve greater macroeconomic risks (including borrowing from the central bank or from abroad). Examples of a rules-based approach can be found in, among others, the United States, Switzerland, and Spain (see Chapter 7 for details).

Finally, in a number of countries, the central government is empowered with direct control over the borrowing of subnational governments. This control may take various forms. These include the setting of annual (or more frequent) limits on the overall debt of individual subnational jurisdictions (or some of its components, such as external borrowing); the review and authorization of individual borrowing operations (including approval of the terms and conditions of the operation); and/or the centralization of all government borrowing, with on-lending to subnational governments for approved purposes (generally investment projects). Control powers generally encompass not only the ex ante authorization of proposed borrowing, but also the ex post monitoring, on a more or less detailed and timely basis, of the financial operations of subnational governments. Direct central government controls are, of course, more common in unitary states (such as the United Kingdom (Chapter 14), France, Japan (Chapter 12), and Korea (Chapter 22)) than in federations. One example for the latter is India, where federal government approval is required for borrowing by the states if they have outstanding debt to the federal government—which is currently the case for virtually all the states (Chapter 21).

Each of these models of control presents advantages and disadvantages, the balance of which would make it more or less suitable to a particular country's circumstances. Moreover, as these circumstances evolve—for example, as fiscal and macroeconomic imbalances improve or worsen—the preferable model may change over time. The review of country experiences presented in Chapter 7 would appear to justify the following main conclusions:

- Although appealing in principle, sole reliance on market discipline for government borrowing is unlikely to be appropriate in many circumstances. This is so, because one or more of the conditions for its effective working frequently are not realized in any particular country. However, market discipline can be a useful complement to other forms of borrowing controls, in particular to help contain resort by subnational governments to practices aimed at circumventing those controls. In this respect, greater transparency and dissemination of information on recent and prospective developments in the finances of subnational governments are highly desirable, and governments should be encouraged to make any necessary changes in the legal and institutional framework to promote these objectives. In countries with a history of bailouts of insolvent subnational governments by the central government, a firm and sustained refusal to engage in further operations of this kind will be necessary to change expectations and behaviors of market participants vis-à-vis subnational government borrowing. It must be recognized that this may be a prolonged process, the more so the longer the previous history of bailouts.

- The ongoing decentralization trend seems likely to come into growing conflict with systems of administrative controls by the central government on subnational borrowing (involving, for instance, a centralization of borrowing or approval of individual loan operations). It would not be surprising to see administrative controls on domestic subnational borrowing decline in importance in the years ahead.
- Rules-based approaches to debt control would appear preferable, in terms of transparency and certainty, to administrative controls and also to statutory limits defined in the context of the annual budget process, the outcome of which may be unduly influenced by short-term political bargaining. There is a clear macroeconomic rationale for barring all levels of government from borrowing from the central bank (or, at a minimum, for severely restricting this type of borrowing). Borrowing abroad by subnational governments should also be strictly limited, in accordance not only with the debt-servicing capacity of the subnational jurisdiction involved, but also with macroeconomic (especially monetary and balance of payments) considerations.
- In principle, a good case can be made for limiting all borrowing to investment purposes. However, the so-called golden rule may not be sufficiently restrictive in countries that need to generate government savings to finance at least a part of public investment. Moreover, it may not be desirable to allow government borrowing to finance investments that do not have adequate rates of economic and social return. Indeed, in many countries, efficient current expenditures on health and education may have higher rates of return than many capital projects. Finally, in practice, it may be

difficult to avoid circumvention of the golden rule through the labeling of certain current expenditures as investments.
- These considerations would seem to argue for setting global limits on the debt of individual subnational jurisdictions on the basis of criteria that mimic market discipline, such as the current and projected levels of service of the debt in relation to the jurisdictions' revenues. It is crucial that the projection of the debt service and of revenues, utilized in testing compliance with the ceiling, be realistic, and indeed preferably conservative. It is equally important that a comprehensive definition of the debt subject to the ceiling be adopted (including, to the extent feasible, extrabudgetary operations, suppliers' credits, and guarantees to credits contracted by the subnational governments' enterprises).
- Finally, even in the context of rules-based approaches, there seems to be scope for increased cooperation for all levels of government in containing (or reversing, if needed) the growth of the public debt. Enhanced involvement of the subnational governments (especially at the regional or state level) in formulating and implementing medium-term fiscal adjustment programs (along the lines discussed in the previous section) should result in greater responsibility of these governments in the conduct of their budgetary affairs, facilitate the recognition of any need for reforms of the existing system of intergovernmental fiscal relations, and help muster adequate political consensus for such reforms.

Concluding Remarks

This chapter has provided a broad survey of the theory and practice of intergovernmental fiscal relations, focusing on key issues and selected country experiences. From this review, a few major conclusions emerge:
- As is well known, the design of intergovernmental fiscal relations is importantly influenced by noneconomic (political, social, and cultural) factors, as well as by economic considerations. Therefore, the limitations of a purely economic analysis of intergovernmental fiscal arrangements should be kept in mind. Within the narrower economic context, the design of these arrangements reflects a balance among different (and not always easily reconcilable) objectives, namely allocative efficiency, income redistribution, and macroeconomic management. The specific balance of these objectives in different countries, and its evolution over time, tend also to reflect the country's social and political history

and current conditions, and the presence or absence of serious macroeconomic imbalances.
- There is broad consensus in the literature that a decentralization of expenditure responsibilities should in principle lead to allocative efficiency gains, by promoting a closer correspondence of expenditure priorities with the preferences of affected citizens. However, it is also increasingly recognized that these theoretical efficiency gains may be negated in practice (or substantially reduced) by administrative weaknesses at the subnational level, especially the lack of modern and transparent public expenditure management systems.
- Country experiences, by and large, bear out the need to accompany a decentralization of spending responsibilities with the assignment to subnational governments of significant own sources of revenue. This is necessary to promote fiscal responsibility by subnational government officials, and their political accountability to the electorate. The best candidates for assignment to the subnational level are taxes characterized by relatively low mobility, a fairly even distribution of the base over the national territory, and relative stability over the cycle. These criteria would tend to argue for total or partial assignment to the regional governments of the personal income tax, general retail sales taxes, and certain excises; and to the local governments of the property tax, business license fees, and user fees. In general, harmonization of the definition of tax bases across the national territory and a not excessive variance of the rates are desirable, to avoid tax-induced distortions.
- As in the case of expenditures, administrative weaknesses may also impair the effectiveness of revenue decentralization. In countries characterized by weak and inexperienced subnational tax administrations, a determined effort to strengthen these entities should be given high priority by the central, as well as the subnational, authorities, and preferably should precede a decentralization of the administration of the taxes devolved to the subnational governments, to safeguard the revenue performance.
- It must be recognized that a high degree of decentralization may come in serious conflict with distributional objectives. This is especially the case, of course, in countries characterized by large regional disparities in income. In these cases, a system of equalization-oriented vertical transfers from the center (as in Australia) or a horizontal redistribution mechanism (as in Germany) are likely to be necessary, to preserve adequate economic and social cohesion in the country. It is important that such mechanisms be

designed, however, so as not to discourage tax effort and cost-effectiveness by the subnational governments.
- Substantial decentralization is also likely to make it more difficult for the central government to carry out macroeconomic stabilization through budgetary policies, for the reasons outlined earlier. Therefore, ceteris paribus, decentralization should progress more slowly in countries facing acute fiscal or macroeconomic imbalances. In these countries, it is especially important that a hard budget constraint be imposed on the subnational governments, through a design of intergovernmental fiscal relations that ensures for the subnational jurisdictions an adequate ex ante balance between expenditure responsibilities and own revenues plus clearly defined transfers from the center; and which bars them from borrowing.
- In countries that do not face serious macroeconomic or fiscal imbalances, it should be recognized that substantial decentralization of revenues and expenditures entails the need for the central government to involve more actively the subnational governments, especially states and large municipalities, in macroeconomic management, and to make them share responsibility for the achievement of national economic objectives (for some suggestions in this respect, see section on Administrative Aspects of Fiscal Decentralization). In these countries, subnational governments can be allowed to borrow, but subject to clearly specified limits, relating to their prospective ability to service the debt. It is important that any such borrowing be carried out by the subnational governments in their own name, without central government guarantee, and that all efforts be made to promote adequate market discipline on such borrowing.

References

Boadway, Robin, Sandra Roberts, and Anwar Shah, 1994, *The Reform of Fiscal Systems in Developing and Emerging Market Economies: A Federalism Perspective*, World Bank Policy Research Working Paper No. 1259 (Washington: World Bank, February).

Huther, J., and Anwar Shah, 1996, *A Simple Measure of Good Governance and Its Application to the Debate on the Appropriate Level of Fiscal Decentralization* (unpublished; Washington: World Bank).

Musgrave, R., 1969, "Theories of Fiscal Federalism," *Public Finance*, Vol. 24, No. 4, pp. 521–32.

Oates, Wallace E., 1972, *Fiscal Federalism* (New York: Harcourt Brace Jovanovich).

Prud'homme, Remy, 1995, "The Dangers of Decentralization," *World Bank Research Observer,* Vol. 10, No. 2 (August), pp. 210–26.

Shah, Anwar, 1994, *A Fiscal Needs Approach to Equalization Transfers in a Decentralized Federation,* World Bank Policy Research Working Paper No. 1289 (Washington: World Bank, April).

Tanzi, Vito, 1996, "Fiscal Federalism and Decentralization: A Review of Some Efficiency and Macroeconomic Aspects," in *Annual World Bank Conference on Development Economics, 1995* (Washington: World Bank).

Tiebout, C.M., 1961, *An Economic Theory of Fiscal Decentralization in Public Finance: Needs, Sources and Utilization* (Princeton, New Jersey: Princeton University Press).

2

Assigning Expenditure Responsibilities

EHTISHAM AHMAD, DANIEL HEWITT, AND EDGARDO RUGGIERO

Economic theory offers limited guidance for assigning expenditure responsibilities among different levels of government. At the micro level, the benefit principle suggests that a given service should be provided by the level of government that most closely represents the region that benefits from such service. For example, local public goods such as municipal services often only benefit persons who live in a given city or township; in these cases, decentralization to the municipal level is feasible and desirable for allocative and administrative efficiency. In contrast, national public goods, such as national defense, macroeconomic stability, and redistribution, require centralized administration and centralized policy.

Most goods that governments supply, however, do not fit neatly into either one of these two categories. For these mixed goods some degree of decentralization coupled with some centralized coordination of policy is both feasible and desirable, owing to unclear benefit regions, externalities, or national redistributional implications. For instance, there are certain efficiency advantages to local supply of primary education and preventive health care, such as possibly better quality through local supervision, and allowance for communities to express cultural and curative preferences. For tertiary education and hospitals, existence of economies of scale and externalities (their benefits accruing to more than one jurisdiction) imply that more centralized control may be warranted. However, the demand for minimum standards often requires that centralized decision making of policies be ensured for all these services. When conflicting goals arise, the analysis of which level should be assigned expenditure responsibility can become quite complicated and subject to normative bias.

The analysis of expenditure assignments is complicated by the fact that centralization-decentralization is a multidimensional choice. Expenditure assignments involve decisions on which level of government should be assigned the formulation, financing, and administration of policies. A number of combinations are possible. Intergovernmental grants allow policymakers to separate expenditure decisions, administration of programs, and their financing. Revenue sharing and grants serve as the coordinating mechanism that allows decentralized expenditure to coexist with centralized tax collection and with redistribution. Since the distributional implications of expenditure decentralization are often undesirable, tensions between expenditure assignments and financing arrangements often arise.

If economic theory provides little guidance on expenditure assignment—apart from purely local and national public goods—the examination of actual practices in this chapter confirms that a wide array of different solutions is possible. There is a great variety of intergovernmental fiscal arrangements and expenditure assignments among different countries, reflecting varying social preferences among the countries involved. Overlapping responsibilities in policy formulation, financing, and administration of services are also common. In general, industrial countries are more decentralized than developing countries, though the former tend to have centralized revenue collection to ensure efficient tax administration (Tanzi, 1994) and to finance redistribution from richer to poorer regions. Not only do intergovernmental fiscal arrangements vary widely across countries, often a specific country's degree of decentralization changes over time. Among the more highly centralized industrial countries—France, Italy, and Spain—significant tendencies toward decentralization are now more evident.

At the macro level, an interesting question arising from expenditure assignments is the interaction between the level of decentralization and macroeconomic stability. This chapter examines the hypothesis that since control of government expenditure is a crucial element in obtaining macroeconomic stability, a more centralized intergovernmental arrangement would be compatible with greater macroeconomic controls. It concludes that macroeconomic control is not contingent on the actual administration of expenditure functions by the central government. A more important element is to have in place appropriate financing mechanisms that provide incentives for expenditure controls. Countries with centralized administration of expenditure functions are as prone to loss of macroeconomic control as those with decentralized administration. However, it appears that decentralized administration with poorly defined policy goals and lax financing mechanisms almost always have negative consequences for macroeconomic control. Thus, establishing a mechanism of expenditure control can be more complicated in a decentralized system that separates expenditure administration from financing responsibilities.

Overall, the findings in this chapter would weigh against major changes in expenditure assignments in most countries if these are sought as a means to achieving improved macroeconomic control. A country's social preference, rather than economic theory, should be the major guide to defining the appropriate level of expenditure decentralization for mixed public goods. Once an administration system is in place, it is difficult and costly to change expenditure assignments. Policymakers having the objective of improving macroeconomic management should perhaps pay more attention to consistency between expenditure assignments and financing arrangements (revenue assignments and the system of intergovernmental transfers), rather than to the extent of centralization or decentralization of expenditure assignments. Increasing administrative and allocative efficiency, as well as matching public expenditure levels to preferences, is more important than the specific intergovernmental expenditure assignments.

This chapter first discusses allocative efficiency and the benefit principle. Then the relationship between expenditure assignments and financing arrangements is examined. Expenditure patterns in various countries for social protection, education, and health are considered next. The chapter concludes with a summary of findings.

Principles of Expenditure Assignment

Although traditional approaches assign allocative expenditure activities to local governments on a benefit principle, distributional and stabilization functions require primary responsibility at the central level.[1] This principle does not lead to a sharp distinction between the expenditure responsibilities of different levels of government.

Shares of Local Expenditures

The systems of intergovernmental finance in the industrial federations have evolved gradually, much like their market and political

---

[1] Musgrave (1959), pp. 181–82.

institutions; the present systems result from historical circumstances and political events and reflect cultural traits. Among the six industrial federations (Australia, Austria, Canada, Germany, Switzerland, and the United States), the share of local (municipal) expenditures in total government expenditures varies from 7 percent in Australia to 24 percent in Switzerland; the state or provincial share of total expenditures varies from 14 percent in Austria to 43 percent in Australia.[2] Transfers from higher-level governments vary from 16 percent of total local (municipal) revenue in Switzerland to 45 percent in Canada; the share of intergovernmental transfers in total receipts of states or provinces varies from 16 percent in Germany to 45 percent in Australia.

Each country has unique features. In Australia, local (municipal) government is of modest importance, and the state governments depend heavily on federal transfers. Switzerland is characterized by strong local governments that meet most expenditures from their own revenues and depend relatively little on transfers.

Expenditure devolution in India can be traced to the Government of India Act of 1935, which provided a degree of political autonomy to the provinces (states). With independence, developmental and infrastructure concerns have been addressed by the extra-constitutional Planning Commission, while the finance commissions have addressed issues of revenue sharing and the financing needs of the states. Expenditure control, given India's federal structure, is a major issue.

In countries in transition to a market economy, such as China and Russia, overall expenditure control and the devolution of expenditure responsibilities are critical to economic stabilization and are of prime policy concern. Existing institutions and methods provide a starting point to determining desirable directions of reform.

Centralized Expenditures

Centralization, that is, vesting the central government or administration with power over policy, facilitates uniformity in the provision of public services.[3] In a number of circumstances, this is necessary. First,

---

[2]Figures in this section are the authors' calculations from data in International Monetary Fund, *Government Finance Statistics Yearbook, 1991*, and refer to the following years: Australia (1990), Austria (1990), Canada (1989), Germany (1990), and Switzerland (1984).

[3]This does not have to be the case, however. If local or regional variety is sought, it is normally desirable to allow subnational levels of government to make the allocation decisions.

certain goods have nonrival consumption within an entire country. Therefore, by definition the level of service, such as through defense and macroeconomic policies, is uniform. Decentralization would lead to an inefficient allocation of resources. Second, when significant economies of scale are present, decentralized administration can be inefficient, depending on the function being considered and the size of the country. Third, undesirable population and capital movements can result from variations in policy and the level of provision between jurisdictions.

In addition to the pursuit of macroeconomic stability, the following activities of government require centralization.

Provision of National Defense and Other National Public Goods

For certain goods, the whole population is affected by a given expenditure decision. Nonrival consumption exists throughout the country, and by definition everyone has access to the same level of service. If decentralization of policy decisions is attempted, each jurisdiction would consider only the direct benefits to its residents and ignore the benefits to residents of other jurisdictions—leading to the free-rider problem. For instance, while localities on the borders of a nation are greatly concerned about national defense, interior communities do not have the same incentives and might simply depend on the frontier regions to protect them. Such behavior, encouraged by an inappropriate system of expenditure assignments, leads to an undersupply and constitutes a misallocation of resources.

Redistribution

The central government is more efficient than local governments in ensuring income redistribution and in establishing minimum standards of public services across regions, because the ability of localities to support low-income groups is severely limited by the localities' revenue bases, as well as the interjurisdictional mobility of the poor, the rich, and businesses. Redistribution by a given locality in isolation can attract the poor from neighboring localities. At the same time, imposing taxes on local factors of production to finance the redistribution can lead to flight of capital and of the wealthy and a consequent shrinkage of the resource base. Fixed factors, such as land and natural resources, vary considerably across regions, and the resulting revenue bases may afford some localities little scope for attaining minimum standards of public services in the absence of transfers from higher levels of government. Though the general government may be more efficient in ensuring income redistribution, the local governments are better able to identify target groups and to mobilize support for them (see the section on Social Protection). In general, the greater the mobility of the populations, the more difficult and costly it is to redistribute income within a locality.

The establishment of minimum access to education, health, and other human services across regions is a socially desirable goal of central government. Such redistributive policy implies substantial expenditure activities—or at least financing responsibility—for the central government.

Provision of Local Public Goods

Government services that benefit a clearly limited geographic region, or local public goods, could be provided by that level. Decentralized provision facilitates regional variety in the mix and the level of local public goods, which can greatly enhance social welfare. For instance, in a high crime area where most of the housing is constructed of stone, the local population will prefer high police expenditures over spending on fire prevention. Alternatively, in a given locality, the road network might need repair, while in another an upgrade of water and sanitary services might be preferable. Once it is accepted that regional variety is desirable, local provision can solve two of the more difficult problems confronting government decision making: the demand revelation problem and efficiency in government production.

The demand revelation problem concerns how much of a given public service to supply. While the market determines the exact quantity of each private good by equating supply and demand, no parallel mechanism exists for public goods. Instead, policymakers need to assess desired levels of supply of each public good, given costs of supply and public preferences. Although democratic elections provide some guidance and polls can also be useful, politicians have their own agendas that may not be in line with the public interest.

Ensuring efficiency in government production relates to public expenditures at all levels of government. For market-supplied goods, competition among producers, the profit motive among managers, and the desire to earn high incomes among workers encourage efficiency and work effort. Although this does not ensure that market production is always efficient, it is clear that competition tends to push the market in that direction. There is no parallel mechanism or motivation for the central government. Instead, a government has to depend on bureaucratic forms of control to induce efficiency.[4] Furthermore, government officials and politicians can benefit by shirking responsibilities and by diverting government resources for personal use. Because this is a serious problem in many countries, more efficient government provision is needed, with streamlined procedures and public surveillance of government bureaucracies.

Decentralization of government promises a partial solution. The Tiebout and tax competition models point out that competition among local governments induces localities to provide an efficient configuration of local public goods. The key to the Tiebout Model is mobility of residents (see Tiebout, 1956; and Gordon, 1983). The framework examines a situation in which numerous localities exist in a metropolitan area. Since residents are mobile between localities, families will tend to choose the area that offers them the best combination of public services and taxes to pay for them. Therefore, local governments must be efficient in the provision of services to retain residents and attract new entrants.

Although problems with these models lie in the imposition of distributional considerations and assumptions regarding mobility, particularly of households, which may not be warranted in practice, they do point to important potential benefits of decentralized provision. On a more intuitive level, the advantages of decentralization stem from possible efficiency gains from smaller operations and the potential gains for consumer choice from variety. Decision making is normally easier in smaller organizations, and a small local government is more likely to cater to local needs and desires. However, large diseconomies of scale are possible in small local government units, as seen, for instance, in Austria. Furthermore, although local bureaucracies may be more efficient than national bureaucracies, the net effects of decentralization on the overall size of the bureaucracy are indeterminate.

With increased decentralization comes the possibility of loss of macroeconomic control as local bureaucracies multiply. Such a proliferation makes monitoring and evaluation more problematic, and the quality of administration may deteriorate, given a shortage of skilled administrators. Tendencies to exaggerate expenditures and to participate in bargaining games with higher levels of government may increase, particularly if financing arrangements are shared.

---

[4]Private businesses, particularly large corporations, can face similar problems and in fact many large corporate bureaucracies are not necessarily more efficient than government bureaucracies.

Assessment of Expenditure Patterns

A difficulty in assigning expenditure responsibilities in some countries lies in unclear distinctions between levels of administration. This is in addition to the difficulties associated with the separation between regulation, financing, and administration of expenditures at a given level. As pointed out in a comprehensive review by Levin (1990), regulation is difficult to measure, and whereas finance and administration can be identified, neither fully represents the complete range of activities carried out by the government. The difference between financing and administration lies in intergovernmental transfers, where the grantor government often has no administrative role in providing goods or services. The financing (administration) of expenditures at a particular level is determined inclusive (exclusive) of grants given and net (inclusive) of grants received. Centralization ratios based on the administration of expenditures are likely to underestimate the role of the central government, particularly with respect to the redistributional transfers generally made by the central authorities. The appropriate classification of extrabudgetary funds, particularly for social security, would also affect the reported degree of centralization.

Some of the resources, such as shared revenues, conditional grants, and borrowing, may provide higher levels of government a degree of control. In some cases, the central government mandates certain expenditures, thus exerting some control over local functions, even when these are administered and fully financed by the lower level of administration. At the opposite extreme, expenditure functions may be mandated and financed by the central government, but administered by the subnational governments, including minimum educational or health standards. Here, the effective control over the level of expenditures rests with the administering lower-level authority (for example, health care in Italy), even though officials of the central administration may be represented at the lower level (for example, social expenditures in Pakistan). The loss of central control in the latter case arises from the effective underwriting by the central government of deficits or expenditure overruns at lower levels of government. Thus, in most cases, the form of transfers from higher levels of government and the associated incentives for limiting expenditure growth appear to be more important in controlling overall expenditures than simplistic categorizations of centralization or decentralization (see Chapter 4).

A wide variety of expenditure patterns and associated financing mechanisms can be observed across the world. Unconditional grants and own resources accord the greatest level of autonomy to local governments in providing local goods and services.

As Table 1 indicates, unconditional grants form a predominant share of transfers in the United Kingdom, France, and Australia—giving local governments the capacity to provide local goods, but not requiring them to do so. On the other hand, only 11 percent of grants in the United States and around 20 percent in the Scandinavian countries and Canada can be classified as free of regulations. Among developing countries, very few distinguish between different types of grants, although a substantial proportion of total expenditures is financed through grants in India (27.8 percent) or Indonesia (17.6 percent), excluding transfers for local expenditures in both cases.

Where identifiable, conditional transfers indicate the extent to which higher levels of government wish to promote a particular activity at the subnational or local level. Conditional grants finance a substantive proportion of expenditures on education in Zimbabwe, the United States, and Canada, but very little in the United Kingdom and Germany. However, in the latter group of countries unconditional grants are more important than in the former—thus indicating that even in a highly "centralized" system, as in the United Kingdom, local authorities have some freedom for maneuver in the allocation of resources for education, despite the establishment of nationwide norms and curriculums.

Financing patterns are relevant to local expenditures, given the empirical phenomenon of fiscal illusion, whereby transfers appear to stimulate expenditures of recipient governments beyond expectations. This phenomenon is observed in several countries for which a reasonably long time series is available (see Winer (1983) for Canada, and Gramlich (1979) for a review of U.S. studies). The evidence is consistent with the hypothesis that the separation of decision making caused by substituting own resources with grants increases local expenditure beyond theoretically expected levels, although the degree of illusion tends to fade over time.

A number of studies point out that the counterpart of fiscal illusion at the local level is the tendency of grants to lead to lower expenditures by higher level governments (see Hewitt, 1986; and Logan, 1986). Therefore, the impact of fiscal illusion on general government expenditures is uncertain. As discussed in Chapter 4, the type of grant and the mechanism whereby it is implemented affect the overall level of local expenditures.

The public choice literature (for example, Brennan and Buchanan, 1980) suggests that decentralization per se might curb the growth of government expenditures—the Leviathan hypothesis, although the

Table 1. Percentages of General Government Expenditure Financed by Intergovernmental Grants
(Average of latest three years available)

	Ending Year	Total Expenditures[1]	Education	Health	Social Security and Welfare	Percent of Intergovernmental Grants Unclassified
Argentina[2]	1987					88.0
Australia	1987	24.5	30.6	8.2	1.4	60.0
Belgium	1987	6.3				0.0
Bolivia	1986	0.4				
Brazil	1987	14.4				
Canada	1987	16.7	50.2	22.9	9.4	21.8
Chile	1987	2.0			0.0	
Colombia	1984	19.1				
Denmark	1986	27.1	9.1	6.2	47.6	23.5
Finland	1987	16.5				
France	1985	6.8	2.7	1.0	1.1	78.0
Germany	1983	10.3	10.9	3.5	3.5	52.6
Hungary	1988	10.4				
India[2]	1986	27.8				
Indonesia[2]	1988	17.6				
Ireland	1987	16.5				
Israel	1986	3.7	18.1	0.7	2.4	51.2
Kenya	1984	4.3				21.1
Luxembourg	1987	11.5	4.9	23.8		
Malawi	1984	6.1				
Mexico	1984	3.3				
Netherlands	1988	23.5				
New Zealand	1981	2.1				
Norway	1986	15.2				16.2
Pakistan	1979	9.7				
Paraguay	1984	0.0				
Poland	1988	10.6				
Romania	1985	10.3				
South Africa	1986	14.9				
Spain	1986	9.8				
Sweden	1987	10.3				21.2
Switzerland	1984	14.9	21.9	7.3	9.4	19.4
Thailand	1982	3.9				9.8
Tunisia	1982	12.1				
United Kingdom	1987	13.3	3.9	0.0	6.5	66.4
United States	1987	14.9	42.8	18.7	13.2	10.9
Yugoslavia	1987	7.2				
Zimbabwe	1986	8.5	37.6	9.3	0.0	2.3

Source: Levin (1990) based on *Government Finance Statistics Yearbook*, Vol. 13 (Washington: International Monetary Fund, 1989).

[1]Includes supranational authorities' share of general government expenditures in Belgium (2.2 percent), Denmark (2.2 percent), France (1.4 percent), Germany (1.8 percent), Luxembourg (2.7 percent), and the United Kingdom (1.9 percent).

[2]Data for general government do not include local government.

evidence is mixed. Cross-sectional analyses based on international data[5] tend to reject the hypothesis. It appears that the form of financing of expenditures is more important in determining expenditure levels than the extent of decentralization. For instance, substitution of own sources with transfers per se can have a stimulative effect on expenditure and could lead to a higher than optimal level of expenditure.[6] The abolition of subnational taxes in 1973 in Italy to centralize tax policy and improve tax administration, coupled with the effective removal of financing responsibility at the subnational level, led to higher expenditure. De facto decentralized revenue and expenditure responsibilities in China in the period up to 1993 have also exacerbated the growth of expenditures and of associated overall budgetary and macroeconomic imbalances. Thus, reduced overall expenditures cannot be taken as an inherent characteristic of decentralization. In fact, the fiscal illusion thesis suggests the opposite.

Brosio, Hyman, and Santagata (1980) found that public per capita expenditure in Italy was indeed positively affected by the separation of the subnational governments' ability to raise own revenue from their expenditure assignments—which had resulted from the fiscal reform in the 1970s. This increase was immediate, although it tended to decline with time owing to the financial problems soon encountered by the subnational governments, as the central government limited the amount of transfers granted to them. Rizzo (1985) also found a positive impact of decentralization on government size in Italy, when coupled with a decline in fiscal responsibility of local administrators. A study of decentralization and government size in Latin America (which controls for a positive correlation between rising income and the size of government (Wagner's hypothesis)) found that decentralization financed by central government transfers, rather than through own revenues, was likely to increase government expenditures (Reid and Winkler, 1992).

Fiscal illusion implies that grants powerfully influence allocation decisions of local government. From the Gramlich (1979) study, it appears that the expenditure elasticity of revenue-sharing grants is approximately unity. This suggests that revenue-sharing grants do not crowd out local revenue collection but instead are put entirely into increased local expenditures. The elasticity associated with matching grants appears to be in the order of two: matching grants approximately double expenditures. Although these empirical results are somewhat

---

[5]Subject to the major caveats concerning the measurement of decentralization, as discussed in the next section.

[6]This is demonstrated theoretically by using a full-information median voter model (Brosio, 1985).

surprising, one explanation offered in Hewitt and Heffley (1989) suggests that the higher expenditures result from an interaction between mobility and grants.

To avoid suboptimal supply, grants are clearly needed when local goods have interregional externalities. In these cases, matching grants can induce localities to take account of the positive benefits afforded to nonresidents. In the resulting arrangement, there are decentralized administration and a sharing of both financing and policy control.

The issue of expenditure assignments and the associated pattern of grants should be viewed in the changing context of a country's macroeconomic conditions. The Italian case reflects the consequence of revenue centralization since 1973, coupled with the assignment to subnational governments of the responsibility for the administration of major expenditure programs, such as health and social assistance, while responsibility for their financing was mostly with the central government (Table 2). There is no local incentive to control costs, and the lack of accountability at the local level has led to an uncontrolled growth of total public expenditure. The grant system developed during the 1970s was meant to be a temporary bridge between the fiscal reform of 1973 and the reform of local taxation and financing—which was started in 1993. In the meantime, ad hoc grants have multiplied as the need arose.

Social Protection, Education, and Health

There is considerable diversity of experience relating to the share of expenditures on social protection, education, and health administered at each level of government, as seen in Table 3. Among industrial countries, education is primarily provided at the central government level, although in the United Kingdom and the United States, it is provided by local governments, and by state governments in Australia[7] and Germany. Among developing countries, education and health care are primarily provided by the central government in some cases, as in Indonesia, but by the state (or provincial) governments in others, such as in India (data on local governments are not available in either country). In other countries, such as Brazil, detailed information is not avail-

---

[7]University education in Australia is assigned to the states under the Constitution. However, most universities are administered by independent syndicates, and almost all the financing comes from the central government through the states. There is thus considerable overlapping of responsibility even where the assignment might seem to be fairly clearly defined.

Table 2. Italy: Arrangements for Financing, Policymaking, and Administration of Major Expenditure Items, 1991

	Financing	Policymaking	Administration
Center			
Health	•	•	
Education	•	•	•
Social welfare[1]	•	•	•
Regions			
Health	•	For own earmarked revenues	
Education			
Social welfare			
Provinces			
Health			
Education	Support personnel, buildings and furniture, for specific schools in secondary education		For functions specified under financing arrangements
Social welfare			
Municipalities			
Health			•
Education	Support personnel, buildings, and furniture in elementary education		For functions specified under financing arrangements
Social welfare	Cash and in-kind benefits to people on the municipal poor list		For functions specified under financing arrangements

[1]Pensions and family allowances.

able for the breakdown of functional expenditures at subnational levels of government, despite the importance of such a classification for overall policymaking.

Social Protection

Social protection mechanisms embody elements of insurance, together with redistribution. This is true in the industrial societies, where formal social insurance instruments cater for old age and loss of income, including unemployment, together with family allowances that limit the risk of poverty due to childbearing, and measures to provide for social assistance. Informal arrangements that mimic the above arrangements are also occasionally found in traditional societies in developing countries—but these suffer from a number of difficulties that mirror the level at which the service is provided (see Ahmad, Dreze, Hills, and Sen, 1991).

Table 3. **Magnitude of General Government Expenditures and Portion Administered by Each Level of Government**[1]
(Average of latest three years available)

Country and Ending Year	Total	Education	Health	Social Security and Welfare	Central government	State government	Local government
	(In percent of GDP)				(In percent of general government)		
Argentina[2] (1987)	33.2	4.0	1.1	9.1	60.3	39.7	
Australia (1987)	39.1	5.5	5.5	9.6	52.9	40.4	6.8
Austria (1987)	51.8				70.4	13.7	16.9
Belgium (1987)	56.7				85.9		11.9
Bolivia (1986)	11.1				85.9	10.6	3.4
Brazil (1987)	34.1				65.8	24.5	9.6
Canada (1987)	46.0	5.8	6.0	12.3	41.3	40.3	18.4
Chile (1987)	32.3	4.9	1.9	8.8	93.8		6.2
Colombia (1984)	18.0	5.5	1.3	3.2	67.4	23.9	8.7
Denmark (1986)	57.6	7.1	5.2	23.1	44.9		52.9
Finland (1987)	43.0				54.7		45.3
France (1985)	49.3	4.6	8.3	20.9	82.2		16.5
Germany (1983)	50.2	4.2	8.0	21.2	58.7	21.5	17.9
Hungary (1988)	64.5	5.7	4.2	18.1	77.8		22.2
India[2] (1986)	22.6	3.4	0.9	2.3	47.5	52.5	
Indonesia[2] (1988)	22.8	3.1	0.5	0.4	88.7	11.3	
Ireland (1987)	55.8				72.5		27.5
Israel (1986)	62.9	5.3	2.0	10.0	90.8		9.2
Kenya (1984)	29.3	5.2	2.1	1.4	94.3		5.7
Luxembourg (1987)	39.1	4.4	0.7	21.3	81.3		15.9
Malawi (1984)	29.1	3.7	2.2	0.6	93.7		6.3
Mexico (1984)	30.2				90.1	7.6	2.3
Netherlands (1988)	59.2				70.1		29.9
New Zealand (1981)	43.2				86.9		13.1
Norway (1986)	47.2				66.4		33.6
Pakistan (1979)	26.1				68.2	28.3	3.5
Paraguay (1984)	11.3				95.1		4.9
Poland (1988)	48.1				71.1		28.9
Romania (1985)	32.3	2.1	2.1	8.9	77.0		23.0
South Africa (1986)	33.3				74.8	12.5	12.7
Spain (1986)	38.2				78.8	9.9	11.3
Sweden (1987)	61.6				59.8		40.2
Switzerland (1984)	37.4	5.3	5.9	13.9	47.5	28.3	24.2
Thailand (1982)	21.2	4.1	1.1	1.2	92.3		7.7
Tunisia (1982)	34.0	5.1	2.5	4.7	94.6		5.4
United Kingdom (1987)	44.8	5.1	5.1	14.3	70.9		27.2
United States (1987)	37.1	5.1	4.3	9.0	60.3	17.3	22.4
Yugoslavia (1987)	25.3	3.2	4.2	7.8	23.2	31.4	45.4
Zimbabwe (1986)	45.0	8.3	2.6	3.0	75.8	24.2	60.2

Source: Levin (1990) based on International Monetary Fund, *Government Finance Statistics Yearbook*, Vol. 13 (Washington: International Monetary Fund, 1989).

[1] Excluding intergovernmental grants.
[2] Data for general government do not include local government.
[3] Includes supranational authorities' share of general government expenditures in Belgium (2.2 percent), Denmark (2.2 percent), France (1.4 percent), Germany (1.8 percent), Luxembourg (2.7 percent), and the United Kingdom (1.9 percent).

	Education			Health			Social Security and Welfare		
	Central government	State government	Local government	Central government	State government	Local government	Central government	State government	Local government
	(In percent of general government)								
	33.3	66.7		24.4	75.6		89.4	10.6	
	8.5	91.3	0.2	43.5	55.6	0.9	92.8	6.2	1.0
	4.8	34.5	60.7	2.6	89.5	7.9	65.8	31.3	2.9
	81.7		18.3	98.1		1.9	100.0		
	55.5	39.2	5.3	49.0	40.2	10.8	90.0	7.8	2.2
	46.8		53.2	7.1		92.9	26.1		73.9
	75.3		24.7	97.0		3.0	91.8		8.2
	1.0	73.8	25.2	74.4	11.2	14.4	79.0	10.9	10.1
	20.0		80.0	39.2		60.8	95.7		4.3
	9.0	90.1		30.2	69.8		0.0		100.0
	65.3	34.7		72.8	27.2		0.0		100.0
	67.2		32.8	97.0		3.0	94.9		5.1
	94.0		6.0	91.9		8.1	75.9		24.1
	74.1		25.9	92.0		8.0	97.4		2.6
	98.7		1.3	82.9		17.1	100.0		0.0
	28.0		72.0	10.3		89.7	99.3		0.7
	6.2	57.5	36.3	45.5	32.1	22.4	88.5	5.6	5.9
	94.8		5.2	93.5		6.5	97.4		2.6
	100.0			100.0		100.0		0.0	
	12.7		87.3	100.0		0.0	84.0		16.0
	4.2	24.5	71.3	50.5	33.8	15.7	78.0	14.6	7.4
	0.0	0.0	100.0	0.0	0.0	100.0	7.3	75.9	16.8
		39.8	86.6		13.4	100.0		0.0	

A major element in the provision of coverage for life-cycle and employment contingencies is the pooling of risk. Thus enterprise-level provision for the aged or the disabled, as was the case in former centrally planned economies, such as China and the countries of the former Soviet Union, imposed on older enterprises major costs that were inconsistent with the efficient functioning of a market economy. Similarly, in several countries (for example, Bangladesh, India, Jordan, Pakistan, and most countries of the former Soviet Union), subsidies to keep inefficient public sector enterprises afloat have proven difficult to remove owing to an absence of effective unemployment insurance. And, while community-based provision for the disabled and aged tends to be effective in identifying the appropriate recipients, because of the lower costs of local information, such methods are not appropriate when the whole community is affected, say, by drought. Thus, by their nature, social insurance mechanisms should not be based on local pooling of risks, and the safety net should be spread as far as administratively possible.

It is clear, however, that the informational advantages of local provision predominate when there is a need for fine targeting, as with most forms of social assistance. The link with local levels of resources (at the margin) is also clear, with the roots of assistance based on charitable provisions by churches, and the more formalized local provisions based on individual wealth in many Middle Eastern and African countries (see Ahmad, 1991). With financing from higher levels of government at the margin, there is a lower incentive to pay, together with a reduced incentive to target the neediest.

The devolution of certain social expenditure responsibilities, for example, for consumer and enterprise subsidies, as in some of the former centrally planned economies in Eastern Europe and Asia, has contributed to an intractable problem of expenditure and revenue bargaining at lower levels of government. This has degenerated into a loss of control over such expenditures, together with an increase in the associated overall deficit. An attempt to introduce a degree of control, by moving to matching earmarked grants, has had a regressive impact, because the system of price and enterprise subsidies is more heavily concentrated in the cities. Moreover, the matching ratios for central grants can be as high as two, and poorer provinces are often unable to comply with the high cofinancing requirements.

Education

Education represents a classic case of conflicting goals and different levels of assignment. Significant cross-country differences can be found between the provision of preschool, primary, secondary, tertiary, and higher levels of education, although standardized information is not available.

In most countries, primary education is supplied free. More developed countries also provide free secondary education and heavily subsidize higher education. The question of why governments choose to subsidize education is not simple. In the first instance, education does not possess the characteristics of a pure public good. Educational benefits mostly accrue to the recipients by increasing their human capital and therefore increasing their expected lifetime income. No strong evidence suggests that the private rewards to education are less than the productivity gain to society and, indeed, private education is to be found at all levels in most countries. The difficulty is that the poor usually have limited access to private education, because of imperfect capital markets and information. Thus, ensuring that low-income persons have at least a minimal level of education is an excellent way of redistributing income. Moreover, the poor in general have a higher discount rate than that of society, and the present value of the future income through education is greater for society than for the poor.

There is thus a prima facie case for public provision of education, although this often coexists with private provision. Education may have to be compulsory since there are private costs involved, for example, the loss of income from child labor, or the reduction in unpaid family services performed by children. Such private costs apply in all countries.

Primary and secondary education is normally administered by the local (that is, municipal) governments. University education is often more centralized to take advantage of economies of scale. There is little question that local administration of primary schools is desirable, although in larger countries there may be diseconomies associated with small-scale operations. First, by definition education services have to be geographically spread out. Second, smaller schools generally provide higher-quality education, although this may be achieved at a higher cost. Third, the direct involvement of parents in schools is observed to be a beneficial determinant of school quality. This benefit can only be achieved through decentralization of administration, as well as local monitoring. Jimenez and others (1988) found that the quality of primary education in the Philippines was higher in localities with higher local participation and monitoring. Despite the desirability of local administration, cost differentials across regions may be substantial. If these differences are due to unavoidable spatial or demographic factors, additional financial support from the central government may be justified.

At the same time, the distributional implications of the quality of education are substantial. Decentralization of financing, as observed in the United States, leads to large differences in educational institutions. Per capita education expenditures in the United States diverge widely in certain geographical regions, leading to a perpetuation of income differences across generations. Most societies consider inequality of educational services unfair. Thus, many societies find it desirable to decentralize control of state-supported schools, while at the same time taking steps to ensure that some minimal quality standards are obtained. In addition, a highly educated population is widely viewed as an important means of promoting development. Therefore, for allocation as well as distributional reasons, the entire nation should be interested in ensuring a minimum educational standard.

The methods used to promote minimum educational quality vary widely among countries. In some, the education program is centralized, with school costs paid entirely by the central government, such as France and Italy. However, at the same time, the staff of schools are required to react to the needs and desires of students and parents. In other countries, schools are effectively supported almost entirely by grants, for example, the United Kingdom. In this case, minimum standards are assured along with local administration, but financed by a block grant. In other circumstances, local financing is supplemented with grants based on needs, although (as with health care in Italy) the respective levels of need and associated responsibility may open up possibilities of bargaining between different levels of government.

Health

Health care affords an interesting example of the interrelationships between public and private provision and the different levels of government at which the public provision would be most effective. Public health facilities, including preventive and diagnostic care, tend to be provided primarily at the local (or municipal) level. Public health facilities and the prevention of communicable diseases have a pure public good characteristic and are best provided by higher levels of government (provinces in some countries or the central government). Curative facilities, particularly at the hospital and specialized levels, have associated economies of scale and are most appropriately provided at higher levels—regions, provinces, or the center, depending on institutional arrangements. Many of these facilities can be provided by private agents, although overlapping insurance and provision can greatly add to overall costs, and to ensure equity, a system of referrals for the poor needs to be devised. As with other forms of mixed provision, the types and forms of health care provision vary widely.

There is a trend toward decentralizing much of health care provision to lower levels of government, although there have been serious problems both with implementation and financing. Managerial ability at the local level is often in short supply (Mills, 1990). In many cases, financing and supervisory mechanisms have had to be reevaluated following decentralization. For instance, Nigeria implemented a National Health Policy in 1988, emphasizing primary health care and secondary facilities to be administered and financed by state and local governments, with the federal government retaining responsibility for teaching and specialty hospitals. Given that shared revenues and grants formed the basis of much of state and local revenues, increasing costs forced a revision in the amounts allocated primarily to local authorities.

The interactions of financing and local provision are seen most clearly in China. Until the late 1970s, preventive and primary health care (for example, with the "barefoot doctors") was organized and financed by localities and communes with remarkable success. The nature of mortality and morbidity in China changed from the typical developing country pattern (with parasitic and infectious diseases predominating) to one associated with middle- and higher-income countries and a virtual eradication of parasitic diseases (see Ahmad and Hussain, 1991). The economic reforms led to a substantial degeneration of the primary health care system and a reliance on payments for services, even for the inoculation of children. Rising incomes, soaring fees, and medicine costs have led to a spiraling cost of health care. At the same time, many of the poor who cannot afford the costs of health care are now effectively excluded from coverage. With the neglect of preventive care, morbidity rates have recently risen for some infectious diseases, such as typhoid and hepatitis, particularly in poorer regions (see Yu Dezhi, 1992). Attempts to introduce private insurance mechanisms in rural areas and in cities suggest that costs per head remain high, and that these mechanisms are applicable mainly in richer areas. Health care services in poorer regions depend crucially on central government transfers, given limitations on own resources of local governments.

Difficulties with financing health care can also be found in industrial countries, such as the United States, where the provision of private care is costly, and large groups of the population are excluded from basic coverage. At the other extreme, the Italian case reflects difficulties with a universal system of multilevel provision, almost entirely financed by transfers from the center until 1993. The central government determines allocations across regions, as well as the establishment of minimum service levels that lower tiers of government are obliged to provide. However, the expenditure norms of the central government's "guaranteed uniform level" are fraught with considerable ambiguity, leading to ad hoc provisions and an erosion of control. Attempts to restrict funding have either led to a lowering of the quality of service or to considerable expenditure overruns.

Without an objective definition of "minimum standards," together with a hard-budget constraint on the local authorities and effective auditing of local and regional expenditures, health care deficits in Italy are likely to continue into the future. Complete centralization, as in the United Kingdom and France, may not provide a full answer. Supervision and associated informational requirements may remain costly, and any attempt to provide a basic minimum is likely to result in implicit rationing and queues. The United Kingdom has experimented with the introduction of competition with respect to supply. The Dutch reforms of their health care system addressed the issue of market structure more than decentralization: maintaining free diagnostic and primary care at the local level, but introducing a greater reliance on market forces for curative care. A system of referrals has been instituted to ensure equity, and government regulations are maintained with respect to quality and cost controls.

The choice of the appropriate level of administration for health care thus depends crucially on the type of service: preventive and public health clearly being provided best at the local level. Others depend crucially on the administrative capabilities of the country, as well as the financing arrangements.

Concluding Remarks

Control of overall expenditure levels is important in a successful macroeconomic strategy. This chapter has attempted to show that this control is not contingent on the actual administration of expenditure functions by the central government, but rather on the adoption, within a system of intergovernmental fiscal relations, of financing mechanisms that provide appropriate incentives for control. Indeed, countries with centralized administration of certain expenditure functions are as prone to loss of macroeconomic control as those in which the administration is decentralized. However, it is also the case that decentralized administration, with poorly defined policy goals and lax financing mechanisms, almost invariably leads to a loss of macroeconomic control. Overall expenditure control, rather than the allocation of responsibilities, would appear to be of most concern from the macroeconomic perspective.

The other main conclusion of this chapter is that the observed wide variety of expenditure assignment patterns reflects varying social preferences among countries—coupled with little theoretical guidance regarding the costs and benefits of decentralization—particularly for mixed goods such as social protection, education, and health. Smaller, decentralized governments have the advantage of being more flexible, administratively simpler, and often able to more closely react to what local residents want. A major disadvantage of decentralization is that its redistributive implications at times lead to unacceptable regional disparities of income. Furthermore, differing social policies can unleash undesirable and inefficient mobility incentives that have contributed at times to an impoverishment of central cities (for example, Washington, D.C.), as persons in need of economic assistance are attracted to relatively more generous localities while high-income families and many businesses are repelled by the steep tax rates needed to support expensive social benefits. Using intergovernmental grants to allow centralized financing along with local expenditure administration is not an entirely satisfactory solution. Some of the advantages of decentralization are lost by such arrangements, as intergovernmental systems can become excessively complicated and nontransparent and can generate their own allocative inefficiencies through fiscal illusion.

These findings imply that substantial reshuffling of expenditure responsibilities, as a means to improving macroeconomic management, is seldom warranted. Existing intergovernmental institutions could generally be retained and reforms should concentrate on ensuring compatibility of expenditures and financing. This will then allow public reforms in the area of public expenditure policy and management to focus attention on more fundamental issues: improving the efficiency of the overall expenditures, increasing administration efficiency, and designing programs that generate little negative economic incentives, including corruption.

There are striking gaps in the information base on expenditure responsibilities and outcomes, even for heavily researched countries, such as Brazil and India. In order to evaluate expenditure programs at each level of government, data should be available on state and local expenditures classified into meaningful functional and economic categories, and on different types of grants and borrowing arrangements at each level of administration. Such information is seldom readily available. Thus, a major effort should be initiated to generate the necessary data at lower levels of government. Such information would help to establish expenditure priorities, to evaluate trade-offs at different levels of government, and to pare off unproductive expenditures—making for a more efficient, equitable, and sustainable public sector.

References

Ahmad, Ehtisham, 1991, "Social Security and the Poor: Choices for Developing Countries," *World Bank Research Observer*, Vol. 6 (January) pp. 105–27.

———, Jean Dreze, John Hills, and Amartya Sen, eds., 1991, *Social Security in Developing Countries* (Oxford: Clarendon Press).

Ahmad, Ehtisham, and Athar Hussain, 1991, "Social Security in China: A Historical Perspective," *Social Security in Developing Countries*, ed. by Ehtisham Ahmad, Jean Dreze, John Hills, and Amartya Sen (Oxford: Clarendon Press).

Bird, Richard M., 1986, *Federal Finance in Comparative Perspective* (Toronto: Canadian Tax Foundation).

Brennan, Geoffrey, and James M. Buchanan, 1980, *The Power to Tax: Analytical Foundations of a Fiscal Constitution* (Cambridge, England: Cambridge University Press).

Brosio, Giorgio, 1985, "Fiscal Autonomy of Non-Central Government and the Problem of Public-Spending Growth," in *Public Expenditure and Government Growth*, ed. by Francesco Forte and Alan Peacock (Oxford: Blackwell).

———, D.N. Hyman, and W. Santagata, 1980, "Revenue Sharing and Local Public Spending: The Italian Experience," *Public Choice*, Vol. 35, No. 1, pp. 3–15.

Buchanan, James M., 1975, *The Limits of Liberty* (Chicago: University of Chicago Press).

Chelliah, R.J., M.G. Rao, and T.K. Sen, 1992, "Issues Before the Tenth Finance Commission," *Economic and Political Weekly*, Vol. 27 (November 21), pp. 2539–50.

Gerber, Robert I., and Daniel P. Hewitt, 1987, "Decentralized Tax Competition for Business Capital and National Economic Efficiency," *Journal of Regional Science*, Vol. 27, No. 3, pp. 451–60.

Gordon, Roger H., 1983, "An Optimal Taxation Approach to Fiscal Federalism," *Quarterly Journal of Economics*, Vol. 98 (November), pp. 567–86.

Gramlich, Edward M., 1979, "Intergovernmental Grants: A Review of the Empirical Literature," in *The Political Economy of Fiscal Federalism*, ed. by Wallace E. Oates (Lexington, Massachussets: Lexington Books).

Hewitt, Daniel, 1986, "Fiscal Illusion from Grants and the Level of State and Federal Expenditures," *National Tax Journal*, Vol. 39 (December), pp. 471–83.

———, 1991, "Transfers to Local Governments," in *Public Expenditure Handbook*, ed. by Ke-young Chu and Richard Hemming (Washington: International Monetary Fund).

———, and Dennis Heffley, 1989, "Unfolding the Flypaper: The Effects of Intergovernmental Grants in an Open Local Economy," IMF Working Paper 89/58 (Washington: International Monetary Fund).

Hewitt, Daniel, and Dubravko Mihaljek, 1992, "Fiscal Federalism," in *Fiscal Policies in Economies in Transition*, ed. by Vito Tanzi (Washington: International Monetary Fund).

Jimenez, Emmanuel, Vicente Paqueo, and Ma. Lourdes de Vera, 1988, "Does Local Financing Make Primary Schools More Efficient? The Philippine Case," PPR Working Paper WPS 69 (Washington: World Bank).

Levin, Jonathan, 1990, "Measuring the Role of Subnational Governments," in *Public Finance with Several Levels of Government*, ed. by Rémy Prud'homme (The Hague: Foundation Journal Public).

Logan, Robert R., 1986, "Fiscal Illusion and the Grantor Government," *Journal of Political Economy*, Vol. 94 (December), pp. 1304–18.

Mieszkowski, Peter, and George Zodrow, 1989, "Taxation and the Tiebout Model: The Differential Effects of Head Taxes, Taxes on Land Rents, and Property Taxes," *Journal of Economic Literature*, Vol. 27 (September), pp. 1098–1146.

Mills, Anne, ed., 1990, *Health System Decentralization: Concepts, Issues and Country Experience* (Geneva: World Health Organization).

Mueller, Dennis C., 1989, *Public Choice II* (New York: Cambridge University Press).

Musgrave, Richard A., 1959, *The Theory of Public Finance: A Study in Public Economy* (New York: McGraw-Hill).

Oates, Wallace E., 1985, "Searching for Leviathan: An Empirical Study," *American Economic Review*, Vol. 75 (September), pp. 748–57.

———, and Robert M. Schwab, 1988, "Economic Competition Among Jurisdictions: Efficiency Enhancing or Distortion Inducing?" *Journal of Public Economics*, Vol. 35 (April), pp. 333–54.

Okun, Arthur M., 1975, *Equality-Efficiency: The Big Trade-Off* (Washington: Brookings Institution).

Pisany-Ferry, J., 1991, "Maintaining a Coherent Macro-Economic Policy in a Highly Decentralized Federal State: The Experience of the EEC," paper prepared at the OECD Conference on Fiscal Federalism in European Economies in Transition (Paris, April).

Reid, Gary, and D.R. Winkler, "Decentralization and Government Size in Latin America" (unpublished; Washington: World Bank, 1992).

Rizzo, Ilde, 1985, "Regional Disparities and Decentralization as Determinants of Public Sector Expenditure Growth in Italy, 1960–1981," in *Public Expenditure and Government Growth*, ed. by Francesco Forte and Alan Peacock (Oxford: Blackwell).

Tanzi, Vito, "Tax Assignments" (unpublished; Washington: International Monetary Fund, 1994).

Tiebout, Charles M., 1956, "A Pure Theory of Local Government Expenditure," *Journal of Political Economy*, Vol. 64 (October), pp. 416–24.

Winer, Stanley L., 1983, "Some Evidence on the Effects of the Separation of Spending and Tax Decisions," *Journal of Political Economy*, Vol. 91 (February), pp. 126–40.

Yu Dezhi, 1992, "Changes in Health Care Financing and Health Status: The Case of China in the 1980s," Innocenti Occasional Papers, EPS 34 (Florence).

Zax, Jeffrey S., 1989, "Is There a Leviathan in Your Neighborhood?" *American Economic Review*, Vol. 79 (June), pp. 560–67.

3

Tax Assignment

JOHN NORREGAARD

A key issue in the literature on fiscal federalism is the question of how subnational authorities might best be financed. This complex issue has no easy solutions, given the wide variety of systems actually applied in different countries and at different times in specific countries. Although there is no ideal system of financing state or regional and local governments, because every country faces different problems and different perspectives, some basic objectives may provide broad guidelines on how tax assignment can best be carried out. Tax assignment can hardly be looked at in isolation. It is an issue intimately related to the question of expenditure assignments across different levels of government, which was discussed in detail in Chapter 2. Even a carefully designed system of intergovernmental expenditure allocation will not work satisfactorily unless it is supported by an equally well-thought-out financing system, and vice versa.

This chapter focuses on the questions to be addressed when decisions are being made on tax assignment among different levels of government. The term "tax assignment" here describes the level of government responsible for determining the level and rate structure of various taxes, whether their revenue is to be collected or received by that level, or shared with others.

Tax Assignment and Tax Sharing

The general principles of decentralization must guide the assignment of taxes to different levels of government. According to these principles, as laid out in the traditional local finance literature, regional and local governments should ideally fulfill mainly allocational functions by providing services that accrue primarily to the local population, services whose costs the local constituency bears as far as possible. In the same vein, because of the degree of openness of local economies, the literature on fiscal federalism argues in favor of limiting regional and local government roles in economic stabilization, as well as in distributional policies.

In very broad terms, the assignment of funds to local jurisdictions may in principle follow one of three options. The first, and probably least attractive, option assigns all tax bases to local jurisdictions and then requires them to transfer upward part of the revenue to allow the national government to meet its spending responsibilities. As this option may hinder effective income redistribution across the national territory, as well as the effectiveness of fiscal stabilization, it may not represent the most efficient way of raising public resources and may provide inadequate incentives for the local jurisdictions to participate in the financing of the national economy. This system resembles that previously in force in the former Yugoslavia and is somewhat similar to the system of negotiated tax-sharing previously practiced in Russia. The system previously in force in China, generally recognized to have inhibited the government's ability to pursue stabilization policies, had analogous features to this extreme model.

A second option, on the other extreme, is to assign all taxing powers to the center, and then finance subcentral governments by grants or other transfers, either by sharing total revenue or by sharing specific taxes. The main disadvantage of this option is that it completely breaks the nexus between the level of tax revenue collected and the decisions to spend that revenue, which constitute the basic prerequisite for a multilevel governmental system that enhances efficiency. Without this connection, the risk is that fiscal illusion will lead to overprovision of local government services. Also, because of the risk of frequent, discretionary cuts in transfers to local levels of governments, this system could also make it difficult to establish a stable system of service provision at the local level. This kind of system bears some resemblance to that once applied in the former Soviet Union and in Hungary. Substantial grant financing of local governments is still practiced in a number of industrial countries, such as France, Italy, and the Netherlands.

The third broad option is the more normal one of assigning some taxing power to the local jurisdictions, if necessary (that is, if vertical imbalances persist) complementing the revenue raised locally with tax-sharing arrangements or other transfers from the central government. This option leads directly to the question of which taxes should be assigned to local jurisdictions and which taxes should remain the responsibility of the national government (the tax assignment problem). By assigning taxes and thus letting the local jurisdictions bear the tax burden at the margin associated with expenditure decisions, the budgetary actions of local governments will be guided by tax-benefit considerations and will in this way improve economic efficiency.[1]

The tax assignment problem is typically not an either/or problem with a specific tax placed clearly and solely under the responsibility of either the local, the state, or the central government: rather, in reality (for most taxes) a spectrum of different designs exists ranging from full and complete local autonomy to systems with some local discretion and to others with no local autonomy whatsoever. In other words, even if a specific tax, such as an income tax, has been assigned to the local level because it is found to satisfy the criteria for a "good local tax" (see below), it is possible to design the income tax with varying levels of local revenue autonomy. Table 1 illustrates this important point in a very general way by providing a ranking of different tax designs with respect to the degree of autonomy that they leave with the local governments. For the sake of illustration, the table also includes the main non-tax sources of revenues for local governments, although obviously a ranking of this nature can only be broadly indicative.

Complete local fiscal autonomy over revenues requires in principle that local governments can change tax rates and set the tax bases. In many countries, however, the central government either defines local tax bases or sets relatively narrow limits to the capacity of local governments to influence the tax base. In some countries (for example, Norway), the central government also sets out limits to the possible variation of local government tax rates.

Taxes assigned to lower levels of government may take the form of own taxes (sometimes referred to as tax separation systems), defined as taxes accruing solely to lower levels of governments, which can determine the rate and, in some cases, also have some autonomy to influence the tax base. An alternative system is represented by overlapping taxes (sometimes called piggybacking systems of local taxation) with the same (or almost the same) tax base for the different levels of government, but with the right of each level of government to set its own tax rate on that common base. This is the system of personal income taxes applied in, for example, the Nordic countries. In Canada, the income tax system used by the provinces involves levying the tax as a percentage of the federal tax revenue accruing within each province. As op-

---

[1]This assumes that there are no substantial externalities associated with the provision of local services, that the tax cannot be shifted to other jurisdictions, and that an efficient equalization scheme is in place.

Table 1. Fiscal Autonomy in Subcentral Governments

Own taxes	Base and rate under local control.
Overlapping taxes	Nationwide tax base, but rates under local control.
Nontax revenues	Fees and charges. Generally, the central government specifies where such charges can be levied and the provisions that govern their calculation.
Shared taxes	Nationwide base and rates, but with a fixed proportion of the tax revenue (on a tax-by-tax basis or on the basis of a "pool" of different tax sources) being allocated to the subcentral government in question, based on (1) the revenue accruing within each jurisdiction (also called the derivation principle) or (2) other criteria, typically population, expenditure needs, and/or tax capacity.
General purpose grant	Subcentral government share is fixed by central government (usually with a redistributive element), but the former is free to determine how the grant should be spent; the amounts received by individual authorities may depend on their tax efforts.
Specific grants	The absolute amount of the grant may be determined by central government or it may be "open-ended" (that is, depend on the expenditure levels decided by lower levels of government), but in either case central government specifies the expenditure programs for which the funds should be spent.

posed to tax separation systems, a system of overlapping taxes may involve administrative advantages with regard to assessing the base and to tax collection. This, however, may be at a potential cost of reduced transparency as the tax levied at each level of government may be less easily identifiable for the taxpayers.

Some, in particular federal, countries prescribe in their constitution the system of tax assignment to be applied. Thus, in India, the Constitution prevents overlapping tax powers so that one type of tax can be levied by only one level of government. Likewise, the modalities of local government taxing powers are specified in the Constitutions of Nigeria and Brazil. In Switzerland, the federal government is prohibited by law from imposing indirect taxes, whereas in Australia a similar rule applies for the states.

The question of local fiscal autonomy may be considered almost completely independent from the question of who actually administers and collects the tax. The allocation of these tasks should be determined on the basis of where they can be carried out most efficiently, although one consideration may be that local accountability may be encouraged if the tax is assessed and collected locally.

Probably the single most critical issue in the discussion of subcentral fiscal autonomy, when looked at from the tax side, is whether the authorities concerned can determine their own tax rates. It could be argued that the case for local discretion, as far as the tax base is concerned, should be limited, because changing tax base definitions (for example, by allowing local governments to set individually the amount of a basic allowance, to introduce special tax reliefs, or to exempt specific sources of income or groups of taxpayers) could lead to distortions in the allocation of resources across localities, and also could have important redistributional consequences—an area in which local autonomy is generally believed to be unwarranted. If local governments cannot alter their tax rates, they cannot alter the level of their services in accordance with local preferences. In some countries, subcentral authorities rely mainly on taxes whose rates are fixed by the central government (for example, the countries with extensive tax-sharing arrangements, such as Portugal and Germany) or whose rate is subject to a ceiling. (Norway is a special case in this regard in that all local governments apply the ceiling rate of the local income tax.)

The importance attached to a lack of discretion in local tax policy depends mainly on the role subcentral authorities are supposed to play. To the extent that they are seen mainly as agents, implementing the policies laid down by other tiers of government, their limited autonomy with respect to tax policy would not appear to be serious. In contrast, if they are meant to implement their own expenditure programs and independently set their service levels in accordance with local preferences, their inability to determine tax rates and thus the level of their own revenues is a serious problem owing to the potential conflict between expectations, needs, and wishes of the local population, and the actual revenue potential available to local governments.

The main arguments against providing subcentral authorities with extensive fiscal autonomy center on the risk of increasing economic disparities between areas or localities and alleged restraints on central government macroeconomic control. Administrative simplicity or administrative economies of scale are also used as arguments for centralized taxes with a specific proportion of tax revenues being allocated to subordinate levels of government.

In what follows, the more specific aspects of tax assignment are dealt with by addressing the basic question of which taxes can be considered good candidates for state and local tax sources and which cannot. What characterizes a good local tax?

A Good Local Tax

A good local tax adequately supports a decentralized public expenditure system. The literature on fiscal federalism and local government finance[2] generally suggests that the following criteria and considerations should form the basis for decisions on which taxes can adequately be assigned to the subcentral level and which should remain at the national level.

- To the extent that the tax in question is aimed at, and is suitable for, economic stabilization or income redistribution objectives, it should be left to the responsibility of the central government.
- The base for taxes assigned to the local level should not be very mobile, otherwise taxpayers will relocate from high to low tax areas, and the freedom of local authorities to vary rates will be constrained. For this reason, general consumption taxes are found at subordinate levels of government only where geographical areas are very large (for example, Canada and the United States). Thus, the more mobile a tax base, the greater the presumption to keep it at the national level.
- Tax bases that are very unevenly distributed among jurisdictions should be left to the central government.
- Local taxes should be visible, in the sense that it should be clear to local taxpayers what the tax liability is, thereby encouraging local government accountability.
- It should not be possible to "export" the tax to nonresidents, thereby weakening the link between payment of the tax and services received.
- Local taxes should be able to raise sufficient revenue to avoid large vertical fiscal imbalances. The yield should ideally be buoyant over time and should not be subject to large fluctuations.
- Taxes assigned to the local level should be fairly easy to administer or, in other words, the more important economies of scale in tax administration are for a given tax, the stronger the argument for leaving the tax base for that tax to the national level. Economies of scale may depend on data requirements, such as a national taxpayer identification number and computerization.
- Taxes and user charges based on the benefit principle can be adequately used at all levels of governments, but are particularly suitable for assignment to the local level, inasmuch as the benefits are "internalized" to the local taxpayers.

This set of broad criteria translates into more specific recommendations regarding which taxes should be assigned to different levels of government, that is, which taxes may be considered good local taxes

---

[2]For general expositions of the principles of fiscal federalism, see Oates (1972) and King (1984).

and which should be left in the domain of the central government. It is generally acknowledged in the literature[3] that the most obvious candidates as good local taxes are land or property taxes and, to some extent, personal income taxes. With some exceptions, turnover or consumption taxes, as well as taxes on capital income, in particular corporate income taxes, are generally considered less appropriate at the local level and in some cases also at the state level[4] because of the mobility of the corresponding tax bases. This broad conclusion derived from principles of local finance seems in very general terms to conform to the financing system actually found in most countries.

The following discussion addresses these questions on a tax-by-tax basis and is intended to cover all the main taxes to which tax assignment is applied in practice (disregarding whether these taxes according to the general principles are considered appropriate at subordinate levels of government or not). The treatment of the different taxes is also intended to be in descending order of importance for subordinate level of governments, although this ordering must necessarily be somewhat subjective (see Tables 2 and 3).[5]

Property Taxes

Property taxes, including in particular land taxes, have historically been widely used as subcentral taxes without any special regard to their alleged incidence. This is the outcome of the perceived advantages of the property tax as a local tax. With a property tax it is always clear which authority is entitled to the revenue it yields, which is not always so for income taxes and other taxes. Administration costs are generally found to be lower for a property tax (provided that there is a registry of properties with updated values) than for an income tax, which requires complex tax returns. The yield of a property tax can be predicted more accurately than for an income tax or a profits tax. Finally, some of the tax will be levied on businesses, which seems reasonable to the extent that businesses derive benefits from subcentral services, such as roads and other infrastructure services.

---

[3]See in particular King (1984), Musgrave and Musgrave (1980), and Oates (1972).

[4]Unless the areas in question are large as is the case in, for example, Canada and the United States.

[5]As illustrated in Tables 2 and 3, the importance of different tax sources varies considerably across countries. Based on more comprehensive information than that presented here, there seems to be a broad tendency for income taxes at subordinate levels of government to increase in importance with increasing level of development, although there are some exceptions to this rule.

Table 2. Distribution of Tax Revenue Among Different Levels of Government

		Total tax			Income tax		
Country and Year	Tax as Percentage of GDP	Central government	State government	Local government	Central government	State government	Local government
Industrial countries							
Federal							
Australia (1991)	30.6	79.7	16.9	3.5	100.0	0.0	0.0
Canada (1989)	34.9	50.9	40.2	8.9	63.5	36.5	0.0
Germany (1991)[1]	41.4	73.4	19.7	6.9	39.1	40.8	20.1
Spain (1990)	34.0	87.0	4.8	8.2	92.9	1.2	6.0
United States (1991)	27.7	65.8	20.5	13.8	81.1	17.1	1.7
Unitary							
Belgium (1990)[1]	45.6	95.6	n.a.	4.4	90.9	n.a.	9.1
France (1991)[1]	43.1	90.5	n.a.	9.5	100.0	n.a.	0.0
Netherlands (1991)[1]	48.5	97.3	n.a.	2.7	100.0	n.a.	0.0
Norway (1990)	45.2	78.8	n.a.	21.2	47.6	n.a.	52.4
Sweden (1991)	54.2	69.6	n.a.	30.4	24.7	n.a.	75.3
United Kingdom (1991)[1]	35.8	96.0	n.a.	4.0	100.0	n.a.	0.0
Developing countries							
Federal							
India (1990)[2]	16.5	65.8	34.2	0.0	100.0	0.0	0.0
Argentina (1989)[2]	14.6	60.4	39.6	0.0	34.2	65.8	0.0
Brazil (1991)	24.5	65.0	30.9	4.1	100.0	0.0	0.0
Mexico (1987)	17.8	85.5	11.6	2.9	98.2	1.3	0.6
Unitary							
Hungary (1990)	48.6	92.4	n.a.	7.6	71.9	n.a.	28.1
Poland (1988)	44.6	78.7	n.a.	21.3	75.9	n.a.	24.1
Israel (1990)	34.7	93.1	n.a.	6.9	100.0	n.a.	0.0
Thailand (1990)	19.7	95.6	n.a.	4.4	100.0	n.a.	0.0
Chile (1988)	20.5	96.2	n.a.	3.8	100.0	n.a.	0.0
Kenya (1991)	23.3	98.3	n.a.	1.7	100.0	n.a.	0.0
South Africa (1990)	27.4	94.5	1.2	4.3	100.0	n.a	0.0
Zimbabwe (1986)	31.3	96.4	n.a.	3.6	100.0	n.a.	0.0

Source: International Monetary Fund, *Government Finance Statistics Yearbook*.
Note: n.a. = not applicable.
[1]Includes supranational authorities' share of general government total tax revenue for Belgium (1.5 percent), France (0.7 percent), Germany (0.9 percent), the Netherlands (1.4 percent), and the United Kingdom (1.2 percent).
[2]Data for general government do not include local government.

An additional argument for the use of property taxes is that, while almost all residents pay directly or indirectly (through rents) the property tax, thus avoiding free-rider problems in local service provision, this is not always the case for local income taxes. It has also been argued that property taxes are guided by the benefit principle of taxation to the extent that the corresponding spending by local govern-

Corresponding General Government Tax								
Property tax			Domestic taxes on goods and services			Other taxes		
Central government	State government	Local government	Central government	State government	Local government	Central government	State government	Local government
2.4	57.8	39.8	72.5	27.5	0.0	45.2	54.8	0.0
0.0	16.2	83.8	40.1	59.4	0.4	60.0	32.4	7.6
2.0	61.2	36.8	79.1	20.8	0.1	100.0	0.0	0.0
5.8	50.5	43.7	81.1	5.7	13.2	99.2	0.0	0.8
6.0	6.7	87.3	16.0	68.3	15.7	97.8	2.2	0.0
100.0	n.a.	0.0	97.0	n.a.	3.0	99.1	n.a.	0.9
100.0	n.a.	0.0	100.0	n.a.	0.0	81.9	n.a.	18.1
65.1	n.a.	34.9	100.0	n.a.	0.0	96.3	n.a.	3.7
37.9	n.a.	62.1	99.6	n.a.	0.4	97.5	n.a.	2.5
100.0	n.a.	0.0	100.0	n.a.	0.0	100.0	n.a.	0.0
99.2	n.a.	0.8	100.0	n.a.	0.0	81.6	n.a.	18.4
33.7	66.3	0.0	49.2	50.8	0.0	88.9	11.1	0.0
49.2	50.8	0.0	85.8	14.2	0.0	61.0	39.0	0.0
2.2	40.5	57.3	37.9	57.8	4.3	94.2	5.3	0.5
1.2	0.0	98.8	99.8	0.1	0.1	5.8	77.0	17.2
100.0	n.a.	0.0	100.0	n.a.	0.0	100.0	n.a.	0.0
48.3	n.a.	51.7	85.8	n.a.	14.2	78.5	n.a.	21.5
12.3	n.a.	87.7	100.0	n.a.	0.0	98.3	n.a.	1.7
81.9	n.a.	18.1	92.1	n.a.	7.9	100.0	n.a.	0.0
19.7	n.a.	80.3	96.5	n.a.	3.5	100.0	n.a.	0.0
0.0	n.a.	100.0	99.5	n.a.	0.5	100.0	n.a.	0.0
25.5	n.a.	74.5	96.7	3.3	0.0	100.0	n.a.	0.0
11.5	n.a.	88.5	98.2	n.a.	1.8	98.7	n.a.	1.3

ments benefits local properties by increasing their value. Against this view, it could be held that, although land and existing structures and thus the tax base cannot move in a physical sense, the tax base can do so in a fiscal sense via the capitalization of property taxes *to the extent* that property taxes are not used for purposes viewed as beneficial to property owners.

Table 3. Distribution of Different Taxes Within Different Levels of Government
(In percent)

Country and Year	Central Government				State Government					Local Government				
	Income tax	Property tax	Domestic taxes on goods and services	Other taxes	Income tax	Property tax	Domestic taxes on goods and services	Other taxes	Grants as percentage of taxes plus grants	Income tax	Property tax	Domestic taxes on goods and services	Other taxes	Grants as percentage of taxes plus grants
Industrial countries														
Federal														
Australia (1991)	71.9	0.3	22.8	5.1	0.0	30.1	40.9	28.9	58.8	0.0	100.0	0.0	0.0	29.9
Canada (1989)	59.3	0.0	21.3	19.4	43.1	3.6	39.9	13.3	21.9	0.0	84.6	1.4	14.0	53.7
Germany[1] (1991)	16.1	0.1	31.5	52.4	62.5	6.6	30.9	0.0	19.2	88.2	11.4	0.4	0.0	44.7
Spain (1990)	33.2	0.4	24.7	41.7	7.6	60.9	31.3	0.2	77.0	22.6	31.1	42.7	3.6	43.1
United States (1991)	55.1	1.1	4.1	39.7	37.4	3.9	55.8	2.9	28.9	5.6	75.3	19.1	0.0	47.6
Unitary[2]														
Belgium[1] (1990)	35.1	2.7	25.6	36.7						75.8	0.0	17.2	7.0	62.1
France[1] (1991)	19.1	2.8	30.6	47.5						0.0	0.0	0.0	100.0	44.7
Netherlands[1] (1991)	33.3	2.3	23.7	40.6						0.0	43.9	0.0	56.1	90.2
Norway (1990)	21.5	1.4	44.7	32.3						87.7	8.6	0.7	3.0	45.9
Sweden (1991)	14.4	4.6	35.5	45.5						100.0	0.0	0.0	0.0	21.5
United Kingdom[1] (1991)	39.1	8.5	33.9	18.4						0.0	1.6	0.0	98.4	85.8
Developing countries														
Federal														
India (1990)[3]	18.6	0.5	44.9	36.0	0.0	1.8	89.5	8.7	48.7					
Argentina (1989)[3]	6.1	5.2	17.1	71.5	17.9	8.2	4.3	69.5	0.0					
Brazil (1991)	22.5	0.1	27.9	49.5	0.0	4.3	89.8	5.9	23.3	0.0	45.5	50.6	3.9	77.5
Mexico (1987)	26.5	0.0	72.5	1.0	2.5	0.0	0.4	97.1	3.3	4.4	7.9	2.3	85.4	5.5
Unitary[2]														
Hungary (1990)	21.2	0.1	37.1	41.6						100.0	0.0	0.0	0.0	59.4
Poland (1988)	32.0	2.2	32.0	33.8						37.5	8.7	19.6	34.2	29.8
Israel (1990)	42.4	1.0	39.1	17.5						0.0	96.0	0.0	4.0	50.0
Thailand (1990)	26.2	3.6	45.0	25.1						0.0	17.0	83.0	0.0	32.9
Chile (1988)	30.7	0.5	48.8	20.0						0.0	56.0	44.0	0.0	52.1
Kenya (1991)	29.3	0.0	53.7	17.0	0.0	0.0	100.0	0.0	91.5	0.0	84.2	15.3	0.5	0.0
South Africa (1990)	54.6	1.6	36.6	7.2						0.0	100.0	0.0	0.0	37.5
Zimbabwe (1986)	47.6	0.4	32.8	19.2						0.0	77.4	15.7	6.9	80.8

Source: International Monetary Fund, *Government Finance Statistics Yearbook.*
[1] Includes supranational authorities' share of general government total tax revenue for Belgium (1.5 percent), France (0.7 percent), Germany (0.9 percent), the Netherlands (1.4 percent), and the United Kingdom (1.2 percent).
[2] There are no state governments in unitary countries.
[3] No data on local governments are available.

The main disadvantage of property taxes lies in the fact that they almost universally realize lower amounts than needed. There are many reasons for this, including the fact that it is a very visible tax (and thus politically unpopular), that it is perceived to have unwanted distributional consequences to the extent that the tax is borne by renters and not by owners of property, and that there are problems associated with the measurement of the tax base, including in particular the "correct" valuation of property, and its updating.

Some countries prefer to distinguish between residential property and commercial and industrial property, with the former being assigned to local taxation, and the latter either to local taxation with a uniform rate or to national taxation only (as is the case in some Nordic countries). In this regard, a particularly contentious issue in many countries (whether industrial, developing, or in transition) has been the taxation of agricultural land. In countries with a general income tax (including income from agriculture), a tax on land could be seen as a discriminatory surcharge on a basic factor input in one sector of the economy, rather than a local benefit tax. In countries without an income tax on agriculture, it has been argued that a land tax on agriculture impedes the development of this important foreign exchange earning sector. Whatever the merits of these arguments may be, the relatively modest tax burden on agriculture found in most countries (which is generally independent of the level of development of the countries in question) seems to reflect the political influence of this sector rather than economic principles or sound fiscal policies.

Other countries apply alternative criteria for the assignment of property taxes to different levels of government. In Brazil, for example, urban property is taxed at the municipal level, while the federal government levies and administers the tax on rural property.

More specifically, at least four important issues relate to the definition and measurement of the base upon which property taxes are levied: the coverage of the base, the use of capital or rental values, the number and nature of exemptions, and the frequency and methods of updating property values. The main issue regarding coverage has been whether land, improvements to land, and buildings should all be subject to tax. The systems applied vary substantially between countries, although most of the countries for which information is available include the unimproved value of land, the value of land improvements, and usually also the value of buildings. The efficiency and equity implications of property taxes have been intensively debated in the literature and will not be pursued further here (see McLure (1977) for an overview of the issues).

In principle, the impact of using rental values or capital values should be the same, assuming well-functioning property and capital markets. It has been argued, however, that there may be major differences in the actual outcome to the extent that rental values reflect mainly the current use of the property, while capital values are said to reflect the value of the property in the best alternative use. Also in this regard, actual methods vary between countries. Capital values are generally based upon market values, although some countries apply corrections to these market values (for example, use a specific proportion of the market value).

Most countries apply a large number of different reliefs under the property tax, for example, in the form of exemption of government property, highways, railways, and other transport or communication facilities, and mining, agriculture, and forestry industries. The subsidies implicit in this kind of treatment, not least with respect to agricultural land, have been increasingly criticized in a number of countries. As indicated above, many countries apply different tax treatment to residential and business property, with residential property usually subject to a more favorable treatment.

A particularly contentious problem in a number of countries has been the frequency and method used to update property values. Thus, in most developing countries, assessment of property values and updating seem to be the major issues. The unpopularity of this type of tax may in some countries be associated with infrequent updates of values, leading to large and abrupt increases in tax liabilities when updating actually takes place. Although property valuations are generally based on market prices, problems are also encountered during certain periods and in areas with modest turnover of property. State and central governments usually perform the valuation of property in order to achieve the necessary coordination between different areas, but the way in which and frequency with which it is done vary substantially across countries.

Although most of the revenue from property taxes generally accrues to subcentral levels of government, state or local governments do not always have complete discretion over the base or the rate. Central governments typically set the rules governing valuations and their frequency and determine exemptions and other reliefs. Also, the central government may impose restrictions on the variations in property tax rates. In practice, local government discretion may be limited in other ways, for example, in the form of earmarking of property revenues, or if higher rates adversely affect grants (as in the United Kingdom before 1989). In Italy, the central government sets a minimum rate for the property tax. If a municipality does not apply the floor rate, transfers to it from the central government are supposed to be reduced correspondingly. Thus, although most of the revenue from property taxes primarily accrues to subcentral authorities in most countries, the respective central governments are generally heavily involved in formulating and administering the provisions of the taxes.

Personal Income Taxes

Most countries assign all or a large proportion of personal income taxes to the central government. Exceptions include the Scandinavian countries, Switzerland, the Baltic countries, Russia, and the other countries of the former Soviet Union. Generally, there are advantages as well as disadvantages of using personal income taxes at the subcentral level. Among the advantages is the fact that personal income taxes generally are buoyant and thus capable of raising the necessary revenue, and in addition they are believed not to fall on businesses, thereby avoiding the risk of subcentral authorities, anxious to attract new industry, indulging in tax-cutting competitions with adverse effects on services provided.

One of the main disadvantages of a local income tax as the main revenue raiser is the fact that, depending on the level of the tax threshold, many people may not pay the tax, although they receive local services.[6] This could have an adverse impact on the way a decentralized system works and has been used as an argument for supplementing an income tax with other tax sources, thereby including the majority of the local constituency in the local tax net. In this regard, two schools of thought may be distinguished. First, many countries (including, for example, most Mediterranean countries and Austria) seem to place considerable weight on income redistribution and on making income tax systems easy to administer by setting a high tax threshold, thereby excluding a large proportion of the population from the tax net. In contrast, other countries (such as New Zealand, Switzerland, and the Scandinavian countries) generally put more emphasis on the inclusion of most of the population in the tax net by setting relatively low tax thresholds, so that more people share the cost of public services.

In the context of financing local governments, there seems to be a case for making a distinction between schedular and global income taxes, since schedular income taxes can in some cases be used by local jurisdictions without great difficulties, in particular if the taxes on, for example, interest income, dividend income, and wages and salaries are withheld at source and constitute the final tax paid. However, the more developed is a country, the higher is the likelihood that individuals re-

---

[6]In some countries, such as Finland and Norway, the income tax threshold in the local tax is much lower than in the central government income tax.

ceive income from different sources, and furthermore that these incomes are derived from different jurisdictions. This may move countries to prefer a global income tax system in which the different income sources are added together for each individual and the tax liability is adjusted according to individual circumstances.[7] For such a system to work well at the local level, it requires flows of information on personal income received from other jurisdictions and thus poses the risk of tax evasion. Against this background, it may be better to leave a global income tax base with the national government, which is in a better position to acquire the necessary information.

However, such a system can be combined with revenue sharing, such as is the case in India, where the states receive about 85 percent of total income tax revenue, allocated on the basis of population, tax effort, and a measure of backwardness. In Brazil, 44 percent of the income tax revenue is transferred to lower level governments under a tax-sharing arrangement, and in Poland, in 1992, 15 percent of the personal income tax revenue was shared with local governments. As part of a recent reform of intergovernmental fiscal relations, shared personal income taxes have also been introduced in Hungary (in 1991, 50 percent of the revenue accrued to local governments). Similar tax-sharing arrangements were also important elements in the financing reform in China in 1980 (under the present financing arrangements, local governments receive all of the yields from personal income taxes).

Notwithstanding these considerations, and to the extent that the administrative capabilities are present at the national level, there is a fairly easy and cost-effective way of taxing a global income tax base in local jurisdictions, namely for the local jurisdictions to use the same statutory tax base as for the national income tax (that is, overlapping taxes or piggybacking). This solution, which reduces administrative as well as compliance cost, is actually used in a number of countries (such as, for example, the Nordic countries and Canada, where the provincial tax is levied as a percentage of the federal tax).[8] However, although it introduces an additional complexity to the tax and thus offsets at least in part some of the administrative savings, some of the countries applying this system (for example, the United States) also use specific tax reliefs in their state and local tax systems. Thus, the extent to which countries using overlapping income taxes coordinate the taxes levied at

---

[7]However, schedular mechanisms such as withholding or minimum contributions may be widely used under a global system for ease of administration.

[8]This particular feature may increase the revenue elasticity of the subcentral tax compared with a normal flat rate system to the extent that subcentral governments will share the gains of any bracket creep effects in the federal tax.

different levels varies considerably. In the Scandinavian countries and Canada, for example, there is a high degree of coordination, while coordination is lacking in Switzerland and the United States.

Generally, because the system requires a fairly advanced administrative system with up-to-date recording of taxpayers' residence, overlapping personal income taxes are generally seen only in developed countries. Combined with an efficient equalization system, such a system is seen, in the countries that apply it, to ensure that variations in tax rates across jurisdictions reflect similar differences in locally determined service levels. Even in industrial countries, however, the administrative recording requirements have been used as an argument against the workability of local income taxes (which, for example, is the case in the United Kingdom).

A special case of overlapping personal income taxes (or partly overlapping income taxes, if some differences in tax bases are allowed) arises when local income taxes, as in the United States, are deductible from federal income tax liability (deductibility is not applied in the majority of countries using overlapping personal income tax systems). The rationale of such a system is the protection it provides for the taxpayer against excessive aggregate marginal tax rates as a result of high local income taxes. An unwarranted side effect may, however, be the incentive for local governments to expand their expenditures, partly financed—at the margin—by nonresidents. It may also reduce the overall level of progressivity of the tax system.

Taxes on income deriving from the activities of small business establishments or from agriculture may often be imposed as efficiently by local governments as national governments, and in some cases local governments may even possess more information than national governments. However, since record keeping by small establishments is often modest or even absent, taxation of such business income has in many cases to rely on presumptive income, based for example on gross sales, on the floor space in which the activity takes place, or on other criteria (for example, in Hungary, the local business tax is levied on the gross turnover of businesses at a maximum rate of 0.3 percent). Taxes on income from small businesses, from self-employed, and from agriculture, with the revenues accruing mostly or solely to local governments, are well known in a number of Central and Eastern European economies in transition, including Poland and Romania, as well as in a number of developing countries, such as India.

Notwithstanding which level of government actually receives the revenue of personal income taxes, practice differs substantially across countries with regard to which level is responsible for the assessment and for the collection of the income taxes at the subordinate level. National or central government responsibility, or—at the most—state responsibility, seems, however, to be the main rule owing principally to the economies of scale involved in the administration of these taxes.

Sales Taxes

The popularity of assigning property taxes—and to some degree also income taxes—to subordinate levels of government is attributable in part to the fact that, with these taxes, differences in tax rates between areas are unlikely to cause serious problems owing to the relative immobility of the tax bases. In contrast, different sales tax rates between different jurisdictions can drive consumers (or rather their purchases) away from high tax areas, as is perhaps best reflected in the serious cross-border trade problems between countries with different tax systems and tax levels (such as between Canada and the United States, and between Ireland and the United Kingdom). A distinction must be made, however, between single-stage sales taxes, such as excises and retail taxes, and multistage sales taxes, such as turnover taxes and value-added taxes (VATs).

Retail sales taxes and excises levied on the final sale to the consumer can be given to local jurisdictions as a revenue source, provided that they do not levy these taxes with highly different tax rates. If they do, citizens will be encouraged to shop in other jurisdictions. The main factors determining the extent to which this will take place are the vicinity of other jurisdictions, the cost of travel, and the value of the goods purchased.[9] Another constraining factor for the use of such taxes at the local level with anything but a modest level of tax rates is the risk of tax evasion, which may be relatively more serious for these (single-stage) sales taxes, especially under high tax rates. However, the existence of, for example, both state and municipal sales taxes in many countries must reflect the fact that these caveats are not universally perceived as serious. Thus, in India, the main revenue source of the states is the sales tax. Turnover taxes and some excises are also important provincial revenue sources in Argentina.

A case can be made for distinguishing between excises on goods, which generally should be assigned to the central level to minimize tax

---

[9]This disregards the problems posed by mail order systems, particularly with regard to the control and setting of tax rates (in the United States, some of these problems have been addressed by applying the rates of the destination states to mail order sales). Although based on a fairly limited sample of countries, Table 3 seems to indicate that the degree of development is also important in this regard, in that there is a tendency for sales taxes to be of larger revenue importance for local governments in developing than in developed countries.

exporting, and excises on selected services, consumed locally, and thus much less prone to tax exporting. Some countries, such as India, assign selected excises to the central government (combined with a tax-sharing scheme), and other excises to state and local governments. A number of countries use local excises or special taxes on automobiles or on fuels, which could be regarded as benefit taxes associated with the costs to local governments of maintaining roads. Municipalities in Brazil are allowed to levy a 3 percent tax on retail sales of fuels and gas. In Poland, own sources of revenue for local governments include a tax on automobiles.

Some countries combine earmarking sales taxes with tax assignment to different levels of government. In Russia, for example, a system of regional and federal road funds is in place, financed in part by excises on fuel and on vehicles, supplemented by taxes on registration and ownership of vehicles.

Sales taxes levied at the manufacturing level should, as a general rule, be assigned to the upper tier of government and to subordinate levels of government only where geographical areas are large.

There seems to be broad albeit not universal consensus in the literature that VATs are most appropriately assigned to the central level of government. This dictum rests on the fairly extensive administrative capabilities required to operate the tax (a requirement that is generally best met by central governments) in combination with the need to make the VAT neutral with respect to the spatial allocation of production and consumption, implying that—generally—the VAT should conform to the destination principle.[10] Implementation of this principle requires, however, border control between jurisdictions if the tax is to be levied by individual provinces or states. This would in most countries be neither feasible nor desirable because of the administrative costs implied and because of the impediments to the free flow of goods and services it would create. In addition, a subnational VAT system would pose problems with regard to which provinces or states should receive the revenues from VAT on imports, and which should bear the burden of VAT refunds on exports.[11] Following this kind of reasoning, comprehensive VATs should be left solely with the national government, as is,

---

[10]Which means that the tax is levied by the jurisdiction in which consumption takes place, independent of the origin of the goods (that is, exports are exempt and imports are liable to tax), as opposed to the origin principle, according to which the VAT is levied by the jurisdiction in which production takes place, that is, interstate exports are taxed and imports are not.

[11]In China and Russia, all import VAT accrues to the federal government, and only domestic VAT revenues are shared with the regions.

in fact, the case in most countries. In some countries (for example, China, Germany, and Russia), central VAT revenues may be shared with subnational levels, although this raises the same kind of problems referred to above, if the tax sharing is based on the derivation principle.

Similar considerations on different aspects of VAT design constitute important elements in the ongoing tax reform discussion in India, which contemplates introducing a comprehensive VAT to replace existing excises and sales taxes, with the aim of sharing the revenue between the three levels of government. However, one of the main questions is whether such a system could function properly without fundamental changes in the present system of intergovernmental fiscal relations in India. According to Bird (1993), it could prove difficult to establish consensus on a formula distributing the VAT proceeds in a context of sharp regional inequalities as the one currently prevailing in that country. Bird also questions the rationale behind sharing the proceeds of any particular tax, because it would seem doubtful that the central government would go through the pain of increasing tax revenues that will accrue in large part to other governments. A more satisfactory alternative—according to Bird—would be to share with the states a fixed share of aggregate central tax revenues.

Brazil offers an example of a VAT assignment system that is generally believed to have had detrimental effects on economic performance. All three levels of government in Brazil are assigned taxing powers on consumption, but with different tax systems, and with the tax covering the widest base, the VAT-type ICMS assigned to state governments and not to the federal government. Furthermore, a large fraction of the federal government consumption tax (the IPI) is transferred to lower levels of governments under a tax-sharing arrangement. This particular design is believed to encourage tax competition between entities of government and to foster tax evasion, which is, furthermore, exacerbated by a large number of different tax rates and exemptions (see Chapter 18 for details).

Corporate Profit Taxes

There seems to be almost universal agreement that the taxation of larger businesses, and in particular corporate profit taxes, should be left to the national level and to provinces or states only where these are very large (as in Canada). This reflects the fact that the economic activities of corporations are typically much more diversified and complex, with factor inputs originating from a number of jurisdictions (and possibly also from abroad), and with sales similarly going to a multitude of jurisdictions. Depending on the nature of the specific markets in question, local taxes on corporate profits would to a large degree be exported or shifted to other jurisdictions in a nontransparent way, thus rendering the associated tax burden almost imperceptible to local citizens. In addition, a high local-tax rate may lead the business entity in question to move the tax base to other jurisdictions, either by physically moving the corporation or by adjusting the internal transfer pricing arrangements.

Leaving the taxation of corporate profits entirely in the hands of local governments would thus create serious informational problems because of the administrative issues associated with the allocation of taxable profits between different jurisdictions in cases of enterprises with economic activity spread over many localities. But also in this case these problems could, at least in part, be overcome by some form of overlapping tax bases between the national and the local level (piggybacking), although the room for tax-rate variations is much smaller for the corporate profits tax than for personal income taxes. In Canada, the base is harmonized to a considerable degree between the provinces and the federal level (although provinces do have the possibility of providing individual investment incentives), while provinces have the flexibility to vary rates. In Brazil, the states can levy a 5 percent surcharge on the corporate income tax.

Some countries have, with the above-mentioned problems in mind, chosen instead to allocate a fixed portion of the profit tax revenue originating within each jurisdiction to the local governments under a tax-sharing arrangement. Thus, Russia allocates 25 percentage points of the 38 percent tax rate on corporate profits to regional governments, while the remaining 13 percentage points remain with the federation.[12] Of the corporate tax revenue in Poland in 1992, 5 percent was shared with local governments. In Nigeria, a special system is in force according to which the federal authority has the legal jurisdiction over the company tax, but the states nevertheless collect the tax and retain the proceeds.

Payroll Taxes

Like VATs and corporate profit taxes, different types of payroll taxes are also generally seen as an appropriate revenue source for the central government only, because different payroll tax rates could drive employers, and jobs, away from high tax areas. In addition, tax exporting is probably significant in the sense that, first, part of the tax may be shifted to prices and thus borne by consumers outside the jurisdiction that receives the revenue, and, second, the tax may be levied on em-

---

[12]Formally, the 25 percent local rate is a maximum, but the large majority of regions are believed to apply the maximum rate.

ployees with residence outside the revenue-receiving jurisdiction. Thus, the tax may not be visible to the local taxpaying constituency, and the relationship may be weak between tax payments and services provided by jurisdictions.[13]

Notwithstanding these general considerations, tax-sharing arrangements for payroll taxes actually exist in a few countries. A relatively small payroll tax is also levied by the states in Australia.

Natural Resource Taxes

Taxes on natural resources are generally perceived as poor candidates for local taxation, since normally the base of these taxes is very unevenly distributed across jurisdictions. In addition, extraction of economic rent from natural resources could be held to be a national prerogative, which should benefit the whole of the nation and not just selected fortunate regions. The taxes in question are also in many cases characterized by a high level of revenue volatility owing to price fluctuations. The associated uncertainty, it could be argued, should be absorbed by the central government, which generally has a number of alternative revenue sources at its disposition, and not by regional or local governments, which are meant primarily to conduct allocative functions (price fluctuations on oil, for example, have created sharp swings in the revenues of states in Nigeria). These theoretical considerations, however, do not take into account the important fact that, in practice, cultural and ethnic differences may be the reason for strong pressures toward regional independence, including regional control over natural resources, as is seen, for example, in Russia.

Alternatively, it could be held that, at least in part, these taxes should be considered as benefit taxes, that is, as payments for the benefits deriving from the provision by local or regional governments of the necessary infrastructure investment without which either exploitation of the natural resources would not be possible, or the return to the investments required could be significantly reduced. In other cases, the taxes may be considered as compensation for the environmental costs associated with the exploitation of natural resources. This might also constitute part of the reason why a number of countries actually operate tax-sharing schemes for natural resource taxation (see country chapters for details). In Russia, local governments in regions rich in natural resources benefit from the retention of a high share of these taxes. Previously, in Nigeria, all taxes accruing from oil production

---

[13]In the majority of countries, provision of regional or local government services is related to the residency of individuals.

went to the states. In Argentina, a revenue-sharing scheme is in place for royalties on mineral extraction.

Import and Export Taxes

Import and export taxes, apart from being generally considered inferior to the taxes dealt with above, should always be imposed by the national government to reduce the possibility of introducing major distortions within the country through differential foreign trade taxes imposed by different jurisdictions. In fact, the large majority of countries assign import duties exclusively to the central government (Nigeria being one exception, with import tax revenue being shared). Nevertheless, in some countries, such as Russia, the formula for sharing important export tax receipts with regions from which the exports originate remains an important tax policy issue (because of the nature of the exports in question, these taxes may as well be considered special cases of taxes on natural resources). India operates a special tax on interstate sales with a maximum rate of 4 percent, and with a number of exemptions (see Chapter 21 for details).

Benefit Taxes and User Charges

In addition to what has been said above about specific sources of taxation, it is generally held that benefit taxes, license fees, and user charges should all be used to the maximum extent feasible at the local level because they are transparent, they minimize the risk of tax exporting, they generally do not involve problems of vertical or horizontal equity, and they increase economic efficiency. Although these charges are significant sources of revenue for the localities, they are generally modest compared with some of the taxes considered above.

Tax Assignment in Practice

A striking feature of the financing of subcentral levels of government is the significant variation in the level and composition of local government taxation across countries. This feature is illustrated in Tables 2 and 3, which for a fairly limited sample of countries show the attribution of total tax revenues to subsectors of general government as percentage of total tax revenue, in federal as well as in unitary countries, and the composition of the tax revenue for each subcentral level of government with respect to different types of taxes (including revenues from the tax-sharing arrangements). These tables by their nature do not indicate the actual degree of state, provincial, or local autonomy over the tax revenues, which, as discussed this chapter, may vary considerably across countries.

Nevertheless, as the tables show, most countries have more than one subcentral tax (although the tables do not distinguish between cases where revenues are solely assigned to the subcentral level and where they are shared under tax-sharing arrangements), and this holds for industrial as well as for developing countries, and for federal as well as for unitary countries. Generally, the personal income tax seems (as expected) to be of greater importance for the subcentral level in industrial countries than in developing countries, although for example in most Anglophone countries the property tax is the dominant tax, especially at the local level (this holds in Australia, Canada, the United States, Ireland, New Zealand, and, until 1990, the United Kingdom).

In some, especially federal, countries, general consumption taxes and in some cases also excises play a considerable role, particularly at the state level (for example, in Austria, Brazil Canada, Germany, India, South Africa, Spain, and the United States). A predominant feature seems to be that these taxes are used by large countries with correspondingly large subcentral areas. Also, in some of these countries, consumption tax systems take the form of tax-sharing arrangements with little or no state or local discretion, as in the case of the Austrian and German VAT.

A common feature not shown in these tables is the dominant use of personal income taxes at the subcentral level as opposed to corporate income taxes, reflecting the fact that corporate income taxes are generally considered unsuitable at the subcentral level owing to the mobility of the tax base.

Although the property tax is among the most popular subcentral taxes, not least in federal industrial countries and unitary developing countries, its revenue measured as a percentage of GDP is generally modest and seldom exceeds about 3 percent. This is probably because it is a highly visible tax, it is hard to evade, there are problems associated with the valuation of property, and it is generally perceived as a regressive tax. For these reasons, the property tax has become increasingly unpopular politically, which may also help to explain why its importance as a revenue source has declined in many countries during the last decade or so.

Concluding Remarks

The theory on fiscal federalism provides some fairly broad guidelines with regard to which taxes can appropriately be assigned to subnational levels of government and which should be kept at the central level. However, although some general patterns in accordance with these guidelines can be identified in country practices, even fairly homogeneous countries at the same level of development have in many cases chosen different solutions to these problems. One of the main reasons for this is that the historical, geographical, ethnic, and constitutional character of each country has profound implications for the range of feasible and efficient tax assignment policies.

Some lessons may nevertheless be drawn from actual country experiences. First is the importance of tax administration: a decentralized fiscal system cannot function satisfactorily without the necessary administrative capabilities at the subcentral level. In other words, the design of tax systems should clearly be adapted to the level and quality of administrative resources that have been found politically appropriate to devote to the subcentral levels of government. Generally, the more complicated the tax in question is made for other reasons (for example, for reasons of revenue or equity), the stronger the argument for placing the tax with a higher or the highest tier of government. As a reflection of this "rule," more complex systems of taxation are generally assigned to subcentral levels of governments only in more developed countries.

Second, in addition to the crucial question of the choice of tax sources at subordinate levels of government, actual experience indicates that a decentralized system will work satisfactorily only if state, provincial, and local governments are given at least one major own source of revenue, that is, a source of revenue over which they have autonomy to determine the revenue (assuming that this system is supported by adequate equalization of tax capacities and expenditure needs). Only then can a multilevel system of government promote accountability and ultimately economic efficiency.

Finally, there are obvious potential gains as well as risks associated with decentralizing taxing powers. The gains include improved mobilization of revenue sources and the potential efficiency gains alluded to above. The risks take the form of leaving the central government in a more vulnerable position with respect to its ability to conduct effective fiscal policies, especially for stabilization purposes.

References

Bird, Richard M., 1993, "Tax Reform in India," *Economic and Political Weekly*, Vol. 28 (December 11), pp. 2721–26.

King, David N., 1984, *Fiscal Tiers: The Economics of Multi-Level Government* (London: Allen & Unwin).

———, 1992, ed., *Local Government Economics in Theory and Practice* (London: Routledge).

McLure, Charles E., Jr., 1977, "The 'New View' of the Property Tax: A Caveat," *National Tax Journal*, Vol. 30, No. 1, pp. 69–75.

Musgrave, Robert A., and Peggy B. Musgrave, 1980, *Public Finance in Theory and Practice* (New York: McGraw-Hill).

Oates, Wallace E., 1972, *Fiscal Federalism* (New York: Harcourt Brace Jovanovich).

Tanzi, Vito, 1996, "Fiscal Federalism and Decentralization: A Review of Some Efficiency and Macroeconomic Aspects," in *Annual World Bank Conference on Development Economics, 1995* (Washington: World Bank).

4

Intergovernmental Transfers

EHTISHAM AHMAD AND JON CRAIG

The revenue and expenditure assignments discussed in the preceding chapters normally give rise to vertical and horizontal imbalances within a nation's intergovernmental finances. A vertical imbalance occurs when the own revenues and expenditures of various levels of government within a federation are unequal. A horizontal imbalance occurs when the own fiscal capacities of various subnational governments of the same level differ. These imbalances must be resolved through a variety of transfer and borrowing mechanisms in order to allow the various levels of government to perform their allotted tasks within a national policy framework.

There are two basic avenues of transferring resources from one level of government to another: sharing of revenues or a system of grants. Revenue sharing can take several forms: tax bases can be shared, or taxes can be pooled and then shared. Tax administration can be seen separately from tax assignments, and revenues collected at one level of government, typically but not exclusively at the central government level, could be assigned in part or entirely to other levels of governments.

A grants system could involve conditional or unconditional transfers. In turn, these transfers can be open ended, or subject to caps. Moreover, some conditional grants may require matching elements by recipient governments. Each alternative approach is examined in this chapter. The choice of transfer mechanism depends on the particular mix of objectives of the policymakers.

Subnational governments play an increasing role in providing infrastructure and lumpy capital outlays in some countries. Such investments may be financed by capital transfers, and/or net advances from the center which may itself borrow to fund such payments. In some cases, subnational governments may be given direct access to capital markets. Unless such markets are highly developed, and other conditions exist that permit market discipline to be maintained on such borrowing, rules may need to be developed to ensure that the scope of such borrowing is consistent with the overall objectives of national macroeconomic policy.

Vertical and Horizontal Imbalances

The existence of a vertical fiscal gap at different levels of government, arising out of own revenue and own expenditure assignments, provides a basic rationale for a system of transfers and borrowing arrangements. In addition, national governments may wish to ensure that citizens in different regions and localities have access to a certain modicum of publicly provided services. Differential subcentral capacities are said to constitute horizontal imbalances. Differential fiscal capacities leading to horizontal imbalances constitute another rationale for the system of transfers between different levels of government. These objectives give rise to different combinations of grants.

Vertical Balances

The vertical fiscal gap is generated by the expenditure and revenue assignments. However, individual policy choices also play a significant role in determining the resulting ex post vertical gap. If a lower level of government chooses to increase spending or not raise assigned taxes, the vertical gap would increase. Thus, if transfers were designed solely to close the vertical gap, there would be little incentive for the lower levels of government to raise own account revenues or restrict or manage expenditures efficiently. Unless there are objective criteria for the determination of transfers, "gap filling" to finance subnational deficits is likely to lead to macroeconomic difficulties as well as indeterminate "bargaining" between the center and lower levels.

Since vertical balances tend to favor the central government, the *size* of the transfers to subnational levels of government often may be a function of macroeconomic stabilization concerns.

Table 1 shows the vertical fiscal gap for different levels of government in a number of federal and unitary countries' governments. Three measures are shown: the vertical fiscal balance as measured by the difference between the own account transactions at the central or all subcentral levels of government; the vertical current balance, which measures the balance on own account current transactions only; and a

Table 1. Vertical Current Balances[1]
(*Ratio of own source revenues to own source current expenditures*)

	Central			State or regional			Local		
	Overall balance	Current balance	Capital balance	Overall balance	Current balance	Capital balance	Overall balance	Current balance	Capital balance
Federal countries									
Australia	1.45	1.48	18.56	0.53	0.59	-2.77	0.83	1.05	0.44
Brazil	0.78	1.15	-0.33	0.82	1.03	0.13	0.28	0.37	-2.11
Canada	1.05	1.08	5.33	0.88	0.93	-1.47	0.53	0.60	-3.57
Germany	1.03	1.08	1.48	0.96	1.09	0.73	0.75	0.94	-0.08
India	0.76	1.20	0.52	0.59	0.82	0.97	n.a.	n.a.	n.a.
Spain	1.05	1.18	2.22	0.28	0.40	-1.38	0.74	0.97	0.02
United States	0.93	0.97	-0.40	1.24	1.41	2.94	0.66	0.75	-2.05
Unitary governments									
Austria	0.97	1.05	0.67	...	...	...	0.90	1.24	0.66
Denmark	1.54	1.61	10.50	...	...	...	0.57	0.59	-6.12
France	1.02	1.07	1.28	...	...	...	0.64	0.91	-0.18
Netherlands	1.26	1.32	7.68	...	...	...	0.26	0.27	-4.59
Sweden	1.21	1.23	16.56	...	...	...	0.76	0.81	-2.43
United Kingdom	1.23	1.26	9.25	...	...	...	0.45	0.46	-3.16

Source: International Monetary Fund, *Government Finance Statistics Yearbook*, 1993.
Note: n.a. = not available.
[1] The data show average ratios over selected periods for each country. The periods chosen are Australia, 1987–91; Austria, 1987–91; Brazil, 1982–91; Canada, 1985–89 (excluding 1987 for capital balance); Denmark, 1987–91; France, 1988–92; Germany, 1983–91; India, 1985–92; Netherlands, 1988–92; Spain, 1987–90; Sweden, 1988–92; United Kingdom, 1985–92; and United States, 1987–92.

vertical capital balance, which shows the extent to which capital spending is financed from own resources and provides an initial insight into the "need to borrow" by different levels of government.

Horizontal Imbalances

In practice, very few countries measure the horizontal imbalances, or fiscal capacities, of their regional governments in a systematic manner. The federations that undertake a comprehensive review of horizontal balances are Australia, Canada, and Germany.[1] An analysis of relative fiscal capacities of the different states in the United States was also prepared in the past, but is not used in determining transfers to states.[2] Among the unitary nations, Denmark and the United Kingdom evaluate the fiscal capacities of their local government authorities in determining grants.

The horizontal imbalances in fiscal capacity may be addressed by equalization transfers from the center (as in Australia, Canada, and Denmark), or between regions (as in Germany). While some countries do not use an explicit "equalization framework," redistributional elements are often introduced into special purpose or conditional grants in order to achieve equity objectives, such as in Indonesia. However, in the absence of an overall framework for determining and evaluating grants, it is often difficult to ascertain whether conditionality of use, with numerous and diverse special purpose grants, is actually inequality decreasing or increasing (see Ahmad, 1997). Empirical evidence from countries as diverse as Australia, Argentina, Canada, and China suggests that there may be substantial differences across regions within the country in terms of revenue bases, as well as cost of provision of services, and that these may necessitate the use of a consistent framework for evaluating and determining grants.

Policy Options

Three different policy responses can be made to this link between vertical and horizontal balances:
- *Correct each imbalance by separate policy measures.* The vertical imbalance at each level is resolved by tax-sharing or grant arrangements. Horizontal imbalances are then resolved by payments from

---

[1]However, the simple formulas used in the equalization exercises in Germany are not based on detailed region-by-region evaluations of fiscal capacity as in Australia and Canada.

[2]See United States, Advisory Commission on Intergovernmental Fiscal Relations (1995).

regions with higher fiscal capacity to poorer regions. This is the approach used in Germany.
- *Implement an integrated system of equalization grants.* The vertical and horizontal balances are dealt with simultaneously through a system of grants, including equalization payments and special purpose grants. This is the Australian and Canadian approach.
- *Correct only the vertical imbalance and ignore horizontal balances.* As under the first option, vertical balances are resolved by tax sharing and grants, but no action is taken to correct horizontal imbalances. Capital and labor migration then responds, not only to earned income differentials, but also to the regional net fiscal benefits (net benefit received from government expenditure and of taxes paid). There may be, however, special purpose grants servicing central government objectives, which may also reduce horizontal imbalances at least in some functional areas. This is broadly the approach in the United States.

The Rationale for Transfer and Borrowing Mechanisms

If the sole concern of central and subnational governments is to fill the vertical fiscal gap created by imbalances in revenue and expenditure assignments, this could be achieved either by sharing revenue from the major taxes on a "derivation" basis (that is, shared in proportion to the revenue collected in each region), or by "gap-filling" unconditional grants. Both approaches may exacerbate horizontal imbalances, and the latter also generates undesirable incentives for recipient governments that could weaken macroeconomic controls.

In practice, both the central and subnational governments normally have diverse objectives to be met through a system of transfers, and these different objectives may need to be met through a combination of policy tools. Typical central government goals include the following:
- Ensure that the overall fiscal stabilization objectives for the national economy are met.
- Provide an acceptable degree of equity between individuals in different regions.
- Encourage the efficient use of resources across the nation.

These goals and the associated policy responses are discussed below.

Stabilization

Aside from variations in its own account revenue, expenditure, and borrowing operations, the central government has two weapons at its disposal in this area: (1) varying the level of transfers and/or revenue shares to subnational governments, and (2) adjusting subnational borrowing, where the subnational governments have separate, but controlled access to the capital markets.[3] In some countries (for example, Canada), the latter option is not available to central governments. But, even in such cases, its relative size and influence may provide the central government with some leverage in persuading subnational governments to participate in coordinated stabilization efforts.

Since economic downturns often have a varying impact on different geographical areas within a nation, the central government may be expected to adjust both the level and geographical composition of its transfers to subnational governments in an anticyclical manner to assist the stabilization task. To the extent that the central government maintains an ongoing vertical current surplus with subnational governments, it can also draw on these resources to boost, or reduce, aggregate spending.

Equity

The term "equity" is often raised in the political debate on intergovernmental finances, especially in federations, and has a number of interpretations. First, there is the need to examine whether each region has the fiscal capacity to deliver an equivalent level of public services to its citizens. Second, there is a question as to which level of government should have primary responsibility for income redistribution.

Horizontal Equity Issues

Some federations (for example, Australia and Canada), but not all, have adopted extensive equalization arrangements. The arguments for such arrangements can be understood at both an intuitive and theoretical level. At the intuitive level, it can be argued that the creation of a national market place, or "economic space," brings with it large benefits in terms of the production, distribution, and administrative scale economies, including common fiscal and monetary policies, common education, health, production and labor standards, and speedy communication and transport facilities. These benefits can be seen as being over and above those that would be available to any individual region,

---

[3] Such controls may spring from constitutional or legal restraints but often simply reflect a broader recognition by subnational governments of the need for such constraints.

and a "fair" distribution of these benefits is often seen as the glue that bonds together the nation-state.[4]

The public finance literature approaches equalization issues from a different viewpoint. The term "horizontal equalization" traditionally related to governments providing equal treatment of individuals who are equally well off. Application of this concept involved an examination of the so-called fiscal residuum (see above).

The concept of horizontal equalization was used by Buchanan (1950) to justify equalizing measures between regions. The problem can be summarized as follows. Even if a central government treats equals equally, while at the same time each regional government treats individuals within its boundaries equally, the overall impact of public policies within a federation is likely to violate the equal treatment of equals principle. The difficulty stems from that fact that even if two communities, one rich and one poor, have identical levels of public goods provision, the wealthier of the two communities will, ceteris paribus, be able to meet its revenue requirements with a lower level of tax rates. This follows because, for a given amount of revenue for each resident, lower tax rates are required in a community with the higher level of per capita income. Therefore, from the standpoint of the federal system, equals are not treated as equals.

The issue can be handled in two ways. First, it can be ignored. Some argue that such an overall equity goal "is not a prime goal in a federation." Others consider that the horizontal equity goal is inconsistent with regional diversity, which is a virtue of federal systems. But Buchanan and others disagree. They call for measures to compensate for such inequality by geographically discriminating tax rates at the central government level, to equalize the total tax bill of individuals, or to make equalizing grants to communities.

These simple theoretical concepts have been the subject of considerable debate. One major criticism has been that the original models used by Buchanan assumed that the total spending of each government is distributed over the relevant citizens in proportion to an assumed (equal) sharing basis and the resulting money amount is taken as a measure of the total individual benefit. But this approach is probably only relevant in the context of universally provided welfare benefits. In the case of public goods, such as education services, it becomes merely a

---

[4]Of course, the separate regional entities may still enjoy some of the benefits via some sort of confederation by participating in a free trade zone (for example, the European Union and the North American Free Trade Agreement), but those benefits may be less substantial than those of a full federation.

cost imputation exercise and cannot serve as a measure of the individual benefits received.

The equalization concept therefore involves many practical measurement difficulties, since particular individuals may choose not to avail themselves of a particular service or avoid payment of a tax or charge by refraining from the activity concerned. For these reasons, even if two regional governments applied the same revenue-raising and expenditure-provision policies, the fiscal residuum of two equally well off individuals would not necessarily be identical. This situation would continue to apply even if the term "individual" was redefined into some concept of family unit or household. The existence of companies and other organizations further complicates application of the principle. An attempt to tackle the application of the "equal treatment of individuals" would also raise a host of practical measurement difficulties, including measures to determine equality between citizens of different regions. All these factors may combine to make the strict "equal fiscal treatment of equals" a difficult objective in either a federation or a unitary state. However, in some countries, increasing interest is being accorded to direct provision of transfers to individuals, for example, through vouchers financed by the central government. These vouchers often allow public services to be provided by private sector contractors. Such contracting out has led to a reevaluation of the role of the state as a service provider, in many countries, without necessarily changing the nature of the public good.

Nevertheless, it can be argued that a central government can achieve an approximation of the equal treatment of equals objective through transfers to different subnational governments. The aim then is to provide each subnational government with the ability to make available a uniform set of public services at a comparable revenue effort.

Three different practical options might be considered:
- The regional government's capacity to provide regional services without having to impose higher taxes and charges than other regions (or regional budget capacity equalization).
- Comparability of the regional government's capacity to provide equally well-off individuals with equal fiscal residuals (or "individual-based" regional government capacity equalization).
- Uniformity across regions in actual standards of service provision and in actual taxes and charges applied (termed performance-based regional government equalization).

Strictly speaking, the third choice might come closer to the desired theoretical objective. However, its achievement would require the central government not only to make the difficult judgments on relative fiscal needs of different regions, but also to impose detailed and binding conditions on the grants paid to regional governments to ensure that those chosen services and taxation norms are implemented. The second choice avoids the conditionality problem but also encounters major measurement problems.

Of the three objectives, the first method may be more acceptable to many democratically elected governments. While it still faces difficulties in quantifying judgments about publicly provided services and taxes, it avoids the subjective measurement of individual differences implicit in the second choice. The equalization of subnational fiscal capacities is likely to be consistent with the actual abilities of governments to achieve the desired objective of equal treatment of equals.

Each of these approaches has strong advocates, and individual preferences are colored by cultural and historical differences. In the United States, for example, there has been an emphasis on performance equalization, at least in respect of specific purpose transfers for public goods such as education. This was also the case in the former Soviet Union and other centrally planned economies, where absolute expenditure norms were used as a basis for regional allocation of funds. By contrast, Canada, Australia, Germany, Denmark, and a number of other countries have favored systems involving varying degrees of capacity equalization. Australia and Canada employ equalization grants from the center, which have the effect of helping to close the vertical gap, while at the same time at least partially correcting for the horizontal imbalances.[5] Another alternative approach involves transfers between subnational levels of government to close horizontal gaps, as employed in Germany.

It is important to recognize that the equalization approach does not necessarily imply full equalization of living standards (as, for example, measured by GDP per head), since private goods are not directly affected by such grant structures, and because subnational capital investment programs are generally managed separately. Even in respect of public programs, inequalities may remain, because different subnational governments may have different priorities. Some may choose to tax at a higher level and use the funds raised to provide a higher standard of public good, whereas others may have a preference for lower taxes and smaller governments.

Income Redistribution in a Regional Context

It is often argued that the role of redistributing incomes within a multilevel state should reside primarily with the central government.

---

[5]Even in Australia and Canada, it can be argued that the systems employed do not provide full equalization, since they cover only a selected portion of the overall state or provincial budgets.

For some, this judgment reflects a view that common standards of redistribution ought to be applied, regardless of where people reside. A contrary view is that the degree of redistribution is essentially a question of taste and that preferences will differ between regions. Horizontal equalization of the type discussed above may provide each region with a capacity to provide some redistribution (which it may choose to use or not). However, there are clearly limits to such regional income distribution arrangements, since large differentials will tend to be thwarted by fiscally induced migration.

Nonetheless, the expenditure and taxation goals of subnational governments will frequently have redistributive consequences, even where the decisions are based on efficiency criteria. The extent to which subnational governments explicitly engage in redistribution across lower tiers depends on the availability of resources, as well as the need. In the United States, for example, within-state variations in incomes and service levels often exceed across-state variations. Thus, there is a role for state-level redistribution, while the federal government focuses on minimum standards. Moreover, the role of the federal government is being reconsidered, with greater autonomy allocated to the states.

Efficiency

As noted previously, theory suggests that, in the absence of externalities, expenditures should be matched to revenue sources, at the level of government at which the benefit is generated. Unfortunately, the adoption of simple guidelines is complicated by the existence of "externalities" in resource allocation, the so-called spillovers. The term spillover refers to instances where the benefits of a service provided by a subnational government spill beyond its own borders to benefit those not contributing to the cost of providing such services. Often-quoted examples are the cost of control of air or water pollution and the cost of educating students who relocate upon graduation to other regions. In each case, the total value of spending by a subnational government on the activities concerned should not necessarily be fully recouped from the residents of the region. In such circumstances, regional governments may consider only benefits to their own citizens and underprovide public services, hence yielding a case for supplementary central government grants for the given purpose.

"Flypaper Effect"

The so-called flypaper effect is an example of the difficulty of analyzing behavior in a multilevel government where the direct link between taxpayer or voter and the service provided is broken. The concept is based on empirical evidence that grants (or revenue shares) provided from one level of government to another tend to "stick" with the recipient government and be used for service provision, and will not be passed on to taxpayers in the form of lower taxes. As a result, the grant leads to a higher level of service provision than would be the case if the payment was made directly to individuals. To illustrate, take the following example. Region A receives a grant of $1,000,000, unrestricted and without matching requirements, which is used to increase expenditure by $800,000 and to provide tax reductions of $200,000. If the grant had been made directly to the individuals of region A, they may have voted to use only, say, $300,000 to increase services, but $700,000 to reduce taxes. The overprovision, or flypaper effect, is then $400,000. In the case of matching grants, the flypaper effect is measured by comparing the level of the public service if the matching rate were applied to the budget and that which would result if matching rates were applied to individual taxpayers. Empirical estimates suggest that the magnitude of the flypaper effect may be considerable in some countries.[6]

Minimum Standards

In practice, many central governments wish to exert some influence over the minimum standards of service provided at subnational level, which affect both efficiency and equity objectives. These programs are advocated for a variety of reasons, such as:
- The national interest, which is seen as being served by achieving some commonality of standards in particular functions (for example, primary school training or roads) mainly provided by subnational government.
- Greater harmony between the programs of subnational governments.
- The assurance of social objectives, such as a politically acceptable minimum living standard. This standard varies from country to country, covering programs such as Aid to Families with Dependent Children in the United States and access to public services, such as housing, in the United Kingdom and Australia.

Such transfers may have some spillover effect—such as implementation of national standards and/or performance guidelines that benefit business expansion. Furthermore, there may also be a desire to use such programs to promote a more equal treatment of the citizens of the country.

---

[6]Musgrave, Musgrave, and Bird (1984).

Of course, central government intervention is not the only possible response to spillovers, nor need it be the most efficient solution. One alternative, seemingly gaining attraction is for subnational governments to work together to operate regional services, such as railways, which yield benefits beyond their respective economic borders.

Conflicts and Complementarity in Objectives for Transfers

The various objectives outlined above for intergovernmental transfers may not be mutually consistent. Some of the issues that may arise are discussed below.

Stabilization and Equity

One example of conflicting objectives is that between the goals of stabilization and equity. This conflict can arise where revenue or expenditure actions taken by the central government to address stabilization concerns have a differential impact on the fiscal capacities of the subnational governments. For example, an income tax imposed by a central government may act to reduce the income and/or consumption tax bases available to subnational governments in a manner that differentially reduces their individual capacities to raise revenue. Similarly, expenditure cutbacks at the center may affect the expenditure needs of subnational governments in a differential manner.

Equity and Efficiency?

Conflicts may also arise between the efficiency and equity goals. Thus, the use of grants to relieve perceived efficiency problems (for example, conditional grants for education requiring the achievement of minimum standards within certain regions) may conflict with fiscal equity goals. This occurs because such grant arrangements ignore the overall fiscal capacity of a region. It is conceivable, therefore, that a region with a relatively high revenue-raising capacity may receive a relatively large education grant simply because it had chosen in the past to spend relatively less on education and, most probably, enjoy a commensurately lower level of taxation. It is possible to reconcile this potential conflict by designing the grants system within an overall equalization framework (see Appendix).

There has been considerable debate about whether efforts to equalize through intergovernmental grants detract or add to the overall efficiency of the economy. There are two strands to this argument. The theoretical debate on this subject[7] centers on the possibility that, in the absence of equalizing transfers, residents in one region will move to another that exhibits higher net fiscal benefits, and whether this "fiscally induced" migration, in turn, creates economic efficiency costs making the nation as a whole worse off.[8]

Boadway and Hobson (1993) provide an intuitive example within the Canadian context,[9] to demonstrate that a free migration equilibrium may be inefficient, when regions have different degrees of access to source-based taxes. This case is important in Canada where the provinces have unequal access to natural resources taxes. Moreover, while the free migration equilibrium will be efficient if residence-based benefits are levied to finance the public provision of private goods, the chances are that such outcomes will not be consistent with the redistributive goals of provincial governments, particularly where regions have to impose taxes on an ability to pay basis. Thus a proportional income tax imposed to finance publicly provided public goods will be redistributive when individuals are heterogeneous with respect to their ability to earn income, and the free migration equilibrium will be inefficient if average per capita incomes differ across regions. Within this model, therefore, efficiency requires that the average per capita income tax revenue be equalized across regions.

Within the model postulated, efficient free migration equilibrium would require either a rearrangement of tax assignments between levels of government to better align types of revenue sources with the types of expenditure to be financed by subnational governments or a system of intergovernmental equalization transfers.

The "efficiency arguments" for equalization are not universally accepted. For example, Swan and Garvey (1992) challenge the view that net fiscal benefits create migration equilibria. In mounting a case

---

[7] See Buchanan and Goetz (1972); Flatters, Henderson, and Mieszkowski (1974); Boadway and Flatters (1982a and 1982b); and Boadway and Hobson (1993).

[8] The equity case for equalization has often been criticized as setting up a disincentive for labor migration out of poorer regions. In the presence of net fiscal benefit differentials, however, such migrations may go too far—so-called fiscally induced migration—and result in an inefficient allocation of labor. To prevent this, full equalization of net fiscal benefits is called for.

[9] The argument is based on a model that distinguishes, on the one hand, between publicly provided private goods (such as health, education, and welfare expenditures, which are assumed to vary proportionately with the population of the region) and pure public goods (where significant economies of scale may exist) and, on the other hand, between source-based taxes and resident-based benefit taxes. Efficiency requires that residence-based taxes should be used to finance the provision of publicly provided private goods, while pure public goods should be financed by source-based taxes.

against equalization, and especially the original analysis of Buchanan (1950), they suggest that a free migration equilibrium is efficient, since the migration process itself would lead to an equalization of incomes. Thus, all individuals would be equally treated from a public policy perspective.

Alternatives to equalization payments by central governments are also discussed in the literature. Cornes and Sandler (1986) draw on the theory of clubs to argue that regions could impose migration taxes on intending migrants. Myers (1990) also investigated the possibility that regions might undertake voluntary lump-sum transfers among themselves in order to deter migration. His results, which assume that migration is costless, suggest that a system of voluntary transfers would suffice and that no central government equalization transfers are required. Hercowitz and Pines (1991) continued this theme by examining the conditions under which a region will voluntarily transfer resources to another in the case where mobility is costly. They showed that, in this case, the interregional transfers will not be socially optimal and that central government transfers will still be required.

A number of empirical studies have also been undertaken in Canada to try to determine whether migrational efficiency distortions are potentially important.[10] These studies confirm that (1) differential net fiscal benefits do exist; (2) resource endowments are a significant contributing factor to these differential net fiscal benefits; (3) inefficient migration does occur in response to these net fiscal benefits; and (4) equalization slows inefficient migration. However, while these studies support the expected direction of change in the relevant variables, they do not provide much guidance on whether the magnitude of change is significant, or that the changes have had a major impact on national welfare.

Ultimately, the issue of whether equalization affects efficiency and growth depends on empirical investigation.

Transfer Options

The main transfer mechanisms used to tackle the various goals of government can be grouped into the following categories: (1) conditional transfers (or specific purpose payments) and (2) unconditional transfers.

---

[10]Courchene (1984), Winer and Gauthier (1982), Norrie and Percy (1984), Watson (1986), and Economic Council of Canada (1982).

Conditional transfers consist of matching grants, nonmatching grants for specific purposes, and block grants. Each of these may be implemented with or without redistribution criteria, which could be either open- or closed-ended.

Unconditional transfers consist of revenue-sharing arrangements, with or without redistribution criteria, and general purpose grants, which may be open-ended or subject to caps. In most countries, a combination of grant mechanisms will be used depending on the objectives of the central government.

General Choices

If grant mechanisms are employed, four levels of choice can be identified.

First, there is a basic choice as to whether the transfers should be made on a conditional or unconditional basis.

In many countries, the central government imposes conditions on some transfers on the use of the funds, and/or the performance achieved in the programs as a means of increasing central government influence over spending, which is primarily the responsibility of regional or local governments but which may also have an impact on matters of vital national concern (for example, air or water pollution control). Similarly, the central government may wish to leave the primary administrative responsibility for certain functions at the regional or local level, but seek to attain national minimum standards in these functions because of a national public concern (for example, on access to health or education programs). The extent of conditions imposed is likely to vary. At one extreme, the regional government may simply be reduced to acting as an agent of the central government. At the other extreme, the conditions may be limited to such matters as information supply, leaving the subnational government with ample scope for innovation and experimentation.

An unconditional grant will often yield a greater increase in utility in the recipient jurisdiction than will a conditional grant. This follows because unconditional grants simply increase community income without altering subnational government spending priorities, which themselves are dictated by local preferences.

The main justification for conditional grants over unconditional grants, therefore, must be that local decision making fails to produce the socially optimal outcome, as in the case of interjurisdictional spillovers discussed earlier. However, many developing countries have relatively weak expenditure management capabilities at the subnational level, and the proliferation of conditionality and performance criteria for special purpose grants is likely to generate confusion and pro forma fulfillment of the needed criteria. Thus, unless they possess the ability to monitor and manage the conditionality for grants, central governments would do better to simplify the design and conditionality of special purpose grants, and to supplement these by lump-sum transfers (which would be seen as own resources by recipient governments).

Second, within the category of conditional transfers, there is also a choice as to whether the central government should require subnational governments to undertake some matching of funding of programs by lower level governments.

Matching conditional grants generally alter local priorities to take account of the central government's spending preferences. They are particularly effective where spillovers are thought to exist. There is extensive literature on this subject. Boadway and Hobson (1993), for example, demonstrate that the optimal matching rate is the rate that will induce the recipient government to provide the socially optimal level of public service—that is, the level for which the marginal social cost is just equal to the marginal social benefit.

Another potential difficulty in administering matching arrangements is that different regions may be able to exert different leverage on the size of the overall grant, because of their different fiscal capacities. In order to limit the ability of any one region to influence the size of the grant, the amount of grant may be tied to total expenditure summed across all provinces. The grant is then tied to expenditures in all provinces, the cost to provincial taxpayers of an additional dollar of expenditure is $\$(1 - s/n)$, where n denotes the number of regions. That is, the additional dollar of expenditure generates a transfer of $\$s$ from the central government but the transfer is spread over all regions, somewhat reducing the leverage of particular provinces as well as the disincentive to use resources effectively.

Third, there is a choice as to whether there is to be some redistribution in the transfer mechanism or whether the transfers will be simply made on an equal per capita basis to each member of the defined population in each region. While formal equalization is usually restricted only to general purpose transfer systems, some element of redistribution between geographic regions is often built into conditional grants (for example, for grants to poorer regions where education or health needs are greater). However, in the absence of an overall framework for evaluating grants, it is not obvious that separately formulated conditional grants (or revenue sharing) with redistributional factors will actually be inequality decreasing or redistributive in an aggregate sense.

Finally, within both conditional and unconditional transfer mechanisms, there is a choice of whether the grants should be open-ended or subject to some limit. Open-ended matching grants encourage local governments with an incentive to internalize identified spillovers and provide the required level of services. At the same time, stabilization considerations often lead central governments to regard such arrangements with some skepticism, and limits to grants are considered desirable on macroeconomic grounds.

Tax and Revenue Sharing

If revenue-sharing or tax-sharing approach is followed, the choices are normally reduced. For example, transfers of shares of major tax collections (such as VAT) are generally made without conditions since they are not related to specific expenditure functions. However, this need not always be the case. For example, excise taxes collected on fuel consumption are often earmarked for conditional transfers for specific road construction. Similarly, most tax-sharing arrangements do not require matching by subnational governments. Most are open-ended in nature, although stabilization policy requirements may induce central governments to impose floors and caps on the amounts transferred.

Generally, tax-sharing arrangements are made on a derivation basis, although formula-based distributions are to be found in many countries. As described above, it is not evident a priori that the overall effect of separately determined redistributive formulas will decrease overall inequality in the absence of a consistent framework for the evaluation of transfers.

Where different sharing ratios are established for different taxes, there may be an incentive for the administering authority to place more effort on taxes that provide greater benefits to its immediate level of government (see Chapter 5 on Tax Administration). India, China, and Russia have experienced such difficulties. There is thus a possibility for "strategic games" between different levels of government that might cloud the transparency of the tax system.[11]

---

[11]Revenue sharing could be determined on a tax-by-tax basis or some pooling arrangement. Under the first choice, a portion x of specific tax (for example, VAT), may accrue to the central government, and the residual $(100 - x)$ to a subnational government in which the revenue was generated. A different share may be used for the enterprise income tax, and so on. Under the pool approach, all shared tax revenues (VAT, enterprise profits tax, and so on) are paid into one fund and then shared according to an established formula. If x percent of the pool is retained by the central government and the rest allocated on a derivation basis (that is, according to the region in which the revenue is generated), then this is equivalent to the $x: (100 - x)$ ratio applied to each shared tax.

Alternatively, a separate "fund" or "pool" may be established, and resources may be distributed automatically on a "formula" basis. The disadvantage with such an arrangement is that the automatic sharing of all revenues could complicate a stabilization package, where it is generally assumed that lower levels would spend all additional resources. Thus, the federal government may have to make a larger own account fiscal adjustment than might otherwise be necessary.

The advantage in tax sharing is that lower levels of governments share in productivity gains leading to enhanced tax collections without having to petition the central government for additional resources (and ensuring that subnational governments have a vested interest in an efficiently functioning economy). This automaticity is not generally assured through a grant system. Moreover, those favoring the tax-sharing approach also often point to the added accountability in public decision making that may be expected to accrue, given that such resources are seen as own revenues of the recipient governments.

Equalization

Unconditional equalization programs are in use in many parts of the world. These may be based solely on differences in revenue (or tax) capacities across subnational levels of government, as in Canada. This approach implicitly assumes that there are no significant differences in cost in the provision of public services across provinces, or those that exist are taken care of by special purpose transfers (see Clark, 1997).

An alternative formulation is based on both the assessment of revenue capacities, as well as an explicit incorporation of expenditure needs (such as in Denmark and Australia). This more general formulation requires more data than the revenue-capacity only option (see Rye and Searle, 1997; and Craig, Chapter 8). It is important that the factors chosen for the estimation of expenditure needs be independent of the actions of individual provinces. If this criterion is ignored, then there is a danger that the process could be manipulated by recipient governments. In this case, the system could degenerate into a variant of gap filling (see Ahmad and Thomas, 1997). Note that even if an elaborate formulation of expenditure needs is adopted, the resulting equalization grant is still untied and the recipient governments could choose to spend it as they wish. For instance, a relatively low level of public services could be provided, with lower-than-standard tax rates, or higher-than-average services with a higher tax effort. This would not affect the amount of the equalization payment, which is lump sum. Provided that the recipient governments are able to vary tax rates and effort, a lump-sum transfer should result in greater accountability, as the policy choices by a spending government would be reflected in the resulting tax rates and burdens.

As with special purpose grants, a choice has to be made whether the equalization estimation should determine (1) the relative amounts going to different provinces; and in addition (2) the total amount to be made available for this purpose.

It is clear that the relative amounts going to each province should be determined by the equalization exercise. This could be based on transfers only to poorer provinces, organized by the central government, of transfers directly from richer to poorer provinces organized on a cooperative basis (as in Germany). Both variants have the advantage that the redistribution is clear and transparent. However, not all countries have the political cohesion that would permit a duplication of the voluntary transfers as in Germany. In addition, the visible redistribution may lead to strong opposition to transfers on the part of the better-off provinces (many of which also have unmet expenditure and investment requirements). Thus, equalization transfers going from the center to all provinces may have certain political advantages. This organizational choice will vary from country to country, depending on political economy realities.

The issue of the amount to be made available under equalization is important. Even in countries that conduct elaborate estimations for the basis of equalization, the amounts for this purpose may be less than that for special-purpose transfers (as in Australia). In some cases, the specification of the formula also determines the amount of the grant. And if this is more than can be justified given macroeconomic constraints, countries such as Canada have resorted to adjusting the formula or imposing caps (see Clark, 1997). The Australian formulation focuses on the determination of relativities for each state, which are then applied to the amounts to be transferred, determined exogenously by the government (see Chapter 8). This arrangement provides greater flexibility and objectivity to the estimation procedures.

Another decision that has to be taken relates to the extent to which special purpose grants are to be incorporated into the equalization process. On their own, numerous special purpose grants may be inequality increasing. Incorporation of such transfers within the equalization process provides a framework for such grants.

A description of a general grant determination process, based on both revenue capacities and expenditure needs, is presented in the Appendix. This draws largely on the Australian model.

Capital Grants

Many countries make extensive use of capital grant systems to finance public investment programs by subnational governments. This is especially the case in countries that do not have well-developed capital markets or where the weak financial position of subnational governments does not permit them to access such markets directly. While most of these grants are for specific purposes or projects, a question arises whether capital needs should be included in an equalization program. This may be of importance when some regions of a developing country lack the basic infrastructure (such as school buildings) necessary for the provision of key public services deemed to be relevant for the equalization exercise. In this context, it would be important to examine the methods of assessing needs, the appropriate mix of grants and advances, as well as the nature of payment arrangements.

As noted earlier, capital needs are normally excluded from equalization exercises because of the difficulties of measuring and assessing relative needs in different regions. Ideally, one might compile a list of projects and conduct cost-benefit analyses on each project. The projects might then be funded in descending order of merit, with a specific capital grant for each functional area, although there are considerable practical difficulties involved in implementing this theoretically appealing approach.

In particular, a difficult area is to decide on the extent to which project financing is to be based on a grant and the portion that should be financed through capital markets. Proxy and sometimes arbitrary measures must therefore be used to allocate funds. In some areas, such as roads and housing, some approximate stock measures may be derived that can serve as a crude basis for evaluation (but see earlier discussion of the varying possible approaches to equalization of capital needs).

These difficulties suggest that a prudent approach to formulating capital grants may argue for providing separate financing for large infrastructure projects (for example, regional airports) and some capital investments of a repetitive nature (for example, rural and district roads and low-income housing), but to leave other smaller enabling investments to be financed by block grants or the general purpose equalization grant (if the relevant activities had been considered in assessing the factors for such a grant).

It must be recognized that capital projects have a long life and that at least a portion of their benefits will be enjoyed by future generations. Moreover, for many large infrastructure projects user charges can be implemented to finance major portions of the total cost. Both these factors make equalization grants an inappropriate tool for financing such capital projects. Consideration should then be given to financing all or part of the projects by advances from the central government at market interest rates that at least cover the center's own cost of borrowing.

In practice, central governments often employ a mix of special purpose grants and advances for large capital projects. The split of advances to grants must again be made on a pragmatic basis, reflecting judgments of the circumstances surrounding each type of expenditure.

Planning and Implementing Transfer Arrangements

The design and monitoring of intergovernment transfers is a complex task as it involves balancing many competing objectives across a wide range of activities. Some general principles emerge from country experiences:

(1) *Stabilization concerns should predominate*. The central government must preserve its capacity to manage the economy. Failure here may jeopardize other goals being pursued by the central and subnational governments.

(2) *Developing a macroeconomic framework*. Individual transfer arrangements should not be negotiated in a vacuum. Ideally, they should be considered in the context of jointly prepared medium-term rolling fiscal plans covering projections of the aggregate revenues and expenditures of all levels of government at least three years ahead.

(3) *Arrangements should contain some flexibility*. While the central government cannot avoid some degree of commitment of medium-term resources, it also needs room to vary overall levels of commitment. Open-ended commitments and variable grants or tax shares with floors or minimal guarantees need to be scrutinized carefully. Indexation arrangements—especially those that might be susceptible to actions by the grant recipient—also need to be handled with care. And while some medium-term funding indications may be unavoidable, a reasonably large component of the total grant should be left for final determination in the annual budget context. So-called sunset clauses should apply to ensure that programs are regularly reviewed.

(4) *Objectives must be clearly spelled out and be capable of being monitored*. The central and subnational governments must be particularly cautious of overlap and duplication in the provision of services. When central governments set conditions on the use of transfers they should have a good idea of how to monitor their objectives, what can be realistically achieved, and what sanctions can be applied in case of nonperformance. Matching requirements in many specific areas may simply

undermine the capacity of the subnational government to manage crucial local services.

(5) *Interrelationships need to be taken into account.* While individual ministries will naturally focus on achieving specific objectives in any program, it is important that the ministry of finance monitor the overall impact of transfers. The consistency between conditional transfers and unconditional grants is important.

(6) *Simplicity is important.* The initial presumption should be that the expenditure needs can be met by the subnational own revenues, including shared taxes, and unconditional grants. The case for a special purpose grant should be clearly spelled out, with simple conditionality and reporting procedures.

(7) *Examine alternatives.* Not all services need to be provided by the state (at any level). In some cases, payments can be made to companies or persons via a voucher or some other mechanism to facilitate access to services such as education. Such measures may be particularly important where the national government seeks to encourage efficiency and diversity in the supply of services.

Concluding Remarks

Most countries need a combination of grants, ranging from special purpose grants, to correct for spillovers and other conditional grants to meet the policy objectives of the central government, to other conditional or unconditional grants, to meet vertical or horizontal imbalances. Each combination of grants will likely have different macroeconomic implications and could affect the incentives of recipient governments to raise their own revenues at the margin or to control own expenditures. A strong lesson from both the theoretical literature and the experiences of other countries (see Ahmad, 1997) is that the design of grants matters for macroeconomic stabilization, as well as efficiency and distributional objectives.

Gap-filling grants to meet the deficits of subnational governments are pernicious and should be avoided to the extent possible, to minimize the danger of fiscal irresponsibility.

Central governments will continue to rely on special purpose grants for a variety of reasons. However, the objectives should be stated clearly, and the conditionality defined in a manner that can be monitored and enforced. It is all too common to find the greatest reliance on special purpose transfers in countries that are unable to monitor effectively the usage of these transfers. Under these circumstances, such grants can induce inefficient resource use, as well as corrupt practices, because of the lack of accountability engendered. In addition, complex conditionality can lead to administrative paralysis at lower levels of government. Moreover, a multitude of special purpose grants bestowed by different agencies can lead to undesirable outcomes, such as an overall increase in horizontal imbalances. Thus, a simple design of special purpose grants, within a consistent overall framework, is to be strongly recommended.

Unconditional equalization grants, provided that these are lump sum and are not influenced by the actions of a recipient government, can be an effective vehicle for financing decentralized expenditures in a manner that encourages accountable resource use. Difficult choices need to be made in relation to the extent and formulation of such transfers, and these need to take into account data and institutional constraints that are to be found in particular contexts.

Appendix. Implementation of Equalization Grants Systems

Subnational governments differ in their fiscal capacities because some can raise more money from their available tax base than others and because the need for and the cost of providing certain services differs among regions.

A number of geographically large countries have felt a need to provide some intergovernment fiscal mechanisms to provide a degree of equity between regions over time. Specifically, full equalization would require that each region should have the capacity to provide the same standard of public services as the other regions, provided it makes the same effort to raise revenue from its own sources and conducts its affairs with an average level of operational efficiency.

If a country anticipated the introduction of a system of grants based on horizontal equalization, a decision would be needed as to the basis for equalization in the medium term: (1) whether to restrict the process to revenue capacities, or (2) whether to include both revenue capacities and expenditure needs.

If the decision is the former, then the revenue capacity equalization could be introduced fairly quickly in most countries. However, in large and diverse countries, there may be a preference to also allow for differences in expenditure needs, particularly if there are substantial differences in the cost of provision of such services and in access to such services.

Whatever is done and no matter how long full implementation might take, the long-term objective must be kept in mind at each stage of the system design, and it is therefore appropriate at the start to set

the principles on which the system is to be based. Some considerations in designing the process and objectives of the system might be as follows:
- Ensure that, as far as possible, the grants do not simply fill fiscal gaps in subnational government budgets. Thus, the recipients of grants should not be able to influence their grant share by their decisions—thereby preventing policy-induced disincentives.
- Achieve an implementable system without imposing too great a burden on government in either the collection or processing of data.
- Involve the subnational governments (especially at the state or provincial level) in the design of the system to achieve a degree of political consensus. This is likely to involve a gradual process in which sharp changes in provincial activity levels are avoided.

With the above considerations, a needs-based capacity equalization may have to be introduced in line with the development of databases and the choice of variables to be included in the exercise. The initial priority might be to introduce revenue equalization as soon as practicable but, since most countries have special purpose grants, these should be examined for inconsistencies with the equalization process and objectives—this too can be effected early on. It should be noted that an equalization process based on needs does not imply that the central government determines what lower levels of government must do. Rather, this should be seen as providing subnational levels of government with the capacity to provide a standard of services, and they may choose to do otherwise. The important aspect is that the equalization grant should be lump sum, thus ensuring that recipient governments have the incentive to use the resources wisely, and to manage their expenditures efficiently.

The steps needed to introduce the full revenue capacity and expenditure needs framework in an administratively manageable fashion are outlined below.

The First Step: The Scope of the Equalization Budget

Ultimately, the objective of an equalization system is to give provincial governments the capacity to provide equal levels of public services if they make equivalent tax efforts. This does not ensure equality in the actual provision of services to each person. An important first step in system design, however, must be to identify the range of public services that a provincial government should have the capacity to equalize.

The initial question would be whether to include both capital and recurrent expenditures and revenue sources within the range of functions to be considered. Typically the equalization process focuses on current expenditures. This however is less defensible in developing countries where the provision of current public services is constrained by the absence of appropriate infrastructure, such as school buildings.

On the other hand, there are major problems with measuring capital needs. Three approaches may be considered:

Flow equalization. This approach would just examine the capacity of each region to deliver a standard increment in own-financed capital stocks in any time period.

Stock equalization without memory of past accumulation. This approach would simply examine the capacity of a region to deliver a standard stock of own-financed capital in any time period without reference to past investment.

Stock equalization with memory of past accumulation. This approach would evaluate a region's capacity to provide own-financed capital over the long-term, making each region bear the consequences of its own past actions.

Aside from the immense statistical difficulty of measuring regional capital stocks, each of the approaches has particular interpretation problems, which may prove insuperable. For example, poorer regions may object strongly to the first approach, on the grounds that the deficiency of the initial stock was due to insufficient transfers. The second approach could be opposed by states that had made a consistent effort to boost their capital stock, and may be penalized by this arrangement. The third approach may find more support among constantly good performers, but would not be favored by regions that had consistently ignored their capital needs.

Two parallel systems could be implemented:
- A system of special purpose capital transfers enabling the central government to target specific infrastructure needs and projects.
- An equalization system for untied transfers to assist in financing recurrent services. It may also be possible to include small capital investments within the equalization formulation on a needs-based approach, such as local public works and rural roads.

Of course, this approach would not necessarily mean that capital needs would be ignored in the equalization exercise. Capital needs may enter in various ways into the assessments. For example, regions may be assessed on their relative debt charges that would take at least some account of the accumulation in capital stock contributing to the present level of debt payments.

Once the range of recurrent services to be covered in the equalization exercise has been decided, this would be related to the own-revenue capacities of the provinces, along with the equalization transfers from the central government. The overall transfers would incorporate an estimated inflation adjustment, and only in very exceptional circumstances would there be ex post adjustments (for example, for major population shifts). The basic relationship is:

> Cost of standardized recurrent services = provincial sources of recurrent revenue (at standardized levels) available to finance these functions + transfers from the central government (both untied and special purpose).

In an important way, therefore, the provincial capacity to link revenue sources to specific expenditure functions has an influence on the scope of the expenditure budget. If provincial revenues are very largely uncommitted, a matching of standardized revenue sources with standardized expenditure functions is impossible. Thus, if only one function is chosen to represent expenditure needs (such as education) and is related to total available own revenues, there would be a large standard budget surplus (B_i), and a danger that the factors for education might misrepresent overall expenditure needs. It would thus be preferable for the standard budget to include as many relevant provincial services as possible. Methods of achieving this (with and without extensive data) are discussed below.

It is seldom possible to completely separate expenditure assignments among various levels of government, given that in each expenditure category there are responsibilities for policy, financing, and administration (see Chapter 2). In Australia, universities are constitutionally assigned to the states. However, all the financing comes from the commonwealth government, which provides funds for this purpose to the states. In policy terms, the universities are fairly independent. For equalization purposes, the universities are not treated as being a state expenditure function, even though the rest of the education sector is included. The definition of a "state-type public service" in the Australian standard budget covers items mainly administered by the states, even if such items are also provided by other levels of government, communities, or public sector enterprises.

In theory, the equalization objective should include all aspects of service provision regardless of the provider. It should not matter how the service provision is arranged or financed. The grants to the provinces can still be determined in such a way as to equalize capacity for them to ensure that, in total, there could be equal provision in each province.

It may be that, in at least some functions, the combined level of activity of the nonprovincial government sources can be assumed to satisfy the same proportion of the eligible group in all provinces. If this assumption holds, then the nonprovincial activity would not affect relativities if excluded from the standard budget and the assessment of disabilities.

If the level of activity of the subprovinces and enterprises is not assumed equal in all provinces, then there are two possible options for proceeding. Either the standard budget, or the expenditure assessment, can be adjusted.

The first option would require the inclusion of the following items in the standard budget:

- The revenue or expenditure in the provincial government accounts.
- The expenditure on the standard budget items included in subprovincial and enterprise accounts.
- The revenue received into subprovincial and enterprise accounts used to finance the standard budget expenditure items (this would normally be equal to expenditure but may be financed from higher levels of government).

The second option of adjusting expenditure assessment approaches is discussed below.

The Second Step: The Structure of the Standard Budget

This step involves the organization of items to be included in the standard budget in a manner that best assists the assessment process.

On the revenue side of the budget, it is probable that a small number of major sources of revenue should be assessed separately. For the others, the task involves distinguishing some common elements that might contribute to differences in revenue capacities and, where they exist, grouping the taxes into one category. For example, although taxes might differ on different types of gambling, it might be decided that income levels are the major source of capacity differences and that all gambling taxes might best be combined into one category.

Similarly, looking at the expenditure functions of government, it might be that some of the small functions such as the registration of births, deaths, and marriages; registration of motor vehicles; and other administrative services could be combined into one single category labeled, say, administrative services. The IMF's Government Finance Statistics classifications provide a good guide to appropriate groupings.

Experience with equalization suggests that there is a tendency for separate categories to be developed in the early assessment stages, because they have attributes (especially availability of some specific data) that appear to lend themselves to separate analysis. On closer inspection, it is often found either that their weight in the total budget is so small as to make separate analysis unwarranted or that they would be better grouped with other items that have common underlying, revenue, demand, or cost influences.

The Third Step: Deriving Standardized Revenues

There are three options for determining the standardized revenue for any source of revenue to be included in the standard budget.

Undertake an "Active" Assessment

This involves the determination of the revenue base using objective data. This may be based on the actual revenue base being accessed by the provinces (such as payrolls) or some overall indicator of economic activity that can be used as an objective measure (such as state gross product on total consumption spending). An important consideration in this task is that the data used should not be simply a reflection of the actual revenues; rather, standard tax policies should be applied to an "independent" provincial tax base to reflect relative revenue capacities (for example, if there are a number of exemptions from the payroll tax base permitted by one province, then an attempt should be made to assess what the base would be if those exemptions had not been made). This difficulty points to the use, where possible, of nationally consistent databases.

Undertake an Equal Per Capita Assessment

This approach is best used when analysis suggests that there is no measurable difference in the per capita capacity of different provinces to raise revenue from a particular revenue source. For example, an equal per capita assessment may be appropriate if provinces collect a poll tax of $100 for each household and demographic data reveal that the number of persons in each household is broadly equivalent in all provinces. Any differences in amounts collected may then be seen to be essentially due to differences in the efficiency of tax administrations, or to policy differences such as particular exemptions granted to some households in some provinces. These differences would imply a need for the provinces concerned to address the efficiency or policy problems leading to lower collections, or make a case to the assessment authority that it suffered an unavoidable disability in the area concerned.

Undertake an Actual Per Capita Assessment

This approach could be taken when analysis suggests that there are few differences in the tax bases, tax rates, or efficiency of collection among provinces in a particular item. The actual collections could then be taken as a sufficiently accurate measure of underlying differences in tax capacity and, therefore, used as a measure of standardized revenue in the overall assessment. An example of successful use of this approach may be a tax item that is collected by the central government (such as VAT) and then shared with the province on a derivation (original source) basis. In that instance, it could be reasonably assumed that the policy and efficiency of the collection authority are broadly the same across all provinces.

There is a danger that the use of actual per capita assessments could be gap filling in that they discourage efficient tax collection practices. It is important, therefore, in any decision to use this approach, to ensure that no significant policy or efficiency differences exist. Revenue trends in any areas assessed by this method should be monitored closely to identify any attempts at grant-share manipulation and, if such action occurs, early steps will be necessary to vary the assessment approach.

The Fourth Step: Deriving Standardized Expenditures

In this area, four alternative approaches are available:

The Factor Assessment Method

This method is used when there is sufficient confidence in an ability to identify provincial differences in the relative underlying demand and/or cost per unit of service provision. The process involves the identification of relevant disability factors and then quantifying their relative influence on the service in question. For example, in the area of primary education, the number of people in the age group of 5 years to 12 years might be seen as a relative measure of demand for the service, and differences in cost due to energy consumption to heat or cool schools might be seen as causing differences in the unit cost of providing education to a student. The Australian experience has been that demand influences are usually easier to quantify than cost influences, either because of the existence of better data or because of greater ease in getting agreement between recipient governments on their relative impact.

A further consideration is that demand factors are likely to be specific to individual expenditure categories in the standard budget—for example, different age or sex—and demographic influences are likely to apply to health and education services. However, cost factors tend to have a more common impact across functional expenditure categories. For example, Australian experience suggests that cost factors, such as variations caused by diseconomies of scale, variations in population density, and dispersion of the population, may have a broadly similar effect on many budget functions. In that context, studies of these broad cost factors, while time-consuming in themselves, may yield benefits for all aspects of distributional policy, including the allocations used in specific purpose grant programs.

Undertake an Assessment Based on a Current Distribution of Specific Purpose or Tied Grants

This approach may be appropriate where there are insufficient data to apply the factor assessment method but there is a specific purpose grant scheme in operation that contains a distribution system that the parties judge to be fair and appropriate (perhaps because of past studies of underlying demand and cost factors). This assessment process simply compares the individual province's per capita share of the specific purpose payment with the national average per capita grant, and uses the relationship between the two as a measure of the global disability that should be applied to the function.

There are two benefits to this approach. First, it does not detrimentally influence the relations between the line ministry currently responsible for the specific purpose grant allocation and those charged with making the equalization grant (in some countries, an independent grants commission, and, in others, the ministry of finance). Second, it does not detrimentally influence the budget flexibility of the provinces by overriding the distribution of the specific purpose payment to which they have become accustomed, without an assessment having been made.

Undertake an Equal Per Capita Assessment—as with Revenue

The assumption is that provinces have no relative demand differences or variations in unit costs of providing services. Standardized expenditure for each province is thus equal to the standard level of expenditure.

Undertake an Actual Per Capita Assessment

Similar in principle to the revenue case mentioned above, the assumption here is that actual costs are an accurate measure of overall relative need. Actual expenditures can therefore be used as an accurate measure of standardized expenditure.

The problem of different contributions to total service provision being made by the nonprovincial suppliers could be overcome in the assessment process. This would avoid the possible difficulty of including subprovincial and enterprise financial transactions in the standard budget. If it was known, or could be estimated that nonprovincial supply of a service across the nation reaches, say, 20 percent of the total relevant population, this could be seen as a standard level of provision. Thus, a province in which more than 20 percent of the eligible population is being served by nonprovincial suppliers would have an advantage. It could be assessed as having a "nonprovincial supplier" factor of less than unity (that is, a relatively lower-than-standard disability). A province in which the nonprovincial suppliers were serving less than 20 percent of the eligible population would have a factor of more than 1.000 (that is, a relatively higher-than-standard disability).

Once such factors are applied, any change in the distribution of services between provincial and other suppliers would need to be closely monitored to ensure that provinces do not use policy decisions to change the balance in an attempt to influence their assessments of relative needs.

This approach may not be adequate for longer-term assessment if provinces are able to change policies in a manner that can affect the assessments. However, it may be acceptable in the short run if the inclusion of the financial activity of nonprovincial suppliers is judged to be too difficult to include in the standard budget.

A further aspect to this solution is that it is effectively excluded when equal per capita assessments are undertaken. This arises because the equal per capita assessments, if nonprovincial expenditure is excluded from the standard, assume an equal provision of nonprovincial supply. It may be that the equal per capita assessments need to be divided into two groups: those in which it is desired to assess a nonprovincial supplier factor in which case that becomes the only factor; and those where a true equal per capita assessment remains.

A nonprovincial supplier allowance, however, is automatically included in actual per capita assessments. This will not present difficulties because any policy action by a province to reduce its expenditure at the expense of a nonprovincial supplier will automatically result in the province being assessed as having a reduced standardized expenditure.

A further consideration to the full equalization process in the environment of a developing country is the realization that some provinces—the ones where infrastructure is less developed—will receive grants to provide recurrent services that cannot be provided because of the absence of the necessary infrastructure. Unless an adjustment or other arrangements are made, these provinces will be able to either raise less than their standardized level of taxation, or provide above-standard services in areas unaffected by their poor infrastructure development. For example, even if there are no school buildings, the provinces would be given funds to employ teachers. These funds could not be spent on teachers, and may be used for other purposes or to reduce taxation as the province sees fit.

Under these conditions, the central government might encourage the provinces to use this part of their equalization grant for infrastructure development to ensure longer-term equalization. Such use of recurrent resources for capital purposes would, along with any funds received for capital investment, enable a province to achieve a standard level of service more rapidly.

References

Ahmad, Ehtisham, Jon Craig, and Dubravko Mihaljek, 1995, "Implementing and Managing Grants—Institutional and Informational Requirements," in *Reforming China's Public Finances*, ed. by Ehtisham, Gao Qiang, and Vito Tanzi (Washington: International Monetary Fund).

Ahmad, Ehtisham, and Ravi Thomas, 1997, "Types of Transfers—A General Formulation," in *Financing Decentralized Expenditures: An International Comparison of Grants*, ed. by Ehtisham Ahmad (Cheltenham, England; Brookfield, Vermont: Edward Elgar).

Ahmad, Ehtisham, ed., 1997, *Financing Decentralized Expenditures: An International Comparison of Grants* (Cheltenham, England; Brookfield, Vermont: Edward Elgar).

———, Gao Qiang, and Vito Tanzi, eds., 1995, *Reforming China's Public Finances* (Washington: International Monetary Fund).

Albon, R.P., 1990, "The Efficiency Implications of Locational-Based Factors in Commonwealth Grants Commission Determinations," Appendix to the Victorian Submission to the *Inquiry into Issues of Methodology*, Victoria's Response to the Discussion Papers, Inquiry into Grants Commission Methodology.

Australian Commonwealth Grants Commission, 1993, *Report on General Revenue Grant Relativities* (Canberra: Australian Government Publishing Service).

Boadway, Robin, 1985, "Federal-Provincial Transfers in Canada: A Critical Review of the Existing Arrangement," in M. Krasnick, K. Norrie, and R. Simeon (research cordinators), *Federalism and the Economic Union: Royal Commission on the Economic Union and Development Prospects for Canada*, Vol. 65 (Ottawa: Canadian Government Publishing Centre).

———, and Flatters, Frank, 1982a, "Efficiency and Equalization Payments in a Federal System of Government: A Synthesis and Extension of Recent Results," *Canadian Journal of Economics*, Vol. 15 (November), pp. 613–33.

———, 1982b, "Equalization in a Federal State," Economic Council of Canada.

Boadway, Robin, and Hobson, Paul A.R., 1993, *Intergovernmental Fiscal Relations in Canada*, Tax Paper No. 96 (Toronto: Canadian Tax Foundation).

Brennan, Geoffrey, and James M. Buchanan, 1980, *The Power to Tax: Analytic Foundations of a Fiscal Constitution* (Cambridge, England: Cambridge University Press).

Brosio, Giorgio, 1992, "The Balance Sheet of the Australian Federation: Some Tentative Estimates," Working Paper No. 24 (Canberra: Federalism Research Centre, Australian National University).

Buchanan, James M., 1950, "Federalism and Fiscal Equity," *American Economic Review*, Vol. 40 (September), pp. 583–99.

———, and Charles J. Goetz, 1972, "Efficiency Limits and Fiscal Mobility: An Assessment of the Tiebout Model," *Journal of Public Economics*, Vol. 1.

Buchanan, James M., and Richard E. Wagner, 1970, "An Efficiency Basis for Federal Fiscal Equalization," in *The Analysis of Public Output*, ed. by Julius Margolis (New York: National Bureau of Economic Research).

Clark, Douglas H., 1997, "The Fiscal Transfer System in Canada," in *Financing Decentralized Expenditures: An International Comparison of Grants*, ed. by Ehtisham Ahmad (Cheltenham, England; Brookfield, Vermont: Edward Elgar).

Commission of the European Communities, 1997, *Report of the Study Group on the Role of Public Finance in European Integration* (MacDougall Report), Vol. 1: General Report (Brussels: Office for Official Publications of the European Communities).

Commonwealth Grants Commission, 1989, *Report on Issues in Fiscal Equalization*, Vols. I and II (Canberra: Australian Government Publishing Service).

Cornes, Richard, and Todd Sandler, 1986, *The Theory of Externalities, Public Goods, and Club Goods* (New York: Cambridge University Press).

Courchene, T., 1970, "Interprovincial Migration and Economic Adjustment," *Canadian Journal of Economics*, Vol. 3, pp. 550–76.

———, 1984, *Equalization Payments: Past, Present and Future* (Toronto: Ontario Economic Council).

Economic Council of Canada, 1982, "Financing Confederation: Today and Tomorrow" (Ottawa: Supply and Services).

Flatters, Frank, Vernon Henderson, and Peter Mieszkowski, 1974, "Public Goods, Efficiency and Regional Fiscal Equalization," *Journal of Public Economics*, Vol. 3 (May), pp. 99–112.

Hercowitz, Zvi, and David Pines, 1991, "Migration with Fiscal Externalities," *Journal of Public Economics*, Vol. 46 (November), pp. 163–80.

King, David N., 1984, *Fiscal Tiers: The Economics of Multi-Level Government* (London; Boston: Allen & Unwin).

Mathews, R.L., 1975, "Fiscal Equalization in Australia: The Methodology of the Grants Commission," *Finanzarchiv*, Vol. 34, No. 1, pp. 66–85.

———, 1982, "Federalism in Retreat: The Abandonment of Tax Sharing and Fiscal Equalization" (Canberra: Centre for Federal Financial Relations, Australian National University).

———, and others, 1981, *Australian Federalism* (Canberra: Centre for Research on Federal Financial Relations, Australian National University).

Mathews, R.L., ed., 1974, *Intergovernmental Relations in Australia* (Sydney: Angus & Robertson).

Maxwell, Judith, and Caroline Pestieau, 1980, *Economic Realities of Contemporary Confederation* (Montreal: C.D. Howe Research Institute).

Musgrave, Richard A., Peggy B. Musgrave, and Richard M. Bird, 1984, *Public Finance in Theory and Practice* (Toronto: McGraw Hill).

Myers, Gordon M., 1990, "Optimality, Free Mobility and the Regional Authority in a Federation," *Journal of Public Economics*, Vol. 43 (October).

Norrie, K.H., and M.B. Percy, 1984, "Province Building and Industrial Structure in a Small Open Economy," in *Economic Adjustment and Public Policy in Canada*. ed. by Douglas D. Purvis (Kingston, Ontario: John Deutsch Institute for the Study of Economic Policy, Queens University).

Oates, Wallace E., 1972, *Fiscal Federalism* (New York: Harcourt, Brace, Jovanovich).

———, and R.M. Schwab, 1988, "Economic Competition Among Jurisdictions: Efficiency Enhancing or Distortion Inducing?" *Journal of Public Economics*, Vol. 35 (April), pp. 333–54.

Petchey, J.D., 1992, 1997, "The Welfare Effects of Fiscal Equalization in a Federal Economy with Different Factor Endowments," Working Paper (Canberra: Federalism Research Centre, Australian National University).

Rye, C. Richard, and Bob Searle, 1997, "Expenditure Needs: Institutions and Data," in *Financing Decentralized Expenditures: An International Comparison of Grants*, ed. by Ehtisham Ahmad (Cheltenham, England; Brookfield, Vermont: Edward Elgar).

Shapiro, P., and J.D. Petchey, 1992, "Guns That Point East Can Point North and South: The Economics of Centralized Federalism," working paper presented in a seminar at the University of Adelaide, September.

Swan, P., and G. Garvey, 1992, "The Equity and Efficiency Implications of Fiscal Equalization," draft working paper, Australian Graduate School of Management, University of New South Wales.

Tanzi, Vito, 1995, "Basic Issues of Decentralization and Tax Assignment," in *Reforming China's Public Finances*, ed. by Ehtisham Ahmad, Gao Qiang, and Vito Tanzi (Washington: International Monetary Fund).

Tresch, Richard, W., *Public Finance: A Normative Theory* (Plano, Texas: Business Publications).

Tiebout, C.M., 1956, "A Pure Theory of Local Expenditures," *Journal of Political Economy*, Vol. 64 (October), pp. 416–24.

United States, Advisory Commission on Intergovernmental Fiscal Relations, 1995, "Measures of State and Local Fiscal Capacity" (Washington).

Walsh, Cliff, and Jeffrey D. Petchey, 1992, "Fiscal Federalism: An Overview of Issues and a Discussion of Their Relevance to the European Community," Discussion Paper No. 12 (Canberra: Federalism Research Centre, Australian National University).

Watson, William G., 1986, "An Estimate of the Welfare Gain from Fiscal Equalization," *Canadian Journal of Economics*, Vol. 19 (May), pp. 298–308.

Winer, S., and D. Gauthier, 1982, *Internal Migration and Fiscal Structure: An Econometric Study of the Determinants of Interprovincial Migration in Canada* (Ottawa: Economic Council of Canada).

5

Tax Administration

CHARLES L. VEHORN AND EHTISHAM AHMAD

In many developing countries efficient or equitable tax policies may fail because the tax administration is not able to implement these policies (Casanegra de Jantscher, 1986). Consideration of the tax administration dimension becomes even more complex when different levels of government are involved in collecting taxes. Central governments, owing to their size and their resources, have a comparative advantage in collecting revenue, but subnational governments have an advantage in providing residents of the locality with the desired amount and mix of local public goods (Oates, 1972 and 1991).

Given the above considerations, intergovernmental relations in the tax area are affected by two key policy decisions. First, how will the collection of taxes be organized—under central government control, control at one governmental level other than the central level, or multilevel government control? Second, how will the central government provide subnational governments with unrestricted revenue—through tax assignment, revenue sharing, or lump-sum transfers—to meet the demand for locally provided public goods?

The mix of policies to address the above questions varies across countries and over time. However, for developing countries and those in transition to market-oriented economies, a simple system of tax policy and administration is likely to be needed to ensure adequate revenue collections. Any undue complications could result in serious ad-

---

With assistance from Kazutomi Kurihara. The authors would like to thank Teresa Ter-Minassian, Milka Casanegra de Jantscher, Carlos Silvani, Parthasarathi Shome, and Tony Pellechio for helpful comments on earlier drafts of the chapter.

ministrative burdens and problems in securing taxpayer compliance, as well as potential revenue loss.

Models of Tax Administration in Multilevel Governments

Tax administration by the central government alone should be distinguished from a structure that allows other levels of government full or partial control of collection. From a macroeconomic perspective, centralized tax administration has clear advantages. If the central government manages all tax administration, tax policies aimed at stabilization of the economy have a higher probability of being implemented as intended. If other levels of government are involved, control over the implementation of tax measures to promote stabilization can be weakened. However, the above argument applies mainly to a subset of taxes, such as the corporate and personal income taxes, and the value-added tax (VAT). Some taxes, such as property taxation, are amenable to local administration without loss of macroeconomic control (see Chapter 3).

There are four basic conceptual models for tax administration among different levels of government: (1) central government tax administration only, with provision of revenue sharing and transfers; (2) central government tax administration only, with assignment of different taxes to different levels of government; (3) multilevel administration, with revenue sharing and transfers; and (4) each level of government administering the taxes assigned to it.[1] The first two options centralize tax administration by maintaining central government control over all tax offices, including tax offices at the regional and local level. The third and fourth options permit tax collection by subnational governments. Whether tax administration is centralized, allocated to one level other than the central level, or spread over various levels of government is as likely to depend on political realities as on technical considerations, but there are technical implications associated with different tax administration structures. The purpose of this chapter is to analyze the advantages and disadvantages of centralized versus subnational or

---

[1]In practice, these four models are not mutually exclusive, so some countries may not fit easily into one category. For example, a country may combine revenue sharing and tax assignment to reach a desired allocation of revenue. However, these conceptual models allow for a more focused evaluation of the tax administration issues. McLure (1983) discusses similar conceptual models to assign the corporate income tax to various levels of government, but does not present a detailed discussion of the administrative dimension.

mixed forms of tax administration. Examples of country experiences will be drawn on where appropriate.

Administrative Objectives and Costs

In assessing how best to collect taxes, it is important to keep in mind two primary objectives of tax administration: (1) to apply the tax laws uniformly to achieve maximum collection at minimum costs, and (2) to promote voluntary compliance by taxpayers (Inter-American Center of Tax Administrators, 1992).

Uniform application of tax laws across taxpayers demonstrates that the tax administration is committed to the fair treatment of taxpayers. This emphasis on fairness has been identified as one factor that helps to enhance confidence in the tax system and to promote voluntary compliance (LeBaube and Vehorn, 1992). However, the promotion of voluntary compliance entails not only a fair treatment of those who comply, but also rigorous enforcement and swift action against those who fail to comply with the tax laws, for example, by failing to file a tax return, failing to file an accurate return, or failing to issue an invoice as required under a VAT. In some countries that levy a VAT, tax officials have the authority to close a business for a few days and post a sign on the door of the establishment, indicating that the closure is due to noncompliance with the VAT law or regulations. Taxpayers will be more inclined to comply voluntarily if they perceive a risk that noncompliance will be detected and punished. A tax administration that simply attempts to minimize its costs of collection, in relation to the potential revenue cannot be viewed as effective unless it fosters a high level of voluntary compliance (Casanegra de Jantscher and Silvani, 1991).[2]

When countries select multilevel or subnational tax administration, authority to collect specific taxes should be given to the level of government that is able to function with the lowest collection and enforcement costs (Rubinfield, 1983). In this perspective, the central government should take full advantage of administrative economies of scale. For example, Rubinfield argues that for the individual and corporate income taxes, tax administration costs will be lower if taxes are collected at the central level than at subnational levels. Collection and enforcement costs for the VAT (especially on a destination basis), customs duties, natural resource taxes, and social security taxes can also be

---

[2] In the tax administration literature, a distinction is made between efficiency—minimizing cost of collection, and effectiveness—promotion of voluntary compliance.

minimized if the central government determines tax policy through legislation, sets uniform regulations, and operates the tax administration. Subnational governments, on the other hand, can collect taxes, such as property taxes, certain excise taxes, and user charges, the administration of which does not present cost advantages associated with the size of government.

Another consideration is the availability of resources, including information, for each level of government. Tax administrations of subnational governments may be less able than the central government to afford the cost of skilled manpower, modern office facilities, and up-to-date technology. However, tax officials at the subnational level have more intimate knowledge of the developments in their geographical area. The knowledge of local conditions is another reason why the property tax is a likely candidate to be administered by local tax officials. As Rubinfield points out, local officials are in a better position than higher-level tax officials to understand the trend of the local real estate market and the effect of zoning and land use regulations on property values.

An argument for the legal framework for some taxes to be set uniformly by the central government is that taxpayers bear an additional cost if they must comply with diverse jurisdictional tax laws. Compliance costs can be especially high for companies that have several branches or subsidiaries operating in different jurisdictional areas. It is not unusual for national corporations in the United States[3] to fill out over 15,000 sales tax returns each year (Bialczak, 1989). Tax autonomy for subnational governments can also open the door to excessive tax competition among jurisdictions, which distorts companies' location decisions, and can involve substantial revenue losses to the competing jurisdictions.

Centralized Tax Administration

Main Features

The option under which all taxes are collected by a central government tax administration provides a minimum amount of administrative complications. In this model, all staff are employed by the central government under one organizational structure. This structure generally

---

[3]In the United States, the retail sales tax is primarily the domain of state governments, which have the legal authority to establish their own tax rate or rates and tax base (see Chapter 15).

encompasses three levels—central, provincial or regional, and local branches of the central tax administration; but there are cases, such as Australia, where the central government tax administration comprises only two levels—the central office and regional branches. In general, all taxes are collected by the central tax administration through their tax offices at the local level, with the regional level playing a supervisory role. This supervisory role includes dealing with taxpayer appeals, collecting the data necessary for an effective management information system, and making sure that the rules and regulations established at the central level are implemented uniformly by the local offices.

Under a centralized tax administration, revenues could be returned to subnational governments through revenue sharing, or transfers, or a combination of both. Revenue-sharing arrangements or assignment of tax bases can take many forms. The simplest arrangement is collection by the central government with sharing determined by a given formula based on some objective criterion, such as origin. A variant of this form is to return a fixed percentage of revenue collected in a given locality back to that locality. However, if an enterprise has factories in many locations but pays all its taxes from its headquarters in a given locality, then that locality may receive more than its fair share, unless some type of formula for apportioning taxes is used.

The major functions of tax administration—taxpayer services, collection, audit, penalties, and appeals—are not affected by the choice between revenue sharing and tax assignment. The revenue-sharing procedures could, however, affect the behavior of the tax staff who may concentrate their efforts on collecting the taxes retained by the central government, at the expense of those shared with the subnational jurisdictions. The choice of a revenue-sharing formula can affect also the motivation and behavior of the tax staff, if tax staff perceive the formula as inequitable. This perception is then reflected in the quality of audits performed, penalties assessed, and appeals reviewed. The formula could also affect the allocation of staff resources (such as highly skilled auditors) if revenues from one tax were primarily distributed to local governments, while revenues from another tax were primarily kept by the central government. It might thus be appropriate to have revenue sharing from a pool of key taxes, including taxes such as VAT, to minimize tax-collection disincentives, rather than to have sharing on a tax-by-tax basis, with varying shares.

With centralized tax administration, it is possible for revenues to be assigned to subnational levels, and for lower levels of government to have legislative control over bases and rate structures. The key issue for lower levels of government is the ability to exercise control over certain tax bases or rates at the "margin." Problems arise when the central tax administration has to cope with varying definitions of the base and different rates of tax—although there are possibilities of "harmonization." However, more complications generally are created when taxpayers have to comply with more than one set of tax rules.

This model of tax administration is, not surprisingly, much more common in unitary countries than in federal countries. The tax administrations of Italy, France, Portugal, many countries in French-speaking West Africa, many formerly socialist countries, and certain Latin American countries fit into this model of centralized tax administration.

Advantages and Disadvantages

Under one organizational structure for all tax administration, clear lines of authority are drawn so that tax staff in local offices realize that they are required to follow the rules and regulations established at the central level. Thus, taxes are collected throughout the country following the same process and procedures. This, inter alia, makes it easier for the tax administration to set up a simple computer system to monitor the collection of various taxes. Taxpayers' records with respect to each type of tax can be consolidated into one database or master file. Stop-filers can be detected quickly, and delinquent accounts can be addressed in an organized fashion. Taxpayers are more likely to receive uniform treatment in assessment, audit, penalties, and appeals, irrespective of where they reside. A well-publicized emphasis on uniform treatment enhances the perception of fairness of the tax system. Enforcement, especially the audit component of enforcement, is simplified if the tax inspector has information, from the taxpayer master file, on every tax for which a given taxpayer is liable. Also, there is no need to establish exchange of information agreements among tax administrations of different governmental units.

The price for this administrative simplicity is that local governments may perceive that they have very little control over receipts. In fact, however, subnational government control over revenues at the margin is more a function of controlling the marginal tax rates than administration per se. Thus, the perception of loss of control with central administration may reflect the balance of political powers between "potentially antagonist" governments, rather than technical constraints.

The assignment of revenues collected by a central tax administration may, however, face a number of difficulties. This is, for instance, the case if the personal income tax is assigned to local governments. Some formerly socialist countries, including most in the former Soviet Union, have decided to assign personal income tax revenue to local jurisdictions (Bell and Regulska, 1992). The problem, in this case, is that income taxes can be levied in principle by the jurisdiction where the income was obtained (source) or the jurisdiction where the taxpayer resides (residency). Assuming that the jurisdiction of residence is entitled to the taxes, the tax administration will have to verify residency. If person X lives in locality A, then all of X's income tax must be transferred from the central government's account to local government A's account. If person X lives in one locality and works in another, say locality B, then either the employer or the tax administration will have to verify that withholding taxes paid by the employer are allocated to the correct account. If, on the other hand, all of the personal income taxes withheld by the employer in locality B go to the local government of locality B, then administrative problems are somewhat reduced. However, if person X also receives income from other sources, such as renting out part of his residence in locality A, tax administration is complicated because person X would presumably fill out a tax return and make payment in locality A. The issue of withheld interest income also poses problems for tax administration if the tax department has to verify the residency of each taxpayer each time interest is paid. If each locality can set its own tax rates, compliance problems for withholders and verification problems for tax officials are further complicated, especially if localities often change these rates.

Piggybacking of a tax by a lower level government on a federal tax base can be one solution to these difficulties, as in Canada. In Canada, with the exception of Quebec, personal income taxes are levied by both the federal and provincial governments, but collected by the federal government. Taxpayers file one unified (federal and provincial) tax return and calculate their provincial tax as a percentage of their federal tax (tax on tax). The percentage may vary depending on the taxpayer's province, because each province has the authority to set its own tax rate.[4] If a taxpayer has moved during the year, the province of residence on December 31 receives the tax revenue for the whole year. The federal government pays an estimated amount to the provinces during the year and calculates a final reconciliation after all tax returns are received.

---

[4] A basically simple system has become excessively complicated as provinces sought more autonomy to respond to voters who demand that local politicians do something to alleviate various perceived problems. Recently, provinces have enacted certain tax credits that have been administered by the central tax administration. Especially controversial are certain proposals that advocates call "province-building" investment credits, which opponents consider beggar-my-neighbor investment provisions (Hartle, 1993). These provisions would move the administratively simple "tax-on-tax" system to a more complicated "tax-on-income" system.

Multilevel Government Tax Administration

Main Features

When a country authorizes one governmental level other than the center, or various levels of government, to levy and collect taxes, administration becomes more complicated than in the case of centralized tax administration. In general, each level of tax administration can create its own organizational structure and processes, which may not be the most efficient from a countrywide perspective. Duplication of effort among levels can easily occur, and effectiveness can suffer if the various tax administrations do not put in place requirements for adequate coordination. While local government officials may have increased autonomy, freedom, and resources to pursue local policy objectives, taxpayers are likely to bear higher compliance costs as each level of tax administration issues different forms, regulations, and procedures.

Under the approach where multiple levels of government are responsible for collecting taxes, the choice between revenue sharing and tax assignment may affect certain functions of tax administration. Normally, revenues are shared downward from central government to subnational governments. However, in a few countries revenue may be shared upward, and subnational governments are authorized to collect all taxes.[5] In this case, certain safeguards are necessary (for example, comprehensive and uniform training of tax officials, strict adherence to audit guidelines) to prevent nonuniform application of the tax laws. If taxes are assigned so that each level of government has authority to legislate and collect its own set of taxes, then problems of coordination among tax administrations are likely, and taxpayer compliance cost may be higher than under other options. Federations such as the United States, Switzerland, and Brazil are examples of countries with multilevel tax administrations and tax assignment (with some control over revenue, administration, and legislation).

Advantages and Disadvantages

Subnational tax administration provides more flexibility with respect to organizational structure and personnel practices than a centralized one. Local officials become more accountable, as a clearer link is established between local decisions to raise revenues and to make ex-

---

[5]Pre-1994 China and Germany are examples of this option. China, as discussed below, is undergoing comprehensive tax administration reform to create a central tax administration, in parallel with provincial tax collection agencies.

penditures. One disadvantage of this system is that some subnational governments, owing to resource constraints, may not be able to staff the various tax administration functions adequately. If some of these governments allocate fewer resources to areas such as taxpayer services, audit, penalties, and appeals, then it is possible that taxpayers in different jurisdictions would not receive uniform treatment with respect to all tax administration functions.

In situations where a jurisdiction surrenders a large net amount of tax revenue to the center, perverse incentives can be created to maintain revenue in the jurisdiction by favorable assessment of taxes due. In pre-1994 China, for example, the central government relied on the local (provincial) tax administration to collect most taxes.[6] Revenue was then shared between the provinces and the center on the basis of an ad hoc revenue-sharing formula, negotiated separately for each province.[7] The temptation was strong to lower the official assessment and then split the difference between the local government and the taxpayer. While the central government officials were aware of this problem, they were unable, with a staff of about 450, to police effectively the activities of more than 500,000 tax staff at the local (provincial) level. Tax administration in China became rule by negotiation rather than rule by law. Changes in tax policy may not be implemented as intended if tax collection becomes a process of negotiation. In order to move closer to rule by law, the Chinese tax structure was overhauled in 1994, with uniform tax laws, a central tax administration for central and shared taxes, as well as parallel provincial or local tax administrations, to remove the perverse incentives from the system.

In some countries, each level of government has tax policy and administration powers over the same tax bases, as in the United States, Switzerland, and Brazil. This arrangement maximizes state or local autonomy and is generally found where states (or provinces) are sovereign bodies. Autonomy is restricted, however, if a higher level of government defines the tax base and rates, or places boundaries on the tax base and/or rates. For further details on tax administration in these countries see below.

---

[6]This reliance created divided loyalties because tax staff, in effect, had to serve two masters—the central government and the provincial or local government. The central tax administration expected each jurisdictional tax administration to follow national tax administration policies, but there were few incentives to ensure that national policies were implemented correctly when the lower-level governments paid the salaries of tax administrators.

[7]Some minor taxes that brought in a relatively small amount of revenue were assigned to local governments.

If taxpayers must deal with several different tax authorities, tax administration can be complicated by duplication of effort among the various tax authorities. Hence, coordination among various tax departments becomes crucial, especially in the area of audits. As part of the federal income tax law in the United States, tax returns and tax return information can generally be disclosed to state tax agencies. If a taxpayer in the United States is audited with respect to federal income taxes, any action taken that changes the taxpayer's liability is automatically transmitted to state tax authorities. States that find state income tax violations also share that information with the Internal Revenue Service (IRS). There is a formal information-sharing agreement between states and the IRS. Detailed guidelines have been published to ensure confidentiality of taxpayer information (United States, Internal Revenue Service, 1993). On the other hand, state tax agencies in Brazil do not share information with Brazil's central government tax agency. Thus, overall tax administration in Brazil is rendered less effective because it becomes more difficult to foster voluntary compliance by ensuring, as much as possible, that taxpayers face a reasonable risk of detection if they do not comply.

Table 1 presents a summary of the advantages and disadvantages under centralized and multilevel tax administration.

Comparisons for Selected Countries

Are there obvious reasons why some countries centralize tax administration, while other countries choose some form of decentralized tax administration? Table 2 shows, for selected countries, the level of government primarily responsible for collecting at least one major tax. Countries in which administration is centralized are more likely to be unitary ones. Many countries with two or three levels of government authorized to collect taxes are federations. Three levels of tax administration are more prevalent in the largest countries. Although the federative or unitary nature of a country and its size appear to be important factors in determining the choice of the model of tax administration, other factors, such as historical trends and the balance of power among government levels, are also likely to play a role in this choice.

The specific circumstances of each country also determine how tax revenue is allocated among the levels. Table 3 illustrates the percentage of tax revenue attributable to (not collected by) each level of government for three specific taxes—income, property, and consumption—and for total tax revenue. Central governments, with the exception of some Scandinavian countries, generally receive most of the revenue

Table 1. Summary of Tax Administration Advantages and Disadvantages

Central Government Tax Administration	
Advantages	Disadvantages
• One organization • Clear lines of authority • Same processes and procedures • Uniform rules and regulations • One computer system, with one taxpayer record for all taxes • No need to exchange information • Stopfilers and delinquent accounts detectable more quickly • Uniform treatment in assessment, audit, penalties, and appeals • Simplifies auditing all taxes of a given taxpayer • Same training and same manuals	• Perception of less local control over revenues, especially if accompanied by central government control over rate structure

Multilevel Government Tax Administration	
Advantages	Disadvantages
• More responsibility of local tax administrators for revenue performance • More flexibility for local tax administrators • May be more appropriate for certain types of tax (e.g., property taxes) • May reflect political/constitutional constraints • More freedom for local policymakers to follow local preferences, if effective administration is feasible	• National policies (including stabilization) may not be implemented correctly • Duplication of effort possible, if more than one administration is used for a single tax base • Potential for nonuniform treatment of taxpayers • Various tax administration functions may not be staffed adequately • Effectiveness may suffer if the various tax administrations do not coordinate among themselves • Taxpayer compliance costs are relatively high

from income taxes. Similarly, central governments generally receive most of the revenue from consumption taxes, with the exceptions of Brazil, India, and the United States. Local governments (and a few state governments) generally receive most of the revenue from property taxes, with the exceptions of some European countries and Chile.

Developed Countries

Germany

Germany employs an extensive revenue-sharing system, characterized by some as the dominant feature of their federalism (Bird, 1986). Taxes are primarily administered at the state (*Länder*) level (with the

Table 2. Selected Countries: Government Responsible for Collecting at Least One Major Tax

	Central	State, Provincial, or Regional	Municipal or Local
Algeria	•		
Belgium	•		
Bulgaria	•		
Chile	•		
China (pre-1994)			•
Côte d'Ivoire	•		
Estonia	•		
France	•		
Guatemala	•		
Iran, Islamic Rep. of	•		
Malawi	•		
Norway	•		
Poland	•		
Portugal	•		
Romania	•		
Sweden	•		
Germany	•	•	
Netherlands	•		•
Paraguay	•		•
Switzerland		•	•
United Kingdom	•		•
Argentina	•	•	•
Australia	•	•	•
Brazil	•	•	•
Canada	•	•	•
Colombia	•	•	•
India	•	•	•
United States	•	•	•

Sources: Information provided by various tax officials and IMF staff; and Bird (1986).

Note: Major taxes include income, sales, VAT, excises, customs, natural resource, and property. In some countries, local governments collect minor taxes, license taxes, and fees, which are not captured in this table.

exception of border taxes), but tax policy is harmonized (Spahn, Steinmetz, and Föttinger, 1996). Tax laws are passed at the federal (*Bund*) level, but state interests are carefully considered because of the unique role played by the Bundesrat (upper house or federal council). Members of the Bundesrat are directly appointed by state governments and vote to protect the interest of their state rather than a political party.

Administration is implemented on a uniform basis, following rule by law. The German administrative system is highly integrated and coordinated. Federal tax officials, in cooperation with state tax officials, determine tax administration processes and procedures. Since some discrepancies in administration are bound to appear, German tax

Table 3. Tax Revenue Attributable to Each Level of Government
(In percent of general government)

Country and Year	Total Tax Revenue			Taxes on Income			Taxes on Property			Domestic Taxes on Goods and Services		
	C	S	L	C	S	L	C	S	L	C	S	L
Netherlands (1988)	97.8		0.8	100.0			100.0			99.4		
Paraguay (1987)	97.6		2.4									
Indonesia (1988)	97.3	2.7		100.0			55.4	44.6		95.4	4.6	
Chile (1987)	96.5		3.5	100.0			100.0			95.5		4.5
Kenya (1986)	96.4		3.6	100.0			1.4		98.6	97.6		2.4
Zimbabwe (1986)	96.3		3.7	100.0			12.3		87.7	98.3		1.7
Ireland (1987)	96.0		2.3	100.0			42.9		57.1	98.7		
Malawi (1984)	95.9		4.1	99.7		0.3	1.9		98.1	99.8		0.2
Israel (1986)	95.5		4.5	100.0			22.9		77.1	100.0		
Thailand (1988)	95.0		5.0	100.0			58.8		41.2	92.8		7.2
South Africa (1986)	94.4	1.5	4.1	100.0			27.7		72.3	95.6	4.4	
Belgium (1987)	93.5		5.0	90.0		10.0	100.0			95.9		3.3
New Zealand (1981)	93.5		6.5	100.0			17.9		82.1	98.8		1.2
Luxembourg (1987)	93.3		6.2	87.6		12.4	92.0		8.0	99.2		0.7
Hungary (1988)	91.7		8.8	73.2		26.8	55.5		45.5	99.2		0.8
France (1988)	90.0		9.2									
United Kingdom (1987)	88.1		10.7	100.0			17.0		83.0	99.8		
Spain (1986)	87.7	3.3	9.0	84.3	1.2	14.4	56.7	23.9	19.4	76.1	7.4	16.5
Mexico (1984)	84.6	12.7	2.7	98.2	1.6	0.2	8.7	52.4	38.9	99.4	0.3	0.3
Australia (1987)	81.1	15.3	3.6	100.0			4.9	49.2	46.0	75.6	24.4	
Norway (1986)	80.9		19.1	57.1		42.9	40.6		59.4	99.8		0.2

Country (Year)												
Poland (1988)	80.9		19.1	79.6					49.2	89.2		10.8
Colombia (1984)	80.3	13.3	6.3	100.0		20.4	50.8		90.5	70.0	30.0	
Bolivia (1986)	78.6	18.4	3.0	99.2	0.8		9.5			60.1	36.2	3.7
Sweden (1987)	77.7		32.6	33.2		66.8				100.0		
Pakistan (1979)	76.9	18.5	4.6				100.0					
Finland (1987)	76.0		25.3									
Austria (1987)	75.8	11.5	12.7	58.0	22.6	19.4	52.1	4.3	43.6	71.3	13.1	15.6
Brazil (1987)	71.4	26.6	1.9	100.0			2.8	51.9	45.3	43.7	53.4	2.8
Denmark (1987)	71.2		28.2	54.0		43.0	57.0		43.0	99.4		0.1
Germany (1988)	69.8	21.7	7.6	39.4	40.5	20.1	5.2	54.5	40.3	69.9	29.4	0.1
India (1986)	67.2	32.8		100.0			39.0	61.0		51.9	48.1	
United States (1987)	66.7	20.6	12.8	81.6	16.8	1.7	5.6	7.2	87.1	17.1	68.0	14.9
Switzerland (1987)	60.5	22.8	16.7	22.8	42.2	35.0	32.6	42.2	25.2	87.7	11.8	0.5
Canada (1988)	50.8	40.0	9.2	63.5	36.5			16.1	83.9	38.7	60.8	0.5

Source: Levin (1991).

Note: C = central government, S = state government, and L = local government; figures are the average of latest three years available.

administrators meet on a periodic basis to harmonize implementation of the tax laws. All tax staff are trained to follow agreed upon processes and procedures, to ensure uniformity in treatment of taxpayers. The German *Länder* also have information-sharing agreements if a business pays taxes in more than one *Land*. However, this information may have to be transmitted in hard copy because the *Länder* do not utilize the same computer systems.

Switzerland

Swiss taxpayers strongly believe that the preferences of each canton have a high priority (Bird, 1986). They are willing to bear the burden of extra compliance costs to ensure that local officials have the necessary own source revenues to meet the demand for local public goods. The canton's taxing powers are relatively broad, within certain constitutional restrictions. For example, double taxation, special taxes on any trade or industry, and unjustified tax relief are prohibited.[8] Jurisdictions within cantons can also levy taxes and set rates, with authorization from the canton.

The tax administrations of the cantons collect income tax for both the canton and the confederation. While taxpayers only need to file one tax return covering both taxes, the definition of taxable income will normally differ between the canton and the confederation because each canton is free to determine levels of exemptions or deductions. So the taxpayer must make two calculations of taxable income, and the tax administration must verify that both calculations are correct. Also, tax auditors must be careful not to confuse the tax rules for cantons with the tax rules for the confederation. While encouragement of diversity is the accepted practice in Switzerland, it does complicate tax administration.

United States

In the United States, the various tax administrations use different methods to collect delinquent taxes. In addition to the traditional method of personal contact by field collection staff, state tax administrations have adopted methods such as (1) new or improved accounts receivable management information systems, (2) updated written billing procedures, (3) telephone collection techniques, and (4) en-

---

[8]The Constitution allows cantons full authority to levy any tax not expressly reserved for the confederation and sets restrictions on the rates of taxes collected by the confederation.

forcement programs that restrict business taxpayer access to certain state licenses and permits if delinquent taxes are not resolved. Some states have modified the roles of revenue officers by reducing the level of personal contact in favor of the above methods. Many states are using modern collection methods not currently used by the IRS. These states have employed private collection companies to collect unpaid taxes and have allowed delinquent taxpayers to use credit cards in paying the taxes due (United States, General Accounting Office, 1994).

Taxpayer compliance costs can be higher with multiple tax administrations than under other options. Currently, 43 states in the United States plus the District of Columbia have adopted a personal income tax.[9] As a result, U.S. taxpayers must file two tax returns, calculating taxable income and tax liability twice, because tax rates, deductions, and exemptions differ between the central level and the state level.[10]

Developing Countries

India

In contrast to tax sharing upward in pre-1994 China and Germany, India is one of a number of countries with multilevel government tax administration, where tax revenue is shared downward. However, the system in India, which provides for revenue sharing on a tax-by-tax basis, also contains some perverse incentives that can reduce the effectiveness of tax administration. For example, central government tax officials collect all individual income taxes on nonagricultural income and then return 85 percent of revenue collected to the states. Even though the tax administration is given a collection target in the budget, the incentive to allocate sufficient enforcement resources and perform high-quality audits for this tax is lower than other taxes, for example, the profit tax or customs duties, where revenue is retained by the central government.

Brazil

In Brazil, the central government levies a VAT on industrial products (IPI), while the states levy a VAT on a broad range of products

---

[9]For further discussion of the U.S. system, see Chapter 15 below.

[10]Three states define state tax liability as a percentage of federal tax liability. Twenty-five states, plus the District of Columbia, use federal adjusted gross income as the starting tax base for taxpayers to calculate their state income taxes; eight states use federal taxable income as the starting base; two states tax only interest and dividend income; and five states use income tax bases that are not related to the federal income tax base (Erard and Vaillancourt, 1993).

(ICMS) (Rodriguez, 1990, and Chapter 18). Both taxes have multiple rates, but the state tax rates cannot exceed a ceiling fixed by the Senate. A committee composed of the financial secretaries of each state (CONFAZ) is responsible for coordination of the VAT, including authorization of exemptions. With respect to interstate transactions, the origin principle is generally applied. The exporting state levies the tax on exports, and the importing state allows a credit to importers, for the tax paid to the exporting state. The distribution of VAT revenue across states depends heavily on the balance of trade with other states.

Tax administration in Brazil is complicated for various reasons. There is an inevitable duplication of effort between the federal and the state governments in the taxation of similar bases under the two VAT-type taxes. Taxpayers must have two taxpayer identification numbers—one for the federal VAT and one for the state VAT—and file two sets of tax returns. The tax administration must also follow two different sets of procedures for invoices of goods shipped between states and goods shipped within a state. Since there is no central statistical database to record sales and purchases for the state VAT, it is impossible to conduct a systematic cross-checking of information. Thus, state auditors are placed in a relatively weak position by a lack of important information. Of course these significant tax administration drawbacks have to be weighed against the gains in increased autonomy for the states.

Countries in Transition

In former socialist countries where tax administrations are still relatively weak, it is essential that adequate resources be allocated to the major functions of collection and audit. These functions were relatively simple to perform with respect to large state-owned enterprises, whose resources, including bank accounts, were closely controlled by their ministries. With a greater market orientation, government control over enterprises still under public ownership is being eroded, and tax administration is even weaker with respect to privatized enterprises or new businesses. Also, for individuals under the socialist system, the tax burden was hidden (the difference between their purchasing power and shadow value of their contribution to production); now the tax burden is explicit, requiring the tax administration to strengthen the audit and collection functions (Ickes and Slemrod, 1992).

The picture is further complicated by the uncertainty surrounding intergovernmental relations in these countries. Both expenditure and tax assignments, as well as the systems of intergovernmental transfers, remain in a state of flux in many formerly centrally planned economies.

Moreover, some of these countries have assigned revenue by ownership rights, rather than by tax. If a local government owns an enterprise, it is entitled to the revenues generated by that enterprise, while a similar enterprise owned by the central government would pay its taxes to the latter. The capacity to enforce taxes on locally owned enterprises is wanting in many instances.

Even though subnational governments are clamoring for autonomy, it makes sense to keep tax administration simple, at least during the transition. A distinction should be drawn between what is technically feasible in the short term and what is a goal to strive for in the long term. In the short term, the most feasible approach may be to establish only one tax administration at the central government level with some type of revenue sharing based on an objective formula.

Issues in Moving from Centralized to Multilevel Tax Administration

General Considerations

Given the trend toward decentralization of expenditures and concomitant financing apparent around the world, steps should be taken to ensure effective tax administration at all levels of government. The first step is to take clear decisions regarding the taxes to be assigned to subnational governments. The knowledge, skills, and abilities needed to administer a property tax, for example, differ from those needed to administer a personal income tax, and the former may be easier to devolve and administer at lower levels of government than the latter. Several key elements should be put in place to establish subnational tax administrations with adequate capacity to collect the devolved taxes. These elements of any successful tax administration reform include a well-defined strategy, a sustained political commitment, a dedicated implementation team, the necessary physical resources, and the provision of appropriate training (Tanzi and Pellechio, 1997).

Subnational tax administrations would have to recruit and train staff to perform various functions within an appropriate organizational structure.[11] The organization should include several basic tax administration functions. One unit should be established to provide taxpayer services

---

[11]In principle, staff should be trained in tax law, the relevant procedural and administrative law, investigative methods, computer technology, economics, and management (Bagchi, Bird, and Das-Gupta, 1995).

(education, information, assistance). Simple collection procedures should be designed to minimize the burden on taxpayers. These procedures could be manual at first, but they should be designed with a view to computerizing taxpayer records as soon as possible.[12] Depending on the type of tax administered, a unit of auditors or land assessors should be established and staff should be trained. Finally, a straightforward system of penalties and appeals should be developed. A separate unit should be responsible for each of these functions (Casanegra de Jantscher, Silvani, and Vehorn, 1992).

In addition to an organizational plan, other preparatory steps should be undertaken. For example, discussions should be held with the central tax administration to provide for some type of information sharing, so that cross-checking activities can be performed. Also, it would be appropriate to form a group of subnational tax administrators, who could meet regularly to discuss common problems and solutions. This group, for instance, could prepare a model tax declaration so that each administration does not have to design its own form. It could also disseminate information on various issues, such as how to strengthen enforcement. State tax administrations in the United States have formed the Federation of Tax Administrators, which performs a number of coordinating and information-disseminating activities.

Administering Subnational Taxes

In this subsection, the type of tax administration choices that would typically face a lower level government is illustrated. Not all possible subnational tax assignments are addressed (for this, see Chapter 3) but the focus is on a key subgroup to show the main choices for some taxes used by lower levels of government in many countries: property taxes, business licenses and user charges, surcharges on the income tax, as well as indirect taxes including excises, the VAT, and the retail sales tax.

Property Taxes

As discussed earlier, property taxes are the prime example of revenues that should be assigned to lower levels of government, particularly to the municipal or local levels. Indeed, the information needed to administer this tax differs substantially from that which would be required say for other direct taxes, such as the corporate or personal in-

---

[12]If possible, subnational tax administrations should use for each taxpayer the same taxpayer identification number as used by the central tax administration.

come taxes, or for indirect taxes, such as the VAT or sales taxes. The focus of a property tax administration is to generate a register of property titles, as well as valuations that are reasonably up to date. Thus, even if there were a single tax administration for all taxes, it is likely that property taxes would be collected separately, for example, from the VAT.

In many developing countries, the greatest difficulty in administering a property tax is to generate comparable and recent information on the property stock, ownership, and valuation. In countries such as Colombia, the maintenance of the property register and updating the valuation is centrally coordinated, although the billing, filing of payments, and auditing of the property tax are carried out at the local level. However, even the centrally maintained property register can prove to be cumbersome and difficult to update in a rapidly changing environment of property development and escalating values, as has been the case in Colombia.

An alternative to the traditional method of property administration based solely on the property register is also to permit self-assessments. Such a method relies on the principles of tax administration enunciated earlier—taxpayer compliance and evaluation, auditing procedures, and penalties and appeals. This method has been applied, for instance, in the Colombian capital, Bogotá, and is seen as a way of circumventing the time-consuming process of updating the property register. Two essential elements with this variant include (1) the collection of information on property sales by the local administration, such as the requirement to register a sale before titles can be transferred; and (2) a visibly unbiased enforcement of sanctions. An example of such a sanction is that the local authority has the right to purchase a property at say between 1 and 1.5 times the declared valuation, in cases where underdeclaration is suspected. Bogotá has had a rapid increase in property tax collections in the two years since the self-valuation scheme was introduced. However, it is important not to come to quick generalizations in this context, since the success of such a method of self-declaration depends crucially on an effective and fair tax administration, with the political will to implement sanctions (without which the scheme could quickly degenerate into revenue loss). To prevent revenue loss, a hybrid administration is also possible, with the traditional property register being maintained as a floor to the property tax liabilities, together with self-declaration based on market values. As has been demonstrated in Bogotá, it is possible to improve property tax collection rapidly by applying tax administration principles judiciously. Bogotá's success would not have been possible if sole reliance had been placed on a property register, which was already better and more sophisticated than those available in most developing countries.

Licenses, Presumptive Taxes, and User Fees

The utilization of *local information* permits the effective local administration of licenses and other presumptive taxes on small businesses and informal sector activities. Such sectors are of great importance in developing and transition economies and are relatively hard to tax given the main tax instruments, such as the income tax or the VAT. The obvious danger with presumptive taxation is the possibility of arbitrariness on the part of the tax administration that could generate more corruption and nuisance than revenues. The various alternatives in this regard seek to minimize discretion on part of the tax administrators and protect the rights of taxpayers, while preserving the revenue base. Some of these options are discussed below.

Standard assessments are one method of imposing presumptive taxes. These are lump sum and could be made a function of occupation or business activity. The lump-sum nature of the tax has positive incentive effects on production. The criteria for imposition of the tax should be clearly defined, and little discretion be given to tax administrators, to minimize corruption. While lump-sum presumptive taxes or licenses are easy to administer, and have positive incentive effects, they generally cannot be easily adjusted for inflation or allow for specific circumstances of taxpayers, and for these reasons may have a limited revenue potential. It is possible also to have *estimated assessments*, which are based on indicators such as the size of business premises, number of employees, installed machinery, electricity use, and so on. In countries such as Italy, coefficients have been developed for particular activities. Procedural aspects have been clearly defined, permitting taxpayers to challenge the applicability of the coefficients, specifying the time period and documentation required (Mercurio, 1994). In countries with local tax administration, there may be some advantage in determining the presumptive base (or coefficients) on a systematic basis (at the regional or perhaps even national level, given the institutional and constitutional arrangements), in order to avoid "nuisance" levies. There is clearly a trade-off between the extent to which the lump-sum nature of the taxes is to be modified, and the discretion available to the tax collectors. Thus, the need to allow taxpayer appeals and ensure rapid and fair adjudication of disputed claims becomes important if taxpayer compliance is to be maintained.

User fees are normally implemented by public service providers and do not generally put pressure on local tax administration resources.

Piggybacked Taxes or Surcharges

The essence of responsible decision making by lower levels of government is the ability to raise own tax rates at the margin to meet additional expenditures. A local tax administration without the ability to influence marginal tax rates does not meet this criterion, but may still be used in cases in which there is distrust of the national tax administration by the lower levels of government. For some mobile tax bases, a simple alternative to an elaborate subnational tax administration is to piggyback on a national tax base, such as the personal income tax. A possible option is a surcharge imposed by the lower level of government on the amount of federal income tax liability. With this form of piggybacking, the distribution of provincial tax revenues would parallel the tax-sharing outcomes. Another option is for the tax to be levied directly on the federal tax base, to avoid tax-on-tax pyramiding. With either variant, the tax would not involve additional tax forms, and the taxpayer would be required simply to fill in an additional line on the federal tax form, permitting the funds to be credited directly by the banks to separate federal and provincial accounts. Lower levels of government could be given the authority to set the rate of the supplementary flat tax or surcharge, subject to a limit (and/or floor), in order to achieve the control over marginal tax rates necessary for local government accountability. Where lower-level auditing capabilities are weak, the central government could perform this function for lower levels of government. However, if there is mistrust of the federal government, separate auditing capabilities could be developed at the lower level, although as argued above, there would be significant benefits from the sharing of information.

For administratively feasible piggybacking by the lower levels of government, the importance of maintaining the same subnational tax base as at the central level cannot be overemphasized. As the Canadian experience suggests, a simple tax can become extremely complicated as lower levels of government indulge in granting various exemptions, thus effectively changing the relevant tax base for piggybacking.

In practice, the federal government would have to inform the subnational governments of the expected tax base, including all federal tax deductions, well in advance of the budget preparation cycle of the provinces or local governments. The subnational levels of government would have to determine their tax rates at about this stage, to allow sufficient time for the central tax administration to inform employers about the local tax rates applying to employees residing in different local or provincial tax jurisdictions. Thus, a single withholding would apply to each taxpayer, to be distributed among different levels of government.

State or Provincial Indirect Taxes

While subnational VATs are feasible, they result in a great deal of administrative complexity if the objective of the subnational government is to tax final consumption, as with the destination-basis VATs. Much of the complexity lies in the treatment of interprovincial sales and zero rating of exports to other provinces under the destination basis. An origin-basis VAT is much simpler to administer: sales to other provinces are taxed, and imports are not. However, in the absence of an interprovincial redistribution mechanism, this system would clearly benefit those provinces where much of the production and refining base is located. Moreover, differences in rates of an origin-basis VAT can promote distortions in location, production, and pricing decisions of national enterprises.

Certain types of excises may also prove difficult to administer at the subnational level. In principle, if an excise is treated as a tax on a final consumer good levied at the point of production, for example, the refinery or the brewery, there should be little difficulty for the provincial or even the local administration in collecting the tax. Usually such production points are few and located in only some of the provinces. There is thus a possibility of increasing horizontal fiscal disparities with such a tax assignment. However, if the tax is levied at the point of consumption, local administration becomes problematic, particularly regarding sales to other provinces. Monitoring sales becomes difficult, and a problem of "domestic contraband" may develop for excisable goods, as in Colombia for example for alcoholic drinks.

A retail sales tax at the subnational level is more feasible than a subnational VAT and, if exemptions are kept to a minimum, provides broader coverage than excise taxes. The United States is one example of a federal system where states depend heavily on the retail sales tax.[13] The heavy reliance is due in part to (1) the relatively limited resistance toward the retail sales tax in comparison with the two major alternatives—the state income tax or the property tax; (2) the belief that the sales tax produces a more stable revenue flow and fewer distortions than the income tax; and (3) the belief that the retail sales tax is relatively easy to administer. The fact that the federal government does not rely on the retail sales tax also encourages states to rely on this tax as a major revenue source. The two major drawbacks of the sales tax are the problem of regressivity and the problem in taxing interstate transactions. Regressivity can be reduced through exemptions or credits, but

---

[13]Forty-five states plus the District of Columbia utilize the retail sales tax with statutory rates varying from 3 percent to 8 percent (Ebel and Zimmerman, 1992).

tax administrators claim that exemptions or credits increase the burden of administration by complicating audits as the tax is often misapplied. Interstate sales will continue to be a problem since states do not have the authority to require out-of-state vendors to collect and remit the sales tax (Due and Mikesell, 1994).

Conclusions

The design of the subnational taxes may have repercussions on tax administration and, conversely, tax policy options and assignments are constrained by tax administration capabilities at each level of government. Thus, there is little benefit for subnational governments in taking on tax tools that they are unable to administer, or others where the ability to influence the marginal tax rates is limited. However, in many parts of the world the search continues for "appropriate" and easily administered subnational revenue sources to match the increasing devolution of expenditure responsibilities to lower levels of government.

Administrative complexity increases when subnational governments attempt to levy and collect taxes on mobile tax bases. This is particularly noticeable in the case of indirect taxes such as the VAT and income taxes. One level of tax administration is to be recommended in such cases (this may be at the provincial level in countries with adequate administrations, such as for the VAT in Germany and Quebec, with central government revenues or shares distributed upward). The more typical case is of a VAT administered by the center, with revenues shared with provinces on a derivation or formula basis. Equalization of revenue or fiscal capacities would come through an explicit grants mechanism or the revenue-sharing formula adopted. Administration can be simplified and, at the same time, provincial control over marginal tax rates can be achieved if piggybacking on a central tax administration and a harmonized tax base (for example, income) is used.

The trade-off between administrative ease and local autonomy has created many different ways in which tax administration is organized. As this chapter has described, some countries rely purely on central government administration; other countries rely on tax administration at lower levels or all levels of government. For subnational tax administration to be effective all the major functions of tax administration (taxpayer services, collection, audit, penalties, and appeals) should be provided. Also, provision should be made for the sharing of information across different levels of tax administration because of the significant efficiency gains that can be achieved. Some functions, for example, certain collection activities, may be contracted out to higher levels of government or the private sector by those subnational governments that lack the capability to provide the function on their own.

Several countries tend to have separate administrations for clearly lower-level tax bases, including, inter alia, property taxes, as well as small businesses and service sector activities. The former is an illustration of an immobile tax base, although problems may exist with the registration of property and its valuation. The latter would be governed by the existence of local information and knowledge that may not be available to higher levels of administration. In such cases, there is a trade-off between simple lump-sum taxes that might have limited revenue potential and more complex formulations that allow some discretion to tax administrators. The choice in most cases is to minimize the discretion to the tax collectors, while raising revenues in as fair a manner as possible. The outcomes vary across countries, reflecting different institutions, administrative capabilities, and political-economy constraints.

Most developing countries and countries in transition to a market economy are likely to face serious complications if they do not place a high priority on the criterion of administrative ease and simplicity of tax design. Many of these countries have not fully developed the institutional capability to successfully operate separate and independent tax administrations at various levels of government (Rice, 1992). This is likely to prove to be a serious bottleneck to responsible governance as expenditure functions continue to be decentralized.

References

Bagchi, Amaresh, Richard Bird, and Arindam Das-Gupta, 1995, "An Economic Approach to Tax Administration Reform," Discussion Paper No. 3 (Toronto: International Center for Tax Studies, University of Toronto, November).

Bell, Michael E., and Joanna Regulska, 1992, "Centralization Versus Decentralization: The Case of Financing Autonomous Local Governments in Poland," in *Public Finance in a World of Transition: Proceedings of the Forty-Seventh Congress of the International Institute of Public Finance, St. Petersburg, 1991*, ed. by Pierre Pestieau, Supplement to *Public Finance*, Vol. 47, pp. 187–201.

Bialczak, J. Elaine, 1989, "Sales Taxation: Local Autonomy Within Sales Taxation and Expense Associated with Disparate Administration," in National Tax Association: Tax Institute of America, *Proceedings of the Eighty-Second Annual Conference*, pp. 127–31.

Bird, Richard M., 1986, *Federal Finance in Comparative Perspective* (Toronto: Canadian Tax Foundation).

Casanegra de Jantscher, Milka, 1986, "Problems in Administering a Value-Added Tax in Developing Countries," IMF Working Paper 86/15 (Washington: International Monetary Fund, December).

———, and Carlos Silvani, 1991, "Guidelines for Administering a VAT," in *Value-Added Tax: Administrative and Policy Issues*, ed. by Alan A. Tait, IMF Occasional Paper 88 (Washington: International Monetary Fund).

———, and Charles L. Vehorn, 1992, "Modernizing Tax Administration," in *Fiscal Policies in Economies in Transition*, ed. by Vito Tanzi (Washington: International Monetary Fund).

Due, John F., and John L. Mikesell, 1994, *Sales Taxation: State and Local Structure and Administration* (Washington: Urban Institute Press).

Ebel, Robert D., and Christopher Zimmerman, 1992, "Sales Tax Trends and Issues," in *Sales Taxation: Critical Issues in Policy and Administration*, ed. by William F. Fox (Westport, Connecticut: Praeger Publishers).

Erard, Brian, and François Vaillancourt, 1993, "The Compliance Costs of a Separate Personal Income Tax System for Ontario: Simulations for 1991," in *Taxation in a Subnational Jurisdiction*, ed. by Allan M. Maslove (Toronto: University of Toronto Press).

Hartle, Douglas P., 1993, "The Federal-Provincial Tax Collection Agreements: Personal Income Tax Coordination," in *Taxation in a Subnational Jurisdiction*, ed. by Allan M. Maslove (Toronto: University of Toronto Press).

Ickes, Barry W., and Joel Slemrod, 1992, "Tax Implementation Issues in the Transition from a Planned Economy," in *Public Finance in a World of Transition: Proceedings of the Forty-Seventh Congress of the International Institute of Public Finance, St. Petersburg 1991*, ed. by Pierre Pestieau, Supplement to *Public Finance*, Vol. 47, pp. 384–99.

Inter-American Center of Tax Administrators, 1992, "Organization of Tax Administration in 27 CIAT Member Countries," *CIAT Review* (December).

LeBaube, Robert A., and Charles L. Vehorn, 1992, "Assisting Taxpayers in Meeting Their Obligations Under the Law," in *Improving Tax Administration in Developing Countries*, ed. by Richard M. Bird and Milka Casanegra de Jantscher (Washington: International Monetary Fund).

Levin, Jonathan, 1991, "Measuring the Role of Subnational Governments," in *Public Finance with Several Levels of Government: Proceedings of the Forty-Sixth Congress of the International Institute of Public Finance, Brussels, 1990*, ed. by Remy Prud'homme, *Public Finance*, 1991, pp. 21–36.

McLure, Jr., Charles E., 1983, "Assignment of Corporate Income Taxes in a Federal System," in *Tax Assignment in Federal Countries*, ed. by Charles E. McLure, Jr. (Canberra: Australian National University).

Mercurio, Domenico, 1994, "Accertamento induttivo per coefficienti presuntivi," *Il Fisco*, Vol. 35, pp. 8379–82.

Oates, Wallace E., 1972, *Fiscal Federalism* (New York: Harcourt Brace Jovanovich).

———, 1991, "An Economist's Perspective on Fiscal Federalism," in *Studies in Fiscal Federalism*, ed. by Wallace E. Oates (Aldershot, England; Brookfield, Vermont: Edward Elgar).

Rice, Eric, 1992, "Public Administration in Post-Socialist Eastern Europe," *Public Administration Review*, Vol. 52, No. 2 (March/April), pp. 116–24.

Rodriguez, Carlos, 1990, "The Origin and Form of Implementation of the Value-Added Tax in Brazil: Some Considerations and Particularities," paper presented at an International Symposium on the Value Added Tax, Istanbul, Turkey, January.

Rubinfield, Daniel L., 1983, "Tax Assignment and Revenue Sharing in the United States," in *Tax Assignment in Federal Countries* ed. by Charles E. McLure, Jr. (Camberra: Australian National University).

Spahn, Paul Bernd, Imke Steinmetz, and Wolfgang Föttinger, 1996, "Tax Assignment and Tax Administration in the German Model of Cooperative Federalism" (unpublished).

Tanzi, Vito, and Anthony J. Pellechio, 1997, "The Reform of Tax Administration," in *Institutions and Economic Development: Growth and Governance in Less-Developed and Post-Socialist Countries*, ed, by Christopher K. Clague (Baltimore: Johns Hopkins University Press).

United States, General Accounting Office, 1994, *Tax Administration: State Tax Administrators' Views on Delinquent Tax Collection Methods*, GAO/GGD-94-59FS (Washington, February).

United States, Internal Revenue Service, 1993, *Tax Information Security Guidelines for Federal State and Local Agencies*, Publication No. 1075 (Washington, January).

6

Budgetary and Financial Management

BARRY POTTER

Whether in a federation or in a unitary state, lower-tier governments play an important role in delivering public policies and services. Their provision of services has an economic impact on overall activity, on the allocation of resources, and on the pursuit of equity objectives. Their financing has an impact on the levels and types of taxation, with allocative and distributional consequences. Their borrowing has an influence on monetary conditions and interest rates. The importance of secondary tiers of government is recognized in the IMF's financial programming exercises that, whenever possible,[1] focus on the financial surplus or deficit of the wider general government sector.

Yet this important macroeconomic dimension of local government activities poses many difficulties for policymakers, particularly when determining annual expenditure budgets and borrowing, both for central and local governments. The institutional arrangements for the determination and conduct of public policies and services need to take appropriate account of macroeconomic goals. The main issues include the following:

- What direction, guidance, or controls—recognizing the range of relationships between the central and local government under different fiscal federalism models—should be given to lower-tier governments, in advance of their budget setting?
- How are the budgets of local governments to be taken into account by the central government, when drawing up its own budget?

---

[1]In practice, poor information about the fiscal position of local governments sometimes requires limiting the programming exercise to the central government.

- What coordination can be put in place to ensure that the respective policies of each tier contribute both to central and local resource allocation and distributional goals?
- What monitoring requirements are needed to ensure that the central government can take into account developments in the delivery of local government budgets, in deciding on any in-year fiscal action?
- How can grant systems, in their size, structure, and payment patterns, best accommodate the need for financial planning and cash management at both levels of government?
- How can the respective plans of both tiers for borrowing best be coordinated to avoid unnecessary borrowing in aggregate or excessive pressures on financial markets at certain times?
- What role, particularly in a unitary state,[2] should the government play in checking not only the aggregate levels of spending by local governments but also the efficiency and effectiveness of that expenditure?

This chapter focuses on the institutional arrangements in intergovernmental relations necessary to meet macroeconomic policy goals. First, some macroeconomic objectives are suggested for the overall conduct of local government budgets and their coordination with central government objectives. Second, some specific approaches are recommended for budget preparation, distinguishing between a federal and unitary (that is, a more agency-type) relationship between local and central government. Third, the need for monitoring of budget implementation and the modalities of corrective fiscal action within the year are considered. Fourth, payment of grants and issues of coordination of cash management and borrowing plans are discussed. Finally, the increasingly important role of audit, inspection, and evaluation in securing objectives on resource allocation and efficient delivery of public services in local governments is discussed.

Public Expenditure Management Objectives for Local Governments

The principal macroeconomic objectives in budget setting and implementation (from a general government perspective) may be described as follows:

---

[2]In federal states, central government control is primarily focused on a design of transfers and control over borrowing. However, even in federal states the central government may exert a degree of control on allocative and distributional aspects of local government through special purpose grants.

- To ensure that aggregate spending and borrowing are consistent with government macroeconomic objectives for inflation, economic growth, and fiscal and monetary stabilization.
- To enable the delivery of public services in an effective way, which meets the allocative and distributional objectives underlying the spending plans.
- To bring about the delivery of services consistent with these plans (and the related budget authorizations and relevant financial regulations), while retaining the ability to modify the plans in the light of evolving fiscal circumstances and in particular revenues available, within the year.
- To ensure that the above objectives are mutually achieved while pursuing effective cash management and minimizing borrowing costs.
- To put in place audit, inspection, and evaluation procedures in order to promote an efficient and effective delivery of public services.

Budget Preparation: Aggregate Expenditure Control

Budget preparation procedures must take into account several macroeconomic dimensions, including (1) the impact of local government budgets on the economy; (2) the interaction between central and local government budgets—for example where some grant expenditure is effectively open-ended; and (3) the need and scope for some coordination between central and local government policies. This last point is particularly important if certain policy objectives are to be secured—for example, where expenditure assignments are such that both tiers of government have policies aimed at the same client group.

Irrespective of the relationship between central and local governments, a precondition for the respective harmonization of budget proposals in this area is adequate information on the public policies, spending plans, revenue projections, and borrowing requirements of each tier of government. For less-developed economies, securing adequate and timely information can be a significant problem. Indeed, lags and inaccuracies, different expenditure (and revenue) classifications, policy misunderstandings (for example, who will pay for a particular service), the absence of a global budget—such that there are important off-budget transactions—can be serious drawbacks to the coordination of budget preparation.

To some extent, the significance of the information problem depends on the local government model in operation. Under a federal arrangement, the central government's main aim is usually to achieve overall macroeconomic control principally through borrowing limits and controls on subnational governments (see Chapter 7). Even then, however, particularly where expenditure assignments have any element of overlap and where central government policies affect local budgets, coordination of policies is highly desirable. Information within the year is essential for monitoring macroeconomic development. Under the unitary model, however, the need for information and coordination, though different as described below, may be just as important. Information requirements vary between the autonomy model—typical of a federal structure as in Germany, the United States, and Canada, for example—and the centralized agency approach, as applied in recent years in the United Kingdom, for example, and described below.

In principle, under either a federal or unitary model, the appropriate fiscal policy from a macroeconomic perspective—that is designed to meet the objectives set out earlier—would have to meet a formidable set of requirements:

- Adequate coordination of spending, revenue raising, and borrowing plans in aggregate to ensure macroeconomic stabilization.
- Agreement on the allocation of resources among spending programs so that, to the extent possible, they reinforce rather than contradict the allocative and redistributional policy goals of each tier.
- Mutually agreed and accurate forecasts of expenditures, revenues, the timing of cash inflows and outflows, and hence borrowing needs.
- Coordination of the timing and amounts of borrowing to avoid undue pressures on the financial markets.

In reality, such a comprehensive approach is difficult to achieve in full. Yet, in a number of countries, the budget preparation procedures incorporate several features designed to meet all or some of these objectives. The approach differs between the federal, more autonomous, models and the unitary, more direct, control arrangements.

The practical experience of federal systems illustrates the importance of having medium-term financial plans that cover all levels of government in the formulation of fiscal policy and plans. For example, in Australia, before the Premiers' Council decides on the overall level of commonwealth (central government) transfers to the states, the Treasury prepares a memorandum for the Cabinet that outlines fiscal developments and prospects in the state or local sectors. These are prepared in the context of forward estimates of outlays for general purpose assistance and the commonwealth's broader objectives for public sector spending and borrowing. This is usually considered alongside updated forward estimates and projections of the economic outlook for Australia as a whole.

In Germany the budget is planned within the framework of a rolling five-year financial plan (covering the current year, the budget year, and three subsequent years). These plans are prepared both by the federal government and by each of the *Länder*. The Financial Planning Council then ensures that these plans are coordinated and that they are consistent with the aggregate fiscal target. This Council is chaired by the Federal Minister of Finance, with finance ministers from each of the *Länder* and representatives of municipalities as members. The work of this Council is complemented by the Committee on Public Borrowing, with similar representation, which coordinates public borrowing and ensures that demands on the market are not excessive or destabilizing. The division of labor is clear: the Council determines the overall level of borrowing consistent with the aggregate fiscal targets, whereas the Committee decides on the phasing of public borrowing. The importance of borrowing controls under this federal system is clear.

The result is a Federal Financial Plan comprising a set of compatible financial plans for the lower levels of government. Based on this financial plan, budget preparation consists of the allocation of funds to line items in the budget of each budget organization in cash terms. Supplementary allocations are rare, and the budget does not include an explicit reserve. This requires a strict cash limit approach to fiscal planning.

With the more centralized government systems under unitary models, the legal powers of the central over local government can make the operation of coordination easier to achieve. Several countries have set up formal procedures and institutions for discussions or negotiations among different levels of government. The impact of these arrangements differs markedly among countries. In the United Kingdom, a Consultative Council on Local Government Finance, established in 1975, acts mainly as a formal notification mechanism for decisions formulated at central government level. The most important negotiations on aggregate local government expenditure and central government grants take place between the Treasury and the sponsoring service ministries for local expenditures. In reality, the Consultative Council has become increasingly redundant with the greater centralization embodied in the post-1990 arrangements for capping local taxes in the United Kingdom (see Chapter 14). While the formal budget plans presented to the U.K. Parliament typically underestimate the level of local government spending—to suggest that the level of local taxes could and should be lower—it is widely understood that the reserve allows for the "overspending" between the notional budgets assumed for presentational reasons and those that the authorities will set (and spend).

Some countries such as Denmark and Sweden have more transparent and effective arrangements, conducting regular negotiations between the ministries of finance and the central organizations representing the regions and the communes. Agreements are reached on targets for the local and regional expenditures. A similar institutional apparatus has been developed in Belgium.

Some countries have also experimented with procedures for specialized negotiations and agreements between central government and individual local units or clusters of such units. Since the tax bases exploited by different levels of government are often the same or related, there are usually strict rules to circumscribe the volume and methods of raising local revenues that must be negotiated with subnational governments. In the early 1970s, the French government began to make planning contracts with large cities (*communautés urbaines*), and in 1974–75 this practice was extended to contracts with middle-sized towns and rural areas (*contrats de pays*). Under such agreements, the central government committed itself to support a multiyear program of local operations and to pay a fixed overall grant.

Against that background, it may be possible to suggest certain requirements for the necessary harmonization of budget plans from a macroeconomic perspective.

- First, the central and local governments need to work on common assumptions for the budget year about the key macroeconomic variables—including prices (and particularly important relative price changes), wages, and the exchange rate. The central government is best placed to formulate these, within the context of its own macroeconomic forecasting function. The central forecasts (and any projected regional variations on prices or wages) need to be circulated to lower-tier authorities in good time for budget preparation.
- Second, a common revenue and expenditure classification is necessary. Most countries have adopted the IMF's classification for Government Finance Statistics for central government programs and it is highly desirable that this classification be extended to state and local government expenditures. A common financial year (often set by law) is essential.
- Third, budget forecasts covering both central and local government revenues, expenditures, and borrowing need to be made well in advance of the budget year if the benefits of coordination from a macroeconomic perspective are to be secured. In addition to guidelines on macroeconomic indicators, the central government should ensure that subnational authorities are given, in good time, an indication of affordability constraints—whether directly

for the unitary model with information on expenditures and revenues or indirectly with guidance on borrowing.
- Fourth, coordination of the budget plans in aggregate is essential for macroeconomic purposes and should ideally be set within a medium-term rolling framework. The form and extent, however, will vary according to the vertical structure of government and in many instances the balance of political and legal powers, as discussed below.

  —For the federal systems, the German and Australian approaches are good examples of the types of coordination that are necessary. Although institutional formats will inevitably vary, and the focus will typically be on borrowing control, the advantages of securing expenditure and revenue data also for macroeconomic monitoring, with the consequent creation of a capacity for fiscal action within the year, are significant.

  —For the unitary model, usually the legal or administrative authority can be relied upon to limit directly or indirectly the expenditure and revenue levels of the lower-tier authorities. But timing is important, if each tier's plans are to take into account the spending plans of the others. In addition, care needs to be taken to avoid the emergence of off-budget transactions or other means of circumventing central controls. Moreover, as the U.K. example suggests, this coordination may not always be achieved with the degree of transparency that is desirable.

  —By contrast, poor coordination is likely to have important economic costs. These include (1) unnecessarily high interest rates (created by excessive or poorly timed borrowing); (2) expensive off-budget transactions (when local government seeks to circumvent central government controls); (3) disruption of expenditure plans (where emergency cutbacks become necessary to maintain overall fiscal stability); and (4) poor resource allocation (because of duplication of effort or gaps in provision between different tiers of government). At worst, fiscal stabilization itself may be threatened.

- Fifth, the coordinated budget projections should be accurate and reliable (in their timing) not least to achieve efficient financial planning. Central and local governments must still be able to exercise flexibility within the year. Expenditures and revenue projections should be kept up to date and, ideally, policies should thus remain stable during the year insofar as possible. The interactions between central and local government expenditures—for example with open-ended specific grants or central government programs directly managed by local governments—should

be taken into account in preparing consolidated budget projections.
- Sixth, given that from a macroeconomic perspective even the best-laid plans are subject to exogenous shocks, there is a case for including contingency reserves within both the local and central government budgets. For the local government budget, such reserves should be used to cope with the normal variations, for example, in demand-led programs. For the central government, the contingency reserve must be large enough to accommodate or offset variations from plans in the local government sector, from a macroeconomic perspective. In some respects, this poses problems. There is a moral hazard problem if some share of the contingency reserve becomes perceived as "belonging" to the local or subnational authorities; it is no longer a genuine contingency reserve but a reflection of nontransparent budget preparation practices.

Budget Preparation: Resource Allocation Among Programs

The other major aspect of budget preparation where some coordination is desirable from a macroeconomic perspective lies in the pursuit of allocative and distributional goals under both federal and unitary models. Central government can be involved in the allocative decisions of lower-tier authorities: (1) to prescribe uniform or minimum standards; (2) to internalize the externalities associated with small areas providing services, with spillover benefits to others; (3) to require local governments to undertake policies that are of national rather than local importance; and (4) to administer central policies where regional organization has efficiency benefits. The precise mechanisms for this central dimension in the delivery of second-tier authority policies will vary, encompassing specific or matching grants, regulation, joint initiatives, and so on.

The essential requirements for efficient resource allocation among expenditure programs were discussed in Chapter 2. In principle, unambiguous, stable expenditure assignments that avoid duplication are to be desired. In practice, however, firm lines of demarcation can be difficult to draw. It is important to distinguish among three aspects: policy, implementation, and financing.
- Policy responsibilities can often be fairly clearly defined. Even here, however, detailed policy issues may be a source of controversy. Stability is generally advantageous but can also be difficult to achieve, not least as political fashion changes. In the United

States the trend has been to give new mandates to the states. In the United Kingdom, on the other hand, the recent history has been of service responsibilities being taken from local government back to the center.
- Implementation can also be a source of difficulty because the line between a policy and an implementation issue may well be hard to draw. Dual implementation, where both tiers are offering a different but related welfare service to the same client groups, may mean that problems of coordination are inevitable. Moreover, as individual welfare cases progress, the service responsibility for the individual may pass from central to local government or vice versa.
- Finally, financing, particularly the award of specific matching or conditional grants, inevitably requires close coordination.

Coordination in service delivery (implementation) in such cases is best achieved at the local level, that is, at the level of the individual lower-tier authority. The need for policy and financing coordination, however, has to be addressed at the budget preparation stage—under any model of local government. Such coordination is often best achieved service by service. Many countries—Australia, Germany, and the United Kingdom, for example—have consultative groups of different kinds for individual services. Their goals include (1) interpretation and elucidation of expenditure assignments; (2) the derivation of detailed service policies and minimum or target service standards that help reinforce their respective policy goals; (3) the drawing up of practical guidance on service implementation; (4) the phasing of expenditures over years (mainly for capital projects) or within the year; (5) discussion of the precise rules for the award and triggering of specific or matching grants; and (6) technical issues, for example, on the recurrent costs of new projects aided by specific grants or of proposed new expenditure assignments.

Such consultative groups can play an important role in helping each tier meet its respective service policy objectives. Yet there are limits to how far such consultation may lead to total accord on policy, implementation, and financing issues. It is inevitable in democracies with more than one tier of government that the political color of central and local government will differ from time to time. The ability of one to enforce or accommodate the policies of the other will depend on the perceived political balance and on the actual (legal) powers of each tier. Views on both resource allocation—say schools versus hospitals—and on redistribution objectives may differ. Not all will accept the primacy of the central government on matters of income distribution that are normally associated with the centralized income taxation and social benefits.

It is also possible that, in the case of specific or matching grants, there may be a less than transparent mechanism for handling grant applications. Indeed, specific grants in themselves raise awkward issues for budget and financial management. First, so long as there is any conditionality in the terms of the grant, there will be uncertainty for budget preparation about the timing and the amounts of receipt. Second, compared with block grants, specific grants can be inefficient in theory, influencing resource allocation decisions of local governments to reflect perceived national priorities rather than local. The implicit resource diversion can result in a net welfare loss. Third, and more practically, there are the administrative costs involved in setting up monitoring and payments of grants. Fourth, to trigger grant receipt on a timely basis requires investment by both central and local government in efficient information systems. But, at worst, the triggering becomes automatic (partly because both sides have incentives to minimize the information checks), leading to inefficient use or misuse of specific grants.

Ideally, therefore, the main objective on both policy and financing, while trying to achieve coordination to the extent possible, must be to ensure that the policy intentions and financing plans of each tier, as reflected in their respective budgets, are accurate, achievable, and—in aggregate—consistent with macroeconomic stability. This also means that the policy pattern should be predictable; that policy changes should be generally avoided within the year, unless they have been taken into account in the budget-setting process; that the intentions on size and timing of specific grants should be as transparent as possible; and that—given some policies are open-ended, for example, for natural disaster expenses—there should be some contingency reserve.

For developing countries, however, this list is likely to represent a rather demanding requirement. The initial focus should be on efficient and accurate budget preparation by all tiers, and putting in place effective budget constraints on the lower-tier authorities, which prevent excessive fiscal deficits, the buildup of arrears, or other off-budget finance. As discussed in the next section, this also means that careful attention must be paid to the implementation of the budget during the year, if the scope for remedial action within the year is to be sustained.

Budget Reporting and Actions Within the Year

In many respects, the requirements for good budget implementation in the local government sector are the same as those for the central government. Starting from clear and well-prepared budget plans, the objective must be to implement the plans in the most efficient manner, with the maximum economy on day-to-day and longer-term borrowing and safeguards to ensure that budget appropriations are held to and not exceeded. This requires (1) clear budget authorization processes internally; (2) efficient payment systems; (3) a suitable accounting framework; and (4) an information system that can cover all the stages of the budget process from budget preparation through commitment, verification, payment authorization, the payment itself, and the accounting for the transaction. Also important are regular, timely, and accurate reporting, built on good information systems, and timeliness and efficiency in both financial planning and the associated borrowing program.

So far as the macroeconomic dimension is concerned, apart from the general need for local authorities to remain within their budgets and manage their budget implementation process in an efficient way, the two main concerns must be the reporting framework and cash planning. The latter, as well as its associated borrowing implications, is especially important where the main financial control over second-tier authorities is exercised through limits on borrowing.

The principal requirements from the reporting system are for timely, consistent, and accurate reporting of the budget implementation. As noted earlier, the revenue and expenditure classification—the latter both in terms of the functional and economic codes—should be consistent with the central government classification so as to allow easy consolidation of the accounts of the whole general government. In many countries, however, it has been possible to go further and ensure that the entire accounting framework is either common between central and local governments (such as in Brazil) or that local government accounting requirements are set by central government law or regulation, as in Germany and the United Kingdom. Many developed countries require their local government authorities to report monthly to the central government on expenditures, revenues, and on borrowing—discussed below. However, such information may not be illuminating, if it cannot be compared with expected patterns to date. Thus, many countries maintain a profile of planned spending—drawn from the aggregate of local governments' own plans and actual patterns of spending in the past. This enables the central government to spot individual localities in trouble, while also allowing trends across subnational authorities to be analyzed.

Whether it is possible and desirable to go further, for example, to monitor expenditure commitments and even verification, will depend on the degree of sophistication of the economy and on the vertical structure. In federal countries, such micromanagement of the affairs of state governments might well be thought unacceptable and unnecessary. In more centralized models, it might appear a logical component of financial planning—particularly in developing countries where there may be concerns about arrears or off-budget financing. For the more advanced economies such monitoring may not be necessary; for the less advanced, including many of the countries of the former Soviet Union at this time, it may well be essential, if macroeconomic problems associated with arrears and off-budget financing are to be avoided. Indeed, in such countries a basic policy dilemma has to be faced: the economic welfare gains available in principle from decentralization can be overwhelmed if there is a loss of control over the macroeconomic position. Despite the political attractions of deepening democracy, the rate of progress may have to be attuned to the rate of institutional improvements in information reporting and budget control.

Although the hope will be that the budget will be delivered as planned, in practice, adverse exogenous economic developments may damage revenue collection, while bad weather or unexpected natural disasters can give rise to additional expenditures in subnational authorities (as well as in the central government). Changes in central government policies, perhaps in response to an exogenous shock, may also have an impact on the delivery of local budgets. In general, it follows from the prime responsibility of the central government to undertake macroeconomic policy coordination that it should have the responsibility for deciding on the need for any countercyclical or other adjustment within the year. The action may be confined only to the central government sector, where it can often be implemented more quickly, sometimes with greater certainty of economic impact. However, the central government action may be partly frustrated by the subnational government reactions. For example, cutting central grants may lead local governments to continue financing a favored project out of reserves or to accumulate arrears. In other cases, such as wage reductions or hiring freezes, it may be necessary or desirable for the second-tier authorities to shoulder part of the fiscal adjustment within the year. Without an adequate reporting system, the need for and targeting of such remedial action can represent a serious obstacle to the efficient conduct of macroeconomic policies.

It is also important, however, that actions within the year to address emerging fiscal problems be appropriate in nature. All attempts should be eschewed that pass the problems of the center to other tiers of government by transferring expenditure assignments, without prior agreement on the policies to be followed and how the resources are to be found. Such "unfunded mandates" should be avoided either within the year or in the annual budget preparation exercise. Also to be avoided are sudden withdrawals or reductions in the amount of general or specific grants of the type attempted in Russia in 1995. The result of these actions will be some delayed or postponed expenditures. But they are also likely to lead to payment arrears, to higher borrowing often from local banks or from suppliers, to poor resource allocation as other plans are disrupted to take on board the new responsibility, and to the growth of extrabudgetary accounts or other creative accounting devices. All such devices evade expenditure control but usually only temporarily: the consequent misallocation of resources can be expensive to resolve later.

Where local governments are required by the central government to take action within the year, it is often best applied on the same basis as for central government—"burden-sharing." That may include hiring freezes, postponement or delay in commencing new capital projects, or reductions in nonwage current expenditures. Once there is agreement on such measures, then it may be sensible to reduce general purpose transfers as the mechanism through which local government will share in the overall fiscal adjustment. In the central government more targeted measures within the year, such as cuts in specific grants, are best avoided except in the context of needing to absorb some unexpected addition that is service specific. An example would be a mandatory but unanticipated increase in teachers' salaries following a court decision or commission of enquiry.

Cash Planning and Borrowing

In the local government sector, just as for central government, efficient financial or cash management and economical borrowing require careful financial planning. Local authorities must be able to project the flows of revenues, both tax and nontax (including central government grants) and cash expenditures and hence the financial deficits and borrowing requirements. At first sight the requirements are clear: for the revenues it is the timing of receipts, and for expenditures it is the timing of cash payments that will determine the borrowing need—setting aside any refinancing. But the interaction between the central and local government sectors poses a number of difficulties:
- Where there is tax sharing, the question of local versus central collection and the speed with which revenues are passed on to, or from, the central government are important.
- The forms of grants—general, specific, and matching—and the need for local governments to demonstrate compliance with the rules determine the timing of the grant receipts in local governments.

- In general, flows of tax revenues and grants from one tier to the other involve improving the cash position of one tier while worsening that of the other. This has led to the development of central treasuries in some countries (such as Italy) with a global consolidated account covering large parts of the general government sector.
- When lower-tier governments borrow from a central government source, there is a need to carefully plan access to markets, and perhaps the need to coordinate with other borrowers has to be factored in. This complicates the interaction between identified cash shortages and borrowing. Many local governments do not have the automatic or quasi-automatic access to financial markets that central governments typically enjoy. However, unfettered access creates other problems as discussed in Chapter 7.

Efficient arrangements for the administration of local tax collection and tax sharing are described in Chapter 5. For grants, the main issues are type and modalities of payment as discussed below.

- In the case of general grants, the normal principle is of payment of grants scheduled according to a profile of estimated expenditures. While this can mean a simple payment of general grants in 12 equal monthly installments, in most countries such grants take into account seasonal patterns of past expenditures, so that profiles over the 12 payments may not lead to equal installments.
- For current expenditures on specific grants, the arrangements may be similar to general grants—for example, when the local government is carrying out a current service essentially on an agency basis. This might be the case for a welfare or education service that is administered by the local government but under central government direction. Others—particularly those that are one-off—may be more difficult. For example, specific grants may be paid to local governments after severe weather damage. Here expenditures will clearly be incurred before the grant is received, and that needs to be factored into cash planning.
- For capital expenditure, arrangements for specific grants again vary. Where receipt of the grant is unconditional, the payments can be linked to the phasing of expenditures, again in line with the seasonal pattern of payments. In some instances, it may be possible to link the payment of the grant to the securing of borrowing for the project. It is also possible to pay such grants only on conclusion of the project. This enhances the financial position of the central government, but only at the cost of increasing the borrowing need of the local authorities. Greater complexities still

may arise where the central government is acting as an intermediary for grants received from foreign donors.
- For matching grants the difficulty is that the requirement to satisfy some conditions of central government, whether for a current or capital grant, injects some uncertainty into the timing of the receipt of the grant. As noted earlier, it is thus in the interests of the local government to put in place efficient reporting systems, which will enable it to trigger a request for the grant payment as soon as warranted.

There are several procedures that would seem to indicate good practice in this area. First, the general principle for all types of grants is that, if neither central or local government is to be given a relative unwarranted financial benefit, grants should be paid as close to the point of financial need as possible. That is, the payments should flow to the local government, just before the local tier needs to start making payment to third parties. For general grants that means phasing according to past patterns of expenditure; for others it means as close a match to the payment as can be achieved. Second, if cash planning is to be efficient, the pattern of such grants across the year should be as predictable as possible. This requires that the rules for the payment of grants should be transparent and unambiguous. This is a further reason why open-ended grants or those with complicated criteria or conditionality should be avoided. Many countries have found this transparency is best achieved through consultative forums. Third, even with transparent rules, however, there is some unpredictability about timing, and sometimes about amount, not least in the case of matching grants. This needs to be taken into account when making cash plans and establishing borrowing requirements.

As noted, the extensive use of both tax sharing and grants in intergovernmental fiscal arrangements means there is an inevitable interrelationship between the cash positions of the respective tiers. All payments of grants initially worsen the financial position of the center, while improving that of the local tier. In some countries the solution has been some form of consolidated bank account that covers both the central and local government sectors—either wholly or in part, for example by including for the local sector only the grant element. This approach has been followed in Italy. The theoretical advantages of consolidation are clear: the general government sector's borrowing requirements are minimized, and to the extent that the center can borrow more cheaply than local government, there is a financial gain available. In practice, however, there has been a risk of the center putting its financial needs before those of the local government. In Italy, in the past, this has led to local governments being forced to borrow from the commercial banks when resources available to them from the central treasury account were insufficient.

Particularly under federal systems, it is desirable for states to borrow in their own name: the terms on which they can borrow signals their creditworthiness to financial markets. By contrast, global borrowing on behalf of states or local governments (as in India) in principle allows some individual local governments to borrow at a rate implicitly subsidized by the more creditworthy. Also, many federal systems would resist, on political as well as legal grounds, any such consolidated approach. Geographical reasons may rule out the approach in other instances.

The alternative is for lower-tier authorities to manage their own finances. The requirements are much the same as for central government:

- Preparing cash expenditure and receipts (excluding borrowing) forecasts by month over the year.
- If the resulting pattern of financing needs is considered undesirable, seeing what can be achieved by rephasing expenditures or accelerating revenues (including grant entitlements).
- Determining a month-by-month borrowing plan, taking account of any refinancing needs.
- Monitoring actual borrowing requirements against the plan.
- Implementing the plan, subject to variation in the light of outturns.

However efficiently this process is conducted by the individual local authority, it means that in the absence of a consolidated approach there can be several local authorities approaching the market at the same time. The central government and even state enterprises may also need to borrow then. In large part, the solution to avoiding the risk of undue financial pressures on the capital market lies in coordination, and perhaps control of access to borrowing, by the central government. The gain from a coordinated approach includes reducing the risk of paying a premium on borrowing because of congestion in financial markets at certain times.

Borrowing constraints thus play an important role in the macroeconomic management of local government expenditure. Indeed, for federal-type systems they represent the main mechanism whereby central control is exercised over states. The main issues related to borrowing policies are discussed in Chapter 7. Here, the main issues relate to the financial management of borrowing—the information requirements covering both stocks and flows, the monitoring systems, and the access to different borrowing "windows," including public and private, domestic and external.

Whatever the borrowing policies (whether market, rules-based, or administrative controls), there are important requirements from a financial management point of view. Many countries monitor the flows of borrowing of individual authorities. On the one hand, this is important for microeconomic purposes as in India—checking that individual authorities are not incurring a level of debt that threatens their solvency. On the other hand, it enables a check on the aggregate position. Ideally, such information should come from monthly reporting of revenues and expenditures by each local government. Alternatively, the central government can rely on "below the line" information from the banking sector, though authorization for the release of such information by the banking sector may need to be established by law. Nonetheless, in less-developed economies this may be the simplest way of securing the necessary information flows.

But even the more developed economies have found that information on debt flows may be insufficient. First, creative accounting and off-budget financing may lead to more expenditure than revealed by the borrowing data. Second, particularly in federal systems, lower-tier governments can be major holders of assets—including financial assets. Many of the problems in recent years have been on the asset side of the accounts—for example, Orange County in the United States and the Western Isles authority in the United Kingdom, where unwise investments eventually resulted in large additional borrowing needs.

One solution is to regard these matters as the inevitable result of market imperfection, leaving the local government to resolve the problem. But this in turn leads to the issue of whether the central government is to be regarded as the guarantor of all subnational government loans. In the past financial markets have often regarded them as such. The moral hazard danger for the central government is that such an approach may ultimately mean it has to "bail out" the authority concerned, as, for instance, in Brazil. An alternative would be to require better information flows on the stocks of debt (the debt register) and of assets held. This may well be politically more acceptable in unitary states, but even for federal countries, it could be required by law with the assessment of financial soundness left to the auditor.

Also, the sources of borrowing have important financial management and macroeconomic implications. Where there is a special "window" for local government borrowing, as in Italy and the United Kingdom, for example, it is easier for the government to coordinate the total borrowing effort. Borrowing is also usually cheaper in these circumstances. Where there is market borrowing, terms and types of borrowing will reflect both the assessment of individual authority's creditworthiness and the degree to which central government is seen as the ultimate guarantor. This last dimension means that the wholly unfettered access to the capital market is unlikely to be prudent—as past country experiences might suggest—and that some coordination of borrowing programs is required.

As regards the forms of borrowing—bonds, loans, and so on—there has been a growing tendency to define the acceptable forms more specifically. One reason for this development was the desire to prevent creative accounting that is outside the normal borrowing controls. A second motive was to tap different sectors of the capital market, essentially for financial or money market development reasons, including the structure of interest rates. A third motive was to discourage long-term borrowing to meet current or short-term expenditure needs.

Even when there is little formal coordination of borrowing, benefits can be gained from the exchange of information. Thus, it is in the interests of all parties that the borrowing plans of the subnational authorities should be known to the center. Combined with the regular flows of information on the monthly finances, whether from an above the line or below the line source, this will enable the center to monitor the financial market implications of borrowing plans closely.[3] For the industrial countries, particularly under federal systems, there may be a case for requiring not only information on debt registers but also on financial assets held, even though there may be no powers to challenge asset-holding ventures. Possible responses to the expected emergence of pressures on the financial markets would include temporary intervention in the money markets so as to ease borrowing conditions or to advise against the proposed timing of a major bond issue.

Audit, Inspection, and Evaluation

Under most fiscal federalism arrangements, the central government plays a major role in financing local services. But it also frequently does more: setting minimum service standards, paying specific grants to secure central government service objectives, requiring local governments to act as an agent in implementing central government policies, and coordinating the services it delivers with those of local government. Ensuring that such services, and the standards at which they are being delivered, meet policy objectives and overall macroeconomic requirements leads central government to play an important role in audit, evaluation, and inspection.

---

[3]Symmetry might suggest that the plans of central government should also be shown to the states, for example, where both tiers can borrow directly. In practice, it may be simpler for the central government to advise states that a planned borrowing might be timed differently.

There has been increasing recognition in recent years that these functions are important. Audit of the traditional propriety or financial types represents the safeguard through which not only the central government, but both local political representatives and the local electorate, can hold the authority accountable for financial performance. Inspection, typically by employees of the central service departments or ministries, enables the center to be sure that mandated service standards are being achieved and to set objective tests of relative service performance. Evaluation, or value-for-money audit, has been the main growth area. It can be seen as combining audit and inspection, by examining not only what financial inputs went into service provision but also (1) what outputs were achieved, (2) what standards of service were provided, and (3) what impact those services had in meeting the policy objective; in short, the economy, efficiency, and effectiveness of services. Moreover, by conducting this exercise on a comparative basis, best practices can be discerned and publicized and other local governments can be encouraged to adopt the same approach. In principle, such evaluations can make an important contribution to improving overall economic performance.

As in public expenditure management more generally, the greatest progress in this area has perhaps been achieved in Australia, New Zealand, and the United Kingdom Some general conclusions may be drawn from their experience.

- The external audit body should be independent of the central government and the local authorities. Ideally it should be attached to the parliament—as for example in Australia where the audit body is appointed by each of the state parliaments. If created by central government, it should have an arm's length relationship from the line ministries and the ministry of finance—as for example with the Audit Commission in the United Kingdom. In short, the audit body needs to be seen as independent of both central and local government.
- The audit body must have "teeth"—the power, through the parliament or the central government, to have its recommendations responded to. Legal sanction (including disbarring members of the local government executive) can be an important ultimate weapon.
- Particularly as local authorities make progress in their accounting formats, often being ahead of central government practices in areas such as accrual accounting, there should be scope for subcontracting the internal propriety audit work to the private sector. This can also help to disseminate private sector accounting practices within the public sector. Also, the external audit body

can often employ private sector experts on a contractual basis to advantage.
- Regularity in audit is important. While most industrial countries have annual propriety audits, this practice is by no means universal in developing countries.
- Inspection can be selective rather than universal and is best directed by the sponsoring ministries. But it should form part of a collaborative effort with value-for-money audit to improve service standards. Increasingly, inspection is by reference to set standards rather than regulations (outputs not inputs) and in part carried out by testing, such as in education.
- It is usually beyond the resources of the external audit body to carry out evaluations of all services every year. Again selectivity is important. The use of structured samples can be important to ensure that the results of any such studies will be representative and universally accepted. Value-for-money studies can be used to identify and then publicize the best practices in service delivery.
- There needs to be a feedback mechanism from evaluation to budget preparation. Thus having publicized best practices in one year, both the external auditors and the service ministry inspectors need to question the local government response in improving service delivery practices in the next. This forms part of the budget cycle in Germany, for example. The authorities for their part need to be feeding in the changes necessary to move toward "best practice" in their budget preparation plans for future years.

Conclusions

This chapter has suggested appropriate institutional arrangements for achieving efficient budget and financial management, under a unitary as well as a federal structure of government. Considerable emphasis has been laid on coordination of both budget policy and implementation and on information sharing, again both for the preparation and implementation phases of the budget. While ideally applying to both the revenue and expenditure sides of the accounts, particular emphasis has been laid on the need for coordination and information sharing on local borrowing plans as a minimum requirement. This latter aspect is particularly important under federal arrangements where there is often reliance on borrowing control as the major instrument of macroeconomic management.

It might be considered that the proposals for greater coordination and information are too idealistic or that they interfere with the actual or perceived policy rights of the states, particularly under federal models. The requirements for both coordination and information sharing in developing countries may also need to be reduced somewhat to cover only the minimum information needs in budget implementation. In reality, however, certainly for the industrial countries and increasingly for the developing countries, the case for such coordination and information sharing is strengthened by a number of developments.

First, there is a general move toward more decentralization of functions because theory suggests a welfare gain from devolving choice closer to the local level. Yet without adequate coordination and control, the macroeconomic consequences may impose costs that overwhelm any resource allocation or efficiency gains. Second, there are efficiency gains to be secured, not least in allocative terms, from cooperation in the policy, implementation, and financing aspects of local and related central services. Third, the closer integration and internationalization of capital markets means that the local and central government sectors need to be aware of their interaction in dealing with the capital markets. That in turn requires more focus on financial planning and on the interaction between central and local finances.

This is an area, however, where there has been relatively little research. In particular, the modal requirements for "joint" financial planning, the case for greater scrutiny of balance sheet developments, and the role of central government actual or perceived guarantees for lower-tier government debts are all areas worthy of further study.

7

Control of Subnational Government Borrowing

TERESA TER-MINASSIAN AND JON CRAIG

In the last two decades, public sector debt has shown a rising trend in relation to GDP in a wide range of countries, both federal and unitary. These increases have reflected high levels of real interest rates on the debt and, in a number of countries, a lack of fiscal discipline, as witnessed by primary deficits in the general government accounts. While these deficits have been recorded most frequently at the central government level—sometimes because of, inter alia, gap-filling transfers to subnational governments—in several countries, especially but not exclusively federations, deficits and debt have emerged and risen over time at the state or provincial and local levels as well.

The growth of subnational public debt is frequently a symptom of an inappropriate design of intergovernmental fiscal relations in the country in question, involving, for example, large vertical or horizontal imbalances or a system of intergovernmental transfers lacking transparent criteria and conducive to ad hoc bargaining or ex post gap filling. A question that arises in this context, and that this chapter attempts to shed some light on, is to what extent the growth of subnational debt may be promoted, or at least facilitated, by a lack of controls and limits on subnational government borrowing.

This chapter reviews a broad range of international experiences with such controls, drawing in particular on the case studies presented in

---

The authors wish to acknowledge helpful comments from a number of colleagues in the IMF, in particular Vito Tanzi and Ehtisham Ahmad.

Chapters 8 through 28. This survey of experiences shows considerable diversity in country approaches to these controls, ranging from virtually sole reliance on market discipline to direct controls by the central government on individual borrowing operations of subnational government entities. The different approaches reflect, among other things, constitutional provisions, the degree of political and administrative control of the central government over the subnational ones, the country's overall tradition of financial discipline, the presence or absence of serious fiscal and macroeconomic imbalances, and the state of development of the country's financial market. In general, central government controls over subnational governments' borrowing tend to be looser, on the one hand, in countries with poor overall financial discipline and as yet unaddressed fiscal and macroeconomic disequilibria, and, on the other, in countries with well-developed and relatively transparent financial systems, which can rely more on the market to discipline the borrowing of subnational governments.

Country approaches to the control of subnational borrowing can be grouped into four broad categories, although most countries utilize a mix of them (Table 1). The four "stylized" categories are (1) sole or primary reliance on market discipline; (2) cooperation by different levels of government in the design and implementation of debt controls; (3) rules-based controls; and (4) administrative controls.

The sections below review, in turn, each of these approaches, followed by some main conclusions.

Reliance on Market Discipline

It has been suggested (Lane, 1993) that a number of conditions need to be satisfied for financial markets to exert effective discipline on subnational government borrowing:
- Markets should be free and open; in particular, there should be no regulations (such as reserve or other portfolio composition requirements) on financial intermediaries that place government in a privileged borrower position.
- Adequate information on the borrower's outstanding debt and repayment capacity should be available to potential lenders.
- There should be no perceived chance of bailout of the lenders in the case of impending default.[1]

---
[1] See Bayoumi, Goldstein, and Woglom (1995).

Table 1. Subnational Borrowing Controls in Selected Countries[1]

	Market Discipline		Cooperative Control		Administrative Control		Rules-Based Control		Borrowing Prohibited	
	Overseas	Domestic	Overseas	Domestic	Overseas	Domestic	Overseas	Domestic	Overseas	Domestic
Industrial countries										
Australia			•	•						
Austria					•	•				
Belgium			•	•						
Canada	•	•								
Denmark			•	•						
Finland	•	•								
France	•	•								
Germany							•	•		
Greece					•	•				
Ireland					•	•				
Italy							•	•		
Japan					•	•			•	
Netherlands							•	•		
Norway					•	•				
Portugal	•	•								
Spain					•	•				
Sweden	•	•								
Switzerland							•	•		
United Kingdom					•	•				
United States							•	•		
Developing countries										
Argentina					•	•				
Brazil					•	•				
Bolivia					•	•				
Chile					•	•				
Colombia					•	•				
Ethiopia					•	•			•	
India					•	•				
Indonesia					•	•				
Korea					•	•				
Mexico					•	•			•	
Peru					•	•				
South Africa			•	•						
Thailand									•	•
Transition economies										
Albania									•	•
Armenia									•	•
Azerbaijan									•	•
Belarus									•	•
Bulgaria									•	•
China									•	•
Estonia					•	•				
Georgia									•	•
Hungary					•	•				
Kazakhstan									•	•
Kyrgyz Republic									•	•
Latvia					•	•				
Lithuania					•	•				
Poland									•	•
Romania									•	•
Russia	•	•								
Slovenia									•	•
Tajikistan									•	•
Ukraine									•	•
Uzbekistan									•	•

[1]Classifications attempt to capture the predominant form of control. In some countries, the approach used may involve a combination of several techniques. See also notes to table below.

Table 1 (continued)

Notes to Table

Industrial Countries

Australia. A cooperative approach is followed in setting annual debt ceilings with state governments within a National Loan Council established for that purpose. The limits set for each state government subsume loan limits for combined local government borrowing within the state concerned. In practice, the limits have been administered flexibly and market discipline plays a major role on final decisions on borrowing targets set by each state (see Chapter 8).

Austria. Domestic borrowing is subject to administrative controls. *Länder* have rules on the purposes for which loans can be raised, and local governments must seek the approval by the supervisory body for each *Land*, except for short-term loans and loans for public enterprises. Loans must be used to finance investment and are judged against the capacity to service debt as evidenced by the current budget balance. The Ministry of Finance must approve overseas loans.

Belgium. Substantial changes in fiscal federalism arrangements were introduced in 1989 with a number of functions devolved to the regions and communities (including local authorities). The arrangements envisage deficits at the subnational level in the early years of a transition period that are reversed toward the end of that period. Borrowing under these arrangements is supervised by a High Finance Council, which has mapped out a program of deficit sharing between the central and subnational governments. The Council subsequently monitors adherence to those targets and can initiate borrowing limitations if needed to meet commitments agreed to by both levels of government to stabilize debt service to revenue levels after 2000 (2010 for the Flemish communities). This debt-to-revenue target constitutes a crude method of capping the relative size of the overall debt burden and the distribution of that burden between central and subnational governments.

Canada. Each province in Canada is free to borrow overseas or domestically without limit. Market ratings have therefore played a crucial discipline on overall borrowing levels by provinces. By contrast, provinces impose strict limits on borrowing by local governments within their own jurisdiction (see Chapter 9).

Denmark. The central government engages in bilateral discussions with subnational governments leading up to the setting of limits on borrowing. Municipalities are allowed to borrow only for investments in certain items (such as water, electricity, urban renewal, housing for aged persons, and land acquisition). Borrowing for other purposes requires the permission of the Ministry of Interior. Strict controls are also set on the terms and conditions of loans. Limited access to overseas markets is permitted.

Finland. No administrative or legal restraints apply to domestic or foreign borrowing. Market discipline is therefore the main form of control.

France. Historically, deficits at subnational level have been small. Following the introduction of Decentralization Laws, subnational authorities are free to contract domestic loans on terms and conditions negotiated with lenders. Overseas loans are permitted subject, in principle, to the approval of the French Treasury.

Germany. Budget laws specify the conditions under which subnational borrowing can be undertaken. Borrowing by the *Länder* is supposedly linked to investment budgets and local authority borrowing to cash flow needs and is subject to approval by the *Länder* authorities. In practice, there are weaknesses in both the formulation and application of the *Länder* laws. The investment requirements are specified ex ante rather than ex post and the interpretation of what constitutes investment is flexible. At the same time, the extent of market discipline is muted by the fact that the federal government has provided assistance to *Länder* experiencing debt-service problems (see Chapter 10).

Greece. The deficits incurred by subnational governments are very small, largely reflecting the administrative control on borrowing by municipalities and communities. In general, loans are linked to investment projects and project studies must be submitted to support loans. No significant foreign borrowing has been undertaken at the subnational level.

Ireland. All domestic borrowing by local authorities is subject to the approval of the Minister of the Environment. Limits on terms and conditions of loans are often specified. Foreign borrowing is not undertaken.

Italy. Subnational governments are subject to legal borrowing limits. Regions are permitted to borrow domestically for capital budgets and share participation with the proviso that debt charges cannot exceed 25 percent of the sum of regional own revenue, net of health contributions and the Common Fund. Regions cannot borrow to fund current expenditure. Municipal and local governments are subject to ex ante ceilings on borrowing, much of which is financed by the Deposit and Loan Fund and other public financial institutions, for investment projects. Foreign borrowing is not permitted (see Chapter 11).

Table 1 (continued)

Japan. The Ministry of Home Affairs supervises and controls all local authority borrowing. Domestic borrowing is generally approved only to finance investment needs or emergency expenditure and local authorities must meet strict debt-service capacity criteria. There is no foreign borrowing at subnational level (see Chapter 12).

Netherlands. The Municipalities Act requires that the current account of subnational governments must be balanced. Borrowing is therefore possible only if interest and depreciation costs can be accommodated within a balanced current account. Loans cannot be denominated in a foreign currency or be linked to a foreign currency. Other restrictions on the terms and conditions of loans may be applied.

Norway. All domestic borrowing must be approved by the authorities. Decisions on access to credit are largely restricted to investment needs and the capacity to service loans is assessed as part of the approval process. Local authorities are not permitted to borrow in foreign currency except with the permission of the Ministry of Finance, but overseas borrowing in Norwegian kroner is permitted.

Portugal. Local governments are free to contract loans without limits from financial institutions including the Treasury. Although requests for debenture issues have to be approved by the Ministry of Finance, few restrictions appear to apply in practice. Medium- to longer-term debentures may be contracted for investment purposes or to redress financial difficulties. There are some restrictions on the amounts raised as annuities.

Spain. Ministry of Finance approval is generally required for domestic borrowing but there are some exceptions, including for those local authorities covered by Autonomous Communities. Long-term loans are generally restricted to investment needs. Overseas loans require Ministry of Finance approval, and the Central Bank and the Inter-Ministerial Committee on Foreign Borrowing may also issue restraints on such borrowing.

Sweden. Domestic borrowing is subject to only two restrictions: (1) real estate alone cannot be used as collateral for mortgages; and (2) in principle, loans should be made only for investment purposes. However, in practice, temporary loans can be made to cover cash flow deficiencies. There are no additional restrictions on overseas borrowing.

Switzerland. Subnational borrowing is normally linked to investment needs. At the canton level, borrowing is normally restricted by laws that require balanced current budgets (including interest payments and amortization of debt). Borrowing to finance investment can proceed only if it does not disturb the current budget balance (see Chapter 13).

United Kingdom. Domestic borrowing approvals are issued annually by the government on the amount that a local authority may borrow. The limit is based on the amounts required to meet capital expenditure needs less provisions for such expenditures and may include an allowance for temporary borrowing to meet cash flow fluctuations. No borrowing from the central bank is permitted, and restrictions may be placed on a number of aspects of loans raised, including the terms and type of loan instruments. Local governments cannot borrow abroad without the consent of the Treasury. In practice, local authorities rarely borrow in foreign currency except in connection with European Union schemes (see Chapter 14).

United States. The subnational sector has been in surplus throughout the 1990s. Virtually all state and local governments require "balanced budgets," but the effective borrowing constraint imposed by such requirements, even when written into the Constitution, is often limited. Often the requirement applies only to the budget, excluding social security and capital spending; in some cases, the requirement only refers ex ante to the formulated rather than the realized budget; and there may be other escape clauses, including extrabudgetary sources of funds. Effectively, therefore, market discipline plays an important role in borrowing discipline (see Chapter 15).

Developing Countries

Argentina. Provincial, municipal, and local governments can borrow domestically subject to certain conditions. Municipal Deliberative Councils must normally authorize borrowing, and approval by provincial legislatures is also often required, particularly if foreign borrowing is contemplated. This is the case, for example, in Buenos Aires, Chaco, and La Pampa. Normally the limits imposed are related to current revenues (for example, in Buenos Aires, Jujuy, and La Pampa the limit is set at 25 percent of revenues) and the borrowing must generally be used to finance capital works (see Chapter 16).

Brazil. Subnational debt reached 17 percent of GDP in 1996 and as a counterpart to restructuring agreements with the central government, strict controls on borrowing have been introduced. A con-

Table 1 (continued)

stitutional amendment prohibits new issues of bonds, and legal rules and central bank regulations prohibit a state from borrowing from state-owned banks. The restructuring agreements with indebted states involve commitment to privatize most of their enterprises and to use the proceeds, among with other measures, to repay existing debt. Under these new arrangements, new borrowing in any year should not exceed the total debt service for the year, or 27 percent of revenue, whichever is greater, and total debt service (including on the new borrowing) should not exceed the states' current surplus for the previous year, or 15 percent of its revenue, whichever is less (see Chapter 18).

Chile. Central government approval is required for all domestic and external borrowing. Specific laws may be passed authorizing borrowing for specific purposes under strict terms and conditions.

Colombia. The degree of central control varies with the type of instrument. While the issuance of bonds by subnational governments requires Ministry of Finance approval (after prior approval by the National Planning Department), other sources, including commercial bank borrowing and various state-owned instrumentalities, are not so regulated (see Chapter 19).

Ethiopia. State governments are legally empowered to borrow domestically subject to terms and conditions set by the center. No external borrowing is permitted (see Chapter 20).

India. The Constitution puts limits on the borrowing powers of the states. Only the central government can borrow abroad. The states are, in principle, entitled to borrow, but they have to get permission from the central government if they have any outstanding debt to the center. All states have such liabilities. Until recently, borrowing was mainly financed by banks under regulations that specified the portion of assets that had to be invested in state securities approved by the central government. Now the Reserve Bank, in effect, allocates state securities to commercial banks. The central government also allots shares in funds from small savings at post offices to states (see Chapter 21).

Indonesia. Subnational government accounts in recent years were close to balance. If borrowing needs arose, they were largely met by loans from the central government.

Korea. Subnational borrowing is regulated centrally. All borrowing proposals require the prior approval of local councils and the Ministry of Home Affairs. The procedures specify which local governments can borrow and which projects are eligible. A portion of the loan funds are raised through compulsory bond placements. Subsidized loans for specific purposes may be also provided by the Ministry of Finance and Economy. The close integration of the borrowing process effectively means that, once approval has been given, the loan is perceived to carry a central government guarantee (see Chapter 22).

Mexico. States and municipalities have the authority to issue securities in domestic capital markets but only the federal government is entitled to borrow abroad. Subnational governments may also borrow from the banking system (see Chapter 23).

Peru. In general, subnational governments are not permitted to borrow. The municipalities of the largest cities (Lima, Cusco, and Arequipa) have incurred debt with international agencies or with other countries to finance infrastructure investments. Their domestic debt has been for short-term credits of lesser amounts. Almost all provincial municipalities have a municipal credit institution that provides such financing.

South Africa. New arrangements have recently been introduced to cover borrowing by the nine provinces. They will be able to borrow on a multiyear basis for capital projects and annually for current expenditures. Borrowing must be approved by the Loan Consultation Committee, which includes the ministers of finance from each of the provinces and the national Minister of Finance (who will retain a veto power). Approvals are based on the debt-service capacities of the provinces, which, in practice, will be assessed against total revenues, including grants from the central government. Local governments will continue to be allowed to borrow (as under the old ordinances) to fund capital projects subject to the oversight of the national Minister of Finance.

Thailand. Subnational (provincial, district, town, and village) governments are legally prohibited from foreign or domestic borrowing.

Transition Economies

Although many transition economies have substantial payment arrears at all levels of government, most do not formally permit borrowing at the subnational level. The exceptions are:

China. Legally, local governments are not permitted to run long-run deficits. However, widespread domestic borrowing occurs, often from commercial banks or financial institutions created by local governments to raise funds for investments. Some subnational governments also borrow abroad through joint ventures, bond issues, and agreements with international lending agencies (see Chapter 26).

Table 1 *(concluded)*

Estonia, Latvia, and Lithuania. The Baltic countries have generally permitted their subnational governments to obtain access to domestic loans in limited amounts, mainly for intrayear financing.

Hungary. Ceilings are imposed by the central government on subnational borrowing, most of which is financed by the state-owned savings institutions. Overseas financing is rare but has been obtained by some municipalities (e.g., Budapest council) from international lending agencies (see Chapter 27).

Russia. Laws passed in 1992 give oblasts, cities, and rayons the right, in principle, to unlimited domestic borrowing. However, in practice, the borrowing has been small both because most subnational governments would not qualify for substantial credit from financial markets and because those markets are themselves undeveloped. Overseas borrowing may become possible—using resources as collateral—but such borrowing would require approval from the central government (see Chapter 28).

- The borrower should have institutional structures that ensure adequate policy responsiveness to market signals before reaching the point of exclusion from new borrowing.

These are indeed stringent conditions, which are unlikely to be realized in the majority of countries. Typically, especially in developing countries, available information on the finances of subnational governments suffers from serious weaknesses in coverage, quality, and timeliness. Many countries still utilize various forms of portfolio constraints on financial intermediaries to facilitate the placement of government securities (including local government ones) at a reduced cost. A number of countries also have experienced various forms of intervention by the central government to prevent default by subnational governments on their debts. Finally, and not least importantly, relatively short electoral cycles tend to make politicians at the subnational government level short-sighted and unresponsive to early warnings by the financial markets.

Recognition of these realities may be a major reason why sole reliance on market discipline to check subnational government borrowing is not usual. A major industrial country that uses this approach is Canada, at least regarding provincial government borrowing.[2] To date, the Canadian provinces have no constitutional or legal limits on their borrowing (both domestic and external), and are not subject to central government controls on it (see Chapter 9). Their debt and debt-servicing capacity are closely monitored by financial markets, in particular by major debt-rating agencies. A review of the trends in provincial government indebtedness in recent years suggests that, even in a well-developed and relatively transparent financial market as in Canada, market discipline on subnational government borrowing has not been

---

[2]Municipalities in most provinces, by contrast, are required to balance their current budgets. Municipal borrowing for investment projects must be approved by the relevant province. Provinces assist municipal borrowing through public financial intermediaries (the municipal finance corporations) and/or through matching grants.

fully effective. Despite a clear deterioration in ratings, and related sizable increase in risk premiums on provincial bonds—more marked for the more indebted provinces—provincial debt has increased steadily over the last several years (reaching about 23 percent of GDP in 1994), and only in the last couple of years have the provincial governments begun to design and implement fiscal retrenchment programs. It may be argued that market discipline is finally starting to work, but only after a "recognition lag" that will necessitate a sharper and more painful retrenchment than would have been necessary if provincial debts, and their service, had not been allowed to rise to their present levels.

Brazil represents another example of a major country that initially shunned legal or administrative controls over state and municipal borrowing, but in recent years has been prompted by the rapid accumulation of subnational government debt to institute such controls (see Chapter 18).

State debt, both domestic and external, grew rapidly in Brazil from the end of the 1960s until the early 1980s. The abrupt drying up of external financing during the debt crisis led to widespread defaults by the states and to the eventual takeover and rescheduling of most of these debts by the federal government in 1989 (for the external portion of the debts) and 1993 (for debts to federal banks). This rescheduling significantly eased the debt-servicing burden on the states. Some of the latter, however, have continued to run up debt to state-owned banks, as well as to suppliers. Finally, a number of states have resorted extensively to the issue of bonds.

The service of this debt came virtually to a halt, and with the high level of real interest rates, especially since the introduction of the *Real Plan* in 1994, the capitalization of interest payments led to an escalation of this debt to the equivalent of around 17 percent of GDP by 1996. The withdrawal of most private investors from the market for state bonds, and the drying up of interbank lending to some state banks, forced various forms of intervention by the federal authorities (including the central bank and federal banks), which de facto shifted most of the default risk on these types of state debt onto the federal government.

As counterpart for the rescheduling of a part of the state debt, limitations have been introduced in recent years on new state borrowing. Specifically, legal rules and central bank regulations now prohibit a state from borrowing from its own commercial banks. New issues of bonds (other than to refinance maturing ones) are prohibited by a constitutional amendment until the end of this decade. At the end of 1995, the federal government through one of its large banks (Caixa Economica Federal) set up lines of credit to provide short-term financial support to the indebted states, as counterpart for the states agreeing to certain adjustment measures. In 1996, the federal government began negotiations with most of the indebted states toward a federally backed restructuring of their not previously rescheduled debt, at reduced interest rates. The counterparts of this restructuring are commitments by the states to privatize most of their enterprises (with the proceeds of sales to be used to reduce the debt), and to implement fiscal adjustment measures aimed at reducing the ratio of their debt to revenues to 1 within a number of years.

This brief overview makes clear that the conditions listed above for the effective working of market discipline on state debt were not, and continue not to be, present in Brazil. While it is unfortunate that the need for controls was not recognized and acted upon before state debts reached their present very high levels, it is encouraging that financial support by the federal government to the states is increasingly being made contingent upon specific commitments by the latter to undertake needed corrective actions. The effectiveness of these adjustment programs will, of course, depend crucially on firmness in their implementation.

A Cooperative Approach to Debt Controls

Closest to sole reliance on market discipline in the spectrum of controls is an approach whereby limits on the indebtedness of subnational governments are not set by law or dictated by the center, but are arrived at through a negotiation process between the federal and the lower levels of government. Variants of this approach may be found in some European countries, such as the Scandinavian ones, and, in recent years, in Australia.

Under this approach, subnational governments are actively involved in formulating macroeconomic objectives and the key fiscal parameters underpinning these objectives. Through this process, agreement is reached on the overall deficit targets for the general government, as well as on the guidelines for growth of main items of revenue and expenditure. Specific limits are then agreed upon for the financing requirements of individual subnational jurisdictions.

In several countries, negotiations are essentially a bilateral process between the center and individual local governments. In Australia, the process is a multilateral one, taking place within the framework of a long-established Loan Council, in which all states, as well as the center, are represented (see Chapter 8). Until 1993, the Loan Council provided the forum for both the negotiation of global debt limits for individual states and the monitoring of compliance with such limits. The experience of widespread attempts by the states to elude these limits through resort to off-budget operations, innovative financing techniques, such as sale and lease-back arrangements, and through borrowing by state-owned enterprises, has prompted the Council in recent years to shift its focus to the ex ante analysis and discussion (as well as ex post monitoring) of the overall net financing requirements of the states, rather than of their outstanding debt. Thus, now the states have to bring to the negotiating table detailed projections of their budgetary operations, and discussions focus on corrective measures, when needed. The Council has also stepped up efforts to promote more effective market discipline on state borrowing, by facilitating the collection and dissemination of timely information on developments in the states' finances.

The cooperative approach has clear advantages in promoting dialogue and exchange of information across various government levels. It also raises the consciousness, in subnational-level policymakers, of macroeconomic implications of their budgetary choices. It seems, however, to work best in countries with an established culture of relative fiscal discipline and conservatism. It may not be effective in preventing a buildup of debt in conditions where either market discipline or the leadership of the central government in economic and fiscal management are weak.

Rules-Based Approaches to the Control of Subnational Borrowing

A number of countries, both federal and unitary, have relied on approaches to the control of subnational government borrowing that are based on standing rules, specified in the constitution or in laws. Some of these rules set limits on the absolute level of indebtedness of subnational jurisdictions; others specify that borrowing can be resorted to only for specified purposes (typically investment projects); yet others stipulate, for instance, that new borrowing is permitted up to a level consistent with a maximum allowed service ratio. Finally, some countries prohibit or severely restrict certain types of borrowing that involve greater macroeconomic risks (such as borrowing from the central bank).[3] Many countries utilize a combination of such rules.

---

[3] Direct government borrowing from the central bank has been prohibited for all European Union members by the Maastricht Treaty. For a review of other countries' experiences in this area, see Cottarelli (1993).

Rules that limit subnational governments' borrowing to investment purposes (the so-called golden rules) are quite common in industrial countries. Examples can be found in Germany (Chapter 10), Switzerland (Chapter 13), and in the majority of the state constitutions in the United States (Chapter 15). Countries that allow short-term borrowing for liquidity purposes generally stipulate that such borrowing has to be repaid by the end of each fiscal year. This is the case, for instance, for some of the states in the United States, and for regional and local governments in Spain.

Examples of rules that "mimic" market discipline by linking limits on the indebtedness of subnational (especially local) governments to the projected debt service on the debt, or to other indicators of their debt-servicing capacity (such as past revenues or the tax base) can also be found in some industrial countries (United States (Chapter 15), Spain, Japan (Chapter 12)), as well as in some developing ones, such as Korea (Chapter 22).

Rules-based approaches have the obvious advantage of transparency and evenhandedness, as well as of avoiding protracted bargaining between the central and the subnational levels of government, a process the outcome of which often ends up being determined more by short-term political factors than by considerations of sound macroeconomic management. On the other hand, by their very nature, rules-based approaches lack flexibility and often end up fostering the development of behavior and practices aimed at circumventing the rules. Such practices include, for instance:

- The reclassification of expenditures from current to capital, to escape current budget balance requirements.
- The creation of entities whose operations—albeit of a governmental nature—are kept off-budget, and whose debts are not counted against the debt ceilings.
- The use of state or local government-owned enterprises to borrow for purposes that should be funded through the relevant government budget.
- The use of debt instruments—such as sale and leaseback arrangements or the so-called private revenue bonds in the United States (see Chapter 15)—that are not included in the debt limits.
- The resort to arrears to suppliers, which are typically difficult to monitor for inclusion in the public debt ceilings.

This nonexhaustive listing suggests that, to be effective, a rules-based approach needs to be supported by clear and uniform accounting standards for government entities, strictly limiting, and preferably eliminating, the scope for off-budget operations; comprehensive definitions of what constitutes debt; and the setting up of a modern government financial management information system, capable of providing timely and reliable data on all phases of expenditure,[4] as well as on financial operations of the various levels of government. Also needed are policies like privatization that minimize the scope for use of financial and nonfinancial enterprises for government purposes.

Direct Controls of the Central Government over Subnational Borrowing

In a number of countries, the central government is empowered with direct control over the borrowing of subnational governments. This control may take alternative forms, including the setting of annual (or more frequent) limits on the overall debt of individual subnational jurisdictions (or some of its components, such as external borrowing); the review and authorization of individual borrowing operations (including approval of the terms and conditions of the operation); and/or the centralization of all government borrowing, with on-lending to subnational governments for approved purposes (generally investment projects). Control powers generally encompass not only the ex ante authorization of proposed borrowing, but also the ex post monitoring, on a more or less detailed and timely basis, of the subnational governments' financial operations.

Direct central government controls are, of course, more common in unitary states than in federations. In the United Kingdom until 1988 the central government exercised direct controls on capital spending of local authorities, which varied according to the source of finance of the project. In recent years, the central government has sought to influence the level of local governments' capital spending through the amount of financial support (grants or loan approvals) provided to them and through a requirement that localities set aside a part of their receipts from asset sales to fund new investment. Credit approvals are determined in two parts: a basic amount set on the basis of need criteria and a supplementary authority earmarked for specific projects.

In Japan, the central government exerts a strong influence on the entire budgetary process of local authorities. Guidelines for borrowing by the latter are set out in the annual Local Government Fiscal Plan, which is approved by the parliament at the same time as the central government budget. Borrowing is generally approved only for invest-

---

[4]As indicated in Chapter 6, timely and reliable information on obligations to pay, as well as on actual payments, is essential to prevent the accumulation of arrears.

ment purposes, paying regard to both the projected debt-service ratio and the overall financing needs of the locality. Much of the financing of local authorities is carried out by the Fiscal Investment and Loan Program, which is effectively a form of government financial intermediation, channeling surplus funds of government entities (such as the postal savings and the social security systems) to the funding of local investment projects.

Tight controls are also exercised by the central government on local government borrowing in France. In Spain, which is not a federation, but has granted considerable autonomy to its regions, central government controls have been tightened in recent years in an attempt to stem the rapid growth of deficits at the regional level. Currently all bond placements by regional governments (as well as most borrowing by local governments) need prior approval by the central government.[5]

Among federal countries, in India central government approval is required for borrowing by states that have outstanding indebtedness to the center (Chapter 21). Virtually all the states are currently indebted to the center, since the large vertical imbalance that characterizes intergovernmental fiscal relations in that country has made all the states dependent on central government support through grants and loans. Moreover, the central government has created, through portfolio coefficients on financial intermediation, a substantial captive market for the placement of state debt, until recently at below-market interest rates. Thus, the extensive control of the center over the state finances has, by and large, failed to impose an effective discipline on the latter. India's experience illustrates well the fact that borrowing controls are not a substitute for a sustainable design of intergovernmental fiscal relations, that is, one that does not give rise to excessive vertical or horizontal imbalances.

Several considerations argue in favor of direct central government controls on the external borrowing of subnational governments. First, external debt policy is intimately linked with other macroeconomic policies (monetary and exchange rate policies and foreign reserve management) that are naturally the responsibility of central-level authorities (in particular, the central bank). Second, a well-coordinated approach to foreign markets for sovereign borrowing is likely to result in

---

[5]Specifically, regional governments have to obtain approval from the central government for the placement of domestic or foreign bonds. They can borrow from banks for investment purposes without central government approval. Local governments can borrow from banks for short-term liquidity purposes and also, without higher level government approval, for investment purposes, as long as their total borrowing for any year does not exceed 25 percent of revenues for the previous year.

better terms and conditions than a fragmented one. Third, a deterioration of foreign ratings for one or more of the subnational borrowers may well have contagion effects on the ratings for other borrowers, both public and private. Finally, foreign lenders frequently require an explicit central government guarantee for subnational borrowing. At a minimum, they tend to count on an implicit guarantee. Thus, the central government is likely, de facto, to bear ultimate responsibility for the subnational governments' foreign debt.

These arguments are less compelling in the case of domestic borrowing of subnational authorities. Detailed administrative control of the latter may involve the central government in micro-level decisions (for example, about the financing of individual investment projects) that would be best left to the relevant subnational jurisdictions. Moreover, administrative approval by the central government of individual borrowing operations of the subnational governments may well make it more difficult for the former to refuse financial support to the latter in the event of impending defaults. On balance, effectively and timely monitored aggregate limits on the overall debt of individual jurisdictions, based on market-type criteria, like maximum ratios of debt service to revenues, would seem preferable to either centralized borrowing or preapproval of individual borrowing operations.

Main Conclusions

The review of selected country experiences with controls on subnational governments' borrowing shows that the nature and coverage of these controls vary widely, reflecting in particular the individual country's history, the balance of power among the different levels of government, macroeconomic and fiscal conditions, and the state of development of financial markets. Each of the "models" of control analyzed in the previous sections presents advantages and disadvantages, the balance of which would make it more or less suitable to a particular country's circumstances. Moreover, as these circumstances evolve—that is, as fiscal and macroeconomic imbalances improve or worsen—the preferable model may change over time.

From the review of country experiences, it would appear that the following main conclusions can be drawn.

Although appealing in principle, sole reliance on market discipline for government borrowing is unlikely to be appropriate in many circumstances. This is so, because one or more of the conditions for its effective working frequently are not realized in any particular country. However, market discipline can be a useful complement to other forms of borrowing controls, in particular to help contain resort by subnational governments to practices aimed at circumventing those controls. In this respect, greater transparency and dissemination of information on recent and prospective developments in the finances of subnational governments are highly desirable, and governments should be encouraged to make any necessary changes in the legal and institutional framework to promote these objectives. Equally desirable—on other grounds as well as that of fostering more effective market discipline—are steps to reduce government intervention in financial markets, such as the privatization of federal and state banks and the elimination, or at least a substantial reduction, of any requirements for financial intermediaries to hold government debt, as well as of other regulatory or fiscal privileges for government borrowers. In countries with a history of bailouts of insolvent subnational governments by the central government, a firm and sustained refusal to engage in further operations of this kind will be necessary to change expectations and behaviors of market participants vis-à-vis subnational government borrowing. It must be recognized that this may be a prolonged process, the more so the longer the previous history of bailouts.

The increasing worldwide trend toward devolution of spending and revenue-raising responsibilities to subnational governments seems likely to come into growing conflict with systems of administrative controls by the central government on subnational borrowing (involving, for example, a centralization of borrowing or approval of individual loan operations). While the case—on macroeconomic management and perhaps cost-effectiveness grounds—for administrative controls appears strong as concerns external financing, it is clearly less so for domestic borrowing, for the reasons indicated in the preceding section. It would not, therefore, be surprising to see administrative controls on domestic subnational borrowing decline in importance in the years ahead.

Rules-based approaches to debt control would appear preferable, in terms of transparency and certainty, to administrative controls and also to statutory limits defined in the context of the annual budget process, the outcome of which may be unduly influenced by short-term political bargaining. There is a clear macroeconomic rationale for barring all levels of government from borrowing from the central bank (or, at a minimum, for severely restricting this type of borrowing). Also, as indicated above, borrowing abroad by subnational governments should be strictly limited, in accordance not only with the debt-servicing capacity of the subnational jurisdiction involved, but also with macroeconomic (especially monetary and balance of payments) considerations.

In principle, a good case can be made for limiting all borrowing to investment purposes. However, the so-called golden rule may not be sufficiently restrictive in countries that need to generate government savings to finance at least a part of public investment. Moreover, it may not be desirable to allow government borrowing to finance investments that do not have an adequate rate of economic and social return. Finally, in practice it may be difficult to avoid circumvention of the rule through the inclusion in investments of certain expenditures for current purposes.

These considerations would seem to argue for setting global limits on the debt of individual subnational jurisdictions on the basis of criteria that mimic market discipline, such as the current and projected levels of service of the debt in relation to the jurisdictions' revenues. It is clearly crucial that the projection of the debt service and of revenues, utilized in testing compliance with the ceiling, be realistic and indeed preferably conservative ones. It is equally important that a comprehensive definition of the debt subject to the ceiling be adopted (including, to the extent feasible, extrabudgetary operations, suppliers' credits, guarantees to credits contracted by the subnational government's enterprises, and relevant financial innovations, such as sale and leaseback arrangements).

Finally, even in the context of rules-based approaches, there seems to be scope for increased cooperation of all levels of government in containing (or reversing, if needed) the growth of public debt. Enhanced involvement of the subnational governments (especially at the regional or state level) in formulating and implementing medium-term fiscal adjustment programs (along the lines of the approach recently adopted in Australia) should result in these governments becoming more responsible in the conduct of their budgetary affairs. A multilateral forum for discussion of budgetary policies and prospects of various levels of government should facilitate the recognition of any need for reforms of the existing system of intergovernmental fiscal relations and help muster adequate political consensus for such reforms. Effective political and intellectual leadership by the central government in such a forum remains essential, and may be viewed as the natural evolution of the traditional administrative controls in an increasingly decentralized world.

References

Bayoumi, Tamim, Morris Goldstein, and Geofrey Woglom, 1995, "Do Credit Markets Discipline Sovereign Borrowers? Evidence from U.S. States," *Journal of Money, Credit and Banking*, Vol. 27 (No. 4), Part 1, pp. 1046–59.

Cottarelli, Carlo, 1993, *Limiting Central Bank Credit to the Government: Theory and Practice*, IMF Occasional Paper 110 (Washington: International Monetary Fund).

Lane, Timothy D., 1993, "Market Discipline," *Staff Papers*, International Monetary Fund, Vol. 40 (March 1993), pp. 53–88.

PART II

Practice: Industrial Countries

8

Australia

JON CRAIG

The Australian federation is distinguished by a large vertical imbalance between revenue and expenditure assignments at the national and subnational level. The central government raises about 70 percent of total public sector revenue but undertakes only about half of public sector expenditures. The resultant "vertical gap" at the state and local government level is filled by grants and loans from the center. The federation also allows state, territory, and local governments and their public enterprises to borrow on their own account, subject to guidelines set jointly with the central government.

While this relatively centralized fiscal system has acted to strengthen the capacity of the central government to implement required stabilization policies, fiscal developments at lower levels of government have occasionally complicated economic management. Some commentators have also argued that the Australian federal system has created disincentives to the introduction of essential structural reforms by subnational governments, as well as wasteful overlap and duplication of services. The Australian authorities have taken new initiatives to tackle these perceived weaknesses, including a medium-term fiscal framework designed to better coordinate fiscal policies and hence permit the public sector to make a contribution to national saving objectives. Although there has been an extensive debate recently about the equalization arrangements in the federation, reviews at the political level suggest that they will continue for the time being.

Structure of Government

The Australian federation was formed in 1901. It comprises the commonwealth government plus the six original colonial state governments and two self-governing mainland territories. There are also about 900 local government bodies.

The Constitution underpinning the federation defines relatively few exclusive powers for the central government, one of which is the power to levy customs and excise duty. However, it does prescribe a number of powers that the commonwealth can exercise concurrently with the states and in which its laws would prevail in the event of a conflict. These powers include defense, taxation, foreign affairs, social welfare benefits and pensions, post and communications, currency, and banking and insurance. Section 96 of the Constitution gives the commonwealth parliament power to make grants on terms and conditions as it sees fit, and the commonwealth has used this power to influence subnational expenditure patterns and administrative priorities and, partly through them, macroeconomic stabilization policy generally.

The six original colonial states, which joined together to construct the original Constitution, retained residual (exclusive) legislative responsibility for a number of service areas including law and order, education, health, housing and urban development, road and rail transport, provision of electricity, gas and water, and a number of industry functions. The Constitution gives no formal recognition to the role of local government, and this level of government falls under state legislative control.

In fiscal and other intergovernmental matters, the two mainland territories—the Northern Territory and the Australian Capital Territory—receive state-like treatment. However, these territories can only attain full statehood by a majority vote of the existing states.[1]

Current Arrangements

In addition to their general government activities, the national and subnational governments operate both nonfinancial and financial public enterprises. In the national accounts, the consolidated public sector is defined to include the general government sector plus the net operating surplus of nonfinancial enterprises; the operations of public financial enterprises are excluded.[2]

---

[1] For convenience, in the remainder of this chapter, the term "states" will be used to encompass the activities of the both the original colonial states and the mainland territories.

[2] In any event, privatization and other factors have significantly diminished the role of public financial enterprises in Australia in recent years.

Expenditure Assignments

As Figure 1a shows, the consolidated commonwealth sector is responsible for just over half of the total public expenditure in Australia and the state government sector for the bulk of the remaining share.

Social welfare and health spending dominates the commonwealth sector's own expenditure budget. Defense also remains an important item, although it has declined relative to GDP over the last decade (see Figure 1b). Of course, the pattern of total spending is different, since the commonwealth also makes large grants to subnational governments for education, health, transport, housing, and social security (see next section).

State government own expenditures are closely aligned with the residual constitutional powers of this level of government—education, health services, housing and community amenities, law, order, and public safety, transport and communications, and social services (see Figure 1c).

Local governments have been given a significant role in the provision of transport services (mainly roads and public transit services), recreational and cultural facilities, and housing and community services such as the provision of local roads and parks (see Figure 1d). About 350 local councils operate nonfinancial public enterprises delivering services such as water, electricity distribution, and transport.

Tax Assignments

Figure 2a shows the dominant position of the commonwealth government sector in total public sector revenues.

The commonwealth's dominance flows from its control of the four major sources of national tax revenue—personal income tax, customs and excise duties, company income tax, and sales tax. Those arrangements flow, in turn, from the commonwealth's constitutional responsibility for customs and excise and the transfer of the right to levy income tax to the commonwealth government during World War II. Almost 90 percent of commonwealth revenue comes from taxation (see Figure 2b), with company and personal income taxes contributing over 60 percent of total revenues, and taxes on goods and services a further 23 percent.[3]

Commonwealth grants and advances constitute about 40 percent of state government sector revenue (see Figure 2c). Tax revenues, which also constitute about 40 percent of total revenue, come from a number

---

[3] Unlike most industrial countries, Australia does not have a value-added tax (VAT).

Figure 1. Australia: Composition of Public Expenditure, 1992/93
(*In percent*)

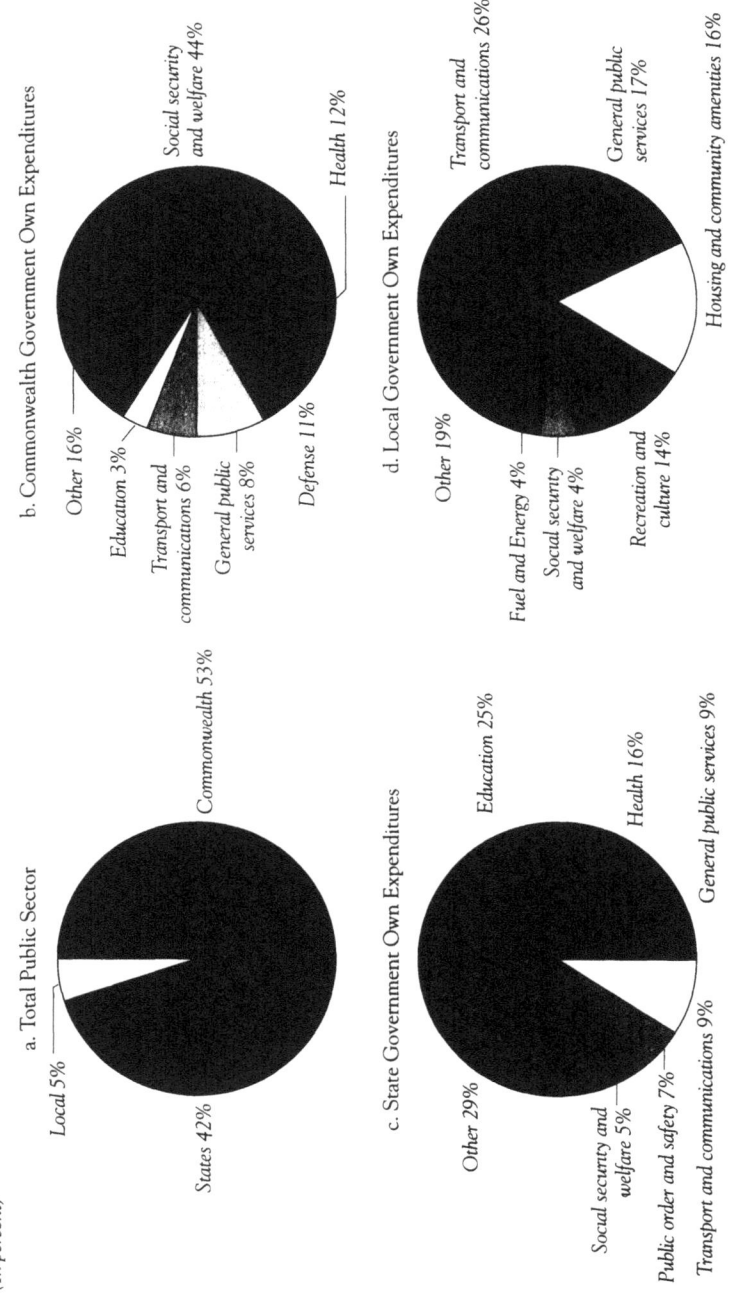

Sources: Australian government budget papers (various issues); Australian Bureau of Statistics, "Government Financial Estimates" (various issues), ABS Catalogue No. 5501; and IMF staff estimates.

of diverse sources. Payroll taxes constitute the largest single source; the remaining tax bases are relatively small, comprising taxes on property—which include stamp duties and land taxes—and a number of indirect taxes—including so-called franchise fees that closely resemble the commonwealth's excise duties, as well as taxes and fees on motor vehicles and gambling and insurance. The tax bases are similar in every state, although the tax rates and base definitions on similar items can vary substantially.

The net operating surplus of state nonfinancial public enterprises accounts for about 12 percent of state revenue. This share is greater than for the commonwealth, and reflects the broad scale of activities undertaken by the state enterprises.

Levies (rates) on residential property provide over half of local government revenue (see Figure 2d). Local governments also rely heavily on transfers from both the state and commonwealth governments, which together contribute close to 30 percent of their revenue. About 80 percent of the state sector payments to local government constitutes the passing on of funds received from the commonwealth. Local governments also raise significant revenues from the various enterprise services they provide (for example, garbage collection services and electricity distribution).

Grants and Advances

Composition of Grants and Advances

Given Australia's considerable vertical imbalance, grants and advances from the center have played a relatively larger role than in similar federations, such as the United States and Canada. The estimated breakdown of these payments in 1997/98 is shown in Figure 3a. Almost all payments are now made in grant form. Over 50 percent of the payments are made in the form of specific purpose (functional) payments to the states, the bulk of which are used by the states themselves but some are simply passed "through" the states, which act as administrative agents, to other recipients (such as universities and local governments) (see Figure 3b). The remaining payments are general purpose payments, mostly in the form of revenue (current) grants to state or local governments. Payments to the subnational governments now total about 8 percent of GDP (Table 1).

General purpose payments to the states and to local governments are made for both recurrent and capital purposes, usually on an unconditional basis. The largest payment to the states is channeled through so-called financial assistance grants, which have generally

180　AUSTRALIA

Figure 2. Australia: Sources of Own Revenue, 1992/93
(In percent)

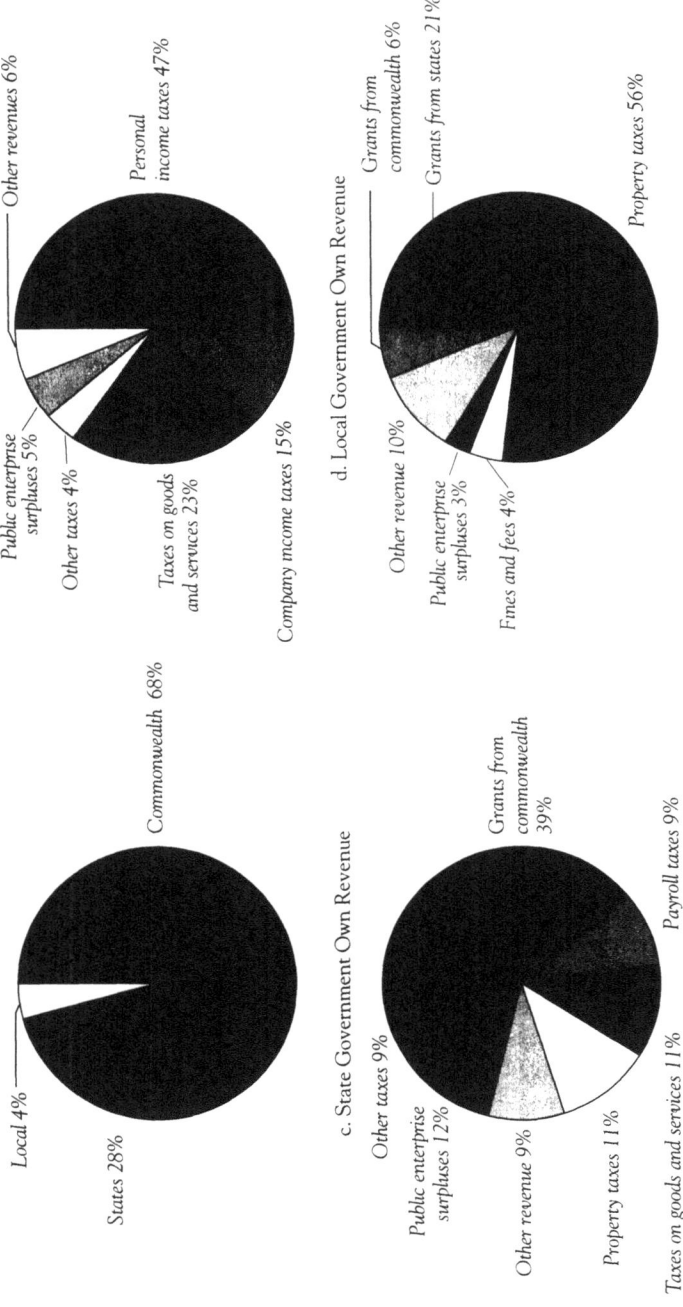

Sources: Australian government budget papers (various issues); Australian Bureau of Statistics, "Government Financial Estimates" (various issues), ABS Catalogue No. 5501; and IMF staff estimates.

Table 1. Australia: Commonwealth Payments to Subnational Government
(In percent of GDP)

	1992/93	1993/94	1994/95	1995/96
Total grants	8.4	8.1	8.0	8.0
Of which: current	7.0	7.1	7.3	7.3
Of which:				
To states				
General purpose	3.7	3.6	3.6	3.6
Of which: financial assistance grants	3.5	3.4	3.4	3.4
Specific purpose	3.3	3.5	3.6	3.6
To states	1.9	2.0	2.0	2.1
Through states	1.4	1.5	1.6	1.6
To local governments	0.0	0.0	0.0	0.1
Capital	1.4	0.9	0.7	0.7
Net advances	−0.7	−0.3	−0.5	−1.0
Total net payments	6.3	6.8	6.8	6.4

Source: Australian Bureau of Statistics (1996).

been set by reference to formula. At present, financial assistance grants are set by reference to actual movements in consumer prices and population.

General purpose recurrent grants to local governments have been made since 1974/75. Grants are determined using a discretionary growth factor each year that tends to yield increases in payments similar in magnitude to those granted under financial assistance grants.

Commonwealth capital grants to the states now consist of relatively small urban development payments, which are distributed according to achievement of performance targets. The former system of capital grants made under the Loan Council arrangements (see below) was abolished in 1993–94. No general purpose capital payments are at present made directly to local governments.

Specific purpose payments cover a wide range of payments made by the commonwealth in pursuit of national policy objectives. They cover both recurrent and capital needs. Most specific purpose payments are subject to conditions on the related state expenditure. In general, these conditions fall into four categories:

• General program requirements, such as the requirement that states provide free public hospital treatment to Medicare patients (that is, those without private insurance) in return for grants made for hospitals.

• Requirements that the payment be spent for a specific purpose, or be passed on to other entities, including universities and nongovernment schools and to local governments.

Figure 3. Australia: Grants to Subnational Governments

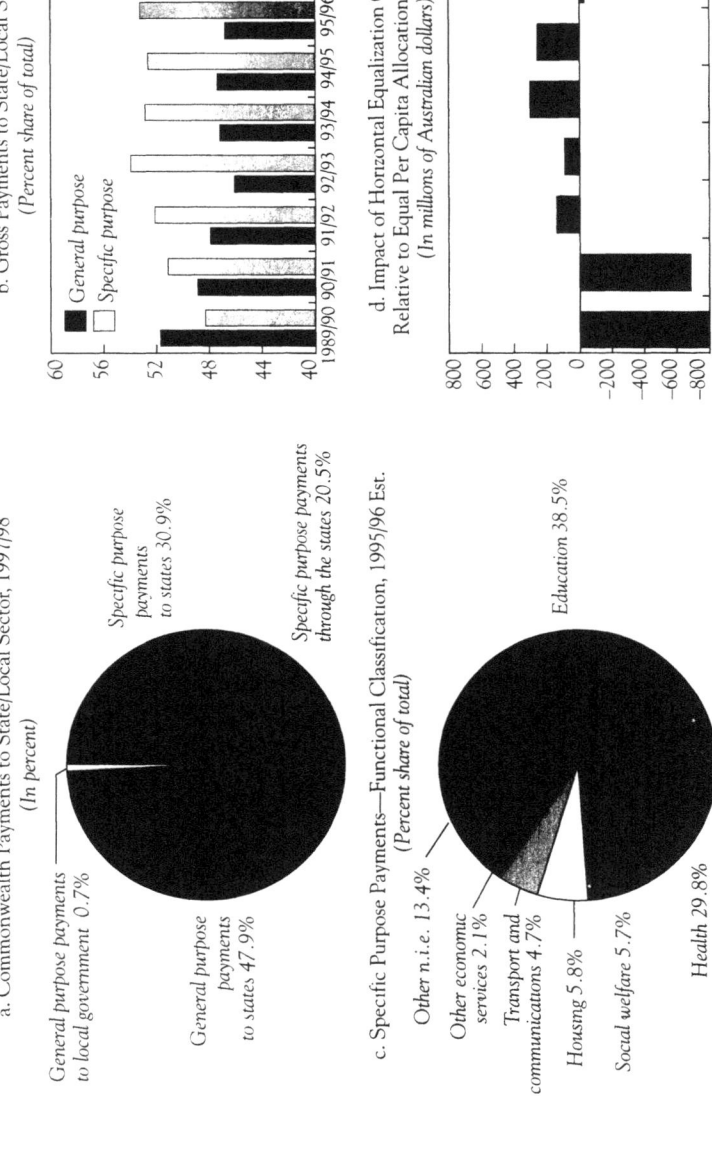

Sources: Australian Government budget papers (various issues); Australian Bureau of Statistics, "Government Financial Estimates" (various issues), ABS Catalogue No. 5501; and IMF staff estimates.
Note: NSW = New South Wales; VIC = Victoria; QLD = Queensland; WA = Western Australia; SA = South Australia; TAS = Tasmania; ACT = Australian Capital Territory; and NT = Northern Territory.

Table 2. Australia: Gross Specific Purpose Payments

	1992/93	1993/94	1994/95
	(In millions of Australian dollars)		
General public services	252.00	276.00	293.00
Defense	—	—	—
Public order and safety	124.00	130.00	131.00
Education	6,395.00	6,583.00	6,695.00
Health	4,413.00	4,840.00	5,089.00
Social security and welfare	561.00	894.00	942.00
Housing and community amenities	1,000.00	1,044.00	1,028.00
Recreation and culture	28.00	23.00	27.00
Fuel and energy	10.00	3.00	2.00
Agriculture, forestry, and fishing	252.00	140.00	227.00
Mining, manufacturing, and construction	15.00	18.00	22.00
Transport and communications	1,885.00	1,059.00	848.00
Other economic affairs	100.00	46.00	39.00
Other purposes	2,130.00	1,625.00	1,698.00
Total	17,165.00	16,681.00	17,041.00
	(Share of total specific purpose payments; in percent)		
General public services	1.47	1.65	1.72
Defense	—	—	—
Public order and safety	0.72	0.78	0.77
Education	37.26	39.46	39.29
Health	25.71	29.02	29.86
Social security and welfare	3.27	5.36	5.53
Housing and community amenities	5.83	6.26	6.03
Recreation and culture	0.16	0.14	0.16
Fuel and energy	0.06	0.02	0.01
Agriculture, forestry, and fishing	1.47	0.84	1.33
Mining, manufacturing, and construction	0.09	0.11	0.13
Transport and communications	10.98	6.35	4.98
Other economic affairs	0.58	0.28	0.23
Other purposes	12.41	9.74	9.96

Source: Australian Government (1996).

- Agreements covering service provision and program delivery mechanisms.
- Detailed conditions on the operation of joint expenditure programs, including program or project approval, arrangements for matching contributions, and information requirements.

The main functional expenditures financed by specific purpose payments are education, health, and housing (see Figure 3c and Table 2).

Most specific purpose payments are indexed for inflation. A review by the Department of Finance in 1995 sought to simplify existing arrangements by developing four "cocktail" indices that combine standard wage and nonwage indices according to different weighting formulas. Each specific purpose payment will be assigned one of the cocktail indices.

The basis of allocation of specific purpose payments among the states varies. Some payments are influenced by historical patterns set when they were negotiated; others are based on the commonwealth's perception of need (for example, hospital funds are distributed on a per capita basis, weighted according to age and sex), while others (such as public housing) are distributed on an equal per capita basis.

Equalization Arrangements

The concern to ensure horizontal equity among the states has long been a distinguishing feature of the Australian federation. This concern arose initially out of dissatisfaction by the states with the financial arrangements instituted after the federation was set up in 1901 and culminated in the establishment in 1933 of a permanent and independent authority—the Commonwealth Grants Commission (CGC)—to assess the claims of the states.

The assessment processes followed by the CGC have changed considerably in both scope and technique since its initial establishment. The present task of the CGC involves making assessments as to the allocation among the states of a large pool of general revenue grants estimated to amount to about 4.5 percent of GDP in 1995/96.

The CGC operates under terms of reference set by the commonwealth after consultation with states and territories. The CGC's investigations aim to determine relative needs according to the principle "that each State should be given the capacity to provide the same standard of state-type services as the other states, if it makes the same effort to raise revenues from its own sources and conducts its affairs with the same operational level of efficiency."

The assessment procedures followed by the CGC are very comprehensive. The assessment of the relative fiscal capacities of states and territories encompasses both revenue-raising capacities and expenditure needs. The assessments are carried out using a representative (or standard) budget that defines the revenue and expenditure items over which the measurement of equalization needs is to be made. National "financial and policy" standards are then calculated for the revenue and expenditure items in the representative budget and objective indicators are used to measure the *relative* revenue-raising capacities and expenditure needs of each state. The assessment process culminates in the recommendation of an index of relative needs ("relativities") that, when weighted by estimated population in each region, provides a basis for allocating the general purpose grant.

The different allocation criteria used for distributing specific purpose payments (described above) can create difficulties for the

CGC in assessing the distribution that should apply to general revenue grants. Since the CGC is charged with examining all sources of revenue for the states in its equalization exercises, including specific purpose payments from the commonwealth, any relative advantage or disadvantage to a particular state or territory conferred through specific purpose payments must be taken into account in the calculations. The most frequent methods used by the CGC have the effect of clawing back any advantage or disadvantage conferred by specific purpose payments.[4] To resolve this potential conflict, the commonwealth has sometimes instructed the CGC to assess relativities on the assumption that existing specific purpose payment distribution patterns are maintained. For example, funds provided to South Australia under a recent financial assistance package (in the wake of large financial losses suffered by public financial institutions in that state) were excluded from the CGC's assessment, to ensure that the benefit of this package was not fully clawed back through CGC assessment of a lower financial assistance grants allocation to that state.

The CGC undertakes a major review of the relativities every five years, with updates in intervening years. The recommendations by the CGC are usually—but not automatically—accepted by the commonwealth and state governments involved.

The extent of redistribution involved in the equalization process can be seen in Figure 3d, which shows the amount by which the recommended grants in 1995/96 exceed (or fall short of) those that would be paid if each state simply received an equal per capita grant.[5] As can be seen, substantial funds are reallocated away from the larger states of New South Wales and Victoria with South Australia, Tasmania, and the Northern Territory being the largest beneficiaries.

General purpose grants to local governments are paid to each state on an equal per capita basis. Each state government maintains a separate grants commission to determine the allocation of these funds among their local governments. These commissions, which are entirely independent of the CGC, base their recommendations on equalization principles, subject to constraints set out in the commonwealth legislation (including a provision that all local authorities should share in the grant).

---

[4]That is, a state receiving a higher share of an "included" specific purpose payment than the CGC considers appropriate to satisfy its needs will be assessed a commensurately lower share of the general revenue distribution pool.

[5]That is, if the allocation to each state varied directly with the population of the state.

Borrowing

A distinctive feature of Australia's federal fiscal arrangements is the Loan Council, a body for coordinating and controlling borrowing by all governments.[6] Initially, the Loan Council operations covered only general government operations, specifying that all borrowing for this sector should be undertaken by the commonwealth government in its own name and then passed on to the states. However, the controls structure was extended, under the so-called Gentlemen's Agreement in 1936, to cover limits on public enterprise borrowing.

The original arrangements continued with only small variations until 1984, when reforms were introduced directed to enable the states to take greater responsibility for their own borrowing. Under the new approach, states began borrowing to finance their budgets and became responsible for refinancing those securities and loans previously raised by the commonwealth on their behalf. In an attempt to retain control of subnational borrowing, global limits were placed on overall public sector borrowing, including the borrowing of public enterprises and local government authorities. Although initially successful, increased use of sophisticated financing techniques by the states (such as sale and leaseback arrangements) saw the intended controls circumvented to such an extent that the global limits approach was abolished in 1992/93.

In its place, the Loan Council has adopted procedures that seek to introduce transparent macroeconomic controls on the overall operations of the public sector. Under the new arrangements, the commonwealth and each state government will present to the Loan Council its *net* financing requirement for the coming financial year. These so-called Loan Council allocations cover the estimated general government balance and certain memorandum items.[7] These proposals are

---

[6]The Loan Council had its origins in the need to coordinate government borrowing in the wake of the debt incurred during World War II. It was initially established on a voluntary basis in 1923 and was given formal status in legislation passed by the commonwealth and the states, in successive stages, from 1927 to 1929, and an amendment to the federal Constitution sanctioned by a referendum in 1928. The Council comprises one representative of the commonwealth—the prime minister or a nominee—and one representative of each state—the state premier or a nominee.

[7]Memorandum items are used to adjust the statistical definitions of deficit and surplus used by the Australian Bureau of Statistics to include some items—such as operating leases or government's risk-weighted exposure to infrastructure projects with private sector involvement—that may have the characteristics of public borrowing but are not included in the formal definition. It has also been agreed that some items should be excluded such as funding of public sector superannuation schemes in excess of expected costs of benefits and borrowing by statutory marketing authorities.

considered by the Loan Council, taking into account each jurisdiction's fiscal position and reasonable infrastructure needs, as well as the macroeconomic implications of the aggregate picture revealed by the Loan Council allocations. If an adjustment is required to meet national macroeconomic objectives, the nature of the adjustment and its allocation across governments will be negotiated within the Loan Council. If questions are raised about the fiscal strategy of any government, further justification for its financing request may be made, and the Loan Council can ask the government concerned to modify its strategy.

The new arrangements are accompanied by more stringent reporting requirements that enable up-to-date monitoring of net financing and debt. If a member becomes aware that it has exceeded, or is likely to exceed, a 3 percent tolerance level in either direction from its endorsed Loan Council allocation, it is obliged to provide an explanation to the Loan Council. This explanation will be made public. While the Loan Council would not be empowered to formally approve the change, it would have the opportunity to pursue any concerns raised by the change in the Loan Council allocation.

Since 1994/95 the arrangements incorporate two important innovations. First, the Loan Council allocations include allowance for public sector risk exposures to infrastructure projects with private sector involvement. Risk exposure calculations are undertaken for all projects with a life of ten years or longer that involve direct provision of services to a public sector entity or the underwriting by the public sector of services provided directly to consumers. The impact is calculated by applying a risk weight to the contingent liability that a project creates for a government. The risk weight is based on project gearing and volatility, and the length of the contract period over that the government faces penalty provisions.

Second, special adjustments are introduced for overfunding or underfunding by governments of the employer component of public sector superannuation scheme liabilities. Briefly, overfunding of the annual cost is to be treated as a form of saving and not as an addition to the Loan Council allocation, even though it may add to the measured deficit. By contrast, underfunding will be treated as a borrowing against Loan Council allocations. The adjustments involved will be handled through memorandum items in the Loan Council allocations calculations.

The initial experience with the new Loan Council allocation approach has been broadly satisfactory, and it appears that the publication of debt details has assisted greater market discipline on borrowing. Developments in borrowing and debt are discussed below.

Administrative Structures

Tax Administration

The commonwealth, state, and local government taxation systems are administered by separate entities. The Australian Taxation Office administers all the major taxes imposed by the commonwealth government, while the state and local governments maintain a number of smaller agencies to administer their taxes and fees. There is no legislative provision for exchange of information between authorities at different levels of government.

Budget Preparation and Implementation

The preparation and execution of budgets by the various levels of government are also conducted by separate agencies. At the commonwealth level, two agencies are involved, the Australian Treasury and the Ministry of Finance. The former has overall macroeconomic policy responsibilities, including the development of overall budget parameters, detailed intergovernment financial policies, and taxation policies, while the latter specializes in expenditure analysis and control.

Separate state treasuries administer state policies, and local governments also maintain their own systems for budget and financial management.

Although one might expect that Australia's federal structure adds to the overall difficulty of formulating and implementing fiscal policies, particularly at the subnational level, several practical efforts have been made to alleviate these problems. First, the budget calendar is carefully arranged so that as many decisions as possible can be made in a sequential order. Thus, the Premiers' Conference and Loan Council meetings between the commonwealth and the states normally take place about two months prior to the presentation of the commonwealth's annual budget and up to six months before the state budgets are introduced. As a result, the resolution of most commonwealth and state financial issues is known well in advance of other budget issues, leaving ample time to make other fiscal adjustments as required. Second, the planning arrangements surrounding grants involve a degree of predictability for a large portion of the commonwealth payments to the states. This is particularly true for education and similar specific purpose payments that are formulated on a multiyear basis. The recent decision by the commonwealth to provide a real terms guarantee for financial assistance grants for the three years to 1996/97 has also improved the ability of state officials to forecast the resources available from the commonwealth for their budgets.

Nonetheless, the introduction of the National Fiscal Outlook program (see next section) has potential to significantly alter the budget preparation procedures followed by each of the participants within the federation, since it places emphasis on coordination of fiscal actions by the various governments within a macroeconomic framework.

Implications

Macroeconomic Management

Macroeconomic management is primarily the responsibility of the commonwealth government in Australia, but it is recognized that successful stabilization policy requires intergovernmental cooperation. Changes in the commonwealth's own account taxes and spending, the level of grants paid to subnational governments, and changes in the access of subnational governments to borrowing are important means by which the commonwealth can seek to influence the overall stance of fiscal policy. However, the state and local governments still maintain a considerable degree of independence in budgetary decision making, flowing from their own substantial sources of revenue. Correct prediction of the likely response of these subnational governments to both economic developments and the commonwealth's own policies is therefore very important in assessing the overall impact of public sector activity.

Although the various levels of government may be expected to work cooperatively over time to achieve satisfactory macroeconomic outcomes, the experiences of the late 1980s and early 1990s have served to demonstrate the difficulties of operating fiscal policy within the Australian federal structure.

With the exception of a brief downturn in 1985/86, the Australian economy experienced relatively rapid growth and falling unemployment in the period from 1982 to 1989. This necessitated a relatively restrictive fiscal policy, and the public sector requirement moved from an "underlying deficit" of 7 percent in 1983/84 to an overall surplus of almost 2 percent in 1988/89 (Figure 4a).[8] Although this change was assisted by a marked reduction in state borrowing, the bulk of the adjustment fell on the commonwealth government sector (Figure 4b). While the commonwealth benefited from rapid growth in its revenues, substantial constraint on own account expenditures and grants to lower

---

[8]The "underlying budget" balance concept used in Australia excludes net advances and hence, the bulk of privatization revenues.

Figure 4. Australia: Nonfinancial Public Sector Operations
(In percent of GDP)

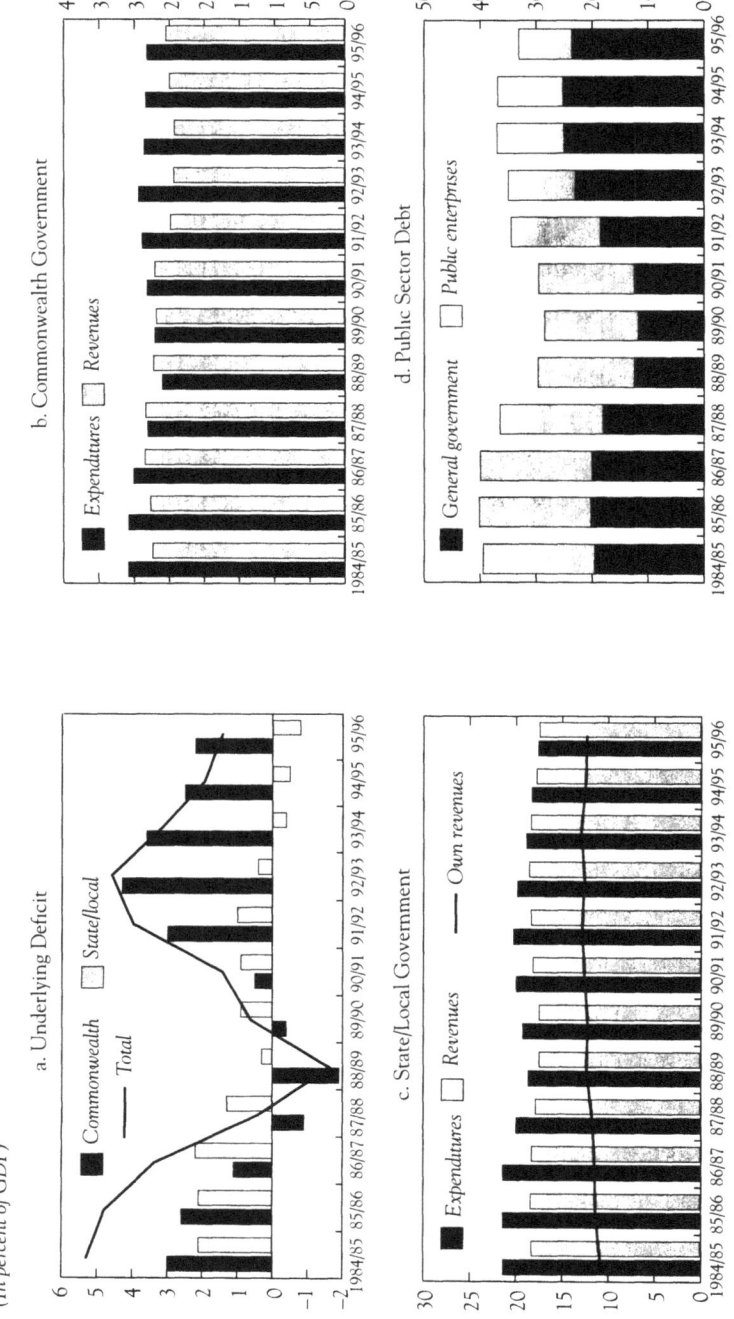

Sources: Australian government budget papers (various issues); Australian Bureau of Statistics, "Government Financial Estimates" (various issues), ABS Catalogue No. 5501; and IMF staff estimates.

level governments was also required. However, during much of this period, subnational governments also experienced a strong growth in their own revenues partly because of robust employment growth (affecting payroll taxes) and a boom in asset prices affecting property and capital asset taxes. As a consequence, subnational expenditures, particularly recurrent expenditures, did not fall substantially relative to GDP during much of the period, notwithstanding the attempt by the commonwealth to restrain grants payments (see Figure 4c). In other words, it can be argued that stabilization efforts may have been less effective than they would otherwise have been because the impact of the cycle enabled subnational governments to sustain a more expansionary policy than might otherwise have been possible.

After the downturn in 1989, opposite pressures came into effect. The collapse of the asset price boom had a particularly significant impact on subnational revenues, and some of the state governments sustained large losses in their overextended state-owned financial institutions. Recession-related demands on subnational expenditures were also substantial, and the ratio of expenditures to GDP rose slightly in the period to 1992. Although a number of subnational governments found themselves constrained by falling debt ratings, their deficits and debt levels rose initially with the total state underlying deficits pushing back up to almost 1 percent of GDP. Meanwhile, the commonwealth found its own revenue growth faltering and demand for its own expenditures, particularly on employment-related activities, rising. The commonwealth also found itself under pressure to assist states with their weakened budget positions. As a consequence of this dual pressure on its finances during the recession, the commonwealth underlying deficit blew out to close to 4 percent of GDP by 1993.

In the subsequent economic recovery, the states have brought about a significant turnaround in their fiscal situation by increasing their own source revenues (chiefly by raising taxes on existing tax bases but also by tapping new tax bases, such as gambling) and by curtailing expenditure growth (with significant reductions in numbers of public employees). They have also embarked on substantial privatization programs. Their underlying balances were in surplus by 1996, and with state debt continuing to fall. By contrast, efforts to stabilize the commonwealth financial position appeared to lag those of the subnational governments—with commonwealth own account expenditure and debt rising through the period to 1996. Overall general government debt rose substantially in the period to 1995 but has since stabilized (Figure 4d).

With Australia's external debt at high levels, there is a continuing need to generate higher savings in the public sector which, in turn, requires improved cooperation and coordination of fiscal policies at the

Table 3. Australia: National Fiscal Outlook; 1997 Version

	1996/97 Estimated	1997/98 Projected	1998/99 Projected	1999/2000 Projected
	(Percent change)			
Economic assumptions				
Real GDP	3.50	3.50	3.50	3.50
Employment	1.75	2.00	2.00	2.25
Wages	4.50	4.00	3.50	3.50
Consumer prices	1.50	1.75	2.50	2.50
	(In percent of GDP)			
Fiscal aggregates[1]				
Revenues				
Commonwealth general government	25.20	24.70	24.70	24.90
States general government	15.20	14.40	14.00	13.60
Of which: commonwealth transfers	8.20	7.90	7.70	7.40
Own source revenue	7.00	6.50	6.30	6.20
Expenditures				
Commonwealth general government	27.0	25.30	24.90	24.40
States general government	15.20	14.30	13.80	13.40
Underlying balance[2]				
Commonwealth general government	–1.80	–0.60	–0.20	0.50
States general government	0.10	0.10	0.20	0.20
Total general government	1.70	0.50	0.00	0.80

Source: National Fiscal Outlook, report to the Premiers' Conference, 1997.
[1] Figures exclude asset sales and commonwealth advances to the states.
[2] The underlying deficit is defined as expenditures (excluding net advances) less revenue. Net advances include new policy lending and net equity injections. Revenues from privatizations are thus excluded.

national level. A recognition of these needs led the commonwealth and the states to embark on joint forecasting and budget planning exercises in 1992. These forecasts were embodied in the preparation of a National Fiscal Outlook document that sought to define a medium-term framework for fiscal policy formulation. Subsequently, it has been successively updated and the published data for the 1997 exercise are shown in Table 3.

Structural Reform

In addition to the need to boost national savings, the Australian authorities have recognized a need to implement a broad range of structural reforms to boost the nation's productivity performance. The system of intergovernment finances has potential to influence success in a number of important structural issues.

Some of these structural issues stem directly from the large vertical imbalance within the federation. Commentators have identified five related problems flowing from this imbalance:

- Reduced accountability by subnational governments to their electorates.
- Duplication and overlap in provision of service.
- Excessive conditionality on payments from the commonwealth.
- Inhibition of taxation reform.
- Slow implementation of microeconomic reforms.

The commonwealth government has made periodic efforts to tackle these issues. In the second half of the 1970s, the government legislated to give the states the right to impose their own personal income tax—which would have piggybacked on the commonwealth tax (as is done in Canada). However, the subnational governments failed to take up the offer with one premier remarking that "the only good tax is a commonwealth tax." Subsequently, the commonwealth agreed to return a fixed share of the proceeds from personal tax, and later a (different) share of the proceeds of all taxes. None of these arrangements survived.

In 1990, the commonwealth launched a proposal for a "closer partnership" with the states that would address the narrowness of the subnational tax base, the conditionality of specific purpose payments, and questions of overlap and duplication.

Some limited progress was made, particularly on the last issue. However, the closer partnership foundered on the unwillingness of the commonwealth to cede any of its control over broader-based taxes or to provide longer-term guarantees to the subnational governments of a fixed share of commonwealth taxation. The need to retain control over macroeconomic policy was cited as the reason for this stance.

Many of the major problems identified in the closer partnership dialogue therefore remain.

Accountability of state governments does not appear to be as strong as in some other federations. In particular, there is a tendency to blame the commonwealth for failures in areas where states have primary service responsibility but funds are provided predominantly by the commonwealth.

State tax reform has been inhibited. State government reports—chaired by Collins (1988) and Nieuwenhuysen (1988)—and other commentators have suggested that state taxes tend to be regressive and to distort incentives.[9] They are narrowly based, subject to variable rates

---

[9]By way of example, Albon (1991) suggests that state taxes have discriminated against housing construction and, within that market, against rental housing in particular. However, Brennan commenting on Albon in the same volume notes that these distortions must be examined in the context of those introduced by commonwealth taxation policies (such as absence of capital gains tax on owner-occupied homes and use of deductible borrowing to achieve high gearing on rental property) that may tend to operate in the opposite direction.

on similar transactions, and involve high costs of compliance. There is also a lack of harmonization in both tax rates and bases across states. In past years, the commonwealth has transferred some taxes to the states—including the payroll tax (1971) and the bank account debit tax (1990/91)—however, these have not had a large impact on state revenue-raising capacity. States face both constitutional and practical restrictions on moving toward more neutral and broad-based systems. In particular, section 90 of the Constitution and associated High Court rulings have been taken as denying the states the capacity to impose taxes on "the manufacture, production, sale or purchase of goods" (Walsh, 1991).[10] These legal restraints are seen as one reason why the states have not attempted to introduce a broadly based sales tax or attempted to impose sales taxes on the largely untaxed service sector in Australia. However, there is also a more general issue as to the practicability of states extending their sales tax bases while the commonwealth has occupied the predominant position in this field. Australia does not possess a broadly based VAT. However, there has been considerable discussion about the desirability of implementing such a tax at the national level, and this may have deterred the states and territories from efforts to extend their indirect taxes.

So long as the commonwealth holds national spending priorities that differ from those of the states, some conditionality cannot be avoided. However, some have argued that the conditions imposed in the past were often overly intrusive and sometimes interfered with the efficient provision of services. There has been some reduction in conditionality (there are few stringent "matching" requirements nowadays). However, some commentators have argued that the conditionality has simply become more sophisticated, not less intrusive. For example, influence can be exerted through a joint planning structure; new untied grants may come with requirements for bilateral negotiations about the purposes for which they will be used; and performance criteria (focusing on outputs) have been introduced for some programs in place of tied funds.

In February 1995, the Australian National Audit Office (ANAO) completed a critical review of the administration of specific purpose payments. The ANAO recommended the introduction of the following:

- Measures to strengthen incentives for greater efficiency of programs, including the identification, measurement, and sharing of potential savings in projects.

---

[10]This issue was tested again in the courts in 1993 and the rulings made again confirmed the supremacy of the commonwealth on this issue.

- In programs where there is a matching requirement, a more detailed specification of the commonwealth's requirements in order to assist states to promote more precise program performance measures.

As noted, there has been progress in the identification and rectification of possible areas of overlap and duplication in the provision of public services. The Council of Australian Government (an intergovernmental body) undertook a major review of arrangements involving areas of shared responsibility, and this has led to some clarification of the roles and responsibilities of commonwealth and subnational governments. For example, the commonwealth withdrew from funding of arterial roads in 1993 and decided it would henceforth restrict its funding to national highways. The amount formerly paid for arterial roads through specific purpose payments was added to the general assistance payments.

The focus of recent intergovernment reform debate has moved to the impact of present taxation and grant arrangements on the incentive of the states to introduce structural reform. This debate has stemmed from the observation that structural reform undertaken by subnational governments should act to boost national production and welfare, but the rewards may flow predominantly to the commonwealth owing to its control over the main taxation instruments. Unless the commonwealth agrees to pass on a portion of any increased revenue generated from higher national output in the form of grants, the states' incentive to participate in such reforms may be diminished (Walsh, 1991).

Two aspects have received particular attention. First, the commonwealth and the states agreed to implement a National Competition Policy recommended by an independent commission headed by Professor Hilmer. The so-called Hilmer report made recommendations to address six major concerns: extension of the existing anticompetitive conduct legislation to cover the unincorporated sector and state government business activities; a review of unjustified regulatory restrictions on competition by governments; development of a set of principles to govern the operation of public monopolies, including proposals mandating separation of regulatory and business functions where competition is introduced into a market previously supplied by a public monopoly; establishing a legally based "access regime" for essential infrastructure facilities that cannot be duplicated economically; restraints on monopoly pricing; and fostering "competitive neutrality" between government and private businesses.

The implementation of these reforms was made difficult by actual and perceived differences in the costs and benefits of reform. While the national, and each subnational, government stood to gain from greater efficiency, some state governments also faced the loss of monopoly rents. Accordingly, in return for agreement by state governments to a clear timetable for reform, in 1994/95 the commonwealth agreed to provide phased compensation payments to the states, conditional on their making satisfactory progress on the agreed reforms.

The reforms are expected to have a substantial impact in five areas of public sector activity, several of which are predominantly under the control of subnational governments: electricity, natural gas, water, telecommunications, and air, sea, rail, and road transportation.

There has also been the question of the consistent taxation treatment of public trading enterprises at different levels of government and the budgetary impact of subsequent action to privatize such enterprises. Historically, publicly owned trading enterprises at both the commonwealth and state level have been exempt from the commonwealth's wholesale sales taxes. The state level enterprises have also been exempt from commonwealth corporate income tax. However, such corporations were widely expected to make higher dividend contributions to the budget to compensate for their preferred treatment. Action to privatize such enterprises therefore had the effect of bringing them within the commonwealth's tax net with direct implications for state revenues via both lost dividend revenue and a reduced sale price.

At the 1994 Premiers' Conference, it was agreed that states will collect tax equivalent payments directly from their wholly owned trading enterprises, while the commonwealth will continue to collect tax from partially privatized state level enterprises and will comprehensively apply the company income tax and wholesale sales tax to its own trading enterprises. Key elements of the agreement are:

- The commonwealth will amend tax legislation to ensure that wholly owned state level enterprises will be exempt from the company income tax and the wholesale sales tax.
- The states will impose a tax equivalent payment on their wholly owned state level enterprises that is uniform among states and matches the commonwealth's tax system.
- Compensation will be provided on a case-by-case basis to ensure that neither the commonwealth nor the states are disadvantaged by the arrangements.

It has been estimated that the amendments to commonwealth legislation will impose a cost of at least $A 680 million a year (about 1.5 percent of GDP) to the commonwealth budget.

These decisions on taxation of public enterprises follow earlier decisions to allow states to impose payroll and other tax and charges on commonwealth public enterprises and should have the desirable effect of creating a more level playing field for competition between public and private enterprises.

In addition to these vertical balance issues, there has been a renewed focus on horizontal balance issues. There are two elements to this debate.

First, notwithstanding considerable simplification efforts by the CGC itself, the assessment measures used in the calculation of per capita relativities have come under sharper scrutiny. In particular, there is debate about the appropriateness of methods of assessing location-specific disabilities, such as dispersion factors, administrative scale factors, urbanization factors, and the possible use of global rather than tax-by-tax assessments of revenue capacity.

Second, there has been a debate about the impact of equalization payments on economic efficiency. On the one hand, some authors (for example, Swan and Garvey, 1992) have suggested that such payments lower potential GDP growth (by discouraging labor from moving from locations where its marginal product is low to places where it is high and diverting funds from more "efficient uses" in those states with higher fiscal capacities), while others (such as Petchey and Walsh, 1993) support such payments on the grounds that they avoid "publicly induced migrational inefficiency." This debate (which finds a counterpart in Canadian literature) remains unresolved.[11]

The focus has been on the CGC's analysis of locational disabilities (including factors such as measures of population dispersion) that tend to lead to higher assessed needs for less populous, more far-flung states and territories within Australia.

Although the debate remains unresolved, it has been pointed out that both the commonwealth and the states tend to practice equalization within their own borders (as, indeed, do most unitary states) because they do not levy higher taxes in higher cost areas or provide lesser services in remote areas. If equalization between states was reduced or abolished, therefore, the impact would be felt statewide and not just in remote areas. In other words, there would be an incentive to move not simply from remote areas to cities but also from smaller state cities to the already large metropolitan areas of Sydney and Melbourne.

Of course, even if it can be demonstrated that there is some trade-off between equalization and efficiency that would not necessarily put an end to the matter since judgments would have to be made as to whether the efficiency cost was a worthwhile sacrifice for a more harmonious federation with open economic space permitting unrestricted competition and development.

---

[11]See, for example, Boadway and Hobson (1993).

The debate over the desirability and sustainability of equalization culminated in the creation of a Heads of Treasury working party in 1992 to examine the adequacy of the current scope and methodology of equalization as well as the principles upon which it is based. The report of the working party, which was presented to the 1994 Premiers' Conference, made a number of recommendations for methodological change. However, it appears that there will be no immediate change to the use of the equalization approach in the distribution of financial assistance grants, and the commonwealth has subsequently strongly endorsed the present role of the CGC.

Conclusions

The operation of economic policy within the Australian federation is circumscribed by constitutional requirements and historical conventions. Although finances are relatively centralized, with a large vertical imbalance favoring the central government, the need to take account of the reactions of state and local governments to commonwealth policies adds to the difficulty of implementing stabilization policies. Moreover, the state and local governments retain considerable influence over structural reforms in a number of key activities. While the commonwealth has the financial power to exert considerable influence on the behavior of subnational governments if it chooses to use it, recent efforts have been directed to achieving better cooperation and coordination of policy through efforts to involve subnational governments in the attainment of important national goals. Meanwhile, despite an active debate on the methodology and economic costs of equalization, the Australian federation seems likely to continue its longstanding emphasis on horizontal fiscal balance.

References

Albon, Robert, 1990, "The Impact of State Taxation: The Case of Housing," in *Issues in State Taxation*, ed. by Cliff Walsh (Canberra: Centre for Research on Federal Financial Relations, Australian National University).

Australian Bureau of Statistics, 1996, "Government Financial Estimates," ABS Catalogue 5510 (Canberra).

Australian Government, 1993, Budget Paper No. 1, 1994/95 and earlier years (Canberra: Australian Government Publishing Service).

———, 1994, "Commonwealth Financial Relations with Other Levels of Government, 1993/94" Budget Paper No. 3 (Canberra: Australian Government Publishing Service).

———, 1995, "Commonwealth Financial Relations with Other Levels of Government, 1994/95," Budget Paper No. 3 (Canberra: Australian Government Publishing Service).

———, 1996, "Commonwealth Financial Relations with Other Levels of Government, 1995/96," Budget Paper No. 3 (Canberra: Australian Government Publishing Service).

Boadway, Robin W., and Paul A.R. Hobson, 1993, *Intergovernmental Fiscal Relations in Canada* (Toronto: Canadian Tax Foundation).

Brennan, Geoffrey, 1990, "State Taxation Issues: Commentary," in *Issues in State Taxation*, ed. by Cliff Walsh (Canberra: Centre for Research on Federal Financial Relations, Australian National University).

———, Bhajan S. Grewal, and Peter Groenewegan, eds., 1988, *Taxation and Fiscal Federalism: Essays in Honor of Russell Mathews* (Sydney; New York: Australian National University Press).

Collins (Chair), 1988, *Report of the New South Wales Tax Task Force 1988—Review of the State Tax System: Tax Reform and NSW Economic Development* (Sydney).

Commonwealth Grants Commission, 1983, *Equity in Diversity—Fifty Years of the Commonwealth Grants Commission* (Canberra: Australian Government Publishing Service).

———, 1991, *Report on Technical Issues* (Canberra: Australian Government Publishing Service).

———, 1993a, *Report on General Revenue Grant Relativities, 1993*, 3 vols. (Canberra: Australian Government Publishing Service).

———, 1993b, *Report on Issues in Fiscal Equalization* (Canberra: Australian Government Publishing Service).

Economic Planning and Advisory Council, 1990, *Towards a More Cooperative Federalism?* Discussion Paper No. 90/04 (Canberra: Australian Government Publishing Service).

Fletcher, Christine, 1991, *Responsive Government: Duplication and Overlap in the Australian Federal System* (Canberra: Federalism Research Center, Australian National University).

Mathews, Russell L., and W.R.C. Jay, 1972, *Federal Finance: Intergovernmental Financial Relations in Australia Since Federation* (Melbourne: Nelson).

———, 1993, *The Theory and Practice of Fiscal Equalization: A Report for the Queensland Government* (Queensland Treasury).

———, eds., 1974, *Intergovernment Relations in Australia* (Sydney: Angus & Robertson).

Niewenhuysen (Chair), 1988, *Committee of Inquiry into Revenue Raising in Victoria* (Melbourne).

Petchey, Jeffrey D., and Cliff Walsh, 1993, *Horizontal Fiscal Equalization in Australia* (Adelaide: South Australian Center for Economic Studies).

Prest, W., and Russell L. Mathews, eds., 1980, *The Development of Australian Fiscal Federalism: Selected Readings* (Canberra; Trumbull, Connecticut: Australian National University Press).

Report of the Heads of Treasuries Working Party, 1994, *Horizontal Fiscal Equalization* (Canberra: Commonwealth Treasury, March).

Rye, C.R., and R.J. Searle, 1994, "The Fiscal Transfer System in Australia," paper presented at the Conference on Fiscal Transfer Systems (Quingdao, China, July).

Swan, P., and G. Garvey, 1992, "The Equity and Efficiency Implications of Fiscal Equalization" (Sydney: Australian Graduate School of Management).

United States, Advisory Commission on Intergovernmental Relations, 1981, *Studies in Comparative Federalism—Australia, Canada, the United States, and West Germany: An Information Report* (Washington: Government Printing Office).

Walsh, Cliff, 1991, "Reform of Commonwealth-State Relations: 'No Representation Without Taxation,'" Discussion Paper No. 2 (Canberra: Federalism Research Center, Australian National University).

———, ed., 1990, *Issues in State Taxation* (Canberra: Federalism Research Center, Australian National University).

9

Canada

RUSSELL KRELOVE, JANET G. STOTSKY, AND CHARLES L. VEHORN

Sparsely populated and stretching from the Atlantic to the Pacific Oceans, Canada is a federal nation composed of heterogeneous provinces. The British North American Act of 1867 established the federal nation, which at that time consisted of only the four provinces of Nova Scotia, New Brunswick, Quebec, and Ontario. Subsequently, other provinces were added; the last was Newfoundland, in 1949. The Northwest Territories and the Yukon Territory were added to the federation at the end of the nineteenth century, but remain under the stewardship of the federal government. Today, Canada consists of 10 provinces, 2 territories, and nearly 5,000 local governments, including cities, towns, villages and townships, counties, and special service districts.

The Government Structure

The current relationship between the federal government and subnational governments can be traced back to the British North American Act of 1867, which enumerated the legislative powers of the federal parliament and the provincial legislatures. The federal powers fall broadly into the area of peace, order, and good government. The federal government is given responsibility for the national public debt and property, the regulation of trade and commerce, defense, money and

---

The authors are grateful to Ehtisham Ahmad, Liam Ebrill, Ron McMorran, and Teresa Ter-Minassian for helpful suggestions and comments.

banking, the criminal law, the raising of money by any type of taxation, and the authority to legislate in any areas not explicitly allocated to the provinces (Boadway and Hobson, 1993). The British North American Act of 1867 gives provincial legislatures the exclusive right to make laws within the province in areas that are generally local or private in nature, such as property and civil rights, public institutions (hospitals, asylums, prisons, and charitable institutions), education, the management and sale of public lands, and the administration of justice. Provincial government activities can be financed through the provincial right to use direct taxation. Provincial activities can also be financed by the "spending power" of the federal government. This power allows the federal government to make expenditures (usually through transfers) on functions under provincial jurisdiction (Clark, 1997). It is also important to note that this act does not contain provisions related to local governments. Instead, local governments are considered "creatures of the provinces" and receive their powers and responsibilities from the provincial legislatures. All provinces, for example, have devolved to local governments the responsibility for primary and secondary education, although in some provinces, responsibility is reverting to the province.[1]

Bird (1990) has pointed out that public sector financing in Canada is unique, because it is one of the most decentralized federations with respect to federal-provincial arrangements and one of the most centralized with respect to provincial-municipal arrangements. The drafters of the British North American Act of 1867 expected the federal government to maintain a dominant position over the provinces, with federal revenue and expenditures about three times those of the provinces. Over time, however, demand grew faster for those public services assigned to the provincial level, and they expanded relative to the federal level.

Table 1 presents government revenue (excluding intergovernmental transfers) as a share of GDP. Revenue of all governments has shown a persistent upward trend in this century, from 19.8 percent of GDP in 1939 to 43.3 percent in 1994. Until the late 1970s, federal revenue exceeded provincial and local revenue (excluding intergovernmental transfers), but since then provincial and local revenue has exceeded federal revenue.

Table 2 shows similar trends for expenditure. Expenditure of all governments has grown from 20.5 percent of GDP in 1939 to 48.6 percent

---

[1]For example, the government of the province of Ontario announced in early 1977 a plan to take control over the provision of education, at the same time devolving to municipalities responsibility for a number of services, including welfare.

Table 1. Canada: Government Revenue[1]
(In percent of GDP)

	Federal (1)	Provincial and Local[2] (2)	Provincial (3)	Local (4)	All Governments[3] (5)
1939	8.2	11.6	5.3	6.3	19.8
1943	21.9	6.9	3.3	3.5	28.7
1950	15.8	8.4	5.0	3.4	24.2
1955	17.1	8.4	4.7	3.7	25.5
1960	16.5	10.6	5.9	4.7	27.1
1965	15.8	13.1	8.6	4.5	29.0
1970	17.5	16.8	11.8	4.3	35.7
1975	18.5	17.2	13.0	4.1	37.4
1980	16.3	19.4	15.0	4.2	37.5
1985	17.4	20.5	16.2	4.1	40.0
1990	19.0	22.0	17.2	4.5	43.3
1994	18.7	22.2	17.0	5.0	43.3

Sources: Canadian Tax Foundation (1994); and Treff and Cook (1995).
[1]Excluding intergovernmental transfers.
[2]Including revenues of public hospitals. The difference between column (2) and the sum of columns (3) and (4) represents the hospital portion.
[3]Including revenues of public hospitals, as well as compulsory contributions to and investment income of the Canada Pension Plan and the Quebec Pension Plan, which are excluded from the other columns. The public pension contributions amounted to 1.5 percent of GDP in 1970; by 1991, they amounted to 4 percent.

in 1994. Federal expenditure increased dramatically around the time of World War II, then fell back to more historical levels. It then grew rapidly until the 1980s and has since stabilized. Federal grants to provinces (almost all grants go to provinces) have been relatively stable between 1970 and the mid-1990s, at around 4 percentage points of GDP. Provincial and local expenditure grew much faster than federal expenditure in the post–World War II period, owing to an increase in spending on the areas for which provinces and local governments are responsible. Resources are transferred to the provincial domain from the federal domain through intergovernmental grants and through shared taxes, most notably, the income tax. The growing gap between revenue and expenditure of general government has led to the accumulation of a sizable debt. This growth in the public sector and in the public debt has raised serious concerns about the ability of Canada to maintain its highly redistributive system of fiscal federalism.

The Constitution Act of 1982 amended and expanded the British North American Act of 1867. It gave constitutional standing to the principles of the welfare state that arose in Canada after World War II. Under the part of the Constitution Act devoted to "Equalization and Regional Disparities," the federal and provincial governments are com-

Table 2. Canada: Government Expenditure
(In percent of GDP)

	Federal Including Grants to Provinces	Federal Grants to Provinces	Federal Excluding Grants to Provinces	Provincial and Local[1]	All Governments[2]
1939	8.2	1.3	6.9	13.6	20.5
1943	39.1	1.3	37.8	6.7	44.5
1950	12.4	1.3	11.1	10.3	21.3
1955	16.4	1.5	14.9	10.7	25.6
1960	17.1	2.4	14.7	14.3	28.8
1965	14.9	2.4	12.6	16.3	28.7
1970	17.2	3.7	13.5	21.4	34.9
1975	20.8	4.4	16.4	23.1	39.9
1980	19.8	4.0	15.7	23.8	40.3
1985	24.0	4.5	19.4	26.0	46.8
1990	22.9	3.9	19.0	26.4	47.3
1994	22.6	4.1	18.5	27.4	48.6

Sources: Canadian Tax Foundation (1994); and Treff and Cook (1995).
[1]Including expenditures of public hospitals.
[2]Including expenditures of the Canada Pension Plan and the Quebec Pension Plan, which together amounted to 2.2 percent of GDP in 1991. Other columns do not include payouts under these compulsory public pension plans but do include pensions paid out of general government revenues (noncontributory schemes, funded from current taxes).

mitted to promote equal opportunities for the well-being of Canadians, to further regional economic development, to reduce disparity in opportunities, and to provide essential public services of reasonable quality to all Canadians (Leslie, 1993). The act also reaffirmed the provincial taxing authority over nonrenewable resources, and instituted certain individual rights, for example, mobility, that could constrain provincial programs from imposing residency requirements. The net effect of this act on fiscal federalism continues to evolve. While one provision advocates reduction in regional disparities as a political principle, another section provides provinces with jurisdiction over nonrenewable resources, which could promote increased regional disparities because these resources are not distributed evenly across provinces.

At the time of federation, the provinces were given the right to provide for health and education. The twentieth century brought federal involvement into these areas, especially through providing grants to provinces and direct programs of income security to the population. The Constitution Act of 1982 reaffirms that the federal government is responsible for equalizing the ability of provincial governments to provide comparable levels of public services at comparable levels of taxation (Leslie, 1993). In this respect, Canadian federalism goes well beyond the redistributional objectives of the U.S. federal system.

To summarize, the last 40 years has seen a steady decentralization of fiscal expenditures in Canada from the federal to the provincial level, reflecting the rapid expansion of expenditures in areas assigned to the provinces, such as health and welfare. This expansion in provincial expenditure brought about a rise in provincial taxation and, until recently, increases in federal grants to the provinces. In recent years, federal grants as a share of GDP have fallen as the federal government has attempted to reduce its budget deficit.

Revenue Sources

The major tax revenue sources in Canada are the personal income tax, the corporate income tax, and the goods and services tax (a value-added tax enacted in 1991 to replace a manufacturers' sales tax) at the federal level; the personal income tax and the corporate income tax (collected by the federal government but remitted in part to provinces), the retail sales tax, and resource taxes at the provincial level; and the property tax at the local level. Table 3 shows the percentage distribution of revenue for the federal, provincial, and local governments in fiscal year 1994.[2] The British North American Act of 1867 gave provinces the power to collect direct taxes. Although a retail sales tax is generally considered by economists to be an indirect tax, Canadian law considers it a direct tax defined as a tax "demanded from the very person who it is intended or desired should pay it." Provincial retail sales taxes are levied on the purchases and collected by the retailer on behalf of the government, so the sales tax is considered a direct tax (Canadian Tax Foundation, 1994).

Personal Income Tax

The personal income tax has evolved over time. Before World War II, the personal income tax system in Canada was fragmented, with both the federal government and provincial governments levying their own taxes with separate bases, rate structure, and residency rules. During the war, the provinces agreed, on a temporary basis, to give up the right to levy the personal income tax and the corporate income tax, in return for cash transfers or "rentals." Some provinces received tax transfers based on forgone revenue, and others received tax transfers based

---

[2]The provincial and local governments are aggregated because the split varies from one province to another. Therefore, the disaggregated figures would be misleading.

Table 3. Canada: Structure of Federal, Provincial, and Local Government Revenue, 1994[1]
(In percent)

	Federal Government	Provincial and Local Government	Total
Income taxes			
Personal	47.1	24.3	33.6
Corporate	8.1	3.0	5.1
On payments to nonresidents	1.0		0.4
Property and related taxes		20.1	11.1
Consumption taxes			
General sales	14.0	12.4	13.2
Motive fuel	2.5	3.6	3.3
Alcoholic beverages and tobacco	2.3	1.5	2.0
Customs duties	2.5	—	1.3
Other	0.6	0.2	0.4
Health and social insurance premiums	14.2	6.1	9.7
Miscellaneous taxes	0.3	2.8	1.7
Natural resource revenues	—	3.5	2.0
Privileges, licenses, and permits	0.3	2.9	1.8
Sales of goods and services	2.8	7.5	5.3
Return on investments and other revenue	4.4	12.1	9.1
Total consolidated own source revenue	100.0	100.0	100.0

Source: Authors' calculations based on data in Treff and Cook (1995).
[1]Estimate.

on the cost of servicing provincial debt, less revenue from death duties (Boadway and Hobson, 1993).

The tax transfer arrangement has undergone several modifications. In 1947, tax transfers were determined on the basis of equal per capita transfers, with various other provisions, such as a minimum yield provision. This modification implicitly brought the concept of equalization into the picture. Provinces that contributed less than the per capita national average would be equalized up to the national norm through a redistribution from those provinces above the per capita national average. However, both the provinces of Quebec and Ontario chose not to participate, under "opting out" provisions. Instead, they received 5 percent of federal personal income taxes collected within their borders.

In 1957, the notion of payments based on equalization was made explicit, along with the concept of fiscal responsibility. Each province received tax rentals based on revenues generated within its own border, initially 10 percent, along with a supplementary payment on the basis of equalization. This arrangement resulted in significant harmonization from a tax policy perspective, in contrast to a country like the United States (see Chapter 15), but prevented provinces from setting their own tax rate structure.

In 1962, the system of tax rentals was replaced with tax collection agreements, whereby the federal government gave tax abatements (or transferred tax room to the provinces). Each province received a standard uniform rate (percent) of federal taxes collected within the province. In addition, each province could set its own rate above the standard rate. Currently, nine provinces and two territories participate in this arrangement. Only Quebec collects its own personal income tax.

The nine provinces that participate in the tax collection agreement set their own tax rate as a rate on federal taxes, with the base defined as basic federal tax. Basic federal tax is different from the federal tax payable in that certain federal surtaxes and tax credits are excluded. Thus, provincial revenue is not affected by changes to the federal tax law outside the basic federal tax provision. This system maintains relative tax harmony while allowing each province to set its own tax-on-tax rate. Two other advantages of this arrangement are ease of administration and a relatively low compliance burden on taxpayers. One tax administration, Revenue Canada, collects both federal and provincial income taxes, allowing taxpayers to file only one return with a few additional lines added to calculate the provincial tax due. Table 4 presents, for 1995, the tax-on-tax rates for each province, which range from 45 percent to 69 percent. As Table 4 indicates, some provinces levy in addition surtaxes on basic federal tax, as well as a separate flat tax on net income.[3]

Quebec has not participated in the federal government's tax collection arrangements, and levies and collects its own personal income tax. In addition to certain federal tax credits, Quebec residents receive a tax abatement (transfer) of 16.5 percent of basic federal personal income tax.

Corporate Income Tax

The federal government collects the corporate income tax for seven provinces, excluding Ontario, Quebec, and Alberta. These three provinces collect their own corporate income tax on bases similar to the federal corporate income tax. The federal government provides a 10 percent tax credit to make room for the provincial corporate income tax. As with the personal income tax, provinces must use the federal tax base, but provinces determine their own tax rates and credits. All

---

[3]For purposes of the personal income tax, the province of residence of a taxpayer is determined by residence on December 31, the last day of the tax year.

Table 4. Canada: Provincial Personal Income Tax Rates in Effect for 1995

Province	Basic Personal Income Tax (In percent of basic federal tax)	Flat Tax (In percent of net income)	Surtaxes (In percent of provincial tax payable)[1]
Newfoundland	69.0	—	—
Prince Edward Island	59.5	—	10.0 on amount payable over Can$12,500
Nova Scotia	59.5	—	20.0 on amount payable over Can$10,000
New Brunswick	64.0	—	8.0 on amount payable over Can$13,500
Quebec	n.a.	n.a.	n.a.
Ontario	58.0	—	20.0 on amount payable between Can$5,500 and Can$8,000
			30.0 on amount payable over Can$8,000
Manitoba	52.0	2.0	2.0 on net income over Can$30,000
Saskatchewan	50.0	2.0	10.0 on sum of basic provincial tax and flat tax up to Can$4,000
			25.0 on sum of basic provincial tax and flat tax over Can$4,000
Alberta	45.5	0.5[2]	8.0 on amount payable over Can$3,500
British Columbia	52.5	—	30.0 on amount between Can$5,300 and Can$9,000
			50.0 on amount payable over Can$9,000
Northwest Territories	45.0	—	—
Yukon	50.0	—	5.0 on amount payable over Can$6,000

Source: Treff and Cook (1995).
n.a. = not applicable.
[1] Except for Manitoba and Saskatchewan.
[2] As a percentage of taxable income.

provinces provide a foreign tax credit, most provide a political contribution tax credit, some provide a research and development tax credit, and others provide a tax credit for the portion of provincial income tax that arises from the disallowance of natural resource royalties as an expense for federal income tax purposes (Canadian Tax Foundation, 1994).

In 1994, a basic federal income tax rate of 28 percent (38 percent before the provincial tax credit) was levied on general business, 21 percent on manufacturing and processing businesses, and 12 percent on small business. A 3 percent surtax was applied to federal tax, bringing the general rate up to 28.84 percent.[4] The general corporate income tax rate for provinces varied from 14 percent to 17 percent, except for Quebec with an 8.9 percent rate for certain general businesses.

---

[4] There is also a tax on large corporations, which the corporate income tax is creditable against.

In order to ensure that corporations with permanent establishments in more than one province are not subject to double taxation, the profit of the consolidated organization is apportioned across provinces using an agreed rule. The allocation formula employed depends on the shares of sales and wage bill in any province. The amount of taxable income allocated to province i is given by

[½ (gross revenue in i/total gross revenue)
+ ½ (wages and salaries in i/total wages and salaries)] × taxable income.

The use of an apportionment rule of this sort reduces the incentive for corporations to engage in tax planning activities, such as transfer pricing, to reduce tax burden (Boadway and Hobson, 1993).

Domestic Indirect Taxes

The major indirect tax of the federal government is the goods and services tax (GST), enacted on January 1, 1991, which replaced an antiquated manufacturers' sales tax (MST). The MST contained some elements of cascading and was applied only to a limited range of manufactured goods, neglecting entirely the service sector, and in its operation had the effect of favoring imports over domestically produced goods. Initially, the federal government proposed to merge the GST with provincial sales taxes to create a national VAT, which would be collected by the federal government and shared with the provinces. However, the provinces did not approve this initiative, so the federal government proceeded alone while continuing to carry on discussions with some provinces. The tax law eventually enacted provided for a single rate of 7 percent, a relatively broad base, and a threshold level of Can$30,000 in annual sales for small traders. Certain sectors, municipalities, universities, schools, and hospitals receive rebates so they would be no worse off under GST than they were under the MST.

The GST represents a significant improvement over the MST from a tax policy perspective; however, it strained intergovernmental relations because the provinces considered it a serious intrusion on their tax territory. The retail sales tax is the second most important revenue source for provinces (excluding property taxes, which are the primary revenue source for municipalities; see Table 3). All provinces except Alberta impose a retail sales tax, with rates varying from 6 percent to 12 percent. There are province-specific exemptions for certain goods, services, or types of purchasers. Food, prescription drugs, medical appliances, and most books are exempt in all provinces. Most provinces exempt certain purchases by municipalities (Canadian Tax Foundation, 1994).

The existence of two separate and different sales taxes has created many intergovernmental problems. The basic issue is designing a way to determine and allocate the provincial portion of GST revenues among the provinces. One compliance burden caused by the failure to obtain provincial approval of the GST is that businesses have to collect two separate sales taxes, provincial and federal, on different bases.[5] Provinces east of Ontario chose to apply their sales tax to the tax-inclusive price, while the other provinces chose to exclude the GST from their sales tax base.

Quebec has agreed to harmonize its retail sales tax with the GST base and collect the tax on behalf of the federal government. This arrangement is the opposite of the traditional income tax agreements whereby the federal government collects tax on behalf of the provinces. In 1996, the provinces of Newfoundland, Nova Scotia, and New Brunswick signed an agreement with the federal government to harmonize the federal and provincial taxes, under which the combined federal-provincial tax rate would be 15 percent. The tax would be collected by a new agency that would involve provincial participation. Other provinces are still opposed to harmonization, although the federal government is continuing discussions on harmonizing the taxes.

Natural Resource Taxes

The federal government has little access to natural resources in the provinces as a revenue source. In the past, it had more access, either through special taxes on resources or indirectly through federal-provincial revenue-sharing agreements. However this access has been gradually ceded to the provinces.[6]

Differences in provincial resource revenues are a major source of interprovincial differences in revenue capacities. While natural resource revenue contributes over 3 percent of provincial and local government revenue (see Table 3), its importance is uneven. Natural resource revenue accounts for one-quarter of Alberta's total general revenue and almost one-tenth of Saskatchewan's. For the other provinces, however, it accounts on average for less than 2 percent of general revenue, and in several provinces it is insignificant (McMillan, 1991).

---

[5]Transnational businesses must collect GST and nine provincial retail sales taxes.

[6]While ownership of natural resources was vested in the provinces by the Constitution, it did not clearly specify how rents arising from these resources might be taxed. The federal government's constitutional claim to revenue arises from its power to control the terms on which interprovincial trade takes place, as well as the power to impose taxes on both the export and import of products.

Other Taxes

The major tax at the municipal level is the property tax. In general, the base is real property—land or things erected on or affixed to the land (Canadian Tax Foundation, 1991). Depending on the province, property tax assessment is conducted by the provincial government, municipal governments, or independent provincial commissions. Assessment is not uniform because of differences in valuation methodologies, definitions of value, and frequency of reassessments. All provinces provide numerous exemptions either through provincial legislation or by authorizing municipalities to exempt certain types of property, such as educational institutions, churches, public hospitals, and charitable organizations. Property tax relief is also given, usually for the elderly. Property taxes are mainly used to support public education.[7]

Expenditure Responsibilities

The major areas of expenditure in Canada are social services, debt charges, and national defense at the federal level, and health, education, social services, and debt charges at the provincial and local levels. Table 5 shows the percentage distribution of expenditure for the federal, provincial, and local governments in fiscal year 1994.[8] The British North American Act of 1876 laid out the basic expenditure responsibilities of the different levels of government. The federal government is responsible for goods and services with national scope, such as defense, international affairs, industrial policy, and research. The provincial and local governments have major responsibility for spending on goods and services that are local in nature, such as public education, health care, and municipal services.[9] The two share responsibilities in areas where both have legitimate interests, such as agriculture, forestry, fishing, and public health.

In the post–World War II era, the federal government has expanded its activities in areas traditionally within the provincial preserve, espe-

---

[7]Since 1972, Canada is one of the few developed countries which has no estate taxes, allowing almost all intergenerational transfers of wealth to escape taxation. As part of tax reform, the federal government vacated this field, opening up additional tax room for the provinces. Tax competition has led to little provincial exploitation of the base.

[8]The provincial and local governments are aggregated because the split varies from one province to another. Therefore, the disaggregated figures would be misleading.

[9]As mentioned earlier, however, the federal government does have concurrent "spending powers" for provincial functions, which it exercises in the form of transfer payments.

Table 5. Canada: Structure of Federal, Provincial, and Local Government Expenditure, 1994[1]
(In percent)

	Federal Government	Provincial and Local Governments	Total
General services	4.4	5.6	5.5
Protection of persons and property	9.3	5.2	7.4
Transportation and communications	2.2	5.9	4.6
Health	4.9	21.8	13.5
Social services	34.8	15.6	24.1
Education	2.9	19.8	12.5
Resource conservation and industrial development	3.9	4.2	4.1
Environment	0.4	3.4	2.3
Recreation and culture	0.8	2.8	2.1
Labor, employment, and immigration	1.6	0.4	1.0
Housing	1.2	0.8	1.1
Foreign affairs and international assistance	2.3	—	1.1
Regional planning and development	0.3	0.6	0.5
Research establishments	0.9	0.2	0.5
Debt charges	22.2	12.5	18.2
General purpose transfers to other governments	6.7	—	—
Other	1.2	1.4	1.4
Total consolidated expenditures	100.0	100.0	100.0

Source: Authors' calculations based on data in Treff and Cook (1995).
[1] Estimated.

cially in the area of the social safety net. The social safety net is complex, consisting of payments made directly to individuals and payments made from one level of government to another to support social safety net activities. The federal government provides a large proportion of transfers to individuals through assistance for the unemployed, family allowances, a universal old age pension, and national health insurance. The federal government also makes transfers to provinces to fund programs in postsecondary education, health care, welfare, and other areas. The rising spending on the social safety net has contributed to budgetary problems for both levels of government.

Overall, expenditure on health care, education, and social services has increased at about the same pace as GDP since the mid-1970s. Expenditure on education has decreased relative to GDP, and expenditure in the other two categories has increased (see Ip, 1991). Provincial-local expenditure on education was the most important function in dollar terms during the 1970s and until the mid-1980s. Nationally, local taxation accounted for about 35 percent of school revenues in

1989, with provincial funding contributing about 60 percent. In recent years, provinces have expanded their role in providing funds for primary and secondary education because of the inability of local governments to raise adequate revenues through the local property tax and because of a desire to equalize spending across local communities within a province.

Intergovernmental Grants

Intergovernmental grants became a significant part of the federal system in the period following World War II at the time that the federal government enacted several major social welfare programs, including unemployment insurance, family allowances, universal old age insurance, and national health insurance. The federal government intended that the latter two programs would be administered by the provincial governments, although it would retain overall control. However, some of the provinces resisted the federal design, and the federal government chose to fund the old age insurance program on its own (Leslie, 1993).

Over the subsequent decades, economic prosperity provided enough revenues for the federal government to expand its programs of family allowances and old age insurance, extend funds to postsecondary education, establish a program of revenue equalization, and fund many shared-cost programs with the provincial governments. In addition, in 1965, the federal government enacted the Canada Pension Plan, a program of compulsory public pensions that includes all provinces except Quebec. Quebec enacted its own plan, the Quebec Pension Plan, which is fully compatible with the federal plan (Leslie, 1993).

The major shared-cost programs introduced in the postwar years were the Medical Care Act and Canada Assistance Plan in 1966. In 1957, the federal government began sharing some hospital care costs with provinces. By 1961, all provinces had hospital insurance plans. The Medical Care Act was made available to any province that agreed to four basic criteria regarding coverage, administration, availability to residents, and portability. By 1971, all provinces had adopted acceptable Medicare plans. The federal grant was open-ended and matching, and varied by province according to per capita costs so that low-cost provinces received more than half their costs and high-cost provinces received less. The Canada Assistance Plan merged four shared-cost programs into one comprehensive program to provide aid to low-income elderly people, the disabled, unemployed people not eligible for unemployment insurance, and the blind. Although the federal government pays half of the cost of the program, the provinces design and administer their own programs. In the mid-1970s, as its fiscal position weakened, the federal government began to restructure the system of grants to provincial governments. In 1977, the Established Programs Financing Act merged hospital insurance, Medicare, and postsecondary education into a block grant, made on an equal per capita basis (Boadway and Hobson, 1993).

Federal funds are distributed by formulas aimed at the equalization of tax capacities, without any explicit attempt to measure expenditure needs in each province. It is implicitly assumed that expenditure needs are equal on a per capita basis. While the issue of expenditure needs has been discussed for many years between federal and provincial officials, no attempt has been made to build an assessment of expenditure needs into the transfer system, owing largely to the technical difficulties involved (Clark, 1997).

Fiscal Imbalances

According to the Conference Board of Canada, revenues as a share of GDP, in 1993 were greater than expenditures at both the federal and the provincial level and less than expenditures at the local level. Specifically, local level own source revenue is only 57 percent of own account expenditures, indicating that local governments are heavily reliant on the transfer system to meet their expenditure responsibilities (Clark, 1997).

While vertical imbalances are mainly significant at the local level, horizontal imbalances in Canada are more pronounced and are exacerbated by the abundance of (taxable) natural resources in a few provinces. Using fiscal capacity indices for 1994–95, Clark has shown that resource-rich provinces have substantially higher fiscal capacities than resource-poor provinces. For example, Alberta's fiscal capacity index of 129.9 was almost twice as high as Newfoundland's index of 65.6, before transfers. Equalization entitlement reduced this disparity significantly as Alberta's fiscal capacity index fell to 122.6 and Newfoundland's rose to 93.6.

Types of Grants

The federal government provides grants to subnational governments in two basic forms: general purpose transfers and special purpose transfers. The major general purpose transfer—equalization payments—is an unconditional grant to only those provinces with below-average tax capacity. The formula, based on 33 revenue sources, is discussed below.

Until 1996, specific purpose transfers comprised the Established Programs Financing (EPF) and the Canada Assistance Plan (CAP). These programs expired at the end of fiscal year 1996, with a new program—Canada Health and Social Transfers—replacing them.

The EPF grants, made to all provinces on an equal per capita basis, contained a cash component and a tax component. Funds from this grant program were allocated solely to health care and postsecondary education. Even though the federal government required that the funds be spent in these two areas, as long as provinces continued to spend more than the allocated amount in both areas, the earmarking requirement could not be enforced.

Transfers under CAP were open-ended and matching, at a 50 percent rate. Assistance was provided to needy persons who are old, blind, disabled, or unemployed, dependent children, or native people, as well as to welfare providing institutions such as nursing homes, homes for unmarried mothers, hostels for transients, and child care institutions. Federal funds covered the costs of direct financial assistance, welfare services, and administration, but did not cover capital costs, or the costs of plant and equipment. The CAP offered a great deal of flexibility to provinces in that they could choose which categories of assistance they would provide. The federal government did not require any means testing, so eligibility was based only on the subjective concept of "need."

Table 6 presents the estimated federal cash and tax transfers, which total almost Can$42 billion for 1995–96. Equalization, EPF, and CAP account for 87 percent of the Can$28.9 billion in cash transfers. Additionally, EPF tax transfers account for 91 percent of the Can$13.0 billion in tax transfers.

Equalization

In Canada, the principle of equalization is part of the Constitution and receives broad support. The three major transfer programs until 1996—equalization payments, EPF, and CAP—attempted to equalize on different bases: capacity, population, and need. The formula for equalization payments distributes federal funds only to the seven "have not" provinces (Newfoundland, Prince Edward Island, Nova Scotia, New Brunswick, Quebec, Manitoba, and Saskatchewan). These provinces have below-average tax capacities defined as the difference between the per capita revenue raised for each specific revenue source on a national basis and the per capita revenue raised by the province for each specific revenue source, using a national average tax rate. The 33 revenue sources include income taxes, payroll taxes, general sales taxes, various excise taxes, resource revenues, property tax revenues,

Table 6. Canada: Estimated Federal Payments to the Provinces, Territories, and Municipalities, 1995/96
(In millions of Canadian dollars)

Cash transfers	
General purpose transfers	
Equalization	8,870.0
Statutory subsidies	38.1
Public utilities income tax transfer	63.0
Youth allowance recovery	−435.2
Territorial financial agreements	1,163.8
Grants in lieu of property taxes	435.3
Total general purpose cash transfers	10,135.0
Established programs financing	
Insured health services	6,891.4
Postsecondary education	2,184.6
Total EPF cash transfers[1]	9,076.0
Other specific purpose transfers	
Canada Assistance Plan	7,226.9
Other	2,237.8
Total specific purpose cash transfers[2]	18,540.7
Total cash transfers	28,886.9
Tax transfers	
EPF tax transfers	
Insured health services	8,041.4
Postsecondary education	3,805.7
Total EPF transfers	11,847.1
Contracting out tax transfers	
8.5 personal income tax points for EPF	—
5.0 personal income tax points for CAP	725.9
3.0 personal income tax points for youth allowances	435.2
Total tax transfers	13,008.2
Total cash and tax transfers	41,895.1
Memorandum items (equalization associated with EPF tax transfers (included in line 1)):	
Insured health services	550.3
Postsecondary education	260.4

Sources: Treff and Cook (1995), based on estimates; and Department of Finance calculations of entitlements under equalization and EDF, October 1995.
[1]Excludes the equalization associated with the tax transfers, already included in line 1.
[2]Includes Can$211.2 million not allocated by provinces.

and so on. The formula, initially based on the national average, was called the representative national average standard (RNAS). It was later changed to the representative five-province standard (RFPS), which includes only British Columbia, Manitoba, Saskatchewan, Ontario, and Quebec. The actual formula is:

$$\sum_j E_{ij} = \sum_j t_j(B_{Rj}/P_R - B_{ij}/P_i)P_i$$

where
- E_{ij} = entitlement under revenue source j in province i,
- B_{Rj} = the tax base for revenue source j in the five provinces,
- P_R = the population in the five representative provinces,
- B_{ij} = tax base for revenue source j in province i,
- P_i = the population in province i, and
- t_j = the national average tax rate for revenue source j:

$$t_j = \sum_i TR_{ij} / \sum_i B_{ij}$$

where TR_{ij} is the actual tax revenue collected from revenue source j in province i.

The equalization grant program embodies gross equalization, in the sense that the have-not provinces are equalized up, while the have provinces are not equalized down as would occur under a net equalization formula. Some redistribution from the have provinces occurs since relatively more of the federal funds came from these provinces, which pay proportionately more in federal taxes (Boadway and Hobson, 1993).

The impact of equalization payments is considerable. Table 7 shows per capita payments to the provinces in 1990/91. Before equalization, the per capita national revenue of the low income provinces varied between 63 percent and 88 percent of the national average. After equalization payments these provinces received 93 percent of the new, higher national average revenue, with a commensurate fall in the relative position of the higher-income provinces. While the equalization formula lowers revenue differentials, it does not, however, eliminate them. In addition, equalization payments equalize revenues, not services; that is, no account is taken of differences in needs (arising, for example, for demographic reasons, or because of differential costs of delivering services).

The formula for EPF was based on the equalized value of tax transfers and a cash transfer that brought the full transfer up to an equal per capita allocation, that is:[10]

Total cash transfer = total entitlement − equalized value of tax transfer.

---

[10] Tax transfers are equalized by providing an additional payment to bring the yield of the transferred taxes up to the level specified in the general equalization formula, discussed above.

Table 7. Per Capita Federal Grants to Provinces, 1990/91
(In billions of Canadian dollars)

Province	National Revenue Yield[1]	Equalization	Established Programs Financing	Canada Assistance Plan[2]
Newfoundland	2,898	1,686	757	177
Prince Edward Island	2,989	1,596	757	184
Nova Scotia	3,518	1,067	757	177
New Brunswick	3,296	1,288	757	221
Quebec	3,973	611	757	251
Ontario	5,086	—	757	199
Manitoba	3,737	867	757	179
Saskatchewan	4,059	525	757	152
Alberta	6,306	—	757	213
British Columbia	4,808	—	757	236

Source: Boadway and Hobson (1993).
[1]The revenue that would be generated using average national tax rates.
[2]Fiscal year 1989/90.

In fiscal year 1996, the federal government gave each province an equalized tax transfer of 13.5 percentage points of basic federal personal income taxes and 1 percentage point of taxable corporate income for EPF.

Table 8 shows the per capita growth in the three major transfer programs from 1980/81 to 1992/93 as well as the split between tax transfers and cash transfers. Equalization, which is a general purpose grant, and EPF, a block grant, grew by 98 percent and 84 percent, respectively. However, the CAP, an open-ended matching grant, grew by 180 percent. The federal government has limited the growth in equalization payments to the growth in GNP. The growth of EPF has also been limited since the 1980s. In the late 1980s, the limit was the rate of growth of GNP less 3 percent. In 1990, the federal government froze EPF transfers at their 1989 per capita levels for two years and extended this freeze for three additional years in the 1991 budget. As a result, the transfers grew only with population growth. Since the limit applied to overall EPF transfers and the tax points continued to grow, the cash component of the EPF fell significantly.

Growth in the CAP was difficult to constrain because of its open-ended nature. The program was little changed since its inception. However, in 1990, the federal government capped the annual rate of growth of CAP transfers to British Columbia, Alberta, and Ontario at 5 percent. Although this was challenged, the Canadian Supreme Court upheld the federal right to restrict the program. This was extended in 1991 for three years (Boadway and Hobson, 1993).

Table 8. Canada: Major Federal Transfers to Provincial Governments
(In Canadian dollars per capita)

	Equalization	Established Programs Financing			Canada Assistance Plan		
		Cash	Value of tax points	Total	Cash	Value of tax points	Total
1980/81	155.5	213.1	194.6	407.7	80.1	12.1	92.2
1982/83	181.1	235.1	218.2	453.3	92.4	13.7	106.0
1982/83	198.1	261.8	241.6	503.3	117.1	14.1	131.2
1983/84	210.7	301.0	244.3	545.3	133.9	13.9	147.8
1984/85	216.4	318.0	265.3	583.2	142.9	15.0	157.9
1985/86	205.0	335.1	288.0	623.1	154.5	16.3	170.8
1986/87	228.5	343.9	315.2	659.1	160.5	17.4	177.9
1987/88	258.6	339.4	350.4	689.8	170.3	19.7	190.0
1988/89	281.3	342.6	378.7	721.3	178.8	20.2	198.9
1989/90	298.4	342.8	415.2	758.0	196.5	22.1	218.6
1990/91	303.6	330.1	427.9	758.0	206.9	23.9	230.8
1991/92	301.1	315.1	437.1	752.2	221.9	24.6	246.6
1992/93	307.3	294.2	458.0	752.2	232.8	25.3	258.1

Source: Leslie (1993).

The February 1994 budget set a joint ceiling on EPF transfers for postsecondary education and CAP transfers. In the 1995 budget, the government chose to combine the CAP and EPF into a single block grant, termed the Canada Health and Social Transfer (CHST), effective in 1996/97. The government postponed defining a formula that would permanently set the size and allocation of the CHST after 1996/97. This new transfer retains the combination of cash and tax transfers. The total entitlement for each is based on national average EPF entitlement and individual CAP cash transfers in an earlier year. The growth of the total entitlement is still linked to national average per capita GDP. From this base, the value of the tax abatement and associated equalization are deducted to arrive at the cash transfer. The federal government has set a floor on cash transfers (Perry, 1996). The system of equalization grants was not amended.

Intergovernmental grants in Canada have a powerful influence on spending. All together, these grants lead to a significant equalization of fiscal capacities across provinces, although they do not entirely eliminate differences. As previously noted, the equalizing formulas do not take into account cost and expenditure need differences. To the extent that services are more costly or there is a greater need for services in some provinces, the grants formulas do not make any explicit provision for these differences. Moreover, the numerous caps on funding imposed by the federal government over the last few years have clearly made long-term budgetary planning more difficult for the provinces.

Local governments are heavily dependent on intergovernmental transfers from the provincial governments and to a lesser extent from the federal government. Most of the grants from provincial governments are in the form of conditional grants for education, health, social services, transportation, and other uses. The remainder are unconditional grants. The mix varies from province to province, depending on the split between provincial and local responsibilities. The major category of conditional grants is for education, which are provided in all provinces except New Brunswick (where funding is entirely a local responsibility). These grants take the form of direct funding and revenue pooling. Typically, education transfers have a redistributive element built into them to equalize the ability of different local jurisdictions to pay for education (Boadway and Hobson, 1993). This, too, is an area where change is occurring.

Borrowing

The size of the public debt has risen rapidly, leading to a heavy debt-service burden for both the federal and provincial governments. This has caused considerable public concern and retrenchment at the federal government level. The federal government began to experience serious budget problems in the mid-1970s, in the aftermath of the first oil shock. These problems continue to the present. Table 9 provides figures on the evolution of public debt in recent years. Federal debt was 70.8 percent of GDP in 1994, up from 33.2 percent in 1980. Provinces also face a heavy debt overhang, although not of the same magnitude as the federal government. Provincial debt was 22.7 percent of GDP in 1994, up from 4.9 percent in 1980. Recently, however, many provinces have introduced debt targets as part of their consolidation efforts. Consolidated public sector debt was 97.1 percent of GDP in 1994, up from 45.5 percent in 1980.

Table 9. Canada: Public Sector Debt
(In percent of GDP)

	Federal	Provincial	Local	Consolidated Public Sector
1980	33.2	4.9	7.4	45.5
1985	45.9	8.0	4.2	58.1
1990	54.6	11.7	3.0	69.3
1993	67.1	20.2	3.4	90.6
1994	70.8	22.7	3.6	97.1

Source: Treff and Cook (1995).

Institutional Features

The federal government can borrow funds for current and capital purposes with no formal constitutional restrictions. The provincial governments can also borrow funds for current and capital purposes with no formal constitutional or federal government restrictions. They are not required to balance their current budgets annually, as is typical in the United States. Alberta, in fact, allows short-term borrowing for current operations up to the amount of the estimated tax revenue for the year. Table 10 provides figures on budget surpluses and deficits in recent years. The federal government and the provinces are subject to some market discipline as their debt is rated by one or more international investment firms, and these ratings are critical in creating a favorable environment for borrowing. In recent years, several of these ratings have been downgraded in response to the large deficits and accumulation of public debt.

The federal government has several sources of borrowing. The major portion of federal debt is borrowed in the traditional bond market (both in Canada and abroad) and consists of marketable bonds, treasury bills, Canada savings bonds, Canada bills, and other debt liabilities. In addition, federal debt consists of borrowing from the Canada Pension Plan (CPP) and from public employee pension plans.

The provincial governments have two major sources of borrowing—the traditional bond market and the CPP. The CPP uses its surplus above current needs to purchase preferentially rated securities from the provinces. The CPP, along with provincial pension plans and provincial government entities, held 56 percent of the outstanding bonds and debentures of provincial governments in 1990 (Canadian Tax Foundation, 1991). Some provinces use the CPP funds themselves, while others act as a conduit for municipal debt.

Table 10. Canada: Government Surplus/Deficit (+/−)[1]
(In percent of GDP)

	Federal	Provincial and Local	Canada and Quebec Pension Plans	Consolidated Public Sector
1980	−3.4	−0.4	1.0	−2.8
1985	−6.6	−0.9	0.7	−6.8
1990	−3.9	−0.5	0.3	−4.1
1993	−4.9	−2.2	−0.2	−7.3
1994	−3.8	−1.2	−0.3	−5.3

Source: Treff and Cook (1995).
[1]All figures include intergovernmental grants.

Unlike provinces, municipal governments are required by the provinces to balance their budgets on a current basis. All provinces, however, provide some type of assistance to local governments in their borrowing activity through public intermediaries (municipal finance corporations) or matching grants. Municipal capital expenditures that involve long-term borrowing must be approved by the province. Many provinces require that local governments submit a capital budget extending over more than one year. Some provinces place limits on total, long-term, or short-term borrowing for the current budget, or some combination of limits to a certain proportion of taxable assessment, the estimated annual tax yield for the locality, or the current budget (Canadian Tax Foundation, 1991).

Macroeconomic Management

Budgets are cyclically sensitive on both the revenue and expenditure sides. Typically, income-based taxes are the most cyclically sensitive form of revenue, although broad-based consumption taxes also exhibit strong cyclical sensitivity. Certain components of expenditure are also cyclically sensitive, especially income transfer and social insurance programs. Interest payments on debt may also exhibit cyclical sensitivity in response to changing market interest rates.

As in other industrial nations, the federal budget has been used as a tool of macroeconomic management in the period following World War II, although in recent decades the rapid rise in government spending not matched by an increase in revenue has led to large structural deficits and a high debt burden. Unlike in the United States, where states impose limits on their ability (and the ability of local governments) to run budget deficits on their current accounts, provincial governments in Canada have more scope for running deficits. This has led not only to a heavier consolidated public debt burden but has also complicated the task of fiscal stabilization for the federal government, because, in principle, the provinces can conduct their own fiscal management, in line with objectives not necessarily compatible with those of the federal government.

The latter, however, has some control over provincial budgets on both the revenue and spending sides. To some commentators, the federal government's motive in expanding its control over the income tax in the early postwar era was to enable it to implement a Keynesian fiscal policy. If the federal government had exclusive access to those revenue sources that were most susceptible to cyclical fluctuations—mainly the personal and corporate income taxes—it would be better able to fine-tune surpluses or deficits as Keynesian principles might prescribe. At the same time, it would be able to shelter the provincial governments from any sudden drop in revenues by financing a large portion of their activities through federal grants. It was thought that the effect would be stabilizing not only over time but also among regions (Leslie, 1993). However, this scheme never fully succeeded because some provinces resisted incorporation into it, most notably Quebec. Subsequently, the federal government transferred some income tax authority back to the provinces, resulting in the current arrangement whereby the government collects the personal income tax for nine provinces and the corporate income tax for seven provinces and transfers it to the provinces. Even the nonparticipating provinces have relatively harmonized personal and corporate income taxes. As a result, the federal government still retains significant control over income taxes.

The cyclical sensitivity of tax revenue also depends on broad-based sales taxes and property taxes. As with the personal and corporate income taxes, the federal government does not have exclusive use of broad-based sales taxes, sharing this authority with the provinces. The switch from the MST to the GST at the federal level has probably acted to reduce the cyclical sensitivity of sales tax revenue. The GST base is broader than the MST base, by including more services and value added of the distribution sector. This would tend to reduce the cyclical sensitivity of the tax, since a more comprehensive measure of spending is likely to be less volatile than one just based on sales of manufactured items. Property taxes are typically less cyclically sensitive than broad-based income or consumption taxes. They move with the business cycle, but generally with a lag. Their concentration at the local and provincial levels is likely to make the provincial and local tax bases less cyclical overall.

Spending on social welfare programs is largely shared between the federal and provincial governments. The cyclical component would come in largely through the individual transfer programs rather than the intergovernmental grant programs, since none of the major intergovernmental grants has an explicitly cyclical element built into it. In this respect, federal spending is likely to be more cyclical than provincial and local spending, emphasizing the importance of sound macroeconomic management at the federal level.

The growth in the provincial and local government sectors in Canada in recent decades may have altered the balance and nature of macroeconomic management. The provincial and local government budgets are likely to be less cyclical than the federal one, and the ability of provincial governments to run budget deficits means that in economic downturns, they need not engage in procyclical cuts in spending and increases in revenues, as in the United States, where states face balanced budget requirements. That same ability, however, as indicated above, covers the task of facilitating the growth of public debt, from an already very high level.

Future Direction of Intergovernmental Relations

The federal system in Canada possesses many of the desirable features of a federal system. Spending and revenue-raising responsibilities are appropriately assigned. An important characteristic has been its flexibility; the federation has proven to be remarkably adept at dealing with economic and social change. Two distinctive features of the Canadian system are that it is decentralized with respect to federal-provincial relations and strongly redistributive. Intergovernmental grants serve to equalize the ability to pay for public services and to correct for spillovers. However, the intergovernmental grants system is being cut back, which poses a problem especially for the provincial governments with lower fiscal capacity. The imbalance between their spending and revenues may grow as the federal government reduces its role. How Canada will reconcile this imbalance with its strong desire for equalization remains an unsolved dilemma.

In addition to fiscal issues, in recent years a number of factors are changing the nature of the federation. These issues include the status of Quebec and possibly the western provinces, within the Canadian federal system; and the free trade agreement with the United States, which may shift the pattern of trade from within Canada to between the United States and provinces of Canada (Boothe, 1992).

References

Bird, Richard M., 1990, "Federal-Provincial Fiscal Arrangements: Is There an Agenda for the 1990s?" in *Canada: The State of the Federation 1990*, ed. by Ronald L. Watts and Douglas M. Brown (Kingston, Ontario: Institute of Intergovernmental Relations, Queen's University).

Boadway, Robin W., and Paul A.R. Hobson, 1993, *Intergovernmental Fiscal Relations in Canada* (Toronto: Canadian Tax Foundation).

Boothe, Paul, 1992, "Constitutional Change and the Provision of Government Goods and Services," in *Alberta and the Economics of Constitutional Change*, ed. by Paul Boothe (Edmonton, Alberta: Western Centre for Economic Research).

Canadian Tax Foundation, 1991 and 1994, *The National Finances: An Analysis of the Revenues and Expenditures of the Government of Canada*, various years (Toronto: Canadian Tax Foundation).

Clark, Douglas H., 1997, "The Fiscal Transfer System in Canada," in *Financing Decentralized Expenditures: An International Comparison of Grants*, ed. by Ehtisham Ahmad (Cheltenham, England; Brookfield, Vermont: Edward Elgar).

Ip, Irene, 1991, "An Overview of Provincial Government Finances," in *Provincial Public Finances: Plaudits, Problems, and Prospects*, Vol. 2, ed. by Melville McMillan (Toronto: Canadian Tax Foundation).

Leslie, Peter M., 1993, "The Fiscal Crisis of Canadian Federalism," in *A Partnership in Trouble: Renegotiating Fiscal Federalism* (Toronto: C.D. Howe Institute).

McMillan, Melville, 1991, *Provincial Public Finances: Plaudits, Problems, and Prospects*, 2 vols. (Toronto: Canadian Tax Foundation).

Perry, David B., 1996, "The Evolution of Federal Finance in Canada," in *Essays on Fiscal Federalism and Federal Finance in Canada*, Discussion Paper No. 6 (Toronto: International Centre for Tax Studies, University of Toronto, July).

Treff, Karin, and Ted Cook, 1995, *Finances of the Nation, 1995* (Toronto: Canadian Tax Foundation).

10

Germany

PAUL BERND SPAHN AND WOLFGANG FÖTTINGER

A cursory analysis of intergovernmental arrangements in Germany points to many features that characterize unitary states: a strong central government with an extensive area of influence, uniformity in legislation on almost all important issues, and a uniform tax system. For the provision of public goods, the German Constitution emphasizes uniformity of living conditions for the whole nation (rather than minimum standards). A further characteristic of German federalism is the strong coordination of policies among different layers of government. To be sure, other elements of the arrangements vindicate the official title of federation: the existence of intermediate levels of governments, 16 *Länder* (or states), and a local government sector the importance of which cannot be overemphasized. Nevertheless, the impression of a "unitary German federation" remains strong.

Structure of Government

The Constitution of 1949 confers primary state powers to the states. However, this tier of government has since experienced a continuous erosion of its original competencies in favor of the federal government. This is the consequence of allowing concurrent legislation for a number of responsibilities (according to Articles 72 and 74 of the Constitution), and of the principle of federal law overriding state law. Even in areas of primary state responsibility, the *Länder's* competence has been reduced by increased sharing of responsibilities and joint decision making.

Although the German Constitution makes some attempt to divide government functions among the tiers vertically (exclusive competencies are defined for the federal government), its approach to federalism differs typically from the models of the Anglo-Saxon world. At the central level, emphasis is laid on legislative functions, the allocation of financial resources, and the formulation of policy guidelines. States and local governments are generally in charge of implementing and administering policies. Lower levels of governments often execute policies on behalf of higher levels, where financing is sometimes tied to the function performed, with corresponding grants or cost restitution. Federal legislation also requires that some functions be financed by the lower tiers from own resources and without compensation (for example, subsidiary welfare, *Sozialhilfe*). Central administration is less developed in general, and the states bear the brunt of administrative responsibilities in Germany (including those for tax administration). This particular division of functions—central decision making with decentralized execution—has been labeled the horizontal approach to federalism in contrast to the vertical model of the Anglo-Saxon world (Spahn, 1978b). However, as in other federations, some important government functions—such as defense—are also assigned in an exclusively vertical fashion.

As regards financial arrangements, the horizontal distribution of functions is matched by the prevalence of revenue sharing. All major taxes (income and corporate income taxes and the value-added tax—VAT) accrue to federal and state governments jointly. Legislation on taxes is uniform and centralized. Parliaments of regional jurisdictions have no power to legislate on national taxes, although some smaller taxes continue to be assigned to state or local governments. All taxes are assessed according to the same national tax code—in particular as regards the tax base.[1] Virtually every law affecting the interests of the states has to pass the Bundesrat (lower house), the states' legislative assembly, which—unlike the equivalent in other federations such as the United States, Canada, or Australia—is a true states' house in the sense that its members are appointed by state governments, recalled by them, and strictly bound to the directions of their respective authorities. The status of the Bundesrat in federal legislation has given the German states jointly a very strong position, which counterbalances the loss of individual state sovereignty in specific areas. Since the political majority in the Bundesrat is often distinct from that of the Bundestag (upper house), party-political confrontations dominate the conflicts between the center and the regions.

---

[1]However, some discretion is accorded to local governments in the setting of tax rates.

Table 1. Germany: Public Expenditures by Level of Government, 1995
(In percent of total expenditures of territorial authorities)

European Community share	3.0
Federal government	34.1
Länder	36.6
Local governments	26.3
Total of territorial	100.0
Memorandum items:	
Social security funds	57.0
Special funds	5.3

Sources: Federal Ministry of Finance (1996, p. 328); and authors' calculations.

Expenditure Assignment

As to the vertical distribution of responsibilities, the Constitution assigns defense, foreign affairs, citizenship, immigration and emigration, international treaties, currency matters, federal transport, and postal and telecommunication services to the federal government. The states are responsible for remaining areas such as culture, education, law and order, environmental and health policies, as well as regional economic policy. Municipalities have responsibility for communal services (sewerage, for example), local health facilities, sports and recreation, school building, housing, and road construction. Yet, given the above-mentioned high degree of horizontal integration of functions, this division of responsibilities is not fully reflected in the distribution of public expenditures across levels of government. Social policy (including health and education), for instance, is implemented at all levels of government. The same is true for investment in infrastructure (roads, communications, and construction) where responsibilities are shared. Since higher levels of government tend to delegate the execution of many of their functions to lower levels, outlays by level of government are a poor indicator of responsibilities. For instance, local governments disburse about two-thirds of all public capital expenditure, much of which is commissioned by higher levels of government.

The current distribution of public expenditures among layers of government is presented in Table 1.

Tax Assignment and Revenue Sharing

In Germany the power to legislate specific taxes has to be seen as totally distinct from the right of each layer of government to appropriate the proceeds from these taxes. Tax legislation is fully centralized. Tax assignment to specific levels of governments is determined by the Constitution, and only minor adjustments in these assignments may be made through federal legislation. Major revisions of federal financial arrangements can be made only through an amendment of the Constitution requiring a two-thirds majority in both houses of the federal parliament.

The significance of taxes directly assigned to each layer of government is small. The main federal taxes (roughly 17 percent of total taxes) are excises, the most important of which are those on mineral oil, tobacco, and alcohol (except beer). The federal government has also the right to levy a surcharge on income taxes, which has become more important recently.[2] The main state taxes (5 percent of total taxes) are the motor vehicle tax and the net wealth tax.[3] Apart from the local business tax,[4] municipalities levy property taxes as well as communal levies on public services (utilities). Local governments collect about 7 percent of all taxes.

All of the most important revenue sources are shared in Germany. The wage and assessed income taxes, the corporation tax, and the VAT, which yield almost three quarters of total tax revenue (71 percent of total taxes in 1995), are all jointly appropriated. In addition, the local business tax—although officially not a joint tax—is shared by all levels of government, and a part of the revenue of the federal mineral oil tax is granted to Länder governments in order to subsidize their regional public transportation. From its share of the VAT, the federal government has to finance Germany's contribution to the budget of the European Union.

The vertical distribution of income taxes is set by the Constitution (Table 2) and, except for grants, any adjustment of the vertical distribution of public funds is exclusively effected through the shares of the VAT to be renegotiated between federal and state governments when-

---

[2]At present (1997), an income tax surcharge of 7.5 percent on all personal and corporate income tax payments is applied to finance costs resulting from German unification ("solidarity levy"). The proceeds of this surcharge accrue solely to the federal government. Initially, surcharges on income taxes were introduced toward the end of the 1960s as a countercyclical device for demand management, but became soon outmoded.

[3]The latter tax is no longer assessed after the Constitutional Court had declared that the rules for defining the tax base discriminate against specific types of assets—which does not conform to the Constitution.

[4]There is strong political demand to abolish the local business tax in order to strengthen private enterprises. The minor part of it, the business tax on working capital, will not be collected from 1998 on if the bill introduced by the federal government passes both houses of parliament. Municipalities would be compensated by a share of VAT revenue, thus intensifying further the integrated system of joint taxation.

Table 2. Germany: Vertical Distribution of Joint Taxes, 1997
(In percent of revenue collected)

Joint Tax	Federal	States	Local
Personal income tax	42.5	42.5	15
Corporate income tax	50.0	50.0	0
Value-added tax	50.5	49.5	0
Local business tax[1]	5	15	80

Sources: *Grundgesetz*; and Federal Ministry of Finance (1996, p. 136).
[1]The shares result from a formula apportionment and are rounded.

ever revenue-expenditure relativities for the federation and the *Länder* will diverge. The result of this bargaining is cast into a federal law requiring the consent of the Bundesrat.

The horizontal distribution of income taxes is based on a derivation principle, that is, it follows the regional pattern of tax yields according to the residence principle, with special rules for the apportionment of the corporation tax. The regional distribution of VAT is mainly on a per capita basis (three quarters), which already implies a strong implicit equalization effect. Moreover, up to 25 percent of the VAT can be used for even more explicit equalization (see section on Horizontal Grants and Equalization).

The vertical distribution of resources, according to source and transfer category, is presented in Table 3 for 1995.

Vertical Grants and Cooperative Federalism

There are vertical grants that imply federal cofinancing of specific state projects. These grants are conditional, and operate within a complex network of interstate cooperation. Such cooperation is governed by a great number of treaties and agreements among authorities, and cannot be discussed in detail here. Only the two most important constitutional provisions for policy coordination may be noted: joint tasks—that imply joint decision making and responsibility sharing, in combination with joint planning and financing—and specific grants-in-aid. These are features peculiar to the German federal arrangements.[5]

These elements of cooperative federalism were introduced in 1969 when it had become clear that federal legislation alone was not sufficient to coordinate policies at the central level. The federal division of functions—with framework legislation assigned to the center and the

---

[5]For a fuller discussion, see, for instance, Reissert (1978).

Table 3. **Germany: Sources of Revenue of the Tiers of Government, 1995**
(In percent of total revenue of each tier)

Revenue Source	Federal	State	Local
Exclusive taxes	30	9	5
Shared taxes[1]	59	63	26
Unconditional grants	—	6	18
Specific purpose grants	—	9	15
Other revenue	11	13	36
Total revenue	100	100	100
Memorandum item:			
Percentage share of total outlays financed by borrowing	10.8	8.3	2.6

Sources: Federal Ministry of Finance (1996); Deutsches Institut für Wirtschaftsforschung (1996); and authors' calculations.

[1]Shared taxes include the full amount of the local business tax, since 20 percent of its revenue are passed from municipalities to the federal and *Länder* governments.

implementation of policies to the lower tiers of government—appeared to be inadequate to ensure coordinated stabilization policies.[6] The model also precluded the federal government from setting guidelines or prerogatives in those areas in which policies cannot be controlled by legislation, namely the provision of public goods and services, especially public infrastructure. It was in these policy domains that the planning and spending functions attributed to the *Länder* proved more important than the legislative functions assigned to the federal government.

As mentioned earlier, the two instruments created in 1969 were joint tasks according to Articles 91a and 91b and grants-in-aid according to Article 104a(4) of the Constitution. Joint tasks are determined for five policy areas.[7] Grants-in-aid are given to the states for regional and local investments within certain policy areas to be defined by federal law or by federal-state agreement. Again, the uniformity-of-living-conditions principle is visible in these arrangements, as the Constitution stipulates that such grants should be used only for equalizing regional disparities, for stabilization, and for stimulating growth.

---

[6]The centralization reached its peak at the end of the 1960s, when Article 109 of the Constitution was amended (1967), the Stability and Growth Law was enacted (1967), a Business Cycle Council and a Financial Planning Council were established, and the principles governing the budgets of federal states governments were harmonized (1969).

[7]These are (1) university construction, (2) regional policy, (3) agricultural structural policy and coast preservation, (4) planning education, and (5) fostering research, to the extent that these are of supraregional importance.

The new provisions have granted a legal basis for earlier practices by which the federal government had provided funds to the *Länder* on a bilateral basis. The new instruments stress multilateral agreement instead—at least for the joint tasks—which is established within so-called planning committees in which the federal government shares the votes with all of the states. All state projects adopted by the federal government and a majority of states are jointly planned and financed. These instruments have increased the scope for central government intervention in many ways—not only through its impact on the planning process itself (in particular on the selection of projects) but also through the potential threat to withdraw federal cofinancing, which usually covers half of the costs.[8]

Among the states, the informal conference of the states' prime ministers is perhaps the most conspicuous example of coordination. Similarly, there are conferences of ministers for special subjects, in particular the conference of the ministers for education and culture, which allows a harmonization of education despite potential political differences among the states.

Furthermore, the German federal system utilizes vertical general revenue grants designed to support the poorer states of the federation. Before unification these unconditional grants, called federal supplementary grants, rendered to the *Länder* by the federal government were only of minor importance. They were made largely redundant by the provision that allows negotiated adjustments in the federal and state shares of the VAT. However, following German unification,[9] asymmetrical vertical grants have become much more important. While taxable capacity was (and still is) significantly lower in the east—because of low productivity, higher unemployment, and short-time work—demands for government services were (and still are) very large. This constitutes a rationale for compensation through interregional fiscal transfers and for stronger involvement of the federal government.

The colossal financial needs of east Germany put the strength of the west German economy to a severe test and had also enormous repercussions on fiscal federal relations. Western states initially resisted pressure to have their eastern counterparts participate in the horizontal

---

[8]The federal contribution varies, though. It is 60 percent for agricultural policy measures, and 70 percent for coast preservation.

[9]On October 3, 1990, five eastern states that had formerly been administered centrally by a socialist government joined the Federal Republic of Germany, adopting its complete legal system. East Berlin was merged with west Berlin that had formerly existed as a west German state under special rule (still being controlled by the Western allies of World War II).

equalization scheme (see the following section). In order to have time for renegotiating intergovernmental financial relations and to achieve a fair burden sharing between tiers of government, vertically and horizontally, the Treaty on Unification stipulated that a new set of rules was to be instituted not earlier than 1995.

For an interim period between 1990 and 1994, the extrabudgetary German Unity Fund was created as a temporary device. It strengthened the inadequate revenue basis of the eastern *Länder* through unconditional grants. During 1990–94, DM 143 billion was channeled through this fund to the eastern states. Of the latter amount, roughly DM 50 billion represented contributions from the federal government, DM 16 billion came from western state budgets, and the remainder was financed through borrowing from capital markets. The federal government and western state and municipal authorities serviced these loans in equal proportions. Further income transfers supporting eastern governments and citizens included specific purpose payments by the federal government, investment credits of the European Recovery Program (ERP), direct transfers from the west German unemployment insurance scheme and the pension funds, and direct payments from the western *Länder*. Table 4 illustrates the transfers and benefits granted by the western governments to the eastern states and their citizens directly (through the channel of social security contributions). These transfers and benefits do not provide a complete picture of the full scale of interregional support accorded to the east German economy. Support was also provided by specific purpose institutions created to facilitate transition from a socialist to a market-oriented economy. The more important of these institutions were the Treuhandanstalt and the Kreditabwicklungsfonds.[10]

---

[10]The Treuhandanstalt was a state agency or government trust in charge of privatizing east German businesses, the formerly state-owned corporations. It was controlled by the federal Ministry of Finance. It had a limited existence and was wound up at the end of 1994. The organization left the federal government with a net debt of DM 270 billion, resulting from the massive subsidies given to private investors as incentives to buy firms and to sustain jobs—the capital stock to be privatized was largely obsolete.

The Kreditabwicklungsfonds was created to wind up debt inherited from the former German Democratic Republic government and from currency conversion. When the German economic, monetary, and social union was inaugurated (July 1990), private demand deposits and savings up to a limit per east German citizen were converted into deutsche mark at parity. Savings above this limit and other financial assets and liabilities were converted at DM 1 = M 2. Since the assets of most banks were transformed into deutsche mark at lower rates than their liabilities, net assets of the banking system had to be topped up by claims against this Conversion Fund. These obligations amounted to approximately DM 102 billion (Deutsche Bundesbank, 1993).

Table 4. Germany: Public Transfers to East Germany

	1991	1992	1993	1994	1995
	(In billions of deutsche mark)				
Federal government	75.7	95.9	117.8	120.4	156.5
States and municipalities of west Germany	5.0	5.0	10.0	14.0	17
German Unity Fund	35.0	33.9	35.2	34.6	9.5
European Union	4.0	5.0	5.0	6.0	7
Social insurance funds[1]					
Pension scheme	5.6	12.3	16.9	22.2	28.5
Unemployment benefits	24.6	38.5	39.5	27.6	23
Total transfers[2]	134.4	164.1	170.8	173.5	211.5
Tax revenue in east Germany[3]	28.7	33.1	34.9	42.6	50.5
Net transfers	105.7	131.0	135.9	130.9	161
	(In percent of GDP)				
Total transfers to the east					
Of west Germany	5.1	5.9	6.0	5.8	6.8
Of east Germany	65.2	62.5	54.4	48.9	55.6
Net transfers					
Of west Germany	4.0	4.7	4.8	4.4	5.2
Of east Germany	51.3	49.9	43.3	36.9	42.3

Sources: Sachverständigenrat (1995, S. 151); and authors' calculations.
[1]Transfers to cover shortfall of social security insurance contributions and outlays of social insurance funds.
[2]Without double-counting of items.
[3]East German tax revenue accruing to the federal government.

Horizontal Grants and Equalization

A closer look at the horizontal distribution of revenue among states shows that equalization occurs through three main processes, also depicted in Table 5:

- First, the allotment of shared revenue to individual states strongly alleviates original differences in regional tax potential—in particular, the distribution of VAT. Up to one quarter of the states' VAT share is used to support financially weaker states. Their fiscal capacity is supplemented up to 92 percent of the states' average tax revenue per capita through these portions. The remainder (three quarters or more) is distributed according to the population of the states.
- Second, there is a particular feature of German federalism, the *Finanzausgleich*, which is a horizontal scheme of interstate equalization without central government interference. Interstate equalization is achieved through a specific set of rules governing a "brotherly" second-round redistribution of means among the states themselves.

Table 5. Germany: Financial Resources of German States—Equalization in Stages

	State Share of	Criteria for Horizontal Distribution	Horizontal Equalization Effect
Primary level	Personal income tax (42.5%)	Residence principle	Weak
	Corporate income tax (50%)	Modified residence principle	Weak
	VAT (35%)		
	Of which 75%	Per capita basis	Strong
	25%	Equalization formula	Very strong
	Local business tax	Regional pattern of tax yield	None
	State taxes (100%)	Regional pattern of tax yield	None
Secondary level	Interstate equalization	Payments to or from states with less or more than average revenues per capita (zero-sum clearing)	Strong
Tertiary level	Asymmetrical vertical grants from federal government		
	Unconditional	Federal supplementary grants	Strong
	Conditional	Joint tasks and grants-in-aid	Moderate

The process starts from a definition of a state and local fiscal capacity measure for each state, which is roughly the sum of state tax revenues with minor corrections for special burdens and local tax revenues adjusted for population density, the degree of urbanization, and so forth. This measure is then related to an equalization standard for the same state, which is derived from the average per capita fiscal capacity of all participating states multiplied by the population of that state. Any shortfall of fiscal capacity in relation to the standard is equalized in steps with graduated rates. A uniform average is not secured, yet there is a guarantee that fiscal capacity (including equalization payments) should reach at least 95 percent of the average for the states as a whole. Equalization payments are made by those states whose fiscal capacity exceeds the standard, again in graduated contributions. The marginal levy is 66.6 percent of per capita fiscal capacity in excess of average fiscal capacity. Fiscal capacity above 110 percent of the average is even "taxed" at a rate of 80 percent. The system works as a clearing mechanism, that is, payments made by the financially stronger states always equal the sum of receipts of the weaker states.

- Third, the federal government provides a variety of asymmetrical vertical grants that favor certain regions. The following types of federal supplementary grants (*Bundesergänzungszuweisungen*) can be distinguished: grants are given to financially weak states in both east and west. These funds make up for the shortfall of revenue, after interstate equalization, of 90 percent of average fiscal capacity per capita. Grants are also given to some of the western states in order to offset losses they suffer as a result of the inclusion of the eastern states in the interstate equalization scheme. Another type of grant is provided in response to the "special needs" of some of the states.[11] Additionally, the severely indebted states of Saarland and Bremen receive financial aid for the amortization of outstanding debt. Finally, the eastern states obtain additional grants-in-aid for a ten year period to enable them to promote investment and economic growth.

Initially, the western states had not allowed their eastern counterparts to participate in the horizontal equalization arrangements. The scheme extended to the eastern states without modification would have turned all the former beneficiaries of equalization payments in the west into contributors. As regards the interstate equalization scheme, it was temporarily effected for the two groups of states in isolation—waiting for a final solution. In order to reduce west-east transfers at the second level of revenue distribution, VAT shares between the federal and the state governments were changed from 63/37 percent to 56/44 percent,[12] which increased significantly the scope of implicit equalization at the first level. The eastern *Länder* were fully integrated in the horizontal equalization scheme beginning in 1995. Each state has its own transfer systems for equalizing fiscal capacity among the local authorities within its jurisdiction (*kommunaler Finanzausgleich*). These schemes take the varying regional economic structure into account, and they are more strongly based on needs than interstate equalization.

Borrowing

Originally, the Law on the Bundesbank had restricted central bank lending to the federal and state governments to a relatively small amount of short-term loans. Institutional limits on deficit financing in Germany now ensue directly from the Maastricht Treaty. Direct government borrowing from the central bank is prohibited, as is privileged

---

[11]These needs reflect the relatively high costs of political administration incurred by small states and the still enormous deficiencies of eastern states as to their public infrastructure.

[12]This differs from the ratio shown in Table 2 because of the impact of a recent technical change in disbursing children's allowances through the tax system, for which the states had to be compensated.

access of public authorities to financing institutions. Furthermore, the Maastricht Treaty—under its excessive deficit procedure—considers whether or not the public deficit of member states exceeds government investment expenditure. This provision was copied from the German Constitution, which restricts federal government borrowing to the "amount of projected outlays for investment purposes in the budget" ("golden rule"). Similar provisions apply to *Länder* budgets in accordance with state constitutions or legislation. Local government borrowing is tied to their cash flow and is subject to state control.

Budget constraints thus appear to be rather stringent in Germany. Notably, the "quasi-constitutional" limits to central bank financing were often praised as being the reason for low inflation, a strong currency, and the financial stability of the German public sector. In principle, this nexus cannot be denied—especially as legislation had rendered the Bundesbank legally independent from federal and state intervention. Yet one could argue that the system had not been put to any severe test in the past and that it had worked largely because it was based on a consensus formed by all political parties and interest groups on the historical experiences of hyperinflation. The test of German unification made it clear, however, that judicial control of budget deficits is difficult to achieve—even *with* constitutional constraints.

However, the budget constraint had been "softened" in many respects even before unification:

- First, it is far from clear what is meant by "investment purposes." In some instances, it is possible to redefine current outlays so as to represent investment outlays without much difficulty.
- Then, an amendment to the Constitution enacted in 1969 permitted the federal government to raise loans to combat "disturbances of general economic equilibrium." This rule is even more difficult to monitor in quantitative terms. The provision was introduced in the heyday of Keynesian demand management. Application of this rule reached its climax only recently, however, when "disturbance of general economic equilibrium" was interpreted as relating to the consequences of unification.
- Recently, the contracting out of public infrastructure investment to private enterprises has become fashionable as a window dressing or deficit-reducing device for public budgets. Private investors who—in view of government guarantees—will bear no entrepreneurial risk are asked to build and prefinance public infrastructure projects, such as roads or bridges. Upon completion of the work, the government redeems the building costs over a certain period and assumes all financial charges related to the project. This accords short-term relief from fiscal pressure under

a public budgeting system that is exclusively based on cash accounting, but at the cost of reducing the room for fiscal maneuver in the future.
- Moreover, it is noteworthy that the tiers of government differ considerably as to the characteristics of their creditors. While the federal stock of debt is mainly in the form of tradable bonds, state governments (to the larger part) and local governments (almost entirely) rely on direct bank loans to finance their deficits. There is no municipal bond market as in the United States, for instance. It is therefore difficult to impose market discipline onto the borrowing of lower levels of government, and this explains the need for more explicit forms of regulation and surveillance.
- Finally, much of the lending comes from state-controlled banks or the local savings banks owned by municipalities.[13] This could be considered a form of "connected borrowing" by public authorities.

Central bank independence has closed the door to easy financing of the budget through money creation, and it has fostered budgetary discipline of the German public sector in the past. Nevertheless, it should be clear that deficit financing is softer than may appear at first sight. Restrictive constitutional rules and monetary policies have not prevented the public sector from running significant deficits since the early 1990s.

Table 6 shows government borrowing and the accumulated debt by level of government. The most important off-budget item is a sinking fund, the so-called Inherited Burden Fund, which carries all debt and liabilities inherited directly or indirectly from the former German Democratic Republic (Treuhandanstalt, Kreditabwicklungsfonds, and East German local housing projects).[14] The repercussions of German unification on deficit financing and public debts become apparent if the gross debt/GDP ratio of 41.8 percent in 1989 is compared with the ratio of 60.3 percent by the end of 1996. Interestingly, *Länder* and local governments only contributed about 2 percentage points to the total increase of the public debt ratio of 18½ percentage points. Thus, the federal government is essentially footing the bill for unification.[15]

---

[13]Often the mayor of a commune is also chairman of the supervisory board of the local savings bank.
[14]For further details, see Föttinger and Spahn (1994).
[15]Off-budget funding is in the domain of the federal government.

Table 6. Germany: Public Debt of Different Levels of Government, End of 1996

	Level of Debt		Deficit	
	In billions of deutsche mark	In percent of GDP	In billions of deutsche mark	In percent of GDP
Levels of government				
Federal	840	23.7	78	2.2
States	560	15.8	43	1.2
Local	205	5.8	13	0.3
Off-budget funding				
Inherited Burden Fund	332	9.4	−7	−0.2
European Recovery Program	34	1.0	3	0.1
German Unity Fund	84	2.4	−3	−0.1
Federal Railways Fund	78	2.2	0	0.0
Other	3	0.0	0	0.0
Total	2,136	60.3	127	3.6

Sources: Deutsche Bundesbank (1997); Sachverständigenrat (1996); and authors' calculations.
Note: Preliminary data. Minus signs indicate surpluses. The Maastricht definition of general government gross debt differs slightly from the data in this table.

Administrative Structure

Tax Administration

In addition to assigning expenditure, revenue, and legislative competencies among the different tiers of government, the Constitution determines (Article 108) which layer shall be responsible for the administration of taxes, that is, who should be in charge of collecting, handling, and spending the budgetary means.

The states bear the brunt of tax administration. The federal government only administers customs duties, fiscal monopolies, excise taxes subject to federal legislation (including VAT on imports), and charges imposed within the framework of the European Union. All other taxes are administered by revenue authorities of the *Länder*. To the extent that taxes accrue wholly or in part to the federal government (joint taxes), state authorities act as agents of the federation. Where the revenues accrue exclusively to local governments, the administration of such taxes is wholly or partly transferred by the states to their municipal authorities.

Both federal and state fiscal administrations are organized along a three-tier structure, comprising overall guiding authorities, intermediate supervisory authorities, and local execution authorities. At the intermediate level, the Regional Finance Offices act as both federal and state authorities. They have departments for taxes, which are designated according to the principles mentioned earlier. The federation assumes the costs related to administering federal taxes; all other costs are the responsibility of the states. Although they work under one roof, the departments of the Regional Finance Offices are strictly separate as to their tasks, organization, staff, and budget.

To ensure uniform standards of tax collecting and auditing throughout the nation, there are several coordinating bodies that work mainly on the basis of informal agreements. The statutes concerning the tax administration personnel and personnel training are also illustrative of the German model of cooperative fiscal federalism: Operating within the framework of a Federal Law on the Training of Revenue Officers, passed in 1961, each state is required to set up, on its own, the institutions and the necessary provisions to train qualified staff.

Budget Formulation and Implementation

The Constitution stipulates in Article 109 that the Federation and the *Länder* will be autonomous and independent from each other as to their fiscal management and budgeting. However, the tiers of government are obliged to take due account of the requirements of overall equilibrium—which is achieved by federal legislation requiring the consent of the Bundesrat.

The Constitution (Article 110), as well as a federal law on budgetary principles for the Federation and the *Länder*,[16] coordinate the budget process by setting uniform principles to be observed by all authorities. Such principles derive from general provisions (such as the principles of gross estimates, comprehensiveness, unity, clarity, periodicity and antecedence, efficiency and cost effectiveness, and authorization to spend and to commit resources) to more specific rules regarding the preparation of the budget, accounting and the rendering of accounts (including the classification of the budget), auditing, and rules applying to special funds set up under federal or state legislation. Also, the budget process has been made more transparent, in order to assess the budget's effects on the economy. The second part of this legislation contains regulations such as multiyear financial planning and the exchange of budget-related information.

The annual budgets (calendar year) are presented as part of a medium-term financial plan, which is established by the Financial

---

[16]This law of 1969 was published in English, together with other relevant material, under the title *Federal German Budget Legislation*, by the Federal Ministry of Finance, Bonn, November 1988.

Planning Council representing all three tiers of government. The Council's objective is to reach agreement on the coordination of general budgetary policy and to support the federal government in its statutory task of ensuring that budgetary policies are consistent with macroeconomic stability. The Council is, however, bound by the Constitution to respect the autonomous and independent fiscal administration of states and the right of self-governance of municipalities. It therefore acts through recommendations that are nonbinding, yet have an impact on budget estimates and budget execution (including the level of borrowing).

Implications

Macroeconomic Management

Toward the end of the 1960s, Germany had pioneered legislation on macroeconomic management. A Stability and Growth Law was enacted that commits the federal government to certain macroeconomic targets[17] and that provides specific instruments enabling the authorities to pursue demand management policies effectively.

Inter alia, the law authorized the federal government to issue decrees, with approval of the Bundestag, to amend the income tax at short notice, including withholding taxes on wages and the corporate income tax. An income tax surcharge or rebate, up to a maximum of 10 percent can be introduced on condition that a disturbance of overall equilibrium exists or is about to emerge. The surcharge benefits the federal budget, not those of states and municipalities. The law also allows the government to accord temporary income tax relief for investment.

In addition, an intergovernmental Business Cycle Council was established to guide governments in coordinating their budgets (apart from medium-term planning), and an attempt was made to influence the social partners through concerted action. Yet, formal coordination essentially failed—except for the very beginning—as the crises of the early 1970s were found to be structural in nature and the range of policy instruments provided by legislation was inappropriate for such purposes. Furthermore, Keynesian demand management had rapidly be-

---

[17]These targets are that the economic and fiscal measures of the Federation and the Länder shall be taken in a way that will, within the framework of a market economy, at the same time help to stabilize prices, maintain a high level of employment, and achieve external balance, accompanied by steady and adequate economic growth.

come unfashionable in Germany, and the instruments provided by the Stability and Growth Law were in the doldrums.

Fiscal federal arrangements allowed the federal government to take a lead in reacting to economic shocks provoked by the oil crises, and budgetary and monetary policies promoted the restoration of macroeconomic stability. During the 1980s, after the second oil crisis, supply-side policies dominated under conservative-liberal federal governments. The rapid expansion of social expenditures was curbed and financial stability was maintained at all levels of government—supported by significant real growth of the economy. However, attempts failed to put the social security system on a sound and sustainable financial basis. Within five years after unification, the consolidation success faded away and the ratio of total general government outlays surpassed 50 percent of GDP—roughly the same level as in 1982.

Moreover, it also became clear in the 1990s that the existing intergovernmental institutions (in particular, the Financial Planning Council) neither were suited to nor had the necessary experience to face the dual challenge of German unification and European integration. One could have expected that the burden of unification would be shouldered by all levels of government in equal proportions. As was discussed earlier, this was not the case and the federal government had to incur disproportionally high expenditures. As a result, the financial and the political weight of lower levels of government in Germany was weakened. Moreover, a coherent economic policy strategy is still lacking that would put the east German economy on a sustainable growth path and allow it to catch up with the west in the foreseeable future.[18]

As massive income transfers to the east are likely to continue for a long time, there is a risk of political tensions between the eastern and the western *Länder*. Additionally, both parts of Germany are plagued by unemployment that has reached record levels unprecedented since World War II.

As to European integration, the federal government has taken the lead in trying to accomplish the macroeconomic and budgetary convergence criteria of the Maastricht Treaty, wich is a precondition for the start of the European Economic and Monetary Union (EMU). Moreover, the German Federal Minister of Finance has sponsored a "Stability Pact" to promote budgetary discipline after the creation of

---

[18]In 1996, economic growth in east Germany slowed down markedly, and was far below projections. Productivity per employee is at 57 percent of the west German level, while net earnings per worker are at 85 percent. See Federal Ministry of Economics (1997, p. 106) for details.

the union. The pact foresees sanctions in the form of fines for member states that exceed the predetermined public deficit limits. Although the federal government is responsible for general government debt in Germany according to the Treaty, it has no power to interfere with the states' autonomous budgeting. So far, there is no agreement with states and municipalities on how a global public sector deficit could be "apportioned" onto tiers of government—both vertically and horizontally.

Structural Reform

The restructuring of intergovernmental financial relations following unification was, at best, a modest alteration. Certainly, it does not constitute a structural reform. Any major revision of federal fiscal arrangements is constrained by the fact that different political majorities reign in both houses of parliament. This form of "divided government" makes it relatively easy for interest groups to block reforms that could jeopardize their privileges by exercising their influence on one of the two largest German parties (the Christian Democrats and Social Democrats). Regional issues rank high on the agenda of the Bundesrat, and this institution is often used as a place for bargaining along party lines.[19]

More recent developments have revealed that German fiscal federal arrangements exhibit serious flaws as regards equity, efficiency, transparency, and accountability (see also Table 7 and Figure 1).

- Although financial settlement among states has had a rather strong equalizing effect in the past, initially the mechanism had worked reasonably well. Yet the burden of the settlements was consistently shifted onto two states—Baden-Württemberg and, in particular, Hesse—while all others either benefited or were exempt from contributing major amounts to the scheme. This had led to political tensions among the states even before unification. At present, the three-stage equalization scheme reverses the order of initial fiscal capacity. The federal supplementary grants provide the eastern states with a fiscal capacity far above the national average. In real terms, they even command greater resources since their costs tend to be below those of their western counterparts. In addition, the dynamics of the debt of the former east German government are staggering: Starting from zero debt in 1990, in only five years the eastern states have reached 70 percent of the

---

[19]See Alesina and Rosenthal (1995, p. 255) for applying the concept of divided government—originally used to analyze the balance of power between the U.S. Congress and the President—to the German federal system.

Table 7. Germany: Fiscal Equalization Among States, 1995

	Relative Fiscal Capacity Per Capita (Average = 100)				
	Public revenue per capita				
	Without VAT	After VAT distribution	After interstate equalization	After federal grants	Rank after equalization
Hamburg	157.5	133.9	102.3	93.4	15
Hesse	118.7	109.7	103.5	94.6	10
Baden-Württemberg	115.7	107.1	103.0	94.2	12
North Rhine-Westphalia	114.2	105.4	102.4	93.7	14
Bavaria	113.8	105.1	102.5	93.7	13
Bremen	111.7	103.0	96.4	141.4	1
Schleswig-Holstein	106.8	100.0	101.3	95.9	9
Lower Saxony	96.2	94.2	97.8	92.9	16
Rhineland-Palatinate	95.7	92.6	96.8	94.3	11
Berlin*	93.3	93.4	95.0	111.0	8
Saarland	83.5	89.1	95.0	129.2	2
Brandenburg*	56.4	84.4	95.0	118.6	6
Saxony*	50.3	83.1	95.0	117.4	7
Mecklenburg-West Pomerania	47.0	82.3	95.0	119.8	3
Saxony-Anhalt*	44.5	82.7	95.0	118.8	5
Thuringia*	43.7	82.6	95.0	118.9	4

Sources: Deutsches Institut für Wirtschaftsforschung (1996); and authors' calculations.
*Eastern states.

per capita debt of their western counterparts; and east German municipalities have attained 80 percent of the per capita debt of their western counterparts.

- Tax sharing and an equalization method that provides resources to each state close to average fiscal capacity per capita entail severe disincentives as to the use and development of own revenue sources. Relatively rich states are "punished" for strengthening their tax base—for example if they promote private investments by delivering appropriate public infrastructure. On the other hand, the poorer states have little incentive to combat structural weaknesses of their regional economies and to pursue prudent fiscal policies that are suited to their taxable capacity. The uniformity of living clause of the Constitution renders it unlikely, however, that this feature of the German federal machinery will be altered.
- Inefficiency through a high degree of interstate equalization is exacerbated by recurrent explicit bailouts of the highly indebted states through the workings of federal supplementary grants. The states of Saarland and Bremen, for instance, receive federal grants that are explicitly aimed at relieving the burden of interest pay-

Figure 1. Germany: Per Capita Fiscal Capacity of States Before and After Equalization
(In percent of average)

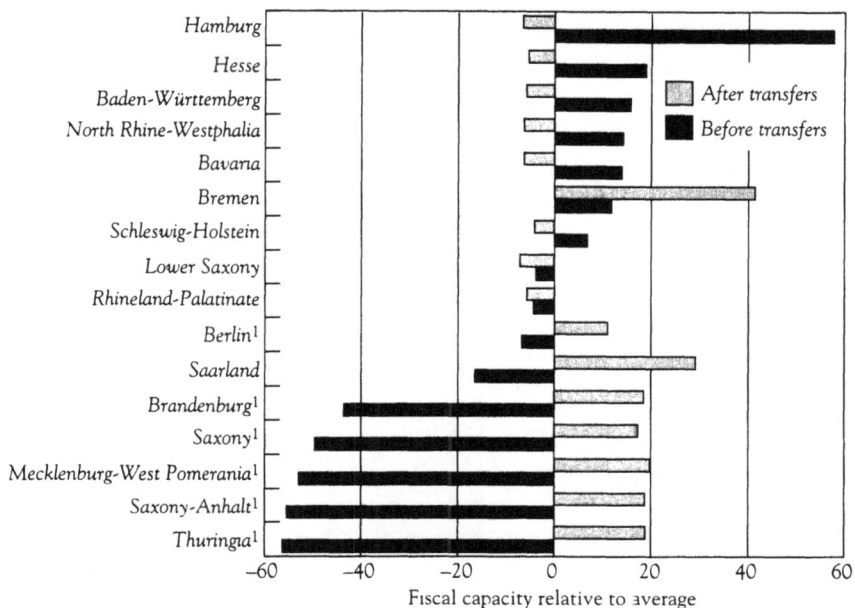

Sources: Federal Ministry of Finance; and authors' calculations.
[1]Eastern states.

ments on their excessive debt.[20] Lack of fiscal discipline on the part of certain states is thus rewarded by larger transfers, which is likely to create moral hazard for other jurisdictions.

- The ever-increasing complexity of an interdependent network of shared taxes and equalization grants and of expenditure functions and decision-making institutions renders it impossible for voters and taxpayers to identify which government spends or taxes, and for what purpose. This breaks the benefit-tax link that is essential for enhancing efficiency in the provision of local public goods. The lack of fiscal accountability by regional authorities is probably one of the most important drawbacks of cooperative federalism.

---

[20]At the end of December 1995, the average debt per capita (including debt of municipalities) of old *Länder* was DM 8,600. The per capita debt of Saarland amounted to DM 14,800 and that of Bremen to DM 24,700.

- Efficiency gains of decentralization are also sacrificed to the extent that taxation is uniform throughout the nation—in spite of some taxing autonomy of municipalities. Own revenue competencies for the *Länder* or discretion to levy state surcharges on federal taxes would contribute to remedy this deficiency, but are unlikely to be considered under the present Constitution. Also, tax-base sharing could be an alternative to relying on joint taxes almost exclusively. The income tax would be a natural candidate. This could enhance efficiency and accountability provided that the corresponding revenue can be used exclusively by the taxing authority—and is immune to attempts to embody it in the interregional equalization machinery.
- Further inefficiencies result from the German system of tax administration. Since the salaries of auditors are paid by the states, *Länder* with an above-average tax capacity have little incentive to detect and prosecute tax evasion. With transfer rates as high as 80 percent onto state tax collections, additional proceeds would be largely siphoned off by higher payments into the *Finanzausgleich*.
- In addition, uniformity in legislation is likely to hamper innovation and structural reform in public management. Competition among governments could encourage authorities to better serve the needs of citizens and to improve the quality of services, but uniform rules, equal salaries for public servants, or invariable prescriptions of a Civil Service Act, and so on are likely to restrict experimentation among jurisdictions and thus hinder public sector reform.

In summary, one may say that interregional solidarity is perverted where the principle of uniformity of living conditions entails a lack of fiscal discipline. This is true to the extent that lack of fiscal discipline is rewarded by larger transfers from federal and state governments. The marginal levies for interstate equalization are much too high. In order to strike a balance between equalization and the legitimate inclination of richer states to spend more of their own tax revenue themselves, one could imagine the equalization formula to incorporate ceilings that would limit the absolute amount of equalization payments for individual states.

Furthermore, there appears to be need for an equalization scheme that works on the basis of objective criteria that cannot be manipulated by recipient governments.[21] And a credible commitment not to bail out state or local authorities in financial difficulties would be an important

---

[21]The authors have proposed a cost-oriented interstate equalization scheme (see Föttinger and Spahn, 1993). For example, they have pointed out that eastern states have a cost advantage in producing public services, since salaries of public employees are still significantly lower in the east.

step to curtail the moral hazard inherent in the financial equalization process.[22]

Finally, the Constitution (Article 29(1)) allows for a reorganization of the federal territory in order to ascertain that states are large enough to provide the functions incumbent on them efficiently. For example, if Hamburg, Bremen, and Saarland would merge with neighboring states, more homogeneous entities could be created that require less interstate equalization. Also, administrative costs could be reduced. However, an interstate treaty aimed at merging Berlin and Brandenburg was rejected by an obligatory referendum in 1996. It is therefore unlikely that politicians will launch further merger projects for the German states in the near future.

Conclusions

German fiscal federal relations have created a high degree of homogeneity as to the regional availability of public infrastructure and government services. This is the basis on which the economy thrives. Financing public services is mainly based on shared taxes and equalization arrangements stressing the uniformity of living conditions in the whole nation, and on horizontal cooperation among layers of government. This has not prevented regional authorities from exerting an influential role within the realm of their own jurisdiction and at the level of the federation.

The spirit of these arrangements has survived the strain placed on the system by German unification. However, the experience has revealed the solidarity among the *Länder* to have limitations. VAT sharing with its implicit equalization effects, as well as asymmetrical vertical grants by the federal government, were preferred to explicit horizontal redistribution as embodied in the interstate equalization scheme. These developments have, however, strengthened the influence of the federal government through its increased role in intergovernmental finance.

However, the German system of intergovernmental fiscal relations has a number of flaws that reduce its efficiency and impinge on interregional equity. They result from a strict interpretation of the uniformity of living conditions mandated by the Constitution. The opportunity to correct the system of fiscal federalism in the wake of German

---

[22]For such a commitment to be credible, regional governments would have to control substantial own resources—which is true for Germany—but it would also require some discretion in taxation—which is generally not the case.

unification was missed. A further chance may appear through the need to reconcile the budget performance of autonomous German governments at all levels with a general criteria for budget discipline as imposed by the project of European Monetary Union.

References

Alesina, Alberto, and Howard Rosenthal, 1995, *Partisan Politics, Divided Government and the Economy* (Cambridge, England: Cambridge University Press).

Deutsche Bundesbank, 1993, "Die Bedeutung von Nebenhaushalten im Zuge der deutschen Vereinigung," *Monthly Report*, No. 5 (May), Frankfurt.

———, 1997, "Die Entwicklung der Staatsverschuldung seit der deutschen Vereinigung," *Monthly Report*, No. 3 (March), Frankfurt.

Deutsches Institut für Wirtschaftsforschung [German Institute for Economic Research], 1996, "Sind die Finanzprobleme in Ostdeutschland durch die Neuordnung des Finanzausgleichs gelöst?" *DIW Wochenbericht*, Vol. 69, No. 17, Berlin.

Federal Ministry of Economics, 1997, *Jahreswirtschaftsbericht* [Annual Report on the Economy], Bonn.

Federal Ministry of Finance, 1996, *Finanzbericht 1997*, Bonn.

Föttinger, Wolfgang, and Paul Bernd Spahn, 1993, "Für einen kostenorientierten Länderfinanzausgleich," *Wirtschaftsdienst*, Vol. 73, No. 5, pp. 237–46.

———, 1994, "German Unification and Its Consequences for Intergovernmental Financial Relations," *Current Politics and Economics of Europe* (NOVA, New York), Vol. 4, No. 1, pp. 37–49.

Reissert, Bernd, 1978, "Responsibility Sharing and Joint Tasks in West German Federalism," in *Principles of Federal Policy Coordination in West Germany: Basic Issues and Annotated Legislation*, Research Monograph No. 25, ed. by Paul Bernd Spahn (Canberra: Centre for Research on Federal Financial Relations, Australian National University).

Sachverständigenrat [German Council of Economic Experts], 1995, *Jahresgutachten 1995/96*, Stuttgart.

———, 1996, *Jahresgutachten 1996/97*, Stuttgart.

Spahn, Paul Bernd, ed., 1978a, *Principles of Federal Policy Coordination in West Germany: Basic Issues and Annotated Legislation*, Research Monograph No. 25 (Canberra: Centre for Research on Federal Financial Relations, Australian National University).

———, 1978b, "The German Model of Horizontal Federal Decentralisation," in *Principles of Federal Policy Coordination in West Germany: Basic Issues and Annotated Legislation*, Research Monograph No. 25, ed. by Paul Bernd Spahn (Canberra: Centre for Research on Federal Financial Relations, Australian National University).

11

Italy

Nicoletta Emiliani, Sergio Lugaresi, and Edgardo Ruggiero

This chapter reviews the Italian experience with decentralization since the 1970s. This experience highlights the following. First, for a decentralization policy to achieve its objectives, several factors—whose roles are often underplayed by the theory of intergovernmental fiscal relations—may be important. These factors include budgetary procedures and transparency, effective accountability of local governments, regional differences in fiscal capacity, and institutional performance. Second, the level and quality of local public expenditure are strongly influenced by other characteristics of intergovernmental fiscal relations—such as the budgetary practices of the central government, tax assignments, transparency of the grants distribution formulas, and appropriate rules promoting fiscal effort—that may in fact be perceived as loosely linked to the delivery of local public services.

In Italy, the fiscal relationship between the central and the subnational governments is characterized by a high degree of vertical fiscal imbalance, ambiguity over responsibility for financing expenditure, and a lack of transparency and stability of policies.[1] The Italian experience of the 1970s and 1980s confirms that expenditure decentralization, when coupled with revenue centralization, may be associated with a loss of accountability at the subnational level. This, in turn, may cause excessive growth of total public expenditure.

---

[1] In this chapter, the term subnational governments refers to regional and local governments. Local governments include provinces, municipalities, and Local Health Units.

The intergovernmental fiscal relations in Italy are based on constitutional laws for expenditure assignments and on ad hoc legislation for revenue and financing. Though piecemeal legislative changes are made in the tax and financing arrangements almost every year, some characteristics remain constant: (1) a marked revenue centralization, (2) a correspondingly high share of grants in revenues of subnational governments, and (3) a marked predominance of conditional grants. The ensuing strong vertical imbalance, together with unrealistic ex ante limits on the amount of transfers to subnational governments, has legitimated the creation of ex post subnational deficits. These unbalanced fiscal relations have often resulted in higher-than-budgeted, contingent liabilities for the central government through the centralization of subnational deficits, debt, and interest costs.

Safeguard mechanisms have been repeatedly introduced and have succeeded in controlling subnational cash expenditure. However, expenditure commitments have been controlled to only a limited extent, because of the lack of local accountability—partly a result of the poor definition of expenditure assignments and financial responsibilities, of effective budgetary procedures and controls, and of hard budget constraints. The particular financing arrangements established between the central and the subnational governments, as well as the budgetary procedures adopted at every level of government, have not provided the incentives to improve expenditure efficiency.

The latest legislative changes have only partially addressed these problems. In 1990, the framework law reforming local administrations established the following three general principles.[2] First, central government grants are to be limited to financing "necessary" expenditures (to be later defined by implementing laws) and corresponding grants are to be allocated to local governments by the central government. The lower levels of government are responsible for raising the resources to pay for other services. Second, to foster fiscal responsibility, new taxes have been transferred to the local governments, and central government grants are reduced by corresponding amounts. Third, managers of subnational entities have been given responsibility for their units' economic results. Similar principles have been adopted in new sectoral laws for the health and transportation sectors, which are a responsibility of the regions. However, these new laws remain ambiguous as to which level of government is ultimately responsible for financing expenditure. This ambiguity is reinforced by the lack of credible threats (that is, bankruptcy procedures) for regions, and the fact that budgetary

---

[2]In the Italian legal system, a framework law establishes general principles that subsequent implementing laws actually put in practice.

practices and subnational governments' accountancy rules have not kept pace with the new legislative framework. These problems have complicated the government's current attempts to reintroduce subnational fiscal responsibility.

This chapter is organized as follows. The structure of government is examined first, followed by discussions on expenditure assignments, revenue assignments and tax administration, and budget formulation and expenditure management. In the final two sections, policy implications and conclusions are drawn, and the latest developments are described.

Structure of Government: Current Arrangements and Main Issues

There are four levels of government in Italy: central, regional, provincial, and municipal. Subnational governments comprise 20 regions, 99 provinces, approximately 8,100 municipalities, and 212 Local Health Units. While provinces and municipalities have long been subnational governments in Italy, regions are a relatively new entity, as the regions were only established under the 1948 Constitution.[3] Five regions are called "special statute" regions (henceforth special regions), as their statutes were issued in the form of constitutional laws that give them considerable legislative autonomy on expenditures: their expenditure assignments are wider and their primary source of revenue is— unlike that of "ordinary statute" regions (henceforth ordinary regions)—shared national taxes (see below). These special regions either are large islands or are areas close to the border that have a sizable foreign population. Four of the five governments were established in 1949 (Friuli-Venezia Giulia in 1964) to reduce the threat of separatist movements and ethnic tensions. The 15 ordinary regions' governments were not formally established until 1970; their process of expenditure devolution was completed only much later (1978), when responsibility for health care was assigned to the regions.

Strong political forces lay behind both the decentralization process and its delays. The largest party in parliament in the 1970s (the Christian Democratic Party) was afraid to lose its grip on regions with a high concentration of support for the opposition parties. Only with the leftist electoral successes of the mid-1970s did the ruling party give in to

---

[3]The Constitution gave regions legislative autonomy in specific areas (see section on Expenditure Assignments). Provinces and municipalities have no legislative autonomy.

decentralization. While the Constitution mandated the devolution of expenditure assignments, it did not specify which level of government would be responsible for financing these expenditures or provide specific guidelines on revenue sources. Therefore, when new expenditure responsibilities were assigned to the regions, the central government was able to establish its control over the new political entities by removing most subnational taxes, centralizing tax administration, and assigning new taxes only to the center. Regions were transferred exactly the amount of grants needed to finance the previous year's cost of the responsibilities newly assigned to them and, for the first years, grants were increased below the rate of inflation. Therefore, while regions achieved expenditure autonomy relatively early, revenue autonomy has never really been achieved, essentially because their financing has been the result of a political compromise.

Expenditure decentralization, coupled with an enhanced redistributive role of the central government, was also viewed as a way to reduce the regional disparity in access to, and quality of, services and in income levels.[4] Italy continues to be characterized by wide regional differences in per capita income, with the northern regions richer than the southern regions. Although this gap has narrowed slightly in the past two decades, it is still considerable; furthermore, the quality of services is still characterized by large regional differences.[5]

Expenditure Assignments

Subnational government expenditure doubled from 1970 (7 percent of GDP) to 1985 (around 14 percent of GDP), reflecting the evolution of the expenditure programs decentralized during the second half of the 1970s (Table 1). It has remained broadly constant since. During 1980–93, the expenditures of the central administration itself increased considerably, from 18 percent to 29 percent of GDP, propelled by wages and interest outlays.[6] Therefore, the share of subnational government expenditure in total public expenditure increased from 22 percent in

---

[4]The Constitution defines health care and education as "universal" rights of citizens. Subsequent legislation has interpreted this to mean that access to health care and education should be uniform for all.

[5]In 1992, the richest Italian region (Lombardy) had a GDP per capita of 126.5 (Italian average equal to 100), compared with 57.7 for the poorest (Calabria). These regions occupied the same relative position in 1982, when the corresponding figures were 128.8 and 58.8 (ISTAT, 1995a).

[6]Interest and personnel outlays are the central government's first and third largest expenditure components, respectively (Table 2).

Table 1. Italy: Operations of General, Central, and Subnational Governments
(In percent of GDP)

	General Government[1]			Central Government[2,3]			Subnational Governments[2,3]		
	Revenue	Expenditure	Deficit	Revenue	Expenditure	Deficit	Revenue	Expenditure	Deficit
				(Revenue, Expenditure, and Deficit)[3]					
1961	...	29.6	...	...	...	...	...	7.0	...
1966	...	36.5	...	...	...	...	...	8.0	...
1970	...	32.5	...	...	...	...	...	7.1	...
1975	...	39.3	...	...	...	...	...	9.2	...
1980	33.6	42.2	8.6	23.5	30.8	7.1	11.7	12.8	1.1
1985	38.6	51.2	12.6	28.8	41.4	12.5	14.0	14.1	0.1
1990	42.5	53.4	10.9	31.0	40.9	9.9	13.2	14.6	1.3
1991	43.6	53.9	10.2	31.4	41.2	9.8	14.0	14.7	0.6
1992	46.3	55.8	9.5	33.1	42.6	9.5	14.1	14.3	0.2
1993	48.0	57.6	9.6	33.7	43.1	9.3	13.6	14.1	0.4

	General Government[1]			Central Government[2,4]			Subnational Governments[2,4]		
	Own revenue	Own expenditure	Deficit	Own revenue	Own expenditure	Vertical balance ratio	Own revenue	Own expenditure	Vertical balance ratio
1961	...	29.6	...	...	...	...	...	7.0	...
1966	...	36.5	...	...	...	...	...	8.0	...
1970	...	32.5	...	...	...	...	...	7.1	...
1975	...	39.3	...	...	...	...	...	9.2	...
1980	33.6	42.0	8.6	20.1	18.2	1.10	1.9	11.3	0.17
1985	38.6	51.2	12.6	24.0	24.0	1.00	2.3	14.0	0.17
1990	42.5	53.4	10.9	26.5	25.4	1.04	2.9	14.5	0.20
1991	43.6	53.9	10.2	27.3	25.6	1.06	3.0	14.6	0.21
1992	46.3	55.8	9.5	29.2	27.0	1.08	3.5	14.2	0.24
1993	48.0	57.6	9.6	29.9	29.0	1.03	4.2	14.0	0.30

Sources: Italian Statistical Institute (ISTAT), National Accounts, Conti delle Amministrazioni Pubbliche e della Protezione Sociale, various issues; data for 1961 and 1966 from Rizzo (1985).

[1]Consolidated figures—data net out flows between levels of government. Includes Social Security Administration.
[2]Excludes Social Security Administration.
[3]Revenue and expenditure for central and subnational governments are gross of grants and transfers between levels of governments. The revenue, expenditure, and deficit of the central and subnational governments do not add up to the corresponding columns of the general government because the latter show consolidated data and include the Social Security Administration.
[4]Revenue and expenditure for central and subnational governments are net of grants and transfers between levels of government. The revenue, expenditure, and deficit of the central and subnational governments do not add up to the corresponding columns of the general government because the latter include the Social Security Administration. The vertical balance ratio is defined as the ratio between own revenue and expenditure, net of grants and transfers to other levels of government.

1970 to above 27 percent in 1985, then decreased to below 26 percent by 1992. This was also due to the fact that, after 1978, no more expenditures were decentralized. In 1979, the central government assumed responsibility for paying the municipal debt—including interest—

Table 2. Italy: Economic Classification of Revenue and Expenditure of
Central Government
(In percent of GDP)

	1990	1991	1992	1993	1994
Total revenue	32.9	32.5	34.4	34.5	32.3
Direct taxes	14.0	14.1	16.0	16.3	14.7
Indirect taxes	11.7	12.1	12.5	11.8	11.7
Other	7.2	6.3	5.9	6.3	5.9
Total expenditure	42.3	43.1	45.0	44.4	41.8
Personnel	8.3	7.6	7.6	7.6	7.4
Purchases of goods and services	1.6	1.4	1.5	1.6	1.6
Interest payments	9.4	10.0	11.2	11.8	10.6
Direct investments	1.0	0.9	0.9	0.9	0.5
Loans and share holdings (net)	0.9	0.5	0.5	0.5	1.0
Of which: local governments[1]	0.8	0.3	0.3	0.2	0.4
Transfers	19.6	20.9	21.7	20.5	19.2
To regions	7.2	7.9	8.0	7.1	6.9
Of which: National Health Fund	5.0	5.7	5.5	5.6	5.7
To provinces and municipalities	2.9	3.0	2.7	2.3	1.8
To others	9.5	10.0	11.0	11.2	10.5
Other expenditure	1.5	1.7	1.6	1.4	1.6
Central government borrowing requirement	9.4	10.5	10.6	9.9	9.5

Source: Bank of Italy, Relazione Annuale, 1994.
[1]Includes regions, provinces, and municipalities.

accumulated prior to 1977, through an increase in grants allocated to municipalities. This rewarded the municipalities that had accumulated more debt. Following this debt-clearing operation, the central government started to impose formal controls on the current budgets of local governments and succeeded in controlling the level of their current cash expenditures.

The central government's interest outlays increased partly because in the 1970s and 1980s, the central government often assumed responsibility for payment of arrears and debt repayment of the subnational governments (see the sections on Conditional Grants, Borrowing, and Budget Formulation and Expenditure Management). For this reason, the budgets of subnational governments report small amounts of interest payments (Tables 3 and 4). By 1981, excluding interest payments and transfers to other entities in the public sector, the central government was the final spender for only 33 percent of total expenditure of the public administration, compared with 65 percent in 1965 (Ghessi, 1984). This 33 percent included wages and was characterized by a high degree of rigidity; this rigidity was partly due to indexation—removed in 1993—and restrictions on the layoffs of civil servants. As a consequence, the scope for the central government to use expenditures as an

Table 3. Italy: Economic Classification of Regional Budgets
(In percent of GDP)

	Ordinary Regions				Special Regions			
	1990	1991	1992	1993	1990	1991	1992	1993
Total revenue	6.76	6.87	6.88	6.22	2.57	2.62	2.43	2.63
Current revenue	5.49	5.96	6.12	5.54	2.23	2.26	2.24	2.41
Direct taxes	—	—	—	—	—	—	—	—
Indirect taxes	0.11	0.15	0.17	0.36	0.01	0.01	0.01	0.01
Transfers	5.36	5.79	5.93	5.15	2.18	2.22	2.21	2.36
Of which: from the state sector	5.31	5.72	5.87	5.08	2.09	2.16	2.16	2.32
Other	0.02	0.03	0.02	0.03	0.03	0.02	0.02	0.03
Capital revenue	1.26	0.91	0.76	0.69	0.34	0.35	0.19	0.22
Transfers	1.25	0.91	0.75	0.68	0.29	0.32	0.18	0.20
From the state sector	1.24	0.89	0.74	0.65	0.29	0.23	0.13	0.17
From other public entities	0.01	0.02	0.01	0.03	—	0.09	0.04	0.02
Other	0.01	—	—	0.01	0.05	0.03	0.01	0.02
Total expenditure	6.94	7.31	6.97	7.82	2.95	3.04	2.94	2.79
Current expenditure	5.69	6.25	6.01	6.87	1.78	1.81	1.84	1.76
Personnel	0.20	0.20	0.19	0.19	0.21	0.23	0.22	0.22
Goods and services	0.17	0.18	0.19	0.16	0.17	0.17	0.16	0.17
Interest payments	0.02	0.03	0.05	0.05	—	—	0.01	0.01
Transfers	5.29	5.80	5.54	5.54	1.39	1.41	1.44	1.35
To families	0.14	0.11	0.09	0.09	0.18	0.18	0.23	0.16
To enterprises	0.41	0.46	0.41	0.43	0.16	0.14	0.13	0.12
To other public entities[1]	4.74	5.23	5.04	5.92	1.06	1.10	1.08	1.08
Other	0.01	0.04	0.04	0.03	—	—	0.02	0.02
Capital expenditure	1.25	1.06	0.96	0.94	1.17	1.23	1.09	1.03
Direct investment	0.20	0.16	0.12	0.12	0.32	0.37	0.26	0.26
Transfers	1.01	0.79	0.73	0.72	0.77	0.73	0.64	0.65
To families	0.07	0.04	0.06	0.06	0.06	0.06	0.06	0.06
To enterprises	0.29	0.32	0.29	0.27	0.22	0.19	0.25	0.26
To other public entities	0.66	0.43	0.39	0.39	0.48	0.47	0.34	0.33
Loans and shareholdings	0.02	0.03	0.02	0.02	0.08	0.13	0.17	0.09
Other	0.01	0.09	0.08	0.08	0.01	0.01	0.02	0.03
Deficit	–0.18	–0.44	–0.09	–1.59	–0.38	–0.43	–0.50	–0.16

Source: Ministry of the Budget (1994).
[1] Includes transfers to Local Health Units.

instrument of macroeconomic stabilization was limited. The functions of the ordinary regions are laid out in the Constitution and in the regional implementing laws, while those of the provinces and municipalities were established in a comprehensive law (1934). The latter has been modified several times by national laws over the years, with the most important recent revisions in 1977 and 1990. Special regions have wider expenditure assignments than ordinary regions; each special region has determined, through constitutional laws, its own additional functions. Regions can delegate their functions, and transfer the necessary resources to perform them, to lower levels of government, although

Table 4. Italy: Economic Classification of Local Governments' Budgets[1]
(In percent of GDP)

	Provinces			Municipalities		
	1990	1991	1992	1990	1991	1992
Total revenue	0.71	0.63	0.61	5.95	5.66	5.50
Current revenue	0.55	0.53	0.52	4.49	4.34	4.35
Direct taxes	0.05	0.04	0.04	0.87	0.83	0.98
Indirect taxes	0.00	0.00	0.00	—	—	—
Transfers	0.47	0.45	0.44	2.92	2.70	2.61
Of which: from the state sector	0.39	0.38	0.36	2.60	2.39	2.30
Other	0.03	0.03	0.04	0.69	0.81	0.76
Capital revenue	0.16	0.10	0.90	1.46	1.32	1.14
Transfers	0.13	0.08	0.07	0.91	0.76	0.65
From state sector	0.02	0.01	0.01	0.26	0.18	0.14
From other public entities	0.11	0.07	0.05	0.47	0.25	0.32
Other	0.03	0.03	0.03	0.55	0.56	0.49
Total expenditure	0.77	0.68	0.66	6.17	6.08	5.71
Current expenditure	0.51	0.50	0.48	4.13	4.11	4.02
Personnel	0.19	0.19	0.18	1.63	1.58	1.50
Goods and services	0.19	0.18	0.17	1.53	1.54	1.55
Interest payments	0.06	0.07	0.06	0.53	0.48	0.47
Transfers	0.05	0.05	0.04	0.40	0.46	0.46
To families	0.02	0.02	0.02	0.16	0.15	0.15
To enterprises	0.01	0.01	0.01	0.02	0.02	0.02
To other public entities[2]	0.02	0.02	0.02	0.22	0.28	0.28
Other	0.02	0.02	0.02	0.05	0.05	0.05
Capital expenditure	0.26	0.19	0.18	2.04	1.97	1.70
Direct investment	0.20	0.15	0.14	1.58	1.50	1.30
Transfers	0.03	0.01	0.02	0.05	0.03	0.04
To families	0.00	0.00	0.00	0.02	0.01	0.01
To enterprises	0.02	0.01	0.01	0.03	0.01	0.03
To other public entities	0.00	0.00	0.01	—	0.01	—
Loans and shareholdings	0.02	0.02	0.01	0.37	0.31	0.31
Other	0.01	0.00	0.01	0.05	0.12	0.04
Deficit	−0.06	−0.05	−0.05	−0.22	−0.42	−0.22

Source: Ministry of the Budget (1994).
[1]Excludes autonomous provinces.
[2]Includes transfers to Local Health Units.

this has been done to only a limited extent—mainly for housing and public works.

Expenditures of the ordinary regions accounted for 7.8 percent of GDP in 1993 (see Table 3). These regions are responsible—directly, or indirectly through the local governments—for most expenditure on health, welfare, agriculture, the handicraft industry, tourism, the environment, public housing, and vocational training. More than two thirds of these regions' expenditures are on health and transportation (for example, they finance most urban and all interurban road transportation (Table 5)).[7] Both are financed mainly through conditional grants (see below). Health alone accounted for around 71 percent of total regional expenditure in 1992 (see Table 5).

Total expenditures of special regions account for about 3 percent of GDP (see Table 3). Special regions have chosen, apart from the functions performed by the ordinary regions, additional expenditure assignments (Table 6). Valle d'Aosta has the most comprehensive additional responsibilities, while Friuli-Venezia Guilia and Sardinia have the least. As is the case for ordinary regions, the largest component of expenditure for special regions is health, which accounts for 33 percent of their total expenditures (see Table 5).

Provinces are assigned relatively limited expenditure responsibilities, although the framework law for reform of local administration stipulates that their main function is to become one of territorial and economic planning and of coordination between the region and the municipalities.[8] Their total expenditures do not exceed 1 percent of GDP (see Table 4). The largest components of provincial expenditure are education and culture (mainly provincial school buildings and their maintenance and provincial museums and libraries) and transportation (mainly maintenance of provincial roads) at around 32 percent and 25 percent, respectively in 1992 (Table 7). Municipal expenditures range between 6 percent and 7 percent of GDP.[9] The largest components of

---

[7]Since 1970, ordinary regions have the legislative authority (within the limits of national laws) for local police, social welfare and related activities, medical and hospital services, labor training, public assistance to school children (the authority for education rests with the central government), urban planning, inland waterways and lake ports, tramways and road systems, water supply, and public works of regional importance. In the economic sphere, these regions are responsible for regulating fishing and hunting, agriculture and forestry, mines, and the handicraft industry, while the central government has retained responsibility for regulating industrial development, labor relations, and salaries of most public employees. Some of these functions (such as local police and social welfare) were assigned in 1977 to local governments, which now receive the corresponding grants from the central government. Other functions (for example, labor training and housing) have been delegated to the local governments by the regions. The grants to finance these functions come from the regional budgets.

[8]The main provincial responsibilities are the maintenance of provincial highways, as well as lake, river, and mountain transportation; environmental protection; nonsolid waste disposal; air and water pollution control; and education of provincial interest.

[9]The main functions assigned to municipalities include local police, public hygiene, social welfare, provision and maintenance of buildings for the judiciary, education, construction and maintenance of municipal streets, solid waste collection, street cleaning, urban planning, zoning and regulation of commerce, operation of urban public transportation, supply of gas and electricity, and often the processing and supply of milk. The last three functions are provided mostly through municipal public enterprises. Some of these functions were statutorily assigned to the municipalities in 1935, others have been gradually transferred to them by the central government and the regions.

Table 5. Italy: Regional Current Revenue and Total Expenditure by Functional Classification[1]

	Ordinary Regions				Special Regions[2]			
	1990	1991	1992	1993	1990	1991	1992	1993
	(In percent of current revenue)							
Own tax revenue	2.0	2.9	2.7	6.6	0.7	0.6	0.6	0.6
Shared taxes	—	—	—	—	58.8	58.3	61.3	65.5
Grants and transfers	97.5	96.6	96.8	92.8	38.8	39.5	36.4	32.0
From the central government	96.7	95.6	95.9	91.8	35.0	37.1	35.0	30.7
Of which: health payroll tax[3]	—	—	—	41.4	—	—	—	15.9
From other public administrations	0.8	1.0	1.0	1.1	3.8	2.4	1.4	1.3
Nontax revenue	0.6	0.5	0.4	0.6	1.7	1.6	1.6	1.9
Total	100.0	100.0	100.0	100.0	100.0	100.0	100.0	100.0
	(In percent of total expenditure)							
General services and public order and safety	5.0	4.6	4.7	4.1	8.7	9.6	8.9	9.0
Education and culture	2.9	3.5	3.1	2.6	9.3	9.2	8.9	9.5
Health	68.5	71.8	71.1	75.0	32.2	32.2	33.3	32.3
Social security and welfare	1.4	1.2	1.4	1.1	3.7	3.4	3.7	3.7
Housing	1.4	1.0	1.3	1.1	4.7	3.9	4.3	4.6
Transportation and communications	7.0	5.8	6.1	5.5	4.2	4.1	4.0	3.8
Other economic services	12.7	10.8	10.3	9.0	26.8	27.3	24.5	26.1
Of which: agricultural	5.8	4.6	4.3	3.5	10.2	9.1	9.2	9.7
Not classified	1.0	1.2	2.0	1.6	10.5	10.4	12.5	11.1
Of which: interest	0.3	0.5	0.8	0.6	0.1	0.1	0.3	0.3
Total	100.0	100.0	100.0	100.0	100.0	100.0	100.0	100.0
Of which:								
Current expenditure	82.0	85.4	86.2	87.9	60.2	59.6	62.9	63.2
Capital expenditure	18.0	14.6	13.8	12.1	39.8	40.4	37.1	36.8
	(In percent of GDP)							
Memorandum items:								
Current revenue	5.5	6.0	6.3	6.1	2.2	2.3	2.2	2.3
Total regional expenditure	6.9	7.3	7.0	7.8	3.0	3.0	2.9	2.8

Source: Ministry of the Budget (1994).
[1]Commitment data.
[2]Includes autonomous provinces.
[3]Starting from 1994, health payroll taxes are classified as regional own revenue.

municipal expenditure are social welfare and housing (around 34 percent in 1991), general public services (21 percent), and transportation and communications—mainly construction and maintenance of local roads—(14 percent) (see Table 7).

Although per capita expenditure levels are quite similar among ordinary regions (Figure 1), the original objective of reducing inequalities in service provision through decentralization has not been achieved. There are still remarkable regional differences in institutional performance

Table 6. Italy: Additional Expenditure Assignments of the Special Regions[1]

	Valle d'Aosta	Trentino Alto Adige	Friuli-Venezia Giulia	Sicily	Sardinia
Disability pensions	•[2]	•			
Primary and secondary education	•	•[2]			•[2]
Subsidies to culture	•	•		•	
Arts	•	•	•[2]	•	•
Registry office		•			
Civil protection and fire department	•	•			•[2]
Transportation	•	•	•	•	
Transfers to local governments	•	•	•	•	•[2]
Subsidies to industry, commerce, and agriculture		•	•	•	
Forestry service	•			•[2]	
Statistics	•				

Sources: Constitutional laws and statutes of regions.
[1] These are the expenditures actually affected. The constitutional laws of the special regions provide for a larger range of responsibilities.
[2] Shared with central government.

(Putnam, Leonardi, and Nanetti, 1992).[10] Both northern regions and northern local governments are consistently better performers than their counterparts in the south. The cost of less efficient public services is borne by the local population. For example, the supply of public health care facilities is considerably lower in the south than in the center-north; nevertheless, utilization rates in public hospitals are lower in the south (ISTAT, 1995a).[11] In the south, household demand for health care met by private suppliers is correspondingly higher, and households spend more out of their own pockets—especially for diagnostic and specialist services (ISTAT, 1995a). In 1977, the central government allocated grants to regions for establishing day care centers, but the regions' response time in utilizing the grants varied considerably. By 1983—six years later—Emilia-Romagna (in the north) had one day care center per 400 children, and Campania (in the south) had one center per 12,560 children (Putnam, Leonardi, and Nanetti, 1992). This suggests that the matching of supply of local public services to local preferences (an objective of decentralization) is not ensured by the current system of

---

[10] This study evaluates institutional performance of subnational governments on the basis of 12 variables expressing the efficiency of their internal operations, the creativeness in their policy initiatives, and the effectiveness in implementing these initiatives.

[11] According to 1992 data, public hospital utilization rates vary from 73.8 percent in Piemonte (in the north) to 59.9 percent in Campania (in the south). Variability is higher among the special regions, ranging from 85.3 percent in Valle d'Aosta (in the north) to 53.3 percent in Sardinia. The Italian average is 69.6 percent.

Table 7. Italy: Local Governments' Current Revenue and Expenditure by Functional Classification[1]

	Provinces[2]					Municipalities				
	1988	1989	1990	1991	1992	1988	1989	1990	1991	1992
	(In percent of current revenue)									
Own tax revenue	8.8	9.1	8.5	8.4	8.2	14.7	19.6	19.5	20.6	22.5
Grants and transfers	84.5	84.3	85.5	85.5	84.7	70.4	64.9	65.1	62.3	60.0
From the central government	73.0	70.2	71.2	71.2	69.0	61.9	57.3	58.0	55.1	52.9
From regions	11.3	11.0	11.1	11.0	12.3	8.1	7.3	6.8	6.8	6.8
From other public administrations	0.3	3.1	3.2	3.3	3.4	0.4	0.4	0.4	0.4	0.4
Nontax revenue	6.6	6.6	6.0	6.0	7.1	14.9	15.5	15.4	17.1	17.4
Total	100.0	100.0	100.0	100.0	100.0	100.0	100.0	100.0	100.0	100.0
	(In percent of total expenditure)									
General public services and public order and safety	15.5	15.2	15.2	17.0	17.2	18.4	19.2	20.6	20.5	21.1
Education and culture	30.4	28.5	28.7	29.7	31.9	15.9	14.6	14.4	14.5	14.6
Social security and housing	8.0	6.5	7.3	6.3	7.7	33.9	33.3	33.8	31.4	34.1
Transportation and communications	30.0	32.9	30.7	28.5	25.3	16.2	15.3	14.1	14.4	13.6
Economic services	10.9	10.7	11.3	11.7	11.5	4.9	5.3	5.2	6.3	5.7
Not classified	5.2	6.2	6.7	6.9	6.3	10.7	12.3	11.9	11.2	11.0
Of which: interest						8.1	8.0	8.6	7.9	8.2
Total	100.0	100.0	100.0	100.0	100.0	100.0	100.0	100.0	100.0	100.0
Of which:										
Current expenditure	65.0	64.4	66.2	72.5	72.5	59.3	60.6	67.1	68.8	70.3
Capital expenditure	35.0	35.6	33.8	27.5	27.5	40.7	39.4	32.9	31.2	29.7
	(In percent of GDP)									
Memorandum items:										
Current revenue	0.5	0.5	0.5	0.5	0.5	4.3	4.4	4.5	4.3	4.4
Total local expenditure	0.8	0.8	0.8	0.7	0.7	6.9	6.8	6.2	6.1	5.7

Source: Ministry of the Budget (1994).
[1] Commitment data.
[2] Excludes autonomous provinces.

Figure 1. Italy: Per Capita Expenditure in Ordinary Regions, 1994
(In thousands of lire)

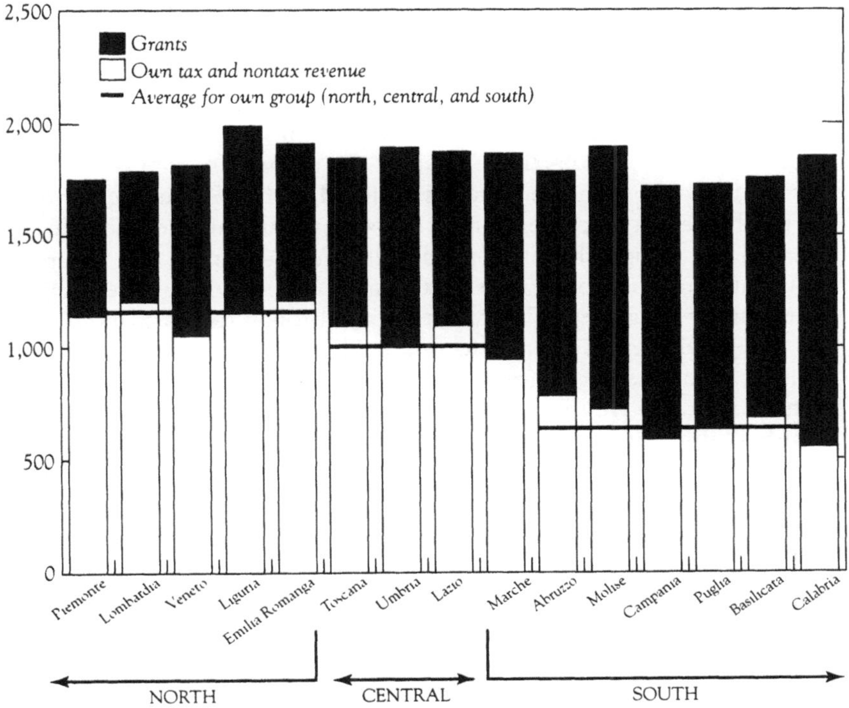

[Bar chart showing per capita expenditure for Italian regions grouped into North (Piemonte, Lombardia, Veneto, Liguria, Emilia Romagna), Central (Toscana, Umbria, Lazio, Marche), and South (Abruzzo, Molise, Campania, Puglia, Basilicata, Calabria). Bars are divided into Grants and Own tax and nontax revenue, with a line showing the Average for own group (north, central, and south).]

Source. Degni and Emiliani (1995).

intergovernmental fiscal relations. As discussed below, the financing arrangements and the budgetary procedures have not created the incentives to improve expenditure efficiency.

Since uniformity in service provision was not being achieved, the framework law reforming local administration stipulated that a standard level of services must be guaranteed to all citizens, as well as the principle of the responsibility of local managers (for example, directors of universities, managers of Local Health Units, and so on). This principle has so far found little practical application, partly because of overlapping expenditure responsibilities. The education sector is a case in point: the central government finances outlays for teachers' salaries, equipment, and some operations and maintenance, while local authorities (provinces and municipalities) finance outlays for buildings and some services (such as energy and water). Responsibilities for administrative and support staff are even more dispersed among the levels of government.[12]

The power of local managers and the room for managerial decisions are limited. Many expenditure decisions are beyond their control, such as the copayment rates for drugs and the salaries of health workers; for hiring and firing, they must follow strict rules and lengthy procedures.[13]

The principle of managerial responsibility has not found easy application in health care partly because of the attempt to supply uniform services throughout the country. As outlined in the 1992 implementing law for the health care reform, the central government is responsible for financing—through the National Health Fund—part of the "guaranteed, nationally uniform" levels of health care services. The regions contribute to financing this standard level through the earmarked payroll tax. The regions "bear the financial consequences of supplying health care above this guaranteed uniform level, of setting up health units and beds above the set standards, and for the deficits of the Local Health Units." Since no agreement was reached on what constitutes "uniform guaranteed levels of health care," the latter have become synonymous with "financially affordable" health services. Each year, the budget law defines what is available for central financing of health expenditure through grants. Of course, the regions argue that their health sector deficits are not the result of poor management, but of supplying nationally uniform levels of health care services, and that the National Health Fund is not sufficient to finance this provision. This has legitimated the central government financing of the regional deficits in the health sector in the subsequent budgetary periods (see the section on Conditional Grants).

---

[12]Municipalities are responsible for the salaries of the nonteaching personnel of kindergartens and of elementary and scientific high schools; the provinces are responsible for the nonteaching personnel of technical high schools; the central government is responsible for nonteaching personnel of junior high schools, teaching institutes, classical high schools, professional and industrial schools, and the administrative personnel of kindergartens and elementary schools.

[13]For example, the 1990 budget appropriated grants for Lit 4.2 billion (3.2 percent of total grants disbursed that year) to pay for the deficit of local transportation companies. That same year, the government agreed to increase the salaries of employees of all—including local—transportation firms. Though the central government appropriated additional transfers, both in 1990 and 1991, to the regions to share the financial burden, the regions were also authorized in 1991 to arrange 15-year bank loans (with interest paid by the central government), to cover the remaining salary costs from 1990. This example highlights two issues. First, poorly defined expenditure responsibilities have affected the transparency of the central government budget. Second, centralized salary negotiations make it impossible to distinguish what share of a local company's deficit is due to a centralized decision or to local mismanagement.

Revenue Arrangements

Regions and local governments rely for revenue on taxes, unconditional grants, specific grants, and borrowing. The current system is the result of over 20 years of legislation, sometimes of an emergency, piecemeal nature. Until 1992, the main feature of the subnational financing system was the low share of own revenue. Conditional grants were the most important source of financing for subnational governments. This was not at all the original constitutional provision, which prescribed own taxes, revenue sharing, and grants as sources of financing; however, the 1974 tax reform, which overlapped with the establishment of the ordinary regions, centralized taxes and their administration.[14] Regional own revenue fell from 8–9 percent of total revenue in 1973 to 2 percent in 1979. Starting from 1992, several national taxes have been assigned to subnational governments, to foster fiscal responsibility at the subnational level. However, the current tax and grants system does not seem to be designed to promote fiscal effort.

Tax Revenue and Tax Administration

Until 1992, regional own tax and nontax revenue amounted to around 3 percent of regional revenue (see Table 5). Regions' tax revenues were either shared taxes (only for special regions) or low-yielding own taxes. Until 1992, subnational governments could not levy taxes or modify tax rates, which were set by the central government.

In 1993, new own revenues were assigned to regional governments, although there were limits on how much local rates could diverge from the national standards. As a consequence, the share of own and overlapping tax and nontax revenue to total revenue of ordinary regions increased to 7.2 percent in 1993—and to 48.6 percent when account is taken of the revenue from the taxes that were transferred to the regions and earmarked to finance health expenditures.[15] The

---

[14]In fact, the actual degree of revenue centralization went beyond the reform plan and taxes originally planned for the subnational governments (local tax on income and capital gains tax on property) were assigned to the central government.

[15]Two kinds of taxes have been earmarked to finance health expenditures (hereafter, health taxes). The health payroll tax is paid by the employer (9.6 percent) and the employee (1 percent). The income health tax is paid on income from self-employment and property and the rate schedule varies from 1.6 percent to 5.6 percent. Since 1993 was considered a transition year, revenues from health taxes were still paid into the central government budget and then transferred to the regions—though the latter had control of their rates. The major regional own revenues are the vehicle tax, the annual vehicle surtax, the special tax on diesel cars, the health taxes, the university fee, and other minor taxes and licenses. In addition to its own taxes, a region may levy the following overlapping taxes: on car registration, on consumption of natural gas, and on gasoline. Rates of own and overlapping taxes may vary within centrally prescribed limits.

health tax rates are set by the central government, though regions can increase them by a maximum of 6 percent. In principle, local rates must be increased if the region has a deficit in the health sector. Although health expenditure is by no means under control, regions have been reluctant to increase rates (Table 8). Since in the past regional deficits have ultimately been borne by the central government, a moral hazard problem has developed.[16] The moral hazard is reinforced by the absence of credible penalties (that is, bankruptcy procedures) for regions.

As for expenditure assignments, revenue arrangements differ among special regions. Most of their revenues come from shared taxes—for example, about 66 percent in 1993 (see Table 5)—whose rates vary, depending on the extent of the region's expenditure responsibilities. In some cases, special regions retain high percentages of the national taxes.[17] All special regions also share in the National Health Fund and in other specific funds. Because tax assignments and shares of taxes differ, when national tax rates are changed, revenues of special regions are affected in different ways. This complicates national tax policy and multiplies claims for larger grants by the regions negatively affected by the tax changes.

To make local governments (provinces and municipalities) fiscally more autonomous, larger own financing sources were assigned to them during 1992–94.[18] The main beneficiaries of this change were the municipalities, as the property tax has become the most important source of local financing (central government grants to municipalities were reduced by an amount equal to property tax collection). In 1992, 40 percent of municipal governments' revenue came from own taxes and nontax revenue (29.6 percent in 1988), with the largest revenue

---

[16]See the section on Conditional Grants for a discussion of the central ex post financing of regional deficits in the health and transportation sectors, and the sections on Borrowing and Budget Formulation and Expenditure Management for central ex post financing of local government borrowing.

[17]For example, Sicily retains 100 percent of the taxes collected in its territory, except from lotto and excise duties. Moreover, it receives a solidarity grant that compensates for its low per capita income.

[18]Municipal own taxes are the municipal property tax (ICI), the municipal tax on enterprises, arts, and professions (ICIAP), the tax on use of public land, the waste disposal fee, the tax on advertising, the surcharge on electricity consumption, the sewer fee, and several minor taxes on concessions. Provincial own taxes are the supplemental fee on waste disposal services, the provincial vehicle registration fee (an amount equal to the national tax), the provincial tax on use of public land, and the provincial surcharge on electricity consumption. Though the government was given in 1993 a parliamentary mandate to draft a regulation for a municipal supplement on the personal income tax, this mandate has not been used.

Table 8. Italy: Main Taxes of Ordinary Regions, 1993

	Registration Licenses and Fees (In percent)	Regional Tax on Gasoline (In lire)	Surcharge on Car Registration Fee (In percent)	Additional Tax on Gas Methane (In lire)	Car Tax (In percent)	Health Taxes (In percent)
National legislation allows rates to be increased by:	20–100	30 lire maximum	20–80	(20–50 lire)/m³	90–110	6% maximum
Piemonte	minimum	30 lire[2]	80	50	100	no
Lombardy	minimum	no	80	20	100	no
Veneto	minimum	no	80	50	100	no
Liguria	100	no	80	50	100	no
Emilia-Romagna	minimum	no	80	30	100	no
Toscana	100[1]	no	80	50	110	no
Umbria	minimum	no	20	20	100	no
Marche	minimum	no	55	30	100	no
Lazio	minimum	no	80	20	100	no
Abruzzo	minimum	no	80	50	100	no
Molise	minimum	no	20	20	100	no
Campania	100[1]	no	80	50	110	no
Puglia	100[1]	30 lire[2]	80	50	110	no
Basilicata	minimum	no	80	50	100	no
Calabria	100[1]	no	80	50	100	no

Source: Giarda (1995).
[1] With some reductions.
[2] Not applied, owing to normative problems.

coming from business tax and local duties and fees (see Table 7). Own revenues of municipalities are estimated to have increased to more than 50 percent in 1994, owing to the municipal property tax becoming their own revenue. The rates of local taxes can generally vary within minimum and maximum limits set by the central government, or overlap with national taxes. Moreover, provincial taxes often overlap with municipal taxes; for example, there are three different fees on electricity consumption and nine taxes on car ownership (Tremonti, 1994).

Tax administration has been fully centralized in Italy since the 1973 tax reform. By the early 1970s, there was broad agreement that a myriad of local taxes and fees had excessively complicated the tax system and contributed to distortions in resource allocation and that local tax administration was not particularly efficient in assessing, collecting, or auditing (Reviglio, 1976; Holmans, 1978). It is likely that this centralization contributed to the substantial tax revenue increase in real terms of the late 1970s and early 1980s (Ghessi, 1984).

Each special region has its own different regulations for tax administration. Sicily autonomously collects all taxes, mostly through private tax collection agencies.[19] In Trentino, taxes are collected by the central government, but nine-tenths of revenue remains with the regional government. Valle d'Aosta and Friuli-Venezia Giulia have a similar arrangement. Sardinia has its own tax collection agency but it is used only for some taxes.

A general problem that arises with revenue centralization is that local residents do not know how much local services cost. With the revenue centralization of the 1970s, the link between taxation and spending was loosened, and fiscal illusion weakened the perception of the real cost of local public goods. This generated excess demand for locally provided public goods, which was initially accommodated. Brosio, Hyman, and Santagata (1980) find that per capita expenditure was positively affected by the removal of taxation powers and the decentralization of expenditures during the early 1970s. Econometric evidence supports the view that expenditure decentralization, without the corresponding fiscal responsibility at the local level, has increased overall public expenditure in Italy (Rizzo, 1985). However, as fiscal illusion declines over time, so does the positive effect of the separation of expenditure and taxing decisions over consolidated public expenditure (Brosio, 1985).

---

[19]In the 1980s, the private collection agency in Sicily retained 10 percent of collection, on account of collection costs, though average collection costs in Italy are estimated at around 3 percent (Stille, 1995).

Unconditional Grants

Ordinary regions receive unconditional grants from two sources: the Common Fund and the Regional Development Projects Fund. Their economic importance is quite small, as they account for only 3 percent of total revenue of ordinary regions.

The Common Fund was originally funded from a quota of excise revenues, to enact the constitutional provision of tax sharing. However, its actual size is in fact determined each year through an informal bargaining process between the central and the regional governments. After reaching an agreement on the size of the fund, the percentage of the mineral oil tax rate that goes into the fund is set to equal that amount. Therefore, the regions do not know the amount of resources available from the Common Fund until the national budget is approved by parliament—which may happen a few months into the financial year. The distribution formula is strongly redistributive.[20] The poorest region, Calabria, which has less than half the per capita income of Lombardy (the richest region), has a per capita transfer from the Common Fund that is 2.4 times greater than that of Lombardy. The weights of the various factors entering the distribution formula—and therefore the regions' shares in the Common Fund—have been frozen since 1976, as the central and regional governments have been unable to agree on different parameters reflecting changed economic and social conditions. Since 1993, regional shares are net of the regional vehicle tax. This has increased the redistributional nature of this grant, since vehicle tax collection is lower in poorer regions.

The Regional Development Projects Fund is financed from general revenue and was set up to equalize the stock of public infrastructure by region. Therefore, 60 percent of its resources was to be distributed to the southern regions. However, since regions have repeatedly not prepared their investment plans, the distribution formula now follows the weights of the Common Fund. The Regional Development Projects Fund is composed mainly of contributions for multiyear expenditure or for the repayment of interest on debt for investments (Degni and Emiliani, 1995).

Following the implementation of the framework law reforming local finances, the grant system to local authorities was restructured in 1994. The amount and distribution of current grants are determined by the previous years' level and distribution of expenditures and are set net of

---

[20]The grant is distributed as follows: 6/10 according to the population of each region, 1/10 according to the territorial size, and 3/10 according to the emigration rate, the unemployment rate, and the inverse of the per capita revenue of the personal income tax.

the collections of municipal property tax. Municipalities now receive three types of current grants: from the recurrent fund (which finances essential ordinary expenditures), the conditional fund (for specific expenditures, such as youth employment), and the equalization fund (which compensates for local differences in the tax base).[21] The recurrent fund is supposed to finance those "essential" services that have been decentralized from the central government to the municipalities.[22] It is distributed according to "objective" criteria that reflect the municipality's population, territory, and socioeconomic conditions—according to parameters of which little is known outside the Ministry of the Interior. The recurrent fund accounted for around 77 percent of current grants to municipalities in 1994. The conditional fund's size and distribution depend on ad hoc laws; this fund accounted for around 25 percent of current grants to municipalities in 1994. To foster fiscal effort, the equalization fund is supposed to be distributed on the basis of the inverse of the tax base of own local taxes. Although the equalization fund was the smallest of the funds in 1994—accounting for around 4 percent of current grants—it will become much more important. While the recurrent fund will be fixed in nominal terms, its increase in line with programmed inflation will be added to the equalization fund. The latter is also supposed to close any local financing gaps that may arise. The conditional fund is supposed to remain fixed in nominal terms.[23]

Two problems are associated with the new system of grants to local governments. First, since the local tax base is mostly unknown, actual collections are used as proxies to determine the distribution of the equalization fund. This distribution mechanism effectively rewards those municipalities opting for lower local tax rates and is a disincentive to fiscal effort—certainly not the result that the reform wanted to achieve. There seems to be an inconsistency between the intention to assign fiscal autonomy to local governments through local taxes and the guarantee of a minimum level of resources, independent from the fiscal effort.

---

[21] The grant system for provinces is effectively the same as for municipalities.

[22] These essential services for the municipalities are the Registry Office, statistical services, local law enforcement, the army draft, and primary and secondary education—for that part under municipal responsibility. The essential services for the provinces are the Office of the Provincial Directorate of Education and expenditures of provincial responsibility within scientific and technical secondary education.

[23] However, since salaries of local government employees were increased in 1995 as part of a collective bargaining agreement settled at the national level, local governments claim that the grant allocations in 1995 were not sufficient to cover recurrent expenditures.

The second problem is the wide disparity in municipalities' ability to generate own resources. For example, the collection of municipal property tax—the largest source of own revenue—varied from Lit 145,000 a person (about US$90) in the central regions, to Lit 71,000 a person (US$44) in the southern regions (the northern regions collected Lit 138,000 (US$86)). While the richer municipalities may actually generate own resources equivalent to around 80 percent of expenditure, the poorer ones may generate only around 20 percent. Therefore, although the new financing arrangements will reduce the importance of grants, their redistributive role may actually increase. This may lead to grievances from the richest local governments with regard to the size and distribution of the equalization fund, and thus to delays in the fund's appropriation. As in previous arrangements, the current grant system does not seem designed to reduce budgeting uncertainty.

Grants for local investments have also changed. Before 1986, the distribution of the Investment Grant—whose size was negotiated between the central and local governments—responded to the applications received from local governments on a first-come, first-served basis. This system suited the administratively more efficient municipalities. Starting in 1994, the central government's contribution to new local investments is limited to a one-time per project amount, set according to the average per capita investment expenditure in 1994. The appropriation for this grant, only 0.02 percent of GDP in 1994, raises questions about its adequacy for new local investment projects. In the past, local governments' investment expenditures have usually been higher than the ex ante available resources—central grants plus own financing. For this reason, local governments have been allowed to borrow from banks and the Deposit and Loan Fund (a government bank), and the central government has picked up a portion of the bill through a new grant established in 1984. The specific grant for repaying these loans (capital plus interest) is larger—at around 0.7 percent of GDP in 1994—than the actual Investment Grant.

Conditional Grants

Conditional grants are by far the largest source of revenue for ordinary regions, accounting for around 87 percent of total revenue in 1992.[24] The central government thought that conditional grants would be better suited for influencing the level and distribution of subnational

---

[24]With the transfer of the payroll tax to regions, the earmarked fund for health expenditure was reduced accordingly in 1993. Nevertheless, conditional grants remain the largest revenue source (around 44 percent of total in 1993).

expenditure of national concern (such as health and public transportation). However, heavy reliance on conditionality has led to lack of accountability of funds spent, because the central government has not been able to clarify its objectives, establish and enforce efficiency criteria, and audit performance.

The National Health Fund and the National Transportation Fund are the two main earmarked funds.[25] Health services and local public transportation are not provided directly by the regions: health services are provided by the Local Health Units, and transportation services by a host of public and private enterprises, most of them municipal corporations. Both also use fees and tariffs but, for social and political reasons, these are never set to finance substantial portions of their expenditures.[26] Though reference was made to "objective" parameters, which were supposed to increase expenditure efficiency (for example, the number of hospital beds or their utilization rates, the coverage of the local bus network, and the age of the existing buses), the size of the funds and their regional distribution is actually determined each year through informal negotiations between the central and regional governments. Essentially, the funds' size and distribution have been set in line with previous years' expenditures (so-called historic expenditure criteria), which implicitly rewarded the inefficient and/or high spenders.

Each year, both funds are deliberately underfunded, to limit the deficit of the general government at the time of budget approval. All negotiating parties are aware of this underfunding. This system has proven useless in stemming the growth of expenditure and deficits and in increasing efficiency in these two sectors. The deficits are financed through arrears to suppliers and through borrowing from banks—which are outside the targeted borrowing of the state sector. These debts are eventually cleared by issuing government bonds, which increases the outstanding debt of the central government without affecting the

---

[25]The economic importance of the other specific purpose grants is small. At present, agriculture, forestry, environmental protection, and mountain communities are the most important destinations for these grants.

[26]The ratio between own income and expenditures for urban public transportation was 25 percent in 1987. The percentage of cost recovery in transportation is highest in the north (34 percent) and lowest in the south (16 percent), with the central regions close to the average (24 percent) (Brosio and Piperno, 1992). Own income of Local Health Units generated by user fees does not exceed 3 percent of their total expenditure (Degni and Emiliani, 1995). Though health contributions represent, on average, 55 percent of the Local Health Units' total income, their importance varies among regions: in Lombardy, it is equal to 67 percent, and in Calabria, 35 percent. The Local Health Units' income from user fees is higher in the north.

Table 9. Italy: National Transportation Fund and National Health Fund—
Budgetary Appropriation and Deficit in Ordinary Regions
(In billions of lira)

	1987	1988	1989	1990	1991	1992	1993[1]
National Transportation Fund							
Budget appropriation	4,051	4,294	4,294	4,207	4,411	4,764	4,764
Deficit	893	1,249	1,809	1,859	2,329	2,725	2,861
Deficit (as percent of budget appropriation)	22.0	29.1	42.1	44.2	52.8	57.2	60.1
National Health Fund							
Budget appropriation		84,019[2]	49,443	55,350	67,184	71,044	71,311
Deficit		13,139[2]	6,235	13,688	9,880	5,316	5,545
Central government loan		11,126[2]	4,784	9,889	8,793	5,316	...
Deficit as percent of budget appropriation		15.6[2]	12.6	24.7	14.7	7.5	7.8
Central government loan (as percent of deficit)		84.7[2]	76.7	72.2	89.0	100.0	...

Source: Degni and Emiliani (1995).
[1]Estimated.
[2]This column refers to 1987–88.

deficit in the current year;[27] it is only in the following years, when the corresponding allocation for interest payments is made in the national budget, that the subnational deficit has an effect on the central level. This has happened every one or two years for health expenditure, and every three to five years for transportation expenditure. The National Transportation Fund deficits of the period 1982–86 were cleared in 1987 by the central government, and the deficit of the 1987–93 period was cleared by a 1995 decree. The percentage of overspending in the transportation sector has been growing steadily since 1987 (Table 9). Starting in 1993, the amounts granted to each region through the National Health Fund have been determined by the region's population size, the difference between the per capita standard costs of providing health services and the regional payroll tax base, and patients' mobility between regions. If a region's health costs are higher than the national average, regional health taxes should be increased to finance the deficit. Though this new formula has been designed to increase efficiency, it has proven difficult to define per capita standard costs, and funds continue to be allocated on the basis of past expenditures. Currently, as in the past, this uncertainty is reason enough for regions to ask that their health deficits be financed by the central government. In-

---

[27] The debt liability so created for the central government is referred to as "hidden debt" in Italy.

deed, this took place in 1993 and 1994, when no region increased the rates of its health taxes, although deficits have since developed. This inaction was also due to the fact that regions did not know the amount of payroll tax that each one would receive, because the first two to three years of the reform were transitory years, during which the health taxes continued to be collected by the central government.

The same problem has arisen in the transportation sector. Though the National Transportation Fund was to be distributed to the transportation enterprises based on deviations from "objective standard costs" (Law 151/1981), these costs have never been defined. Therefore, actual average costs came to be used; actual costs, however, are ill suited to improving efficiency. Moreover, the National Transportation Fund was often distributed to the regions with long delays into the financial year, making it impossible to distribute it ex ante to the transportation companies. As in the health sector, these delays have substantiated regions' demands to the central government for additional allocations (at end-year) to finance the deficits of the transportation enterprises.

The current grants system is at odds with the central government's objective of reducing interregional differences in service levels. Most grants are demand driven, as the size and distribution of most are decided on the basis of past expenditure. Demand-driven grants reward inefficiencies in expenditure—particularly if, as in Italy, there is no appropriate system of expenditure monitoring and budgetary constraints (see the sections on Borrowing and Budget Formulation and Expenditure Management).[28]

Borrowing

Although legal limits on borrowing by subnational governments exist, they are bypassed by resorting to temporary arrears accumulation, recourse to bank credit by entities supplying local public services (for example, Local Health Units and transportation enterprises) to the

---

[28]Starting from 1996, the National Transportation Fund (and other smaller conditional grants), the Common Fund, and the Regional Development Projects Fund have been removed and replaced by unconditional financial resources funded through a quota of the excise on gasoline and by an equalization fund. In 1996, these two new financing sources together equal the amounts that would have been allocated through the replaced funds. From 1997, each region will receive the quota of excise collected in its territory. The allocation for the equalization fund will increase with programmed inflation. This increase will be distributed approximately as an inverse function of the excise on gasoline collected in each region. This new system provides more certainty to regions with regard to their revenue and reduces the scope for bargaining, although the distribution formula of the increase of the equalization fund is complex and lacks transparency.

Table 10. Italy: Composition of the Stock of General and
Local Governments' Debt
(In percent of GDP)

	1985	1986	1987	1988	1989	1990	1991	1992	1993	1994
General government	82.3	86.3	90.5	92.6	95.6	97.7	101.2	108.3	117.3	121.4
Medium- and long-term bonds	35.9	41.0	42.7	43.4	44.3	46.3	50.6	53.0	61.4	66.7
Short-term bonds	18.8	18.0	19.6	22.0	24.1	24.6	23.7	26.2	25.8	24.2
Post office deposits	7.4	7.9	8.5	8.7	9.2	9.4	9.4	9.7	10.3	11.2
Bank loans	4.1	3.9	3.7	3.5	3.5	3.5	4.3	4.7	5.5	5.5
Of which: subnational governments[1]	3.5	3.3	3.1	2.8	2.8	2.9	3.5	3.6	4.5	4.3
Other domestic debt	0.3	0.3	0.3	0.3	0.2	0.2	0.2	0.2	0.2	0.2
Debt issued abroad	1.5	1.4	1.8	2.0	2.3	3.0	3.1	3.4	4.7	5.1
Debt to Bank of Italy	14.3	13.8	13.8	12.8	11.9	10.7	9.9	11.0	9.3	8.4
Memorandum items:										
Debt of subnational governments to Deposit and Loan Fund[2]	...	...	...	5.3	6.6	6.8	6.6	6.5	6.5	6.6
Total debt of subnational governments	...	...	...	8.1	9.4	9.7	10.1	10.1	11.0	10.9

Source: Bank of Italy (1994).
[1] Includes regions, provinces, and municipalities' debts to banks.
[2] The Deposit and Loan Fund is included in the general government; therefore, the debt of subnational governments to the Deposit and Loan Fund is netted out when the debt of the general government is consolidated.

subnational governments and by later shifting responsibility for the deficits to the center. For these reasons, the magnitude of the debt of subnational governments—around 11 percent of GDP in 1993–94—is not large (Table 10).

Currently, regions are permitted to borrow only for the capital budget and for share participation in regional enterprises, with the proviso that capital charges (interest plus principal repayment) not exceed 25 percent of the sum of regional own revenue, net of health contributions, and the Common Fund. Regions cannot borrow to finance current expenditure. However, the Local Health Units and transportation companies (which account, through the National Health Fund and National Transportation Fund, for around 80 percent of regional expenditure) can borrow from commercial banks, and eventually it is the central government that foots the bill, through periodic deficit clearing (see the section on Conditional Grants). Therefore, regional budgets report little interest outlays.

The previous section discussed how payment arrears to suppliers in the health sector have been allowed to build up and how Local Health Units have been authorized to borrow from commercial banks to pay suppliers' bills.[29] This is usually timed so that arrears are not paid until the following financial year, at the earliest, and until additional financing is forthcoming. This occurred in 1983, 1986, and 1987, then every one to two years until 1993. As in previous years, in 1993 the regions were authorized to borrow from the Deposit and Loan Fund to repay outstanding arrears, but this resulted instead in higher current spending, and outstanding arrears were not reduced. The interest on the 20-year loans contracted by the regions with the Deposit and Loan Fund is borne by the central government. The 1993 settlement of overdue debt is supposed to be the last one for the health care sector and was considered a precondition for Local Health Unit managers—and ultimately regions—to assume responsibility for their units' economic results. Similar problems were encountered by some transport authorities.

For local governments, in the early 1970s, there were few controls on the sources, amounts, and conditions of their borrowing, which led to the accumulation of large commitments for interest payments.[30] Rising domestic interest rates required emergency financing from the Treasury in 1976, and, in March 1977, parliament decided to convert all short-term debt of local governments into 10-year treasury bonds.

Since the financial crisis of the 1970s, local governments have not been allowed to borrow short term from the banking system to finance current expenditures—except for temporary liquidity shortages; strict limits have been imposed on the rate of spending increases—especially for personnel; and a balanced budget requirement—including grants—has been introduced. During the 1980s, a system of ex ante determination of the overall available revenue, including grants, was introduced. This system of ex ante ceilings was effective in reducing local government expenditures. For investment projects, provinces and municipalities may borrow from banks, the Deposit and Loan Fund, and other public banking institutions, if they provide a repayment plan. Local governments have often been encouraged to divert some borrowing from the Deposit and Loan Fund indirectly to the suppliers through arrears, again, to meet the targeted borrowing figures by pushing more borrowing outside the budget concept. Suppliers obtain loans from

---

[29]For example, the average delay between the delivery of drugs by suppliers and the issue of payment warrants by Local Health Units is around one year (average for the period 1991–94). However, Piemonte (in the north) paid in 146 days, on average, while Campania (in the south) paid within 597 days. Before the 1993 debt-clearing operation, one region in the south had recorded payment delays of 720 days (Carli, 1995).

[30]In 1975, about 50 percent of the subnational government deficit was financed by banks and special credit institutions; around 42 percent was financed by the Deposit and Loan Fund.

banks to finance these arrears and use the local governments' commitments to secure these loans.

The current system of ineffective controls on borrowing has serious economic costs. Uncertainty about the actual availability of cash resources for program managers undermines normal budget management discipline. Delaying provision for local capital projects can increase their costs, when it results in suboptimal phasing of work or the expensive renegotiation of contracts. Diverting borrowing from the Deposit and Loan Fund to commercial banks adds to financing costs and may allow uneconomic capital projects to proceed if commercial banks believe there is an implicit government guarantee on the loan. Allowing Local Health Units to go into arrears not only adds to borrowing costs but encourages suppliers to add a premium to their prices, in the expectation of delayed payment.

Budget Formulation and Expenditure Management

Regional budget formulation often ends nearly three months after the new fiscal year begins.[31] Only when the central government budget is approved by parliament and grant amounts and reference rates of regional taxes are known can the regional administrations estimate their total revenues and finalize their budgets. Regional budgets are transmitted to the central government, which has a 30-day statutory period to approve or comment on them—with no power to reject them. Meanwhile, the first quarter's operations are conducted on the basis of the appropriations for the first quarter of the previous fiscal year. This lengthy process creates uncertainties for budgeting.

Although grants from the central government should be released regularly, in practice, the releases require protracted correspondence and continuous prodding by the regional governments. The Treasury account regularly provides advances to cover the deficit of the national pension system. One source of these advances is the delayed access of other agencies, including subnational governments, to their funds deposited in the account.

All controls on the regional expenditure process are formal, rather than substantial. Regional quarterly cash reports are sent to the General Accounting Office for information purposes only. There is no standard reporting format, and budgetary practices have evolved regionally

---

[31]During 1979–85, the average approval date for regional budgets ranged from January 27 (Friuli-Venezia Giulia, in the north) to August 7 (Calabria, in the south) (Putnam, Leonardi, and Nanetti, 1992).

to satisfy specific needs. Each region's budget is different, so they are almost impossible to compare.[32] Transparency of budgetary information and, therefore, expenditure control and management, have suffered.

The format and the accounting rules of provinces and municipalities' budgets are specified by law in minute detail. Data are collected on a cash basis, and reporting formats do not distinguish costs from expenditures, so that it is difficult to know the actual economic cost of any specific service. Budgets, once approved, are reported to the General Accounting Office for information purposes only and to the Regional Control Committee for formal control—basically, to verify that the budget has violated no laws. Although a local accounting officer has to authorize that spending is formally consistent with the budget, no organization has jurisdiction on budget substance.

Auditing, under the guidelines of the 1934 comprehensive law, was strictly internal, performed by three elected councillors (not necessarily professional accountants or auditors), and essentially of a formal and financial nature—at best, checking that public money was spent in accordance with the budget. The 1990 framework law provided for an external Board of Auditors, consisting of professionals who are to evaluate results achieved and advance proposals to the municipal and provincial councils to improve performance. All public entities should use cost accounting and, while still retaining the cash reporting, also use accrual accounting. However, apart from a few attempts limited to few services, these mandates have not been put into action.[33] As a consequence, the auditors—in those municipalities that have actually established an external Board of Auditors—do not have the essential accounting tools for managerial control or for evaluating efficiency of expenditure programs, and the political representatives are not in a

---

[32]For example, each region classifies grants from the central government in different ways. Some regions include their share of the National Health Fund under one heading only, while others split it among headings. Another example relates to the transfers from the central government to meet the outstanding arrears of the Local Health Units. These are entered in the regional budgets as revenue in a variety of ways, sometimes simply as "transfers in accordance with law x" (the decree allowing that particular transfer), sometimes simply as "transfers to cover deficit"; never do these budgetary entries report the amount of transfers that covers interest payments to banks as opposed to payments to suppliers. The Italian Statistical Institute (ISTAT) collects the revised budgets of the subnational governments, but these are published with a delay of more than two years (March 1995 for 1992 outcome).

[33]Local government accounting is still regulated by a 1934 state law, which means that additional national implementing legislation is needed to establish accrual accounting. Though cost accounting is mandated by an implementing law (29/1993) of the framework law, local administrators have generally been unable to solve the technical difficulties in implementing a cost-based accounting system (Mussari, 1994).

position to take into consideration the economic consequences of their choices.[34]

Subnational governments are therefore not accountable—apart from a general, formal accountability—to local taxpayers. As discussed above, lack of accountability also stems from the limited ability of the former to make economic choices (their financial resources being largely provided by the state through conditional grants, and the rules and methods of service provision imposed from above). Citizens have diverted their dissatisfaction with the services rendered by the subnational governments to the central government, which they blame for cutting and delaying grant disbursements and for imposing inflexible rules on the use of these funds and the provision of services. To be sure, regions do accumulate substantial uncommitted allocations, but this is partly due to the fact that all expenditures are committed to specific objectives and funds cannot, in principle, be shifted from one expenditure chapter (for example, personnel, drugs, and machinery) to another. This problem is more acute in the areas where central government grants are conditional because the grant appropriation law usually specifies—in minute detail—how funds should be spent.

Another consequence of these arrangements has been that the innovative ability of the subnational governments—one of the presumed advantages of decentralization—could not be fostered. The subnational governments' managers were accountable only if they failed to guarantee financial compliance with formal rules. Issues of quality, efficiency, and effectiveness in the provision of services needed to be raised by the managers on their own initiative; since they were concerned instead with measuring the financial compliance with legislative standards, little interest to innovate has been generated. However, in this area as well there have been considerable differences between the northern and southern regions' ability to produce innovative legislation.[35] To be fair, the traditional concept of accountability is changing due to the latest reform laws on local administration: the tasks of managers and politicians are now, at least in principle, separate, and the managers are directly responsible for administrative fairness and efficiency in obtaining their units' objectives. However, accounting methods and budgetary practices have not yet changed, and

---

[34]The new "Audit Handbook" (a guideline for the Board of Auditors), which was to be prepared by June 1993, is not yet available.
[35]Putnam, Leonardi, and Nanetti (1992) track 12 areas of regional competence on which similar laws appeared in many regions and find that most regions were either consistent leaders or consistent laggards in introducing new legislation. The highest score was recorded by Emilia-Romagna (in the north) and the lowest by Calabria (in the south).

the local politicians have not yet fully used their expanded revenue-raising powers.

Regional and local authorities are the major providers of public services, and their expenditures are an important element of public spending; yet, the institutional and regulatory setup is such that the central government does not collate information on their aggregate budgets nor monitor prospective or actual spending in-year. Although the unified treasury account for subnational governments allows a quarterly reporting of their cash positions and it enables a certain control over local authorities' cash sources by regulating disbursements of the central government's grants and transfers, this does not constitute control over their spending because of the lack of reporting of and controls on commitments. Responsibility for distributing grants to, for collecting data on, and for controlling regional and local governments rests with the Treasury and the Ministry of the Interior, respectively; however, there is little coordination or exchange of information on subnational government matters between the two. At the beginning of each year, the Treasury (for the regional governments) and the Ministry of the Interior (for the local governments) know the subnational governments' expenditure commitments from their budget estimates. However, during the course of the year, the ministries collect no information on changes in expenditure commitments. Subnational expenditure data are not satisfactorily broken down by economic and functional categories, making expenditure analysis difficult.

Conclusions and Policy Implications

The system of intergovernmental fiscal relations in Italy has impaired allocative efficiency and accountability in the use of public resources and has contributed to the growth of public expenditure, deficit, and debt by promoting fiscal irresponsibility at the subnational level. Decentralization has not yet yielded the results predicted by theory. What has instead happened is the following. First, subnational governments have been able to match the supply of local public goods with local preferences with varying degrees of success—higher in the north. Second, decentralization per se may have not allowed greater experimentation in the provision of output, because the degree of central government control on resource allocation has remained high and because local administrative capabilities are not uniformly distributed. Third, subnational management practices have not evolved: budgetary practices, expenditure monitoring and control, and budget transparency have not improved. Indeed, it is arguable that these have worsened as expenditure was decentralized.

In fact, intergovernmental fiscal relations have contributed to various structural macroeconomic problems. First, subnational governments have been a source of hidden debt for the central government. Second, the central government has had less margin to use expenditures for fiscal policy, as most of these are either of subnational responsibility or entitlement and interest outlays. Third, national budget transparency and the national public expenditure management system have suffered, as the central government resorted to accounting expedients to limit its cash borrowing requirements.

Although the latest measures taken to foster subnational fiscal responsibility may not suffice in dramatically changing subnational fiscal behavior, there is a considerable degree of consensus in Italy in favor of a further expansion of regional expenditure competencies and tax autonomy and of a reduction in conditional grants. However, in the political debate on how to achieve these objectives, three crucial elements are missing: the administrative constraints, the budget management and the issue of accountability, and the regional disparities.

The first element, administrative constraints, is virtually lacking in the Italian debate on how to achieve further decentralization. Most proposals tend to allocate new functions to the regions without taking into consideration that administrative support may be unevenly distributed at the subnational level: overstaffing and poor training, inability to tap available funds (especially those provided by the European Union), lack of development plans in key economic (for example, agriculture, transportation, and environment) and social (for example, health and vocational training) sectors. Also, the capacity of regional and local government to administer current and potential resources of revenue needs to be strengthened. Administrative capabilities at the subnational level may prove to be an obstacle to further devolution of expenditure responsibilities.

The second element is budget management and accountability. Fiscal responsibility may be difficult to achieve without a marked improvement in budgetary practices. The first step could be the publication of the subnational budgets, so that the taxpayers would clearly see the connection between their fiscal efforts and the public goods and services supplied to them, and local administrators would become more subject to public scrutiny. To prevent subnational autonomy from becoming synonymous with incomprehensible policies, uniform standards for transparent budget classification and new accountancy rules need to be set. For example, there is a clear link between the transparency of the budget and the control of subnational borrowing. The cost of borrowing should be transparent and made known to the citizen/taxpayer as well as to the central government. Improvements in national budgetary practices and expenditure management are also necessary. For example, the first National Health Plans that were prepared were approved only after long delays, were ambiguous in their prescriptions, and difficult to implement. The distribution of the National Health Fund continued, therefore, to be based on past expenditure levels and bargaining. Likewise, central monitoring of subnational budget execution has not adjusted to the reality of an increasingly decentralized government.

Related to the budgetary practices is the issue of accountability of individual managers (at both the central and the subnational levels). Too much emphasis is currently placed on legal compliance. Managers should be made responsible for their respective cost centers, and the accountancy rules should be modified to allow them to monitor costs—rather than cash expenditures and formal application of the law. External auditing and a value-for-money approach to performance should be used to facilitate the evaluation of efficiency and effectiveness in service provision. A central value-for-money agency could be responsible for making reviews and comparisons, drawing out the best practices, and offering general guidance on how to improve management.

With increased accountability should come the imposition of harder budget constraints on regional and local governments, including tighter controls on borrowing and a firm refusal of bailout by the central government. These limits should be set in standing rules, incorporated in the law rather than through the annual budget process, which offers opportunities for bargaining. These standing rules cannot be effectively applied until the monitoring system of the consolidated budget is first improved. Accurate and timely information on borrowing of all levels of government should be disseminated to financial markets. Arrears and debts to suppliers should be centrally monitored.

The third element is the constraint imposed on further decentralization by the large disparities in income and in institutional performance between the northern and the southern regions—even after 20 years of a decentralization policy designed to reduce these differences. Although the transfer system, notwithstanding large differences in fiscal capacity, has resulted in a rather uniform level of per capita expenditure in the ordinary regions, this has not implied the same level of effectiveness in the delivery of local public services. The policy implication is that it is meaningless to prescribe a guaranteed standard level of expenditure for each person. The recent reform of health care financing has explicitly set government grants at a level that ensures a uniform per capita expenditure, independent from the revenue collected by each region through the health taxes and from the level of effectiveness in providing health services. Rather than referring to an as yet undefined level of "necessary" services that the central government should finance, a definition in terms of functions, for example preventive and public health, should be sought.

The literature on fiscal federalism offers considerable theoretical and practical guidance concerning the assignment of tax and expenditure responsibilities to the subnational governments and the appropriate systems of intergovernmental transfers designed to support them (see Chapters 2 and 3 for an extensive discussion of these issues). Here, only some observations relevant to Italy are presented. First, progress in building an effective revenue-raising capacity and in strengthening budget management and accountability at the subnational level should precede further devolution of expenditures.

Second, given the existing marked regional differences highlighted above, if a path of increased decentralization is chosen, it should also be openly recognized and accepted that even more pronounced regional differences in the delivery of local public services may result. It should be realized that there is an inherent inconsistency between the current desire for both increased decentralization and service uniformity throughout the country. Disparity in the provision of local public services is a normal occurrence in a decentralized system; and it is even more so in a country characterized by sharp regional differences in fiscal capacity, unless the system relies on large-scale interregional redistribution of resources.

Thus, it is crucial that the government decides on the objectives of increased decentralization. Only then can the instruments for achieving such objectives be designed. For example, the government should first choose what degree of regional disparity in the provision of local public services is acceptable; then it can determine what tax assignments, tax sharing arrangements, and equalizing grants would be appropriate to support that choice.

Latest Developments

With the 1997 Financial Law, and the accompanying laws, parliament has delegated the government to change, with effect from 1998, the regional financing system through the establishment of (1) a regional income tax surcharge (between 0.5 percent and 1 percent); (2) a regional tax on productive activities (with a rate variable between

3.5 percent and 4.5 percent);[36] and (3) an interregional equalization transfer system (whose revenue sources and objectives are yet to be specified). These new taxes will replace all regional taxes on business income, the health payroll tax, the health income tax, and several other minor regional taxes. During a transitory period of three years (1998–2000), the new taxes will be managed by the central government, which will set the tax rates and allocate the revenue among regions according to parameters yet to be specified. Only after the year 2000 will regions be able to set rates—within the centrally mandated limits.[37] Between 65 percent and 90 percent of the IREP will be earmarked to finance regional health care expenditures. Any resulting ex ante financing gap for National Health Fund will be financed through transfers by the central government, as in the current system. Finally, the government has approved the creation of a Bicameral Commission aimed at elaborating reforms in intergovernmental fiscal relations by June 1997.

It is too early to assess the implication of these measures, as several crucial aspects have yet to be determined. However, a few general observations can be made. First, the introduction of the IREP and income surcharge are a step in the right direction, as these should simplify the tax system and make it less distortionary and will provide regions with large and autonomous revenue sources—although the autonomy to set rates will be reached only in 2001. Second, crucial to the success of the reform is that several key aspects currently undetermined be solved expeditiously, including how to distribute the new revenue among regions, and the interregional equalization transfer system. In particular, as discussed in the previous section, the government should first choose what degree of regional disparity in the provision of local public services is acceptable; only then can it determine the parameters that should be chosen to calculate a region's payments or withdrawals from the equalization fund. As in recent years, failure to settle these issues may lead to a distribution of revenue and of equalization funds on the basis of the past trends. Third, the recent measures still fail to address the concerns raised in this chapter with regard to budget management and the issue of accountability (both of them are problematic at the central and decentralized level). In particular, the recent measures do

---

[36]IREP (the Italian acronym for this tax) is a direct tax on the value added produced by enterprises and the self-employed. Local governments will share—a yet undefined—portion of the IREP revenue to compensate for the abolition of the local tax on enterprises, arts, and professions (ICIAP).

[37]It has not yet been decided if the regions will administer the new taxes.

not reduce budgetary uncertainty for the regions, nor do they reduce moral hazard for regions.

References

Bank of Italy, *Relazione Annuale* (Rome), various issues.

Bin, R., M. Cammelli, A. DiPietro, and G. Falcon, 1995, *Una proposta federalista per l'Italia Regione Emilia-Romagna* (Bologna, March).

Brosio, G., 1985, "Fiscal Autonomy of Non-Central Government and the Problem of Public-Spending Growth," in *Public Expenditure and Government Growth*, ed. by F. Forte and A. Peacock (Oxford: Blackwell).

———, 1994, "Financing Regional and Local Governments by Means of Transfers: The Case of Italy and Spain," paper prepared for the Conference on Fiscal Transfers Systems, Qingdao, China, July.

———, D.N. Hyman, and W. Santagata, 1980, "Revenue Sharing and Local Public Spending: The Italian Experience," *Public Choice* (Amsterdam), Vol. 35, No. 1, pp. 3–15.

Brosio, G., and S. Piperno, 1992, "La Spesa Pubblica per i Trasporti," in *I Trasporti e l'Industria*, ed. by Marco Ponti (Bologna: Il Mulino).

Brosio, G., G. Pola, and D. Bondonio, 1994, "Una proposta di federalismo fiscale" (unpublished; Turin: Fondazione Giovanni Agnelli).

Buglione, E., and G. France, 1984, "Skewed Fiscal Federalism in Italy: Implications for Public Expenditure Control," in *Comparative International Budgeting and Finance*, ed. by A. Premchand and J. Burkhead (New Brunswick: Transaction Books).

Carli, S., 1995, "Nuove USL, far finte di essere sane," *La Republica* (Rome), June 19.

Centro Studi di Politiche Economiche (CESPE), 1994, "La Scelta Federalista," *Schede e Contributi*, No. 12 (Rome).

Ceriani, V., 1995, "Gli Aspetti Economici del Federalismo," in *Il Principio Federativo*, ed. by A. Cantaro and M. Degni (Bari: La Meridiana).

Degni, M., and N. Emiliani, 1995, "Perspectives of Fiscal Federalism in Italy," Commissione Tecnica per la Spesa Publica (unpublished; Rome: Ministry of the Treasury, May).

Ghessi, Giuseppe, 1984, "Bilancio dello Stato: l'Accentramento del Deficit," *Il Deficit Publico: Origini e Problemi*, ed. by E. Gerelli and A. Majocchi (Milan: Franco Angeli).

Giarda, P., 1994, "Status-Quo and Federalism: A Hypothesis of Regional Financing Reform" (unpublished; Rome: Commission for the Regional Financing Reform, Ministry of Regional Affairs, May).

———, 1995, *Regioni e Federalismo Fiscale* (Bologna: Il Mulino).

———, and N. Emiliani, 1994, "La Spesa Pubblica non fa Privilegi," *Il Sole 24 Ore* (Rome), January 6, p. 7.

Holmans, Stephanie K., 1978, "The Italian Public Expenditure System," HMS Working Paper No. 3 (London, May).

ISTAT (Italian Statistical Institute), *National Accounts, Conti delle Administrazioni Pubbliche e della Protezione Sociale*, various issues (Rome).

———, 1995a, *Relazione Annuale 1994* (Rome).

———, 1995b, *Conti Economici Regionali Anno 1992* (Rome, May).

Ministry of the Budget, *Relazione Generale sulla Situazione Economica del Paese*, various issues.

Ministry for Institutional Reforms, 1994, "Commissione Speroni per una Proposta di Riforma della Costituzione sulla Forma di Stato" (unpublished; Rome).

Ministry of the Interior, 1994, "Commissione Maroni per i Problemi Finanziari degli Enti Locali" (Rome).

Ministry of the Treasury, 1994, *Trasferimenti Statali Alle Regioni 1993* (Rome).

Mussari, Riccardo, 1994, "Accounting and Accountability in Italian Local Governments: Recent Changes and Challenges for the Future," *Public Budgeting and Finance* (New Brunswick), Vol. 14, No. 4 (Winter), pp. 54–70.

Putnam, Robert D., Robert Leonardi, and Rafaella Y. Nanetti, 1992, *Making Democracy Work: Civic Traditions in Modern Italy* (Princeton, New Jersey: Princeton University Press).

Reviglio, Franco, 1976, *Lezioni sulla Riforma Tributaria* (Turin: Giappichelli).

Rizzo, Ilde, 1985, "Regional Disparities and Decentralization as Determinants of Public Sector Expenditure Growth in Italy (1860–81)," in *Public Expenditure and Government Growth*, ed. by F. Forte and A. Peacock (Oxford: Blackwell).

Ruggiero, E., 1983, "Italy: Expenditure Assignments and Financing Arrangements" (unpublished; Washington: International Monetary Fund, March).

Stille, Alexander, 1995, *Excellent Cadavers* (New York: Pantheon Books).

Tanzi, Vito, 1996, "Fiscal Federalism and Decentralization: A Review of Some Efficiency and Macroeconomic Aspects," in *World Bank Annual Conference on Development Economics, 1995* (Washington: World Bank).

Tremonti, G., 1994, *La Riforma Fiscale: Il Libro Bianco del Nuovo Fisco* (Milan: Il Sole 24 Ore).

———, and G. Vitaletti, 1994, *Il Federalismo Fiscale* (Bari: Laterza).

12

Japan

DUBRAVKO MIHALJEK

After almost half a century of status quo, decentralization has become a major issue on Japan's political and economic agenda in recent years. Soon after his inauguration in 1996, Prime Minister Ryutaro Hashimoto outlined four challenges that Japan must tackle: deregulation, administrative reform, devolution of authority, and relocating the capital city. These challenges are closely interrelated. The local public sector, which in 1995 accounted for about 16 percent of gross domestic product and employed over 3 million people, is one of the most regulated sectors in the Japanese economy. The central government exercises detailed and stringent controls over the revenues of local governments and a wide range of local expenditures. As a result, the degree of effective revenue and expenditure centralization in Japan is among the highest in industrial countries.

There seems to be broad agreement in both the government and the private sector that the rigid system of local public finance and intergovernmental relations needs to be reformed, but consensus on the direction of reforms has yet to emerge. Meanwhile, pressures for decentralization are on the rise, stemming from the need for fiscal consolidation and the process of deregulation and structural reform, as well as from the wave of decentralization efforts in other industrial countries. Fiscal decentralization is likely to improve welfare because central government control may interfere with the efficient supply of local public goods and services and not provide incentives for local governments to act respon-

---

The author is grateful to Teresa Ter-Minassian, Guy Meredith, Nobuki Mochida, Masatsugu Asakawa, and Kenji Okamura for helpful comments.

sibly. Local governments in Japan also show a high degree of "grant dependency," which in the fiscal federalism literature has been associated with an inefficient size of the public sector and distortions in the allocation and financing of public goods. Empirical estimates of the relationship between historical changes in the degree of centralization and the size of Japan's public sector presented in this chapter suggest that the tendency of general government to expand as a result of higher revenue and expenditure centralization is much stronger in Japan than in other industrial countries. These expansionary effects operate to an important degree through transfers to local governments.

This chapter analyzes the system of local public finance and intergovernmental relations in Japan, with a view to assessing the strengths and weaknesses of this system and identifying possible approaches to fiscal decentralization. Of special interest to the fiscal federalism literature are the unique features of Japan's intergovernmental relations, such as the use of local borrowing as a tool of macrofiscal policy, the use of a local public finance program as a policy coordination tool, and the institutional representation of the interests of local governments in policy bargaining with other ministries, in particular the Ministry of Finance.

This chapter first provides a historical overview of the Japanese system of local government and describes the key constitutional, sociopolitical, and organizational aspects of the system that has emerged after World War II. Next, the basic structure of the present system of intergovernmental finances is analyzed, including the assignment of policy functions, expenditure responsibilities and revenue sources, and the grants system and local borrowing. The following section summarizes the views of Japanese policymakers and public finance experts on the problems of local public finances, reviews government reform initiatives, and elaborates on the need for fiscal decentralization on the basis of empirical evidence on the size and growth of the public sector in Japan. The chapter concludes with an outline of possible approaches to fiscal decentralization. An appendix summarizes the main statistical data on local public finance in Japan, compares them with the data on local expenditure and revenue in major industrial countries, and describes in more detail the local tax system and intergovernmental grants.

Intergovernmental Relations in Japan

Historical Background

Prior to World War II, local governments in Japan had little or no independence and were generally treated as administrative arms of the national government.[1] There was no basic constitutional recognition of local autonomy, and the legal existence of local governments rested on a few basic statutes. Governors of prefectures were local agents of the national government, appointed by the Emperor and responsible to him. Local governments' affairs were for the most part supervised by the Ministry of Interior and, where relevant, by other ministries (transport, education, agriculture, and so on).

Under a complex set of nationally established rules, local governments were responsible for sharing the costs of all national government programs, but had little or no say in the policies that defined them or even the manner of their implementation. Municipalities were fully subordinated to prefectural governors in all but the most minor local issues. The electoral base was very narrow, being primarily male land- or property owners.[2] Political leadership tended to be an elite of minor nobility and landowners who viewed themselves not as public servants but as officials of the crown.

The process of urbanization fostered by the national government from the 1880s until World War II had an important impact on relations between the central and local governments. As millions of people left the countryside, the old-style concepts of paternalistic local government proved inadequate to meet the burgeoning demands for housing, sanitation, health care, transportation, electric power, and other elements of a modern infrastructure. Local authorities did not have the revenue resources to meet these growing needs, and they soon realized that they had to require the national government to pay for its own demands. At the same time, a broader base of educated people began to insist on a greater political voice in their own affairs, and were able to exert more direct influence on the political elite that ran the national government. These trends were interrupted by World War II, but they were a powerful influence toward democratization, which established a climate for the rethinking of Japanese government.

Constitutional Aspects

The new Constitution of 1947 emphasized the basic principle of democratic government and fundamental rights, drawing heavily from European and American traditions. It established for the first time the principle of a government of the people, in contrast to a government loyal to the Emperor. Japan committed itself to a structure that carried

---

[1]This section draws on Bingman (1989). For a more detailed analysis, see Mochida (1985).
[2]Universal suffrage for men was achieved in 1927, and for women in 1947.

representative government down to the prefectural level and cities, towns, and villages. The Constitution itself gave a recognition to these bodies equal to that of the national government, and it further stipulated that: "Regulations concerning organization and operations of local public entities shall be fixed in accordance with the principle of local autonomy" (Article 92).

The Local Autonomy Law (1947) defined a two-tiered structure of local government consisting of prefectures and municipalities. While each level has equal status under the Constitution, national policies have continued to be paramount, and the national government retains a superior position: "Each local public body shall, in addition to its own community affairs, and the affairs required by national law or by cabinet order, perform other administrative affairs within its area insofar as such affairs are not reserved to the State" (that is, the national government) (Article 12).

Local authority in Japan is thus conveyed in a form directly opposite to the concept of residual states' rights in federations—that is, specific authorities not given to the national government are reserved to the states. In contrast, the Local Autonomy Law makes specific designations of roles that the national government authorizes local governments to exercise.

In addition to its authorizing role, the Local Autonomy Law defines the authorities of local legislative bodies and local officials, establishes many uniform rules that must be obeyed, and final approvals that are retained by the national government.[3] The Local Autonomy Law also cites some 550 other national laws that define an estimated 70–80 percent of all the activities of local governments.[4] The system that emerged is very "public administration" oriented, in the sense that it contains many elements that also define how the administration or management of public functions is to be carried out (Bingman, 1989).

One of the more striking features of Japan's system in this regard was the mandamus proceedings. Until 1991, when the Local Autonomy Law was revised, the relevant minister in the national government could directly order a prefectural governor—who is an elected official—to carry out certain actions, and if the governor did not obey such

---

[3]For example, the law defines the powers and authorities of chief executives, including the number, name, and responsibilities of all major subdivisions of local governments.

[4]These laws are not just major statutes such as the City Planning Law or the Environmental Preservation Law, but also such acts as the Law for School Meals for Night Courses of Senior High Schools, or the Laundry Law, which sets forth detailed procedures for licensing, registration, and examination of laundries and their workers (Bingman, 1989, p. 52).

orders, he or she could be removed from office by the national minister, subject to certain legal appeals.[5]

Sociopolitical Aspects

The defining characteristic of Japan's system of intergovernmental relations is the strong collective preference for equal access to public goods. The Japanese people and government were willing to commit themselves after World War II to the evolution of autonomy for their newly defined structure of local government. However, they would not do so in a pattern that would reject their history and tradition of strong central government and allow for substantial regional differences to emerge. Equal access to public goods and fair sharing of the burden to finance these goods were viewed as essential for economic and social development. Hence, local governments were willing to sacrifice autonomy to maintain regional equity.

To implement these principles, local autonomy would have to function within a framework of uniform structure and ground rules defined by the central government. Interregional redistribution—the extent to which populations of different regions are supplied with the same level of public services and subjected to same burdens of taxation—is, therefore, the central issue for Japan's system of intergovernmental fiscal relations. In this respect, Japan is similar to Germany, where the constitution guarantees "equality of living standards" to all Germans, and unlike the United States, where the federal government pursues a largely hands-off regional policy.

Organization

There are currently 47 prefectures and 3,281 municipalities in Japan. Forty-three prefectures and four equivalent bodies (Tokyo, Osaka, Kyoto, and Hokkaido) correspond to U.S. states, while three large cities have been given special authorities equivalent to prefectures. Municipalities include cities, "designated" cities (those with populations of 500,000 or more), towns, and villages. Currently there are 10 designated cities, 663 cities, 1,994 towns, and 577 villages. In addition, there are several thousand "special" local public entities, including the 23 wards of metropolitan Tokyo and over 7,000 functional associations of

---

[5]National ministers are themselves elected officials: the Constitution requires that the prime minister and at least half of the cabinet come from either house of the Diet. In practice, almost all of them are Diet members, primarily from the house of representatives, whose 511 members are elected for four-year terms.

public bodies such as property wards and unions of local public enterprises.

The basic structure and authorities of local governments have not been defined by those governments themselves, but by a series of national laws that mandate essentially the same institutional setup at all three levels. Each prefecture has a bicameral legislative assembly, whose members are elected for four-year terms. In general, all activities of the prefecture are under the direct authority of the governor as chief executive. Governors submit a high proportion of new legislation each year (including the budget) and have veto powers on bills. Governors appoint and supervise all public employees, and organize and manage the departments of the government, including ownership and management of all public facilities. They may also let contracts or establish and supervise public enterprises to carry out the public's business. The assembly may pass a resolution of nonconfidence by vote of two thirds of the membership. Governors, in turn, may dissolve the assembly.

Municipal assemblies have basically the same structure as prefectural assemblies, and mayors as chief executives have duties and powers similar to those of governors of prefectures.

Financial Relations Between the Central and Local Governments

Assignment of Policy Functions

In view of the unitary structure of government and a highly integrated national economy, stabilization policy in Japan is the sole responsibility of the central government. Redistribution policy in Japan is also centralized, given the high degree of homogeneity in preferences for core public services, the mix of taxes, and the degree of interpersonal and interregional redistribution that has evolved over time. However, even the allocation function in Japan remains highly centralized, although—as discussed below—there are strong efficiency arguments for a more decentralized provision of public goods and services.

Vertical Fiscal Imbalance

Like in other unitary states, financial relations between the central and local governments in Japan are marked by a substantial vertical fiscal imbalance—that is, revenues generally exceed expenditures at the central level and fall short at the local level. The central government

Table 1. Japan: Ratio of Own Tax Revenue to Own Expenditure[1]
(In percent)

	1975	1985	1990	1994	1975-94 Average
Central government	119.3	112.7	134.7	103.5	115.6
Local governments	32.1	41.9	43.3	42.4	39.1

Source: Ministry of Home Affairs (1994).
[1] Own expenditure does not include transfers to local (central) governments. Own revenue includes all revenue collected by the central government (that is, before revenue sharing with local governments).

receives tax revenue that typically exceeds by 15 percent the amount that it spends for its activities (Table 1). By contrast, the tax revenue of local governments amounts to less than 40 percent of the funds necessary to perform their functions.

To fill the financing gap at the local level, the central government transfers part of its "excess" tax revenue to local governments; these transfers amount to about 35 percent of local revenue (6½ percent of GDP). Prefectures and municipalities raise the remaining funds through nontax revenue and borrowing.

Division of Expenditure Responsibilities

The vertical fiscal imbalance results from the division of expenditure responsibilities and revenue-raising powers between the central and local governments. In Japan, the central government performs relatively few public functions directly. These include defense, national law and order, judiciary affairs, postal service, national hospitals and medical facilities, and institutions of higher education and research. Local governments are responsible for a major share of public spending, including that on education and culture, infrastructure, health and welfare, and public law and order. On average, central government expenditure accounts for about 10 percent of GDP, and local expenditure for about 18 percent of GDP (Table 2; see also Table 6 in the Appendix).

Municipalities are responsible for slightly over half of total expenditure (Table 3). The share of municipal spending increased substantially between 1970 and 1980, but has remained stable at about 51 percent of local spending since.

As regards the nature of local expenditure, about two-thirds is current spending and the rest is capital spending. The largest expenditures of local governments are on education and culture (26 percent of local

Table 2. Japan: Shares of Central and Local Expenditure[1]

	1975	1985	1990	1994	1975–94 Average
	(In percent of total expenditure)				
Central government	32.4	38.4	37.6	41.2	37.2
Local governments	67.6	61.6	62.4	58.8	62.8
	(In percent of fiscal year GDP)				
Central government	8.0	10.7	10.8	11.4	10.5
Local governments	16.7	17.2	17.9	16.3	17.6

Sources: Ministry of Home Affairs (1994); and national accounts.
[1]Including expenditure financed by transfers from central or local governments.

spending), infrastructure (21 percent), health and welfare (17 percent), and law and order (9 percent).[6]

Although considerably more public spending takes place at the local level than at the central level, the central government remains heavily involved in almost every aspect of local public spending. Unlike in most unitary states and federations, the Local Autonomy Law does not clearly distinguish between the responsibilities of the central government and those of local governments. Rather, the law provides that prefectures perform those functions that "require uniformity in performance, cover a wide geographical area, are deemed too extensive for management by municipalities, or require efforts to coordinate two or more cities, towns, or villages." Major programs (such as education, health, and infrastructure) are in practice formulated by national ministries and financed directly or indirectly by the central government. National ministries also retain numerous bureaucratic authorities with respect to local governments.[7] Local governments in principle have large administrative responsibilities—over planning, construction and maintenance of facilities, regulation and zoning, management, inspection, and monitoring of compliance—but in practice national direction can be so detailed that it can severely constrain the authority of local officials and leave them with the job—but not the power—to satisfy public needs.

---

[6]For a breakdown of expenditure by function and level of government, see the Appendix.

[7]These authorities include the right to demand reports and evaluations of performance; the right to conduct investigations, inspections, and audits of local government activities; and the right to impose various corrective measures (Bingman, 1989).

Table 3. Japan: Shares of Prefectural and Municipal Expenditure[1]

	1970	1980	1985	1990	Average[2]
	(In percent of local expenditure)				
Prefectures	55.3	48.3	49.0	48.8	50.0
Municipalities	44.7	51.7	51.0	51.2	50.0
	(In percent of fiscal year GDP)				
Prefectures	7.2	8.6	9.0	8.5	8.6
Municipalities	5.8	8.3	9.6	8.9	8.6

Sources: Jichi Sogo Center (1993); and national accounts.
[1] Including expenditure financed by transfers from higher-level governments; expenditure by prefectures excludes transfers to municipalities.
[2] For 1970, 1975, 1980, and 1985–90.

Revenue Assignment

As noted above, the main sources of local revenue are local taxes (on average, 37 percent of local revenue), transfers from the central government (35 percent), nontax revenue (20 percent), and bonds (9 percent). Excluding transfers, local governments' own revenue accounts for about 42 percent of consolidated government revenue (11 percent of GDP) (Table 4).

At the local level, prefectures raise about 55 percent of revenue (9½ percent of GDP) (Table 5). While the share of local taxes in revenues of prefectures and municipalities is about the same (35 percent of prefectural or municipal revenue), municipalities raise relatively more funds from nontax sources (20 percent of total revenue, compared with 15 percent for prefectures) and local bonds (10 percent, compared with 7½ percent for prefectures). Prefectures receive more transfers from the

Table 4. Japan: Shares of Central and Local Revenue[1]

	1970	1980	1985	1990	Average[2]
	(In percent of total revenue)				
Central government	58.0	61.4	59.3	57.1	58.6
Local governments	42.0	38.6	40.7	42.9	41.9
	(In percent of fiscal year GDP)				
Central government	11.2	17.9	16.7	16.6	16.0
Local governments	8.1	11.3	11.5	12.4	11.3

Sources: Jichi Sogo Center (1993); and national accounts.
[1] Includes tax revenue, nontax revenue, and borrowing; local revenue does not include transfers from the central government.
[2] For 1970, 1975, 1980, and 1985–90.

Table 5. Japan: Shares of Prefectural and Municipal Revenue[1]

	1970	1980	1985	1990	Average[2]
	(In percent of local revenue)				
Prefectures	59.9	53.2	53.6	54.0	54.7
Municipalities	40.1	46.8	46.4	46.0	45.3
	(In percent of fiscal year GDP)				
Prefectures	8.0	10.1	9.5	10.0	9.6
Municipalities	5.4	8.9	8.2	8.5	8.0

Sources: Jichi Sogo Center (1993); and national accounts.
[1]Includes transfers from the central government. Municipal revenue does not include transfers from prefectures.
[2]For 1970, 1975, 1980, and 1985–90.

central government (42 percent, compared with 36 percent for municipalities). Details of the assignment of major national and local taxes are provided in the Appendix.

Although local taxes represent one of the most important revenue sources for local governments, the tax bases and tax rates cannot be determined by the independent initiative of local governments. The Local Tax Law—which was, significantly, enacted by the National Diet—prescribes in great detail the taxes that can be imposed by local governments, defines the tax base in each case, and determines the tax rates. While local governments are given some flexibility with certain taxes, any discretion that local governments may have must be exercised with the approval or informal agreement of the central government.

Grants and Fiscal Equalization

To transfer its "excess" revenue to local governments, the central government uses revenue-sharing grants, referred to in Japan as the "local allocation tax," and a large number of specific purpose grants, known as "central government disbursements." The local allocation tax accounts for 50–60 percent of all transfers to local governments (15–20 percent of local revenue). Central government disbursements account for 45–60 percent of central government transfers (up to 15 percent of local revenue), while local transfer taxes account for 3–7 percent of all transfers (up to 2 percent of local revenue).[8] Details of the grants system are described in the Appendix.

---

[8]Local governments also make (small) payments for specific purposes to the central government, mainly toward improvements for public works carried out by the central government.

A major purpose of the local allocation tax is to equalize the fiscal capacity of local governments. The Japanese equalization model takes into account the inherent differences in both revenue-raising capacities and expenditure needs of local governments, an approach that is very similar to General Revenue Assistance in Australia. A prefecture or municipality that enjoys a high revenue-raising capacity and has a low cost of providing services is considered fiscally strong, and vice versa. The index of fiscal capacity and, hence, the amount of equalization payment depend on the ratio of "basic financial needs" over "basic financial revenue." Where basic revenue exceeds basic financial needs (this is generally the case in large metropolitan areas), the local government receives no transfer but is entitled to retain its excess. By contrast, low-capacity governments (generally those situated in rural areas) receive large per capita equalization payments.

Basic financial need is not equivalent to the actual expenditure of a local government, but rather represents a standardized amount deemed necessary to provide public services at the level prescribed by the national government. The basic financial need for each public service is calculated according to the following formula:

Basic financial need = unit of measurement × unit cost × cost differential.

The total financial need of a local government is the sum of the basic financial needs for all expenditure items. The unit of measurement in the above formula is generally local population, or length and area of roads or other public facilities. Unit costs for public services are determined each year by the Local Finance Bureau of the Ministry of Home Affairs, taking into account price changes and changes in the demand for services. Finally, cost differentials depend on factors such as population density and growth, climate, area and geography, degree of urbanization, and industrial diversification.[9] These factors reflect the differential costs of providing standard services that arise due to unavoidable circumstances in which local governments operate. The local allocation tax is on the whole administered in a fairly neutral manner, but inevitably there are occasional political pressures to include as many expenditures as possible in the unit of measurement when calculating standard fiscal needs.

Basic financial revenue is defined as general revenue that can be appropriated to meet the basic financial need. It is calculated as the sum of the local transfer tax and a prescribed percentage of the "standardized" local revenue—80 percent of such revenue for prefectures, and 75 per-

---

[9]For details, see Yonehara (1981 and 1993).

cent for municipalities.[10] Standardized revenue is the local tax revenue that can be obtained under the "standard" tax rate determined by the central government. If a local government levies taxes at lower rates and experiences a revenue shortfall, its basic financial revenue will not be considered inadequate (such a government may, therefore, receive no transfer). Conversely, if a local government levies taxes at higher-than-standard rates, it will not be penalized—the amount of transfer will be calculated as if the local government applied the standard rate.

The equalization impact of the local allocation tax is quite strong. For example, in FY 1992, per capita local tax revenue in Tokyo (the wealthiest prefecture) was ¥262,000, but only ¥61,000 in Okinawa, the poorest prefecture. After the transfer of the local allocation tax, however, per capita revenue in Okinawa rose to ¥217,000.

The main objective of specific purpose grants is to achieve uniformity in the provision of local public services. Unlike the local allocation tax, most of the national specific purpose grants are allocated among local governments at the discretion of the central government; there are only a few formula-based grants. Specific purpose grants are mainly designed as cost-sharing programs, that is, they subsidize a certain percentage of the standard cost prescribed by the national government. The rate of subsidy differs from program to program, depending on the financial burden of the program and the interest the central government has in the program. Almost 35 percent of the total amount of specific purpose grants are subsidies for public construction projects.

The system of specific purpose grants creates a close link between corresponding departments of national and local governments. For example, an officer in the public works department of a local government may come under the control of an officer of the Ministry of Construction, and that control may be more direct than that exerted by the head of the local government body itself. These links and the fact that similar subsidies are handled by different ministries often lead to administrative inefficiency. For example, a mayor of a small village may be forced to purchase two different makes of new buses simply because different ministries have different specifications for the use of buses.

Borrowing

Local borrowing accounts for about 9 percent of local revenue. The approach to local public finance in Japan has regarded borrowing as a

---

[10]The full amount of standardized revenue is not used in this formula in order to provide incentives to local governments to enlarge their tax bases, and also to take into account special local needs that require nonstandard amounts of revenue.

source of funds to be resorted to only in case of special financial need (Yonehara, 1981; Ishihara, 1993). Because it gives rise to future financial claims against the local government, borrowing is generally limited to capital outlays. Local governments are prohibited from raising loans without the approval of the central government. The Local Loan Program, drawn up by the central government each year, lays down the rules governing approvals for local borrowing. This program is drawn up at the same time as the Local Public Finance Program, which determines local governments' shares of the local allocation tax and specific purpose grants.

The main creditors of local governments are the central government, public enterprise loan funds, and the private sector. The central government funds, which provided finance for about 60 percent of local borrowing in the late 1980s, were provided through the Fiscal Investment and Loan Program (FILP), that is, indirectly from Post Office savings accounts, Post Office Life Insurance, and Annuity Systems (Ministry of Home Affairs, Local Autonomy College, 1995). The Japan Finance Corporation for Municipal Enterprises' Fund (JFM) lends both short-term and long-term funds to local authorities that run public enterprises. It financed about 12 percent of local borrowing in the late 1980s, mainly by issuing its own bonds, which are held by either securities companies and other financial institutions, or organizations with special links to local governments (for example, the Local Government Employees Mutual Aid Corporation).

As for private funds, which financed about 28 percent of local borrowing in the late 1980s, a number of large local governments (including Tokyo Metropolis and Osaka Prefecture and City) sold their bonds in the open bond market, or floated loans in foreign countries. Most local authorities, however, borrowed long-term funds from commercial banks, insurance companies, and agricultural cooperatives (sometimes without issuing marketable bonds), as well as from the central government and the JFM. The FILP and the JFM usually lend to local governments at a lower rate and for a longer term than private financial institutions.[11] Consequently, local governments generally see more advantage in borrowing from these sources. This is one of the reasons why an allocation of funds by the central government is necessary in connection with local loans (see below).

The use of local loans to assist in the implementation of fiscal policy has increased in recent years. Given the relative size of the local public

---

[11]In the past few years, the interest rate charged by private financial institutions has been lower than the FILP rate; however, the former is floating, while the latter is more or less fixed.

sector, the central government must rely on local governments to implement its fiscal policy. It is impracticable to alter the local tax system or the local allocation tax to compensate for changes arising out of the business cycle. The local tax system and the proportion of national taxes allocated to local governments are fixed by statutes, which can be amended only by the Diet. The size of local borrowing, on the other hand, can be changed by executive action, and such changes are accompanied by an easing or tightening of fiscal policy. In view of this flexibility, the proportion of local loans in local revenue tends to increase in years when the national government adopts expansionary fiscal policy, and vice versa.

Local Public Finance Program

The involvement of the central government in the determination of local revenue and expenditure makes the budgets of the central and local governments in Japan much more closely linked than is the case in other unitary states. But the Local Public Finance Program links the central and local budgets even more closely together.

The Local Public Finance Program is assembled by the Ministry of Home Affairs, which bargains on behalf of local governments with the Ministry of Finance and the Cabinet. Each year, the central government makes an official estimate of the revenues and expenditures of local governments. On the revenue side, this estimate covers revenues from local taxes and nontax revenues, the local allocation tax, local transfer taxes, the national specific purpose grants, and local loans. On the expenditure side, the estimate covers wages and salaries, expenditure on goods and services, capital outlays, interest payments, and subsidies to public corporations. These estimates are then combined with an array of national policies and programs such as the FILP in order to produce, for each local expenditure program, an "acceptable" income-expenditure plan. The most important feature of this process is how revenues and expenditures are balanced through the local allocation tax and local borrowing. The Ministry of Home Affairs is responsible for ensuring that local governments have enough revenue to balance the program, and it bargains hard with the Ministry of Finance to secure the sources of revenue for local governments. The Local Public Finance Program is thus a unique mechanism for coordinating national and local fiscal policies.

From a public choice perspective, the Local Public Finance Program is subject to all the vagaries of the budget process. But when the program is approved by the Cabinet, it locks in local governments in terms of their own local taxes, their local loan programs, their employment and general administrative expenses, and most important, the levels of funding for almost all public programs.

Issues in Intergovernmental Finance

Views from Japan

Despite the slow progress toward fiscal decentralization, public debate in Japan on the reform of intergovernmental fiscal relations has been lively. In 1979, the Local Government System Research Council, an advisory organ of the Prime Minister's Office, proposed decentralization for the first time in its 30-year history. The council noted that the Ministry of Home Affairs and the Ministry of Finance shared a common interest, although from different standpoints (Shindo, 1984). The Ministry of Home Affairs was keen on promoting decentralization in order to respond to the growing demands by the public for a more responsive and flexible local government that would be able to address such issues as urban congestion and environmental problems. At the same time, the Ministry of Finance, facing the urgent need to reduce the administrative expenses of national ministries, was searching for government organs and agencies to which national administrative affairs and projects could be transferred. In this context, the Ministry of Finance did not oppose decentralization initiatives.

Subsequently, the Ministry of Home Affairs has argued that the most significant theme for both central and local governments for the foreseeable future would be to obtain the cooperation and understanding of the general public for higher taxes (Ministry of Home Affairs, 1984). In the view of this ministry, the level of Japan's public services compared favorably with that of other major countries; however, the average Japanese citizen's tax burden was still one of the lowest among developed countries. The ministry therefore proposed measures to increase local tax revenue from existing taxes, reduce tax incentives for large corporations and capital income, and increase the reliance on user charges.

Opinions about fiscal decentralization have differed sharply at the local government level. Financially stronger governments have favored decentralization as a way of mobilizing larger resources for their growing expenditures. They have demanded greater flexibility to determine both revenues and expenditures, and have generally been in favor of greater freedom of initiative in policymaking. Financially weaker local governments have been concerned that any shift in the regime might decrease the local allocation tax to which they would be entitled in the future. Therefore, they were in favor of reforms that would result in either larger transfers from the central government or smaller expenditure responsibilities for local governments, noting that, for the public bodies lacking the ability to raise revenues, decentralization may mean the "freedom to go bankrupt." Meanwhile, the central government, reflecting the resistance of the Japanese public to horizontal inequality, was concerned that fiscal decentralization might increase regional fiscal disparities, and eventually increase the need for resource transfers to local governments.

In contrast to the government, Japanese industry and financial institutions have generally associated decentralization with smaller, more efficient government, emphasizing the need to reduce the tax burden and improve public infrastructure. Opinions about fiscal decentralization among public finance experts have been sharply divided. While many have pointed to the need to restore local self-government as a means of enhancing government responsiveness to citizens' needs and improving efficiency of resource allocation, others have questioned the emphasis on individual preferences and local accountability, given the widely shared ideas of fairness in Japan.[12] Finally, the opposition parties recently raised the issue of decentralization in political debate, arguing that the clear division of responsibilities between different levels of government was essential for reinvigorating the Japanese society and economy (Ozawa, 1996).

Government Reform Initiatives

Historically, government initiatives to reform intergovernmental finances have arisen largely as a result of macroeconomic pressures. Thus, in the mid-1950s, Japan's local public finance system nearly collapsed under the burden of heavy borrowing to finance the rapidly rising local budget deficits, which prompted the central government to make a special temporary grant and create the system of fiscal equalization grants in 1954 (Mochida, 1997). Owing to buoyant economic growth and more stable revenues, the financial situation of local governments improved considerably between the mid-1950s and mid-1970s. Since then, however, both the central and local governments have been faced with declining revenue buoyancies and expanding expenditure requirements. Most recently, the recession of 1992–95 has led to a sharp slowdown in the growth of central and local revenues, while at the same time giving rise to the need for fiscal expenditures

---

[12]For a review of the academic debate on decentralization, see Mochida (1995).

to stimulate the economy. As a temporary measure, the central government allowed local governments to issue far more bonds than in "ordinary" years, and encouraged them at the same time to increase their capital spending to offset weak private spending. To place the additional bonds, local governments had to tap private sector funds, hence raising their indebtedness. The reform of local public finances has thus become intertwined with and dependent upon the progress of overall fiscal consolidation.

Partly in response to the growing strains of local public finance, in 1993 the Diet passed a resolution calling for greater decentralization, and in 1995, the Murayama coalition government enacted the Decentralization Promotion Law, which obliged the government to draw up a five-year decentralization plan and set up a committee in the Prime Minister's Office to advise on and monitor the decentralization process. While it represents an important step in political and administrative terms, the Decentralization Promotion Law remains vague on the overall objectives of decentralization and the methods for their implementation. Recent pronouncements by the government suggest that future reform initiatives are likely to focus on administrative reforms, in particular, further rationalization of expenditures.

Other recent reform initiatives include promotion of so-called hometown development projects (locally designed and implemented regional development projects); greater involvement of local governments in the design of social welfare programs that correspond to local needs and circumstances; and the debate on the relocation of the capital, which has highlighted the need to devolve authority to the local level and enhance the transparency, simplicity, and efficiency of government.[13]

Need for Reform

The need for fiscal decentralization arises not only from macroeconomic pressures but also from theoretical and empirical considerations of public sector efficiency. In particular, the decentralization hypothesis developed within the framework of public choice theory provides a strong efficiency rationale for fiscal decentralization. In addition, there is fairly strong empirical evidence on the tendency of the public sector in Japan to expand faster than in less centralized economies as a result of higher revenue and expenditure centralization.

---

[13]See Ministry of Home Affairs (1994) and Hashiyama (1996).

One of the clearest statements of the decentralization hypothesis was provided by Brennan and Buchanan (1980): the greater the extent to which taxes and expenditures are decentralized, the smaller should be, ceteris paribus, the overall involvement of the government in the economy. One set of arguments in support of this hypothesis rests on the premise of greater political competition between various fiscal jurisdictions (Tiebout, 1956). Thus, in a centralized setting, the monopoly power to extract resources through tax legislation is less challenged than within a decentralized, multilayer government, where citizens' access to comparative political "shopping" introduces a dimension of contestability on the political markets. This argument is believed to be particularly relevant at the local level (municipalities, counties) because of the influence of alternative tax-and-services packages on the locational choice of residents and businesses.

Another set of arguments focuses on the status of the budget constraint for different levels of government. In general, all levels of government are involved in allocation, but the opportunity for deficit spending through public borrowing and seigniorage creates a softer budget constraint for the central government than for lower levels of government. In a representative democracy, it is expected that the legislative representatives, after election, will articulate the fiscal preferences of their voters (including special interest groups) to safeguard their re-election. Under a soft budget constraint, the proportion of budgetary means available for discretionary use can generally be expected to be higher, and the political decision makers should, therefore, be able to give in more easily to the demands of interest groups and bureaucrats, as generally only a part of the tax bill has to be presented to voters or taxpayers. Therefore, one may expect that, other things being equal, the size of the public sector will be larger in a centralized setting.

The decentralization hypothesis has received fairly strong empirical support. In a recent study commissioned by the European Union, Moesen (1993) showed that an increase in the ratio of central government revenue to GNP by 1 percent raises the overall size of the public sector in industrial countries by 0.18 percent of GNP, while an increase in the ratio of central government expenditure to GNP of 1 percent raises the size of general government expenditure by 0.22 percent of GNP.[14] As predicted by the decentralization hypothesis, the degree of centralization is also found to have a strong positive effect on expenditure for transfers and subsidies.

---

[14]The sample included five federations and ten European unitary countries during the 1980s. See also Saunders (1988) and Moesen and Van Rompuy (1990).

Estimates of the relationship between historical changes in the degree of centralization and the size of the public sector in Japan yielded the following equations:

$$TEG = -0.3077 + 0.9253\ LDV + 0.5164\ CENR$$
$$(1.82)\quad\ \ (8.50)\qquad\quad\ (2.25)$$

$$\text{Adj. } R^2 = 0.83 \qquad SEE = 1.33$$

$$TEG = -0.4428 + 0.9475\ LDV + 0.7228\ CENE$$
$$(2.50)\quad\ \ (9.72)\qquad\quad\ (2.91)$$

$$\text{Adj. } R^2 = 0.85 \qquad SEE = 1.25$$

where
- TEG = total government expenditure (central plus local) in percent of GDP,
- LDV = five-period moving average of the dependent variable, TEG,
- $CENR$ = a measure of revenue centralization, that is, total revenue of central government (before transfers to local governments) in percent of total revenue (central plus local), and
- $CENE$ = a measure of expenditure centralization, that is, total expenditure of central government (including transfers to local governments) in percent of total expenditure (central plus local).

Both equations were estimated by OLS on the FY 1970–93 (settlement) data;[15] t-statistics are shown in parentheses.

The above regressions suggest that a 1 percent increase in the revenue centralization ratio increases the size of Japan's public sector by 0.52 percent of GDP, while a 1 percent increase in the expenditure centralization ratio increases the size of the public sector by 0.72 percent of GDP. These results indicate that the tendency of general government to expand as a result of higher revenue and expenditure centralization is much stronger in Japan than in other industrial countries.

Subsidiary regressions, where the above explanatory variables are regressed on the transfers-to-GDP ratio, indicate that these expansionary effects operate to an important degree through transfers to local governments: a 1 percent increase in the revenue centralization ratio increases the size of transfers to local governments by 0.2 percent of GDP, while a 1 percent increase in the expenditure centralization ratio increases the size of these transfers by 0.36 percent of GDP. Again, these

---

[15]For a detailed description of variables and sources of data, see the Appendix.

effects are considerably stronger than those obtained by Moesen (1993) and Moesen and Van Rompuy (1990) for industrial countries other than Japan.[16]

Options for Reform

The preceding sections identified several problems of local public finance in Japan: excessively tight expenditure controls, lack of freedom of local governments to determine local tax rates, and a relatively high dependence of local governments on grants and borrowing. This section outlines possible approaches to fiscal decentralization, taking into account the strengths of Japan's system of intergovernmental fiscal relations, in particular, its effectiveness in horizontal fiscal equalization and implementation of macrofiscal policy.

Relaxing Expenditure Controls

It seems fair to say that the devolution of powers to local governments that occurred after World War II has been largely aimed at achieving the goals of the central government (that is, to improve national welfare as a whole). The alternative would, therefore, seem to be freeing local governments from central controls (that is, improving *local* welfare). As discussed above, economic analysis, as well as political theory, does provide a strong rationale for the establishment of local governments that are responsive to the wishes of their citizens, instead of being simply the agencies of the central government. So long as there are local variations in preferences and costs, there are clearly efficiency gains from carrying out public sector activities in as decentralized a fashion as possible. The only services that should be provided centrally are those for which there are no differences in demands in different localities, where there are substantial spillovers between jurisdictions that cannot be handled in some other way (for example, by negotiation or by grant design), or for which the additional costs of local administration are sufficiently higher to outweigh its advantages.

The assignment of expenditure responsibilities in Japan formally conforms, to a large extent, to these principles. Therefore, the issue is not so much to change the assignments themselves, as to redefine responsibilities for designing, implementing, and financing these assign-

---

[16]Transfers include the local allocation tax, local transfer taxes, and specific-purpose grants to local governments. For details of these regressions, see the Appendix.

ments. One concern that is often expressed in this context is that local governments would allow the level and quality of public services to deteriorate below the standard considered desirable. This may be to a large extent a misplaced concern. If the service in question is of national importance (for example, health, education, or research) or one in which there is a strong national interest in maintaining standards (for example, poverty alleviation or some other distributional goal), such a service should remain nationally funded (at least in part) and its implementation monitored. If it is not a matter of national interest (for example, local roads or sewerage system), why should the national government be concerned? If the local electorate does not like what the local government does—or does not do—the government can be voted out of office at the next election. As is frequently emphasized in the public choice literature, the freedom to make mistakes and to bear the consequences of those mistakes is an important component of local autonomy (Bird, 1994).

A more effective devolution of spending responsibilities should be accompanied and supported by a strengthening of the capacities of the local authorities to manage expenditures. As in many countries, local government in Japan is generally considered to be less efficient than the central government. An important role in overcoming this efficiency gap could initially be played by local offices of the national administration, which in most cases possess the required skills and expertise—but not necessarily the sufficient workforce—to administer local spending programs effectively.

Managing Tax Diversity

As regards the local revenue system, prima facie there seems to be a strong case for allowing local governments more freedom in determining local taxes. In principle, local governments should not only have access to those revenue sources that they are best equipped to exploit—such as residential property taxes, income taxes, and user charges for local services—but they should also be both encouraged and permitted to exploit these sources without undue central supervision.

Local governments in Japan have relatively large receipts from what appear to be local taxes, but since they can neither set the tax rates nor determine the tax bases, it is difficult to see how they can be accountable to their constituents at the margin, as both efficiency and local autonomy require. As the economic role of local government is to provide to local residents those public services for which they are willing to pay, accountability is essentially the public sector equivalent of the "bottom line" in the private sector.

Large urban centers, which have a strong revenue base, usually also have much larger expenditure needs. Uniformity of the local tax code may thus prevent them from raising additional revenue that they need—and are able to raise. Although the central government allows local governments to vary the tax rate, the degree of flexibility is small: prefectures can raise the standard tax rate of the personal income tax up to 1.2 times the standard rate, and municipalities up to 1.5 times (up to 1.1 times and 1.2 times, respectively, in the case of the enterprise tax); but they cannot levy a tax rate lower than the standard rate (see the Appendix). Some flexibility in setting the consumption tax rate would also seem warranted. Such tax diversity takes account of different circumstances in which local governments operate, and different preferences over the mix of taxes and public goods.

It should be noted that most elements of the existing tax system—including the assignment of taxes, harmonized tax bases, and centralized collection and revenue sharing of certain taxes—can and should be preserved while allowing for the greater freedom of the local governments to determine the tax rates. In particular, the local allocation tax has proved quite effective as a tool of horizontal fiscal adjustment and should continue to be administered in as neutral a manner as possible. Finally, local governments should be encouraged to rely on user charges and fees for providing public services as much as possible.

A major concern that is expressed with respect to local tax diversity is that unharmonized tax structures can lead to distortions such as reduced tax neutrality, increased administrative and compliance costs, and tax exporting. However, recent empirical research has tended to reduce the validity of the case for tax centralization, partly because of a more favorable academic perception of the competitive process, and partly because more sophisticated empirical studies suggested that the quantitative importance of the potentially distorting effects from unharmonized tax structures was exaggerated in the traditional literature. In particular, the empirical work surveyed by Groenewegen (1988) indicates that differences in taxes were generally too small an element in business costs (or individuals' locational decisions); that tax differentials reflecting differential quality and costs in local public services were not necessarily perceived as inefficient; and that subnational tax policymakers often had real fear of the potential effects of tax competition and, hence, were not keen on creating tax havens.

Reducing Dependency on Grants and Borrowing

Local governments raise about 50 percent of revenue from local taxes and nontax sources, while another 20 percent comes from the local allocation tax, a revenue-sharing grant that can be regarded as essentially local governments' "own" revenue (albeit collected and distributed by the central government). Of the remainder, about 17 percent are specific purpose disbursements by the central government, designed to cover the costs of providing certain functions on behalf of the central government, and another 2 percent are earmarked revenue-sharing grants. Hence, if revenue-sharing grants are treated as local governments' own revenue, the level of grant dependency is about 17 percent of local revenue, and the overall revenue deficiency, that is, the amount raised through local borrowing, amounts to about 10 percent of local revenue. These ratios are, indeed, high—about 2¼ percent and 1¼ percent of GDP, respectively.

It is largely a matter of structural fiscal reform how to reduce the dependency of local governments on grant money and borrowing. The fiscal federalism theory cannot offer much guidance on this issue, except noting that promoting local autonomy is likely to help reduce the inefficient size of the local public sector. It should be recognized, however, that the need for large local borrowing arises to a certain extent because of the way the central government conducts macrofiscal policy. Given the flexibility that such an arrangement allows the policymakers, it is not entirely clear that the revenue gap should be closed completely through, for example, larger permanent transfers from the central government. Another point to note is that local borrowing is used almost exclusively to finance capital projects. Hence, to the extent that these projects are cost-effective and raise the long-run productivity of social capital, they do not necessarily have to be financed by taxes on the current generation of taxpayers.

As for the design of specific purpose grants and the modalities of borrowing, a number of improvements could be achieved. The main problem with specific purpose grants, recognized for a long time by the Japanese experts (see, for example, Yonehara, 1981; and Jichi Sogo Center, 1993) is that, although (or perhaps because) they contain very detailed provisions, they do not sufficiently take into account local circumstances and needs.[17] As noted earlier, the detailed nature of the these grants and their overall large volume can lead to inefficiency and frustration for both the central and local governments. The number of specific purpose grants should, therefore, be reduced to a few important expenditure areas. Other expenditures presently financed by specific purpose grants could be either devolved to local governments (and,

---

[17]In the case of construction works, for example, even the brands of construction materials and parts are sometimes specified by the central government.

hence, financed from their general revenue resources, including the local allocation tax) or, to the extent that they remain a central government responsibility, financed by grants-in-aid to local authorities, which would encourage local governments to take a more active role in implementing the activities deemed important by the national government.

From the perspective of the local authorities, the main issues concerning local borrowing are that procedures for loan applications are too complicated and time consuming, and that, in conducting countercyclical policy through variations in local borrowing, the central government does not take into account the burden of future interest payments by local governments. If local governments are to become more autonomous in their spending and taxation decisions, local borrowing should be facilitated through simplification of procedures for raising local loans. Given that financial markets in Japan are highly developed, there is no reason why the central government should be involved in almost every step of local loan raising.

The existence of ceilings on local borrowing has played an important role in maintaining the soundness of local government finances compared with the central government finances. However, such limits could be set more flexibly, for example, on the stock of debt at the local level rather than annual deficits, so as to allow local governments greater flexibility in responding to regional economic shocks. In this context, one should stress the need for transparent standing rules—linked, for example, to the projected ratio of debt service to revenue—for setting limits on the overall debt of local jurisdictions.

Given how tightly most aspects of local public finance in Japan are controlled, fiscal decentralization is not likely to produce exactly the pattern the central government—or local governments—would choose to implement if left to their own devices, except in the unlikely case that their goals precisely coincided. Conflicts between the central and local governments as to what should be decentralized are, therefore, inevitable. It should also be recognized that, in an economy as highly regulated as Japan's, the overall public sector efficiency may not simply increase as a result of shifting the expenditure responsibilities to local governments. Fiscal decentralization therefore must be accompanied by overall deregulation of economic activity. But if accessibility, local responsibility, and the effectiveness of government are to be improved, it is of fundamental importance that governments that are responsible for expenditure decisions should be responsible for raising the revenue to fund them and should have control over—and responsibility for—revenue sources adequate to enable them to do so.

Appendix. Summary of Local Public Finance in Japan

Expenditures

Table 6 illustrates the scale of public expenditure and intergovernmental transfers effected by the central and local governments in FY 1992.

On a net basis, the central government was responsible for about one-third of total expenditure (10 percent of GDP), and local governments for two-thirds (19 percent of GDP) in FY 1992. Transfers from the central to local governments consisted of the local allocation tax (52 percent), local transfer taxes (6 percent), and specific purpose grants (42 percent). Transfers from local governments to the central government were payments for certain public works carried out by the central government. Total transfers amounted to about 7 percent of GDP in FY 1992.

A standard classification of government expenditure by function in the IMF's Government Finance statistics framework is not available for Japan's local governments. Table 7 compiles such data on the basis of expenditure categories used in Japanese budgetary statistics. The entries for the central government are based on the initial budget for FY 1992; the entries for local governments are based on the settlement data. Both sets of data refer to gross expenditure (detailed breakdown on a net expenditure basis is not available). In view of these data limitations, the expenditure shares presented in Table 7 (as well as in Tables 9 and 10, which contain international comparisons of expenditure shares) should be regarded as illustrative only.

Table 8 presents a breakdown of expenditure by function at the level of prefectures and municipalities for FY 1990. The breakdown covers

Table 6. Japan: Central and Local Government Expenditure, FY 1992

	In Billions of Yen	In Percent of Total	In Percent of GDP
Gross expenditure	167,700	100.0	35.8
Central	77,141	46.0	16.5
Local	89,560	54.0	19.3
Transfers from			
Central to local	30,622	...	6.6
Local to central	1,274	...	0.3
Net expenditure	134,804	100.0	28.9
Central	46,518	34.5	10.0
Local	88,285	65.5	18.9

Source: Ministry of Home Affairs, Local Autonomy College (1995).

Table 7. Japan: Expenditure by Function and Level of Government, FY 1992

	Central[1]	Local[2]	Total	Central	Local	Total
	(In billions of yen)			(In percent)		
General public services, public order, and safety[3]	4,577	15,228	19,805	23.1	76.9	12.2
Defense	4,552	—	4,552	100.0	—	2.8
Education	5,683	18,406	24,089	23.6	76.4	14.9
Health[4]	4,104	5,614	9,664	42.2	57.8	6.0
Social security, welfare, and housing[5]	11,351	9,935	20,408	53.3	46.7	13.2
Economic affairs[6]	9,015	32,294	41,309	22.5	77.2	25.8
Debt service	16,447	7,115	23,562	69.8	30.2	14.6
Other[7]	16,122	968	17,090	94.3	5.7	10.6
Total	72,218	89,560	161,778	44.6	55.4	100.0

Sources: IMF staff estimates based on Ministry of Finance (1994); Ministry of Home Affairs, Local Autonomy College (1995); and Ministry of Home Affairs (1994).
[1]Based on the initial budget for FY 1992; gross expenditure basis.
[2]Based on settlement data for FY 1992; gross expenditure basis.
[3]For central government, includes miscellaneous expenditure; for local governments, includes local assembly, general administration, fire protection, and police.
[4]For central government, includes public health, government-managed health insurance, seamen's insurance, and subsidies to National Health Insurance.
[5]For central government, includes public assistance, social welfare, measures for the unemployed, employees' pension insurance, national pension, "pensions and others," children's allowance, other social insurance, and housing expenditure from the public works budget.
[6]For central government, includes public works (except housing), economic cooperation, and measures for small businesses, energy, and foodstuff control; for local governments, includes public works and measures for employment, agriculture, and trade and industry.
[7]For central government, includes local allocation tax and contingency; for local governments, includes disaster relief and miscellaneous.

expenditure financed by central government transfers, as well as prefectural transfers to municipal governments.

On the whole, prefectures had a slightly higher share in (gross) expenditure than municipalities in FY 1990 (52 percent, compared with 48 percent of total local expenditure). Prefectures carried out a higher proportion of expenditure on education and economic affairs than municipalities, while municipalities carried out a higher proportion of expenditure on social security, welfare, and health. Economic affairs were the main expenditure item for both prefectures and municipalities; education, general public services and public safety, and social security and welfare were the other major spending categories. Debt service accounted for a relatively high proportion of both prefectural and municipal spending.

To compare the composition of expenditure at the central and local levels of government in Japan with other countries, data from Table 7 were used along with the data from the IMF's *Government Finance Sta-*

Table 8. Japan: Local Expenditure by Function, FY 1990[1]
(In percent)

	Share in Gross Expenditure		Composition by Level of Government		
	Prefectures	Municipalities	Total local governments	Prefectures	Municipalities
General public services, public order, and safety[2]	47.3	52.7	18.9	17.3	20.6
Social security and welfare	29.0	71.0	10.6	6.0	15.5
Health	33.5	66.5	5.7	3.7	7.8
Education	64.2	35.8	20.1	25.0	14.8
Economic affairs[3]	54.9	45.1	34.0	36.2	31.7
Debt service	46.7	53.3	8.0	7.2	8.8
Other[4]	86.4	13.6	2.8	4.7	0.8
Total	51.6	48.4	100.0	100.0	100.0

Source: Jichi Sogo Center (1993).
[1] Based on settlement data for FY 1990; gross expenditure basis.
[2] Includes local assembly, general administration, fire protection, and police.
[3] Includes public works; employment and industrial relations; agriculture, forestry, and fisheries; and trade and industry.
[4] Includes disaster relief and miscellaneous.

tistics Yearbook for two unitary states—France and the United Kingdom—and two federations—the United States and Germany. As the data for Japan were not compiled on the same basis, these comparisons only illustrate an approximate order of magnitude of central and local expenditure shares (Table 9).

In interpreting the data in Table 9, it is important to note that, while the proportion of local government spending in Japan is relatively high for both total expenditure and individual spending categories (such as general administration and safety, education, health, and economic affairs), local governments have little effective control over the scope of spending that takes place at the local level. As discussed above, major programs (such as education, health, and public works) are in practice formulated by national ministries and financed directly or indirectly by the central government. Local governments in Japan execute these expenditure programs under detailed national direction, and, therefore, the degree of effective centralization of expenditure functions is higher than suggested by the above figures.

Table 10 compares the composition of expenditure at each level of government in Japan and four other industrial countries. As in Table 9, these comparisons are only an illustration of expenditure shares at each level of government, given that local government data for Japan are not available in the IMF's Government Finance Statistics format.

Table 9. Japan: International Comparison of Expenditure Shares by Level of Government and Function[1]
(In percent of expenditure on each function)

	Japan		France		United Kingdom		United States			Germany		
	Central	Local	Central	Local	Central	Local	Central	State	Local	Central	State	Local
General public services, public order, and safety	23	77	74	26	54	46	45	18	37	30	47	23
Defense	100	—	100	—	100	—	100	—	—	100	—	—
Education	24	76	74	26	15	85	4	25	72	2	75	23
Health	42	58	98	2	100	—	50	35	15	73	12	15
Social security, welfare, and housing	53	47	83	17	74	26	75	15	10	72	12	17
Economic affairs	23	77	71	29	74	26	42	36	22	46	27	26
Other	...	...	—	—	83	17	68	14	18	66	24	9
Total	44	56	83	18	71	29	59	18	23	61	22	18

Sources: International Monetary Fund (1990); and IMF staff estimates based on Ministry of Finance (1994) and Ministry of Home Affairs, Local Autonomy College (1995).

[1] Data for Japan are IMF staff estimates, based on Table 7. Data refer to the following years: FY 1992 for Japan, 1985 for France, 1988 for the United Kingdom and the United States, and 1987 for Germany.

Table 10. Japan: International Comparison of Expenditure Shares by Function and Level of Government[1]
(In percent of central or local expenditure)

	Japan		France		United Kingdom		United States			Germany		
	Central	Local	Central	Local	Central	Local	Central	State	Local	Central	State	Local
General public services, public order, and safety	6	17	8	13	7	14	7	9	15	4	18	11
Defense	6	—	7	—	12	—	27	—	—	9	—	—
Education	8	21	9	14	3	37	1	19	43	—	27	10
Health	6	6	24	3	14	—	10	23	8	19	9	13
Social security, welfare, and housing	16	11	45	42	34	30	30	19	10	51	23	40
Economic affairs	13	36	6	11	7	7	6	17	8	7	11	13
Other[2]	45	9	—	16	22	13	17	12	15	9	12	13

Sources: International Monetary Fund (1990); and IMF staff estimates based on Ministry of Finance (1994) and Ministry of Home Affairs, Local Autonomy College (1995).

[1] Data for Japan are IMF staff estimates, based on Table 7. Data refer to the following years: FY 1992 for Japan, 1985 for France, 1988 for the United Kingdom and the United States, and 1987 for Germany.

[2] For Japan, includes debt service, local allocation tax grants, and contingency.

Table 11. Japan: Local Government Revenue, FY 1990
(In percent of total)

	Prefectures	Municipalities	Total
Local taxes	39.9	38.7	41.6
Transfers from central government	36.8	25.6	33.1
Local transfer tax	1.8	2.1	2.1
Local allocation tax	18.2	15.5	17.8
Specific purpose grants	16.8	8.0	13.3
Charges and fees	2.2	2.4	2.4
Other revenue[1]	13.7	25.5	15.1
Local bonds[1]	7.3	7.8	7.8
Total	51.1	48.9	100.0
Memorandum items:			
Total revenue			
In billions of yen[1]	43,455	41,582	80,410
In percent of GDP	10.0	9.6	18.5

Source: Jichi Sogo Center (1993).
[1]Transfers from prefectures to municipalities are netted out from the total.

Compared with other industrial countries, local governments in Japan spend a relatively higher proportion of their budgets on general public services, safety, and economic affairs and a relatively lower proportion on social security, welfare, and health. Also, spending on education as a proportion of local budgets is lower in Japan than in the United Kingdom, the United States, and Germany. At the central level, the government in Japan spends about the same proportion on administration, defense, and education as the central government in France. The share of health and social security spending in Japan's central government budget is, however, lower than in the other industrial countries, while the share of expenditure on economic affairs (public infrastructure, agriculture, and energy) is higher.

Revenues

Total revenue of local governments consists of local taxes, central government transfers, nontax revenue, and local borrowing. The distribution of the main sources of revenue among prefectures and municipalities in FY 1990 is shown in Table 11.

Prefectures and municipalities raised roughly the same proportion of their revenue from local taxes, charges and fees, and local bonds. Central government transfers represent a higher proportion of prefectural revenue because prefectures carry out more functions on behalf of the central government than municipalities. On the other hand, munici-

Table 12. Japan: Major Taxes

	Local Taxes	
National taxes	Prefectural taxes	Municipal taxes
Income tax	Prefectural inhabitants tax	Municipal inhabitants tax
Corporation tax	Enterprise tax	Fixed assets tax
Inheritance tax	Real property acquisition tax	Light vehicle tax
Consumption tax[1]	Prefectural tobacco tax	Municipal tobacco tax
Liquor tax	Golf course usage tax	
Tobacco tax	Special local consumption tax	
Gasoline tax	Automobile tax	
Securities trade tax	Automobile acquisition tax	
Stamp tax	Light oil delivery tax	

[1]Twenty percent of the consumption tax is transferred directly to local governments.

palities raise more revenue from nontax sources such as income from properties, shares, reimbursements, and contributions.

The major national and local taxes assigned to the three levels of government are shown in Table 12.

Local taxes are generally levied on an identical tax base as national taxes. Some representative tax rates follow.[18]

Prefectural Taxes

- Prefectural inhabitants tax

    If filing as an individual:
    ¥700 a person (standard per capita tax)
    For annual income of ¥7 million or less: 2 percent
    For annual income over ¥7 million: 4 percent
    If filing as a corporation:
    Standard per capita tax: ¥20,000–800,000 per corporation, depending on capital plus reserve funds
    Standard tax rate: 5 percent of the national corporation tax
    Maximum tax rate: 6 percent of the national corporation tax

- Prefectural enterprise tax

    For ordinary corporations:

Taxable income	Standard tax rate	Maximum tax rate
Less than ¥3.5 million	6 percent	6.6 percent
¥3.5–7.0 million	9 percent	9.9 percent
Over ¥7 million	12 percent	13.2 percent

[18]For details, see Ministry of Finance, Tax Bureau (1996).

For cooperative associations:

Taxable income	Standard tax rate	Maximum tax rate
Less than ¥3.5 million	6 percent	6.6 percent
Over ¥3.5 million	8 percent	3.2 percent

- Real property acquisition tax

  Standard tax rate: 4 percent of the appraised value of land or house at the time of acquisition. Special deductions apply for certain residential properties.

Municipal Taxes

- Municipal inhabitants tax
  If filing as an individual:
  Per capita tax: ¥1,500–2,500 (maximum ¥2,000–3,200), depending on the size of municipality

Income tax	Standard rate	Maximum rate
For annual income up to ¥2 million	3 percent	4.5 percent
For annual income of ¥2–7 million	8 percent	12.0 percent
For annual income over ¥7 million	11 percent	16.5 percent

  If filing as a corporation:
  Lump sum tax: ¥50,000–3 million (maximum tax is 1.2 times the standard tax), depending on corporate capital plus reserve fund and the number of employees.
  Standard tax rate: 12.3 percent of the national corporation tax
  Maximum tax rate: 14.7 percent of the national corporation tax
  Capital gains from the sale of property are taxed separately.

- Municipal property tax: The standard tax rate is 1.4 percent (up to 2.1 percent maximum) of the cadastral value of land, houses, and depreciable assets. Special deductions and exemptions apply to certain residential properties.

Local governments are also assigned a large number of minor taxes, whose yield is small (0.1 percent of local tax revenue):

- Minor prefectural taxes: Local entertainment tax, meals and hotel tax, mine lot tax, hunter's registration tax, fixed assets tax, nonlegal ordinary tax, hunting tax, and water utilization and land benefit tax.

- Minor municipal taxes: Electricity tax, gas tax, mineral product tax, timber delivery tax, special landholding tax, nonlegal ordinary tax, spa tax, business office tax, city planning tax, water utilization and

Table 13. Japan: Central and Local Government Taxes, FY 1990

	In Billions of Yen	In Percent of Total	In Percent of GDP
Total collections	96,230	100.0	22.2
Central	62,780	65.2	14.5
Local	33,450	34.8	7.7
Prefectural	17,353	18.0	4.0
Municipal	16,097	16.8	3.7
Transfers from			
Central to local[1]	27,600	...	6.4
Local to central[2]	1,132	...	0.3
Prefectural to municipal[3]	1,868	...	0.4
Net allocation	96,230	100.0	22.2
Central	36,312	37.7	8.4
Local	59,918	62.3	13.8
Prefectural[4]	31,657	32.9	7.3
Municipal[5]	28,439	29.4	6.5

Sources: Ministry of Home Affairs, Local Autonomy College (1995); Jichi Sogo Center (1993); and IMF staff estimates.
[1] Includes local allocation tax, local transfer tax, and specific purpose grants to local governments.
[2] Contributions for central government projects.
[3] Includes municipal taxes collected by prefectures.
[4] Includes prefectural share of the local allocation tax, local transfer tax, and specific purpose grants.
[5] Includes municipal share of the local allocation tax, local transfer tax, and specific purpose grants.

land benefit tax, common facilities tax, land development tax, and national health insurance tax.

Table 13 describes the allocation of the tax revenue among the three levels of government in FY 1990.

The breakdown of prefectural and municipal taxes in FY 1992 is illustrated in Table 14.

On the whole, the share of municipalities in local taxes was higher than that of prefectures in FY 1992 (57 percent compared with 43 percent). Municipalities raised a higher proportion of their tax revenue from personal income and property taxes, while prefectures raised more tax revenue from corporate income and automobile taxes. Taxes raised by local governments amounted to 8 percent of GDP in FY 1992. As discussed below, this represents a relatively high proportion of total revenue by international standards.

Unlike the expenditure data, the revenue data compiled in Japan are fully comparable internationally. Table 15 presents the shares of three main revenue sources—taxes, nontax revenue, and grants—at each level of government in Japan and five other industrial countries.

The share of Japan's local governments in total tax revenue is about one-third, the same as in France but significantly higher than in the

Table 14. Japan: Local Tax Collections by Source, FY 1992
(In percent of total)

	Prefectural	Municipal	Total
Inhabitants tax	33.0	51.6	43.6
Individuals	19.8	37.7	30.0
Corporations	5.5	13.9	10.3
Interest income	7.7	...	3.3
Corporation tax	38.3	...	16.4
Property taxes[1]	4.6	37.2	23.2
Automobile taxes	13.4	0.5	6.0
Other	10.7	10.7	10.7
Total	43.0	57.0	100.0
Memorandum items:			
Total taxes			
In billions of yen	14,883	19,735	34,618
In percent of GDP	3.4	4.5	8.0

Source: Ministry of Home Affairs, Local Autonomy College (1995).
[1]For prefectures, includes real property acquisition tax and prefectural fixed assets tax; for municipalities, includes municipal fixed assets tax and special landholding tax.

United Kingdom and Italy. In terms of the share in total nontax revenue, Japanese local governments are comparable with states and local governments in the United States and Germany. Central governments in all industrial countries shown (except Italy) raise about 88 percent of their revenue from taxes. The share of grants in local revenue is roughly the same in Japan, France, and Italy. Finally, in terms of the GDP shares, local taxes in Japan amounted to about 7¾ percent of GDP in FY 1990, about one-third lower than in France (10½ percent of GDP in 1988), but higher than in the United Kingdom and Italy. The proportion of nontax revenue raised by local governments in Japan is highest among the countries shown (5¾ percent of GDP). Grants to subnational levels accounted for about 5 percent of GDP in all the countries shown except Italy.

Intergovernmental Transfers

Japan's central government makes three basic types of grants to local governments:

(1) Unconditional, general purpose revenue-sharing grants, referred to in Japan as the local allocation tax. These grants are essentially mandatory transfers of revenue from a number of national taxes (in whole or in part) to local governments. Specifically, the local allocation

Table 15. Japan: International Comparison of Revenue Assignment by Level of Government[1]

	Tax Revenue	Nontax Revenue	Grants	Tax Revenue	Nontax Revenue	Grants	Tax Revenue	Nontax Revenue	Grants
	(In percent, by source)			(In percent, by level)			(In percent of GDP)		
Japan									
Central	65.2	23.8	4.9	88	10	2	22.1	7.5	5.3
Prefectural	18.0	30.8	49.2	40	23	37	14.4	1.8	0.3
Municipal	16.7	45.4	45.9	39	35	26	4.0	2.3	2.6
							3.7	3.4	2.4
France									
Central	66.3	39.5	4.5	85	13	2	31.5	8.1	8.8
Local	33.7	60.5	95.5	44	21	35	20.9	3.2	0.4
							10.6	4.9	8.4
United Kingdom									
Central	87.0	60.3	3.7	88	12	1	29.9	5.8	5.4
Local	13.0	39.7	96.3	34	20	46	26.0	3.5	0.2
							3.9	2.3	5.2
Italy									
Central	97.2	40.9	4.7	93	3	3	24.6	2.2	17.1
Local	2.8	59.1	95.3	4	7	89	23.9	0.9	0.8
							0.7	1.3	16.3
United States									
Central	56.0	27.0	—	87	13	—	20.9	6.3	5.1
State	26.8	41.3	39.2	55	26	20	11.7	1.7	—
Local	17.2	31.7	60.8	42	22	36	5.6	2.6	2.0
							3.6	2.0	3.1
Germany									
Central	50.2	21.7	2.3	89	10	1	23.1	6	4.3
State	35.5	25.0	41.9	71	13	16	11.6	1.3	0.1
Local	14.3	53.3	55.8	37	36	27	8.2	1.5	1.8
							3.3	3.2	2.4

Sources: Organization for Economic Cooperation and Development (1990); and Jichi Sogo Center (1993).
[1] Data for Japan are for FY 1990, data for the United States are for 1987, and all other data are for 1988.

tax consists of 32 percent of the yield of the income tax, the corporation tax, and the liquor tax; 24 percent of the yield of the consumption tax;[19] and 25 percent of the yield of the tobacco tax.

The local allocation tax is divided into the ordinary allocation tax (94 percent of the total) and the special allocation tax (6 percent of the total), which is intended to compensate for shortfalls in the ordinary allocation tax. Local governments can spend the local allocation tax for any purpose, but the amounts transferred are designed so as equalize the fiscal capacity of local governments (see discussion below).

(2) Specific purpose grants, that is, transfers designed to finance (in whole or in part) the expenses related to specific local expenditure programs. The main objective of specific purpose grants is to achieve uniformity in the provision of local public services. Specific purpose grants are of two types: central government disbursements, which are further divided into: payments for "agency delegated tasks," that is, for tasks that are essentially central government responsibility but their execution is entrusted to local governments (for example, administration of health insurance and the provision of national pensions); the central government's obligatory share in certain local expenses (for example, salaries of public school teachers, contributions to construction work and disaster relief); and grants-in-aid to local authorities, that is, incentive subsidies used to encourage local governments to perform the activities deemed important by the national government.

(3) Local transfer taxes, which are essentially specific purpose, revenue-sharing grants, that is, taxes levied and collected by the national government on behalf of the prefectural and municipal governments (for example, vehicle tonnage and certain fuel taxes) and earmarked, for the most part, for specific purposes (such as local expenditure on roads).

Regression Variables and Data Sources

The variables used in the regressions reported in the section on Issues in Intergovernmental Finance were defined as follows:

> TEG = the sum of: central government expenditure on general account (settled), minus expenditure on transfers (local allocation tax, local transfer taxes, and specific purpose grants), plus local government expenditure in local public

---

[19]This percentage is applied to the central government's share of the consumption tax (that is, to the 80 percent of the yield of the tax). Local governments get an additional 20 percent of the total yield of the consumption tax as a direct transfer; this portion, however, falls outside the scope of the local allocation tax.

finance program; divided by fiscal year GDP. This variable represents general government net expenditure.

CENR = central government revenue on general account (settled), divided by the sum of: central government revenue on general account (settled), minus transfers to local governments (local allocation tax, local transfer taxes, and specific purpose grants), plus local government revenue in local public finance program. This variable measures the revenue centralization ratio.

CENE = central government expenditure on general account (settled), divided by the sum of: central government expenditure on general account (settled), minus expenditure on transfers (local allocation tax, local transfer taxes, and specific purpose grants), plus local government expenditure in local public finance program. This variable measures the expenditure centralization ratio.

All variables were obtained from Nomura Research Institute's 1994 database.

The following subsidiary regressions were also referred to in that section:

$$TRANS = -0.0919 + 0.1037\ LDV + 0.2044\ CENR$$
$$(0.90)\quad (1.58)\quad\quad (1.47)$$

Adj. $R^2 = 0.11$ SEE = 0.80

$$TRANS = -0.1984 + 0.1343\ LDV + 0.3606\ CENE$$
$$(1.88)\quad (2.32)\quad\quad (2.44)$$

Adj. $R^2 = 0.16$ SEE = 0.74

where the dependent variable, TRANS, is central government transfers to local governments (local allocation tax, local transfer taxes, and specific purpose grants) in percent of fiscal year GDP. Parameter estimates in the first equation are statistically significant at the 10 percent level (except the intercept); parameter estimates in the second equation are statistically significant at the 5 percent level.

References

Bingman, Charles F., 1989, *Japanese Government Leadership and Management* (New York: Macmillan).

Bird, Richard M, 1994, "Threading the Fiscal Labyrinth: Some Issues in Fiscal Decentralization," *National Tax Journal*, Vol. 46 (June), pp. 207–27.

Brennan, Geoffrey, and James M. Buchanan, 1980, *The Power to Tax: Analytic Foundations of a Fiscal Constitution* (Cambridge, England: Cambridge University Press).

Groenewegen, Peter, 1988, "Taxation and Decentralization: A Reconsideration of the Costs and Benefits of a Decentralized Tax System," in *Taxation and Fiscal Federalism: Essays in Honour of Russell Matthews*, ed. by Geoffrey Brennan, Bhajan S. Grewal, and Peter Groenewegen (Sydney: Australian National University).

Hashiyama, Reijiro, 1996, "Whither the New Capital," *Look Japan* (June), pp. 14–15.

International Monetary Fund, 1990, *Government Finance Statistics Yearbook 1990* (Washington: International Monetary Fund).

Ishihara, Nobuo, 1993, "The Local Public Finance System," in *Japan's Public Sector: How the Government Is Financed*, ed. by Tokue Shibata (Tokyo: University of Tokyo Press).

Jichi Sogo Center, 1989, *Statistical Abstract of Japanese Local Public Finance* (Tokyo: Jichi Sogo Center).

———, 1993, *The Situation of Local Public Finance in Japan* (Tokyo: Jichi Sogo Center).

Ministry of Finance, Budget Bureau, 1994, *The Japanese Budget in Brief* (Tokyo: Ministry of Finance).

———, Tax Bureau, 1996, *An Outline of Japanese Taxes, 1995* (Tokyo: Ministry of Finance).

Ministry of Home Affairs, 1984, "Local Administration and Finance," in *Public Administration in Japan*, ed. by Kiyoaki Tsuji (Tokyo: University of Tokyo Press).

———, 1994, *The Japanese Local Public Finance System* (Tokyo: Ministry of Home Affairs).

———, General Affairs Office, 1995, *Source Material on the Bill on the Promotion of Regional Decentralization* (in Japanese) (Tokyo: Ministry of Home Affairs).

Ministry of Home Affairs, Local Autonomy College, 1995, *Local Public Finance in Japan* (Tokyo: Ministry of Home Affairs).

Mochida, Nobuki, 1985, "The Role of Local Government Expenditures in Pre-War Japan," *Annals of the Institute of Social Science*, Vol. 26, March.

———, 1995, "Balancing Equity and Decentralization," *Social Science Japan* (November), pp. 10–11.

———, 1997, "Revenue, Expenditure, and Intergovernmental Transfers in Japan," paper presented at the World Bank/Economic Development Institute Workshop on Local Government and Economic Development in Japan, Kobe, Japan, January 3–5.

Moesen, Wim A., 1993, "Community Public Finance in the Perspective of EMU: Assignment Rules, the Status of the Budget Constraint, and Young Fiscal Federalism in Belgium," in Commission of the European Communities, *The Economics of Community Public Finance, European Economy*, Vol. 5.

———, and Paul Van Rompuy, 1990, "The Growth of Government Size and Fiscal Decentralization," in *Public Finance With Several Layers of Government*, ed. by Rémy Prud'homme (Brussels: Foundation Journal of Public Finance).

Organization for Economic Cooperation and Development, 1990, *Revenue Statistics 1965–89* (Paris: Organization for Economic Cooperation and Development).

Ozawa, Ichiro, 1996, "Reforming Japan: The Third Opening," *The Economist* (March 9), pp. 21–23.

Saunders, Peter, 1988, "Explaining International Differences in Public Expenditure: An Empirical Study," *Public Finance*, Vol. 43, pp. 271–94.

Shindo, Muneyuki, 1984, "Relations Between National and Local Government," in *Public Administration in Japan*, ed. by Kiyoaki Tsuji (Tokyo: University of Tokyo Press).

Tiebout, Charles, 1956, "A Pure Theory of Local Expenditures," *Journal of Political Economy*, Vol. 64 (October), pp. 416–24.

Yonehara, Junshichiro, 1981, *Local Public Finance in Japan* (Canberra: Centre for Research on Federal Financial Relations, Australian National University).

———, 1993, "Financial Relations Between the National and Local Governments," in *Japan's Public Sector: How the Government Is Financed*, ed. by Tokue Shibata (Tokyo: University of Tokyo Press).

13

Switzerland

Paul Bernd Spahn

Switzerland is a confederation composed of 26 cantons (and half cantons) of unequal size, topography, and economic potential. Its population exhibits a great variety of cultural backgrounds, languages, religions, settlement characteristics, and economic activities. While some regions at the crossroads between Italy, France, and Germany have benefited from international trade for centuries, others remained more secluded because of mountainous conditions and geographical isolation.[1] These factors account for large regional disparities and imbalances within the Swiss economy. In recent times, some formerly remote areas have experienced dramatic changes to their economies owing to transalpine traffic and tourism, with a notable impact on the ecology. Swiss attitudes are thus characterized by the protection of minority groups, the preservation of cultural diversity, mutual consideration and assistance, and the care for the environment—which has constitutional rank. Such attitudes have also shaped institutional political arrangements.

Switzerland has one of the oldest federal traditions dating back to the Everlasting Alliance of 1291, when three cantons formed a union

---

[1] Recently, the discrepancies between the German, French, and Italian cantons have widened sharply. This is true both in terms of economic performance (for example, unemployment is much higher in the French- and Italian-speaking cantons than in German-speaking cantons), as well as in terms of international orientation on the key question of membership in the European Union. Whereas the French- and Italian-speaking cantons favor membership, the German-speaking cantons oppose it strongly. These increasing economic and political diversities have put pressure on intergovernmental relations.

to resist Habsburg rule. In 1815, Switzerland's independent political status was confirmed by the Congress of Vienna, and the Swiss Confederation was constituted in its present boundaries. In 1848 a formal federal Constitution was adopted for Switzerland, which until then had consisted of a loose confederacy of regions. The present arrangements are based on this first Constitution, which, however, has been amended several times, notably through the important overhaul of 1874, which was strongly influenced by the U.S. model of federalism.

Structure of Government

The basic elements of Swiss federalism are the following:
- The cantons[2] are legally sovereign states, unless their sovereignty is explicitly limited by the Constitution (Article 3 of the Constitution). Likewise, municipalities have considerable legal autonomy and political power although they are not fully sovereign.
- The confederation is based on the idea of equality between its constituents, the cantons, which is reflected in the role of the Council of States, the upper house of parliament. Its voting procedure accords equal weight to each canton, large or small.[3]
- The Constitution provides for a vertical distribution of responsibilities among layers of government, yet, as in Germany, the lower tiers of government also perform functions that are delegated from above. Thus, it is difficult to discern a clear vertical distribution of functions among the authorities. There are also elements of cooperative federalism, horizontal cooperation (through ministerial conferences), and expert-based discussions and consulting procedures (*Vernehmlassungsverfahren*), whereby government agencies of different levels, political parties, and economic and social groups are involved in preparing legislation. Formal collective decision-making bodies are lacking, however.
- Revenue as well as expenditure functions are distributed independently among the tiers of government. Each authority has its own

---

[2]Three of the 23 cantons are divided into half cantons. In addition, there is a municipal substructure of about 3,000 communes that are under cantonal control. As in Germany—and contrary to Australia—this latter layer of government is very important in Switzerland. Since the cantons may delegate government functions to their communities at extremely varying degrees, it is best to treat the state level in Switzerland inclusive of communal services (and revenues).

[3]Each of the 20 full cantons has two representatives in the Council of States; the six half cantons have one representative each.

budget, yet the budgets are interrelated through a network of intergovernmental transfers.
- Constraints are imposed on both expenditures and revenues by the political system of direct democracy. Voters are not only asked to elect representatives, they are frequently called to the polls to decide on all proposed constitutional changes and on specific pieces of legislation (including projects to amend federal tax financing). Federal referendums must not only be approved by a majority of voters, but also by a majority of the cantons.
- Regional diversity, in combination with cantonal sovereignty and direct democracy, has led to different levels in the provision of regional public goods and to significant variations in regional tax laws.[4] The communes—which have no independent tax sovereignty—may levy surcharges on cantonal taxes with varying annual coefficients.

The Swiss model of federalism is complex not only because of the complicated network of intergovernmental relations but also because it interacts with the system of semidirect democracy and proportional representation of parties, which aims at maintaining close links between authorities and citizen-voters. Such arrangements reflect the importance accorded to the protection of minorities, and they entail specific forms of constitutional and legislative procedures (see below).

Current Arrangements

Expenditure Assignment

The Constitution attributes to each layer of government so-called principal responsibilities. Article 8 of the Constitution empowers the confederation to deal with foreign affairs, but cantons are also allowed to enter into international agreements "on matters of neighborly relations" (Article 9).

The exclusive responsibilities of the confederation are in defense, external relations, citizenship and the status of foreigners, political asylum, civil and penal law, social protection, policies on property, economic order, money and currency, energy policy, and national transportation and telecommunication (see Table 1 for a list of constitutional provisions). Exclusive competences of the cantons are in the

---
[4]For income tax, for instance, where sovereignty is shared by the confederation and the cantons, there are 26 + 1 different tax codes with varying definitions for tax bases, exemptions, and deductible items, as well as for tax rates.

maintenance of public order, public welfare, establishments of health care, schools and education, the relationship between state and church, regional and local land planning, roads, and the use of water and other resources. All other domains—the Constitution mentions in particular health, the protection of the environment, culture, the fostering of research, science and arts, universities and vocational education—are presumed to be the responsibility of cantons unless federal law assigns functions otherwise. Where responsibility in such areas is conferred to the confederation, policies are generally implemented at the cantonal level. But even where the Constitution assigns functions to the central government, it often provides a "fallback" position at the local level, for example, for public welfare for the needy (Article 48).

This division of responsibilities is, however, not easily discernible from the budget or financial accounts and certainly not fully reflected in the structure of government expenditures. As in the case of Germany, cooperation among authorities and the delegation of executive functions to lower levels of government—in combination with intergovernmental transfers of resources—make it difficult to assess the political significance of public authority from the vertical breakdown of public outlays as shown in Table 2.[5]

The extensive network of payments, subsidies, incentives, joint financing, and delegation of competences that has evolved over the years tends to blur the identification of spending authorities, as well as their accountability. Such complexities may also have contributed to hoisting particular private interests over national or regional policy objectives in some instances (Bieri, 1979, p. 48).

Tax Assignment

The Swiss Constitution is very explicit in separating taxing powers vertically. Originally, the center government collected all the indirect taxes (customs duties and excises), and cantonal and municipal governments were ascribed direct taxes (income and wealth taxes). Over the years, the confederation has, however, acquired powers in the realm of income taxation as well. This was mainly dictated by vertical fiscal imbalances and diverging revenue needs—not by stabilization policies. In the Swiss case, the federal income tax was introduced during World War I—in the disguise of a defense tax. World War II saw the introduction of yet another important federal tax, the turnover tax (a

---

[5]The sum of outlays of each level of government exceeded the consolidated total by more than 20 percent in 1993.

Table 1. Switzerland: Exclusive Responsibilities of the Confederation According to the Swiss Constitution

Category	Rule in Favor of the Confederation	Restrictions in Favor of the Cantons
General provisions	Articles 2 and 5.	Articles 3, 6, and 7.
Defense and civil protection	Articles 8 (general), 20 (military corps), 22 (military camps), and 22[bis] (civil protection).	Exception: Article 9 ("neighborly relations").
External relations	Articles 8 (general) and 28 (customs).	
Macroeconomic policies	Article 31[quinquies] (countercyclical policy and employment policies).	
Money and currency	Articles 31[quater] (banking), 38 (coining), and 39 (banknotes).	
Citizenship and status of foreigners	Articles 44 and 45[bis] (citizenship), 66 (loss of civil rights), 68 (stateless), 69[ter] (status of foreigners), and 70 (expulsion of foreigners).	Cooperation of cantons is generally required. Articles 60 and 61 (reciprocity, equality of status mandate).
Law and order	Article 64[bis] (penal law).	Article 50 (public order, religious freedom) and 56 (regulation of associations).
Welfare and social protection	Articles 34[bis] (health and accident insurance), 34[ter] (labor relations), 34[quater] (old-age pensions and insurance), 34[quinquies] (family policies), 34[sexies] and [septies] (housing), and 34[novies] (unemployment insurance).	Article 48 (subsidiary aid to the needy).
Policies on property and territory	Articles 22[ter] (protection of property rights), 22[quater] (use of property), and 23 (public interest and expropriation).	
Economic order	Articles 24 and 24[bis] (water and forestry), 24[ter] (shipping), 25 (fishing, hunting), 31 (freedom of commerce), 31[bis] (restrictions on the freedom of commerce), 31 (consumer protection), 31[septies] (price controls), 34 (child labor, labor protection), 40 (measures), and 64 (trade in mobile property).	Articles 31 and 31[ter] (business regulations), 32 (cooperation for price controls), and 33 (certification of scientific personnel). Responsibility for implementation.
Energy policies	Articles 24[quater] (electricity) and 24[quinquies] (nuclear energy).	
National transportation and telecommunications	Articles 26 (railways), 26[bis] (pipelines), 36 (postal and telecommunication policies), 36[bis] (national roads), 36[ter] (earmarking of mineral oil tax), 37 (control on cantonal roads and bridges), and 37[ter] (air traffic).	Article 36[bis] (implementation and maintenance of roads, national roads) and 27[bis] (restrictions on traffic).

Table 1 *(concluded)*

Category	Rule in Favor of the Confederation	Restrictions in Favor of the Cantons
Environment	Articles 24[septies] and [octies] (pollution control, renewable energy), 24[novies] (abuse of genetic engineering), and 36[sexies] (transit traffic and ecology).	Article 24[sexies] (protection of the natural environment). Implementation is responsibility of cantons.
Promotion of culture, radio, and television	Articles 27[ter] (film), 27[quater] (stipends and aid to students), 27[quinquies] (sports), 27[sexies] (promotion of science), and 55[bis] (radio, television).	Cooperation with cantons needed.
Intergovernmental relations	Articles 42[ter] (equalization among cantons) and 42[quinquies] (tax harmonization).	
Special issues	Articles 32[bis] and [ter] (liquor: quality control, production, and import), 40[bis], and 41 (abuse of weapons and ammunition), 69 and 69[bis] (health protection, infectious diseases).	Articles 32[quater] (regulation of liquor trading) and 35 (gambling).

wholesale sales tax). Both "emergency taxes" stayed on, and their introduction was later sanctioned by a constitutional amendment. However, the law fixes maximum rates for these federal taxes, and "sunset" dates were established for their expiry.[6]

As to present arrangements, the following vertical assignment of taxes prevails in Switzerland:

- Indirect taxation on private expenditures (value-added tax), excises, and customs duties are exclusively federal.
- Tax bases of direct taxes on personal income and wealth and on business income and wealth are exploited concurrently by all levels of government, including municipalities—with priority given to the cantons.[7]

---

[6]The constitutional basis for the confederation's direct tax and turnover tax ended in 1994. A proposal for a tax reform securing revenue for the confederation was rejected in 1991, forcing the government to embark on an emergency program and, later, on a fourth referendum on introducing a value-added tax (VAT) in Switzerland. This referendum was accepted in November 1993 granting the adoption of VAT at the beginning of 1995. Again, a sunset date was established (the year 2006), and the vote, once again, limits the rate by the Constitution, at 6.5 percent, which is significantly lower than that in neighboring countries and well below the minimum rate established for members of the European Union (15 percent) (see Article 41[ter] of the Constitution).

[7]There is opposition against the federal government exploiting direct taxes, however, and a conforming constitutional initiative was lodged in November 1993.

Table 2. Switzerland: Government Budgets, 1995

	Confederation	Cantons	Communes	Total[1]
	(In percent of consolidated total outlays)			
Outlays	36.7	47.2	34.6	100.0
Revenues	32.7	45.4	33.9	93.5
Deficit	4.1	1.8	0.7	6.5
	(In percent of GDP)			
Outlays	11.2	14.4	10.5	30.5
Revenues	10.0	13.9	10.3	28.5
Deficit	1.2	0.5	0.2	2.0

Source: International Monetary Fund, *Government Finance Statistics Yearbook*, 1996.
[1] Items may not add up to 100 owing to the elimination of double-accounting for the total. Budgeted figures may not coincide with financial accounts.

- As a matter of principle "each tier of government is endowed with a full or partial tax authority for a number of taxes and not only one. Cantons and communes have also the right to levy user charges and fees for those services where this is appropriate" (Dafflon, 1991).
- The cantons have an exclusive right to tax motor vehicles.

The bestowal of independent taxing powers to each layer of government enables the federal as well as regional governments to discharge their functions effectively without being dependent on each other. Contrary to Australia, for instance, cantonal dependence on grants is low in Switzerland, amounting to an average of roughly 20 percent of their budgets. If revenue sharing is included, it is about 27 percent. It should be noted, however, that the figure for grants comprises 7½ percent of municipal contributions to cantonal services—hence upward-oriented vertical grants. If these grants are deducted, the total dependency of cantons on the confederation is below 20 percent of their budget receipts (Dafflon, 1991).

Competing taxing powers at the two levels of government and diversity in fiscal federal arrangements create enormous problems of tax coordination, tax competition, and harmonization in Switzerland (Dafflon, 1986). Although the Constitution mandates the avoidance of cantonal double-taxation, legislation was slow to respond, and the principles governing horizontal tax coordination were largely developed by the Courts of Justice. The variety and complexity of subnational tax systems is only rivaled by that of the United States where tax competition as well as vertical and horizontal tax coordination has been a major concern for years. In Switzerland, case law has, however, established a uniform practice as regards which canton is allowed to tax which part of the income of individuals and companies.[8] Some of the constitutional provisions attempting to cope with intercantonal double taxation or prohibiting special taxation of industries (Articles 46(2) and 31 of the Swiss Constitution) evoke conforming instruments embodied in the U.S. federal arrangements (like the "immunity doctrine" or the "due process of law clause" of the Fifth Amendment).

Equalization, Revenue Sharing, and Grants

Switzerland has a strong tendency to equalize differences in taxable capacity through asymmetrical vertical grants provided by the central government. The objective is to enable the cantons to provide similar levels of services without forcing them to levy taxes that are significantly more onerous than in other cantons. This prescript is firmly entrenched in the federal law on equalization of 1959. The principle of "uniformity of living conditions"—typical for German equalization arrangements—is not adhered to in Switzerland, however (Bieri, 1979, p. 12).

The redistributive aims are mainly achieved through three types of vertical financial adjustments: federal tax reimbursements, tax sharing, and specific purpose grants (usually conditional grants-in-aid).

Similar to Australia at the inception of the federation, the Swiss Confederation reimburses part of the revenues collected from customs duties (yet only on fuel and petrol). This reflects the fact that the confederation has delegated certain responsibilities (especially road building) to the cantons to be administered by them on behalf of the central government. The horizontal incidence of these payments is very complex, since they are mainly related to cantonal expenditures on road construction and improvement. Although financial assistance is calculated in accordance with these functions—and on a fiscal capacity indicator, which is discussed below—these transfers are essentially unconditional.

Tax sharing is often portrayed in Switzerland as a means to compensate the cantons for their tax sovereignties forgone as these were transferred to the confederation (Higy, 1973, p. 8). Such means, which have recently become more important under pressure from cantonal governments, can also be interpreted to form unconditional general revenue grants. They are basically distributed in accordance with regional revenue collection, population, and the canton's relative fiscal needs, measured in terms of a statistical indicator. Tax-sharing revenues thus form

---

[8]For a further discussion see, for instance, Dafflon (1977), pp. 88ff.

part of an asymmetrical vertical perequation scheme that is closed ended.

The scheme can be imagined to work in two steps: (1) the federal contribution may be thought of as constituting a "closed pool"; and (2) horizontal perequation is then achieved through rules similar to those of the German *Finanzausgleich* (equalization among states).[9]

In 1992, tax sharing encompassed three revenue sources. The cantons received 30 percent of the federal direct tax on income and profits, 10 percent of the withholding tax, and 20 percent of a tax on exemption from military service.[10] The latter tax share is distributed among the cantons on a derivation basis without equalization provisions. The direct tax share is allocated partly on the same basis and partly according to the fiscal capacity indicator discussed below. Revenue sharing from the withholding tax is allocated to the cantons according to population for one half, and according to fiscal capacity for the other half.

Traditionally, vertical intergovernmental transfers have been dominated by conditional grants-in-aid to be applied in accordance with policy priorities of the federal government. Conditional grants given to cantons by the confederation are usually closed ended with matching requirements. Some grants are provided with "pass through" obligations, that is, they have to be handed down to municipalities, sometimes together with mandatory additional funding of the canton.

In addition to providing funds for specific state functions according to national priorities, federal conditional grants are also intended to have some equalizing effect. As for tax reimbursement grants and for tax sharing, their horizontal allocation is partly based on a cantonal fiscal capacity measure.

In order to stabilize its own budget, the confederation has frequently reduced its grants to the cantons in equal proportions. This has diminished the equalization effects embedded in the arrangements because poorer cantons are harder hit under this approach. It also renders the distribution scheme inflexible and does not allow setting priorities that vary across regions. Moreover, the specific purpose grants have been

---

[9]The federal government's contribution to such a "pool" was zero in Germany before unification, hence the pool must be filled through contributions made by the richer states. As to its impact on horizontal fiscal incidence the Swiss model is, however, rather similar to that of the German *Finanzausgleich*. In particular, if a canton's fiscal capacity falls, the compensating fiscal effect of the revenue-sharing grant is made up by other cantons, not by the confederation.

[10]This tax is paid by male Swiss citizens exempted from military service. It is essentially a poll tax that is proportional to income and inversely related to the number of days of military service completed.

criticized as rendering cantonal budgets rigid and entailing waste of resources. A major reform project was therefore initiated at the end of 1996 that aims to separate more clearly general revenue grants and equalization, on the one hand, and specific purpose payments and political control, on the other. It also attempts to render the grants system more efficient.

Fiscal Capacity and Equalization

Measurement of the cantons' fiscal capacity has been modified several times. The actual formula comprises four ingredients (Dafflon, 1991).
- *The canton's (adjusted) fiscal revenue per capita.* This includes cantonal and local tax revenue from all sources (adjusted for differences in tax effort in order to obtain comparable figures).
- *The canton's GDP per capita.* Not only fiscal resources are stressed in the formula, but also private income (which seems to be a natural indicator of fiscal capacity); this is different from Germany or Australia where only public revenue is considered in the formulas for horizontal perequation.
- *Regional (cantonal and local) tax effort.* In a federation that accords a large degree of tax discretion to regional governments, no canton can be allowed to benefit from higher grants by reducing its own fiscal effort below an acceptable level.[11]
- *The canton's specific expenditure requirements.* These enter the formula in a rather modest way—similar to expenditure needs in the German *Finanzausgleich*. Differences in the costs of providing services in mountainous regions are expressed by an indicator measuring the relative importance of agricultural areas below 800 meters; another proxy for differences in costs is relative population density. These indicators may appear to be quite crude, especially in comparison to the criteria developed by the Commonwealth Grants Commission in Australia.

Despite these provisions for horizontal perequation through asymmetrical vertical revenue sharing and grants, equalization is generally less important in Switzerland than in other Western federations—except the United States. The main outcome has been to increase the amount of subsidies given to poorer cantons, a virtually self-perpetuating category (Frey, 1977, pp. 98–100). As one prominent writer on

---

[11]A similar correction is made for horizontal perequation through special grants in Australia. In Germany—with its uniformity in taxation—such a criterion is not applied (and would not make much sense).

Swiss federalism has concluded: "equalization in grant programs is of subsidiary interest only" in Switzerland (Dafflon, 1989, p. 213).

Borrowing

In principle, each public constituency is autonomous and independent in its budgetary procedures in Switzerland, including borrowing. Yet this does not mean that there is no effective budget constraint on deficit spending. The idea of "sound financing" of public budgets is firmly entrenched in people's minds, and this consensus view governs fiscal federal arrangements in general. Moreover, direct democracy has secured that soft financing through money creation is prohibited by law, and obligatory finance referendums—or the mere threat of calling to the polls in the case of facultative referendums—act as an effective constraint on loan finance, as they do on taxation. The "golden rule" is formally established, which permits borrowing only for investment purposes on a pay-as-you-use basis. Article 42bis of the Constitution obliges the federal government to consolidate budget deficits with due "consideration for the state of the economy." At the local level, borrowing is limited by law in most cantons, which apply the golden rule to their municipalities as well.

According to the Constitution, cantonal laws, or municipal decrees, the following can be subject to referendums: "engagement credits or project appropriations, the estimates (of the budget) as a whole, individual payment credits or annual appropriations, or loans" (Bieri, 1979, p. 70). Although the importance of finance referendums has declined, the eventuality of such referendums and a broad consensus on the issue seems to have worked, in the past, as an effective constraint on public borrowing. During the 1980s, Swiss governments produced even small financial surpluses. At the beginning of the 1990s, however, public budgets started to drift into deficits that reached 4.6 percent of GDP in 1993. This was mainly owing to cyclical aspects that predominantly affected the budget of the confederation, while municipalities were able to improve their fiscal position during this time.

Although budget deficits have recently been reduced significantly for the total public sector (2½ percent of GDP in 1996), despite continued economic stagnation, the experience of rising public borrowing requirements has spurred a discussion on constitutional limitations of deficit spending. An initiative was started in 1995 with a *Vernehmlassungsverfahren* (procedure to consult all interest groups involved) that recommended to reduce and stabilize the ratio of public expenditures to GDP rather than the deficit ratio itself. This may eventually find its way into the Constitution although it is yet unclear which form it may take.

Administrative Structure

Tax Administration

As in Germany, the administration of taxes is highly decentralized in Switzerland. Each layer of government administers its own taxes, with some compensation for administrative costs incurred for shared taxes. This reflects independent taxing autonomy of subcentral governments and the multiplicity of cantonal tax laws that have sprung from it. Unlike in Germany, however, tax administration is not necessarily guided by uniform rules and procedures, as tax legislation for one and the same tax might differ significantly among regions. The assessment of multicantonal companies is a burdensome task both for the private sector and for tax administrators, since the rules to avoid double taxation among regions have become rather complex over the years. Significant cooperation and exchange of information among fiscal administrations is required, rendering the process of tax assessment and verification very cumbersome. The notion of a "tax jungle" is often used in connection with Swiss taxation and its administrative intricacies.

Attempts made in Switzerland in the mid-1970s to introduce a uniform federal income tax with cantonal participation or to impose uniform cantonal direct taxes throughout the nation were both defeated. Following a constitutional amendment in 1977, the confederation has chosen the avenue of some formal tax harmonization of income taxes, and, more recently, harmonization of direct cantonal and communal taxation was successful to some extent, following conforming legislation.[12] Furthermore, a referendum on the introduction of a VAT held in November 1993 was positive. This illustrates both the Swiss electorate's willingness to accept basic reforms and a mounting disposition toward centralization and harmonization. Such change might also have been spurred by developments in neighboring countries, notably in the European Union, as well as by recent tendencies in world capital markets and international tax competition.

Budget Formulation and Implementation

Budgetary procedures in Switzerland differ significantly from those in other countries. Items to be included in the budget must have been legislated upon beforehand, and budget appropriations cannot be intro-

---

[12]*Loi fédérale du 14 décembre 1990 sur l'harmonisation des impôts directs des cantons et des communes.* The cantons and communes were given eight years to adapt their respective legislation. After this term, federal rules will apply automatically. At the same time, the federal law on direct taxation has been coordinated.

duced in their own right. In other words, "public budgets are not material financial laws enacted by Parliament, but only documents or formal laws that are established by the government and discussed by Parliament. The power of the Legislature to decide priorities and the amounts of public outlays is limited" (Dafflon, 1977, p. 72).

The budget as well as medium-term financial planning—a planning tool of the Federal Council—serve mainly to establish a coherent view on public finances and on its macroeconomic impact. Its classification is by government function and types of expenditure as well as economic categories and modes of financing. The budget is established both on a cash flow and an accrual basis, and it also allows monitoring of government commitments.

The peculiarity of Swiss public budgeting shifts political responsibilities on to legislative and constitutional procedures rather than parliament and the budget itself. It is through these procedures that direct democracy comes into play. Although legislation is normally initiated by the parliament, the Constitution allows the electorate to challenge any proposition by constitutional initiatives, and the demand must eventually be put to the nation in a referendum. Similarly, any cantonal government can compel the government to examine draft legislation by the Councils.

Examination typically leads to the appointment of a Select Committee that opens consultation with public authorities, political parties, special interest groups, and organizations (*Vernehmlassungsverfahren*).[13] While this process allows some particular interests to creep in, it also ensures that legislation is based on a broad social consensus.

Implications

Macroeconomic Management

Traditional theory of federalism suggests that macroeconomic management rests on a degree of centralization of government spending functions, as well as on the power (and willingness) to use the budget as a fiscal policy instrument. In Switzerland, the Constitution obliges the federal government to make provisions for balanced economic growth and all tiers of government to consider conjunctural aspects when establishing their budgets (Article 31^{quinquies}); however, a highly decentralized public sector, as well as complex budgeting procedures, do

---

[13]For a further discussion of constitutional and legislative procedures in Switzerland, see Laufenburger (1961) or a summary in Dafflon (1977), p. 72ff.

not seem to be auspicious for macroeconomic stability. The lack of fiscal cooperation among the cantons and between the cantons and the federation appears to impede fiscal policy coordination even further. Moreover, built-in stabilizers are relatively weak given a considerable time lag between accrual of income and the collection of direct taxes. The only self-acting stabilization effect derives from federal unemployment insurance, which was introduced in 1977, and from social security contributions. The gross turnover tax, which also taxed investment and intermediate inputs, was even procyclical, and Swiss taxation has sometimes been characterized as an "automatic destabilizer" (Organization for Economic Cooperation and Development, 1993, p. 55). However, the introduction of VAT has significantly enhanced the stabilizing function of fiscal revenue.

Nevertheless, Switzerland has experienced remarkable fiscal stability over the postwar period, with relative price stability, full employment, and a strong currency. Apart from monetary and wage policies, migration, transborder commuters and seasonal workers, as well as fluctuating labor participation rates, especially before the introduction of federal unemployment insurance, seem to have cushioned cyclical shocks until more recently. However, unemployment—which stood at only ½ of 1 percent in 1990—has significantly risen since then (to about 4½ percent in mid-1996). This is mainly attributed to the institutional change of unemployment insurance and the behavior of labor supply (Organization for Economic Cooperation and Development, 1993, p. 98), apart from a recession and structural difficulties of the Swiss economy.

Recession and structural problems have also affected public budgets, which had deteriorated over the years. In the early 1990s, expenditure growth strongly exceeded revenues, forcing governments of all tiers into debt, although the debt was less for the local sector. The federal government has responded by submitting to parliament an extensive fiscal consolidation package, yet the very nature of the budgeting procedure has rendered its implementation difficult. This is the reason for suggesting a constitutional amendment in order to limit parliamentary spending powers as they exceed the proposal of the executive (*frein aux dépenses*).

The introduction of a modern broad-based consumption tax on goods and services in 1995 has strengthened the revenue side of the budget and removed the procyclical conduct of the turnover tax. It has also eliminated some of the structural handicaps of the old tax system, which discriminated against investment and exports—besides impeding effective decentralization and contracting out. Yet the VAT rate is limited by the Constitution, and the medium-term financial plan anticipated a continuing and widening structural budget deficit for 1996–97 (Gygi, 1994, p. 15). Excessive deficits were, however, successfully avoided mainly through a reduction of expenditures, which fell from 32.2 percent of GDP in 1993 to 30.5 percent in 1995. All layers of government took part in this consolidation exercise.

Structural Reform

Structural reform in Switzerland has centered around one principal theme: how to adapt to a changing economic environment, in particular the creation of the single market in Europe, and how to preserve Swiss competitiveness in world markets for industrial products and (mainly financial) services. Despite the rejection by Swiss voters in December 1992 of a proposal on entry into the European economic area, the Swiss government continues its policy aiming at adapting Swiss law to European Union law, in accordance with the treaty negotiated between the member countries of the European Community and the European Free Trade Association. A revised legislative package, "Swisslex," which was based on elements of the former "Eurolex" package rejected by the referendum, was formally presented to parliament in early 1993. Most of this legislation was adopted rapidly, and some of it became effective as early as 1994.

Furthermore, the central government has embarked on a revitalization program that covers "competition policy, immigration, education, and research as well as the removal of obstacles to international trade and to the intercantonal exchange of services and goods" (Organization for Economic Cooperation and Development, 1993, p. 61). It is also adapting tax policies to the principles applying in the European Union, mainly in the realm of taxing income and of corporate law, besides the introduction of a VAT and the dismantling of customs duties and their revenue-neutral incorporation into excises.

Initiatives in structural reform are typically taken by the central government. This is not to say that cantons and municipalities lack ingenuity in structural reform—on the contrary, they are often the first to notice the need for change and to react to regional economic challenge, yet their policies are often uncoordinated as they attempt "to solve their own economic problems by offering taxation incentives for industry (in the form of temporary tax reductions for new investment, deferment of taxes and depreciation concessions). . . . All these factors lead to undesirable competition and structural distortions." (Bieri, 1979, p. 92). It has also been argued that the cantons' wide-ranging powers to regulate at the local level is a major obstacle to needed structural reform. Furthermore, lower levels of government are often constrained by particular private interests that may impinge on collective decision making. Swiss constitutional and legislative procedures thus have costs which ensue from widespread horizontal and vertical cartellization, restrictions on competition through regulations and public procurement practices, collusive behavior among firms, and protective attitudes of government agencies (Organization for Economic Cooperation and Development, 1992, p. 71ff).

The Swiss Constitution confers the right to counteract "harmful economic and social effects" stemming from such behavior to the confederation, which has engaged in more active competition policy more recently, and the general public seems to be well aware of the challenge and the need for reform. Many, however, view the European Union as a threat to the very nature of Switzerland's political system. This is less true for the vertical distribution of power, which is also found in other Western European countries, notably in Germany. However, it is felt that European integration would jeopardize the very machinery of direct democracy and reconciliatory maneuvers between private and public interests as established in the traditional constitutional and legislative procedures.

Conclusions

If a lesson can be learned from the Swiss experience it is that "systems based on a strong reliance on cantonal sovereignty *can* work, even though it will likely result in wildly different—though widely accepted—personal (and other) tax systems" (Bird, 1986, p. 67). The picture of a "tax jungle" and lack of coordination is thus inappropriate. It may have been created by centralist interest groups to evoke resentments against a decentralized public decision-making process, yet it fails the test of an objective scrutiny into the workings of such a diversified system.

One feature of Swiss federalism is to be stressed in particular: an inherent tendency toward consensus and compromise and a strong commitment to safeguarding minority interests. Political decisions are seldom reached without prior consensus among all parties, and it would not be acceptable to decide on policy issues that are likely to meet resistance from substantial minority groups. Helvetian cooperative federalism means effective coordination at the horizontal level and institutionalized vertical consulting among political parties, economic and social groups, and government bodies at all levels. Established coordinating bodies (as in Germany) are missing, however. The Helvetian brand of "cooperative" federalism resembles more the Japanese system of consensus building and collective choice. In the past, this philosophy brought about effective policy coordination within a highly diversified policy structure, as it fostered political and economic stability, as well as growth and general welfare, without much formal demand management.

Yet the constitutional and legislative procedures have recently come under strain mainly through the process of European integration and increased competition in international markets. The need for structural reform of the Swiss economy is obvious. A comprehensive reform of fiscal federalism is currently being discussed. General economic trends are likely to strengthen central government involvement. Yet government authority at all levels remains subject to scrutiny by the Swiss electorate, and conservative trends have often impeded government action on issues sensitive to Switzerland's neighbors (such as transalpine traffic). Thus, the Swiss model of political decision making remains antagonistic to the approach taken by the Maastricht Treaty for the European Union—despite its principle of subsidiarity. It remains to be seen whether Helvetian federalism can survive in an environment that calls for greater coordination at the supranational level and whether the principle of subsidiarity is sufficient to protect devolution of power and direct democracy in Switzerland.

References

Bieri, S., 1979, *Fiscal Federalism in Switzerland*, Research Monograph No. 26 (Canberra: Centre for Research on Federal Financial Relations, Australian National University).

Bird, Richard, 1986, *Federal Finance in Comparative Perspective* (Toronto: Canadian Tax Foundation).

Dafflon, Bernard, 1977, *Federal Finance in Theory and Practice: With Special Reference to Switzerland* (Bern and Stuttgart: Paul Haupt).

———, 1986, "Fédéralisme, coordination et harmonisation fiscales: étude du cas suisse," *Recherches Economiques de Louvain*, Vol. 52, No. 1.

———, 1989, "Calcul de la capacité financière des cantons: synthèse et évolution," *Wirtschaft und Recht*, Zürich, pp. 210–220.

———, 1991, "Revenue Sharing in Switzerland" (unpublished).

Frey, René L., 1977, "The Interregional Income Gap as a Problem of Swiss Federalism," in *The Political Economy of Federalism*, ed. by Wallace E. Oates (Lexington, Massachusetts: Lexington Books).

Gygi, Ulrich, 1994, "Die Bundesfinanzen nach dem Mehrwertsteuerentscheid," *Die Volkswirtschaft*, Vol. 67, No. 2, pp. 14–20.

Higy, Camille, 1973, *Le système fiscal suisse* (Berne: Administration fédérale des contributions).

Laufenburger, H., 1961, *Economie des finances suisses* (Geneva: Librairie de l'Université).

Organization for Economic Cooperation and Development, 1992, *Economic Surveys—Switzerland* (Paris: Organization for Economic Cooperation and Development).

———, 1993, *Economic Surveys—Switzerland* (Paris: Organization for Economic Cooperation and Development).

Wischard, Jean-Pierre, 1994, "Die Voranschläge von Bund, Kantonen und Gemeinden für das Jahr 1994," *Die Volkswirtschaft*, Vol. 67, No. 2, pp. 37–45.

14

United Kingdom

BARRY POTTER

The United Kingdom had a well-established system of local government finance and intergovernment fiscal relations, which remained relatively stable from Victorian times until the late 1980s. Over the last 15 years, however (and particularly since 1988), significant reforms in the functions, structures, and above all, the financing of local government have begun to reduce the role of local government within the economy. The functions and hence the size of local government has diminished, and the structure is being simplified.

The reforms pursued over the 1980s (which culminated in the introduction of the community charge or poll tax) were intended to encourage greater local accountability and to devolve financial responsibility. But the reforms failed: indeed, the result, by the early 1990s, was the reverse of the original intention. Local governments' freedom to set their own budgets and to determine local taxes have been progressively circumscribed by the central government. Contrary to developments elsewhere in Europe, the principle of subsidiarity (often cited as desirable by the U.K. government in other contexts) has been clearly subordinated to greater central control over macroeconomic aggregates and the local tax burden.

Structure of Government

Local government structures differ in each of the three countries within Great Britain (England, Wales, and Scotland).[1] Historically, the

---

[1] Northern Ireland is excluded from this chapter; the structural and financial arrangements there have been largely untouched by the reforms introduced elsewhere in the United Kingdom over the last few years.

emergence of powerful city councils is often traced back to the late nineteenth century but the traditional shire authorities in rural areas stretch back much longer, to before the Middle Ages. The most recent comprehensive structural changes were undertaken in 1974, following the Redcliffe-Maude report. In both England and Wales, a two-tier system of elected local governments was established, covering shire counties and districts in rural areas, and metropolitan boroughs and districts in urban areas. (In Scotland, except for a few single-tier island authorities, the senior tier was referred to as a region rather than a county or borough.)

Under the 1974 reforms, the main local authority functions in England and Wales were split between the two tiers. The principal services allocated to the lower tier included housing, environmental services, and certain local transport responsibilities. The upper tier was given responsibility for education (which accounted for about 50 percent of total local government spending), police, fire, social services, and structural planning. The 1974 reorganization of local government was widely recognized to have been expensive, leading to a general levering up in salaries and numbers of personnel.

Nonetheless, in the light of the decreasing functions being undertaken by local authorities over the course of the 1980s, the government announced in 1992 that a new Local Government Commission would review the local government structure in England. (Separate reviews were established for Scotland and Wales.) Initially the broad policy intent seems to have been to shift toward more unitary councils but, in practice, the commission in England has largely favored retention of the status quo with some boundary changes, plus the creation of a few additional single-tier authorities, for example in areas of rapid population growth, such as new towns. Apprehension about the possible "cost of change" consequences in terms of higher personnel expenditures has discouraged a more extensive reform of the present structure. By contrast, in Scotland and Wales, a different approach was pursued: single-tier authorities were reintroduced in 1996, reflecting a widespread sentiment that the two-tier arrangement was too cumbersome for small countries.

Current Arrangements

Expenditure Assignment

After a progressive addition of new responsibilities following World War II, particularly in social areas, transport, and planning, since 1979 there has been a considerable reduction in local authorities' powers and

Table 1. United Kingdom: Local Authorities' Current Spending by Function
(In millions of pounds)

	1979		1983		1989		1993	
	Current account	Percent of total	Current account	Percent of total	Current account	Percent of total	Current account	Percent of total
Education[1]	7,532	61.3	11,955	59.9	17,561	56.9	20,102	49.4
Housing	85	0.7	168	0.8	233	0.8	443	1.1
Personal social services	1,504	12.2	2,606	13.1	4,395	14.2	6,909	17.0
Fire services and police	1,814	14.8	3,274	16.4	5,412	17.5	8,148	20.0
Transport and communications	829	6.8	1,291	6.5	1,616	5.2	2,225	5.5
Other economic affairs and services	516	4.2	651	3.3	1,634	5.3	2,890	7.1
Total	12,280	100.0	19,945	100.0	30,851	100.0	40,717	100.0

Source: Central Statistical Office, National Accounts (Tables 8.2 and 8.3).
[1] Current account data exclude expenditure of polytechnics in England from April 1989 and FE sixth form colleges from April 1993.

functions. Whereas local government accounted for 42 percent of total government spending in 1979, by 1994 that figure was reduced to 36 percent.

The main changes have taken place in housing, education, and transport (see Tables 1 and 2). In housing, the extensive sale of social rented housing to existing tenants, the elimination of the right of local authorities to build or buy houses, and the substitution of housing associations as the main provider of social housing have substantially reduced local government net capital expenditure. In education, the removal of polytechnics, sixth-form colleges, and colleges of education from local authorities' control and the transfer of some schools to grant-maintained status (run by the Department of Education rather than local authorities) have cut back local authority capital spending and reduced the growth of current expenditures on education. In transportation, the privatization of local bus services and removal of local rail and bus subsidies have also been significant in lowering local government spending. In Scotland, in 1996 water services were also taken away from local authorities' control and privatized. Indeed, over the last 15 years only one major new service has been entrusted to local authorities—community care (essentially care of the elderly). Even that decision seems to have been taken somewhat reluctantly by the government (it was delayed for several years), and in the absence of a better alternative.

Table 2. United Kingdom: Local Authorities' Gross Capital Expenditure in England
(In millions of pounds)

	1987/88	1988/89	1989/90	1990/91	1991/92	1992/93	1993/94
Education[1]	592	766	890	813	798	767	853
Housing[2]	3,246	3,431	4,908	2,939	2,521	2,246	2,278
Personal social services	144	171	218	168	160	160	198
Fire services and police	53	60	69	48	51	57	72
Transport and communications	775	961	1,134	964	1,087	1,261	1,447
Other economic affairs and services	1,199	1,530	2,177	1,346	1,180	1,018	1,243
Total	6,009	6,919	9,396	6,278	5,797	5,509	6,091

Sources: H.M. Treasury, *Public Expenditure*, Statistical Supplement to the Financial Statement and Budget Report 1994-95, and Statistical Supplement to the 1992 Autumn Statement.
[1] Includes housing association grant.
[2] Capital account data exclude houses for specific services (for example, police); these appear under the service concerned. Data are net of receipts from sales of council houses and other.

Tax Assignment

In principle, two local taxes are now raised by local authorities—the national nondomestic rate (also known as uniform business rate) and the council tax. Until 1988, there were separate domestic rates for households and nondomestic rates for businesses. Rate payments were the product of a rateable value per property, estimated on rental values revised every five years ("revaluation"), and a rate poundage set by each local authority. After a hostile public reaction to the revaluation of properties in Scotland in 1985, a political commitment was announced to find a replacement. The outcome—which was to have fundamental repercussions for central and local government—was the introduction in 1989 in Scotland of a community charge (colloquially referred to as the poll tax); this community charge was introduced a year later in England and Wales.

The community charge was a poll tax, levied on all adults (over 18 years) in each household. Community charge rebates were available to poorer adults, including students, but all adults were required to pay a minimum of 20 percent of the community charge set by the local authority. The universality of the community charge was designed to promote local accountability: since all adults paid the charge for local government services, they were expected to take account of the size of the charge and quality of local services in casting their votes. However, the community charge created immense practical and policy problems:

there were widespread campaigns against the tax on the grounds that it was regressive, excessive in size, and inequitable. There were riots on its introduction; noncompliance and noncollection proved to be serious problems. After two years, the abolition of the community charge was announced.

In its place, the domestic tax base returned to a modified form of domestic rates, termed the council tax. But the modifications were substantial. First, the tax base was changed from rental values to capital values; as under domestic rates, however, the tax liability falls on the householder (that is the occupant, whether tenant or owner) in the property, rather than on the owner. This was intended to retain the household principle that each adult should contribute to the tax payment—although it is unenforceable and tax liability in practice falls on the head of household. Second, the council tax was based on a broad banding of properties into eight categories, rather than a specific capital value. Third, a reduction in council tax liability was made available for single person households, despite the obvious disincentive to optimize the use of housing. This feature of lower liability for single adult households was also held over from the community charge. Fourth, more extensive income-related subsidies were available to householders than there were under domestic rates and the community charge.

More difficult to define is the nature of the national nondomestic rate. When the community charge was introduced in the late 1980s, this replaced the local nondomestic rate. Previously, this nondomestic or business rate had been set locally and formed part of the local authorities' tax base. Under the post-1988 regime, a single national rate poundage was set separately in Scotland, England, and Wales. (The rate poundage is indexed year by year.) The proceeds of the tax payments were pooled nationally and redistributed on a per capita basis to the local authorities. This arrangement was broadly unchanged under the 1993 regime, although the precise basis for distributing the pool to local authorities is determined annually by the central government.

In practice, therefore, the national nondomestic rate is better seen as a central government tax whose proceeds are earmarked through a current grant to the local authorities. A single national nondomestic rate in each of the three countries has not been achieved, however. There remain subsidies paid to businesses to prevent rate bills from rising faster than inflation in areas where the switch to a national basis raised tax payments. There are also special arrangements in Scotland to enable gradual harmonization between the Scottish and English rate poundages.

Grants

The grant systems are separate in England, Wales, and Scotland. All are highly complex, but are based on the same general approach. In essence, there are two kind of grants: a block grant, termed revenue support grant in England and Wales, and a series of specific grants. The annual block grant is determined as follows.

First, the central government sets a guideline figure for total standard spending for local authority current expenditure, determined essentially on macroeconomic grounds in the context of setting the annual public expenditure budget. The total standard spending is then split between categories of authority within each county in England, for example, between metropolitan districts, metropolitan counties, rural districts, and rural counties. Second, for each local authority, there is a standard spending assessment. This is the amount the government estimates should cost the local authority to provide a common level of local services, consistent with the aggregate total standard spending. The revenue support grant is distributed so that, if a local authority spends at its approved standard spending assessment, the authority can charge a standard council tax (a government-set norm) for a household in a middle-band property. Thus,

Revenue support grant = standard spending assessment – distributed share of national nondomestic rate income
– council tax revenue at standard council tax.

The standard spending assessment for each authority is built up on a service-by-service basis, usually by multiplying the numbers in the client group (for example, pupils for education) by an estimated unit cost, allowing for additional costs (for example, transport of pupils in remote areas). These allowances for additional costs are based on cross-section regression analysis, which is used to attach weights to factors such as climate and population density, that influence unit costs.

The determination of standard spending assessments is not carried out by an independent body,[2] but rather by the responsible government department in each of the three countries, in consultation with the local authorities. The distribution of the grant in each country has thus, in part, become a political, rather than a fully objective process. There are several opportunities for this political input. First, the share of total standard spending for each the four types of councils can be varied. Second, the weight given to each of the seven main services within the total can

---

[2]This is in contrast to the Australian government's approach, which relies on an independent Grants Commission.

also be changed, for example, by boosting the total standard spending assessments for education, while compressing that for environmental services. Third, the weight attached to the factors determining relative needs for services can also be varied. Indeed, it is common for individual authorities or groups of authorities to lobby for the inclusion of new factors (a recent example is miles of coastline as a determinant of the cost of fire services) or for greater weight to be attached to existing factors. One result of such lobbying is a proliferation in the number of service programs or subprograms for which needs indicators are specified; moreover, the number and complexity of such indicators have also increased. A cycle has developed whereby the government (or more accurately government officials) reduce the number of programs or subprograms and indicators, most recently in 1989, in the interest of transparency. Then programs are subdivided over time in the name of greater sensitivity and fine-tuning, until the resultant complexity again overwhelms understanding. In early 1996, the government announced that the Institute of Fiscal Studies would review the formulas again.

In practice, as the complexity grew, relatively small shifts in the share of types of council or services or in the weights attached to specific needs indicators produced considerable movements in grant entitlement. This lack of stability in year-to-year grants received is acknowledged to be undesirable, since it prevents careful planning of future service delivery. Dampening mechanisms have therefore been introduced from time to time to prevent sharp year-on-year changes to individual authority grants. Thus, in 1994–95, an additional specific grant—the standard spending assessment reduction grant—was paid to local authorities whose standard spending assessment fell by more than 2 percent.

While the grant entitlements are built up from the service-specific indicators of need, the general grant is not hypothecated by service. Thus, grant receipts justified, for example, by greater unit costs for primary school education need not be spent on primary schools or even on education: they could be used to finance more spending on the police. The central government determines total revenue support grant transfers, but individual local authorities still control the distribution of grants among local services.

Over the last 15 years, however, there has also been a shift away from the revenue support grant toward more use of specific grants (although the revenue support grant still accounts for the bulk of grants received; see Table 3). Such specific grants are paid over and above the block grant, thus boosting to a higher level the grant percentage covering the relevant expenditure item. In origin, specific grants were conceived as a means of ensuring that a particular service item to which the central government gave priority was likely to be fully supported by local gov-

Table 3. United Kingdom: Financing of Local Government
(In millions of pounds unless otherwise indicated)

	1987/88	1988/89	1989/90	1990/91	1991/92	1992/93	1993/94
Revenue support grant[1]	12,554	12,776	12,982	13,127	13,603	21,795	22,332
Specific grants	2,622	2,811	3,236	3,798	9,705	5,069	5,228
Other current grants[2]	6,292	6,099	6,495	8,466	10,061	12,233	13,007
Nondomestic rate payments[3]	9,764	10,537	11,338	12,093	14,235	14,055	13,215
Capital	4,545	4,386	4,292	5,043	5,727	6,079	5,922
Total central government support to local authorities[3]	35,777	36,609	38,342	42,527	53,331	59,230	59,705
Local authority financed by local taxes and from asset sales[4]	9,227	10,711	15,515	15,085	10,780	10,192	10,500
Local payment as a percent total local authority expenditure[5]	42.2	44.9	28.8	26.2	16.8	14.7	15.0
Total local authority expenditure	45,004	47,320	53,857	57,612	64,111	69,422	70,200

Sources: H.M. Treasury, *Public Expenditure*, Statistical Supplement to the Financial Statement and Budget Report 1993-94, and Statistical Supplement to the 1992 Autumn Statement.

Note: Components may not add to totals because of rounding.

[1] Rate support grant for the years up to 1989/90 (1988/89 in Scotland).

[2] Mostly current grants outside aggregate external finance wholly, expenditure on certain national policies that local authorities administer, such as community charge benefit, housing benefit, and student awards.

[3] For 1989/90 (1988/89 in Scotland) and earlier years the estimated yield of nondomestic rates has been used as a proxy for nondomestic rate payments.

[4] For 1987/88 and 1988/89 adjusted to exclude nondomestic rate payments.

[5] For 1987/88 and 1988/89 includes nondomestic rate payments. For 1989/90 through 1992/93, includes community charge grant. For 1993/94, includes council tax.

ernment—for example, a specific grant to encourage the purchase of computers. In addition, tight grant conditionality could ensure that the money was spent in precisely the ways that the central government intended. The disadvantage is that such specific grants involve centralized determination of relative priorities. Moreover, the greater the percentage of total grant allocated to specific grants, the less local authorities can switch resource allocations to reflect local conditions—for example, in the above case the availability of used, but up to date, computers from a nearby computer business at no cost.

Capping

No account of the current U.K. arrangements could be complete without consideration of capping. In the early 1980s, a series of measures was taken intended to discourage additional spending above the guideline (a then similar concept to the standard spending assessment) set by the central government for each authority. Various models at first reduced the proportionate amount of extra grant on such extra spending,[3] but culminated in systems that withdrew grant for spending above the government guidelines. None of these systems proved effective.

In their place, rate capping was introduced from 1986, initially as an emergency measure. Its purpose was to enable the government to judge as excessive either the absolute expenditure level relative to the guideline or the year-on-year increase in spending plans. If the expenditure was found excessive, the government could cap the size of the local tax set. Between 1985 and 1989 relatively limited use of these powers was made, with typically no more than a dozen authorities (out of more than 200) capped annually. Although the caps and, more specifically, the government's interpretation of "excessive" was challenged in the British courts, no such court case brought against the government was successful.

It was widely assumed that with the introduction of the community charge in the late 1980s capping would be dropped. The thesis upon which the community charge was introduced was greater electoral accountability. Unlike domestic rates, all adults would pay (even the poorest would contribute). All spending above government guideline by a local authority would be highly geared at 4:1; that is, with no extra grant available for spending above the standard spending assessment, a 1 percent increase in spending would require a 4 percent rise in the community charge. In these circumstances, the accountability of local government to the electorate would dissuade the local council from excessive spending. In logic, there was no need for capping: in practice, it was retained, at the insistence of the then U.K. Chancellor as a fallback.[4]

Faced with very high local taxes when the community charge was introduced, the government realized that the legislation permitted the capping procedures to be extensively applied.[5] Capping has now become a permanent feature of the local government fiscal regime, including under the 1992 Local Government Act that introduced the new council tax. Actual application of the caps is rare: it is the threat,

---

[3]Under the pre-1988 systems, the amount of revenue support grant received depended on actual spending rather than the standard spending assessment or equivalent spending guidelines.

[4]See Lawson (1992).

[5]For an interesting description of how "accidental" this key policy mechanism was, see Thatcher (1993), the chapter on "The Community Charge."

via the preannouncement of the likely criteria for applying caps, which encourages local authorities to moderate their budget plans. The threat has become more effective over time: only three local authorities had their budgets capped in 1993–94. Although the cap is formally applied to the local tax, the impact is on holding local government expenditure to levels deemed appropriate by central government. In short, a high grant percentage (over 80 percent of total local authority current expenditure), combined with an actual or threatened cap on local taxes that pay for the rest, enables central government to exercise a high degree of control over total local government current spending.

Borrowing

In the United Kingdom, local governments are prevented by law from borrowing for current expenditure purposes. Local authorities are permitted to borrow for capital spending and may do so either through a commercial bank or from the Public Work Loans Board—a body with access to funds from the U.K. National Loans Fund and therefore able to offer better borrowing rates than the commercial banks.

The regime to control local authority capital spending and borrowing has become highly complex. Starting in the mid-1980s, local authorities were first encouraged and then required to sell social rented houses to existing tenants on demand (the "right to buy"), at a large discount against the market price, although often at prices much higher than historical building costs and the associated debts. This flood of asset sales provided local authorities with the capital revenues needed to finance much of their capital programs. From the mid-1980s onward the central government imposed limitations on the rate at which such capital revenues could be used. In addition, under the 1989 Local Government and Housing Act, comprehensive controls were put in place on borrowing. (In part, this was necessary to stop a number of abuses adopted by local authorities to reclassify current as capital spending and vice versa.)

There are now tight controls over the spending from capital receipts: only 25 percent of capital receipts from housing and 50 percent of other capital receipts may be used for capital expenditure, with the residual to be set aside for debt repayment. Each authority is also given an annual capital guideline. Part of this comprises an assessment of its ability to finance capital spending from asset sales, known as receipts taken into account. The remainder of the annual capital guideline is issued in the form of credit approvals (basically permissions to borrow), comprising basic credit approvals and supplementary credit approvals. (The latter are earmarked for particular services or projects.) Finally, there are also limitations set on each authority's overall net indebtedness, based on marginal additions consistent with the annual credit approvals and the stock of outstanding debt.

Administrative Structure

Tax Administration

Much of the administration of the council tax lies in the hands of the lower-tier district authorities. In addition to setting a council tax for their own services, these authorities levy a precept charge (that is, council tax) on behalf of the upper tier. The key accounting concept—the collection fund—receives all grants (including receipts from the national nondomestic rate) and council taxes and allocates funds to each tier. Determination of the tax base lies with the central government through the government Valuation Office, an agency that compiles and maintains valuation lists. For the creation of the new council tax bands, nearly 60 percent of the valuation work was contracted out to the private sector. Appeals can be made both by householders (against their band) and by businesses: if no settlement is reached within six months, a formal hearing is given at a Valuation Tribunal. There is of course much less need for precision under this banding arrangement for the council tax than under the previous domestic rating regime. Nonetheless, hundreds of thousands of appeals have been registered in the first few years.

The payment of income-related subsidies to council taxpayers is also administered by the lower-tier authorities, in cooperation with the Department of Social Security. However, the relevant income scales and rates of subsidy are determined nationally. Partly in reaction to what were seen as inadequate subsidies under the preceding community charge regime, the subsidies are now more generous. In particular, 100 percent subsidies are available to the poorest households, whereas only 80 percent was paid under the community charge. Subsidies extend well up the income scale and are paid to households in the first four income deciles.

Implications

Macroeconomic Management

The present local government fiscal regime in the United Kingdom does not lead to any significant problems from a macroeconomic management perspective. This reflects the paramount importance attached

Table 4. United Kingdom: Growth Rates in Total Expenditure on Goods and Services at 1990 Market Prices

	Average 1983–87	Average 1988–93
Local government[1]	2.0	0.8
Central government	1.1	2.3
General government	1.7	1.8

Source: Central Statistical Office, National Accounts..
[1] Total final consumption plus expenditure on fixed assets.

by the government (from the mid-1980s onward) to achieving macroeconomic control of general government expenditure. The very high percentage of local authorities' current spending now financed by central government grant (more than 80 percent) combined with the tight capping on the remainder financed through local taxes and borrowing limits enables tight overall control of local authorities' current spending.

Throughout much of the early to mid-1980s, it was argued that local government spending was increasing faster than other kinds of government spending. This was partly fueled by capital revenues from asset sales. Whatever the cause, as Table 4 shows, the growth in local authority spending was faster than that of central government. Total local government spending is now under firm control. As the table also shows, since 1988 local government spending has grown at less than half the rate of central government spending.

A different macroeconomic problem was generated during the second half of the 1980s and early 1990s by the sales of local authority assets, particularly housing. Despite the discount against current market value, house sales were profitable for the local authority when measured against historic cost and associated debt. Moreover, the debt had often been contracted at relatively low interest rates; as interest rates throughout the economy rose in the latter half of the 1980s and early 1990s, local authorities appreciated the scope for a form of "round tripping." Rather than repay the debts with the proceeds of asset sales, local authorities placed large amounts into the U.K. money markets. So large were these deposits that they were sufficient to generate extra liquidity in the banking system; this made it more difficult for the Bank of England to keep the banking system short of funds so as to control interest rates, and threatened to require additional issue of government debt. While various solutions were proposed, the subsequent reduction in interest rates and gradual dissipation of the deposits through higher capital spending have largely removed this problem.

While macroeconomic management may not be a problem, it would be wrong to think there are no wider economic problems associated with the current local government fiscal regime. On the contrary, several issues arise.

First, the high percentage of local authorities' spending supported by government grant has injected a very high gearing level for marginal spending. As pointed out in a Institute for Fiscal Studies paper,[6] if local authorities spend at 10 percent above the standard spending assessment, this will lead to an addition of nearly 70 percent on the council tax above the government norm—a ratio of 7:1. Moreover, unlike the community charge where the more modest ratio of 4:1 was widely criticized, the gearing is no longer common to all local authorities. For some authorities, the ratio can be as high as 12:1. Now that the tax base plays an important part in the grant determination and only partial resource equalization is achieved,[7] this gearing ratio puts a considerable burden on the needs assessment for determining standard spending assessment and thus grant entitlement. Arguably, it is more than regression-based analysis can bear, particularly when the analysis is further refined by a political input. The smallest error in determining standard spending assessment can have a sizable fiscal impact on low-resource (and often high-need) areas.

Second, the failure of the community charge has had a lasting impact on the overall tax structure of the United Kingdom. Because the community charge was judged to have reached an unacceptable level, the 1991 budget included a switch from community charges to VAT; by raising the latter by 2½ percentage points, it was possible to reduce the level of community charges by around one-third. Earlier, in 1989–90, the "nationalization" of the nondomestic rates, severely cut back the size of the genuinely local tax base (see Table 3). Finally, when the council tax replaced the community charge in 1993, to ensure a smooth introduction, the level of the council tax was held below that of the community charge, measured on a comparable basis. This substantial contraction of the local tax base and growth in central taxes over the last five years is the counterpart to the high grant percentage. Resistance to local taxes has grown. In 1995–96, the government cut back central government grant so as to raise local taxes. It is proving politically very difficult to raise local taxes because of troubled recent history. Local government is now more able to make public the link in public pronouncements between grant received and the local tax burden.

---

[6]Giles and Ridge (1993).
[7]Full resource equalization applies only for spending at standard spending assessment.

Third, in political terms, the reforms introduced in 1988 and 1989 to promote local accountability and good stewardship of resources have led to a fiscal regime in which such accountability has been very largely dissipated. Each council on average collects less than 20 percent of the resources it spends: the rest is determined by the central government, and any addition judged excessive can be negated by the central government through actual or potential capping. Far from enhancing local democratic accountability, the reforms have made local authorities less accountable for the local taxes they set.

Fourth, despite the reintroduction of a property-based tax, the current council tax, like its predecessor, the community charge, is still regressive in income terms. Many households living in properties within the same council tax band have significant differences in total income. This situation arises, in particular, for multiple-adult households and two-income households. Even to the extent that there is a broad correlation between household income and capital values, an overall limit has been set on the size of the maximum council tax bill at three times that in the lowest band. Since the relationship between capital values and income seems to be greater than three to one, the council tax can be judged regressive. However, the availability of extensive subsidies to some degree limits the regressivity at the lower end of the income scale: it is certainly less regressive than the community charge.

Structural Reform

The most interesting structural issues on local government can best be considered under functions, the configuration of local councils, and local democracy.

Functions

Over the last 15 years, as noted, local authority functions have been progressively diminished. In some cases, the changes have been clear and clean, for example, the removal of colleges of further education from local authorities' control and their transfer to the central government. But the change in other functions is less clear-cut, for example, that with regard to schools. Local authority schools have been allowed to opt out of local council control and into grant maintained status, that is, broadly under the control of the Department of Education. As the numbers of such schools have grown, the original formula for their financing (equal to the amount while in the local authority sector) has become less satisfactory. Their financing is now to be based on a separate formula, so there is an obvious link back into the question of assessing local authorities' financial needs for education in the context of determining the revenue support grant. Uncertainty over the future status of individual schools makes the planning of school place requirements more complex.

Similarly, in housing the transfer of functions has not been clear-cut. Local authorities retain responsibility for the management and maintenance of large social housing estates, yet new building is in the hands of housing associations. Again, the basis upon which these associations make their decisions about relative needs and the feedback of their activity into housing-need indicators for local authorities have not been resolved satisfactorily. In other areas—local transport, social services, and environmental services—many responsibilities have passed to central government, which funds service provision through an agency that is nominally private but is largely financed by the central government. The assessment and coordination of relative service needs, the establishment of local cross-service priorities, and the accountability for service standards all seem to have been weakened under the present arrangements. The current position in areas such as education is also widely seen as unstable, a temporary solution at best.

Structure

On structure, there is much political controversy about the need for change. The possible introduction of a new regional government tier ("devolution") in Scotland and in Wales with varying powers over local services is proposed by the two political opposition parties. That would require a thorough review again of the fiscal environment for local government though the reintroduction of unitary authorities, and exclusive administrative devolution already in place (the Scottish and Welsh offices) has simplified the task of such reform. In any case, the progressive reduction of the functions of the senior tier (metropolitan and shire counties) in England has raised questions about their future role especially because Scotland and Wales have now moved to a single-tier regime. In particular, any further contraction of education responsibilities might make it difficult to defend a two-tier structure.

Local Democracy

Finally, there is a broader issue of the loss of local democracy, the counterpart to the centralization of powers and control. The role of local democracy is reduced to the effective stewardship of given resources—getting value for money and the best service standards. Local authorities are assisted both by the work of the service inspectorates, for example, on education, policy, and fire services, and by value-for-money reports by the Audit Commission, which compare, contrast, and can identify set service practice. Yet, major elements of local services, including part of education and provision of social housing, are now under the command of private associations—essentially spending agencies financed by the central government. These associations are managed by boards appointed by the central government. Moreover, government ministers with central government have emphasized the arm's-length relationship of boards. Complaints about service standards thus have to be pursued fundamentally through the courts rather than through political representation. There are also no fixed requirements for the coordination of policy between such associations and the relevant local authorities. The loss of information may damage future capacity planning.

Conclusion

Despite the many reforms of the last 15 years, it is difficult to believe that the present intergovernment fiscal relations in the United Kingdom are stable. The arrangements for financing current expenditure owe more to the problems encountered in introducing the community charge and the need to find a hurried alternative, than to a carefully delineated scheme based on well-argued or widely accepted economic principles. For example, it is acknowledged that the new arrangements involve a high degree of central government control and that, despite stated objectives, they have failed to introduce more electoral accountability in local government. On the contrary, the reforms have set back further the cause of greater accountability.

Also, the transfer of part or all of certain functions from elected local authorities to unelected private associations, under the direct financial control of the central government, can be only an intermediate solution. The accounting and reporting requirements on such associations, the precision of their mandates, and the arrangements with local government for coordination in assessing service needs and agreeing on service delivery all lack transparency. Whether such transfers proceed further or, on the contrary, functions are reintegrated within the local authority network will in part depend on political developments.

Whatever the wider macroeconomic advantages, the United Kingdom has been unusual in the extent to which centralization and control of formerly local services has proceeded. It can be argued that, even with the capping regime in place to limit total expenditures, local authorities can shift priorities and change and improve the means of service delivery; thus, the role of the central government in determining levels and patterns of service delivery should not be exaggerated. But the direction of change over the last 15 years in the United Kingdom has been unequivocally toward centralization and restriction on local government action. Elsewhere in Europe, there has been a tendency toward more fiscal federalism and greater freedom, for example, in Germany and Italy. The arguments for greater fiscal freedoms for local government are familiar: the better assessment of local needs, the ability to choose between local priorities, and the delegation of greater fiscal responsibilities—the broad principle of subsidiarity. The deepening of democracy is also cited as an advantage. In economic terms, such greater fiscal federalism may lead to different standards of local services, and different local tax payments encouraging further factor mobility. By contrast, the United Kingdom has proceeded down an altogether different course, striving to achieve commonality of local services through strong and dirigiste financial controls. The logic and structure of these systems also point toward similar local tax burdens. The current systems seem to reflect a deep-rooted lack of confidence in local government and in local democracy.

References

Butler, David, Andrew Adonis, and Tony Travers, 1994, *Failure in British Government: The Politics of the Poll Tax* (Oxford: Oxford University Press).

Department of the Environment, 1994, *Annual Report* (London: HMSO).

Giles, Christopher, and Michael Ridge, 1993, *Right This Time? An Analysis of the First Year's Council Tax Figures* (London: Institute for Fiscal Studies).

Lawson, Nigel, 1992, *The View from No. 11: Memoirs of a Tory Radical* (London: Bantam Press).

Thatcher, Margaret H., 1993, *The Downing Street Years* (NewYork: HarperCollins).

15

United States

JANET G. STOTSKY AND EMIL M. SUNLEY

The federalist system of government in the United States is an overlapping structure of federal, state, and local governments. Subnational governments play a much larger role in American political life than in most other countries, reflecting the country's historical roots in a tradition based on participatory democracy and checks and balances on the power of government. In 1990, there were 50 states and 83,186 local governments, encompassing municipalities, townships, counties, school districts, and special service districts. The clear demarcation of the roles of the general purpose and limited purpose local governments (school districts and special service districts) is unusual.

Structure of Government

Although local governments are subordinate to the state governments, the nature of the relationship between state and local governments varies from state to state. In some states (for example, New Hampshire), local governments play the dominant role in terms of expenditure and revenue assignment, whereas in others (for example, Hawaii), they play a minor role.

In addition, the relationship among local governments varies from state to state. In some states (for example, Massachusetts), municipali-

---

The authors wish to thank Ehtisham Ahmad, Robert Ebel, Richard Hemming, Teresa Ter-Minassian, and the IMF's Western Hemisphere Department for helpful comments.

ties are the dominant form of local government, while in others (for example, Maryland), counties are more significant.

The federalist system in the United States today bears little relation to that envisioned by the founders of the country more than 200 years ago. The Constitution of the United States, ratified in 1787, established the legitimate spheres of the federal and state governments. Nevertheless, the Constitution, reflecting the conflict between those in favor of stronger federal rights and those in favor of stronger state rights, intentionally leaves unclear many issues regarding the assignment of roles and responsibilities among governments. As a result, over the years, the role of the federal, state, and local governments has evolved in response to changing conditions.

In this century, the government sector, including federal, state, and local governments, has expanded. One dominant change in the federalist system stands out. This is the growth in importance of the federal and state governments as the source of funds for public expenditures, with the corresponding decline in the importance of local governments. The federal government has over time expanded its role in many areas that had traditionally been the responsibility of the state and local governments. This growth accelerated during the 1960s with the introduction of the Great Society programs, which expanded income transfers to the poor and to the elderly. State governments have similarly expanded their role in areas that had traditionally been the responsibility of the local governments.

Corresponding to this evolution in the federalist system, there has been a growth in the level of intergovernmental grants (generally categorical or special purpose grants) from higher to lower levels of government. Although the federal government assumed increased financial responsibility for government programs, it did not directly spend all of this money. Instead, it transferred considerable funds to the state and local governments, allowing them to retain administrative control over their traditional programs. A similar evolution has occurred between state and local governments, with state governments transferring money to local governments for education and other purposes.

Federal intergovernmental grants grew most rapidly at a time when the federal government was in a strong fiscal position relative to the state and local governments. Persuasive arguments were offered that intergovernmental grants would produce a more efficient and equitable government system. But the vertical fiscal imbalance between the federal and lower levels of government no longer exists, as a result of the weakening of the federal government's budgetary position during the 1980s. This weakening has led to cutbacks in federal aid programs and responsibilities.

In contrast to other industrial countries, the United States has no general purpose grants to the states aimed at achieving horizontal equalization. The various categorical grants to the states, although containing equalization factors in their formulas, primarily are used by the federal government to ensure minimum standards. These categorical grants impose federal mandates on states receiving federal assistance, and today the states want the federal government to limit unfunded mandates; that is, spending requirements imposed by the federal government with only partial federal funding, if any.

Administrative Structure

Tax Administration

The United States has a decentralized tax administration with each federal, state, and local government having its own tax administration to collect the taxes it imposes. This decentralization gives each government maximum fiscal independence and control over the base and rates of its taxes. This independence, however, results in higher compliance costs for taxpayers and higher administrative costs for the tax authorities.

Most individuals and businesses file both federal and state income tax returns. They first complete their federal income tax returns before beginning their state return. The burden in filling out their state returns depends largely on the degree of conformity between the state and federal income tax laws. There can be considerable horizontal tax overlapping when an individual lives in one jurisdiction and works or earns income in another, or when an individual moves from one jurisdiction to another. This overlapping is alleviated by one jurisdiction allowing a credit for taxes paid to another. Businesses that operate in more than one state must allocate and apportion the interstate income among the states. The most common apportionment formula is a three-factor formula of sales, property, and payroll with each factor equally weighted. But some states double-weight sales, use only two factors, or use only sales to apportion income. As a result, the same income can be taxed in more than one state, and some income may not be apportioned to any state and thus escape taxation at the state level. A strong case can be made for states using a single, uniform formula for apportioning business income; however, the federal government has no power to enforce this uniformity.

Income tax administration is coordinated between the federal government and each of the 50 states (and the District of Columbia) through agreements to exchange information. This permits states, for example, to follow up on taxpayers who file a federal income tax return but not a state tax return. Also, the state income tax returns of many states ask whether the taxpayer had been audited or had filed an amended federal return.

In 1972, Congress enacted a provision that would have permitted states to elect to have the federal Internal Revenue Service collect the state income tax. A state could piggyback its tax only if the state taxable income conformed to federal taxable income with a few adjustments. States would have been able to set their own tax rates. No state ever elected to piggyback its tax, and Congress repealed the provision in 1990. Among the reasons no state elected piggybacking is the high degree of conformity required under the federal law, the fact that state revenues would change whenever the federal tax base is changed, the states' unwillingness to rely on federal auditing and enforcement, and the loss of state jobs.

Budget Formulation and Implementation

The federal fiscal year runs from October 1 to September 30, with a specific timetable for completing each part of the budget process. This timetable is not always adhered to, and at times the federal government has entered the new fiscal year without a budget in place.

State budgets operate generally on a July 1 to June 30 fiscal year and an annual basis. Unlike the federal government, states cannot generally submit a budget that will be balanced by the issuance of debt. Also unlike the federal government, state governments separate their budgets into a current (or operating) budget and a capital budget. The operating budget refers to expenditures and revenues for the current year. Operating expenditures include general expenditures for all functions, some utilities expenditures, pension contributions, and payments for debt service. Operating revenue include taxes, fees, intergovernmental aid, and interest on investments. The capital budget refers to expenditures and revenues for long-term capital projects, such as the construction of schools and highways. Capital projects are typically financed by long-term borrowing.

Stringency of the balanced-budget requirement varies from state to state. There are four restrictions that generally apply: the governor must present a balanced current budget, the legislature must pass a balanced budget, the governor must sign a balanced budget, and the state cannot roll over a deficit into the next fiscal year. Most typically, states must satisfy all four requirements, although states practice virtually every other combination. Most states face some requirement to either submit or sign a balanced budget, but some states are not required to realize a balanced budget at year-end, thereby allowing them to carry over an operating deficit into the next fiscal year.[1] This gives states more budget flexibility in that they need not act immediately to bring their budgets into balance if expenditures exceed or revenues fall short of expectations. The disadvantage, however, is that states may not address their budget problems immediately and compound fiscal woes by pushing off deficits into the future. Regardless of the specific statutory or constitutional rules that apply to state governments, the municipal bond market ultimately imposes discipline on state budgets.

To avert cash-flow problems under normal budgetary conditions, some state governments may issue short-term debt. But states may create fiscal dilemmas if they issue large volumes of short-term debt and carry this debt over into subsequent years to hide persistent deficits. This practice, also used by local governments, led New York City to the brink of default in 1975.[2]

States may face many statutory and constitutional limitations on their taxing and spending powers, which complicate the budget process. The most common restriction is to limit the growth of revenues or expenditures to the growth of state personal income. Several states limit growth to the sum of the inflation rate and the growth of population, or to fixed percentage increases. State governments in turn limit local governments, typically by imposing a limit on property tax rates, although some states also limit property tax revenues. Evidence suggests that these limitations have not been very effective in constraining state governments, although they have been more effective in constraining local governments.[3]

Current Arrangements

Expenditure Assignment

The state and local governments have traditionally been responsible for the provision of basic government goods and services, primarily elementary and secondary education, and police and fire services at the local level, and transportation, public works, public welfare, and higher education at the state level. The federal government has traditionally been responsible for providing national defense and public welfare. Today, however, the state governments have acquired a much more important role in funding public education, even though the provision of

---

[1] Advisory Commission on Intergovernmental Relations (1994c).
[2] Inman (1983).
[3] See Kenyon and Benker (1984) and Preston and Ichniowski (1991).

these services still remains largely in local hands. The federal government has acquired a much more important role in funding most spheres of public activity, especially public welfare and public works, although again, with the exception of income transfers to the elderly, the provision of these services remains largely in state hands. There is thus considerable expenditure overlapping between the different levels of government on virtually all public activities.

Total government expenditures in 1990 were 40.0 percent of gross domestic product (GDP).[4] Federal government expenditures (including intergovernmental grants) were 25.1 percent of GDP, state expenditures (including intergovernmental grants) were 10.3 percent of GDP, and local expenditures were 10.5 percent of GDP (Table 1). Over time, the relative importance of the different levels of government and the mix of spending and revenues at each level has changed (Tables 1, 2, and 3).

The largest components of federal expenditures are for insurance trust programs (largely Social Security and Medicare), national defense, interest on government debt, and intergovernmental aid. In recent years, Social Security and Medicare and interest on government debt have increased dramatically as a share of federal spending, while national defense and intergovernmental aid have declined. The largest components of state and local expenditures are for education and public welfare. State and local governments have increased spending most dramatically on health, prisons, and interest on debt in recent years.[5]

Tax Assignment

The U.S. Constitution grants the federal and state governments independent taxing powers, while local governments derive their powers to tax from the state governments. Each government imposes its own taxes. There are no shared taxes, although more than one government may exploit the major revenue sources.

Total government revenues in 1990 were 36.9 percent of GDP. Federal government revenues were 20.8 percent of GDP, state revenues (including intergovernmental grants) were 11.4 percent of GDP, and local revenues (including intergovernmental grants) were 10.5 percent of GDP (see Table 2). As with expenditures, over time, the relative im-

---

[4]This total excludes duplicative intergovernmental transactions; thus, it is less than the sum of the federal, state, and local totals.

[5]State and local governments are typically aggregated because the breakdown between state and local governments varies from state to state. Thus, the precise breakdown between state and local governments is less meaningful than the aggregate. See Advisory Commission on Intergovernmental Relations (1994c).

Table 1. United States: Total Government Expenditures, Selected Years
(In percent of GDP)

	All Governments	Federal			State			Local		U.S. GDP (In billions
Year	Total[1] (1)	Total (2)	Direct[2] (3)	Intergovernmental (4)	Total (5)	Direct[3] (6)	Intergovernmental (7)	Total (8)	Direct (9)	of U.S. dollars) (10)
1962	30.6	19.7	18.4	1.3	6.3	4.4	1.9	7.9	7.8	575.8
1967	31.4	20.4	18.5	1.8	7.2	4.8	2.3	8.1	8.1	819.8
1970	32.7	20.5	18.2	2.3	8.4	5.5	2.8	9.1	9.0	1,017.1
1975	35.0	21.4	18.3	3.1	9.9	6.7	3.3	10.2	10.1	1,599.1
1980	35.0	22.5	19.2	3.3	9.4	6.3	3.1	9.5	9.4	2,742.1
1985	39.0	25.5	22.8	2.6	9.6	6.6	3.0	9.6	9.5	4,053.6
1990	40.0	25.1	22.5	2.7	10.3	7.2	3.2	10.5	10.4	5,542.9

Source: Advisory Commission on Intergovernmental Relations (1994c).

[1] Excludes duplicative intergovernmental transactions; it is less than the sum of the federal, state, and local totals in columns 2, 5, and 8.
[2] Includes Social Security and Medicare insurance, employee retirement, railroad retirement, veterans' life insurance, and unemployment compensation.
[3] Includes utility expenditure, employee retirement, unemployment compensation, workers' compensation, and other insurance trust expenditure.

Table 2. United States: Total Government Revenues, Selected Years
(In percent of GDP)

	All Governments	Federal	State					Local				U.S. GDP
				Intergovernmental					Intergovernmental			(In billions
Year	Total[1] (1)	Total (2)	Total (3)	Federal (4)	Local (5)	Own source[2] (6)	Total (7)		Federal (8)	State[3] (9)	Own source[2] (10)	of U.S. dollars) (11)
1962	29.2	18.5	6.5	1.2	0.1	5.2	7.5		0.1	1.9	5.5	575.8
1967	30.8	19.7	7.5	1.7	0.1	5.7	7.9		0.2	2.2	5.4	819.8
1970	32.8	20.2	8.7	1.9	0.1	6.8	8.8		0.3	2.6	5.9	1,017.1
1975	32.5	19.0	9.8	2.3	0.1	7.5	10.0		0.7	3.2	6.1	1,599.1
1980	34.0	20.6	10.1	2.3	0.1	7.8	9.4		0.8	3.0	5.7	2,742.1
1985	35.0	19.9	10.8	2.1	0.1	8.6	9.9		0.5	2.9	6.5	4,053.6
1990	36.9	20.8	11.4	2.1	0.1	9.1	10.5		0.3	3.1	7.0	5,542.9

Source: Advisory Commission on Intergovernmental Relations (1994c).
[1] Excludes duplicative intergovernmental transactions; it is less than the sum of the federal, state, and local totals in columns 2, 3, and 7.
[2] Includes taxes, user charges, miscellaneous general revenue, utility revenue, liquor store revenue, and social insurance revenue.
[3] Includes substantial but unknown amounts of federal grants to states that are "passed through" by the states to local governments.

Table 3. United States: Federal, State, and Local Revenues and Expenditures
(In percent of GDP unless otherwise noted)

	1970	1980	1990
Total federal revenues (in percent)	20.2	20.6	20.8
General	16.1	15.2	14.1
Intergovernmental	—	0.1	0.1
General from own sources	16.1	15.2	14.1
Taxes	14.4	12.8	11.4
Individual income	8.9	8.9	8.4
Corporation income	3.2	2.4	1.7
Sales, gross receipts, and customs duties	1.8	1.2	1.0
Other	0.4	0.4	0.3
Charges and miscellaneous	1.7	2.4	2.7
Insurance trust	4.1	5.3	6.7
Total federal expenditures (in percent)	20.5	22.5	25.1
General	16.4	16.3	18.1
Intergovernmental	2.3	3.3	2.7
Direct general	14.1	13.0	15.4
National defense and international relations	8.3	5.5	6.2
Interest on general debt	1.4	2.2	3.4
Other	4.1	6.5	7.1
Insurance trust	4.1	6.2	7.1
Total state and local revenues (in percent)	14.8	16.5	18.6
General	12.9	13.9	15.3
Intergovernmental from federal	2.1	3.0	2.5
Own source	10.7	10.9	12.9
Taxes	8.5	8.1	9.0
Property	3.3	2.5	2.8
Sales and gross receipts	3.0	2.9	3.2
Individual income	1.1	1.5	1.9
Corporation income	0.4	0.5	0.4
Other	0.8	0.7	0.7
Charges and miscellaneous	2.2	2.8	3.8
Utilities and liquor stores	0.8	0.9	1.1
Insurance trust	1.1	1.6	2.2
Total state and local expenditures (in percent)	14.6	15.8	17.6
General	12.9	13.5	15.1
Education	5.2	4.9	5.2
Public welfare	1.4	1.7	2.0
Hospitals	0.8	0.9	0.9
Health	0.2	0.3	0.4
Highways	1.6	1.2	1.1
Police protection	0.4	0.5	0.6
Corrections	0.2	0.2	0.4
Sewerage and solid waste	0.3	0.5	0.5
Interest on general debt	0.4	0.5	0.9
Other	2.4	2.7	3.0
Utilities and liquor stores	0.9	1.3	1.4
Insurance trust	0.7	1.1	1.1

Source: Advisory Commission on Intergovernmental Relations (1994c).

portance of the different levels of government and the mix of revenues at each level has changed (see Tables 1, 2, and 3).

At the federal level, the personal income tax and payroll taxes have become the most important sources of tax revenue while the corporate income tax and selective sales taxes have diminished in importance in recent years, reflecting a combination of political and economic factors.[6] Unlike most developed countries, there is no broad-based consumption tax at the federal level.[7]

At the state level, the general sales tax has traditionally been the most important source of tax revenue. The personal income tax has, however, now essentially reached parity with the general sales tax. Similar to the federal level, the shares of corporate income tax and selective sales taxes have diminished in recent years.[8]

States exhibit considerable variation in their tax structure. Most states impose their own personal and corporate income taxes, sales taxes, and wealth transfer taxes. Broad-based state personal income taxes are imposed by 43 states, while corporate income taxes are imposed by 44 states. Michigan replaced its corporate income tax with a value-added tax (which differs from the value-added taxes in place elsewhere in that it is based on the additive method).[9] General sales taxes are imposed by 45 states. Alaska and New Hampshire impose no broad-based personal income taxes or general sales taxes.

At the local level, the property tax remains the predominant form of tax revenue, though it has diminished in importance in recent years. Frequently, more than one local jurisdiction levies a property tax, with each local jurisdiction levying its own rate with respect to its definition of the property tax base. In some states, local governments impose sales and income taxes.

Intergovernmental Grants

Intergovernmental grants create a complex web of transfers from one level of government to another.[10] State and local governments are heavily dependent on transfers from the federal government to meet

---

[6]Increased demands for redistribution through the tax code and the need for a buoyant source of revenues has led to the increase in personal income taxes, while payroll taxes have risen to support increased Social Security and Medicare responsibilities.

[7]Messere (1993).

[8]Advisory Commission on Intergovernmental Relations (1994c).

[9]Under the additive method the tax base is determined by adding (1) wages and (2) profits before taxes and debt service with certain adjustments.

[10]See Department of the Treasury, Office of State and Local Finance (1985) for a comprehensive discussion of the intergovernmental grants system in the United States.

Table 4. United States: Grants and General Expenditures

Year	Federal Grants as a Percentage of State and Local General Expenditures	State Grants as a Percentage of Local General Expenditures
1972	19.9	34.3
1973	22.8	35.5
1974	21.5	36.6
1975	21.5	35.9
1976	26.9	35.8
1977	27.0	36.1
1978	26.7	36.3
1979	26.1	37.4
1980	27.6	37.5
1981	23.2	37.7
1982	19.7	37.1
1983	19.0	35.7
1984	19.6	35.5
1985	19.4	36.5
1986	19.1	36.3
1987	17.0	35.7
1988	16.9	35.5
1989	16.7	35.9
1990	17.6	34.7
1991	17.6	34.4

Source: Advisory Commission on Intergovernmental Relations (1994c).

their financial needs. Federal grants as a percent of state and local expenditures increased greatly in the 1960s and early 1970s.[11] Federal government grants peaked in 1980 when these funds accounted for 27.6 percent of state and local general expenditures. Federal grants then declined as a proportion of expenditures, reaching a low of 16.7 percent in 1989, but have risen more recently, reflecting an increase in income transfers (Table 4). An increasingly large share of federal grant outlays are direct payments to individuals through income-transfer programs, administered by state governments.

A large proportion of the federal grants are passed through from state governments to local governments. In addition, state governments provide their own grants to local governments. Local governments are heavily dependent on this aid. Total state grants to local governments (including federal pass-through grants) were 34.4 percent of local expenditures in 1991 (see Table 4).[12]

---

[11]Federal grants are best expressed as a share of combined state and local outlays because an unknown amount of federal grants are passed on from state to local governments and the breakdown of responsibilities between state and local governments varies from state to state.

[12]Advisory Commission on Intergovernmental Relations (1994c).

Grant programs in the United States are either nonconditional or conditional. The main nonconditional program was revenue sharing, which was based on equalization principles. General revenue sharing was provided by the federal government to local governments from 1972 to 1986 and to state governments from 1972 to 1981.[13] This money was distributed by statutory formula with few restrictions on its use.[14] State governments still provide some nonconditional support to local governments.

There are two types of conditional grants. Block grants apply to broad categories of related functions and impose few restrictions on how states and localities allocate funds to activities within the block. There are block grants for health, social services, and other areas of expenditures.

Categorical grants provide money for a specific program, and several major types of categorical grant programs are used at the federal level. Formula-based grants distribute money to states and localities according to legislatively or administratively defined criteria. These criteria include factors that measure the needs of the community, its capacity to provide public services, the cost of providing public services, and the tax effort the community is already making to provide public services. These formulas vary from the most simple to very complicated but are typically related to population and per capita income of the community. The simplest formula might provide a fixed amount to each grant recipient regardless of the costs of providing that service. More typically, formulas provide amounts related to the costs of providing the service so the formula would have a variable amount (or a fixed and variable amount) related to the total population in the grant recipient's jurisdiction. For special purpose grants for education, the formula might vary with school enrollment; for prisons, the formula might vary with prison population, and so on.[15]

Formula grants include both open-ended, matching grants, and closed-end, matching and nonmatching grants. Medicaid (medical assistance for the poor) is the largest open-ended, matching program. The matching rate varies across states in inverse fashion to per capita

---

[13] Federal budgetary problems led to the erosion of support for this program, leading to its termination.

[14] The revenue-sharing formula included a mixture of factors reflecting expenditure needs and fiscal capacity. In the case of local governments, there was a "tiering" of the allocation process, with funds allocated first to counties and then to local governments within counties, disadvantaging poor jurisdictions in rich counties. See Department of the Treasury, Office of State and Local Finance (1985), pp. 183–93.

[15] Department of the Treasury, Office of State and Local Finance (1985), pp. 176–82.

income with the federal share ranging from 50 percent to roughly 80 percent.[16]

Project grants do not distribute money in a general manner. Governments solicit applications for these grants and award the funds selectively. These grants are closed-end and may or may not have matching requirements. There are also mixed formula and project grants, which are discretionary grants that are constrained by a formula.

Approximately half of the categorical grants require matching funds from the state and local governments, although the number of programs requiring matching funds has tended to decline in recent years. The state matching rate is usually quite low, covering far less than half of expenditures for most matching programs.

In 1993, the federal government had 593 grant programs—15 block grants and 578 categorical grants. Even though the federal government has made efforts, particularly in the early 1980s, to decrease the number of grant programs, these programs continue to proliferate, rising from 404 grant programs in 1984 to 593 programs in 1993.

In 1993, 1.1 percent of federal grant outlays were for general purpose grants (payments to Puerto Rico and the District of Columbia), 10.6 percent for broad-based grants (mostly block grants), and 88.3 percent for categorical grants. In 1993, project grants were 72.5 percent of federal categorical grant outlays, the highest percentage since 1975.[17]

Federal grant programs encompass the full range of government activities. The largest number of grants are for education, social services, health, transportation, pollution control, and regional development. In terms of expenditures, the greatest growth in recent decades has been for health, rising from 9.0 percent of federal grant expenditures in 1966 to 41.0 percent in 1994. This increase largely reflected the growth of Medicaid, which began in 1966 with $0.8 billion of expenditures (6.0 percent of expenditures) and reached $82.0 billion in 1994 (39.0 percent of expenditures). The increase in Medicaid spending has resulted from rapid increases in health care costs and in the number of people served by Medicaid, new services mandated by the federal government, and the discovery of strategies by states to enhance the federal contribution. Income support dropped from 27.8 percent to 24.5 percent of outlays over this period, while transportation dropped from 31.6 per-

---

[16] Aid to Families with Dependent Children (income support for poor families, generally headed by a single mother) was until 1996 the other large open-ended matching grant program.

[17] Advisory Commission on Intergovernmental Relations (1994a).

cent to 11.2 percent and education dropped from 20.0 percent to 15.5 percent.[18]

The distribution of federal grants has changed significantly over time among states. On a per capita basis, states that at one time were the largest recipients of aid have fallen relative to other states. The link between federal aid and state fiscal capacity—the potential ability to raise revenue relative to the cost of service—is weak. In the United States, however, intrastate disparities in fiscal capacity tend to be even larger than interstate disparities. Comparing counties within a state, federal aid does appear to reduce disparities in fiscal capacity.[19]

Although the state governments employ the same types of grants, their number and function are more limited. Well over half of state grant outlays to local governments are formula-based grants for public elementary and secondary education. The formulas on which this aid is based are usually related to local tax effort and expenditure needs and are intended to equalize spending on education across school districts. The states make only limited use of project grants in addition to general budgetary support. In addition to education, state governments provide funds for public welfare and other public services.

Considerable research has examined the effect of intergovernmental grants on the nature of state and local fiscal decisions.[20] The main conclusion of econometric research is that grants exert a powerful influence on both the level and composition of spending by recipient governments, emphasizing the importance of incorporating intergovernmental grants into an analysis of fiscal decision making.[21] In addition, this research has found that matching grants stimulate more spending than nonmatching grants, consistent with the predictions of the positive theory of grant response. These empirical findings suggest the importance of intergovernmental grants in determining the level and mix of public goods and services in the United States.

---

[18]Offfice of Management and Budget (1996).

[19]Department of the Treasury, Office of State and Local Finance (1985), pp. 193–206.

[20]See Craig and Inman (1982, 1986), Gramlich (1977, 1982), Inman (1979), and Stotsky (1991).

[21]Although intergovernmental grants are one mechanism by which the federal and state governments influence the actions of lower levels of government, mandates, particularly by the federal government, are another important mechanism. The receipt of grants may be premised on state and local governments meeting certain federally determined conditions. These mandates may be unfunded requiring state outlays to meet the federal requirements.

Tax Expenditures

Two features of the federal tax code are similar to grant programs, even though they do not involve direct transfers of funds to state and local governments. The federal government allows taxpayers who itemize personal expenses on their federal income tax returns to deduct the state and local income taxes and property taxes from gross income in computing federal income tax liabilities. Deductibility lowers the cost of these taxes for taxpayers who itemize. In effect, these taxpayers do not pay federal taxes on income used to pay these taxes. Deductibility allows state and local governments to shift part of the burden of these taxes to the federal government and thereby to make this deductibility equivalent to an open-ended, matching grant to state and local governments. Deductibility is an inefficient way to subsidize lower levels of government. The same support for state or local government spending could be achieved through direct transfers at lower cost to the federal treasury. Deductibility also reduces the progressivity of the federal tax code. In 1986, the federal government eliminated the deductibility of state and local sales taxes and contemplated eliminating all deductible taxes. The federal tax expenditure from this deductibility was estimated at $38.1 billion in 1994, representing one of the largest tax expenditures in the federal tax code. In some cases, states allow deductibility of federal income taxes, as well.

Interest on state and local debt is generally exempt from federal income taxes. The tax exempt feature of this debt allows state and local governments to issue it at a lower interest rate than prevails in the market because its return must only be competitive with the after-tax return to taxable debt. This exemption also functions like an open-ended, matching grant to state and local governments. This exemption is criticized as inefficient because it provides a higher return than is necessary for all but the marginal taxpayer and as inequitable in that the benefits largely accrue to higher-income taxpayers. In the early 1980s, state governments greatly expanded the use of municipal debt for private purposes. Encouraged by the tax exempt status of municipal debt, state governments borrow to subsidize private investments for the purpose of promoting economic development. This borrowing generally takes the form of revenue bonds, which are backed only by revenues from the project they are intended to finance. The rapid increase in this borrowing led Congress in 1986 to enact a cap on the amount of private purpose bonds each state can issue. The tax expenditure from the exemption of interest on municipal debt in 1994 was $12.0 billion for public purposes and $7.6 billion for private purposes.

Borrowing

The federal government is not required to run a balanced budget, but may issue debt to finance its deficit.[22] In 1991, the federal government's debt was $3,683.1 billion, equal to 65.0 percent of GDP.[23]

In 1991, aggregate state and local debt was $915.8 billion, equivalent to 16.2 percent of GDP. This figure has increased in recent decades, rising from 14.3 percent of GDP in 1970. Most of the growth has come in state government debt, which rose from 4.2 percent to 6.1 percent of GDP over this period.[24] State and local governments, which must generally have a balanced operating budget, primarily borrow to finance capital projects, such as public works and schools. They also borrow to subsidize private capital investments and to ease short-term cash flow problems. State and local borrowing is generally governed by constitutional and statutory provisions that vary across states and localities. The largest share of state and local government borrowing has typically financed the construction of highways, followed by education facilities, water and sewerage facilities, and other utilities. In recent decades, borrowing for highways and education has declined while that for utilities has risen. State and local governments also borrow to meet short-term cash flow needs. Since revenues and expenditures do not always match, governments borrow to cover short-term revenue shortfalls. Some governments have abused this privilege by using short-term borrowing to conceal deficits in their operating budgets, although requiring governments to adhere to generally accepted accounting practices constrains this activity. States also borrow to subsidize private industry. However, the 1986 Tax Reform Act's limitations on the use of tax-exempt borrowing for private purposes has dampened some of this activity.

In recent decades, large city governments in the United States, particularly in the East and Midwest, have encountered serious budget problems. As middle-income residents and businesses left for the suburbs, tax bases declined rapidly and needs for social welfare and other income-related public services rose rapidly. Several cities have used debt to buy time, but have in the process come close to default or bankruptcy (for example, Cleveland, New York, and Philadelphia). These problems have led to useful mechanisms to avoid such crises in the fu-

---

[22]There have been proposals for a Constitutional amendment to require a balanced budget. In the spring of 1995, one balanced budget amendment received the required two-thirds vote in the House but failed in the Senate by one vote. It is not clear whether three-fourths of the states would ratify an amendment proposed by the Congress.

[23]Advisory Commission on Intergovernmental Relations (1994c).

[24]Advisory Commission on Intergovernmental Relations (1994c).

ture, in particular, the development of stricter accounting standards for governments. Hard-pressed cities have looked to the state governments (and secondarily to the federal government) for assistance and in the process have become heavily dependent on state (and federal) funds.[25]

State and local governments are, in principle, free to borrow without federal government interference, and, in fact, the federal government subsidizes state and local borrowing by exempting the interest on state and local bonds from federal income taxation. In the case of state and local borrowing to finance private activities, such as home mortgages, student loans, airports, and water facilities, the exemption from income tax is limited to "qualified private activity bonds."

State and local borrowing also is limited, in part, by the requirements that state and local governments run balanced operating budgets and by the stricter accounting standards mentioned above. An even more important factor, however, is that the federal government does not guarantee state and local bonds. These bonds must be floated on the private capital market and meet the market test for soundness. Moreover, investors in state and local bonds rely on private bond rating agencies that grade the quality of bonds issued by the various state and local governments which, in turn, are quite sensitive to the risk their bonds will be downgraded as this affects borrowing costs.

Implications

Macroeconomic Management

Economic slowdowns cause budget problems for government by reducing revenues and increasing some expenditures above expected levels. During slowdowns, government spending rises above expected levels as people lose their jobs or face reduced workweeks, retire, and become eligible for unemployment compensation, welfare, pensions, and other income-transfer programs. The federal and state governments share the impact of these cyclical changes because they share funding responsibilities for the main income-transfer programs. Although the states administer Aid to Families with Dependent Children and Medicaid, the largest income-transfer programs available to the nonelderly, the federal government pays more than half of the cost of these programs. This raises the issue of what is the appropriate role of the federal and state governments in providing income insurance. The federal government has been seen as the principal provider of this insurance be-

---

[25]Ladd and Yinger (1989).

cause it has greater capacity for countercyclical spending and a broader tax base.[26]

The sensitivity of revenues to change in the level of economic output or income is measured by the income elasticity of revenues. Corporate and personal income taxes are generally regarded as having the greatest income elasticities, followed by the general sales tax, wealth taxes, and selective sales taxes. Since the federal government derives a large part of its revenue from income taxes, federal tax revenues tend to be income elastic. Since state governments derive a large part of their tax revenues from a mix of income taxes and the general sales tax, their tax revenues tend to be elastic but not as much as federal taxes. The U.S. Treasury estimated the weighted-average income elasticity of own source federal revenues as 1.14, state revenues as 1.10, and local revenues as 0.97, in 1984.[27]

This dependence on income-elastic taxes exerts a destabilizing influence on the budget because revenues grow more rapidly than income in expansions and revenues shrink more rapidly than income in recessions.[28] In recent decades, the federal government and state governments have relied increasingly on income and payroll taxes, making their tax revenues more sensitive to economic fluctuations.

Local governments, in contrast, for own source revenues rely primarily on property taxes, which are among the least elastic taxes. This exerts a stabilizing influence on local budgets during economic downturns, unless, as may sometimes be the case, an economic downturn coincides with a crash in the real estate market. In addition, with the exception of only a few local jurisdictions, local governments do not bear any direct responsibility for Aid to Families with Dependent Children and Medicaid, and hence do not face the same spending pressures in a downturn. Nevertheless, in a prolonged downturn, even the property tax may exhibit some income elasticity as nonpayment of taxes increases and property values are lowered to reflect the decline in economic activity, resulting in a drop in tax revenues (it is not always possible for local governments to raise tax rates to compensate for a decline in the base). In addition, in a growing economy, the inelasticity of the local government tax base results in a tax base that may grow relatively slowly compared with the income tax base, causing long-term problems for local governments.

Since the federal government can run a budget deficit, its budget tends to exert a countercyclical influence on economic activity. When

---

[26]Oates (1972).
[27]Department of the Treasury, Office of State and Local Finance (1985), p. 341.
[28]In contrast, income-elastic taxes exert a stabilizing effect on economic performance.

economic activity slows, the budget deficit widens, moderating a downturn. When economic activity increases rapidly, the budget deficit shrinks, moderating the stimulus. In principle, federal grants (as distinct from entitlement programs) could be used for explicitly countercyclical purposes, increasing during downturns and decreasing during upturns. There does not, however, appear to be any conscious policy of countercyclicality built into federal grant programs. In addition, the lags between recognition of an economic downturn, approval of additional spending, and actual spending may be too long for "public works" spending to be an effective countercyclical policy. Nevertheless, since a large share of grants are for income-transfer programs, such as Medicaid, these grants would tend to exert a countercyclical influence on the economy. But since the income-transfer programs require matching funds from state governments, this countercyclicality would not necessarily lead to a marked improvement in state and local budget problems. Other potentially countercyclical elements in federal grant policy have diminished in recent years with the fiscal retrenchment taking place at the federal level.

Since state and local governments generally cannot run a budget deficit on the current budget, their budgets have both countercyclical and procyclical elements. When economic downturns occur, state and local governments must move rapidly to eliminate any emerging deficit caused by falling revenues and rising expenditures. There are a variety of ways to finance a deficit.[29]

One way is to draw down reserve funds. Many states have Rainy Day Funds in which they hold surplus revenues for times of budgetary stress. A generally accepted rule of thumb in state government budgeting is that reserve be equal to approximately 5 percent of the current budget. Cash reserves can be used to conduct a countercyclical fiscal policy. As revenues fall in a downturn, previously accumulated cash reserves can be used to cushion the impact of this shortfall. As revenues rise in an upturn, surpluses can be allowed to accumulate. In recent years, the arrangements for Rainy Day Funds have become more formalized, even though most states have not met their reserve goals.[30] As a practical matter, it is difficult for state governments to maintain reserves, since there are always pressing needs and political pressure for government spending. In principle, reserves could play an important countercyclical role, but in practice, they have not been important in recent years.

---

[29]Eckl (1987).
[30]National Governors' Association (1994).

Large deficits, however, require spending and revenue adjustments that can either be short or long term in nature. On the spending side, the main problem is that states have little flexibility for cutting their budgets in the short term. A large proportion of state spending goes for goods and services, including contractual wages and salaries, leaving state governments with little room for discretionary spending cuts. Since state governments provide sizable aid to local governments, this is one area in which they may have some flexibility in cutting spending, although, in the case of education, the largest aid component, they may face restrictions on short-term cuts. In addition, reducing aid to local governments may help a state government avert a budget problem, but it ends up pushing the problem onto local governments. One tactic is to shift expenditures—such as the last paycheck of the fiscal year to state government employees, to vendors, or to local governments—into the next fiscal year. However, this is at best a stop-gap strategy because the additional revenues must be raised in the following year. States may also defer or eliminate capital expenditures, although delaying needed projects may raise their ultimate cost. Other methods include undermaintaining the infrastructure and underfunding the contribution to the employees' pension system or borrowing from it. But these tactics only thrust the problems onto future taxpayers.

On the revenue side, a large deficit may require governments to take short-term measures, such as accelerating the collection of taxes or raising taxes or other revenues. State governments can accelerate tax collection by reducing the interval for collection, creating a one-time revenue gain. State governments may also increase tax revenues by raising the rate of existing taxes, by broadening the base to which a tax applies, or by instituting a new source of tax revenues altogether. Unless the tax change is reflected in withholding or current payments, the change will not, however, increase revenues in the current fiscal year. Another way to raise revenues is by charging or increasing user fees for services.

The extent to which state budget management results in a counter-cyclical or procyclical influence depends in part on whether the stimulative effects of additional spending outweigh the depressing effects of higher taxes and charges required to balance the budget. In the most recent recession, state budgets were viewed as exerting a markedly more procyclical stance than in the past, reflecting the many pressures placed upon state governments these days.

While short-term state budget problems may largely reflect cyclical forces in the economy, to the extent that these problems represent longer-term structural budget problems, they require states to supplement short-term measures with more fundamental reforms of expenditures and revenues. These reforms may take the form of cuts in the scope or extent of expenditure programs, greater efficiency in the provision of public services, expansion of the tax base, increases in tax rates, or introduction of a new tax. States faced with persistent revenue shortfalls have taken a variety of adjustment measures, depending on the political and economic situation. States where voters are already discontented with the high level of taxes may have to rely on expenditure cuts. Elsewhere, state voters may find tax hikes more palatable.

Structural Reform

In recent decades, an important source of pressure on state governments has come from local governments to assume responsibilities for certain programs and to increase intergovernmental aid. The pressures stem primarily from demands of the poorer communities for redistribution from wealthier communities.

Public education is one area where most state governments are under pressure to increase their funding responsibilities because of inequalities in spending levels across communities within a state. Public elementary and secondary education was once largely the responsibility of local governments, with most funding coming from the local property tax. Since the local property tax is the main source of tax revenue for localities, the variation in wealth across communities within a state, reflected in property values, leads to similar variation in local government ability to fund local public services. State governments have reduced this variation through intergovernmental grants to the local governments for funding public elementary and secondary education and other public services. Nevertheless, these efforts have been inadequate to satisfy critics of the system of funding public education.

Since the 1971 *Serrano vs. Priest* decision in California, under which the state supreme court ordered the state to devise a grant program to equalize per pupil spending across California school districts, courts in the majority of states have ordered state governments to reform their public education financing system, leading to far-reaching changes in state tax systems to finance the additional responsibilities. In recent decades, the states have assumed a more important role in this funding. Since the 1970s, state governments have financed a larger share of this education than local governments. Nevertheless, 25 years after *Serrano*, there are still many inequalities in public education financing and the court cases continue. Ultimately, state governments may have to assume most of the role of funding elementary and secondary education, requiring stronger taxing powers.

Strengthening the taxing powers of the state government generally entails reforming both the general sales tax and the personal income tax.[31] The main problem with the general sales tax is that it often taxes business services while exempting a significant fraction of personal consumption. In particular, most general sales taxes do not tax consumer services in any comprehensive way and efforts on the part of state governments to extend the sales tax to services have at times met with significant opposition, although some extension to services has occurred in recent years. Despite the low overall reliance on consumption taxes in the United States relative to other developed countries,[32] the personal income tax remains the most promising prospect for state governments to expand their taxing powers. This tax has grown rapidly in recent decades as a share of state government revenues and is best suited to meet the demands for increased redistribution between communities in a state.

There have also been important structural changes in the intergovernmental grants system. In the early 1980s, the Reagan administration suggested major changes in the system of distributing federal grant money. It proposed eliminating the general revenue-sharing program to the state governments and consolidating many smaller categorical grants into larger block grants, both of which were enacted. The administration's more dramatic proposals were to shift responsibility for the major health and public assistance programs. It proposed that the federal government assume all responsibility for Medicaid and return almost all responsibility for Aid to Families with Dependent Children and food stamps (in-kind food aid to the poor) to the state and local governments. These proposals were not enacted, although given the growth of Medicaid spending, the states may wish that they had disposed of any responsibility for this program.

In 1986, the Reagan administration eliminated local revenue sharing and the deductibility of sales taxes and limited the use of tax exempt municipal bonds. Since then, there have been no major shifts in the federalist system, although, both Presidents Bush and Clinton have proposed various changes.

The year 1996 has proven to be a watershed for U.S. intergovernmental fiscal relations. In 1996, the Republican-controlled Congress enacted legislation to end the federal entitlement for Aid to Families with Dependent Children. The bill replaces this program with a block grant to states and allows them to set their own eligibility standards.

---

[31]Break (1994), pp. 1–5.
[32]Messere (1993).

The amount a state can receive depends on the amount it was receiving under Aid to Families with Dependent Children. The bill restricts eligibility for individuals who remain unemployed, requiring recipients to find a job within two years of first receiving aid. It also restricts lifetime benefits to five years of aid. This change will have major ramifications for state and local governments. The main change is a greatly increased role for state governments. This strategy is designed to shift budgetary pressures from the federal government to the state and local governments and to give state and local governments more discretion in how they design and administer welfare programs. State and local governments will feel budgetary pressures most acutely in any future recessions when the need for entitlements grows rapidly. The likely result is that state spending on entitlements will decline in the face of diminished resources and an increase in the effective "price" of these entitlements with the loss of the matching grant.

Still remaining on the Republican agenda are legislation to amend the Constitution to require a balanced budget, and to replace the federal income tax with a flat tax or consumption-based tax.[33] If the federal government adopts a balanced budget amendment, this could also lead to cuts in intergovernmental aid, adding further stress on the state and local governments.

Recent proposals for federal tax reform could also have a significant effect on state and local finances. Several of these proposals would eliminate any remaining deductibility of state and local taxes under the federal income tax. Adoption by the federal government of any proposal for a broad-based consumption tax to replace the federal income tax likely would force states to abandon their corporate income taxes inasmuch as these taxes conform to the federal tax base. With repeal of the federal tax, the state tax bases would diverge, imposing much higher compliance costs on companies that operate in many states. Taken together, federal changes in intergovernmental grant policy, budget policy, and tax policy could imply radical changes in the nature of fiscal federalism in the United States in years ahead.

References

Advisory Commission on Intergovernmental Relations, 1994a *Characteristics of Federal Grant-in-Aid Programs to State and Local Governments: Grants Funded FY 1993* (Washington: Advisory Commission on Intergovernmental Relations, January).

---

[33]Gold (1995).

———, 1994b, *Significant Features of Fiscal Federalism*, Vol. 1 (Washington: Advisory Commission on Intergovernmental Relations, June).

———, 1994c, *Significant Features of Fiscal Federalism*, Vol. 2 (Washington: Advisory Commission on Intergovernmental Relations, December).

Break, George F., 1994, "The Big Four of State-Local Tax Finance: Under Siege in a Changing World," *NTA Forum*, Spring/Summer, pp. 1–5.

Craig, Steven G., and Robert P. Inman, 1982, "Federal Aid and Public Education: An Empirical Look at the New Fiscal Federalism," *Review of Economics and Statistics*, Vol. 64, pp. 541–52.

———, 1986, "Education, Welfare and the 'New' Federalism: State Budgeting in a Federalist Public Economy," *Studies in State and Local Public Finance*, ed. by Harvey S. Rosen (Chicago: University of Chicago Press for the National Bureau of Economic Research).

Department of Commerce, Bureau of the Census, *Government Finances*, various issues.

Department of the Treasury, Office of State and Local Finance, 1985, *Federal-State-Local Fiscal Relations* (Washington: U.S. Government Printing Office).

Eckl, Corina L., 1987, *State Deficit Management Strategies* (Denver: National Conference of State Legislatures, November).

Gold, Steven D., 1995, "Impacts of the Revolution in Federal Policies on State and Local Government," *NTA Forum*, Summer, pp. 1–6.

Gramlich, Edward M., 1977, "Intergovernmental Grants: A Review of the Empirical Literature," in *The Political Economy of Fiscal Federalism*, ed. by Wallace E. Oates (Lexington, Massachusetts: Lexington Books).

———, 1982, "An Econometric Examination of the New Federalism," *Brookings Papers on Economic Activity*, Vol. 2, pp. 327–60.

Inman, Robert P., 1979, "The Fiscal Performance of Local Governments: An Interpretive Review," in *Current Issues in Urban Economics*, ed. by Peter Mieszkowski and Mahlon Straszheim (Baltimore: Johns Hopkins University Press).

———, 1983, "Anatomy of a Fiscal Crisis," *Business Review: Federal Reserve Bank of Philadelphia*, September/October, pp. 15–22.

Kenyon, Daphne A., and Karen M. Benker, 1984, "Fiscal Discipline: Lessons from the State Experience," *National Tax Journal*, Vol. 37, No. 3, pp. 433–46.

Ladd, Helen F., and John Yinger, 1989, *America's Ailing Cities* (Baltimore: Johns Hopkins University Press, 1989).

Messere, Ken, 1993, *Tax Policy in OECD Countries* (Amsterdam: IBFD Publications BV).

National Governors' Association, 1994, *The Fiscal Survey of the States* (Washington: National Governors' Association, April).

Oates, Wallace E., 1972, *Fiscal Federalism* (New York: Harcourt Brace Jovanovich).

Office of Management and Budget, 1996, *Budget of the United States Government: Historical Tables* (Washington: Office of Management and Budget).

Preston, Anne E., and Casey Ichniowski, 1991, "A National Perspective on the Nature and Effects of the Local Property Tax Revolt, 1976–1986," *National Tax Journal*, Vol. 44, No. 2, pp. 123–45.

Stotsky, Janet G., 1991, "State Fiscal Responses to Federal Government Grants," *Growth and Change*, Summer, pp. 17–31.

PART III

Practice: Developing Countries

16

Argentina

GERD SCHWARTZ AND CLAIRE LIUKSILA

Argentina is a large and decentralized country with significant constitutional powers bestowed to the provincial level of government. As defined in Article 1 of its National Constitution, there are three main levels of administration: federal, provincial, and municipal. The general constitutional organizing principle is that the provinces hold all powers that they have not delegated to the federal level.

At the same time, Argentina has large regional concentrations of population, and strong regional disparities in levels of economic development. Given such disparities, the ability of subnational governments to provide goods and services to the population and finance these out of own resources differ considerably. As a result, the federal government has faced, and continues to face, very different demands from the different provinces.

Until the mid-1970s, Argentina was characterized by extensive centralization of various aspects of public policymaking, particularly in the areas of taxation and the exercise of regulatory functions. Since then, substantial decentralization of spending responsibilities has taken place; revenue-raising powers, however, remain largely concentrated at the federal level, with attendant large vertical imbalances and heavy dependence of the provincial and local governments on transfers from the central government, including revenue sharing. A reform of the

---

We would like to thank Ehtisham Ahmad, Jerald Schiff, Ernesto Stein, Teresa Ter-Minassian, and the participants of a Fiscal Affairs Department seminar on "Argentina: Fiscal Federalism and Provincial Tax Issues" for helpful comments and suggestions, and Lina Annab and Derek Bills for excellent research support.

current system of intergovernmental fiscal relations is clearly a high priority for Argentina, and one that the authorities will need to face in the near term.

This chapter describes the main features and characteristics of Argentina's system of fiscal federalism, analyzes key policy issues and problems, and discusses various reform options, focusing on revenue and expenditure assignments and responsibilities, the system of transfers, borrowing, and the federal-provincial fiscal pacts. Some aspects of tax administration and public expenditure management are also discussed. The concluding section analyzes major implications of the existing system for macroeconomic management and structural reform.

Structure of Argentina's Public Sector

Notwithstanding substantial progress with privatization, deregulation, and other structural reforms over the last several years, Argentina's public sector remains fairly extensive. Its principal public sector entities are three levels of public administration (that is, the *federal* administration, 23 *provincial* administrations plus the administration of the municipality of Buenos Aires, and 1,110 *municipal* administrations), the quasi-public health funds, and the financial public sector. The federal administration includes the central government, various decentralized agencies, federally owned nonfinancial public enterprises, and the national social security system. Provincial governments, including the municipality of Buenos Aires, have their own nonfinancial public enterprises and social security systems for provincial government workers.[1] In March 1996, the financial public sector included the Central Bank, 6 national official banks, and 21 provincial and municipal banks.

The National Constitution stipulates that provinces must organize and assure in their territories an effective municipal system. The concrete design of this system is left to each province to decide, but it has to be outlined in the respective provincial constitutions. In practice, provinces have granted varying degrees of independence to their municipalities; most, but not all, have granted autonomy to their municipalities, implying that municipalities are free to establish their own procedures for government, including, at least in theory, the right to

---

[1]Many of the social security systems for provincial government employees are being incorporated into the national social security system, a process that started in 1994.

establish and administer their own taxes. A significant development in this regard is the direct election of mayors, a process that was initiated in the municipality of Buenos Aires in June 1996.

Fiscal Federalism: Main Aspects and Recent Reforms

The major policy shaping Argentina's system of fiscal federalism since the mid-1970s has been "re-decentralization," which has been intensified over the last several years and is expected to continue over the short to medium term. While, according to the National Constitution, provincial governments hold significant powers, historically, more and more decision-making authority had gradually been transferred to the federal level. For example, according to the National Constitution, the provinces are to guarantee basic education, while other levels of education are understood to be the joint responsibility of the federal and provincial administrations. Over time, however, federal educational policy had gradually come to encompass all levels of schooling and largely absorbed provincial powers in this area (Artana and others, 1995). Since the mid-1970s, this process is being reversed, and more and more responsibilities in the education sector have been transferred back to the provinces. Similar processes of centralization and subsequent decentralization have also taken place in other sectors, particularly in health care.

One of the more notable features of the current system of fiscal federalism in Argentina is the imbalance between own resources and spending at the different levels of government (Artana and López Murphy, 1994; Artana and others, 1995; and Fundación de Investigaciones Económicas Latinoamericanas (FIEL), 1993). Table 1 shows that, in 1995, for example, provinces carried out 54 percent of all national and provincial expenditures, while own revenues of provincial governments accounted only for about 20 percent of total provincial and national revenue. Overall, provincial government own revenues only covered about 40 percent of provincial government expenditure in 1995 (Table 2).

These own revenue and expenditure imbalances have meant that revenue-sharing mechanisms have traditionally been a central element of fiscal federalism in Argentina. Decentralization initiatives on the expenditure side increased even further the importance of various revenue-sharing mechanisms, and they featured prominently in two recent federal-provincial fiscal pacts. In 1995, federal transfers covered about 50 percent of provincial government expenditure, and provincial transfers covered roughly 55 percent of municipal government spending

Table 1. **Argentina: Revenue and Expenditure Shares of Federal and Provincial Levels of Government**
(In percent of total)

	1991	1992	1993	1994	Est. 1995
Revenue shares					
Before transfers	100	100	100	100	100
Federal level[1]	84	82	80	80	80
Provincial level	16	18	20	20	20
After transfers	100	100	100	100	100
Federal level[1]	56	54	56	56	55
Provincial level	44	46	44	44	45
Expenditure shares	100	100	100	100	100
Federal level[1]	48	42	42	44	46
Provincial level	52	58	58	56	54
Memorandum items:					
Provincial own revenues in percent of provincial expenditure	34	39	42	41	41
Transfers in percent of total federal and provincial revenue[2]	28	28	24	24	25

Sources: Government of Argentina; and authors' calculations.
[1]The federal level comprises the federal government, decentralized agencies, the national social security system, and the operating surplus of national public enterprises. Operations to clear expenditure arrears to suppliers, provinces, and pensioners are excluded from expenditures.
[2]Based on the consolidated accounts of the 23 provinces plus the municipality of Buenos Aires.

(Artana and others, 1995). The 1994 Constitution stipulated that a new revenue-sharing agreement was to go into effect on January 1, 1997, but that date has been postponed.

Argentina's revenue-sharing mechanisms have a redistributive character, that is, they are meant to benefit poorer provinces more than richer provinces. Table 3 shows per capita revenue and expenditure for various groups of provinces relative to the average for all provinces. In per capita terms, advanced (that is, richer) provinces had significantly lower total revenue and expenditure than less-developed provinces, received less funds through revenue sharing mechanisms, but raised more revenue from own sources.

Interestingly, the wedge between advanced and less-developed provinces may have widened over the period 1972–91. For example, data in Table 3 show that, during 1972–91, per capita own revenues of advanced provinces increased relative to the average for all provinces from 111 percent to 121 percent, but fell in less-developed provinces from 48 percent to 42 percent. Over the same period, however, per capita expenditure in advanced provinces fell relative to the average of all provinces from 86 percent to 78 percent, but increased in less-developed provinces

Table 2. Argentina: Provincial Government Finances[1]
(In percent of GDP)

	1989	1990	1991	1992	1993	1994	Est. 1995
Total revenues	7.9	7.1	8.2	9.7	9.7	9.6	9.3
From own sources[2]	2.6	2.4	3.0	3.8	4.4	4.3	4.1
Federal transfers	5.2	4.7	5.2	5.9	5.3	5.2	5.2
Coparticipation	3.2	2.9	3.8	4.4	4.0	3.8	3.7
Housing Fund (FONAVI)	0.4	0.5	0.4	0.3	0.3	0.3	0.3
Tax advances	0.5	0.2	0.1	—	—	—	—
Other	1.2	0.8	0.9	1.1	1.0	1.2	1.1
Total expenditures	8.4	8.5	9.0	9.9	10.5	10.5	10.2
Current expenditures	7.1	7.2	7.8	8.8	9.2	9.1	9.0
Wages	4.1	4.4	4.7	5.3	5.5	5.3	5.4
Goods and services	0.9	0.9	1.0	1.0	1.1	1.1	1.0
Interest	0.3	0.1	0.1	0.2	0.2	0.2	0.2
Transfers to municipalities	0.8	0.8	1.0	1.1	1.2	1.1	1.0
Other	0.9	1.0	1.0	1.3	1.3	1.3	1.3
Capital expenditures	1.3	1.3	1.2	1.1	1.3	1.4	1.2
Overall balance	−0.5	−1.4	−0.7	−0.2	−0.8	−0.9	−0.9
Memorandum item:							
Overall balance excluding federal transfers	−5.7	−6.1	−5.9	−6.1	−6.1	−6.1	−6.1

Sources: Government of Argentina; and authors' calculations.
[1]Consolidated accounts of 23 provinces and the municipality of Buenos Aires.
[2]In addition to own revenue (current and capital), contains nonclassified revenue. Privatization receipts are excluded

from 121 percent to 145 percent; this may point to a widening gap in expenditure efficiency and productivity across provinces.[2]

Expenditure Assignments

Expenditure assignments in Argentina are not dissimilar to those in other federal countries. The central government is exclusively responsible for matters concerning defense, foreign affairs, international trade, the regulation of interstate trade, monetary policy, immigration policy, and provision of unemployment insurance[3] (Table 4). Responsibility for health care and primary and secondary education rests jointly with fed-

---

[2]Low-density provinces have been separated out because they may be considered as a special case. For example, many low-density provinces have relatively high per capita own revenue due to natural resource rents. They also have high per capita expenditure due to indivisibilities; that is, basic infrastructure and services have to be provided independent of population density.

[3]Unemployment insurance is also provided by the private sector.

Table 3. Argentina: Per Capita Revenue and Expenditure in Different Groups of Provinces

(Average for all provinces = 100)

	1972	1981	1991
Total revenue			
Advanced provinces	78	81	82
Low-density provinces	217	216	208
Intermediate provinces	123	113	121
Less-developed provinces	127	149	143
Own revenues			
Advanced provinces	111	113	121
Low-density provinces	151	93	146
Intermediate provinces	70	68	70
Less-developed provinces	48	60	42
Coparticipation transfer revenue			
Advanced provinces	83	74	66
Low-density provinces	216	200	169
Intermediate provinces	128	143	157
Less-developed provinces	140	166	192
Other transfer revenue			
Advanced provinces	21	40	38
Low-density provinces	319	422	499
Intermediate provinces	198	151	130
Less-developed provinces	236	271	228
Total expenditure			
Advanced provinces	86	84	78
Low-density provinces	235	205	230
Intermediate provinces	121	110	116
Less-developed provinces	121	143	145

Sources: Fundación de Investigaciones Económicas Latinoamericanas (1993); and authors' calculations.

Note: The advanced provinces are the Province of Buenos Aires, the Municipality of Buenos Aires, Santa Fé, Córdoba, and Mendoza; the low-density provinces are Chubut, Santa Cruz, La Pampa, Río Negro, Neuquén, and Tierra del Fuego; the intermediate provinces are San Juan, San Luis, Entre Ríos, Tucumán, and Salta; and the less-developed provinces are Catamarca, Chaco, Corrientes, Formosa, Jujuy, La Rioja, Misiones, and Santiago del Estero.

eral, provincial, and municipal governments; responsibilities for social welfare services, police, and highways are shared between federal and provincial levels of government.

Consolidated nonfinancial public sector expenditure increased by over 3 percentage points of GDP during 1989–95 and amounted to 23 percent of GDP in 1995 (Table 5). The federal level accounted for about 55 percent of this total.[4] However, after subtracting interest

---

[4]As defined here, the federal level includes the federal government, decentralized agencies, the national social security system, and the operating surplus of national public enterprises.

Table 4. Argentina: Selected Expenditure Assignments of Federal, Provincial, and Municipal Governments

Expenditure	Delivery of Service	Financing	Regulatory Powers
Defense	F	F	F
Environmental policy	F, P, M	F, P, M	F, P, M
Education			
Primary	P, M	P, M	F, P, M
Secondary	P	P	F, P, M
University	F	F	F
Foreign affairs	F	F	F
Health	F, P, M	F, P, M	F, P
Health insurance	F, P	F, P, M	F, P
Immigration policy	F	F	F
International trade	F	F	F
Interstate trade regulation	F	F	F
Justice	F, P, M	F, P, M	F, P, M
Monetary policy	F	F	F
Public safety			
Prisons	F, P	F, P	F, P
Police	F, P	F, P	F, P
Roads	F, P, M	F, P, M	F, P
Social housing	P	F, P	
Social welfare	F, P	F, P	F, P
Transport			
Sea	F	F	F
Rail (passengers)	P	F	F, P
Air	P	...	F, P
Unemployment insurance	F	F	F

Sources: Shah (1994); and Artana and others (1995).
Note. F = federal level of government; P = provincial level of government; and M = municipal level of government. In addition, there is private sector provision for different expenditure categories alongside public sector provision, as in the case of unemployment insurance.

payments, mandated social security transfers, and other entitlement programs, the federal level had discretion over only about 12 percent of total spending of the nonfinancial public sector. The increase in expenditures that occurred during 1989–95 was about evenly distributed between the federal level and the provincial level. While, for the provincial level, the increase in expenditures was largely due to the transfer of responsibilities from the federal level, the increase in expenditures of the federal level was mostly because of growing pension spending, and occurred notwithstanding the ongoing transfer of responsibilities—in health and education—to the provinces.

Since the mid-1970s, and reflecting efforts to improve public sector efficiency, the policy of devolving spending from the federal to subnational levels of government and to the private sector has resulted in important changes in the structure of public expenditures. Examples of

Table 5. Argentina: Consolidated Nonfinancial Public Sector[1]
(In percent of GDP)

	1989	1990	1991	1992	1993	1994	Est. 1995
Consolidated nonfinancial public sector							
Revenue	16.4	16.2	18.8	21.0	22.2	21.6	20.7
Expenditure	19.7	20.3	22.1	21.4	22.1	23.0	23.0
Balance	−3.3	−4.1	−3.2	−0.4	0.1	−1.4	−2.2
National nonfinancial public sector							
Revenue	13.7	13.8	15.8	17.2	17.8	17.3	16.6
Tax revenue	11.2	11.9	14.3	16.1	16.5	16.2	15.5
Non-tax revenue	1.7	1.0	1.2	0.9	1.0	1.1	1.1
Operating surplus of state enterprises	0.8	0.9	0.3	0.2	0.3	—	—
Expenditure	16.5	16.5	18.3	17.4	16.9	17.8	18.0
Transfers to provinces[2]	5.2	4.7	5.2	5.9	5.3	5.2	5.2
Own spending	11.3	12.1	13.1	11.5	11.6	12.6	12.8
Balance	−2.8	−2.7	−2.5	−0.2	0.9	−0.5	−1.4
Provincial nonfinancial public sector							
Total revenue	7.9	7.1	8.2	9.7	9.7	9.6	9.3
Own revenue	2.7	2.4	3.0	3.8	4.4	4.3	4.1
Transfers to provinces[2]	5.2	4.7	5.2	5.9	5.3	5.2	5.2
Expenditure	8.4	8.5	9.0	9.9	10.5	10.5	10.2
Balance	−0.5	−1.4	−0.7	−0.2	−0.8	−0.9	−0.9

Sources: Argentine authorities; and authors' calculations.

[1] As defined in this table, the consolidated nonfinancial public sector comprises the national and the provincial nonfinancial public sector; it excludes the municipal nonfinancial public sector. The national nonfinancial public sector comprises the federal government, decentralized agencies, the national social security system, and the operating surplus of national nonfinancial state enterprises. The provincial nonfinancial public sector reported here only comprises the consolidated operations of the provincial governments. Federal government operations to clear expenditure arrears to suppliers, provinces, and pensioners, financed by bond issues (BOCONs) are excluded from expenditures.

[2] Based on the data reported in the consolidated accounts of the provincial nonfinancial public sector.

these changes are provided in Table 6. For instance, while in 1983 the federal level carried out 44 percent of all education spending, in 1992 its share was reduced to 22 percent, reflecting the ongoing devolution of spending responsibilities for primary and secondary education to the provinces; the share of provincial expenditures increased correspondingly. A similar pattern is found in health care spending, with the difference that municipal rather than provincial government spending was increased, at the expense of federal level spending. Similar reductions of the share of federal level spending were also observed in other expenditure categories, such as social assistance, public housing, and spending on infrastructure and general services. In all these cases, the major increase in expenditure responsibilities occurred at the provincial level of government.

Table 6. Argentina: Use and Provision of Public Funds for Selected Expenditure Items

	1983	1992	Change in Shares 1983–92	Real Growth Rate During 1983–92
	(In percent of total)		(In percent)	
Education				
Spending of public funds	100	100	—	+28
Federal level	44	22	–22	–36
Provincial level	49	70	+21	+82
Municipal level	2	2	—	+76
Private sector	5	6	+1	+56
Provision of financing	100	100	—	+28
Federal level	49	27	–22	–30
Provincial level	49	71	+22	+84
Municipal level	2	2	—	+76
Health care				
Spending of public funds	100	100	—	+24
Federal level	17	11	–6	–19
Provincial level	74	74	—	+24
Municipal level	9	15	+6	+114
Private sector	—	—	—	—
Provision of financing	100	100	—	+24
Federal level	24	14	–10	–30
Provincial level	67	72	+5	+32
Municipal level	9	15	+6	+114
Social assistance				
Spending of public funds	100	100	—	+38
Federal level	19	2	–17	–85
Provincial level	18	37	+19	+188
Municipal level	7	9	+2	+82
Private sector	56	52	–4	+28
Provision of financing	100	100	—	+38
Federal level	81	65	–16	+10
Provincial level	12	26	+14	+203
Municipal level	7	9	+2	+82
Public housing				
Spending of public funds	100	100	—	–24
Federal level	18	7	–11	–70
Provincial level	82	93	+11	–14
Municipal level	—	—	—	—
Private sector	—	—	—	—
Provision of financing	100	100	—	–24
Federal level	84	79	–5	–28
Provincial level	16	21	+5	–5
Municipal level	—	—	—	
Infrastructure and services				
Spending of public funds	100	100	—	–50
Federal level	68	39	–29	–72
Provincial level	30	57	+27	–6
Municipal level	2	4	+2	+32
Private sector	—	—	—	—
Provision of financing	100	100	—	–50
Federal level	72	58	–14	–60
Provincial level	26	38	+12	–27
Municipal level	2	4	+2	+32

Source: Authors' calculations based on data in Artana and others (1995).

The devolution of expenditure responsibilities in areas such as primary education, hospitals, water, electricity, and adult education, need not affect the financing of these expenditures, that is, while spending responsibilities are transferred to subnational levels, the federal level could continue to provide financing via transfers. In Argentina, this only held true in some cases. For example, for social assistance, which grew by 38 percent in real terms during 1983–92, the federal level reduced dramatically its own spending, but increased its overall provision of financing, although by much less than the overall increase in spending (see Table 6).

In many cases, however, the devolution of expenditure responsibilities to subnational levels of government took place without a comparable transfer of funds to finance these activities, even though some compensating transfer payments were and are being made. For example, in the case of health care spending, which grew by 24 percent in real terms during 1983–92, the federal level decreased its own spending and its provision of financing, suggesting that expenditure responsibilities were devolved without providing full financing for the transfer of responsibilities. Similar patterns existed for education spending, public housing, and infrastructure and services (see Table 6).

To face the increased expenditure responsibilities, subnational governments resorted, among other things, to financing from provincial banks or commercial banks (often collateralized by future receipts from revenue-sharing agreements), or issued IOUs in lieu of paying wages; provinces also received discretionary aid from the central government in the form of loans or grants.

In general, though, the devolution of expenditure responsibilities forced subnational governments to prioritize spending. As a result, the structure of subnational government expenditures underwent significant changes. The observed real growth of health and education spending, for example, reflected a redirection of spending by the municipal and provincial administrations that more than compensated for the decision by the federal government to reduce its own funding of these functions. The increased spending on health and education by provincial and municipal governments was matched by substantial expenditure cuts elsewhere, such as public housing and public infrastructure and services. This view is corroborated by evidence of neglect of public infrastructures in various Argentine provinces (see Schuler, 1995).

Tax Assignments

The National Constitution establishes the principles of separation of tax sources between the federal government and the provinces. However, ever since the federal government experienced a fiscal crisis in the late nineteenth century, a number of tax sources, notably consumption, have been shared between the federal and provincial governments. In theory, the current system is rather simple: the federal government has exclusive powers to set import and export duties, and, for a limited period of time, may also establish direct taxes; indirect taxes are concurrent taxes that can be imposed by the federal and/or provincial governments; the provinces have the exclusive right to impose permanent direct taxes.[5]

In practice, the provinces have delegated much of their responsibility for legislating, administrating, and collecting taxes to the central government, but receive a share from these taxes. Two key reasons for this delegation of power are that the central government can collect most taxes more efficiently than provincial governments, and that the potential tax bases differ significantly from province to province. Taxes collected by the federal government include the income tax, the value-added tax (VAT), excise taxes, foreign trade taxes, liquid fuel and energy taxes, the gross assets tax (which was levied on companies but has recently been eliminated), the personal assets tax (levied on individuals), social security taxes, and a number of minor levies. Taxes collected by provincial and municipal governments are the real estate tax, the automobile tax, road taxes, and the provincial turnover tax, which, in 1993, accounted for over 50 percent of all own revenue of the provinces and is levied in addition to the federal VAT.

Total revenue of the consolidated nonfinancial public sector increased by 4.3 percent of GDP during 1989–95 to a level of 20.7 percent of GDP in 1995 (see Table 5). About two-thirds (2.9 percent of GDP) of the increase in overall revenue occurred at the federal level, which experienced a rapid growth of tax revenue (by 4.3 percent of GDP), but reductions in nontax revenue (by 0.6 percent of GDP) and in operating surpluses of state enterprises (by 0.8 percent of GDP), the latter reflecting extensive privatization. In 1995, about 80 percent of all revenue was collected at the federal level, slightly less than in 1989.

As already suggested, the centralization of revenue-raising functions at the federal level reflects, to some extent, the different capacities of different provinces to raise their own revenue, which in turn is mainly due to differences in provincial tax bases, and, to a lesser extent, to differences in the strength of provincial tax administrations. Overall, provincial own revenues represented about 45 percent of total provin-

---

[5]Sales taxes, such as the provincial turnover tax, are defined as "direct taxes" in Argentina.

cial government revenue in 1993; the remainder came from various federal transfer mechanisms. In 1992, Argentina's most advanced subnational entity, the municipality of Buenos Aires, with 9 percent of the country's population (according to the 1991 census), accounted for 27 percent of all tax revenue collected by the provincial administrations. In contrast, 6 poorer provinces,[6] that together also accounted for 9 percent of the country's population, raised only 3 percent of all tax revenue collected by the provincial administrations.[7] Other evidence also points to the different taxing abilities of different provinces according to their level of economic development (see Table 3): in 1991, for example, per capita own revenue of the economically advanced provinces exceeded the average for all provinces by about 20 percent; in contrast, the less-developed provinces only collected 42 percent of the average per capita own revenue for all provinces.

If own tax collections are taken as an indicator, economic differences between the advanced and the less-developed provinces have been increasing (see Table 3): in 1991, advanced provinces exceeded the national average for per capita revenue from own sources by more than they did 20 years earlier, whereas the less-developed provinces fell short of the national per capita average by more than they did 20 years earlier. The mirror image is that, in per capita terms, the less developed provinces had to rely more and the advanced provinces less on transfers from the federal level in 1991 than they did in 1972.

Intergovernmental Transfers

Argentina has elaborate federal-provincial transfer mechanisms, which are necessary given that revenue-raising functions continue to be fairly centralized while expenditure functions are being gradually decentralized. There are similarly elaborate provincial-municipal transfer mechanisms, but these differ from province to province. As shown in Table 1, in 1995, transfers from the federal level to the provinces amounted to 25 percent of the total national and provincial revenue collected. However, the quantitative importance of federal-provincial revenue transfers differs significantly across provinces. While, for example, in the province of Buenos Aires transfers represented only 51 percent of provincial expenditures in 1993, in four provinces (Cata-

---

[6]Catamarca, Corrientes, Formosa, Jujuy, La Rioja, and Santiago del Estero.
[7]For details, see Gómez Sabaini (1993); data for earlier periods are shown in Fundación de Investigaciones Económicas Latinoamericanas (1993).

marca, Formosa, La Rioja, and Santiago del Estero) they accounted for more than 90 percent.

Improving the structure of the federal-provincial transfer mechanisms is of key importance for improving Argentina's public sector efficiency: given the wide regional economic disparities, a transfer system will always remain a central element of Argentina's system of fiscal federalism, no matter by how much provincial tax bases and tax administrations can be improved.

It has sometimes been argued that the redistributive effect of transfers falls short of what would be needed to address Argentina's significant regional differences. For example, the World Bank (1996), based on data presented by Porto and Sanguinetti (1993), argues that per capita transfers to the poorest provinces (Chaco, Formosa, and Santiago del Estero), where close to 40 percent of the population lived below the poverty line in 1991, are only slightly higher than the average per capita transfer to all provinces, whereas some wealthier provinces received almost double the average per capita transfer. While the data presented in Table 3 and other available evidence do not support this statement, they do suggest that interregional redistribution may be insufficient. For example, the correlation coefficient between a poverty headcount index and per capita shared tax revenue, calculated on the basis of data presented in Rezk and others (1996), was only about 0.31 in 1994; this is, however, better than the 0.15 that prevailed in 1984. Similarly, during 1981–90, the share of less-developed provinces in total federal revenue transfers to the provinces rose from 19 percent to 24 percent. This improvement came mainly at the expense of the advanced provinces which saw their share in the total decline from 50 percent to 42 percent over this period.

Currently, there are three basic mechanisms for revenue sharing between the national and the provincial level: (1) the "coparticipation" scheme, which provides automatic, nonearmarked transfers; (2) other automatic transfers, all of which are earmarked for specific purposes; and (3) discretionary, that is, nonautomatic, transfers and grants that may be either earmarked or nonearmarked. The detailed structure of the system is shown in Figure 1.[8] Accordingly, excise taxes, income taxes, and the VAT (and, before being phased out in 1995, also the gross assets tax) are subject to revenue sharing under the coparticipation scheme. However, the provinces receive a certain share of the income tax and the gross assets tax under separate arrangements prior to the distribution of tax rev-

---

[8]Figure 1 is a revised and updated version of a similar chart in Cetrangolo (1993); also see Ministry of the Interior (1996).

Figure 1. Argentina: Assignment of Federal Revenue Collections in 1996

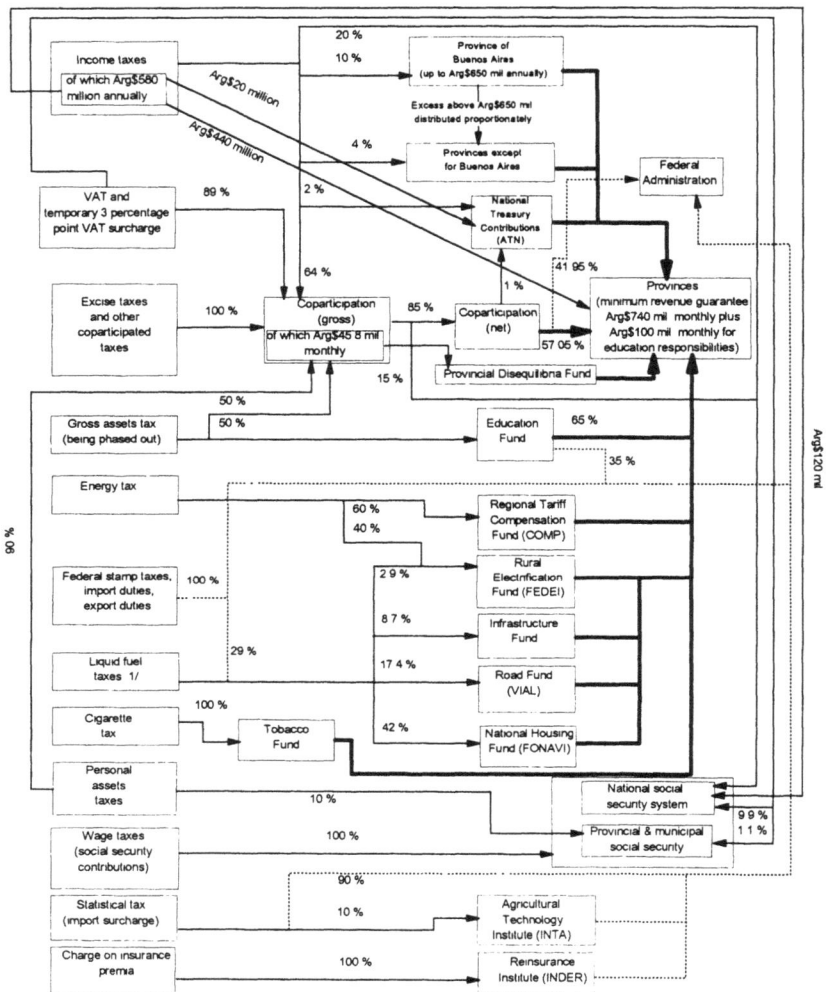

enue under the coparticipation scheme, just as 11 percent of VAT revenue is given to the social security system prior to entering into the coparticipation scheme. Other taxes, such as the fuel tax, the energy tax, the personal assets tax, wage taxes, the import surcharge (called the "statistical" tax), and charges on insurance premiums are shared according to separate earmarking rules outside of the coparticipation scheme. In principle, all discretionary transfers and grants are provided in the form of National Treasury Contributions (ATN), which is a mechanism to allocate in discretionary fashion to the provinces 2 percent of income tax revenue and 1 percent of "net" coparticipation revenue.[9] The various transfer arrangements have undergone numerous changes, partly reflecting changes in the tax system. For example, the introduction in 1995 of the personal assets tax (for individuals) and the phasing out of the gross assets tax (for companies) also had implications for the revenue-sharing arrangements (see Figure 1).

The coparticipation scheme is the centerpiece of the transfer system, and currently responsible for over two-thirds of all federal-provincial transfers. The basic structure of the scheme, under which the provinces entrust the federal government with the task of administering a number of taxes, the revenues of which are then shared, has existed since 1935. Since its inception it has seen frequent changes, reflecting both the continuing devolution of expenditures and the distributional issues that have arisen in this context. Since 1980, coparticipated revenue is not only shared between the federal and the provincial governments but also with the social security system.

During 1980–96, the primary distribution of coparticipated revenue has been governed by three major regimes, successively. In the early 1980s, and based on a 1973 legal regime, the provinces received 48.5 percent of coparticipated revenue directly and a further 3 percent through the Regional Development Fund. The remaining 48.5 percent was retained by the federal government. However, by 1983, various "pre-coparticipation" arrangements had reduced the effective share of the coparticipated revenue going to the provinces to 29 percent.

When the 1973 law expired at the end of 1984, it took until 1988 to approve a new coparticipation law, and the three-year period 1985–87 was characterized by the absence of a legal regime for "coparticipating" tax revenue between the federal and provincial levels. In practice, each year the various provinces negotiated bilateral agreements with the federal government. The overall revenue share of the provinces grew dur-

---

[9]In some instances, provinces received other discretionary transfers in the form of reimbursable advances against future coparticipation revenue.

ing 1985–87, and this higher share was by and large validated by a new "transitory" coparticipation law in 1988, which stipulated that 56.66 percent of coparticipated revenue accrue directly to the provinces, with an additional 1.0 percent allocated for discretionary distribution to the provinces in the form of ATNs, while the remaining 42.34 percent are retained by the central government.

The main features of the 1988 coparticipation scheme essentially prevail until today, even though there have been numerous changes and adjustments. The two major changes have been to establish "precoparticipations," that is, to redirect parts of the tax revenue originally destined toward the coparticipation scheme toward other purposes, and to provide some fixed-sum transfers and a minimum transfer guarantee to the provinces.

The secondary distribution of coparticipated revenue, which has the explicit objective of redistributing income among the provinces, has remained by and large unchanged since 1984. The allocation among the provinces is based on the following basic criteria: 65 percent is distributed according to the number of inhabitants, 10 percent according to population density (inhabitants per square kilometer), and 25 percent according to the inverse of the number of houses and automobiles per inhabitant and the inverse of the average level of education per inhabitant. As shown in Table 3, in 1991, per capita coparticipation transfers to less-developed provinces exceeded the average for all provinces by 92 percent, whereas in advanced provinces they amounted only to 66 percent of the average for all provinces.

There are various other automatic transfers apart from the coparticipation scheme, as shown in Figure 1. These include transfers earmarked for different funds that are under either the spending responsibility of the provincial governments (for instance, the National Housing Fund (FONAVI), the Road Fund, and the Rural Electrification Fund), or the federal administration (for example, the Agricultural Technology Institute and the Reinsurance Institute). They also include direct transfers to the provinces (from part of income tax revenue) and the social security system (from part of the VAT and income tax revenue). For example, provinces (excluding the municipality of Buenos Aires) receive 4 percent of all income tax revenue directly, but they also receive part of the 64 percent of income tax revenue that enters into the coparticipation scheme.

There are also discretionary transfers, mostly in the form of (nonreimbursable) grants. The main purpose of these transfers is to fill resource gaps at the provincial level. During the first half of the 1980s, grants rose sharply and peaked at 3 percent of GDP in 1983, representing one-third of total provincial revenue. During this period, grants were not conditioned on improvements in the financial performance of provincial governments, but they were allocated in direct proportion to the size of the provincial deficit, thus penalizing provinces with prudent fiscal policies and rewarding those with weak fiscal discipline.

Finally, there are discretionary transfers that are reimbursable, at least in principle. These include those made through FONAVI, and Treasury advances against future tax revenues. FONAVI obtains earmarked resources in the form of 42 percent of fuel tax revenue (around 1 percent of GDP). These funds are lent to the provinces, which then onlend the money through provincial housing organizations to individuals to finance housing construction. FONAVI transfers, though nominally reimbursable, are effectively nonreimbursable because of low repayment levels—the loan recovery rate is less than 10 percent. In addition, FONAVI does not reach the very poor, and, in fact, it has evolved into a mechanism for subsidizing middle-class housing.

Historically, the existence of the transfer system has been a source of instability. The many changes in the system made it difficult for the provinces to forecast the funds available to them each year, which did not, however, prevent individual provinces from embarking on expansionary expenditure policies. Particularly in the early 1980s, when the funds channeled through the coparticipation arrangement were reduced via pre-coparticipation arrangements, the provinces began to rely more heavily on discretionary ATN transfers to fill financing gaps. In 1983, for example, ATN transfers exceeded coparticipation transfers by 75 percent. As originally designed, ATN funds had the objective of providing reimbursable grants to the provinces in the case of "unusual events"; it was an emergency "gap-filling" transfer mechanism that provided advances against future tax revenue in exceptional circumstances, and advances were supposed to be repaid by the provinces at the time they received funds through the regular revenue-sharing arrangements. In practice, ATN funds became the major mechanism for providing discretionary funds to provinces, largely reflecting their respective relative political leverage.

During 1985–87, after the 1973 coparticipation law had expired and a new accord could not be reached, all transfers to the provinces were channeled through the ATN mechanism. Sanguinetti (1993) argues that, during this period, political factors played the dominant role in allocating transfers across provinces. He found that provinces ruled by the federal opposition party received higher per capita transfers from the federal government than those ruled by the same party governing the federal level. He attributed this to "coordination failure," where the federal government was generally unable to ensure fiscal discipline (which is reflected in higher overall transfers to the provinces during this period), but was particularly unable to do so in provinces ruled by the opposition party, and therefore was forced to cover the higher deficits of these provinces via higher discretionary transfers.

The new coparticipation agreement that came into effect in 1988, capped discretionary ATN funds at 1 percent of coparticipated revenue (in addition to 2 percent of income tax revenue going toward ATN). Thus, it greatly enhanced the importance of fixed rules in the federal-provincial revenue-sharing arrangements, even though, during 1989 and 1990, when provincial finances came under severe pressure, tax advances were again increased. These tax advances reached 6.2 percent of provincial revenues in 1989, and were repaid in nominal terms during a period when the annual inflation rate was 3,000 percent. Even until today, and within the general environment of relative economic stability that has been prevailing during the last few years, the federal government has been forced sometimes to provide extraordinary discretionary transfers to provinces, outside of the normal transfer framework, for instance in the form of advances against future tax revenue.

Subnational Borrowing and Debt

Within Argentina's federal structure, all levels of government are generally permitted to borrow both domestically and abroad to cover their deficits. During the 1980s, both federal and local governments borrowed extensively, reflecting the weak fiscal management during the period. In addition to direct borrowing, both federal and local governments accumulated sizable arrears on payments for wages and pensions, to suppliers, and for debt service. During 1991–95, the federal government tried to clear its accumulated expenditure arrears to pensioners, suppliers, and to the provinces by issuing "consolidation bonds" (BOCONs) and other government debt instruments. These federal arrears clearance operations added up to a total of about 9 percent of Argentina's 1995 GDP.[10]

Lack of financial control prevailed in particular at the provincial level and was an important source of financial and macroeconomic instability throughout the 1980s. In the late 1980s, and before discretionary ATN transfers, the provinces accounted for roughly 40 percent of the deficit of the consolidated nonfinancial public sector. These deficits were financed by discretionary ATN transfers and loans from the federal government, but also by loans from the provincial banks and

---

[10]Also see Teijeiro (1996).

other parts of the financial system, arrears to suppliers, and delays in wage payments to provincial government employees (Fundación de Investigaciones Económicas Latinoamericanas, 1993).

Provincial banks, in particular, acted as captive sources of financing. The provincial government banks were considered to be akin to the central bank of each province: they provided funds to the provincial governments upon demand, and in turn, received rediscounts from the Central Bank of Argentina. During 1983–90, for example, these central bank rediscounts amounted to over 2 percent of annual provincial spending (Fundación de Investigaciones Económicas Latinoamericanas, 1993). Given their portfolio of bad assets and assets of doubtful quality, resulting to a significant extent from lending to provincial governments, provincial banks were among the prime candidates for the bank restructuring and consolidation exercises that started in earnest in 1995.

By establishing a currency board arrangement for monetary management, the Convertibility Law of March 1991 ended inflationary central bank financing of public sector deficits at all levels. This also meant that new rediscounts from the central bank to the provincial banks were eliminated, and the central bank began to recover outstanding rediscounts. To strengthen further control over provincial bank operations, in 1993 the reserve requirement on deposits of provincial entities held at provincial banks was gradually raised to equal that for ordinary bank deposits. In cooperation with provincial governments, the federal government has begun to restructure, privatize, or liquidate provincial banks. As of March 1996, six provincial banks had been privatized, and seven other provincial banks were in the process of being privatized. Also, since the beginning of 1994, provincial governments have been required to obtain congressional approval for borrowing in foreign currencies. So far, only 0.2 percent of GDP of foreign borrowing by the provinces has been authorized.

Still, while the currency board arrangement reduced, among other things, the degrees of freedom for carrying out extraordinary financing operations, it has not been sufficient to bring about financial discipline at the provincial level. There are no legal limits on domestic currency borrowing operations of the provinces, and provincial governments have continued the practice of pledging future transfer receipts from co-participation as a collateral for borrowing from commercial banks. In addition, provincial governments have sometimes developed alternative sources of financing. For example, when faced with a cash crisis in 1995, several provinces issued "coupons" in lieu of wage payments.[11]

---

[11]See, for example, Vernango (1995).

Given these continued problems with financial discipline, many provinces remain overindebted. Provincial debt per capita averaged Arg$430 in 1995 (which compared to an average of US$400 for the U.S. states),[12] ranging from Arg$50 in the province of San Luis to Arg$2,200 in La Rioja. Total provincial debt amounted to 58 percent of total provincial revenue in 1995, and while in six provinces (La Pampa, Neuquén, San Luis, Santa Cruz, Santa Fé, and Tierra del Fuego) provincial debt was less than 20 percent of total revenue, in nine provinces (municipality of Buenos Aires, Chaco, Córdoba, Corrientes, Formosa, La Rioja, Mendoza, Misiones, and Rio Negro) it exceeded 80 percent.

The fact that many provincial governments had to resort to extraordinary financing operations and remain heavily indebted suggests that further adjustment and reform are needed. This would be supported by the disaggregated provincial fiscal accounts, as shown in the World Bank report (1996), which suggest that only two provinces (Mendoza and the municipality of Buenos Aires) had a primary fiscal surplus in 1995, whereas nine provinces had a primary fiscal deficit between 20–36 percent of their total revenue, and eight other provinces had a primary deficit between 10–19 percent of their total revenue. Such fiscal positions are clearly unsustainable.

Main Aspects of the Federal-Provincial Fiscal Pacts

By the early 1990s it had become clear that economic reform efforts by one level of government alone, regardless of how well designed, would not be sufficient to yield the desired fiscal and macroeconomic adjustment. To coordinate their reform efforts, two successive fiscal pacts were negotiated between the provincial and federal authorities in the 1990s. While these two pacts provided a starting point, they will need to be succeeded by further adjustment measures by the provinces.

The first federal-provincial fiscal pact, which was agreed in August 1992, aimed at (1) further decentralization by transferring expenditure responsibilities for public health, education, and housing from the federal to the provincial governments; (2) getting the provincial governments to shoulder part of the burden of improving the financial situation of the national social security system that had accumulated enormous payment arrears to pensioners; and (3) promoting tax reform

---

[12]Arg$1 equals US$1.

at the provincial level. In this context, the pact also sought to ensure that the transfer windfall for the provinces from the strengthened revenue performance would be used efficiently. A key change under this first pact was to divert to the national social security system a portion of the revenue transferred to the provinces under the coparticipation scheme. It was agreed that 15 percent of all coparticipated tax revenue would be transferred to the social security system in a precoparticipation arrangement (see Figure 1). This change effectively reduced the share of coparticipated revenues allocated to the provinces from 57.7 percent to 49.0 percent, but it also cut the coparticipated revenue retained by the federal government from 42.3 percent to 36 percent.[13]

At the same time, the pact's fiscal decentralization policies were implemented. In 1992, spending responsibilities in education, health, and social expenditure equivalent to roughly 1 percent of GDP were transferred from the federal government to the provincial administrations. In the area of health care, all hospitals and clinics operated by the federal government were transferred to the provincial governments. While most social welfare programs were transferred to the provinces, about two-thirds of the remainder of the budget of the Ministry of Health and Social Welfare (about 1 percent of GDP) was channeled to the provinces through FONAVI, which was transferred to the provinces in 1992. While nominal responsibility for secondary education was transferred to the provincial administrations in 1992, the actual transfer was arranged separately with each province over a two-year transition period. The provinces already had responsibility for primary education before the pact went into effect, so that with these additional changes, postsecondary education is now the only level of education remaining under the responsibility of the federal government.

Notwithstanding the transfer of spending responsibilities to the provinces, concerns about the need to rein in provincial spending resulted in an agreement that current expenditures that were financed by coparticipated revenues, including outlays for public services transferred to the provinces, could only grow by 10 percent in nominal terms in 1993, the same rate as the projected growth of nominal GDP at the time. Any coparticipated revenue in excess of the projected amount would have to be used to cancel provincial government debt or to finance capital expenditure. In addition, provinces would be responsible

---

[13]At the federal level, however, there was a clear overall gain as the national social security system is part of the federal public sector.

for the debt service on loans contracted with international organizations for infrastructure projects executed in their territories.

The second federal-provincial fiscal pact, which was proposed in August 1993 and went into effect in 1994, carried the reforms a step further by (1) encouraging the provinces to carry out deregulation and privatization; (2) offering provinces an option to shift their troubled social security systems for provincial government employees to the national system; and (3) supporting the reduction or elimination of provincial taxes that affect enterprise costs or may impede the development of financial markets.

Tax reform was clearly the centerpiece of the second fiscal pact, as shown in Tables 7, 8, and 9. Provinces adhering to the pact committed themselves to eliminating stamp taxes on checking accounts, taxes on the transfer of fuel, gas, and electricity, and, most important, phasing out the provincial turnover tax. While the provincial turnover tax constitutes the largest source of provincial own tax revenue, it is a cascading tax, constitutes a drag on enterprise costs, benefits imports over domestic products and increases the cost of exports, has a tax base that overlaps with the federal VAT, and makes it difficult to audit interprovincial transactions.

Initially, the provinces were slow to join this second pact, largely because of the revenue implications of the tax reforms, particularly the initial stipulation to abolish the provincial turnover tax before June 1995. While the provinces were free to replace the turnover tax with other taxes, many have not yet done so. Some provinces have begun to replace the turnover tax with a provincial tax on final retail sales. While this would preserve revenue, it is not most efficient as it exploits the same tax base twice, by the federal level (VAT) and the provincial level (turnover/sales tax), and with separate administrative structures. Also, a retail sales tax is notoriously difficult to administer, especially in a country with a very fragmented retail sector.

Overall, there is no easy short-term alternative for replacing the provincial turnover tax. Various possible alternatives (such as a provincial level VAT (PVAT), a provincial final retail sales tax, a provincial wholesale and retail sales tax, a provincial income tax, or increased reliance on real estate taxes) have their own specific drawbacks.[14]

Other alternatives for improving provincial revenue would be beneficial in the long run, but would not yield short-term results. For example, as Crotty and dos Santos (1996) point out, broadening federal

---

[14]See Crotty and dos Santos (1996) for an elaboration of advantages and disadvantages of different alternatives.

Table 7. Argentina: The Second Fiscal Pact—An Overview

(1) Provinces that are signatories receive:

- The minimum amount of coparticipated revenues is increased to Arg$740 million a month, compared with a minimum of Arg$725 million a month that was established under the previous federal pact that was in force during 1993.
- To the extent that they eliminate stamp duty and taxes on gross income for productive activities, provinces are not required to refund advances made by the Treasury since August 1992 to comply with the guaranteed coparticipation minimum (during September 1992 to June 1993; advances from the federal government amounted to Arg$0.9 billion).
- The option to transfer their pension funds to the national system, including the deficits they generate, that is, approximately Arg$1.2 billion a year.
- Political guarantees to negotiate the offsetting of claims and debts between the provinces and the federal government.

(2) Productive sectors[1] receive:

- Exemptions from the provincial turnover tax—the process must be completed by June 30, 1995, the provinces having the option to apply it partially and gradually—or primary production; industry; mining; tourism; financial services; savings and investment companies and mortgage security companies; the provision of electricity, water, and gas services, except for those generated in homes for domestic use.
- Exemptions from stamp duties for financial or insurance operations for the agricultural, industrial, mining, or construction sectors, with the commitment that this will fully apply to the remaining operations and sectors by June 30, 1995.
- Exemptions from specific provincial taxes levied on transfers of fuel, gas, electricity, including taxes on self-generated energy, and domestic services.
- The elimination of rates or taxes that are levied directly or indirectly on the flow of goods among jurisdictions or the use of physical space, including airspace, for services.
- Waiver for the taxes on interest earned on fixed term and savings bank deposits, banking debts, and gradually all taxes levied on payroll, with completion of this waiver process by June 30, 1995.
- Relief from the assets tax, to the extent that they are affected by the repeals and exemptions arranged by each province in connection with stamp tax.
- Reductions of 30–80 percent in rates of employers' social security contributions, applying only to those sectors that are exempt from stamp duties and turnover taxes.

(3) Provinces are also required to:

- As of January 1, 1994, revise taxes on real estate property, so that in no case they exceed, for rural real estate, 1.2 percent; suburban real estate, 1.35 percent; and urban real estate, 1.5 percent of the taxable base. The taxable base may not exceed 80 percent of the market value of the real estate.
- As far as possible, strengthen the tasks of auditing and supervising compliance with tax obligations, implementing standard systems that give precedence to regimes of at-source withholding and collection or payment on account.
- Within three years, replace provincial turnover taxes with a general consumption tax, with a view to ensuring tax neutrality and an improved competitiveness of the economy.
- Move toward the full or partial privatization, or leasing/concessions to the private sector of provincial public enterprises.
- Undertake deregulation, removing the restrictions on the supply of goods and services and on interventions in the various markets.
- Adopt rules consistent with national legislation on occupational accidents.

Source: *Ambito Financiero* of January 21, 1994.
[1] Agricultural production, industry, construction, mining, tourism, and scientific and technological research.

Table 8. Argentina: Tax Stipulations of the Second Fiscal Pact of August 1993—Obligations of the Provinces[1,2]

Tax	Measures Adopted	Sector or Activity
Stamp tax	Repeal	Any institutionalized financial or insurance operation for the agricultural, industrial, mining, or construction sectors.
Specific provincial taxes and municipal taxes	Repeal	Transfers of fuel, gas, electricity, including taxes on self-generated energy, and similar services.[3]
Taxes on interest on fixed term and savings bank deposits and on banking debts	Repeal	
Provincial turnover taxes	Eliminate	• Primary production, financial services provided by financial institutions. • Savings and investment companies, mortgage security issuing companies, private pension funds (AFJPs). • Mutual fund management companies. • Insurance companies, with respect to income from their specific activity. • Currency transactions, with respect to income from such activity. • Production of goods, not including income from sales to consumers.[4] • Provision of electricity, water, and gas services for commercial and/or industrial purposes. • Real estate construction. The elimination process should be completed by June 30, 1995.
Real estate property taxes	Revise	As from January 1, 1994: • Average tax rates should not exceed, for rural real estate, 1.2 percent; suburban real estate, 1.35 percent; and urban real estate, 1.5 percent. • The taxable base should not exceed 80 percent of the market value of urban and suburban real estate or the value of undeveloped land in the case of rural real estate.

VAT and income tax bases, and tackling evasion through a soundly based and well-executed program of audit and enforcement measures at the federal level have the potential in the long term to produce more revenue for the provinces through revenue sharing or through a provincial surcharge on these taxes, but would not yield short-term results. Similarly, improving real estate taxation would require substantial initial efforts, including, for example, improving property mapping and property registries; providing better and more consistent application of valuation techniques; improving the exchange of information between local tax offices, property registries, local building license au-

Table 8 (concluded)

Tax	Measures Adopted	Sector or Activity
Road taxes and road maintenance taxes	Revise	It is recommended to municipal governments that these or similar taxes not exceed 0.40 percent of the value of the provincial taxable base and be adjusted to reflect the cost generated by the actual provision of the service.
Taxes on driver's licenses	Revise and coordinate	The obligation will be to ensure the uniformity of valuations or applicable tax rates among all jurisdictions as of 1994. Valuations published by the Directorate General of Taxation (DGI) are to serve as reference.[5]

Sources: Based on information provided by Instituto de Estudios Económicos sobre la Realidad Argentina y Latinoamericana (IEERAL); and Fundación Mediterránea.

[1]It was also agreed to work toward a repeal of those municipal taxes that are applicable to the same tax bases as provincial taxes.

[2]In addition to the measures mentioned in the table, the provinces also accept the obligations to (1) move toward the partial or complete privatization of services, works, or projects that are the responsibility of provincial or municipal governments; (2) remove the restrictions on the supply of goods and services and on interventions in the various markets; and (3) adopt the rule established in Article 16 of Law No. 24,028, for determining jurisdiction in occupational accident cases.

[3]The inclusion of the remaining operations and sectors should be gradual, and to be completed by June 30, 1995, in accordance with the schedule to be determined by each province.

[4]These will be treated in the same way as the retail sector.

[5]If this tax is wholly or partly the responsibility of municipal governments, then it will be proposed to these governments that they align themselves with this system.

thorities, and public utilities; and improving collection and enforcement procedures.[15]

The announcement in December 1993 that federal payroll taxes levied on employers would be reduced, depending on region and sector, in those provinces participating in the second pact, increased pressure on provincial governments to join. By May 1994, all but one provincial legislature had ratified the second fiscal pact, and most had taken at least some initial steps toward implementation. Also, the provinces were given a minimum revenue guarantee and some other guaranteed

---

[15]Still, there is considerable room for improving the effective tax base of real estate taxes, which in 1995 accounted for only 18 percent of all own revenue of the provinces. For example, in the city of Santa Fe, a recent survey showed that two-thirds of the lots that were vacant according to the tax roll actually had buildings on them, and 56 percent of all properties were underrecorded in the sense that the extent of the construction that was recorded was less than what was actually on the lot. A similar survey in the municipality of Santo Tomé found 52 percent of all properties to be underrecorded. Also, a 1994 tax amnesty in the province of Buenos Aires led 400,000 taxpayers, including 170,000 whose land was vacant according to the tax roll, to report 30 million square meters of construction previously unknown to the tax authorities (Provincia de Buenos Aires, 1994).

Table 9. Argentina: Tax Stipulations of the Second Fiscal Pact of August 1993—Obligations of the Federal Government[1]

Tax	Measures Adopted	Content
Gross assets tax	Repeal	Assets earmarked for productive processes in the specific priority sectors affected by the repeal and exemptions of provincial stamp taxes.
Payroll taxes	Repeal	Reduction in employers' social security contributions for specific sectors. This will be effected in keeping with the sectoral priorities established for the elimination of provincial turnover taxes.
VAT	Revise	Adjustment of the rules relating to VAT withholdings and payments on account, so that in no case shall taxpayers be liable for an effective tax rate exceeding 18 percent.
Other commitments		• To accept the transfer of provincial pension funds to the National Social Security System.[2,3] • To organize and implement the system of rural mortgage bonds and negotiable bonds backed by urban mortgages. • 60-day suspension of the withholding of coparticipation surpluses in excess of Arg$725 million.[4] • The guaranteed minimum monthly revenue transfer to the provinces is increased from Arg$725 million to Arg$740 million as of January 1994.

Sources: Based on information provided by Instituto de Estudios Económicos sobre la Realidad Argentina y Latinoamericana (IEERAL); and Fundación Mediterránea.

[1]The federal authorities agree to revise the taxes collected by the Municipality of Buenos Aires (MCBA) along the same lines and on the same terms as those undertaken by the provinces.

[2]Excluding the professional funds stipulated by Article 56 of Law No. 10,038.

[3]In cases where provincial social security systems are included in the new social security arrangements approved by the federal authorities.

[4]This guarantee amount was established under the fiscal pact concluded on August 12, 1992 and ratified by Law No. 24,130. This suspension was to be valid provisionally for 60 days and permanently once the provinces have met the obligations for immediate application undertaken pursuant to this agreement.

fixed payments that provided a floor of federal transfers equivalent to about 4.5 percent of GDP annually.

The second fiscal pact clearly shows the "horse-trading" that is involved in implementing structural reforms of the system of fiscal federalism, that is reminiscent of the old adage "two steps forward, one step back." An example is the reduction in federal employer payroll taxes, which reduced enterprise costs ("the two steps forward"), but came at the expense of making payroll taxes an explicit instrument of regional and sectoral policies, and contributed further to the growing social security deficit ("the one step back").

The reduction in the federal employer payroll tax rate became a centerpiece of the second fiscal pact, even though initially it was somewhat of an afterthought largely designed to induce provinces to participate.

Previously, the employer payroll tax had amounted to 33 percent, with the exception of three provinces, where it was 28.5 percent. The new rates, which began to take effect in most provinces in early 1994, implied reductions from anywhere between 0 to 80 percent, depending on region and sector of production. Economically weak regions received larger reductions, and these reductions were restricted to the agriculture, industry, construction, mining, and scientific and technological research sectors. Tourism and the service sectors (basically all nontradables) received no reductions. About 50 percent of the labor force was affected by these reductions in employer payroll taxes.

The new system of employer payroll tax rates was excessively complicated and distortive, as it meant that different industries in the same province could have different employer payroll tax rates, and the same industry in different provinces could have different tax rates. Even within the same province, employer payroll contributions were differentiated according to rural or urban location. For example, in the province of Entre Ríos, the new employer payroll tax rate was 18.2 percent in the capital city, 13.2 percent in the district of Feliciano y Federación, and 16.5 percent in the rest of the province.

In March 1995, the new system of employer payroll tax rates was simplified, and tax rates were generally unified across sectors at a level of 16.5 percent, half the previous rate, with some differentiation according to provinces still being maintained. This involved rate reductions in the services and tourism sectors, and a partial rollback of previous reductions in most other sectors.

The second fiscal pact gave to provincial governments the option to transfer to the federal social security system the public pensions systems for provincial government employees. These systems all had actuarial deficits.[16] This option implied that the federal government had to be ready to absorb additional social security deficits of about 0.5 percent of GDP initially, but, given the large actuarial deficits in some provinces, over time, the cash deficits would become even more significant. Another example was the agreement under the second pact that the federal government would forgo provincial government repayment obligations equivalent to 0.4 percent of GDP, which were related to higher-than-mandated coparticipation transfers,[17] and to increase, al-

---

[16]Many provincial social security systems had more generous benefits than the federal system. Provincial social security systems that would be transferred to the federal system would operate henceforth under the same regulations as the federal system.

[17]Coparticipated revenue transfers in excess of the monthly minimum contained contingent repayment obligations by the provinces. The federal government elected to waive this repayment obligation as part of the second pact.

beit only by a small amount (Arg$17 million a month), the fixed minimum guaranteed coparticipation transfer.

Tax Administration and Expenditure Management

Weak tax administration and expenditure management systems contributed to large fiscal imbalances at all levels of government during the 1980s. Since then, major improvements have been made at the federal level; it remains a major challenge to translate these into improvements at subnational levels of government.

Since 1989, major efforts have been made to strengthen tax administration, particularly at the federal level, and these helped to boost tax revenue collections, which rose to 15.5–16.5 percent of GDP during 1993–95, from about 11–12 percent of GDP at the beginning of the decade.[18] VAT compliance, for example, increased from an estimated 34 percent in 1989 to 64 percent in 1992, but dropped back to 60 percent in 1993, and to 55 percent in 1994 (Crotty and dos Santos, 1996). Own revenues of the provinces also improved during this period, by about 1.5 percent of GDP. In both cases, however, some of the improvement may not have been due to better tax administration, but to the reversed Tanzi effect that set in when inflation was drastically reduced under the convertibility scheme. In addition, Argentina still falls short of the tax compliance levels that prevail in neighboring countries, such as Chile (where VAT compliance, for example, is over 80 percent) or Uruguay (where it is over 70 percent) (Crotty and dos Santos, 1996).[19] Similarly, several revenue sources still appear underexploited in Argentina, like, for example, income taxes, which yielded 2.2 percent of GDP in Argentina in 1995, but yielded over 4 percent of GDP in neighboring Brazil and Chile.

Still, the growth in national tax revenue was remarkable, also in light of the fact that over 20 taxes, mainly inefficient and distortive tax handles, were abolished during that period. Among the administrative measures that contributed to this growth were the strengthen-

---

[18]Since inflation was drastically reduced at the same time that tax administration was being improved, it is difficult to separate out revenue increases that are due strictly to the reduction in inflation (through the reversed Tanzi effect), and revenue increases that are only due to improvements in tax administration.

[19]The task of improving tax compliance in Argentina has been complicated by frequent tax amnesties that have been used by federal, provincial, and municipal authorities to allow people to pay previously underreported or delinquent taxes with reduced penalties. As a result, a prevailing attitude has been: "why should I pay my taxes if I can wait for the next amnesty?" (Crotty and dos Santos, 1996).

ing of penalties for evasion, computerization of tax returns, and improved training of auditors. In April 1993, responsibility for collecting social security contributions was transferred from the social security system to the national tax service, which helped significantly to improve compliance. However, in contrast with all these improvements at the federal level, most provincial and municipal tax administrations remain weak.

A further current problem is reporting systems that make it difficult to consolidate the accounts of different levels of government. Some of the fundamentals for improving the flow of information are being put in place, though. In particular, the integrated financial information system (SIDIF) of the national administration has developed into a powerful tool for controlling the execution of the federal budget. Unfortunately, it only covers the federal level: provincial and municipal governments formulate their budgets independently from the federal government and are not required to consult with the federal government or even to provide data on budget execution.

To be sure, coordination between different levels of government, particularly between the federal and provincial levels, has been intensified over the last couple of years (also in the context of the two federal-provincial fiscal pacts). However, because of the statutory independence of provinces and municipalities, federal government attempts to coordinate the operations of subnational governments in line with national macroeconomic stabilization and adjustment objectives usually required lengthy negotiations and many compromises.

Given the need for further reform and adjustment at all levels of government and given that decentralization will continue, it would seem desirable to strengthen provincial and municipal government reporting and management systems along the lines of the federal system. The key purpose of such systems would be to provide a comprehensive tool for all levels of government to help with cash management, financial planning, and public debt management. Such systems have worked well in other federal states, including neighboring Brazil, where one has been in existence for over a decade.

Implications for Macroeconomic Management and Structural Reform

In 1990, the World Bank, in analyzing provincial government finances in Argentina and their macroeconomic implications, concluded that "provincial-national financial practices have contributed to unsustainable public sector fiscal and quasi-fiscal deficits, and their continu-

Table 10. Argentina: Changes in Consolidated Nonfinancial Public Balances During Four Time Periods
(In percentage points of GDP)[1]

	1970–75	1975–80	1980–83	1983–87	1990–94
Overall change	–13.6	7.9	–8.1	7.3	2.7
Provinces	–5.9	4.8	–3.3	–1.9	0.5
Other	–7.6	3.1	–4.9	9.3	2.2
Federal government	–5.5	3.3	–2.8	7.4	0.7
State enterprises	–2.3	0.1	–1.3	2.0	–0.9[2]
Social security	0.2	–0.3	–0.8	–0.1	—
Other[3]	...	...	...	...	2.4

Sources: Sanguinetti (1994); Argentine authorities; and authors' estimates.

[1] An improvement in the balance is denoted by a positive number; a worsening by a negative number.

[2] Data for 1990–94 refer only to the operating surplus of nonfinancial state enterprises.

[3] Primarily consists of the balance of decentralized agencies and the balance of quasi-fiscal operations of the central bank.

ation would undermine national efforts to attain price stability and to promote sustainable economic development."[20]

Since then, the efforts of the federal government to stabilize and restructure the economy have met with considerable success. Similarly, as a result of substantial progress in restructuring the system of fiscal federalism, it is no longer true that "Argentina provides a good illustration of the 'fiscal perversity' of subnational governments" (Prud'homme, 1995, p. 206), as had been the case during much of the 1970s and 1980s.

Often, the provinces have been blamed for a large part of Argentina's problems with macroeconomic management. Sanguinetti (1994), for example, has suggested that the fiscal behavior of the provinces was a major culprit in various failed stabilization attempts of the past, particularly the fiscal crises of 1975 and 1983, and the failed stabilization attempt during 1985–87 under the Austral Plan. This claim is supported by the data shown in Table 10. From 1970 to 1975, the balance of the consolidated nonfinancial public sector worsened by 13.6 percentage points of GDP, to which the provinces contributed the most. Similarly, from 1980 to 1983, when the balance of the consolidated nonfinancial public sector worsened again by about 8 percentage points of GDP, the provinces again contributed the most. During 1983–87, when the overall balance of the consolidated nonfinancial public sector improved by over 7 percentage points of GDP, the overall balance of the provinces continued to deteriorate by almost 2 percentage points of GDP. By contrast, during 1975–80, provincial finances

---

[20] World Bank (1990). Similar arguments can also be found in World Bank (1992).

improved significantly more than those of the rest of the nonfinancial public sector.

It may be argued that the failure of provincial governments to adjust was partly a reflection of distorted incentive systems. For example, as Tanzi (1996) has pointed out, historically, four provinces used to have legal authority to grant exemptions from the national VAT. At least in the short run, using their authority was clearly in the best self-interest of these four provinces, but it resulted in a considerable erosion of VAT revenue at the federal level, and aggravated national fiscal problems.

Also, for the more recent period of 1990–94, Table 10 would suggest that both provincial governments and the federal government contributed to the adjustment of the finances of the consolidated nonfinancial public sector, but that other factors, such as ending quasi-fiscal operations of the central bank under the convertibility law, contributed the most.

Finally, without underestimating the efforts of the federal government to increase tax revenue at the federal level, and while recognizing the revenue windfall that this created for the provinces (via the automatic revenue-sharing arrangements), it should also be noted that the improved fiscal performance of the central government has reflected in part the policy of decentralizing expenditure responsibilities without a corresponding decentralization of revenue-raising powers or tax bases.

Clearly, numerous problems remain to be addressed. In particular, macroeconomic management has been complicated by the fact that adjustment initiatives usually originated at the federal level, and, up to now, have largely failed to translate into similar adjustment initiatives at the provincial level. As Tanzi (1996) has suggested, by and large, the attitude of provincial and municipal governments has been that economic stabilization is a national public good and is thus the sole responsibility of the federal government. One reason for this may be that the nature of the revenue-sharing arrangements has allowed provincial government to delay adjustment, and thereby water down the macroeconomic impact of federal initiatives. For example, faced with the need to correct large macroeconomic imbalances, the federal government introduced major tax and administrative reforms that succeeded in raising sharply the ratio of taxes to GDP. Through these efforts at the federal level, provinces received an automatic revenue windfall via the various revenue transfer mechanisms. The financial problems the provinces experienced during the 1995 recession reflected difficulties in cutting back expenditures in line with reduced transfers, particularly from coparticipation.

It has been suggested that not only the vertical revenue-expenditure assignment imbalance but also the deficient design of the transfer system itself remain fundamental weak points in the otherwise successful stabilization program now under way (López Murphy and others, 1995). The current revenue sharing arrangements rely almost exclusively on fixed shares, that is, a certain percentage of whatever is collected is transferred to the provinces (Figure 1).[21] Hence, when economic activity is high or when reforms at the federal level increase tax revenue, transfers are high, thus allowing provinces to increase spending; when economic activity is low or tax evasion or avoidance is on the increase, transfers are low (but not below the minimum guarantee). This tends to exacerbate cyclical fluctuations in activity and to frustrate in part restrictive budgetary policies at the federal level.

At the same time, and given the need to raise revenue, the federal government has had an incentive to focus its efforts on those taxes that mainly accrue to the federal level. As Tanzi (1996) has suggested, this may easily lead to a situation where nonshared taxes will acquire a greater weight in the tax system, even when they are less efficient. In Argentina, the incentives to focus on nonshared taxes for increasing revenue efforts have prompted the federal government to raise import-related revenues, including through a temporary import surcharge in the form of a "statistical tax" or by increasing to the permitted maximum the list of MERCOSUR imports that still have to pay import duty. Also, there has been a tendency to implement different pre-coparticipations (most recently, in the form of a temporary 3 percentage point increase in the VAT that was initially excluded from the revenue-sharing arrangements and given directly to the federal level). As argued by Porto and Sanguinetti (1993), these pre-coparticipations are reminiscent of the early 1980s, when similar arrangements undermined the revenue-sharing mechanism that was in place and contributed to its demise at the end of 1984.

A new revenue-sharing mechanism needs to be put into place in the near future. While it is difficult to envision that a radically different mechanism could be negotiated easily, it would clearly be desirable to address the major shortcomings of the current mechanism. This would include addressing the need further to reduce discretionary elements, broaden the taxes included in the revenue-sharing arrangement (ideally, all taxes should be shared to an equal extent), and to reduce the procyclicality of transfers, maybe by establishing a stabilization fund (even though it should be made clear that this fund would not be available for discretionary transfers).

---

[21]However, the provinces have a minimum guarantee under the coparticipation scheme, that is, they are legally guaranteed a minimum transfer each month, even if total revenues collected were to fall to zero.

Similarly, problems remain concerning progress with structural reform, particularly at provincial and municipal levels. Notwithstanding substantial progress in restructuring Argentina's system of fiscal federalism, most recently under the two federal-provincial fiscal pacts, structural reforms at subnational levels have been lagging; a key issue in this regard is government employment, particularly at the provincial level. During 1983–90, when the provinces enjoyed relatively easy access to extraordinary financing, provincial civil service employment expanded by about 48 percent, and made provincial governments an employer of last resort, particularly in the poorer provinces. For example, of the four provinces that in 1992 raised less than 10 percent of their total expenditure through own revenues (Catamarca, Formosa, La Rioja, and Santiago del Estero), three ranked highest with regard to the level of public employees per 100 inhabitants. Similarly, the four provinces that raised more than 30 percent of their total expenditures through own revenues in 1992 (Buenos Aires, Córdoba, Mendoza, and Santa Fé) were the only ones that had less than ten public employees per 100 inhabitants. In general, provinces with the lowest level of own revenue mobilization (relative to total expenditures) are also the ones where civil service employment (per 100 inhabitants) is highest, and vice versa: during the 1990s, the correlation coefficient between own revenue mobilization (relative to total expenditure) and civil service employment of the various provinces has remained fairly stable at about −0.70.

In conjunction with the federal-provincial fiscal pacts, various programs were developed to encourage the provinces to downsize provincial government employment through incentives payable to government employees and to private firms that might be prepared to hire them. The most innovative of these schemes, the BOCEP program, functions as a marginal employment subsidy. BOCEPs, or bonds for the creation of private employment, are bonds given to provincial public sector employees who are retrenched on a voluntary basis. The retrenched workers are to hand over their BOCEPs to their new private sector employers, who can, in turn, use these bonds to obtain a loan for investment purposes from the state-owned National Bank; BOCEPs are then amortized over five years.[22]

However, so far, provincial public sector employment reduction schemes have all met with only limited success. On average, provinces continued to spend over 50 percent of their total expenditure on wages and salaries (see Table 2), and, even though, according to newspaper re-

---

[22]For a detailed description of this scheme, see Montoya (1994).

ports, about ten provinces have been experiencing repeated problems in paying civil service wages on time, major employment adjustments remain yet to be made.

To be sure, federal government efforts to improve macroeconomic management and introduce various structural reforms have forced adjustment upon subnational levels of government, as, for example, evidenced in the fact that own revenues of the provinces grew by over 50 percent in real terms during 1989–95. At least for some provinces, the need to adjust may have arrived faster than anticipated, as suggested, for example, by recent strikes of public servants in several provinces. Usually, the less-developed provinces were the ones that had the most trouble adjusting, even though, as shown, for example, by the salary arrears public workers in Córdoba (Argentina's second largest city) and other parts of the country had to endure mid-1995,[23] adjustment has been difficult pretty much everywhere.

Fundamental reforms of the system of fiscal federalism in Argentina are inevitable. These reforms need to take into account the complex interests and needs of the various participants: the central government, the richer provinces, and the poorer provinces. In a first step, a possible reform package could comprise three main elements: (1) strengthening the own tax base of the provinces; this could include passing on to the provinces the federal income tax for natural persons (personal income tax) or creating a "piggyback" provincial income tax, and improving real estate taxation, maybe with guidance provided by the federal level; (2) reducing the overall degree of revenue sharing, and, in this context, replacing the complicated revenue-sharing arrangements that currently exist for each specific tax by a more simple system where the provinces receive a certain fixed (but lower) share of all revenue collected; and (3) establishing an explicit equalization scheme among the provinces that supports the poorer provinces.

References

Ambito Financiero, 1994, issue of January 21.

Artana, Daniel, and Ricardo López Murphy, 1994, "Fiscal Decentralization: Some Lessons for Latin America," paper presented at the annual meeting of the Latin American Econometric Society, Caracas.

Artana, Daniel, Oscar Libonatti, Cynthia Moskovits, and Mario Salinardi, 1995, "Argentina," in *Fiscal Decentralization in Latin America*, ed. by Ricardo López Murphy (Washington: Inter-American Development Bank).

---

[23]See, for example, Vernango (1995).

Cetrangolo, Oscar, 1993, "El Pacto Fiscal y las Relaciones Financieras entre la Nación y las Provincias" (Buenos Aires: Fundación Union Industrial Argentina, October).

Crotty, John, and Paulo dos Santos, 1996, "Provincial Tax Issues," paper presented at a seminar on Fiscal Federalism and Provincial Tax Issues (Washington: Fiscal Affairs Department, Internatinal Monetary Fund, July).

Fundación de Investigaciones Económicas Latinoamericanas (FIEL), 1993, *Hacia una Nueva Organización del Federalismo Fiscal en la Argentina* (Buenos Aires: Fundación de Investigaciones Económicas Latinoamericanas).

Gómez Sabaini, Juan C., 1993, "Coordinación de la Imposición General a los Consumos entre Nación y Provincias (Argentina)," *Serie Política Fiscal*, No. 47 (Santiago: United Nations Economic Commission for Latin America and the Caribbean).

López Murphy, Ricardo, Oscar Libonatti, and Mario Salinardi, 1995, "Overview and Comparison of Fiscal Decentralization Experiences," in *Fiscal Decentralization in Latin America*, ed. by Ricardo López Murphy (Washington: Inter-American Development Bank).

Ministry of the Interior, Undersecretary for Assistance to the Provinces, 1996, *Coparticipación Federal de Impuestos—Un Tema de Todos y Para Todos* (Buenos Aires, November 26).

Montoya, Silvia, 1994, "Diagnóstico y Perspectivas del Empleo Público Provincial," *Novedades Economicas*, January–February, pp. 45–55.

Porto, Alberto, and Pablo Sanguinetti, 1993, "Descentralización Fiscal en America Latina: El Caso Argentino," *Serie Política Fiscal*, No. 45 (Santiago: United Nations Economic Commission for Latin American and the Caribbean).

Provincia de Buenos Aires, 1994, *Noticias de Economia*, September/October.

Prud'homme, Rémy, 1995, "The Dangers of Decentralization," *World Bank Research Observer*, Vol. 10, No. 2 (August), pp. 201–220.

Rezk, Ernesto, Marcelo Capello, and Carlos Alberto Ponce, 1996, "Arreglos Fiscales Intergubernamentales en Argentina," draft presented at the International Seminar on Fiscal Federalism and Federal Finances in Córdoba, Argentina, June 27–28.

Sanguinetti, Pablo J., 1993, "The Politics of Intergovernmental Transfers and Local Government Deficits: Theory and Evidence," *Estudios Economicos* (Mexico), pp. 87–109.

———, 1994, "Intergovernmental Transfers and Public Sector Expenditures: A Game-Theoretic Approach," *Estudios de Economía* (Chile), Vol. 21, No. 2 (December), pp. 181–212.

Schuler, Karl, 1995, "Rauher Wind Über der Pampa," *Mosquito*, No. 9/10 (December), pp. 34–37.

Shah, Anwar, 1994, "The Reform of Intergovernmental Fiscal Relations in Developing and Emerging Market Economies," Policy and Research Series No. 23 (Washington: World Bank, June).

Tanzi, Vito, 1996, "Fiscal Federalism and Decentralization: A Review of Some Efficiency and Macroeconomic Aspects," in *Annual World Bank Conference on Development Economics, 1995* (Washington: World Bank).

Teijeiro, Mario, 1996, "La Política Fiscal Durante la Convertibilidad" (unpublished; Buenos Aires: Centro de Estudios Públicos, April).

Ter-Minassian, Teresa, 1996, "The Role of the Treasury in the Financial Management of Government Operations: The Brazilian Experience in an International Perspective," paper presented at the First Brazil Seminar on Public Finance, Brasilia, September 2.

Vernango, Javier, 1995, "Diez Provincias sin Dinero Para Sueldos," *Ambito Financiero* (January 24, 1995).

World Bank, 1990, "Argentina: Provincial Government Finance Study," World Bank Report No. 8176-AR (Washington: World Bank).

―――, 1992, "Argentina: Towards a New Federalism," World Bank Report No. 10612-AR (Washington: World Bank, June).

―――, 1996, "Argentina: Provincial Finances Study," World Bank Report No. 15487-AR (Washington: World Bank, June).

17

Bolivia

G.A. MACKENZIE AND JOSÉ-LUÍS RUIZ

As previous chapters have related, the major objective of recent reforms of intergovernmental financial relations in countries around the world has been the decentralization of government operations from the central to the regional and local levels. This is especially true of Latin American reforms. The experience of Mexico and Brazil, where reforms have affected mainly regional-center arrangements, and that of Colombia, where reforms have affected arrangements of the center with both regional and local governments, have elicited much interest. The decentralization movement is not confined, however, to the larger countries of the region. Bolivia's recent reform has resulted in a quite substantial increase in the financial autonomy and responsibilities of local governments. The lessons that can be drawn from it could apply to the many countries where the second tier of government is comparatively unimportant—and, in particular, those countries where government is relatively centralized. This was Bolivia's starting point.

Center-Local Government Financial Arrangements Prior to the Reforms

General government in Bolivia consists of the national government, nine departments, and approximately 310 cities and towns. In recent years, total general government expenditures have amounted to about 25 percent of GDP (Table 1). Prior to the reforms that began in 1994, however, there was effectively no middle layer between the national government and the municipalities, since the nine departments were

Table 1. Bolivia: Financial Operations of the General Government
(In percent of GDP)

	1992	1993	1994	1995	1996
Revenue and grants	21.6	21.4	23.5	23.5	23.6
Current revenue	17.3	17.7	18.3	18.5	18.7
Tax revenue	16.5	16.9	17.2	17.3	17.4
Domestic taxes	15.2	15.5	15.7	15.9	16.1
Custom duties	1.3	1.3	1.4	1.4	1.2
Nontax revenue	0.8	0.9	1.2	1.2	1.3
Current transfers from	1.7	1.9	2.2	3.0	1.8
Public enterprises	0.4	0.5	0.7	1.4	0.3
Private sector[1]	1.3	1.5	1.5	1.5	1.5
Capital revenue	0.2	0.3	0.6	0.6	1.0
Foreign grants	2.4	1.5	2.4	1.5	2.1
Expenditure	24.5	26.5	26.8	25.7	25.9
Current expenditure	18.4	20.0	19.8	19.2	19.1
Wages and salaries	8.5	9.0	9.2	9.0	8.9
Goods and services	2.6	2.4	2.0	2.3	2.3
Interest	2.6	2.6	2.5	2.9	2.7
Transfers to	2.6	3.0	4.3	3.3	3.7
Public enterprises	0.4	0.7	1.2	0.4	0.3
Private sector	2.1	2.3	3.1	2.9	3.4
Other	2.2	3.0	1.8	1.7	1.6
Capital expenditure	6.1	6.5	6.9	6.5	6.8
Fixed capital formation	5.9	5.9	6.3	6.1	6.4
Transfers to public enterprises	—	0.4	0.1	—	0.1
Other	0.1	0.3	0.5	0.4	0.4
Overall balance	−2.8	−5.1	−3.2	−2.1	−2.3

Sources: Ministry of Finance; Integrated System of Financial Administration and Government Control (SAFCO); Central Bank of Bolivia; and IMF staff estimates.

[1]Comprises social security contribution paid by the private sector and public enterprises.

essentially administrative entities. Each department did have a Regional Development Corporation (RDC), which played an important role in the provision of infrastructural investment. In respect of its organization and financial structure, however, the RDC was essentially like an investment fund, or a decentralized agency of the central government, without financial autonomy.

The centralized character of the Bolivian state prior to the recent reforms is reflected in the national government's near monopoly of expenditure assignments. The nine RDCs were not responsible for the administration of current expenditure programs. Most current expenditure, including social expenditure, was the responsibility of the national government.[1] Municipal governments, with the exception of the

---

[1]The larger municipalities undoubtedly undertook some expenditure on social programs, although there is no readily available information on the composition of their expenditures.

largest cities—La Paz, Santa Cruz, Cochabamba, and El Alto—had little revenue of their own, and of 310 cities and towns only about 30—the larger ones—benefited from the revenue-sharing scheme then in effect.[2] As the foregoing suggests, there is a huge variation in the size of Bolivian municipalities, despite their common legal status: the four largest cities have between them roughly 2¼ million of the country's 7½ million inhabitants, but a large number of towns have less than 1,000 inhabitants.

The limited role in the provision of public services played by the municipalities is borne out by the fact that in 1993 noninterest expenditures (primary expenditure) of the municipalities amounted to only 8 percent of general government primary expenditure or 2 percent of GDP (Table 2). Even this modest expenditure level was financed largely by statutory or discretionary transfers from the center. Own revenues of the municipalities (excluding discretionary transfers and revenues received under the then existing revenue-sharing arrangement) amounted to about 20 percent of their total revenues, or just 0.3 percent of GDP. Their comparatively small size and limited access to either domestic or external credit meant that the finances of the municipalities as a group were more or less balanced from one year to the next.

The Impact of Reform

The Popular Participation Law, which was promulgated in 1994, and the Decentralization Law, which became effective at the beginning of 1996, reflect not only a desire for financial decentralization but, as the name of the first piece of legislation suggests, a grassroots sentiment for more local participation in the political process. Although the discussion of this chapter is limited to their economic and financial content, these aspects of the reforms are better appreciated when the political sentiments motivating the reform are kept in mind.

Briefly put, the reforms have resulted in a substantial devolution of expenditure responsibilities to the municipalities. All municipalities, even the smallest, benefit from the new revenue-sharing scheme, which is the source of the revenue that finances the increase in local govern-

---

[2]The smaller cities and towns were not denied participation in the scheme by law. However, the administrative and bureaucratic requirements for participation were apparently onerous for small towns, and the incentives to participate may not have been compelling, at least if the increase in revenue that participation entailed would have come at the cost of central government provision of certain public services.

Table 2. Bolivia: Financial Operations of the Municipalities
(In percent of GDP)

	1992	1993	1994	1995	1996
Revenue and grants	1.5	1.7	2.6	3.4	3.6
Current revenue	1.4	1.5	2.4	3.2	3.2
Revenue sharing	1.1	1.2	2.0	2.8	2.9
Other	0.3	0.3	0.3	0.4	0.4
Other revenue and grants	—	0.1	—	0.2	—
Capital transfers from rest of public sector	—	0.1	0.2	0.1	0.3
Expenditure	1.5	1.9	2.4	3.5	3.8
Current expenditure	1.1	1.2	1.2	1.4	1.6
Wages and salaries	0.6	0.6	0.6	0.7	0.8
Goods and services	0.2	0.3	0.2	0.3	0.4
Interest	—	—	—	—	0.1
Other	0.2	0.3	0.2	0.3	0.2
Current transfers to rest of public sector	0.1	0.1	0.1	0.1	0.1
Capital expenditure	0.4	0.6	1.2	2.0	2.2
Fixed capital formation	0.4	0.6	1.2	1.9	2.0
Capital transfers to rest of public sector	—	—	—	0.1	0.2
Overall balance	0.1	−0.2	0.2	—	−0.2
Memorandum items:					
Noninterest expenditure as percent of GDP	1.5	1.8	2.4	3.4	3.7
Noninterest expenditure as percent of general government noninterest expenditure	6.6	7.7	9.9	14.9	16.1
Capital expenditure as percent of noninterest expenditure	26.7	33.3	50.0	58.8	59.5
Current revenue as percent of general government current revenue	8.1	8.5	13.1	17.3	17.1

Sources: Ministry of Finance; Integrated System of Financial Administration and Government Control (SAFCO); Central Bank of Bolivia; and IMF staff estimates.

ment expenditure.[3] The RDCs have been eliminated, and their expenditure program responsibilities, plus some additional ones, have been assigned either to the departmental government (*prefectura*) or to the municipalities of the department, to be financed by tax earmarking and revenue sharing. These observations are elaborated in what follows.

Municipalities

Expenditure Assignments

Municipalities are now responsible for the provision of education through the secondary level and virtually for all health services. They have also been assigned responsibility for sports facilities (with certain

---
[3]Revenues are transferred via the banking system on an almost daily basis from the Treasury's account to those of the municipalities. Small towns band together and open a collective account.

exceptions), micro-irrigation, local roads, and most cultural facilities. This substantial devolution of expenditure responsibilities has entailed a very marked increase in the share of general government primary expenditure executed by the municipalities, from the 8 percent share in 1993 already noted to 16 percent in 1996. Although the reforms have certainly boosted municipalities' current expenditure, their capital expenditure has increased remarkably, and its share in primary expenditure has increased from 33 percent in 1993 to 59 percent in 1996 (see Table 2). This is mainly a reflection of the transfer of local investment projects from the old RDCs to local governments.

Despite the municipalities' enhanced role in the provision of education and health programs, among other public services, they continue to share some responsibility in these areas with the national government. This is particularly true of the health sector, where the national government (through the *prefecturas*) is responsible not only for paying the salaries of medical and technical personnel but also for managing them (Popular Participation Law, Article 3). In general, there is considerable potential for an overlap in expenditure responsibilities, as well as potential for a conflict between levels of government managing different facets of the same service.

The legislation embodies a concern that some municipalities are simply too small to be able to carry out their expenditure assignments effectively. For this reason, it stipulates that such municipalities should be provided technical assistance. The law also requires that towns whose populations fall short of 5,000 form an association (*mancomunidad*) whose total population will at least reach that figure.

Revenue Arrangements

The revenue-sharing (coparticipation) agreement provides that 20 percent of the revenue generated by the taxes assigned to the national government should be transferred to the municipalities, and that this amount should be distributed according to the share of each in total population, as established by the 1992 census.[4] Thus, if town A has

---

[4]The taxes assigned to the national government are basically all taxes on goods and services and on domestic income and profits, plus taxes on international trade and on inheritances. Each department is divided up into provinces, and each province into a section, which for the purposes of the law is considered to be the territorial limits of the municipality that is located in it. Consequently, all inhabitants of Bolivia are effectively assigned to one municipality or another, even if they live in the country. The law also provides that 5 percent of the national government's revenue should be transferred automatically to the public universities. Mineral, petroleum, and forestry royalties are assigned to the departments.

seven times the population of town B, its share of coparticipated revenues is seven times as great. The municipalities are also assigned certain tax bases; namely, property taxes and business licenses (*patentes*). The reform has entailed an increase in the ratio of local government current revenue to GDP from less than 2 percent in 1993 to more than 3 percent in 1996, and an increase in its share of general government current revenue over the same period from 8 percent to 17 percent (Table 2).

There is no obvious reason for believing that the resources that have been assigned to the average-sized municipality are not enough to finance the additional expenditure programs for which it is now responsible. That said, to the extent that the supply of public goods and services is subject to economies of scale, the proportional formula favors the larger cities, at least relative to a formula with a lump-sum element, or one where revenue increases with city size, but by less than proportionately.[5] In addition to taking no account of economies of scale, the revenue-sharing formula makes no allowance for the fact that municipalities will differ in their capacity to raise revenue. Again, the larger cities and towns would probably benefit from economies of scale with respect to the tax collection function, and incomes in the larger cities would in any case tend to be higher than those in the smaller towns.

The laws impose restrictions on the use of the shared revenues. In particular, 85 percent of the coparticipated revenues are to be devoted to investment expenditure. For the purpose of the law, investment is defined very broadly: it includes effectively *all* the expenditures associated with the new expenditure assignments of the municipalities, except for wages and salaries and other personnel expenditure. (Popular Participation Law, Article 23V). Debt service can be included under the investment expenditure umbrella, up to a limit of 90 percent of coparticipated revenues, but only if the debt being serviced is deemed to have been financing investment projects. Expenditures incurred for training may also be included (Special Decree 23813, Article 16). It is not clear whether these limitations are binding, since municipalities are effectively given a good deal of latitude in their application.

The assignment of property taxes to the municipalities is in line with the general principle of tax assignment that stipulates that local gov-

---

[5]The proportional formula for the transfer to a given town can be expressed simply as X bolivianos times the number of the town's inhabitants as established by the 1992 census where X = total shared revenue divided by the total population of Bolivia (also from the 1992 census).

ernments should be allowed to exploit only the most immobile bases. To the extent that the incidence of the *patente* falls on business activity, and not on the property at which the business is located, it is less well suited than the property tax to finance local government, because its base will be more mobile. These taxes are, however, typically levied at moderate rates, and are not a significant source of revenue.

One feature of the revenue-sharing arrangement that is problematic is the fact that local governments receive 20 centavos of every additional boliviano raised by the national government. This holds even when the national government is obliged to increase taxes as part of an adjustment effort. It receives only 80 centavos for each extra boliviano it raises. When financial conditions are stable and the economy is growing more or less at its trend rate, this system of revenue sharing can function reasonably well. Assuming that tax revenues grow pari passu with GDP, the system provides the lower level governments with a source of finance that bears some relationship to their expenditure needs. It does not function well, however, in periods of fiscal crisis, when the central government is forced to tighten its belt. Paradoxically, the revenue-raising efforts of the central government in these circumstances allow the local governments to spend more, thus thwarting the adjustment effort. In the Bolivian case, the national government must overadjust—for each boliviano in extra revenue it seeks to raise to reduce the deficit, it must raise 1.25 bolivianos, assuming that the local governments will spend all the extra revenue that they get.[6]

This feature of the revenue-sharing arrangement is similar to that which governs the sharing of revenue between the federal government and provinces of Argentina, except that Argentina's "coparticipation coefficient" is much higher than that of Bolivia.[7] More than half of each peso raised by Buenos Aires goes to the provinces. Consequently, the Bolivian arrangement does not have the same potentially serious consequences as the Argentinean arrangement. Another difference of note between the two systems is that, in Bolivia's case, the pool of revenues shared includes revenue from all the taxes that are assigned to the national government, whereas in Argentina's case, the pool of shared revenues excludes the taxes on international trade. In consequence, the Argentine revenue-sharing arrangement creates an incentive for the federal government to rely more on taxes that are less efficient but not

---

[6]Taking account of the 5 percent transfer to the public universities, the gross yield of new tax measures must increase to 1.43 bolivianos.

[7]Argentina's coparticipation coefficient is actually an average, since, unlike the Bolivian revenue-sharing mechanism, the coefficient differs by type of tax.

shared. The Bolivian arrangement has the merit of not creating this rather perverse incentive.

Prefecturas

Expenditure Assignments

The *prefecturas*, like the RDCs they replaced, are expected to play an important role in the provision of new infrastructure; specifically, in the areas of road construction, rural electrification, irrigation infrastructure, environmental preservation, tourism, social assistance programs, institution-building (for municipalities), and other projects in conjunction with municipalities. However, they have relinquished responsibility for the infrastructural investments that are now undertaken by the cities and towns.

Unlike the RDCs, the *prefecturas* also have responsibilities for current programs. The national government delegates to them the responsibilities for human resource management and administration in the health, education and social assistance areas, although, as noted above, the wage bill in these sectors is financed by a transfer from the national government. The *prefecturas* are also responsible for the provision of public services in the areas of social assistance, sports, culture, tourism, agriculture and pisciculture, and local roads unless these are the responsibility of the municipalities. It is important to stress, however, that in political and constitutional terms, the *prefecturas* are simply an arm of the central government. The senior official of the *prefectura* is appointed by the government; he is not elected by the residents of his department. On balance, the recent reforms have not had a significant impact on total expenditure by the *prefecturas*. It is, if anything, lower than it was prereform (Table 3).

Revenue Arrangements

The *prefecturas* continue to be assigned the royalties from forestry and petroleum and minerals extraction. The major change brought about by the recent reforms has been the creation of the Departmental Equalization Fund (Fondo Compensatorio Departmental), under which those *prefecturas* whose per capita revenues from royalties are lower than the national average receive a compensatory transfer from the national government that effectively brings them up to the average. Those *prefecturas* that are relatively resource-rich receive nothing from the Fund. Another important aspect of the reform was the introduction of a special coparticipation arrangement, under which the *prefecturas*

Table 3. Bolivia: Financial Operations of the Regional Development Corporations and *Prefecturas*
(In percent of GDP)

	1992	1993	1994	1995	1996
Revenue and grants	2.3	2.5	1.9	1.6	2.4
Current revenue	1.6	1.6	1.1	0.7	1.4
Revenue sharing	0.8	0.9	0.4	—	0.4
Hydrocarbon taxes	0.7	0.6	0.6	0.6	0.6
Other	0.1	0.1	0.1	0.1	0.4
Current transfers from rest of public sector	—	0.1	0.1	0.2	0.1
Capital revenue	0.1	0.1	—	0.1	0.4
Capital transfers from rest of public sector	0.3	0.4	0.5	0.3	0.2
Foreign grants	0.2	0.3	0.2	0.3	0.2
Expenditure	2.9	2.7	2.2	1.8	2.4
Current expenditure	0.9	0.8	0.8	0.5	0.8
Wages and salaries	0.3	0.4	0.4	0.2	0.4
Goods and services	0.3	0.1	0.1	0.1	0.2
Interest	—	—	0.1	—	0.1
Other	0.2	0.2	0.2	0.1	—
Current transfers to rest of public sector	0.1	0.1	0.1	—	0.1
Capital expenditure	2.0	1.9	1.4	1.3	1.6
Fixed capital formation	1.8	1.7	1.3	1.1	1.5
Capital transfers to rest of public sector	0.2	0.1	0.1	0.2	0.2
Overall balance	–0.6	–0.1	0.3	–0.2	—
Memorandum item:					
Noninterest expenditure as percent of GDP	2.9	2.7	2.1	1.8	2.3

Sources: Ministry of Finance; Integrated System of Financial Administration and Government Control (SAFCO); Central Bank of Bolivia; and IMF staff estimates.

collectively receive 25 percent of collections of the Special Tax on Hydrocarbons (Impuesto Especial a los Hidrocarburos—IEH) (the RDCs shared in the earlier coparticipation arrangement).[8] These two revenue sources, together with royalty income, make up the lion's share of their revenue. Total revenues are now little changed from their prereform ratio with respect to GDP (see Table 3).

There is a certain inconsistency between the assignment of revenue to the *prefecturas* and their lack of political autonomy. In general, entities that are components of central government should be financed via

---

[8]The revenue from the IEH is distributed as follows: 50 percent is divided among the *prefecturas* in proportion to their relative population sizes; and 50 percent is divided in nine equal parts, one for each department. Thus, if a given department's share of total population is x, and total revenue from the IEH is R, that department's share (S), in bolivianos, of total revenue from the IEH would be given by:

$$S = ((x*0.5*R) + ((0.5*R)/9))$$
$$= ((x + (1/9))*(0.5*R)).$$

budgetary transfers, since it is logical that their operations should be subject to the same degree or kind of scrutiny as any central government operation. There is no reason, in other words, why the coverage of the budget should not encompass them. However, these considerations are not reflected in the new financing arrangements for the *prefecturas*.

One possible rationale for the assignment of taxes and the revenue-sharing arrangements is to ensure that the national government pays due regard to regional interests. These revenue arrangements may work to reduce regional disparities, and may be appropriate if the budgetary process at the national level were not to work well for the smaller or more disadvantaged regions. However, it is possible to imagine a more centralized arrangement—with no assignment or sharing of revenues—that guaranteed, say, a minimum level of social spending per inhabitant while nonetheless ensuring that the financial operations of the *prefectura* were included in the national government's budget.

Implications of the Recent Reform

There is much to praise in Bolivia's reforms. To point out just two of their merits, they address a heartfelt need for greater participation in the governance of the country at the community levels, and they achieve a sorely needed redistribution of revenue to the poorer areas of the country.

Certain features of the reforms may, however, make the gains from decentralization of expenditure less than they otherwise would be. In particular, they appear to entail some overlap of expenditure responsibilities. The reforms may also have created some horizontal imbalance, in the sense that the increase in the expenditure responsibilities of some municipalities may have outstripped the increase in revenue they receive under the coparticipation agreement.[9] Further, the reforms have greatly increased the number of jurisdictions in Bolivia with both the motive and the opportunity to borrow. Local government indebtedness, up until now negligible, may start to grow. Finally, the devolution of expenditure responsibilities to small jurisdictions that may not be ready for them may contribute to wasteful expenditure.

---

[9]If national government expenditure in the areas for which municipalities now have responsibility was very low before the reform, then the lack of balance need not prevent an increase in expenditure, but pressures for increased spending may be created nonetheless.

Overlapping expenditure responsibilities. Current expenditure assignments are either not entirely clear-cut, or entail two jurisdictions being responsible for two different economic expenditure categories in the same program. In particular:
- The laws assign certain specific investment responsibilities to the *prefecturas*. However, they also assign a residual category of investment—any investment—if it is not the responsibility of the municipality. This approach does not really give clear guidance. Does it mean, for example, that the *prefecturas* will undertake investment in the rural areas of a municipality's jurisdiction?
- The assignment of health programs has the central government (through the *prefecturas*) being responsible for administering certain program inputs—for example, salaries of professional personnel—while the municipality is responsible for maintaining the physical plant and also for materials and supplies. This arrangement risks being inefficient.
- There is scope for rationalization of the road construction and maintenance programs of *prefecturas* and municipalities, according to informed sources.
- There is apparently some confusion on the part of officials at different levels of government about their current expenditure assignments.

Risk of horizontal inequity. Decentralization has increased both the local governments' expenditure responsibilities and the revenue they need to carry them out. Revenue and expenditure increases may match in the aggregate, but this is not necessarily true of each and every city and town. Those in a surplus position may well spend more than they need to, while those whose revenue increase has fallen short of what is needed to finance their additional expenditure responsibilities will have an incentive to borrow. In other words, there is likely to be an asymmetry in the response of local government. The result is that both the gross and the net indebtedness of the local government sector increases.

This is simply a conjecture at this stage, and it is not possible to hazard a guess as to whether horizonal inequity is significant and whether it could have these kinds of consequences. Nonetheless, the signs of emerging horizontal imbalances bear watching.

Increase in the number of jurisdictions able to borrow. Although the total amount of revenue shared with the municipalities is allocated on the basis of a fixed amount per head, the agreement has had a dramatic effect on the revenue of the smaller towns, which previously were getting next to nothing, or nothing. As an example, one small town has seen its annual revenues increase from Bs 7,000 (less than US$1,500) to Bs 2 million. By increasing the stream of revenues to the smaller municipalities, coparticipation makes them more attractive to potential lenders. It has also resulted in a quantum jump in the *number* of municipalities borrowing from the National Fund for Regional Development (a central government agency), from a handful to over 50. Although these entities are too small at present for their financial operations to have macroeconomic effects, and may in any case have been unable to borrow, their size and borrowing capacity will grow over time. The potential increase in the number of debtors may have implications for the national government's debt management systems. Since the national government's monitoring system has been geared to the largest cities and the *prefecturas*, its present coverage is not broad enough to respond to an increase in borrowing by smaller municipalities.

Potential for and consequences of unwise spending decisions by local governments. Anecdotal evidence suggests, as could be expected, that there is considerable variation in the abilities of the smaller towns to carry out expenditure projects. Reported cases range from that of a small community that had been able to implement a school building project successfully to another that had wasted a large sum of money on unusable cellular phones. Perhaps needless to say, if too much money is wasted at the local level, there may be pressure for additional expenditure, which might increase the debt of either level of government.

The point of these observations is not to argue that the recent impressive reforms of local government in Bolivia should be reversed. Indeed, most of these observations could be made of any reform that devolves a substantial share of expenditure to local authorities. The point is rather that it is only sensible to be aware of the potential pitfalls and snares surrounding a reform of this type.

Directions for Further Reform

The decentralization of government services may well improve substantially the efficiency with which public services, especially health and education, are provided, since they will involve directly the people who will most benefit. The question arises as to how the beneficial impact of these reforms can be enhanced by measures that would minimize or neutralize the potentially harmful side effects of the reform. On the basis of the foregoing discussion, the major risks to the reform may be summarized as follows:

- *Overlaps.* Inefficiency resulting from overlaps (or gaps) in the provision of services, and from problems stemming from the joint management of a given activity by two levels of government.

- *Problems of technical competence.* Inefficiency resulting from a lack of technical competence in the design, execution of projects, and in the provision of services by the local governments.
- *Excessive incentives and opportunities for indebtedness.* Excessive indebtedness at the local government level resulting from the combination of increased access to borrowed resources by the municipalities, a lack of incentives for fiscal prudence, and problems with the national government's control systems.

Expenditure overlaps. It may be that there will be problems coordinating the operations of the *prefecturas* and municipalities. If so, these may well be amenable to being addressed bilaterally. The joint management of certain services by the national government and the municipalities, which could also lead to coordination problems, might also be addressed in this way. If, as experience is gained with the new arrangements, this informal approach proves unsuccessful, the problem of overlaps may ultimately have to be addressed through an amendment to the legislation that aims at a sharper delineation of the responsibilities of the various levels of government.

Lack of expertise. As noted above, the law recognizes the possibility that municipalities may require assistance, at least initially, in carrying out their new responsibilities. Given the disparities in size of Bolivian municipalities, and their lack of experience in the provision of many public services, a good deal of technical assistance will probably have to be provided by the national government. This can be seen as an initial investment that will benefit the country as a whole once the smaller cities and towns have become more adept at managing their expenditure programs. That said, it may be that some towns will be too small to provide the services expected of them. If so, some special arrangement may have to be made, where the *prefectura* assumes responsibility for certain services. The question then arises as to whether the legislation might distinguish explicitly between classes of municipalities according to their capacity to deliver basic public services or whether ad hoc arrangements will suffice.

Debt issues. Local government indebtedness has to date not been a problem in Bolivia. The total debt of the municipalities in 1996 was only 1.2 percent of GDP, and most of this was concentrated in the three largest cities. Under the new arrangements, however, indebtedness is quite likely to grow. Local government borrowing will need to be controlled, either directly or indirectly, by the national government since the market model is not well suited for the Bolivian setting. Market-based systems are found in comparatively few countries. The requirements for their successful operation are heavy. In particular, they require well-functioning and comparatively broad financial markets and reliable, comprehensive, and timely information on the government's financial operations.

At present, domestic borrowing is subject to formal controls, but borrowing does take place without formal authorization. The national government monitors the financial operations of the 10 or so largest cities, but not those of the remaining 300.

Two basic components of an effective management system for local government debt are a good information system and a system of local government budget review by the relevant financial agency of the national government. Under such a system, the local governments, at least the largest of them, prepare a budget using standard procedures, which they discuss with the national government (the Ministry of Finance) before the start of the fiscal year.

In vetting municipal budgets, the Finance Ministry can rely on a rules-based system, a discretionary approach, or a combination of the two. For example, the ministry could assign maximum values to indicators of the ability of local governments to service their debt. Two such indicators could be the ratio of the stock of debt to current revenue, and the ratio of the flow of debt service to current revenue. Under a rules-based approach, all municipalities would have to submit budgets that respect the particular values chosen for these indicators (and any other thought to be necessary to control local government finances). The indicators would be revised from time to time, but not necessarily annually.

In addition to this, however, the Finance Ministry should require that the budgets submitted to it respect an *annual* limit on borrowing. The annual limit is necessary because the current level of indebtedness is low, so that even a moderate limit on the ratio of debt or debt service to revenue will not suffice to prevent large increases in indebtedness (and large deficits) from one year to the next. Put another way, it is not simply the *level* of indebtedness that matters, but its *rate of change*.

In Bolivia's case, the annual limit could be negotiated on a case-by-case basis with the larger municipalities, and would be renegotiated each year. It would not be feasible to negotiate individual limits with each of the more than 300 municipalities in the country. For the smaller municipalities, an all rules-based approach would probably be necessary. For example, in addition to the requirement that the two debt-service capacity indicators be respected, a limit could be imposed on the annual increase in the nominal value of debt, for which one value would be chosen that would apply to all of the smaller towns.

For the *prefecturas*, it can be argued that if expenditure needs in a particular year clearly exceed revenue, the national government should finance the excess, to the extent that it is deemed desirable and affordable, by discretionary transfers. This approach is consistent with the legal and political status of the *prefecturas*. Alternatively, the national government could give them the same treatment it would give to the larger cities and towns.

The coparticipation formula. A final issue to address is whether the revenue-sharing formula can or should be altered to eliminate the scope it provides local governments to increase spending when taxes at the national level are being increased to reduce the deficit. One possibility might be to redefine the revenue base subject to revenue sharing so that it does not include the revenue generated by tax increases and other measures adopted to promote a reduction in the deficit. Thus, for example, if the rate of the value-added tax (VAT) is increased from 13 percent to 15 percent, the revenue-sharing formula could be modified so that it applies to only (13/15*100) or 87 percent of VAT revenue, meaning that the additional revenue deemed to be generated by the tax rate increase would accrue in its entirety to the national government. This procedure would have to be symmetric, however; a reduction in the rate of the tax from 15 percent to 13 percent would then result in the national government's giving up the 2 percentage points of VAT revenue that was going directly to it, without being subject to revenue sharing. This procedure would only work well when the adjustment measures take the form of a rate increase, or some other form that allows a simple calculation of the amount of revenue that would not be subject to the coparticipation formula.

Another possibility might be to assume that the agreement would apply only to tax revenue up to some stipulated ceiling. For example, it could be assumed at the beginning of the year that all revenue exceeding 115 percent of the previous year's figure would not be shared, but would go entirely to the national government. The threshold value of 115 percent would be determined on the basis of some formula or method; for example, by making a projection of the revenue increase that could be expected with real GDP growing at its trend rate, and inflation at its underlying rate. Both of these proposals would detract to some degree from the simplicity of the current arrangement, and it may be that given the relatively modest share of revenue going to the municipalities, the pro-cyclical nature of the revenue-sharing rule may not be a problem.

As a final observation, the low share in their total revenue of taxes raised by the municipalities themselves suggests that it would be highly desirable to encourage them to exploit their own tax bases more fully. The higher the value of the coparticipation coefficient, however, the less the incentive the municipalities have to finance themselves.

18

Brazil

TERESA TER-MINASSIAN

The history of intergovernmental fiscal relations in Brazil has been characterized by alternating phases of decentralization and recentralization. The period of the dictatorship, from the mid-1960s to the mid-1980s, was marked by strong centralist tendencies, with a clearly dominant role of the federal government and its enterprises in the management of public resources, as well as in the economy as a whole. The democratization process, culminating in the enactment of the 1988 Constitution, was accompanied by a resurgence of decentralization trends. These tendencies have been especially marked on the revenue side, resulting in a relatively high degree of control over revenue sources by the state and local governments, compared with other large federations around the world.

In 1995, own tax revenues of the subnational governments accounted for nearly 38 percent of total tax revenues (including social security contributions) and were equivalent to 10.5 percent of GDP. The share of tax revenues at the disposal of subnational governments (defined to include own plus shared revenues) represented nearly 50 percent of total tax revenues (Tables 1 and 2). In the same year, state and local governments accounted for about 60 percent of public consumption and for 63 percent of public investments. By contrast, the federal government (mainly through the social security system) maintained a preponderant (over 80 percent) share in social transfers (Table 3).

The author wishes to thank Trevor Alleyne, Adrienne Cheasty, Isaias Coelho, João Oliveira do Carmo, Lorenzo Perez, Tej Prakash, and Gerd Schwartz for useful information and comments.

Table 1. Brazil: Operations of the General Government[1]
(In percent of GDP)

	1991	1992	1993	1994	1995
Nonfinancial revenue	26.7	24.4	25.9	28.8	28.7
Tax revenue	24.0	22.2	23.6	26.4	28.0
Direct taxes	3.9	3.5	4.1	3.8	4.2
Value-added taxes	9.3	8.9	8.3	8.9	9.2
Social security taxes	4.8	4.6	5.0	5.3	5.2
Trade taxes	0.4	0.4	0.4	0.5	0.7
Other tax revenue	5.6	4.9	5.8	8.0	8.6
Nontax revenues	2.8	2.2	2.3	2.4	0.7
Nonfinancial expenditure	24.4	22.7	24.0	25.3	28.3
Current expenditure	24.9	22.9	23.2	23.8	26.7
Gross wages	11.6	10.3	11.0	11.0	12.0
Transfers	5.1	5.3	4.6	5.1	5.6
Pension benefits	4.5	4.8	4.0	4.7	4.9
Subsidies and grants	0.6	0.5	0.6	0.5	0.6
Other current expenditure	8.2	7.3	7.6	7.7	9.1
Capital expenditure	5.0	3.0	3.5	2.9	2.4
Float and statistical adjustment	−5.5	−3.2	−2.8	−1.4	−0.8
Primary balance (deficit −)	2.3	1.7	2.0	3.5	0.4
Real net interest payments	0.8	3.3	1.7	2.9	4.3
Operational balance (deficit −)	1.5	−1.6	0.2	0.6	−4.0
Public sector borrowing requirement	15.2	31.3	44.9	35.8	5.8

Sources: Ministry of Finance of Brazil; Central Bank of Brazil; and IMF staff estimates.
[1] Figures may not add to totals due to rounding.

The Brazilian federation encompasses three levels of government: the Union, 26 states plus the Federal District,[1] and about 5,000 municipalities of widely ranging sizes. It is noteworthy that, in the 1988 Constitution, the municipalities have been formally granted a status of members of the federation. Although the operational implications of such a status are not spelled out, it appears to confer greater autonomy to the municipalities in Brazil than is the case in most other countries.

In recent years, there has been a rapid increase in the number of municipalities, quite divorced from economic and financial viability considerations. The increase reflected the lack of clearly specified criteria for the creation of new municipalities, and the fact that the

---

[1] The states are grouped, mainly for analytical purposes, into five regions: North, Northeast, Center-West, South, and Southeast. These regional groups are also relevant for the distribution of certain transfers from the federal government.

Table 2. Brazil: Summary Operations of State and Municipal Governments
(In percent of GDP)

	1991	1992	1993	1994	1995
Revenue	14.2	13.0	13.0	13.7	14.1
Tax revenue	8.5	7.9	7.6	8.5	10.5
VAT ICMS	6.9	6.7	6.0	6.8	7.2
Other	1.6	1.2	1.5	1.7	3.3
Nontax revenue	2.3	1.7	1.9	1.7	0.0
Transfers	3.3	3.4	3.5	3.6	3.6
Tax transfers	3.1	3.3	3.3	3.4	3.4
Other central government transfers	0.2	0.2	0.2	0.2	0.2
Expenditure	12.7	12.7	12.4	13.3	14.3
Current expenditure	12.7	12.2	12.4	11.5	12.7
Gross wages	6.7	6.5	6.8	5.9	7.0
Materials and supplies	2.5	2.5	2.5	2.3	5.7
Transfers and subsidies	3.5	3.3	3.2	3.3	0.0
To enterprises	0.1	0.2	0.1	0.0	0.0
Pensions and welfare	0.6	0.5	0.5	0.5	0.0
Subsidies and other current expenditures	2.9	2.6	2.5	2.8	0.0
Capital expenditure	2.3	2.1	2.1	1.9	1.5
Adjustment	−2.3	−1.6	−2.0	−0.1	0.1
Primary balance (deficit −)	1.5	0.4	0.6	0.5	−0.2
Net interest payments[1]	0.2	1.1	0.3	1.4	2.1
Operational balance (deficit −)	1.3	−0.8	0.2	−1.0	−2.3

Sources: Ministry of Finance; Central Bank of Brazil; and IMF staff estimates.
[1]Comprises interest payments on external debt, plus the real component of interest payments on domestic debt.

revenue-sharing mechanism involves financial incentives to this creation.[2]

Despite longstanding efforts at income redistribution, Brazil remains a country characterized by major disparities, both among regions and in the size of incomes. In 1992, the eight states in the South and Southeastern regions, where 57 percent of the country's population lives, accounted for virtually three quarters of the national GDP. Per capita incomes ranged from the equivalent of less than US$600 a year in the poorest state (Piaui) to more than US$4,200 in the richest (São Paulo) (Affonso, 1995). Social indicators show an equally wide range across the country (Table 4).

---

[2]The Constitution stipulates that any newly created municipality must receive transfers from the federal and state governments adequate to ensure its basic functions. These transfers are, however, financed through a redirection of funds previously allocated to other municipalities in the relevant state.

Table 3. Brazil: Federal Government Operations[1]
(In percent of GDP)

	1991	1992	1993	1994	1995
Revenue[2]	15.9	14.8	16.5	18.6	18.2
Taxes	15.4	14.4	16.1	17.9	17.5
Direct	3.9	3.5	4.1	3.8	4.2
Individual	3.1	2.4	2.9	2.6	2.9
Corporate	0.7	1.1	1.3	1.2	1.4
Indirect	3.0	2.8	3.1	3.8	2.5
IPI	2.3	2.2	2.3	2.1	2.0
IOF	0.6	0.6	0.7	0.8	0.5
IPMF	0.0	0.0	0.1	1.0	0.0
Taxes on trade	0.4	0.4	0.4	0.5	0.7
Earmarked social taxes	3.1	2.9	3.2	4.1	4.4
Social security contributions	4.8	4.6	5.0	5.3	5.2
Other taxes	0.3	0.2	0.2	0.4	0.4
Nontax revenues	0.4	0.4	0.4	0.7	0.7
Expenditure	15.0	13.5	15.0	15.6	17.6
Current expenditure	15.5	14.1	14.3	15.9	17.6
Gross wages	4.9	3.8	4.2	5.1	5.0
Social security benefits	4.5	4.8	4.0	4.7	4.9
Transfers	3.8	3.9	4.0	3.9	3.9
To states and municipalities	3.1	3.3	3.3	3.4	3.4
Other	0.6	0.6	0.6	0.5	0.5
Subsidies and grants	0.2	0.1	0.1	0.1	0.4
Other current expenditure	2.2	1.5	2.0	2.1	3.4
Capital expenditure	2.7	1.0	1.4	1.0	0.9
Direct	2.2	0.9	1.4	1.0	0.8
Investment	1.2	0.6	1.0	0.8	0.7
Other capital expenditure	1.0	0.2	0.4	0.3	0.1
Capital transfers to public enterprises	0.5	0.1	0.0	0.0	0.0
VAT adjustment	–0.8	–0.6	–0.3	–0.4	–0.2
Float and adjustment	–2.4	–0.9	–0.4	–0.9	–0.7
Primary balance (deficit –)	0.8	1.3	1.4	3.0	0.6
Net interest payments[3]	0.6	2.1	1.4	1.5	2.2
Operational balance (deficit –)	0.3	–0.8	0.0	1.6	–1.6

Sources: Ministry of Finance; Central Bank of Brazil; and IMF staff estimates.
[1]Includes the central administration, social security system, and Central Bank of Brazil.
[2]Excludes proceeds from privatization.
[3]Comprises interest payments on external debt, plus the real component of interest payments on domestic debt.

Expenditure Assignment

The 1988 Constitution assigns relatively few functions exclusively to each level of government. Specifically, it reserves to the federal level its traditional functions, notably defense, foreign affairs, control of the money supply and of the financial system, and the exploitation of certain monopolies, currently in the process of being dismantled. It re-

Table 4. Brazil: Regional Disparities in Social Indicators
(In percent unless otherwise indicated)

Social Indicator	North	Regions				National average
		North-east	Center-West	South-east	South	
Infant mortality rate (per thousand; 1989)	55	98	41	40	38	59
Years of life expectancy (1985)	64.5	55.7	67.7	65.3	65.7	62.6
Child malnutrition rate (1989)	42.3	46.1	25.7	21.7	17.8	31.0
Rate of elementary school attendance (1987)	88.7[1]	77.9	84.6	87.1	82.7	83.2
Rate of first grade repetition	...	31.3	...	14.4[2]	8.3[3]	19.8
Illiteracy rate	19.8[1]	43.3	22.5	16.4	16.2	24.6
Percentage of dwellings with running water	80.0[1]	48.4	62.0	84.4	68.4	70.9

Source: Afonso (1996).
[1] Urban areas only.
[2] State of São Paulo only.
[3] State of Santa Catarina only.

serves to the state and municipal levels the provision of police and other security services, as well as a few other services, in their respective geographical areas. For the vast majority of public expenditures, however, the Constitution envisages concurrent responsibilities, to be further specified by a federal law—which so far has not been proposed (Table 5). This lack of clarity in the assignment of spending responsibilities contributed to duplication and waste of resources in the provision of goods and services. Thus, for example, the federal government continues to be actively involved in the provision of basic education, which in principle should be carried out by the local level, albeit with financial support by higher levels of government to the extent needed to ensure adequate minimum standards nationwide.

Despite the lack of legal definition of spending responsibilities, in practice, there has been a clear trend toward a decentralization of public expenditures. This trend has been, however, more a response to the fiscal stress on the federal budget—resulting from the decentralization of revenues and the adverse macroeconomic conditions of the early 1990s—than the result of a planned and orderly devolution of spending responsibilities. As a result of this decentralization, the share of the federal government (including the social security system) in total noninterest expenditures of the general government has declined significantly since 1988. The limited information available on the functional classification of expenditures by different levels of government in Brazil indicates that the federal government spends the bulk (nearly 80 percent) of its resources on social security and social assistance, general ad-

Table 5. Brazil: Expenditure Assignments

Expenditure Function	Responsibility for Policy and Control	Responsibility for Provision
Defense	F	F
Foreign affairs	F	F
Foreign trade	F	F
Monetary and financial policies	F	F
Social security	F	F, S
Sectoral policies	F, S	F, S
Immigration	F	F
Railroads and airports	F	F, S
Natural resources	F	F, S
Environmental protection	F, S	F, S
Education	F, S, L	F, S, L
Health	F, S	F, S, L
Social assistance	F, S	F, S, L
Police	F, S	F, S, L
Water and sewerage	F	S, L
Fire protection	F, S	S
Parks and recreation	L	L
Roads		
National	F	F
State	S	S
Interstate	F	F, S
Local	S	L

Source: Afonso and Ramundo (1996).
Note: F = federal, S = state, and L = local.

ministration, and interest on the public debt. State spending is concentrated on general administration, education, social assistance, and health. Municipal spending focuses on general administration, housing and urban services, primary education, health, and local public transport (Figure 1).

It is interesting to note that 71 percent of total expenditures of the state and local governments are carried out by the eight relatively rich states of the South and Southeast (Afonso, 1994). This suggests that, despite the substantial redistributive role of the federal transfers, the wide disparities in own revenue-raising capacities of the states continue to substantially affect the regional distribution of state and local spending.

Revenue Assignment

The current assignment of revenue sources in Brazil departs in several respects from the traditional prescriptions of the fiscal federalism literature, especially regarding indirect taxes. The federal government is currently assigned the following main taxes: the personal and corpo-

Figure 1. Brazil: Structure of Government Spending
(In percent)

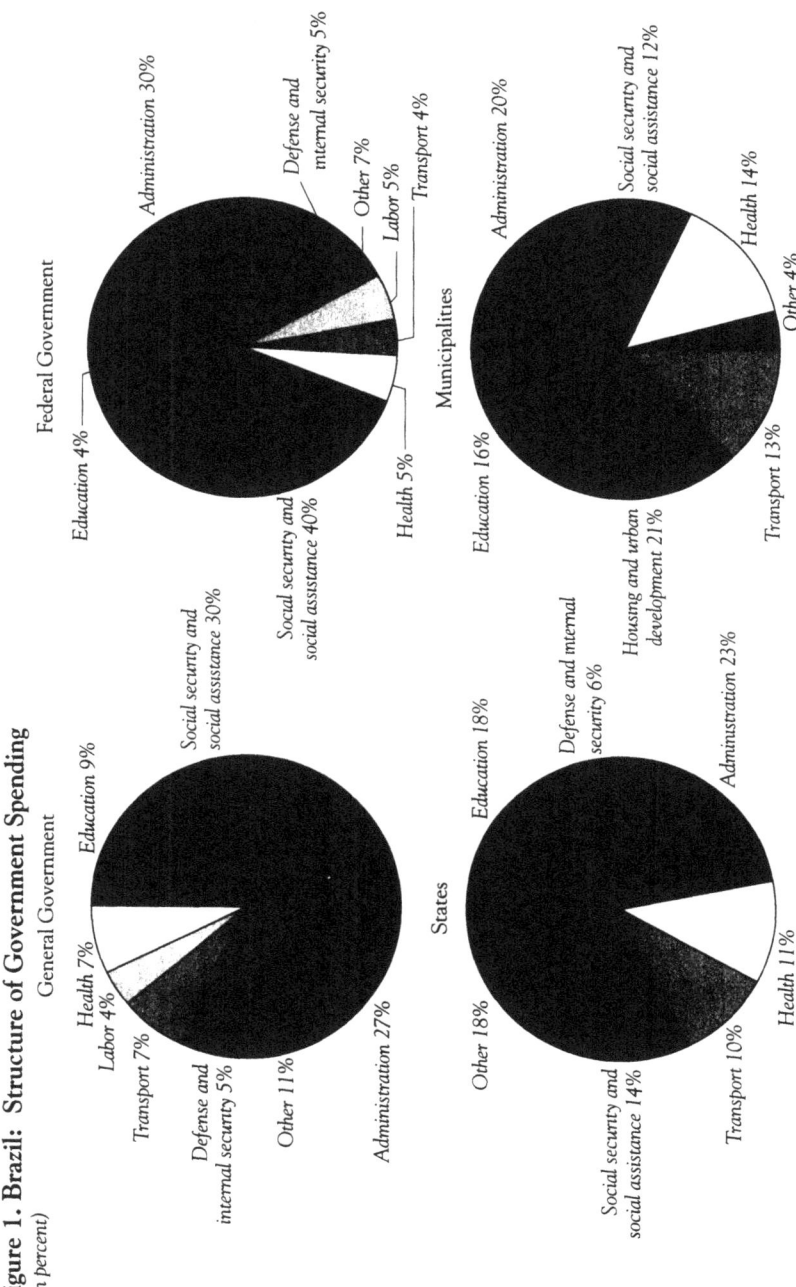

Source: Afonso and Ramundo (1996).

Table 6. Brazil: Tax Assignments

	Responsibility for		
Tax Category	Definition of base	Setting of rate	Administration
Foreign trade	F	F	F
Corporate income	F	F	F
Capital gains	F	F	F
Personal income	F	F	F
Transfers of property	S, L	F, S, L	S, L
Vehicles	S	S	S
Property	L	L	L
Rural property	F	F	F
Payroll	F	F	F
Civil servants' payroll	F, S, L	F, S, L	F, S, L
Sales taxes			
IPI	F	F	F
ICMS	F, S	F, S	S
ISS	F, L	F, L	L
Fees, royalties	F, S, L	F, S, L	F, S, L

Source: Afonso and Ramundo (1996).
Note: F = federal, S = state, and L = local.

rate income taxes (which are, however, shared with the states and municipalities—see section on Intergovernmental Transfers); a selective value-added-type of tax (the IPI), which is in essence a series of excises with different rates and a credit mechanism, and which is also subject to revenue sharing; a tax on rural property (shared 50 percent with the municipalities); various types of social security contributions levied on payroll or turnover of enterprises; taxes on foreign trade; and certain taxes on financial operations (Table 6). The last three categories are not shared with the lower-level governments. The states are assigned a broad-based value-added-type tax (the ICMS), a tax on motor vehicles, and estate and gift taxes. The municipalities are assigned a tax on services (the ISS), a tax on transfers of immovable properties, and a tax on urban real estate property.

The ICMS has traditionally suffered from a number of shortcomings (Affonso and Silva, 1996), some of which were eliminated in 1966 through a major reform. Specifically:

- The ICMS is levied at different rates on different categories of goods: reduced rates on "essential necessities," 17 percent on most goods,[3] and 25 percent on luxury goods. These rates are levied on a tax-inclusive base, resulting in higher rates on a net-of-tax basis. All interstate transactions are taxed on an origin basis. The rate

---

[3] 18 percent in three states.

on these transactions is set by the federal senate at 12 percent, except for exports from the states in the South and Southeast to states in the other regions, which are taxed at 7 percent. The difference in rates on interstate and intrastate transactions complicates administration and provides an incentive to misclassify transactions, to reduce the tax liability.
- Until the 1996 reform, exports of nonmanufactured goods were not zero rated, and credit was not allowed for the purchase of capital goods.
- The base of the ICMS has been eroded by the granting of widespread, but not necessarily uniform across the country, exemptions and other preferential treatments for selected sectors.[4]
- The superimposition of the ICMS with the selective federal (IPI) and municipal (ISS) taxes has given rise to cascading and distortions in the tax burden across sectors and localities. This cascading is reinforced by the fact that some sizable contributions earmarked for the social security system (COFINS and PIS/PASEP) are levied on turnover.

Following the 1996 reform, which zero rated all exports and introduced a credit for capital goods, the federal government has proposed a more comprehensive reform, which would replace the present ICMS and IPI with both a federal and a state-level VAT, levied on the same tax base and at homogeneous rates for interstate as well as intrastate transactions. It has also been proposed that this tax should be levied on a destination basis. Although the proposed mechanism[5] is in principle

---

[4]Tax preferences under the ICMS have to be approved unanimously by a committee of the Secretaries of Finance of the states (CONFAZ), chaired by the Deputy Minister of Finance. The unanimity rule has helped moderate, but far from eliminated, the proliferation of preferences under the ICMS.

[5]Specifically, the proposed system would work as follows. Under the hypothesis of a move to a full destination principle, intrastate transactions and imports from abroad would be taxed under the federal and the state-level VAT in the state of the transactions. Exports abroad would be zero rated under both taxes. Exports to another state would be subject to a VAT levied federally at a rate equivalent to the sum of the rates of the federal and state VATs. Imports from another state would pay both the federal and the state VAT in the state of destination, but the importer would be entitled to a credit for the combined VAT paid by the exporter. Under this scheme, the full revenue of the state VAT would accrue to the destination state. The system could be adjusted to allow for different revenue sharing between the states of origin and destination by modifying the respective rates of tax, and adjusting correspondingly the federal component of the combined rate.

The proposed system would eliminate the scope for evasion created, under the current system, by the differential in the rates levied on intrastate and interstate transactions. To remain administratively manageable, it would require uniformity of the state VAT rates across the country, as well as little or no differentiation of the rates by type of commodity. See Varsano (1996) and Silvani and dos Santos (1996) for further details.

compatible with different arrangements for the sharing of revenues among the states, any move from the current origin principle is bound to have a significant impact on the distribution across the states of their major revenue source, entailing losses for states that are net exporters to the rest of the country and gains for those that are net importers. It is, therefore, unclear whether and how the political consensus needed to implement such a reform—which would require a constitutional amendment—can be mustered.

The distribution of revenue across levels of government and by type of tax has undergone significant changes in recent years, with the share of the federal government (before revenue sharing) in total tax revenues declining by about 5.5 percentage points between 1988 and 1995 (to around 62 percent of total). Currently, various forms of social security contributions account for about 55 percent of own revenues of the federal government, the ICMS for nearly 93 percent of those of the states, and the ISS for nearly half of those of municipalities.

Intergovernmental Transfers

As in other countries, intergovernmental transfers in Brazil fulfill several functions: fill a "vertical" imbalance between expenditure and own revenue assignments that, albeit smaller than in the majority of federal, as well as unitary, countries, remains significant, especially as regards the municipalities; help moderate horizontal imbalances; and promote specific objectives through special purpose grants.

The changing balance between these, not necessarily always compatible, goals has shaped the evolution of the system of intergovernmental transfers over time, in particular the relative weights of revenue sharing versus grants and the composition of the latter. The democratization process and the attendant decentralization trend have been reflected in a marked increase in the share of nonconditional transfers (revenue sharing and block grants) at the expense of special purpose grants. The 1988 Constitution set specific criteria for revenue sharing, both among different levels of government and among different governments of the same level (see below). As a result of these trends, the federal government has seen the share of tax revenues at its disposal[6] decline from about 66 percent at the beginning of the 1980s to about 54 percent by the mid-1990s. The corresponding shares of state and

---

[6]For each level of government, this is defined as the ratio of own tax revenues (plus revenue shared with upper levels, minus revenue shared with lower levels) to total tax revenues. It is an indicator of relative fiscal autonomy of each level of government.

local governments have risen from 24.5 percent to nearly 29 percent (for the states) and from 9.5 percent to over 17 percent (for the municipalities) over the same period.

Revenue Sharing

The main vehicles for revenue sharing are two funds: the Fundo de Participação dos Estados (FPE) and the Fundo de Participação dos Municipios (FPM). The FPE is constituted with 21.5 percent of the net[7] revenues of the three main federal taxes, namely the personal (IRPF) and corporate (IRPJ) income taxes and the selective VAT (IPI). The distribution of the fund among the states is fixed by a law of 1989 that determines a coefficient for each state. These coefficients are mainly based on redistributive criteria, which attribute higher weights to the three poorer regions (North, Northeast, and Center-West). The coefficients vary between 9.4 percent for the state of Bahia (the largest and most populous state in the Northeast) to 1 percent for São Paulo (the state with the highest per capita income). Altogether, the above-mentioned poorer regions account for 85 percent of the FPE.

The FPM is constituted with 22.5 percent of the net revenues of the income taxes and the IPI. Its distribution formula is more complex than that of the FPE. Specifically, 10 percent of the fund is distributed to the capitals of each state, 86.4 percent to other municipalities with populations of less than 156,216, and the rest to the remaining municipalities. Within these shares, the coefficient of each municipality is determined by two criteria: the state to which the municipality belongs and the size of its population (as determined by periodic census). The regional allocation of the FPM is less redistributive than that of the FPE, given the importance of population size in the formula. Accordingly, the combined share of municipalities in the three poorer regions is around 51 percent in the FPM, compared with 85 percent in the FPE.

In addition, the 1988 Constitution mandated the following:
- Ten percent of the IPI be transferred to a fund (FPEX) intended to compensate the states for the loss of revenue entailed by the zero rating of exports of manufactured products under the ICMS. The distribution of this fund among the states reflects their relative shares in manufactured exports.
- Three percent of the IPI be earmarked for the financing of investment credits to the private sector in the three poorer regions of the country.

---

[7]Net revenues exclude refunds and fiscal incentives.

- The revenue from a tax on financial operations on gold be fully devolved to the states and municipalities in which these operations take place.
- Fifty percent of the revenue from the federal tax on rural property (ITR) be devolved to the municipalities.

As regards revenue sharing between the states and the municipalities, the 1988 Constitution raised the percentage of the ICMS to be transferred by the states to the municipalities from 20 percent to 25 percent, and stipulated that 75 percent of these transfers should be distributed among the municipalities of each state on a derivation basis, that is, on the basis of the contribution of each municipality to the value added of the state. The balance is distributed according to criteria decided by the individual states.[8]

The mechanism of revenue sharing was temporarily amended in 1994, in preparation for the introduction of the stabilization plan (Plano Real), to reduce the earmarking of federal revenues, and the percentage of these revenues to be transferred to state and local governments. Specifically, a constitutional amendment created a special fund (Fundo Social de Emergencia, FSE) fed by various types for revenues[9] that would not be subject to sharing or earmarking. The FSE expired at the end of 1995, but was extended—with the new name of Fiscal Stabilization Fund (Fundo Estabilização Fiscal, FEF)—through the end of June 1997 by a second constitutional amendment. It is estimated that this mechanism increased significantly the portion of federal revenues not subject to earmarking or sharing.

Grants

As indicated above, the weight of grants in total intergovernmental transfers has tended to decline over the last several years, reflecting the reaction of the federal government—in a context of growing fiscal stress—to the increase in the share of its revenues transferred to the lower levels of government, especially the municipalities. There remain, nevertheless, a wide variety of grants, some of a block, some of a special purpose nature, some more or less regular, others ad hoc (the so-called *convenios*). Grants are a main vehicle for federal funding of programs in the education, health, and social areas. Together with

---

[8]See Barrera and Roarelli (1996).

[9]These included, among others, income taxes withheld on the salaries of federal employees, a social contribution (PIS) paid by financial institutions, the revenue from an increase in the rate of another contribution paid by the same institutions, and 20 percent of federal revenues transferred to the FPE and the FPM.

own spending by the federal government on education programs, they contribute to meeting the constitutional mandate that 18 percent of federal revenue be spent on education.[10] The revenue of a special contribution levied on enterprise turnover (COFINS) is earmarked for the financing of health and other social programs, including—through the *convenios*—some programs carried out by state and local governments.

Some Weaknesses of the Current System of Intergovernmental Transfers

The brief overview above of the current system of intergovernmental transfers in Brazil points to a number of weaknesses in the system:

- Some federal sources of revenue are subject to sharing with subnational governments, while others are not. This has led to undue reliance of the federal government on these latter sources, which tend to have substantial efficiency costs (for example, contributions on salaries or on enterprise turnover, or taxes on financial transactions);
- The coefficients of vertical distribution are fixed in the Constitution, which has the advantage, from the standpoint of the recipient governments, of facilitating their budgetary and financial planning. However, this also imparts considerable rigidity to the federal budget, thereby constraining the scope for using the shared taxes as instruments of fiscal adjustment or stabilization.
- The coefficients of horizontal distribution are the result of political bargaining, and bear no clear and systematic relation with either relative tax capacities and tax efforts, or relative expenditure needs of the individual states and municipalities.[11]
- Although a quantitative assessment of the redistributive impact of block and special purpose grants across and within states is extremely complex (due to spillover effects, lack of adequate data, and so on), available studies suggest that the incidence of many of these programs has been both highly variable over time and not clearly related to the level of development of the states (see Barrera and Roarelli, 1996).

---

[10]In addition, the full revenue of a special 2.5 percent payroll tax (the so-called *contribuição do Salario-Educação*) is earmarked for elementary school education.

[11]For example, there appears to be no clear relation between the level of transfers per capita from the FPE to the different states and the level of per capita income, or indicators of tax efforts or of expenditure "disabilities" of the state.

Subnational Borrowing and Debt

Past experience with borrowing by state and local governments in Brazil illustrates well the risk of a lack of limits and controls on such borrowing in an environment not conducive to the effective working of market discipline.

Background

State borrowing, primarily to finance public infrastructure, began in earnest in the second half of the 1960s, and was initially financed mainly by federal financial institutions that channeled to state utilities and other state enterprises funds collected through a variety of forced savings schemes, based on payroll taxes. As these funds dwindled during the 1970s, reflecting the adverse impact of the first oil shock on the economy, resort by the states, as well as the federal government, to external borrowing increased sharply. This source of finance came, however, also to a virtual end in the early 1980s. These events, in combination with a deepening recession in the economy, led to widespread default by the states on the service of both their external and internal debt. After nearly a decade of negotiations and ad hoc interventions by the federal government, Law 7976 of 1989 and Law 8727 of 1993 formalized the rescheduling by the federal government of state debts to external creditors and to federal financial intermediaries, respectively. The debts were rescheduled over a 20-year period, with varying grace periods on payment of principal and somewhat more favorable interest rate terms, including an annual cap (initially 9 percent, later 11 percent) on the ratio of debt service to state revenues and automatic capitalization of debt-service obligations exceeding this cap.[12]

This rescheduling eased the cash flow problem of the states, by shifting onto the federal Treasury the cost of temporarily financing the difference between actual debt service and the cap. The evolution of interest rates and the revenue performance over the period of rescheduling will determine the size of the outstanding obligations for the states at the end of that period (the year 2013).

These debt rescheduling operations were not accompanied by firm steps to improve the budgetary performance of the states, in particular to rein back their noninterest spending, which continued to rise through the mid-1990s. The deterioration in the primary balance of the states was especially marked in 1995, when the fiscal dividends for dis-

---

[12]See the World Bank (1995) and Oliveira do Carmo (1996) for a more detailed account of developments in state debt during the 1980s and early 1990s.

inflation were mostly dissipated through large salary increases to state and local employees.

The deterioration in the primary balance was accompanied by a rapid increase in real interest rates on nonrescheduled debt (mainly debt to state banks and bonds).[13] With the service of this debt having come to a virtual halt, the capitalization of interest payments led to an escalation of debt. The domestic bonded debt of the states rose from the equivalent of 2.3 percent of GDP in 1991 to 5.4 percent of GDP by mid-1996. The withdrawal of private investors from the market for state bonds and the drying up of interbank lending to some state banks forced various forms of intervention by the federal authorities (including the Central Bank), which effectively shifted most of the default risk on these types of state debt onto the federal government.

In addition to their funded debt, a number of states accumulated various forms of so-called fluctuating debt, including short-term borrowing from commercial banks secured with future revenues (the so-called revenue anticipation loans, AROs), arrears to suppliers or employees, and guarantees (or comfort letters) for bank borrowing by contractors for state infrastructure projects. It is estimated that by the end of September 1996 the total indebtedness of the states and other public entities under their control had reached the equivalent of 17.5 percent of GDP.

Recent Developments

Growing concerns about the seriousness of the problem of state debt has led to a tightening of controls on new state borrowing in recent years. Specifically, central bank regulations now prohibit a state from borrowing from its own banks.[14] This prohibition has been interpreted not to cover the increase of the debt resulting from the capitalization of unpaid interest. New issues of bonds (other than to refinance maturing ones) are prohibited by a constitutional amendment until the end of this decade. Senate Resolution 11 of 1994 sets guidelines restricting new borrowing on the basis of two criteria, relating to the size of borrowing and the coverage of the overall debt service.[15] These guidelines

---

[13]These debts are especially concentrated in four large states: São Paulo, Rio de Janeiro, Minas Gerais, and Rio Grande do Sul.

[14]The prohibition does not extend to borrowing from other state banks. This represents a loophole, which, however, does not appear to have been significantly exploited to date.

[15]Specifically, in any particular year, new borrowing should not exceed the total debt service for the year or 27 percent of revenue, whichever is greater, and total debt service (including on the new borrowing) should not exceed the state's current surplus for the previous year or 15 percent of its revenue, whichever is less.

appear, however, to be relatively generous, and not to be enforced consistently. In particular, they do not cover the growth of debt resulting from capitalized interest.

At the end of 1995, the federal government, through one of its large banks (the Caixa Economica Federal), set up lines of credit to provide short-term financial support to indebted states, in exchange for commitments by the latter to undertake fiscal adjustment programs (including a retrenchment of payrolls). Preliminary information suggests that, although some of the larger indebted states did indeed undertake initial adjustment steps, the overall financial position of the states continued to worsen in 1996, partly reflecting one-time expenditures in connection with the payroll retrenchment and a clearance of wage arrears.

A more comprehensive approach to the restructuring of state debt was undertaken in the last months of 1996, through the negotiation of federal-state agreements. These involved the following:

- The replacement of state debts to banks and of bonded debt with debt to the Treasury, mostly of 30-year maturity and with a real interest rate of 6 percent[16] a year, well below current average levels. In addition, the agreements contemplate a cap of 13 percent (15 percent for some states) in the annual debt-service ratio, with automatic rescheduling of service in excess of this cap.
- The sale of state assets (mainly state-owned enterprises and banks) equivalent to at least 20 percent of the debt.
- Commitments by the states to adjustment programs aimed at securing a reduction of the ratio of the state debts to their projected revenues to a maximum of 100 percent within a prespecified period (ranging from 6 to 19 years, depending on the state).

Once approved by the federal and state legislatures, the agreements will involve a pledging of own and shared revenues of the states as guarantees to the federal government for the scheduled service of the restructured debt. About 16 such agreements had been signed by early 1997.

These agreements represent an important step in the right direction in addressing the problem of state debt in Brazil. Especially positive features are the provision for privatization of state banks and enterprises, with the proceeds used to reduce the debt, and the stipulation of guarantees for the federal government, through the pledges of state revenues. Nevertheless, the agreements remain so far rather unspecific re-

---

[16]The rate is 7.5 percent a year for some states that have chosen to limit the sale of assets to 10 percent of their outstanding debt.

garding the adjustment measures that the states will need to take to reduce their debt-revenue ratios within the prespecified (for the major part, relatively lengthy) periods. Moreover, the stipulation of a cap on debt-service payments creates an undesirable element of moral hazard.

As part of the effort to strengthen the state finances, the federal government has recently begun an active program of technical and financial assistance (with the support of international financial institutions) to modernize the tax administration and financial management systems of the states. This effort should help the states improve the management of their finances, as well as ensure the availability of more timely and reliable information on developments in the latter.

Concluding Remarks

This brief review has made it clear that Brazil's system of intergovernmental fiscal relations has both positive and negative elements. On the positive side, the Brazilian states, and to a lesser extent the municipalities, have substantial own revenue-raising powers, a fact that should foster fiscal responsibility and political accountability for their budgetary policies. The current system of tax assignments is, however, inconsistent in some respects with the received wisdom in the literature and with prevailing international practice in this area.

In particular, the coexistence of a broad-based state VAT with a more narrowly based multirate federal VAT is awkward and has given rise to cascading and distortions in the tax burden across sectors and localities. Also, the state VAT is plagued by erosion of the base and by substantial difficulties in administration. A reform of the entire VAT system along the lines proposed by the federal government in late 1995 would address many of these weaknesses. Any move away from the current origin-based system would have, however, substantial implications for the distribution of revenue and is unlikely to be accepted by the losing states, unless accompanied by compensating measures. Such measures could involve, for instance, changes in the current system of horizontal distribution of shared revenues.

A more fundamental reform—but one that may be less acceptable to the states and municipalities—could involve replacing the existing system of sales and excise taxes with a more standard VAT with a single rate or two rates, levied at the federal level on a broad base including services, with the proceeds shared with states and municipalities on a derivation basis, and complemented by a narrow range of excises. To provide them with a degree of fiscal autonomy, the states could be assigned the personal income tax, or a part thereof (with a piggybacking mechanism), while maintaining the existing vehicle taxes. The municipalities should have full control of the bases for property taxation, and could also be allowed to levy a modest surcharge on the personal income tax, as well as business license fees.

Given the existing wide disparities in income levels, tax capacities, and expenditure needs across states and municipalities, intergovernmental transfers aimed at equalization will need to continue to play an important role in Brazil in the foreseeable future. The present system of revenue sharing is based on rigid coefficients, for both vertical and horizontal distribution, which are not based on transparent criteria linked to tax capacities, tax efforts, and expenditure needs. A reform of the intergovernmental transfer system should ideally aim at:

- Eliminating the incentives that the system currently provides to the federal government to rely on nonshared but distortive taxes.
- Introducing elements of flexibility in the coefficients of vertical distribution, to help smooth out the impact of cyclical fluctuations in revenues.[17]
- Redesigning the criteria for horizontal distribution, to gear the amount of transfers to each subnational jurisdiction to allowing it to provide an average level of the services it is responsible for, with an average degree of tax effort.[18]

A reform of this type would be a medium- to long-term project. It would necessitate as preliminary steps a clearer definition of expenditure responsibilities assigned to each level of government and a major effort to gather, on a systematic basis, the information needed for a realistic assessment of tax capacities, efforts, and expenditure needs (see Appendix of Chapter 4 for details). In the shorter run, more approximate indicators of tax capacities and spending needs could be utilized, such as those used in other countries surveyed in this book,[19] to introduce greater transparency and a more explicit equalization orientation into the system. Brazil could also consider the creation of an independent commission (such as those in Australia and India) to regularly monitor and advise on the implementation of a reformed, more transparent and flexible, system of intergovernmental transfers.

Brazil's experience until recently with state debt illustrates well the dangers of a lack of control on subnational government borrowing, in a situation where the conditions for the effective working of market dis-

---

[17]At a rate of 7.5 percent a year for some states that have chosen to limit the sale of assets to 10 percent of their outstanding debt.

[18]A system of this type is implemented, among others, in Australia (see Chapters 4 and 8).

[19]See, for example, the chapters on Canada, Germany, Japan, and Korea.

cipline are not present. The steps already taken by the authorities to restrict such borrowing and to link the restructuring of past debts with adjustment programs of the states are certainly in the right direction. Firm political will—at the federal as well as the state levels—will be needed to ensure that these programs are strictly adhered to over the short and the medium term. The successful implementation of certain needed structural reforms (in particular of the civil service and of the social security system, as well as the privatization of financial and nonfinancial public enterprises) would greatly help the targeted adjustment in the finances of all levels of government in Brazil.

References

Affonso, R., 1995, *Os Estados e a Descentralização no Brasil* (unpublished; December).

———, and P.L. Silva, eds., 1995, *A Federação em Perspectiva: Ensaios Selecionados–FUNDAP* (São Paulo).

———, eds., 1996, *Reforma Tributável e Federação–FUNDAP–UNESP* (São Paulo).

Afonso, J.R., 1994, *Descentralização Fiscal na América Latina: Estudo de Caso do Brasil*, Serie de Política Fiscal No. 61 (Santiago: United Nations Economic Commission for Latin America and the Caribbean).

———, and J.C. Ramundo, 1996, *Federalismo Fiscal no Brasil–Breves Notas–Ministério da Fazenda–Seminário sobre Gestão da Despesa Pública* (Brasília, March).

Barrera, A.W., and M.L. Roarelli, 1996, "Relações Fiscais Intergovernamentais," in *A Federação em Perspectiva: Ensaios Selecionados–FUNDAP*, ed. by R. Affonso and P.L. Silva (São Paulo).

Oliveira do Carmo, J., 1996, "Controle do Endeudamento dos Governos Estaduais e Municipais," paper presented at the first Seminar on Public Finance (Brasília, September).

Silvani, C., and P. dos Santos, 1996, "Administrative Aspects of Brazil's Consumption Tax Reform," *VAT Monitor*, Vol. 7, No. 3 (May/June).

Varsano, R., 1996, "A Proposta de Reforma Tributária em Discussão no Brasil," paper presented to the Eighth Regional Seminar on Fiscal Policy of CEPAL (Santiago, January).

World Bank, 1995, *Brazil State Debt: Crisis and Reform Report* (Washington, June).

19

Colombia

EHTISHAM AHMAD AND KATHERINE BAER

This chapter provides an overview of the major issues in the area of fiscal decentralization and local government finances in Colombia, an evaluation of the current systems, and a summary of options for reform.

Colombia's local government finance system has undergone fundamental changes in the recent past aimed at decentralizing the public sector, increasing the autonomy of local and regional governments, and improving the quality of public services provided to the local population.[1] Although there has been a gradual shift toward a decentralization of revenue and expenditure responsibilities in Colombia for many years,[2] the 1991 Constitution provided a major impulse to the process of decentralization.[3] In addition, the popular election of municipal mayors and departmental governors has introduced a dynamic political constituency in favor of decentralization.

This chapter is based on developments in Colombian intergovernmental finances through the mid-1990s, and draws on two earlier papers by E. Ahmad, G. Brosio, P. Bernd Spahn, and C. Vehorn and by E. Ahmad, J.-L. Ruiz, and I. Garrido. Comments on these papers were received from Jose Antonio Ocampo, Guillermo Perry, Armando Rodríguez, Emil Sunley, Teresa Ter-Minassian, Andrew Tweedie, and Nestor Urrea.

[1] In this paper, state-level governments are generally referred to as departments (or *departamentos*, as they are known in Colombia), and local governments are generally referred to as municipalities.

[2] The debate about whether Colombia should have a federal or a unitary structure of government has raged for over a hundred years.

[3] See for example Bird (1984) and Wiesner-Duran (1992). The legal aspects of recent reforms are discussed in Perry and Rodríguez (1991), pp. 65–83.

At the same time, reform of local public finances has acquired increased importance as the regional and local governments have begun to contribute to macroeconomic imbalances over time. The contribution of transfers to fiscal imbalances is most evident at the level of the central administration, whose overall position deteriorated significantly between 1991 and 1996. The largest source of growth in central administration expenditure during 1991–96 has been current transfers;[4] of this, transfers to the regional and local governments have accounted for a steadily growing percentage. Thus, a great deal still needs to be done to reform the structure of the existing transfer system and to provide lower levels of government with the ability to utilize own resources at the margin, and thus to engender accountability. This involves effective tax administration, as well as appropriately designed transfers, budget, and information systems, together with controls on borrowing.

Colombia has a three-tier structure of government—including the national government, departments, and municipalities—with expenditure responsibilities, as well as own sources of finance for each tier. In Colombia, each level of government is defined as having central, decentralized, and state-owned components. Many of the smaller municipalities do not so far have the capacity to manage own taxes, or to finance current expenditures out of disposable revenues. Many of the larger municipalities have modern systems of tax administration and appear to be in a better position to take on expenditure functions and raise own revenues than most departments. The departments have a limited capacity to take on the expenditure responsibilities in the areas of health and education that are assigned to them, and the national government has created special funds for these purposes, so that the transfers for these expenditures do not even enter departmental budgets. Thus, both departmental and municipal accountability are fairly limited.

Expenditure and Revenue Assignments

Expenditure Assignment

The 1991 Constitution devolved substantial expenditure responsibilities to municipalities and departments, in a manner that is consistent with the benefit principle of expenditure assignment.[5] The objec-

---

[4]Includes transfers to the regional and local governments and to the public social security system.

[5]For a description of the benefit principle and the current expenditure assignments (in theory) in Colombia, see Ferreira and Valenzuela (1993).

tive is to achieve outcomes that are responsive to local needs, and thus better targeting as well as efficiency in provision. However, the decentralization process in Colombia is still in its infancy. The departments and most municipalities lack the institutional capacity to effectively perform assigned expenditure functions.[6] Decentralization is further constrained by a continuation of the strong tradition of centrally determined norms for expenditures, such as education and health.

Perhaps the greatest constraint facing the effective assumption of expenditure responsibilities at the territorial level is that neither departments nor municipalities have sources of own revenues fully under their control—many of the ceded taxes and transfers are earmarked. Moreover, there is uncertainty concerning the total cost implications of the decentralized responsibilities. This is partly because expenditure policies continue to be determined by the national government, and there is a danger of ending up with unfunded mandates.

The widespread use of earmarking is a result of accountability problems—the national government is not sure that public monies will be used for "appropriate" purposes. In theory, a vertical hierarchy, with a number of special funds and earmarking, should ensure that resources are properly spent according to centrally made decisions. However, decentralized implementation in the absence of proper information flows and budgetary procedures, in a country like Colombia, can severely hamper the task of monitoring outcomes or of assessing policy priorities correctly. As in many countries, arbitrariness and corruption are also possible.

Moreover, centrally determined funding of public functions through earmarked taxes results in budgetary inflexibility and runs the risk of inefficiency and waste. Resources channeled through funded programs may diverge from local needs in the longer run, and it is politically difficult to abolish strings once they have been attached. Moreover, earmarking allows specific interest groups to secure a share of public resources for long periods. And finally, the centrally determined funding of public activities reduces the scope for autonomous public policy at the local level, as it often implies the predominance of national goals. This runs counter to the objectives and spirit of decentralization.

Tax Assignment

The tax assignments of the national government accord largely with basic principles of intergovernmental finance and appropriate tax ad-

---

[6]See Cárdenas (1994).

ministration.[7] The structure of intergovernmental fiscal relations in the early 1990s is described in detail in Wiesner-Duran (1992). The Constitution of 1991 replaced the municipal share of the value-added tax (VAT) by a share in current revenues (the *Participación*, described below).

Current System

National Taxes

All major taxes are assigned to the national government, including the VAT, international trade, and personal and corporate income taxes. This assignment corresponds to international practice and also facilitates administrative efficiency—given the functional structure of DIAN (the tax administration and customs department). Altogether, the national government raised about 11 percent of GDP in 1996 (or Col$10,210 billion) in tax revenue from these sources.

The structure of national taxation is shown in Table 1. Income taxes and the VAT contribute roughly equal shares to total national tax revenue (slightly above 40 percent each). Taxes on foreign trade add another 10 percent, and among the remaining taxes, only the tax on gasoline plays an important role, with about 6 percent of total tax collection.

Departmental Taxes[8]

The national government has ceded all excise taxes on the consumption of liquor, beer, and tobacco to the departments (Table 2). The departments also administer these taxes, with the exception of the beer tax, which continues to be administered by the national government. In addition, the departments administer and collect a tax on motor vehicles *(impuesto de timbre)*, which is similar to a tax at the municipal level with the same base *(impuesto de circulación y tránsito)*. Furthermore, the departments are assigned a registration tax *(impuesto de registro y anotación)* on official documents such as inheritances and property transactions (where the tax is based on the intrinsic value of the document), as well as lump-sum transactions such as the certification of diplomas. The registration tax is thus a blend of a stamp tax and a traditional transactions tax and is similar to an inheritance and gift tax, or a property transaction tax.

---

[7]See Tanzi (1995).
[8]The departmental tax system and options for its reform are discussed in Appendix I.

Table 1. Colombia: Selected Tax Revenues at National, Departmental, and Municipal Levels

	1993	1994	1995	1993	1994	1995
	(In billions of pesos)			(In percent of GDP)		
National taxes						
Income taxes	2,317	2,870	3,390	5.1	5.2	4.7
Value-added tax	2,241	2,749	3,433	4.9	5.0	4.7
Trade taxes	552	706	882	1.2	1.3	1.2
Other taxes	341	419	484	0.8	0.8	0.7
Total	5,451	6,744	8,189	11.9	12.3	11.3
Departmental taxes						
Liquor	234	304	269	0.51	0.53	0.38
Beer	190	165	215	0.42	0.29	0.31
Cigarettes	103	59	75	0.23	0.10	0.12
Motor vehicles	159	55	70	0.35	0.10	0.11
Others	95	57	85	0.21	0.10	0.12
Total	781	641	715	1.71	1.14	1.02
Municipal taxes						
Industry and commerce	199	376	1,047	0.44	0.66	1.49
Property	204	279	356	0.45	0.50	0.51
Motor vehicles	37	51	14	0.08	0.09	0.02
Others	76	160	260	0.16	0.28	0.37
Total	516	866	1,677	1.13	1.54	2.38
Total (all levels)	6,748	8,251	9,951	14.81	14.62	14.15
GDP	45,567	56,402	70,281			

Source: Ministry of Finance.
Note: These data do not include payroll taxes.

There are a number of smaller taxes on gambling with a great variety of tax bases, lottery premiums, lottery ticket sales, horse racing, and betting games, each with a complicated set of rules. Similar taxes on gambling exist also at the municipal level. The departments also operate a slaughter tax, again in parallel with municipalities. The revenue picture of the departments is further complicated by the fact that they operate regional monopolies in major sectors. This is true for lotteries, and for the consumption of specific goods, like liquor.

Altogether, the departments raised 1 percent of GDP in taxes in 1995. The structure of departmental taxation is shown in Table 2. Excises provide the major source of revenue to the departments and accounted for more than three-fourths of total tax revenue in 1995.

The liquor tax is particularly important, with nearly 40 percent of total departmental revenue. The other major departmental tax, on the registration of motor vehicles, raised about 10 percent of total depart-

Table 2. Colombia: Individual Taxes as a Share of Departmental Tax Revenues

	Antioquia			Caldas			Córdoba		
	1990	1993	1996	1990	1993	1996	1990	1993	1996
Tax revenue[1]	0.89	0.87	0.56	0.44	0.36	0.58	0.96	0.95	0.95
Tobacco	0.16	0.15	0.04	0.24	0.23	0.32	0.28	0.31	0.04
Beer	0.09	0.09	0.10	0.12	0.12	0.30	0.26	0.25	0.40
Vehicle tax	0.06	0.07	0.06	0.06	0.34	0.11	—	—	0.04
Liquor	0.52	0.58	0.69	0.01	–0.011	0.04	0.27	0.23	0.44
Registration	0.03	0.03	0.09	—	—	0.20	—	—	0.01

Source: Ministry of Finance.
[1]As a proportion of departmental current revenues.

mental tax revenue in 1995. The registration tax, which could be a substantial revenue raiser in view of increasing values for property transactions, contributed only about 2½ percent to total departmental tax revenue in 1995, significantly less than the revenues generated by one of the taxed consumption goods. All other departmental taxes provided about 10 percent of total revenue.

Municipal Taxes[9]

Municipal taxation in Colombia rests on two main pillars: a property tax *(impuesto predial unificado)* and a business tax *(impuesto de industria y comercio)*. Each of these taxes contributed from 20 percent to 60 percent of total municipal tax revenue in 1995 (see Table 3). The municipal motor vehicle tax raised about 2 percent of total municipal tax revenue.

Apart from these major taxes, municipal governments in Colombia operate a host of smaller taxes, some of which were introduced on an ad hoc basis. Among these are the slaughter tax, a tax on public performances, a tax on club sales, a tax on the extraction of sand, gravel and stones, gambling taxes, and stamp taxes. Some taxes generate very little tax revenue, complicate the administration, and render the municipal tax system unwieldy.

Among the taxes with a fair revenue-raising potential is the *contribución de valorización*. This is a betterment levy (rather than a tax), by which the costs of specific public works projects are shared among direct beneficiaries. This levy is based on the benefit principle and could eventually raise more significant amounts of municipal revenue than in the past, if more widely applied. Another potentially important revenue source could be a surcharge on the price of gasoline. Medellín

---

[9]The municipal tax system and options for its reform are discussed in Appendix II.

Table 3. Colombia: Municipal Taxes
(As a share of municipal current revenue)

	1990	1993	1995
Antioquia			
Tax revenue	0.52	0.51	0.59
Property tax	0.21	0.20	0.24
Business tax	0.23	0.21	0.26
Vehicle tax	0.004	0.003	0.01
Santafé de Bogotá			
Tax revenue	0.87	0.85	0.85
Property tax	0.15	0.14	0.21
Business tax	0.34	0.34	0.36
Vehicle tax	0.12	0.15	0.00
Caldas			
Tax revenue	0.34	0.61[1]	0.51
Property tax	0.19	0.37	0.22
Business tax	0.11	0.21	0.13
Vehicle tax	0.02	0.04	0.02
Córdoba			
Tax revenue	0.21	0.21	0.52
Property tax	0.11	0.13	0.33
Business tax	0.06	0.06	0.10
Vehicle tax	0.006	0.006	0.01

Source: Ministry of Finance.
[1] The large increase is due to a negative number for other taxes, probably a redistribution to other departments.

uses this instrument to finance its metro project, and other municipalities have followed suit recently.

All local taxes raised only about 2 percent of GDP in 1995. Given their much higher expenditure responsibilities (about 6.1 percent of GDP in 1995), municipalities have to rely to a large extent on national support through grants and cofinancing arrangements. Given assured and increasing intergovernmental transfers, as stipulated under the Constitution, municipalities have resorted to borrowing, as discussed below.

Vertical Imbalances

Taxes, such as the VAT, and the corporate and personal income tax, are assigned and administered at the national level as in many countries. This leads to the problem of vertical imbalances, as illustrated in Table 4. For example, in 1994 municipal government tax revenues were only 32 percent of municipal expenditures, while national government tax revenue was 87 percent of national expenditures.

Despite the vertical imbalance in its favor, the national government has been increasingly constrained by the constitutional stipulation on

Table 4. Colombia: Vertical Fiscal Imbalance Between Levels of Government, 1994

	In Billions of Pesos	In Percent of Own Level Expenditures	In Percent of Total Expenditures
National level			
Expenditures	9,463	100.0	66.0
Own revenue	9,549	100.9	80.1
Taxes	8,189	86.5	57.1
Nontax revenue	931	9.8	6.5
Departmental level			
Expenditures	1,574	100.0	10.9
Own revenue	1,001	63.7	8.4
Taxes	715	45.4	5.0
Nontax revenue	287	18.3	2.0
Municipal level			
Expenditures	3,296	100.0	22.9
Own revenue	1,367	41.5	11.4
Taxes	1,047	31.8	7.3
Nontax revenue	369	9.7	2.6
Total			
Expenditures	14,333		100.0
Own revenue	11,918		83.2
Taxes	9,951		69.4
Nontax revenue	1,587		11.1

Source: Ministry of Finance, National Planning Department.
Note: Expenditures include operational surplus or deficits of public enterprises at each level. Expenditures do not include transfers to other levels of government. Net outlays of public enterprises are consolidated with the expenditures at each level of government.

increasing transfers to the territorial governments. However, since decentralization is not yet fully functional, the national government continues to bear expenditure responsibilities that have not been effectively devolved to territorial governments (for example, teachers' salaries). On the other hand, Table 4 may understate the extent of the potential vertical imbalance, given the degree of earmarking that exists in Colombia—that is, mandated expenditures that have to be met out of the own resources of departments. Part of the difficulty is that the national government retains control over overall wages and salaries, which together with other contingent liabilities and the limited own resources (own revenues plus untied transfers) of the local governments, make it difficult for the local authorities to assume the expenditure responsibilities fully.

Problems Associated with Current Revenue Assignments

The tax assignments of the territorial governments are designed to strengthen their autonomy based on own resources. However, own revenue collections of departments and municipalities combined represented a little over 3 percent of GDP in 1995. The social and economic conditions among the different regions of Colombia vary widely, as reflected in GDP per capita among departments. The standard deviation of per capita income among departments is 42 percent of the mean value, which is high compared with industrial countries. The dispersion of per capita income affects regional taxable capacity, as well as the differentials in basic needs for public services of departments and municipalities.

Recent legislation assigns royalties on natural resources (such as petroleum) mainly to producing municipalities and departments. Despite the redistributing role of the Fondo Nacional de Regalías, horizontal fiscal imbalances are likely to have been exacerbated by this legislation, with associated efficiency costs in the longer run.

Horizontal Tax Competition

Colombia faces a number of problems relating to horizontal tax competition, at both the departmental and the municipal level. The departmental system of specific consumer taxes generates domestic contraband of taxable goods (such as liquor and tobacco). The local surcharge on gasoline consumption also encourages tax competition. A redesign of these taxes would be necessary to reduce illegal trafficking and easy avoidance, and to facilitate administration and increase revenue capacities.

Intergovernmental Transfer System

To correct the vertical imbalance, a system of national government transfers to departments and municipalities has been used since the late 1960s.[10]

Tax Sharing

In the past, Colombia shared the VAT with municipalities, but now practices tax sharing on a more comprehensive base. The sharing of a comprehensive revenue pool avoids several disadvantages that result from sharing separate revenue bases (as described above). However, the shared revenue base is not as comprehensive as might appear at first

---

[10]For a detailed account of the evolution of the transfer system to territorial governments in Colombia, see Sanchez and Gutiérrez (1994) and Acosta and Yaker (1994).

sight. For instance, for the first year in which they are in force, the national government does not include in the pool surtaxes on the income tax, the resources resulting from broadening the base of shared taxes, and increases in the consumption tax.[11] To introduce greater flexibility to resource allocation and use, tax sharing should be untied. The a priori earmarking of tax revenue causes complications for a revenue-sharing scheme.

There are four main mechanisms for revenue sharing between the national, regional (*departamentos*), and local governments (*municipios*): (1) the *situado fiscal*, which provides automatic transfers to the regional governments earmarked for current expenditure in health and education; (2) the *participación municipal*, which earmarks transfers to the local governments for current and investment expenditure on basic services including education, health, and water supply; (3) the system of cofinancing funds; and (4) the National Royalties' Fund. Under the first two mechanisms, all central government tax and nontax revenue is subject to revenue sharing. As required by the 1991 Constitution, which mandated steady increases in transfers to the end of the decade, revenue shared with the regions under these two systems has increased steadily in the last four years as a share of central government current revenue (Table 5). In 1991, approximately 12 percent of the central government's current revenue was transferred to the local governments;[12] this rose to 18 percent in 1997, and is scheduled to reach 22 percent by 2001. In 1996, central government revenues transferred to both the regional and local governments accounted for 41.5 percent of total central government current revenue.

Since 1993, the size of the *situado fiscal* has been set as a minimum share of the central government's total current revenues, and has varied from 23 percent in 1994 to 24.5 percent in 1996. The 1991 Constitution stipulates that neither the *situado* nor the *participaciones (regional and local transfers)* can diminish as a share of central government current revenue in relation to the previous year's share. Moreover, in the event of a shortfall in the national government's current revenue, transfers cannot be automatically reduced in the same proportion. This inflexibility in budget rules significantly constrains the fiscal management of national revenues.

---

[11]Also, the earmarked parts of VAT (on cement), the *Cajas de Previsión* (Social Security Funds), and the old *intendencias* and *comisarías* (other subnational revenues) do not enter the pool.

[12]According to the transition rules established in the 1991 Constitution, local governments could not receive less revenue under the new revenue-sharing system than that which they had received under the previous revenue-sharing system.

Table 5. Colombia: Transfers of Central Administration Current Revenue
(In percent of total current revenue)

	1993	1994	1995	1996	1997	1998	1999	2000
To municipal governments (participaciones)	14.0	15.0	16.0	17.0	18.0	19.0	20.0	21.0
To regional governments (situado)	22.5	23.0	23.5	24.5	24.5	24.5	24.5	24.5
Total	36.5	38.0	39.5	41.5	42.5	43.5	44.5	45.5

Source: Ministry of Finance.

Transfers to Departments: Situado Fiscal

The 1968 Constitution introduced the *situado fiscal*, a system of transfers that has continued to be the central pillar of departmental finances. The basic features of the *situado* remain as the fundamental precepts of the current transfer system. The distribution formula was as follows: 30 percent of the total revenue was distributed in equal shares among departments, territories, and the national capital of Bogotá and the remaining 70 percent was distributed according to the population.

The transfer was earmarked for health and education. At the same time, a complete reorganization of the provision of these services was made through the creation of the Regional Education and Health Funds (Fondos Educativos Regionales and Fondos Seccionales de Salud), mainly dependent on the national government. These agencies received direct payments from the *situado fiscal*, without a line item in the budgets of the departments. In other words, the role of departments in their two most important areas of responsibility was reduced to supplementing funds, if any, from their own sources to these agencies.

Law 60 of 1993 provides additional legislation on transfers, pursuant to the 1991 Constitution: the total amount of the *situado* will be determined as a minimum share of the nation's total current revenues, ranging from 23 percent in 1994 to 24.5 percent in 1996. A new law is thus needed for 1997. Law 60 defines the distribution formula for the *situado* as follows: 15 percent of the total revenue is to be distributed in equal shares among departments, territories, and the national capital of Bogotá and the remaining 85 percent is to be distributed according to the population. This distribution clearly favors the smaller departments, and may have some net distributional impact. For example, in 1995 the smallest departments received the largest transfers in per capita terms for health and education. In the same year, the largest share of transfers earmarked for education went to finance primary and secondary education, as determined by Law 60.[13] The distribution criteria set by Law 60 have varied from year to year to ensure a smooth transition from the previous system to the new one, which was originally scheduled to be in place by 1997. However, during the first half of 1997, no legislative initiatives had been taken to determine the amount of the increase (or decrease) in the *situado* or to redefine distribution criteria.

As mentioned above, departments may use the *situado* for education and health only. According to Law 60, departments are required to devote at least 60 percent of the *situado* to education and 20 percent to health. Departments may at their discretion allocate the remaining 20 percent according to their priorities, but only within these two sectors. In effect, the local discretion is limited, and the *situado* is essentially a special purpose transfer. From the departments' perspective, there is a reluctance to assume directly their expenditure responsibilities since they have no clear perception of their future spending obligations.[14] The problem is particularly acute in education.

Transfers to Municipalities: *Participación Municipal*

The second major transfer scheme is the *participación municipal*, a special purpose transfer to the local governments established by the 1991 Constitution to finance recurrent and investment expenditure for basic services. Between 1968 and 1991, these transfers were general purpose transfers to the municipalities. An important restriction in the Constitution is that the transfers are to be determined on the basis of total current (tax and nontax) revenues of the national government,[15] and that the share of these revenues going to local governments is to increase from 14 percent in 1993 to 22 percent in 2002. The Constitution also stipulates that the transfers be distributed 60 percent according to the number of poor people and people with unsatisfied basic needs; the remaining 40 percent according to population, "fiscal and administrative efficiency," and progress made by municipalities in improving the quality of life in their territory. Again, Law 60 of 1993 specifies the formula and determines the share of current revenues to be distributed each year. It also sets the criteria for the use of funds.

---

[13]The law stipulates that at a minimum, 50 percent of *situado* transfers for health are to be used to finance primary health care. In 1995 Col$238 billion, equivalent to 50.5 percent of the *situado*, went to finance primary health services.

[14]According to Law 60, the transfer of responsibilities should be completed by 1997.

[15]Revenues deriving from new taxes are not included, for the first year, in the amount to be distributed to the municipalities, as well as those coming from increases in the existing tax rates and from changes dictated by "economic emergencies."

During a transition period for the distribution of *participación* transfers, every municipality received annually a basic transfer, equal, in constant prices, to the transfer received in 1992. The remaining amount of the transfer was distributed as follows: 40 percent in direct proportion with the number of persons with unsatisfied basic needs; 20 percent according to a poverty index; 22 percent according to population; 6 percent according to a fiscal efficiency index, measured by the increase over two years of per capita municipal own revenues weighed by a relative unsatisfied basic need index; and 6 percent according to an administrative efficiency index, measured by the ratio between the rate of increase over two years of current expenditures (other than on education, health, and infrastructure) and the number of inhabitants with water and sewer services. A special provision was made for small municipalities (less than 50,000 inhabitants), by allocating to them a share of 5 percent of the total transfer, net of its basic component.

Participación funds are earmarked for the following uses: 30 percent for education; 25 percent for health; 20 percent for water provision, in case the share of population serviced is less than 70 percent; and 5 percent for sports, recreation, and culture.

A transition period was introduced by Law 60, according to which municipalities were given time to adjust the structure of their expenditures to this norm.[16] Since the 1995 ruling by the constitutional court declaring this norm unconstitutional, a number of municipalities have been unable to finance their operating and debt-servicing expenditure out of own tax resources.

The Cofinancing Funds

To complement the system of specific purpose grants described in the sections above, a system of cofinancing funds was gradually introduced over the years.[17] Cofinancing resources were expanded until 1996, and in 1995 represented almost 40 percent of transfers to municipalities. As in the case of other countries, specific purpose grants allow the donor, here the national government, to pursue specific priorities in the various fields. These transfers are made mostly on

---

[16]Furthermore, a general constraint has been imposed in favor of rural areas. They have the right to a share of the expenditure not less than the share of their population in the total population of the municipality.

[17]Among the most important funds created during the 1980s are the DRI (for rural development), the PNR (destined to rural areas with high incidence of poverty and violence), INURBE (for low-income housing), Fondo de Caminos Vecinales (for rural roads), and FINDETER, a development bank primarily aimed at financing urban infrastructure projects at the local and regional level.

a matching basis. Providing technical assistance to beneficiary governments has also been an important function of the cofinancing arrangements.

Until recently, the main cofinancing funds have included: the Fondo de Cofinanciación para la Infraestructura Vial, for intermunicipal roads; the Fondo de Cofinanciación para la Infraestructura Urbana, mainly for municipal transport; the Fondo de Inversión Social, for social investment projects (such as education); and the Fondo del Desarrollo Rural Integrado, for infrastructure projects in rural areas. The principles for distribution of the cofinancing resources are similar to those of other transfers, including the number of persons with unsatisfied basic needs in each department and the share of other transfers going to the municipalities in each department. A needs indicator is combined with a fiscal capacity indicator. There are different matching shares, for which recipients may use either their current revenues or borrowed resources, ranging from 10 percent for poor municipalities to 40 percent for rich municipalities and to 50 percent for big cities.

While beneficial to the local governments, the cofinancing system has had important flaws. These are related to the lack of coordination, and the ad hoc objectives assigned to the funds. Annual programs are independently formulated by each agency, with indeterminate criteria for project selection and cost sharing. There are no consistent directives for guiding the agencies in their operation. Moreover, the grants are distributed among various regions more in order to correct perceived weaknesses of the transfer system than to implement national priorities in given fields of activity. In some municipalities and departments, monies allocated for cofinancing in some fields, such as preschool education, are not used. This is partly an information problem, particularly in the smaller municipalities. In other areas, projects are formulated solely to obtain access to financing.

In contrast to the *situado* and the *participaciones*, the 1991 Constitution does not stipulate that the cofinancing funds must increase at a certain rate in relation to central government current revenue. Therefore, the national government has much greater flexibility in determining the level and allocation of these funds to the regional and local governments. As a reflection of this flexibility and as a result of recent measures to reduce 1997 budgetary outlays, the cofinancing system has recently undergone significant changes. In early 1997, a series of measures were announced affecting the cofinancing system. These measures included: (1) a change in the basis of allocation of funds from grant funds to loanable funds on concessionary terms; (2) a significant reduction in the budget allocation for cofinancing; and (3) a reduction in the number of cofinancing funds to one.

The National Royalties' Fund

The National Royalties' Fund also represents an important source of revenue for the local governments, particularly in the wake of the large oil discoveries in the early 1990s.[18] Royalties distributed in 1995 were nearly equivalent to the cofinancing funds. This Fund, established by the 1991 Constitution and further regulated through legislation passed in 1994, was set up to distribute natural resource royalties primarily to the producing regions for purposes of investment.[19] The distribution of royalties among the various regions is on a presumptive equal per capita share, but the skewness of the actual distribution is striking. Despite the right of producing departments for a claim on royalties generated in their territory, small departments with a tiny population, like Arauca, get a large amount of royalties, giving ground to charges of misuse of resources.

Evaluation of the Present System

The overall distribution of transfers is shown in Table 6. Leaving aside royalties, transfers seem advantageous to departments with low per capita GDP (these are marked with an asterisk in Table 6). However, the overall redistributive impact is not clear. Rich departments include in their jurisdictions the biggest cities, with a high concentration of poor migrants and of unemployment. The distribution of royalties has a major impact on the distribution of the entire system of transfers to territorial governments. Small oil producing departments benefit from higher per capita sums than big departments, further clouding the overall effect of transfers and royalties.

Links Between Revenue and Expenditures

Decentralization in Colombia has clearly enhanced the revenue side of the budget of territorial governments. The overall sense of constitutional provisions in this field is that the nation considers allocating to territorial governments a large and rapidly growing share of its own revenues as an essential step for putting the decentralization process on the right path. Devolution of expenditure responsibilities has been mostly

---

[18]Natural resource taxation exclusively at the local level entails severe risks of misallocation. In practice, a balance has to be struck between the local government's interests and those of the nation to avoid large regional inequities and to make more efficient use of resources in the longer term. This usually calls for some revenue-sharing arrangement between the local and the national governments—which can take various forms, such as production sharing or royalties, and rests ultimately on political negotiation.

[19]About 90 percent of the National Royalties' Fund's resources are from oil production.

Table 6. Colombia: Transfers to Departments and Municipalities
(In billions of pesos unless otherwise indicated)

	Situado Fiscal		Transfers to Municipalities		Royalties		Total		Per Capita (In pesos)	
	1994	1996	1994	1996	1994	1996	1994	1996	1994	1996
Amazonas	5.8	9.8	1.1	1.9	131	...	7.1	11.7	201,474	208,188
Antioquia	170.5	272.5	119.7	202.8	16.1	17.4	306.3	492.7	70,648	100,157
Arauca	8.7	16.7	3.5	6.3	105.3	91.7	117.5	114.7	1,238,920	616,913
Atlántico	27.2	47.6	18.0	32.8	2.3	...	47.6	80.5	74,101	115,028
Barranquilla (Distr.)	22.9	35.7	16.7	27.8	3.6	0.06	43.3	63.7	43,835	56,017
Santafé de Bogotá (Distr.)	163.2	258.2	74.7	121.7	17.5	...	255.5	380.0	54,181	69,296
Bolívar	38.0	55.3	28.6	52.9	2.5	6.7	69.1	114.9	92,686	126,591
Boyacá	74.0	118.8	48.8	91.5	2.7	5.3	125.5	215.6	100,474	163,902
Caldas	52.4	84.9	27.8	44.3	3.3	0.3	83.6	129.6	93,120	125,834
Caquetá	19.5	33.0	10.3	17.9	1.1	...	30.9	50.9	104,889	138,523
Cartagena (Distr. of)	17.4	48.6	10.5	18.9	2.4	1.5	30.3	69.0	46,612	86,944
Casanare	10.8	18.0	6.5	14.5	27.5	101.5	44.8	133.9	267,588	633,818
Cauca	45.8	78.3	30.0	51.2	3.4	3.3	79.2	132.8	86,887	117,822
Cesar	34.4	57.7	23.0	40.4	1.1	2.0	58.6	100.2	76,576	121,090
Chocó	26.1	41.2	12.4	22.6	1.3	0.6	39.8	64.5	117,721	158,668
Córdoba	47.1	75.6	34.3	58.4	4.0	5.1	85.4	139.1	79,039	109,083
Cundinamarca	92.0	147.1	56.8	106.3	5.9	0.6	54.8	254.2	96,649	135,546
Guainía	5.3	8.7	0.5	0.9	0.04	0.04	5.8	9.7	499,969	341,424
Guaviare	5.4	9.7	1.7	3.2	0.2	...	7.4	12.9	117,661	133,138
Huila	37.0	59.2	23.7	42.7	27.0	28.8	87.7	130.7	116,962	154,980
La Guajira	18.9	33.9	10.9	17.8	10.0	21.1	39.9	72.8	119,925	168,199
Magdalena	31.5	45.4	22.9	40.5	2.5	0.0	57.0	85.8	84,101	108,283
Meta	23.4	39.1	15.3	28.8	26.8	26.2	65.6	94.1	122,643	1,932,949
Nariño	59.9	100.0	38.1	68.1	3.9	5.0	101.9	173.1	87,957	119,907
Norte de Santander	53.2	88.3	28.9	50.2	3.6	3.4	85.7	141.9	87,855	122,114

Putumayo	12.2	20.7	7.1	12.6	8.9	6.9	28.2	40.2	127,068	152,338
Quindío	27.5	46.5	11.1	18.0	1.5	0.0	40.1	64.5	98,812	130,336
Risaralda	36.5	59.7	17.2	28.0	2.6	0.03	56.3	87.7	79,400	103,952
San Andrés	5.8	10.0	1.0	2.2	0.1	0.06	6.9	12.3	174,426	202,699
Santa Marta	9.9	24.8	4.8	8.1	1.0	0.14	15.7	33.0	58,056	98,835
Santander	83.9	135.9	47.9	86.4	22.6	20.7	154.4	243.1	96,122	134,208
Sucre	26.9	47.8	19.2	35.0	0.9	27.0	47.2	109.9	79,520	156,855
Tolima	59.6	97.0	38.4	65.4	5.6	5.6	103.6	168.0	88,279	130,637
Valle del Cauca	115.5	189.0	72.3	118.9	12.7	0.42	200.6	308.3	62,064	482,543
Vaupés	5.2	9.2	0.8	1.8	0.07	0.08	6.2	10.9	310,324	445,313
Vichada	5.3	9.0	0.6	1.5	0.04	...	6.0	10.5	560,688	169,794
Total	1,480	2,434	886	1,543	331	381	2,698	4,359	83,463	117,506

left to ordinary legislation. This weak correspondence between revenue and expenditures appears to be a major problem for the overall equilibrium of the public sector, especially if account is taken of the fact that territorial governments are encouraged to use their transfers as a leverage to increase their reliance on debt financing.

The share of the nation's current revenues allocated to territorial governments is presently close to 50 percent and will grow if the trend is to proceed along the guidelines provided by the Constitution. However, these percentages are typical of fully fledged federal systems, where responsibilities of subnational governments are much wider. The earmarking of these transfers appears to hinder effective decentralization. Thus, the central government continues to bear much of the expenditure responsibilities, although resources have been transferred to territorial levels of government.

Constraints on the Use of Transfers

While territorial governments now have more resources to spend than under the previous system, discretion in the use of funds has been even more curtailed by fixing distinct percentages to be spent for every function. The Colombian approach to decentralization seems to still favor the model of functional administration, typical of highly centralized systems, in which the center sets the priorities and decentralized institutions are mainly asked to implement them.

There are clear reasons for this approach, but the problems are also evident. On the one hand, newly elected mayors, governors, and local councils frequently lack administrative experience, political and bureaucratic misuse of resources is still widespread, and control by voters is still in its infancy, particularly in the rural areas. On the other hand, excessive constraints may be counterproductive. They tend to reduce responsibility at the local level, when, as is usually the case, local priorities diverge to a certain extent from national priorities. In fact, one of the main advantages of decentralization is the geographical differentiation of policies, according to locally perceived priorities and voters' preferences in the sphere of autonomy delegated to territorial governments.

When rigid constraints impede satisfaction of first-level priorities, local authorities will turn to second- or third-level priorities. School buildings will be constructed when there is no additional need, whereas the extension of aqueducts is badly needed, since tap water covers only a tiny percentage of the population. Rigid, detailed rules are not followed, weakening cooperation and coordination between national and local authorities. The former are then tempted to issue new, even more rigid, constraints.

In all countries, there are national priorities within the spheres left to local authorities. These priorities may be better pursued by using specific purpose grants, with simple criteria, rather than complicated criteria (more suited for general grants), which are difficult to monitor.

The Emergence of New Territorial Rents

Although the 1991 Constitution set up a framework for a more equitable distribution of royalties, legislation seems to have ceded excessive ground to pressures coming from producing areas. No basic change has been introduced over the previous allocation system, since producing departments and municipalities still retain their shares of the royalties within realistic levels of production, and new rents have been created for ports and other areas marginally affected by the production of natural resources. Whereas there is certainly an argument for compensating local jurisdictions, where production and transportation of natural, polluting resources takes place, the distribution rules for royalties go beyond this necessity, depriving the nation of an important source of revenues for the implementation of its priorities. Moreover, royalties exert a distorting effect on the overall design of transfers, creating areas of privilege and inefficiency.

Problems Related to the Formulas

A number of countries, particularly in Latin America, rely on special purpose transfer mechanisms similar to those examined in the Colombian context. Some of the shortcomings of such transfers are discussed below.

Incentives for Fragmentation

The 15 percent "equal share" provision of the *situado fiscal* provides an incentive to create new jurisdictions. A similar effect is induced by the special provision for small municipalities, jointly with the rapid increase of the total amounts transferred to them. International experience shows that the positive effects of decentralization do not derive from the number of local jurisdictions, but from their ability to provide public services to their citizens, which implies a minimum size for efficient operation of local governments.

Inadequate Information

A problem frequently found by countries using formulas, as in Colombia, for funding territorial (especially municipal) governments is the lack of up-to-date information. Colombia seems to present many problems in this respect. Population and other data used for the formulas are available only at census years. The high mobility of the Colombian population makes census data projections problematic. The last census took place in 1993, and total population figures were published in 1997. From 1985 to 1997, the formulas utilized (controversial) projections for population, based on data from the previous two censuses for the most important indicator, that is, the number of poor and of persons with unsatisfied basic needs. Thus, the 1985 census has been used to estimate this number,[20] and the rates of change between the 1973 and 1985 censuses were used to project changes to the current period. This favors static areas, or areas with a declining population, and penalizes those areas, including the big cities, experiencing massive inflows of new migrants.

The Use of the Same Indicators for Different Transfers

The same indicators, or slightly different versions thereof, are used for the distribution of transfers.[21] This contradicts one of the basic rules for economic policy, according to which the number of instruments should be correlated to the number of objectives. In other words, if every category of transfers uses the same criteria for allocating funds, there is no need to use different transfers—one grossed up would be enough. If the nation really desires to pursue distinct specific objectives with its transfer system, it should have recourse to distinct indicators for each category of transfers, properly targeted to its aims and priorities.

Local Tax Administration

The problems discussed above with the structure of the existing revenue-sharing system must be viewed in the context of the local governments' capacity to raise and manage their own revenue. The structure of the departmental and municipal tax systems is discussed in greater detail in Appendices I and II, respectively. This section focuses on the status of tax administration at the local level.

In Colombia the capacity of departmental and municipal tax administrations varies widely. A few tax administrations, usually in large

---

[20]Population data for 1993 will be used in the formulas beginning in 1998.

[21]Appendix III contains a detailed description of the main indices used to distribute tax revenue among departments and municipalities.

Table 7. Colombia: Tax Administration Functions for Selected Departments

	Antioquia	Caldas	Córdoba
Number of tax staff	196	102	92
Organizational structure			
By collection and enforcement functions	X	X	X
Annual plan	—	—	—
Taxpayer services (information, assistance, and education)			
Walk-in	X	X	X
Newspaper	X	X	X
Radio	X	X	X
Collection			
Computerized	X	X	X
Manual	X	—	—
Payment at banks	—	X	X
Payment at tax office	X	X	—
Cross-checking			
Manual	X	X	—
Computerized	—	—	—
Enforcement	X	X	X
Penalties			
Specific tax sanctions	X	X	O
Confiscation	X	X	X
Payment incentives[1]	O	X	O

Source: Discussions with tax officials.
Note: X = exists; — = does not exist; and O = unknown.
[1] Tax officials receive a share of the cash value of goods confiscated.

municipalities, are in the process of establishing modern procedures. However, many tax administrations at the departmental level, and in the smaller municipalities, lack the capacity to perform basic tax administration functions in an effective manner. Almost half (44 percent) of the 1,048 municipalities in 1993 had a population size of less than 10,000. For these municipalities, there are certain diseconomies of scale associated with developing a modern tax administration. Summaries of tax administration procedures in 1994, for selected departments and municipalities, are presented in Tables 7 and 8, respectively.

Taxpayer Services

The large municipalities address the tax administration function of providing such taxpayer services as information, assistance, and education in varying degrees. Officials in these municipalities are well aware of the importance of taxpayer services. In small municipalities, however, the capacity does not exist to provide a full range of basic services.

Table 8. Colombia: Tax Administration Functions for Selected Municipalities

	Bogotá	Medellín	Manizales	Lorica	Sasaima
Number of tax staff	240	300	37	38	4
Number of taxpayers					
Property tax	1,400,000	300,000	51,000	30,000	10,400
Industry and commerce tax	56,000	50,000	10,000	1,110	120
Organizational structure					
By function	X	—	—	—	—
By type of tax	—	X	X	X	—[1]
Annual plan	X	X	X	—	—
Taxpayer services (information, assistance, and education)					
Walk-in	X	X	X	X	X
Correspondence	X	X	X	—	—
Telephone	X	X	—	—	—
Newspaper	X	X	X	X	O
Radio	X	X	X	X	X
Collection					
Computerized	X	X	X	X[2]	X
Manual	—	—	—	—	X
Payment at banks	X	X[3]	X	X	—
Detection of stop filers	X	X	X	—	—
Cross-checking[4]	X	X	X	—	—
Audit					
Number of auditors[5]	17	20	5	0	0
Skill level	medium	medium	low	n.a.	n.a.
Penalties	X	X	X	X	—
Appeals	X	X	X	X	—
Self assessment					
Property tax	X	—	—	—	—
Industry and commerce tax	X	X	X	X	X

Source: Discussions with tax officials.
Note: X = exists; — = does not exist; O = unknown; and n.a. = not applicable.
[1] In Sasaima, the tax office is part of the Treasury Department.
[2] Accounts of taxpayers for both the property tax and the industry and commerce tax have been computerized by contracting out to firms that specialize in this technology.
[3] Payment is also allowed at the tax office, by cash or credit card.
[4] The municipal taxpayer identification number for business is the same as the national taxpayer identification number, which facilitates cross-checking with DIAN.
[5] In Bogotá another 40 auditors, and in Medellín another 30, were available on a contractual basis.

In departments too, only a few of the basic services are provided. Taxpayers are forced to wait in line to obtain necessary information. In some cases, especially with respect to the excise taxes, taxpayers must follow several time-consuming steps before payment is completed. Many of the officials do not appear to be concerned about taxpayer inconvenience.

An important component in the strengthening of tax administration is awareness of the taxpayers' perspective. Important steps include the development of a more comprehensive taxpayer services function and the streamlining of procedures to reduce the compliance burden on taxpayers. In addition, various tax forms should be simplified as much as possible.

Collection

The collection process, in general, is relatively strong in the local tax administration in Colombia. Although some medium-sized municipalities have not computerized collections, most small municipalities have received computers and special software (SIAM) from the national government. Many tax administrations have developed units that monitor the payments of large taxpayers, since a sizable percentage of the revenue comes from a small number of large taxpayers. For those tax administrations that cannot quickly detect stopfilers, a first step would be to identify the large taxpayers (say the top 10 percent) and begin to monitor (even on a manual basis) their payments.

Audit

Small municipalities and departments lack an audit function. Departments focus on deterring smuggling as their primary enforcement tool. They do not focus on the taxpayer. Small municipalities have little capacity to question the information provided by the taxpayer on the industry and commerce tax return. As the decentralization process unfolds, it will be in the best interest of each level to establish an audit function. A first step may be to follow the action taken in large municipalities, which is to hire contractual auditors for specified periods of time.[22] Regular staff could observe these contractual auditors performing desk audits, and accompany them on field audits to learn how to conduct an audit. Additional training is another step. Observance of audits should be accompanied with classroom training in accounting and audit techniques.

Audits alone will not create a climate of voluntary payment of taxes. Taxpayers must know that there is a risk of detection if they fail to register, fail to file a return, or fail to pay the correct amount on time.

---

[22]In principle, prolonged use of private auditors may lead to situations of conflict of interest. Thus, this initial use of private auditors has to include the training of tax staff so that, eventually, they will be able to conduct audits on their own.

Cross-checking of information with other sources through use of the computer is an important enforcement tool. Some municipalities have cross-checked information with the national tax administration (DIAN). But this effort has largely been on a case-by-case basis, rather than a systematic initiative that would encompass all taxpayers. The municipalities visited are interested in systematic cross-checking and plan to explore with DIAN ways to achieve this objective.

Penalties and Appeals

A speedy and well-designed appeals process protects taxpayers' rights, while complementing the penalty structure. Small municipalities do not seem to be able to apply penalties. They try to provide an incentive by discounting the tax bill if paid by a certain date. They lack a simple system of penalties and appeals, along with the experience to design and implement such a system. Without such a system and the resolve to apply it, the tax administration in small municipalities will be unable to raise adequate own source revenue.

Appeals can be resolved within two years at the national level, but appeals at the departmental and municipal levels go to the civil courts, and may take up to ten years to resolve.

Other Issues

Development of an Annual Plan

The larger municipalities have a planning process, and Bogotá has a very sophisticated one. However, the smaller municipalities lack a clear sense of priorities and goals. It is important for staff in these tax administrations to develop a better perspective of the overall goals of tax administration, and how their specific tasks help to attain the goals. Development of an annual plan can be an initial step in a process to modernize tax administration at the municipal level.

Dissemination of Information

Given that tax administrations at each level deal with a common set of concerns regarding taxes at that level, it would be important to develop a network to share innovative ideas. For example, large municipalities could meet with medium-sized municipalities to explain how they have implemented modern procedures. The medium-sized municipalities could then, in turn, meet with the small municipalities to discuss administration advances they have made. In order to realize an organized dissemination of information, which would include techniques to develop an annual plan, a coordinating body is needed which could profit from technical support from the national tax administration.

Adjustment for Inflation

One final tax administration issue to consider is the problem of collection lags. Currently, municipalities, except for Bogotá, collect the industry and commerce tax based on annual sales of the previous year. With inflation, the real value of the taxes collected is reduced. One way to address the problem of collection lags would be to increase the sales of the previous year by expected inflation for this year. Another way would be to apply periodically an inflation adjustment mechanism to tax liabilities.

Territorial Debt and Expenditure Management

As observed above, earmarked own revenues, with nationally determined use of transfers, limit the effective decentralization of expenditures envisaged in the 1991 Constitution, and encourage the use of credit. Banks have an incentive to lend on the strength of constitutionally increasing transfers from the nation. While there is concern that growing territorial borrowing could pose a threat to the country's macroeconomic stability, the data available from various sources are partial and inconsistent.

Weaknesses in expenditure reporting and control mechanisms at the territorial levels severely hamper prospects for "accountability" in subnational spending. Progress in this area is of high priority if the full benefits of decentralization are to be realized.

Territorial Debt

Territorial borrowing by the administrations at each level increased rapidly in nominal terms from 1993 to 1996 at an average annual rate of 67 percent for the departments and at a rate of around 55 percent for municipalities. When public sector enterprises are included, the overall growth rate of territorial debt was lower at 16 percent for 1994. During the same period, the stock of debt nearly doubled, from around 1 percent to nearly 2 percent of GDP in 1996.

It is curious that departments, in particular, appear to have maintained positive net asset balances with the banking system at a time when borrowing has increased sharply. This paradoxical situation is due to the high degree of earmarking of transfers from the national government and of own revenues, together with the legal requirements to maintain separate accounts for each source. Given weaknesses in monitoring, commercial credit acts as a more "fungible" resource for the territorial governments.

Budgets for three municipalities and two departments for 1995 show that in each case there have been increasing deficits, with inelastic revenue sources and additional expenditure responsibilities associated with the increasing decentralization envisaged under the 1991 Constitution, as well as contingent liabilities under the recent pension reform plan.

The government's macroeconomic plan for 1994–98 is predicated on a central government deficit counterbalanced by surpluses at the territorial and public enterprise levels. However, as a whole the territorial governments have been in a deficit position from 1994 to 1996, and the prospects for improvement in the near future are not encouraging, given present trends.

Policy Initiatives

The Ministry of Finance has taken several measures that should effectively curtail the rate of increase in territorial borrowing. First, a decree was issued in mid-1995 increasing the amount of revenues that might be used as collateral, from 130 percent to 150 percent of the guaranteed loans. Moreover, credit institutions have to increase the ratio of net worth to loans to territorial entities. While increasing the cost of credit, these measures should reduce both the supply of credit, as well as the demand (although one-term mayors and governors do not appear to be particularly interest-sensitive).

Second, a new law on local government borrowing (*Ley de Endeudamiento Territorial*) was approved in early 1997. While falling short of requiring an independent evaluation of the borrowers' credit risk directly, the law establishes a system of warning signs based on stock and flow indicators of the regional and local governments' repayment capacity, and specifies the jurisdiction that must approve the requests. However, under the law's new rules some local governments have actually increased their borrowing capacity. The two indicators are (1) interest payments as a percentage of (current) savings; and (2) the stock of debt as a percentage of current revenue. In addition, local governments cannot borrow to cover current expenditure. The agencies designated to supervise the new borrowing rules are the banking superintendency, the Ministry of Finance, and the commercial banks.

At the same time, the Ministry of Finance has begun to implement a program aimed at improving local government fiscal and debt management. The program requires local governments with weak finances to undergo an adjustment process that might include freezing salaries and undertaking other austerity measures. However, the main lacuna in the proposed measures is that the national government does not have the means to implement the controls—given sporadic flows of information and nonexisting external audit mechanisms. Thus, reforms in the management of debt and public expenditures are extremely urgent.

Management of Debt and Public Expenditures

Given that there are over a thousand municipalities, considerable variation in expenditure management practices is possible. However, an examination of the current budgetary situations and practices in some of the largest and more modern municipalities, as well as small and more remote ones, and two departments suggests that even the more advanced administrations suffer from serious shortcomings.

Cartagena and Manizales are among the larger municipalities, and do not lack qualified staff or management capabilities. Manizales, in particular, and Bogotá have made impressive improvements in their tax administrations in recent years. However, difficulties in the public expenditure management aspects are apparent in all municipalities, and these are magnified in the smaller municipalities. Expenditure reporting and control weaknesses in the municipalities severely constrain the effectiveness of the decentralization process.

The territorial authorities face a number of vastly differing reporting formats that are required by a number of national government agencies. In many cases, these reporting requirements lead to a paralysis of the capabilities of the municipalities, with a resulting deterioration in the quality of the information generated. The differing formats also detract from the assessment of the budgetary situation of the territorial governments—needed for an effective management of territorial public finances.

Some of the "standard" formats preclude a meaningful assessment of the overall budgetary situation of individual territorial governments. For instance, there are problems in the classification and formats used for municipal budgets, with an unfortunate confusion between revenues and financing items. Thus, municipalities systematically lack a clear perception of their overall deficit outcomes or prospect and are unable to gauge the extent of their difficulties.

An even greater difficulty is the absence of reliable information on budgetary outcomes. In Cartagena, even cash spending data are seen as unreliable, an issue complicated by the legal requirement to maintain unrelated separate funds and earmarked revenues. The Treasury does not keep a register of spending, and consequently does not have an accurate picture of the overall level of cash spending, or of its destination.

The problem of expenditure monitoring is exacerbated at all municipal levels by the absence of "impartial" and technically qualified controllers. Existing controllers are appointed by local legislatures and are subject to bias. The smaller municipalities do not have adequate own tax revenues to qualify for a controller, and reliance on the departmental controller is tantamount to the absence of any form of control or accountability.

Thus the absence of verifiable expenditure outcomes is likely to have repercussions on possibilities for restraining territorial indebtedness (for example, through measures such as "current savings" that rely on expenditure outcomes as well as revenues raised). All the municipal and departmental data suggest inconsistencies between the financing available and the implied primary and overall deficits.

Departments tend to have weaker management capabilities than the larger municipalities or districts (for example, Bogotá). Thus, the problems seen in the latter level of government are magnified at the departmental level. As in the municipalities, a particular lacuna exists in the inadequate generation of information on expenditure outcomes. And with the inability of the territorial governments to monitor actual spending, the systems of control are nonfunctional. In the departments, as in the case of municipalities, attempts to tie resources and transfers to particular ends because of weak local controls may prove ineffective precisely because relatively stronger controls and reporting mechanisms are required for special purpose grants and tied revenues. Paradoxically, the existence of such "tying" of resources, through special bank accounts, may actually impede the introduction of effective local controls or effective fiscal management, since the overall expenditure situation is not transparent.

Prospects for Territorial Governments

The dynamics of the decentralization process, with weak expenditure management, inadequate incentives to raise own revenues, and easy access to debt finance do not bode well for macroeconomic stability in Colombia.

Banks are keen to lend, given that many territorial governments have earmarked resources that they are unable to utilize together with assured increases in transfers and royalties. And loans to territorial governments are perceived as sovereign debt.

On their part, the territorial governments are keen to borrow, since this provides a potential source of "untied finance." Also, with the three-year electoral cycle, with no reelection possible for mayors and governors, there is relatively little concern about the consequences of borrowing—this will be someone else's problem. Indeed, the assessment of budgetary profiles for selected territorial governments bears this out. In Manizales, the stock of debt increased from 69 percent of current revenues in 1994 to 79 percent in 1995, with interest payments increasing by nearly 80 percent in nominal terms in 1995 over 1994 levels. The municipality in 1995 was close to breaching the 30 percent debt service to current revenues criterion. Cartagena, on the other hand, had a stock of debt of 150 percent of current revenues in 1993, and this had risen to 180 percent in 1994. The 1995 budgets indicated that the financing gap may be more than twice as large as current revenues, but because there had been an aggressive refinancing campaign (as well as an indeterminate buildup of arrears), the municipality was comfortably placed vis-à-vis the debt service to current revenues criterion.

The national government was thus correct in seeking to establish a more stringent criterion of unsustainable debt increase at the territorial level, based as a proportion of disposable savings. This indicator would indeed bring attention to bear on the problem territories before the financing difficulties become unsustainable. However, to make the limit functional, improved information systems are needed, vis-à-vis both the banking system and larger municipalities, as well as the monitoring of budgetary trends at the territorial level. Limits to territorial borrowing, together with less earmarking of transfers and enhanced local tax administration, are also crucial in ensuring that greater accountability accompanies the decentralization process.

Appendix I. The Departmental Tax System

Current Taxes

Excise Taxes

The departmental tax system rests mainly on specific taxes on local consumption. Revenue from excises is also earmarked, which reduces the scope for autonomous policy at the departmental level.[23] Excise tax-

---

[23]Revenue from the liquor tax is assigned to the financing of university and regional hospitals (Decree 1222/86, Article 134), the revenue from the gasoline tax to the financing of roads (Decree 1222/86, Article 151), and 8 percentage points of a 48 percent tax rate on beer to the provision of health services (Decree 1222/86, Article 160).

ation at the departmental level requires the definition of domestic "exports" and "imports" of taxable goods, such as liquor and tobacco, which in turn necessitates internal "fiscal borders" for appropriate monitoring. Moreover, intraregional purchases of taxable goods can be effected only on the basis of mutual agreements among departments. This generates legal and administrative complexities. Although producing factories keep a record of their deliveries to their customers by department, this does not guarantee that the "imported" goods will be taxed by the consuming department. It creates scope for "internal contraband," which is at odds with the notion of a common Colombian market.

The problem is exacerbated by foreign competition for excisable goods. The importer is required to pay the excises to the department in which the imported goods are sold,[24] but there is large scope for tax evasion. Thus, foreign contraband competes with local production of excisable goods. Furthermore, excisable goods are "exported" to other departments "duty free" and this may de facto constitute a loophole through which the goods are eventually "reimported" to the department without the payment of excises.

In order to reduce the incentive for smuggling, the national government in 1994 lowered the tax rate on tobacco, simultaneously creating a Fondo Tabacalero de Compensación Tributaria in order to indemnify producing departments for the loss of revenue. This experience illustrates the fundamental deficiencies of a system of decentralized excise taxation that remains subject to national policy decisions.

The system was further complicated by the fact that the departments were given regional monopolies on the introduction and the sale of excisable goods, for instance for the distribution of liquor (Decree 1222/86, Article 123). This allows the departments to benefit from a monopoly rent as well as from the excise. Recent developments illustrate that regional monopolies and regional taxation of consumer goods cannot exist without the support of national government policy. In order to protect monopoly rents, the national government had to impose customs tariffs on imports. Moreover, the revaluation of the peso, relative to the U.S. dollar, rendered imports more competitive in the Colombian market, putting pressure on monopoly rents and affecting the level of excises.

Other issues of excise taxation in Colombia relate to the tax base and to the rate structure. The tax base for liquor, for instance, refers to the average value of a 750 cc. bottle of spirits sold in Colombia. This

---

[24]Although the national Dirección de Impuestos y Aduanas is responsible for collecting customs duties on imported goods, it is not in charge of excise duties that have to be paid to the departments (Article 125 of Decree 1222/86).

value is uniformly fixed by DIAN, the national tax administration and customs department and is updated regularly according to market developments. The tax base is thus a quantity independent of the commercial value of a specific product. A bottle of imported high-quality liquor bears the same tax as a cheap bottle of domestic liquor.

Furthermore, a relatively high tax rate of 35 percent applies to liquors, while *aperitivos* (aperitifs) carry a much lower rate of 10 percent. The delineation of these product categories by alcohol content (above and below 28 degrees vol.) is arbitrary. The maximum alcohol content of *aperitivos* is also high, and this induces the production of liquor up to the critical mark, which may not be in the public interest.

The Motor Vehicle Tax

The Colombian departments operate a motor vehicle tax in parallel with the municipal *impuesto de circulación y tránsito*, using essentially the same tax base. This base is the commercial value of the motor vehicle as established annually by the Instituto Nacional del Transporte (INTRA). The rate structure is progressive and certain exemptions apply (vehicles of the public service and public law enforcement, school buses, agricultural machinery, and so on). Again, a large part of revenue from this tax is earmarked.[25] The revenue potential of the motor vehicle tax is substantial. The complexities resulting from the assignment to two tiers of government, with two tax administrations managing the same tax base could, however, be resolved by consolidating the tax at the department level, through a piggybacking or a revenue-sharing mechanism.

Some countries use the motor vehicle tax to monitor and discourage pollution and noise, and in Colombia, the tax is lower on older cars. However, the commercial value of a vehicle does not reflect relevant environmental criteria. Carbon emissions by older cars, with a lower commercial value, may be higher than that on new cars, and a reduced tax on older cars is not warranted on ecological grounds.

The Registration Tax

The registration tax (*impuesto de registro y anotación*) is levied on the issuance of official documents and the certification of legal acts. The law defines a great number of such acts, some of which are taxed on a

---

[25]Eighty percent of tax collections from the motor vehicle tax are assigned to investment expenditures or to the servicing of debt for road programs.

lump-sum basis (like a fee), while others are taxed on their intrinsic value. The latter renders the registration tax similar to taxes on gifts and inheritances, for instance, or to taxes on the transaction of property, which exist in other countries.

In principle, the registration tax operates at all levels of government, in accordance with the nature of the act registered. It also competes with a host of *estampillas*, or stamp taxes, that all tiers can apply on top of the registration tax. The departments are, in particular, entitled to levy—within limits—revenue through stamp taxes for departmental development and rural electrification. Revenue from the stamp taxes is also earmarked. Furthermore, there is a 10 percent surcharge on the registration tax and the local property tax (*impuesto predial*), tied to the financing of military, agricultural, and cadastral maps. This surcharge has, however, been handed over to the departments, and the surcharge on the property tax was abolished in 1990. All increases of the basic registration tax are also earmarked to finance programs of social assistance.

Given the potentially high base of the registration tax for property transactions, including the separation of property in the case of divorce, and for inheritances and gifts, the revenue from this tax is comparably small—and is only a fraction of the tax on motor vehicles. This is an indicator of administrative complexities and poor enforcement of the tax. It may be worthwhile to simplify the registration tax, in conjunction with that of stamp taxes, and to target the former to the more important economic transactions and legal acts.

Gambling Taxes

Various taxes on gambling (including monopolies) have grown into a very complex system that is difficult to administer. Given the relatively low yield (which may nevertheless be important for some departments), a simpler structure should be sought that is easier to monitor and to administer.

Reforming Departmental Taxation

Existing Excises

A policy change shifting the collection of excises to the producer level could simplify administration and improve revenue collections. This would eliminate problems relating to "internal contraband." One option is a national excise administration (by DIAN), with the assignment of revenues to departments. Given that departments express little confidence that the national tax administration would be diligent in collecting departmental taxes, DIAN could offer its services for a fee—to promote effectiveness in collection.

Another option is for decentralized excise taxation at the production level, imposed by departments on enterprises within their own jurisdiction. However, this arrangement would favor the producing departments and could exacerbate regional inequities.[26] A redistribution mechanism would need to be established to compensate the losing departments.

Excise taxation at the producer level would facilitate tax administration by reducing the number of taxpayers to those with generally well-kept records. Given the production basis of the excise applying to the producer or importer, it would be possible to cross-check the value of total sales with the various departments and the declarations for the VAT. An appropriate margin for the distributor would have to be added in order to approximate distribution based on consumption. Imported excisable goods should face the same treatment as domestically produced goods—with taxation at point of entry—rendering DIAN responsible for collecting the departmental excises on imported goods, in addition to customs duties.

Additional Excises

There is scope for an excise on industrial nonalcoholic beverages administered by the departments at the producer level—with tax collection at the point of origin (importer or producer). This should pose no particularly complex administrative problems for industrially produced drinks. A similar redistribution mechanism could be achieved as for alcoholic beverages.

The Gasoline Tax

At the departmental levels, gasoline tax could be a major source of revenue. Since domestic prices for gasoline are low in Colombia com-

---

[26]It is interesting to note that this reasoning applies to excise taxation, but *not* to royalties on natural resources in Colombia where the producing departments and municipalities are granted almost full access to a tax base the regional distribution of which is highly inequitable. It is also doubtful whether the present system of excise taxation achieves the objective of distributing the proceeds among departments according to consumption. The per capita distribution of the excise on liquor, for instance, shows a highly unequal pattern among departments in 1990, which is, of course, partly explained by variations in consumer behavior. The fact that two of the main producing departments—Antioquia and Cundinamarca—also collect the highest per capita liquor tax might indicate that the tax is mainly distributed according to production even now.

pared with international prices, the scope for gasoline taxation is potentially high. In some European countries, revenues from the gasoline tax rank closely behind the VAT and income taxes. In Colombia, however, the scope of a gasoline excise is limited by a national energy policy. As long as the consumer price of gasoline is administered, any increase in the tax rate would be shifted backward onto suppliers—and would realistically be feasible only if the consumer price of gasoline is allowed to reflect the tax.

Departmental Sharing of Tax Bases with National Level

The sharing of tax bases among governments has to be distinguished from tax sharing. The sharing of tax bases gives the lower tiers direct access to a substantial tax base, such as the income tax, which, for administrative purposes, may be collected by the national administration. Lower level governments are, in principle, free to set their own rates in these cases, which is not possible in the case of tax sharing.

The sharing of the VAT base among levels of government entails severe administrative complexities and regional inequities, owing to the tax credit mechanism and the zero-rating of exports. Such an arrangement would be further complicated if departments were allowed to set their own tax rates.

The simplest surcharge would be for the personal income tax—with the same definition of taxable income as for national taxation. Such a surcharge would benefit most the already better-off departments, given the high correlation with higher income taxpayers, and some of the poorer departments might not benefit as much—thus increasing horizontal fiscal imbalances. The departments would decide on a surtax rate, which may be subject to a national "floor," to be applied on the national income tax base. The tax rate could also be limited by a ceiling in order to reduce locational distortions resulting from tax-induced migration.[27] Initially, there could be a mandatory uniform rate, to allow departments to gain experience with their new tax base, and to register taxpayers. Variable rates could be introduced in a couple of years.

If the total tax burden is to be kept constant, the national government would have to make room for departmental taxation by revising its own rate structure. This would have implications for national expenditures, as well as transfers; the surcharge should not be introduced if these adjustments are not possible.

---

[27]In this case, a ceiling would be preferable, because tax competition is less visible than in the case of excise taxation or surtaxes on the consumption of goods.

Revenues generated by the surcharge should accrue on the basis of residence according to the benefit principle of taxation. Withholding taxes should be treated on the same basis. The same taxpayer identifier number is available for the withholding tax as for self-assessment, making allocations to departments possible. Departmental tax collections would not be practical,[28] although responsibilities for accounting, auditing, and enforcement could be at the departmental level.

Surtax on Company Income Tax

A surtax on the company income tax, based on the residence criterion for firms, would pose administrative difficulties, given the problems of distinguishing returns at company headquarters from the income's department of origin. Nevertheless, it is possible to apportion total profits taxable on the basis of simple formulas.[29]

Environmental Taxes

Ecological taxes are usually linked to negative externalities, to "internalize" the social costs of production and consumption. The price of goods produced and consumed should reflect their "full" costs, not only private costs. Negative externalities may be global, national, departmental, or municipal. Each level of government should have appropriate instruments to contain environmental damage within its territory. Given that the effects may be spread over a number of regions, the charges generally operate within a common framework of national standards. However, administration is often decentralized, also permitting enhanced local revenues.

In order to reduce excessive packaging, a tax could be used to render it more costly, and to finance the disposal of non-recyclable containers. Such a tax could apply to the producers of containers, bottles, cans, cardboard boxes, and similar packaging products. Since the location of such firms is highly arbitrary across the country, the tax would be best administered and collected by the national government. This does not

---

[28]This is because of the possible lack of correspondence between the residence of the taxpayer and the location of his sources of income.

[29]California had operated a scheme that identified the state's share in the worldwide profits of multinational companies on the basis of weighted criteria such as the local wage bill, capital, and turnover. In Germany, where the corporate tax is shared between the federal government and the states, a similar formula is used to apportion a globalized amount of tax paid by firms to regions. Portugal operates a municipal surcharge on the company tax, the *derrama*.

preclude the transfer of the proceeds to those territorial entities that face the daily problems of garbage collection and removal.

There is a scope for further surcharges on utilities, for instance, on telephone bills, electricity bills, or the supply of water. These are easily administered, and generate stable and secure revenues for departments or municipalities. Some of these surcharges relate to local ability to pay (telephone bills), others are broadly connected with environmental damage as caused by the use of energy and water.

Appendix II. The Municipal Tax System

A local tax system should encourage accountability and obey the benefit principle in order to be efficient. In principle, the Colombian property tax (*impuesto predial unificado*) and the business tax (*impuesto de industria y comercio*) meet the required criteria. The former can be seen as equivalent to the consumption of local services by local residents and the latter constitutes an equivalent of public services consumed by local business. Furthermore, user charges and fees, as well as betterment levies for the financing of local projects, are particularly suited to the financing of local projects, the benefits of which are more visible and tangible at lower than at higher levels of government.

The Property Tax

The Colombian property tax is essentially ad valorem. In 1990, various taxes on local property were merged into the *impuesto predial unificado*, which now covers all local properties of households, public establishments, and industrial and commercial enterprises. A part of the tax, 10 percent, is tied to housing construction, and there is a surcharge on the tax (between 15 percent and 25.9 percent), tied to programs for protecting the environment and natural resource bases, 50 percent of which must be spent within the jurisdiction of the local government that collects the surcharge.

The base of the property tax is the cadastral value or, alternatively, a self-assessed value of such property. The latter cannot be lower than the cadastral value. The cadastral value is established officially by the national Instituto Geográfico Agustín Codazzi (IGAC) at regular intervals.[30] This institute also provides other services to local governments,

---

[30]The department of Antioquia as well as the cities of Bogotá, Medellín, and Cali maintain their own cadasters. By law, the cadasters have to be updated at least every seven years (Law 75/86, Article 174).

such as the dissemination of information and training of officials. A minimum tax base applies, which is calculated in terms of square meters of the land or the building times a minimum price, which varies in accordance with location and social characteristics of the population.

The updating of values is based on information obtained from the register of property transactions and other documentation, which fix reference prices for selected property (*predios testigos*). These reference prices are used to evaluate neighboring properties across the more homogeneous areas, where various characteristics are taken into account and consolidated on the basis of weights obtained from regression analyses. For intermittent years, the cadastral value is actualized on the basis of the average national consumer price index, as determined by the national Statistical Office (DANE). The National Council for Economic and Social Policy (CONPES) decides on the degree of adjustment to the price deflator, which may range between 70 percent and 100 percent. Special restrictions apply to the adjustment of property values for agricultural land.

In general, property values are significantly undervalued in Colombia and do not reflect market developments. This is explained by various factors: deficiencies in the register of property transactions (the market value is seldom declared); significant time lags in updating the cadastral values; a preponderance of social factors in the evaluation process; limitations on the annual increment of the tax; and concessions expressed in less than full indexing of property values for intermittent years.

Besides the cadastral value, the law allows self-assessment of the property tax value, which cannot be below the former. One would expect that self-assessment would be seldom evoked. There are incentives to induce an automatic adjustment by the taxpayer. For instance, when the property is used as a collateral for a loan, banks are obliged to report the mortgaged value to tax authorities. There are also fiscal incentives that should encourage self-adjustment of property values. The national capital gains tax on realized property transactions acknowledges the registered value of a property for the *predial* as a fictitious "purchase" price that is deductible from the sale price. By adjusting the registered value for the property tax, the taxpayer can thus reduce his capital gains tax liability. Of course, this incentive works only in the case of intended sale of the property, and it rests on the assumption that transactions prices are declared honestly.

Another problem related to the property tax base is its comprehensiveness. While IGAC claims to cover 97 percent of the properties it is responsible for, the coverage ratio for Bogotá was said to be only in the order of 30 percent. Such figures have to be interpreted with caution, however, since the coverage rate hinges on complete information and timely updating. Every change in the use of property, and every modification of buildings, for instance the partitioning into subunits, may entail a change in the total number of properties. This can only be known after a complete and comprehensive update.

The *impuesto predial unificado* is the cornerstone of municipal finance and should be strengthened as far as possible. There are essentially two main areas where the property tax needs reform: the valuation of the tax base, and strengthening of tax administration (in particular enforcement of the tax laws). A reform of the rate structure is meaningful once these basic problems have been resolved.

Valuation of Property

The IGAC is the central body in charge of setting the official value of most properties in Colombia (with the exception of Antioquia, Bogotá, Cali, and Medellín). It could be converted into a more flexible and responsive fee-for-service institution that is subject to competition.

A first step could be a decentralization of IGAC, where the 7 regional, 21 sectional, and 44 delegated offices obtain greater autonomy and are allowed to compete with each other. While the IGAC may retain the monopoly to determine officially property values in the country, valuation itself could be performed by municipalities, the regional bodies of the IGAC, and even private institutions (trust funds, banks, and insurance companies). A fee for service could be based on the increment in the value of the property, which would create an incentive to update values on a timely basis. Valuations could be contested by the taxpayer, through reconciliation and legal procedures.

A next step would be a much closer cooperation between IGAC (specifically its autonomous regional bodies) and municipalities. In principle, any municipality can ask IGAC to revise the valuation of any property at any time, based on documented evidence such as the price of a contracted property transaction. In practice, however, most municipalities tend to wait for a more comprehensive revision, stipulated to take place every seven years.

On-line access, or exchange of information, between the IGAC and the municipalities would significantly enhance the quality of the database. Revisions to the value of a representative property should automatically lead to an adjustment of all properties in a given property zone. This would be possible if IGAC procedures for the comprehensive routine revisions based on *predios testigos* are adhered to. If the cadastre of IGAC is not available on a database, an appropriate project to develop such a system should be initiated. Since the technology for managing the cadastre is sophisticated, and demands highly qualified staff, the cadastre itself should perhaps best be administered centrally.

The evaluation procedures should be subject to competition and debate. At present, the IGAC bases its evaluation mainly on transaction prices which, for various reasons, are often defective. Alternatives are possible, through banks and insurance companies that finance the acquisition of properties or mortgages, based on procedures that include, inter alia, a minimum rate of return, expected rentals, the current costs of construction (in the case of an existing building), and socioeconomic and risk factors.

The national government may also want to reform the legal and procedural framework for property transactions in Colombia, in particular, registration. It is possible to obtain or falsify titles of property, which are used to obtain credits and/or "sell" land. Furthermore, it is common to declare transaction values well below actual market prices. An effective system of penalties would have to be put in place.

A penalty could also be imposed in the form of the government's right to enter any pending contract at the declared price, plus an appropriate margin. This right would have to be exerted from time to time and should be widely publicized in the media, in order to have a deterrent effect. It may also be prudent to require the payment of all pending taxes relating to property prior to the registration of a change in ownership.

Self-Assessment of Property Values

In 1994, Bogotá introduced self-evaluation of properties, with a remarkable success in terms of revenue raised. Tax collections for 1994 exceeded those of the previous year by roughly 100 percent. This can be explained by a number of factors, the most important of which is the much wider coverage of taxpayers, a consequence of the previously low coverage rate of the cadastre in Bogotá. A further effect relates to previously very low cadastral values with regard to market levels. Such revenue increases may not occur in other municipalities, where the coverage of the cadastre is more comprehensive and where cadastral values have recently been updated. To be fully effective, however, the municipality must exercise its prerogative to purchase property it considers to be undervalued.

The mandatory use of self-assessment has been proposed, but may be premature, particularly given the constraints on tax administration capabilities in many municipalities. Even in Bogotá, a number of administrative issues remain to be solved, and the initial success needs to be sustainable over the medium term. Bogotá, through its policy, has generated a large amount of information that is now unrelated to the cadastre. This creates the need to establish a separate database, requiring new management tools and procedures to keep the new database current.[31] Municipalities should therefore remain free to evoke the option of self-assessment whenever they feel to be in a position to handle the flow of information this would entail. If Bogotá can display a well-functioning system in the medium term, the demonstration effect would make a mandate unnecessary.

Rate Structure of the Property Tax

At present, the law allows municipalities to vary property tax rates between 1 and 16 per thousand, which is a relatively wide range. But municipalities usually do not exploit the full scope of potential offered by the law. On the contrary, there is evidence that some municipalities have reduced their rates as property values were reassessed upward. This indicates a lack of volition to use the property tax on the part of some municipalities, where private concerns of local land owners may collide with public interest. The taxable capacity of local governments can also be enhanced by establishing a higher tax rate floor by national legislation. The rate structure of the property tax could also be simplified by eliminating the progressivity according to property use and socioeconomic characteristics of the owner. Such criteria should already be taken care of in a proper evaluation of the property.

A distinction has to be made between rural and urban properties. Rural properties are often small in Colombia, they generate little revenue, and they provide subsistence incomes to poorer families. The strain on tax administration would be considerably reduced by exempting such farms. A marginal adjustment in the tax rate would more than compensate for the reduced number of farms covered. The annual output on the farms greatly exceeds the assessed values per hectare from the cadastre. This suggests that a revision in property values could be mandated on the basis of potential output—greatly increasing revenues, without affecting the poorer farmers. The commercial use of land, for instance, for greenhouses, should not benefit from the exemption.

The Business Tax

The local business tax covers all industrial and commercial activities, as well as services, including banks, savings institutions, financial

---

[31]This does not mean that the self-assessed values in Bogotá are true market prices. This is partly because, as an initial incentive, Bogotá announced it would be satisfied with values at about 50 percent of the true market price.

corporations, and insurance companies. With the exception of Bogotá, the tax base is the average monthly value of gross receipts of the year preceding the tax period. The distributors of petroleum derivatives are taxed only on their distribution margin, which is fixed by the national government. The proceeds from the sale of assets and from exports are exempt from the tax.

The tax rate is set at the discretion of the municipality, and can vary between two and seven per thousand for industrial activities, and between two and ten per thousand for commercial activities and services. There is a surcharge of 15 percent on the amount of business tax collected, which is motivated by the intention to tax advertisements and publicity. This is only a presumptive surcharge since the level of gross sales may not be correlated with this type of activity.

The Colombian business tax has a number of conceptual problems: there is uncertainty with regard to the tax base in the case where a firm produces industrial goods and performs commercial activities (or provides services) at the same time. According to the law, this would give rise to double or even triple taxation. The courts had to clarify that the tax is due only once when production and distribution are carried out by the same firm in the same municipality. Double taxation persists, however, when production and distribution do not take place in the same community.

Of course, double taxation applies for each transaction among *different* firms, which entails cascading of the tax. This tends to encourage vertical integration of industries, but it is not at all clear how the tax would treat interregional trade within one business conglomerate that operates in various municipalities. The law is silent on the sharing of the tax base in these cases, and the courts may well rule that such transactions be treated like those among independent firms.

Cascading is highly distortive and inefficient, and it favors foreign suppliers over domestic producers and suppliers, in that the former have to pay the tax only once. This bias embedded in the tax base may be tolerable in view of the low tax rates, and given that the total revenue of the tax is low on average (0.4 percent of GDP in 1993), although the tax burden may be heavier on certain sectors. If the tax is to produce higher revenue in the future, however, some reform of the tax base would be desirable.

Options for Reform of the Municipal Tax System: The Business Tax

The local business tax employed in Colombia is essentially a gross turnover tax. Options for the reform of the base of this tax are considered below.

Net Turnover Tax

In order to eliminate the distortive effects of cascading, the business tax could be converted into a net turnover tax. Such a tax is employed, for example, by municipalities in Hungary. The tax base is normally the sales revenue of products sold and services provided, reduced by the purchase value of the goods sold, and the value of services provided by subcontractors.

This option mitigates some of the distortions related to cascading. It is also different from the VAT and it captures both exporters as well as suppliers to the domestic market—in line with the benefit-principle. There are also rules that allow the apportionment of the tax base among different municipalities, if the entrepreneur's activity extends over more than one locality and if local turnover cannot be defined separately. If this option were to be adopted by Colombian municipalities, it would require the revision of tax rates, since the tax base of a net turnover tax is narrower than that of a gross turnover tax. It is also somewhat more complicated in administrative terms.

Retail Sales Tax (Wholesale Sales Tax)

Cascading could also be avoided if the business tax were levied only at one stage of processing, for instance, at the retail or at the wholesale stage. A retail sales tax (a wholesale sales tax) has a number of problems. It favors municipalities where commerce is predominant, and it disfavors local governments with agriculture, industry, and services, because these activities would remain untaxed. This can lead to severe regional imbalances if the tax is levied at the municipal level. It would also violate the principle of benefit taxation at the local tier, because some business firms would be allowed to consume local services without contributing to their financing.

From a tax administration perspective, a retail sales tax can be far more complicated than the industry and commerce tax. Currently taxpayers report annual sales from the previous year, and pay $1/12$ of that amount each month. With a retail sales tax, taxpayers would have to report sales each month (based on the cash register receipts for audit purposes), and segment products sold, if some are exempt or taxed at different rates. The taxpayers' compliance burden is further complicated if the sales tax base is different from the VAT base. Given the limited audit capacity of most municipalities, a retail sales tax would be more difficult to administer than the current industry and commerce tax.

Taxation of Factors of Production

Some European countries tax the use of factors of production rather than output. The business tax is considered to form part of the production costs, which include the use of local public services. Often the factors of production are combined in a schedular tariff with a wage and a capital component. This avoids factor distortions.

The payroll taxes on the wage bill are already high in Colombia and were increased recently to cope with new demands for health services and old-age pensions. There is thus limited scope for utilizing this base for local taxation.

Taxation of Local Profits

Another possibility is to tax local business profits. As mentioned earlier, Portugal employs such a tax at the municipal level, the *derrama*, where the local tax base is derived from global profits within the nation by an apportionment formula. Germany's business tax also has a profit component (apart from local business capital) that is, however, defined in gross terms. In particular, the deductibility of interest payments is disallowed—which is different from the logic of the company tax.

Presumptive Business Taxation

There are various forms of presumptive business taxation based on objective criteria, such as the number of employees, square meters used, electricity consumption, and the telephone bill. Such forms of taxation are, of course, only approximations to a fully fledged business tax, and their use is mainly motivated by administrative considerations. Since each of these indicators will have a different significance for various business activities, a presumptive tax system has to classify such activities and attribute different weights to the criteria for each class of activities. This introduces a degree of arbitrariness, it creates severe delineation problems in practice (with a potential for conflict and legal disputes), and it complicates the administration of the tax. It should be noted that in Colombia, an unwieldy system of presumptive taxation has already been replaced by a more standardized approach across the whole nation.

A particular form of presumptive taxation could be considered, however. Some municipalities employ a lump-sum minimum tax for small businesses, which acts as a "license tax." This facilitates tax administration enormously, as it can be controlled even for the occasional street vendor, who would have to carry his "license" issued only after payment of the tax—eventually to be renewed every month.

Local Surcharges

Local surcharges on national or departmental taxes can simplify tax administration, while leaving municipalities their full fiscal autonomy, in particular the discretion to set their own tax rates. Municipalities should avoid application of such surcharges on smaller tax bases, which renders the tax system unwieldy, and could become a nuisance to the taxpayer.

Some municipalities have introduced (or are considering the introduction of) a local surcharge on gasoline sales within their constituency. National laws allow municipal governments to use such a surcharge up to a ceiling of 20 percent. This surcharge, while constituting a potentially important revenue base, could create severe problems of horizontal tax competition, if levied at the municipal level. The problems are similar to those discussed at length for excises. Consumers could evade the surcharge by purchasing gasoline in nontaxing or low-taxing municipalities, where distances are not too great.

In the case of Medellín, the tax is levied on the sales of the main local producer or distributor, not at the local gasoline stations. This creates an incentive for gasoline stations to purchase their supplies outside Medellín, where wholesale distribution of gasoline is untaxed, and they reap an extra margin on their sales in Medellín where the normal retail price would include the tax. Not only is the local surcharge avoided in this case, but the tax wedge is appropriated by private firms at the retail level.[32]

There are difficulties faced by regional suppliers-distributors with electricity-based surcharges. Such difficulties may be explained partly by administered pricing, partly by the need for heavy investments that amortize only over a longer time period. Again, a more market-oriented approach in the energy sector, combined with targeted social assistance to the poor, is preferable to the subsidizing of production and distribution, but this would require prior adjustments of sectoral policies at the national level.

Slaughter Tax

Given the limited revenue sources for municipalities, the slaughter tax is important at the local level. However, the base is split, with departments being assigned the revenues from the slaughter of large animals, and municipalities getting revenues from the slaughter of smaller animals. This tax should be consolidated at the municipal level.

---

[32]Petroleum prices are fixed nationally.

Appendix III. Revenue-Sharing Indices

Index of Unsatisfied Basic Needs

The index of unsatisfied basic needs is used as a tool for the redistribution of resources from rich to poor areas. This index, widely used for similar purposes in a number of other Latin American countries, is also taken into account for the distribution of cofinancing funds. In Colombia, the index includes the number of people without health and education services, and a few characteristics related to the conditions of housing. While there is clearly no general objection to the use of indicators of need for redistributing resources among levels of government, there are some problems associated with its introduction in the formulas in the Colombian case.

In a diverse country, different factors reflecting need may have more or less significance in various regions (for example, the absence of heating and proper roofing may be more important in the mountainous regions than in the sierra or the coastal areas, where thatched housing without heating would be quite adequate). Moreover, individual jurisdictions have different problems and priorities. Some departments may have adequate provision of access to education and to basic health, and may have other priorities not foreseen in the centrally determined formulas. Since equal weights are given to different components of the index, the formula cannot take into account these diversities and the corresponding needs. The NBI index also excludes other basic needs relevant to the operation of territorial governments, such as infant mortality, unemployment, or the nutritional content of the diet of the poorest strata of the population.

In part, some of the problems may be solved by a reconsideration of the index, based on effective experiences in the various areas of the country. An option is to revise the entire framework of transfers to territorial governments by making this consistent with the decentralization objectives, for example, by making territorial governments more able to respond to local conditions, through an enhanced reliance on general transfers and own revenues at the margin. Specific purpose grants should use indicators (other than the unsatisfied basic needs) better targeted at the specific problems they aim to solve.

Fiscal Effort Index

A fiscal effort index is used for distributing the *situado fiscal*. This index has a small quantitative impact, but its use may have a severely distorting influence.[33] The index is calculated as the increase over the previous year of expenditures on health and education, financed by revenues other than the *situado fiscal*, that is taxes, fees, profits from locally owned firms, and borrowing. Departments may thus increase their indebtedness, increase their expenditures and obtain a substantial increase in their transfers, even with a reduction in their own tax revenues. Moreover, this index is very sensitive to changes from one year to the other.

Proper fiscal effort indices should measure the actual use by territorial governments of their potential tax base, taking into account differences in the latter across jurisdictions.

Fiscal Efficiency Index

This index is used for distributing the participation transfers to municipalities. Here also, the index has a small quantitative impact. The index is calculated as the rate of change, over two years, of tax collections. This percentage is then weighted by the unsatisfied basic needs index, to favor the poorest jurisdictions. While this index is better than that used for departments (since municipalities have a wider and more standardized tax base than departments), there are still some problems to be solved. Here again, fiscal efficiency is not properly measured. For example, municipalities with a high increase in population, or with new economic activities, may have a huge increase in their tax revenues (and be correspondently rewarded by this index) even if there is reduced effort in tax collections.

Administrative Efficiency Index

The formula for transfers to municipalities uses this index, which is measured as the ratio between per capita operating expenditures and the number of inhabitants with water, sanitary, and sewerage services. It is aimed at stimulating expenditure for these services, since for equal levels of expenditures, it rewards those jurisdictions that have a smaller number of inhabitants serviced. Here again, there is a clear incentive to expand borrowing instead of tax revenues, and to reward jurisdictions with higher degrees of inefficiency in their expenditure.

---

[33]This index has determined the allocation of less than 1 percent of shared revenue, on average, and has thus far been ineffective in encouraging a greater fiscal effort on behalf of the local governments.

References

Acosta, O., and I. Yaker, 1994, "El Proceso Reciente de Descentralización Fiscal en Colombia y sus Perspectivas" (Santafé de Bogotá).

Bird, R., 1984, "Intergovernmental Finance in Colombia" (Cambridge, Massachusetts: Harvard Law School).

Cárdenas, Juan Camilo, 1994, "Informe del Estudio de Caso—Municipio de Valledupar; Municipio de Zapatoca" (Washington: Banco Mundial y Departamento Nacional de Planeación).

Ferreira, A.M., and E.G. Valenzuela, 1993, "Descentralización Fiscal: el Caso Colombiano" (CEPAL/GTZ, Proyecto Regional de Descentralización Fiscal).

Perry, G. and J. A. Rodríguez, 1991, "Las Finanzas Intergubernamentales en la Constitución de 1991," Cuadernos de Economía.

Sanchez, F., and C. Gutiérrez, 1994, "La Descentralización Fiscal en Colombia: Problemas y Perspectivas" (Santafé de Bogotá).

Tanzi, Vito, 1995, "Tax Assignments and Administration," in *Reforming China's Public Finances*, ed. by Ehtisham Ahmad, Gao Qiang, and Vito Tanzi (Washington: International Monetary Fund).

Wiesner-Duran, E., 1992, "Colombia: Descentralización y Federalismo Fiscal"(Presidencia de la República, Santafé de Bogotá).

20

Ethiopia

GIORGIO BROSIO AND SANJEEV GUPTA

The process of fiscal decentralization in Ethiopia began in 1992. Proclamations were issued during 1992–93 to establish federal and regional self-governments and to define both the revenue-sharing arrangements and the powers of the federal and the regional governments (henceforth referred to as states).[1] These elements of a federal structure have been embraced by the National Constitution, which was approved in December 1994. The National Constitution lists nine states, but there are two other jurisdictions that currently have the status of provisional administration. Interstate boundaries reflect ethnic or linguistic groups, and states vary considerably in terms of land area and population.

Since the 1993/94 budget, expenditures devolved to the states have increased gradually to about 40 percent of total consolidated expenditures, whereas the federal government has continued to account for most of the revenues under the tax-assignment arrangements. Transfers from the federal government are thus the major source of support of states' expenditures. Expenditure devolution has taken place in four core areas: agriculture, education, health, and road construction.

This chapter first describes the main characteristics of intergovernmental relations in Ethiopia, particularly the fiscal structure of

---

The authors wish to thank Ehtisham Ahmad, Benedict Clements, Dawn Rehm, Edgardo Ruggiero, Gerd Schwartz, and Teresa Ter-Minassian for many helpful comments, and Manfred Koch for his assistance and advice.

[1]Proclamation numbers 7/1992, 33/1992, and 41/1993. The decentralized subnational units are referred to as states in the Constitution. Although proclamations preceding the Constitution label the decentralized subnational units as regions, this chapter refers to them as states, in keeping with the usage in the Constitution.

Ethiopia. It then reviews the current grant system, highlighting the major drawbacks in its design and the way it is implemented. Finally, it presents options to strengthen it.

Main Characteristics of Intergovernmental Relations

The following characteristics of Ethiopia's federal structure are particularly noteworthy.

First, revenues are categorized as central, state, and joint (Table 1). The most important revenues are assigned to the federal government. As the sharing of revenues jointly levied and collected by federal and state governments is still to be defined, they are collected by the federal government. The revenue assignment of the state governments is concentrated in direct tax revenue, including most personal income taxes; however, there is no historical evidence in Ethiopia of sustained growth of these taxes. As a result, there is a large and growing vertical fiscal imbalance between the state share of revenue and expenditures, which has widened from 14.7 percent in 1993/94 to 28.5 percent in the 1995/96 budget (Table 2). Under present trends, this vertical fiscal imbalance is likely to persist in the foreseeable future.

The principal reason for the large share of the federal government in total revenue is the dominance of indirect taxes in total revenue and the federal government's high share of these taxes under revenue assignments. For instance, the federal government collects about 90 percent of all indirect taxes, with over 80 percent of sales taxes and 100 percent of import duties. One important revenue source, excises, is not legally assigned to either level of government, but is being collected by the federal government. Consequently, the average proportion of spending covered by a state's own resources was about one-third in 1994/95. With the exception of the provisional administration of Addis Ababa, all states had deficits in 1994/95, and required federal transfers.

Second, revenue collections are highly concentrated in a few states; four states accounted for 84 percent of total revenue in 1994/95, while the smallest four contributed a mere 2.2 percent (Table 3). This illustrates the states' widely divergent revenue-raising capacities. The per capita revenue effort in 1994/95 varied between Br 5.7 in Afar and Br 125 in Dire Dawa.

Third, the expenditure responsibilities assigned to the federal and state governments in the Constitution are close to what is found in a highly decentralized system. For instance, the Constitution calls on the federal government to establish and administer national defense; administer monetary policy, currency, and banking; formulate and imple-

Table 1. Ethiopia: Revenue Sharing Between the Federal and State Governments

Federal	State	Joint
Duties, taxes, and other charges on imports and exports.	—	—
Personal income tax of employees in federal government, international organizations, and those working in enterprises owned by federal government.	Personal income tax of state government employees and those working in enterprises owned by states and in the private sector.	Personal income tax of employees working in enterprises owned jointly by federal and state governments.
Profits tax and sales tax from federal government-owned enterprises and those operating across regional boundaries.[1]	Profits tax and sales tax from the state government-owned enterprises.	Profits tax and sales tax of enterprises owned jointly by federal and state governments.
—	Income tax, royalties, and land rent from small-scale mining enterprises.	Profits tax, royalties, and rent from large-scale mining, petroleum, and gas enterprises that are incorporated.
—	Agricultural income tax from private and incorporated farmers.	—
Taxes on national lottery prizes and gambling.	—	—
Taxes from air, rail, and marine transport.	Fees from water transportation within the state.	—
Taxes from rent of property owned by the federal government.	Taxes from rent of property owned by the state government and income from private properties within the state.	—
Charges and fees on licenses and services of federal government; stamp duties; and rents of federally owned government houses and properties.	Charges and fees on licenses and services of the state government; rents on state-owned houses and properties; and fees on the use of land.	—
—	Profits and sales taxes from individual merchants who are residents of the state.	Profits tax on corporations and tax on dividends paid to shareholders.
—	Forest royalties.	—

Sources: Ethiopian Government Proclamation 33/1992; and Constitution of Ethiopia, December 8, 1994.

[1]Excise taxes are not mentioned in the Proclamation and the Constitution.

Table 2. Ethiopia: Expenditures and Revenue of the Federal and State Governments[1]
(In percent of total)

	1993/94 Preliminary Actual[2]	1994/95 Preliminary Actual[2]	1995/96 Budget
Federal government			
Expenditure share	68.5	60.1	55.4
Revenue share	83.2	85.3	83.9
Difference[3]	14.7	25.2	28.5
State governments			
Expenditure share	31.5	39.9	44.6
Revenue share	16.8	14.7	16.1
Difference[2]	−14.7	−25.2	−28.5

Sources: Ministry of Finance; and authors' estimates.
[1]The fiscal year runs from July 8 to July 7.
[2]Excludes in-kind grants and project grants, data on which will become available after fiscal accounts are closed.
[3]This difference is between revenue and expenditure shares.

ment foreign policy; be responsible for the development, administration, and regulation of air, rail, waterways, and sea transport and major roads, as well as for postal and telecommunications services; and regulate interstate and foreign commerce. Furthermore, the federal government is asked to formulate the country's policies in respect of overall economic and social development, and draw up and implement plans and strategies of development. The Constitution also calls for the federal government to set national standards for policies in, inter alia, public health and education.

Table 4 shows state expenditures by function, as a percent of total consolidated expenditure, for 1993/94, 1994/95, and 1995/96. The share of the states in total public expenditure has increased steadily. Whereas in 1993/94 states were responsible for 31.5 percent of total consolidated expenditure, their share is budgeted to rise to 44.6 percent in 1995/96. The increase is composed of a 6 percentage point increase in the recurrent budget and a 24 percentage point increase in the capital budget. Thus, there has been a strong shift toward devolution of the capital budget to the states since 1993/94.

The shift in expenditure responsibilities between the preliminary outcome for 1993/94 and the budget for 1995/96 was greater in some areas of public expenditure. For instance, the states' share of economic services in recurrent expenditures increased by 8.4 percentage points, owing to devolution in agriculture and natural resources, industry, trade, and tourism, as well as transport and communications. Furthermore, around four-fifths of total consolidated recurrent expenditure on

Table 3. Ethiopia: Revenue Shares of States and Per Capita Revenue Effort

States and Provisional Administrations	State Revenue Shares (In percent of total)				State Per Capita Revenue Collection[1] (In birr)			
	1993/94		1994/95		1993/94		1994/95	
	Budget	Preliminary Actual	Budget	Preliminary Actual	Budget	Preliminary Actual	Budget	Preliminary Actual
Tigray (region 1)	7.1	6.1	5.9	6.8	17.7	12.1	16.0	17.9
Afar (region 2)	1.0	0.9	1.0	0.5	9.7	7.6	10.8	5.7
Amara (region 3)	14.1	14.8	13.7	14.3	8.3	6.9	8.9	9.0
Oromiya (region 4)	23.0	31.5	26.7	29.2	10.9	11.8	13.8	14.6
Somali (region 5)	3.9	5.9	5.4	4.5	17.7	21.3	27.2	21.6
Benishangul/Gumuz (region 6)	0.6	0.5	0.5	0.6	9.3	6.7	9.9	10.6
SEPA[2]	10.3	10.1	10.9	11.5	7.9	6.1	9.1	9.3
Gambela (region 12)	0.3	0.4	0.3	0.5	23.7	22.9	27.7	36.4
Harari (region 13)	2.3	...	0.9	0.6	209.7	...	87.2	55.1
Addis Ababa (region 14)	34.5	27.6	32.5	29.3	133.2	84.6	137.4	119.7
Dire Dawa (region 15)	2.9	2.2	2.2	2.1	169.9	102.9	140.7	125.0

Sources: Ministry of Finance; and authors' estimates.
[1] Based on population data used in 1991/92 elections.
[2] Southern Ethiopian People's Administrative region (formerly regions 7, 8, 9, 10, and 11).

the judiciary, agriculture and natural resources, transport and communications, education and training, and public health were incurred by states in 1994/95 and are budgeted for 1995/96.

The bulk of capital spending on agriculture, water and natural resources, education, public health, and community services is also undertaken by the states. For education, the state share is two-thirds, compared with 80 percent and more in the other three areas. There is a national plan to increase rural roads by 1,000 kilometers annually. The states' 1995/96 capital budget for roads, transport, and communications is designed to meet this target.[2]

Fourth, the states vary widely in population, land area, and economic circumstances. For instance, Oromiya is estimated to have a population of 17.1 million and a land area of about 0.32 million square kilometers, while both Gambela and Harari have populations of only 0.1 million each and land areas of 27,300 square kilometers and 3,000 square kilometers, respectively. Severe economic disparities exist between war- and

---

[2] Ethiopia has about 15,000 kilometers of trunk and link roads and about 8,000 kilometers of rural roads. No major extension of trunk roads is planned by the federal government.

Table 4. Ethiopia: State Expenditures by Function
(In percent of consolidated total expenditure)

	1993/94		1994/95		1995/96
	Budget	Preliminary	Budget	Preliminary	Budget
Total expenditure	39.4	31.5	38.1	38.8	44.6
Total recurrent expenditure	39.1	37.8	41.0	42.1	43.6
General service	28.6	25.4	29.8	33.9	30.6
Organs of state	83.9	56.0	81.9	76.1	77.0
Judiciary	74.2	81.3	75.3	84.9	82.4
Defense	...	...	...	...	...
Public order and security	67.9	64.3	71.2	65.6	71.4
General services	27.7	28.5	29.7	38.3	32.3
Economic services	60.9	57.8	61.6	64.3	66.2
Agriculture and natural resources	78.3	81.1	81.8	83.5	85.0
Industry	56.3	54.7	63.4	68.0	67.0
Mines and energy	27.6	22.0	22.5	29.7	28.7
Trade and tourism	53.0	54.4	61.9	69.6	67.3
Transport and communications	75.8	27.2	77.9	92.2	88.8
Urban development and construction	27.4	18.6	23.4	24.3	22.9
Social services	79.8	72.9	79.4	75.3	81.4
Education and training	86.0	82.7	87.4	86.8	88.3
Culture and sports	58.9	57.6	59.2	64.1	63.8
Public health	83.6	82.0	82.8	84.2	84.3
Labor and social welfare	23.7	32.3	26.1	29.2	30.9
Relief and rehabilitation	28.9	15.1	21.9	10.8	23.5
Pension payments	58.6	59.5	55.8	57.7	52.7
Interest and charges	...	...	...	...	...
Miscellaneous	...	...	...	16.0	15.2
Total capital expenditure	39.8	22.0	34.9	33.0	46.0
Economic development	29.8	16.1	24.1	23.4	38.8
Agriculture, water, and natural resources	57.7	32.7	65.9	54.0	79.8
Mining, industry, commerce, and tourism	26.2	6.4	0.3	5.2	0.6
Electric power	...	...	0.9	0.7	0.4
Roads, transport, and communications	24.9	9.3	9.4	16.0	25.1
Social development	78.9	39.1	79.0	69.0	77.4
Education	73.7	40.3	70.4	59.2	67.5
Public health	87.9	37.5	95.3	85.6	88.1
Community services	78.1	38.9	77.8	69.4	83.9
General services	100.0	43.4	31.6	22.8	28.4
Compensation payments	...	1.6	...	...	...

Source: Ministry of Finance.

drought-affected states. This implies that expenditure needs also vary widely, as do revenue-raising and, hence, fiscal capacities.

Fifth, there are vast differences in per capita expenditure of states with an annual average of about Br 42 per capita for the recurrent budget and Br 19 per capita for the capital budget in 1994/95. The variation among states in per capita recurrent expenditure is between Br 17.3 in Afar and Br 300.3 in Gambela; for per capita capital expenditure, it is between Br 10.6 in Amara and Br 204.6 in Gambela (Table 5). This suggests that the present grant system does not fully capture relative expenditure needs. It further suggests that a reform of the grant system alone is likely to be inadequate to correct historical inequities in Ethiopia, and therefore, an adjustment in the revenue assignments would also be needed. However, such an adjustment may not be feasible in the near term, since the Constitution was approved only at end-1994.

Sixth, state governments in Ethiopia are legally empowered by the Constitution to borrow domestically. The Constitution requires the federal government to determine conditions and terms under which states may borrow from domestic sources. The initial proclamation issued in 1992 set these conditions. Any form of external borrowing by the states is disallowed.

According to the 1992 proclamation, a state could borrow only for projects that have a feasibility study showing its ability to repay the debt, and submit their request for borrowing to the Ministry of Finance or the Ministry for Economic Development and Cooperation.[3] The likely impact of such borrowing on the national budget is an important consideration in granting the approval.

The new Constitution and the 1992 proclamation are unclear on who the lender is (whether the National Bank of Ethiopia or any other commercial bank or financial institution) and what instruments of debt are open to states (for example, treasury bills or bonds). According to proclamations on banking and monetary matters (No. 83 and No. 84 of 1994), commercial banks are not permitted to lend to state governments; and the National Bank may not extend direct credit to any person other than federal government, commercial banks, or other financial institutions.

Finally, there is a wide variation in administrative capacities of the states. For instance, the provisional administrations of Addis Ababa and Oromiya have a relatively better infrastructure and personnel to formulate and implement public programs. By contrast, some states need to be assisted by the federal government.

Differing administrative capacities of the states have important implications for the federal government seeking to exercise adequate control over the country's financial operations and macroeconomic policy. Expenditure devolution in Ethiopia has resulted in diffusion of financial information away from the center. States have, in turn, devolved

---

[3]The study should also include a forecast of income generated by the project, based on realistic economic indicators.

much of the responsibility of the payment to the lower levels of government. But the communication between these levels and a state, and between the states and the center, is often less than satisfactory. The lower levels of government in some states lack both telephones and electricity. Reliability of service is also a problem where such facilities exist, and travel to some areas can take several days.

The Grant System

The Constitution gives state governments four distinct sources of revenue: own taxes, fees, and user charges; taxes shared with the federal government; grants from the federal government; and domestic borrowing. The states have relied principally on federal transfers to support their expenditures because states' own taxes accounted for only 16 percent of consolidated total revenues in the 1995/96 budget, the sharing of revenues from taxes jointly levied and collected by the federal and state governments is still to be defined, and domestic borrowing by the states is yet to assume any role. Until now, only general, nonconditional grants have been extended. The grant system has been modified twice since 1993/94, following the devolution of staff, offices, and responsibilities to regional governments.

As state governments were not able to prepare their own recurrent and capital budgets in 1993/94, allocations were decided mainly by the federal government. Transfers for recurrent expenditure to the states were based on the number of bureaus and staff and on the expenditure needed to maintain the infrastructure. The interstate allocation for the capital budget was made on the basis of the ongoing projects transferred from the federal government to the state governments and an assessment of the states' capacities to implement projects.

The method adopted in 1994/95 and 1995/96 for grants follows a pattern frequently found in other developed and developing countries, combining a formula with ad hoc adjustments. More precisely, the overall size of grants to states was determined by taking into account all important macroeconomic variables (Box 1). First, the size of total resources available to support expenditures of both the federal and the state governments was estimated. The resource envelope for these expenditures included total tax and nontax revenues, counterpart funds, and other foreign assistance to the states. The total resources were then divided between the federal and the state governments on the basis of existing expenditure assignments.

In 1994/95, allocations from the states' overall expenditure ceiling to individual states were made separately for the recurrent budgets and for

Table 5. Ethiopia: Per Capita Expenditure by State and Function, 1994/95[1]
(In birr)

	Tigray	Afar	Amara	Oromiya	Somali	Benishangul/Gumuz	SEPA[2]	Gambela	Harari	Addis Ababa	Dire Dawa
Total expenditure	96.2	37.2	41.1	53.7	57.9	138.0	48.6	508.5	326.8	187.6	193.9
Total recurrent expenditure	51.4	17.3	30.5	42.3	35.9	79.0	32.1	303.8	300.3	111.5	165.6
General service	12.0	7.5	6.1	11.2	17.6	24.7	6.9	139.4	67.9	44.3	39.2
Organs of state	4.8	2.9	1.6	5.9	0.5	7.7	1.6	28.6	11.5	10.1	7.3
Judiciary	1.1	2.3	0.5	0.8	3.2	2.0	0.8	12.5	5.8	3.0	2.2
Defense	...	...	...	...	...	...	...	...	...	...	...
Public order and security	4.4	0.3	2.4	2.8	12.8	8.9	2.8	32.2	36.8	13.6	18.2
General services	1.7	2.0	1.5	1.7	1.2	6.1	1.7	66.1	13.8	17.6	11.6
Economic services	11.2	4.8	6.2	6.3	5.6	15.8	6.6	66.1	21.9	13.2	26.9
Agriculture and natural resources	6.5	2.5	5.5	5.6	1.6	10.5	5.5	44.7	9.2	6.1	21.8
Industry	0.1	0.4	0.1	0.1	1.1	0.4	0.2	2.7	2.3	0.9	0.7
Mines and energy	0.1	0.4	...	0.1	0.1	0.6	0.1	1.8	1.2	0.3	...
Trade and tourism	0.3	0.9	0.2	0.2	2.2	1.4	0.2	7.1	1.2	1.3	2.9
Transport and communcations	0.1	0.1	0.1	...	0.4	0.6	0.2	3.6	3.5	1.6	...
Urban development and construction	4.2	0.5	0.2	0.4	0.2	2.2	0.4	6.3	4.6	3.1	1.5
Social services	24.6	4.5	15.0	20.5	12.1	37.8	16.8	98.3	149.6	53.5	72.6
Education and training	15.0	2.5	10.5	15.8	0.8	19.8	12.4	44.7	80.6	32.2	42.1
Culture and sports	0.3	0.3	0.2	0.2	0.2	1.0	0.4	2.7	2.3	2.3	1.5
Public health	8.5	0.4	3.8	4.2	10.6	14.1	3.5	40.2	63.3	16.9	25.4
Labor and social welfare	0.2	0.4	0.2	0.1	0.2	0.8	0.2	4.5	2.3	1.5	1.5
Relief and rehabiltration	0.6	0.9	0.3	0.2	0.3	2.0	0.3	6.3	1.2	0.5	2.2
Pension payments	3.6	0.5	3.1	4.3	0.6	0.8	1.7	...	61.0	0.5	26.9
Interest and charges	...	...	...	...	...	...	...	...	...	...	...
Miscellaneous	...	...	0.1	...	...	...	...	...	...	...	...

Total capital expenditure	44.8	19.9	10.6	11.4	22.0	59.0	16.5	204.6	26.5	76.2	28.3
Economic development	25.9	16.0	6.2	7.8	11.8	15.4	6.9	110.8	18.4	21.6	8.7
Agriculture, water, and natural resources	14.7	13.8	4.1	5.8	11.3	9.9	4.7	97.4	18.4	16.9	8.7
Mining, industry, commerce, and tourism	0.1	...	0.1	0.3	...	2.2	...	...	...	3.6	...
Electric power	...	...	0.1	...	...	...	...	...	...	...	...
Roads, transport, and communications	11.2	2.3	1.9	1.7	0.6	3.2	2.1	13.4	...	1.1	...
Social development	18.9	3.8	3.9	3.2	9.4	39.6	8.0	76.0	8.1	53.8	19.6
Education	10.2	2.3	1.3	1.1	5.3	12.5	2.6	15.2	2.3	1.9	4.4
Public health	5.3	1.0	1.6	0.9	2.6	8.3	2.7	31.3	4.6	0.3	5.1
Community services	3.4	0.5	1.0	1.2	1.4	18.8	2.7	29.5	1.2	51.7	10.2
General services	...	...	0.5	0.4	0.7	4.0	1.7	17.9	...	0.7	...

Sources: Ministry of Finance; and authors' calculations.
[1] Based on population data used in 1991/92 elections.
[2] Southern Ethiopian People's Administrative region.

> **Box 1. The Grant Framework**
>
> (a) *Federal and state expenditure*
>
> $FR + SR + DD + FFA + SFA = TE = FE + SE$
> $FE = FR + DD + FFA - TR$
> $SE = SR + SFA + TR$
>
> where,
> FR is federal government tax revenue,
> SR is state government tax revenue,
> DD is domestic borrowing,
> FFA is foreign assistance to the federal government,
> SFA is foreign assistance to the states,
> TE is Ethiopia's total public expenditure,
> FE is federal government expenditure,
> SE is state government expenditure, and
> TR are the net transfers from federal to state governments.
>
> (b) *The formula for allocating gross grants in 1995/96*
>
> $TR_i = \frac{1}{3} TR \times [POP_i/POP + ID_i/ID \times POP_i/POP + SRB_i/SRB]$
>
> where,
> i stands for state i,
> POP is population,
> ID is the I-distance indicator,
> SRB is budgeted revenues of state i.

the capital budgets. No precise formula was used for the recurrent expenditure grant. Instead, five broad criteria were used: the number of existing "*weredas*" and "zones" in each state,[4] the 1993/94 allocations, the length of rural roads, the number of state agricultural demonstration centers, and the 1993/94 state expenditure for education and public health. Thus, the authorities have been mainly concerned, it appears, with providing each state with no fewer resources than they received the previous year. A formula was experimented with for capital expenditure in the same year. It included five indicators, with weights shown in parentheses: population (30 percent), I-distance[5] (25 per-

---

[4]The lowest level of subnational government in Ethiopia is *weredas*, followed by zones.

[5]The I-distance indicator is a synthetic variable that seeks to capture the differences in the levels of social and economic development among the states. It is based on eight distinct, quite heterogeneous, variables: length of rural roads, share of rural population in total population, per capita industrial production, per capita crop food production, density of telephone lines, number of post offices, hospital beds in relation to total population, and

cent), regional tax effort (20 percent), 1992/93 capital expenditure (15 percent), and area (10 percent).

In 1995/96, by contrast, the entire state allocation was distributed by means of a general formula, with no distinction between current and capital allocations. It included three variables: population, the state revenues budgeted, and the *I*-distance indicator weighted by population. An equal weight of 33.3 percent was assigned to each (see Box 1). Because of the concern for providing states with no less resources than in the preceding year, the historical levels of expenditures were not very much affected.

Net transfers, that is, actual disbursements from the federal treasury, are the difference between the gross grants determined by the formula and budgeted own revenues of states. The application of the formula means that if actual revenues fall short of budgeted revenues, the states' budgets can face severe expenditure compression.

As in 1994/95, substantial differences between the allocation generated by the formula and the amounts allocated in the previous year emerged for a number of states in 1995/96. They were adjusted with supplementary discretionary allocations, so that the impact on state allocations would be gradual (Table 6). Allocations for 1995/96 show a redistributive pattern, where the poorest states receive a net per capita amount well above the national average; in part, this redistribution arises from a hidden factor, that is, the poorest states are also the smallest. The substantial gross grants that benefit Addis Ababa and, to a lesser extent, Dire Dawa are explained by their city-state characteristics, that is, by their high revenue-generating capacity.

While the poorest states benefit from higher per capita transfers than the rest of the country, the overall redistributive impact of the present system is difficult to ascertain. This is because of the lack of information on extrabudgetary donor assistance and because redistribution and equity aspects have to be evaluated in Ethiopia according to inter-ethnic fairness, historical neglect of certain regions, and the differing impact of war, drought, and famine on various parts of the country.

Problems with the Existing Grant Formula

Establishing a grant system that is simple, fair, and transparent is difficult for any federal country. The problems are compounded in

---

pupils in elementary schools in relation to total population. These variables are combined by means of a rather awkward formula aimed at minimizing the intercorrelation between variables. This indicator is weighted by population. In other words, the choice of the *I*-distance indicator is dictated by the desire to achieve interstate equity in the distribution of grants, against the background of uneven revenue-generating capacities.

Table 6. Ethiopia: Allocation of Grants to States, 1995/1996
(In millions of birr unless otherwise indicated)

States and Provisional Administrations	According to the Formula	Difference over 1994/95	Discretionary Adjustment	Initial Budget Allocation	Additional Allocation	Final Allocation	From Domestic Sources	Foreign Grants and Loans	Final Allocation Per Capita (In birr)
Tigray	295.9	−31.9	32.6	328.5	14.4	342.9	319.3	23.6	105.5
Afar	128.3	−13.5	13.8	142.1	6.3	148.4	121.6	26.8	189.0
Amara	811.8	70.4	1.9	813.7	39.6	853.3	766.7	86.6	62.5
Oromiya	1,076.4	36.9	2.6	1,079.0	52.4	1,131.4	982.2	148.6	66.5
Somali	164.1	−1.2	1.6	165.7	7.9	173.6	151.1	22.5	98.7
Benishangul/Gumuz	32.4	−74.3	74.4	106.8	1.6	108.4	82.5	25.9	219.1
SEPA[1]	649.0	41.0	1.5	650.5	31.5	682.0	615.6	66.4	64.8
Gambela	9.6	−80.6	80.6	90.2	0.5	90.7	72.7	18.0	810.5
Harari	15.0	−25.7	25.7	40.7	0.7	41.4	38.0	3.4	476.4
Addis Ababa	480.1	109.7	1.1	481.2	23.4	504.6	397.8	106.8	241.1
Dire Dawa	33.2	−3.3	3.4	36.6	1.6	38.2	32.8	5.4	277.4
Total	3,695.8	...	239.2	3,935.0	179.9	4,115.0	3,580.9	534.0	82.4

Sources: Ministry of Economic Development and Cooperation; and authors' calculations.
[1]Southern Ethiopian People's Administrative region.

Ethiopia by the lack of adequate and up-to-date information, the shortcomings of the *I*-distance indicator, the lack of incentives for enhancing states' tax efforts, the need for interstate equity, and the need for encouraging the implementation of minimum standards. The reform options examined in the following section seek to remedy these weaknesses.

Lack of Adequate and Up-to-Date Information

In Ethiopia, population plays a dominant role in the existing formula, but population data are outdated. For 1995/96 allocations, the population data from the 1991/92 elections were used. The mobility of the population and differences in the rate of population growth among states since the last census are not taken into account in the present grant system. The use of old population data thus favors static states and penalizes the states, including the cities, that experience inflows of migrants. The same problem carries over to most variables used for calculating the *I*-distance. Many of these variables are compiled through surveys, often conducted at long intervals.

Shortcomings of the *I*-Distance Indicator

The *I*-distance indicator in use in Ethiopia suffers from a number of shortcomings:
- The variables included in the index are highly heterogeneous. Variables, such as per capita food crop and industrial production, are related to the level of economic development. Others reflect the existing level of public services, both national and states, such as post offices and hospital beds, thereby capturing expenditure needs. But the use of the share of urban population in total population has no clear meaning in the Ethiopian context. Urban development is an indicator of growth, but then expenditure needs also tend to be concentrated in urban areas.
- A given indicator could have a different meaning for different states. A case in point is the road density in sparsely populated (desert) and highly populated (urban) areas;
- Many needs-based indicators are excluded from the *I*-distance index, such as the share of population with access to clean water, the number of victims of war, the rate of infant mortality, and the proportion of population below the poverty line.
- The construction of the index is not transparent and its application is discretionary. The formula, which is quite complex, is questionable on both economic and statistical grounds. Indeed, the

final value of *I*-distance appears to be highly dependent on the choice of the first variable fed into the computer program.

Lack of Incentive for Revenue Enhancement

The formula does not necessarily stimulate the states' revenue efforts. This is because greater revenue efforts will lead to higher gross grants, and, at the same time, this revenue will be deducted from the gross grants to determine the net transfer to each state.[6]

The present formula could also create competition among states to overstate their budgeted revenue. It could lead them to embark on ambitious expenditure plans to have a larger entitlement from the common pool. The cost of the revenue shortfall might then have to be borne by the whole country if the state exercised its right to borrow domestically. This problem would be obviated to some extent if actual revenue collected in the preceding year were used instead of budgeted revenue.

Need for Interstate Equity

This goal has the highest priority in the present grant system of Ethiopia. Each state should perceive that the formula provides an equitable distribution of national resources. As in most developing countries, Ethiopia's effort to reduce disparities in levels of public services in different states is plagued by the problems of identifying indicators of need and by severe data limitations, compounded by the continuing redefinition of interstate boundaries.

Need to Encourage the Implementation of Minimum Standards

Ethiopia's Constitution (Article 51) mandates that the federal government establish national standards in health and education. The federal government is also committed to foreign donors to spend the counterpart funds on social programs. In 1995/96, counterpart funds generated resources for the budget amounting to 3.3 percent of GDP. This would require some built-in incentive in the formula for the state to spend more on these areas. Since grants to the states in Ethiopia are

---

[6]The following example clarifies this point. Suppose a state has no own tax revenue. In this case, gross grants will coincide with the net grant amount. As this state starts to collect revenue, it will receive larger gross grants. An increase in own tax revenue will have a negative impact on the net grants; this effect is greater than the positive impact on gross grants. States with rapidly expanding revenue will eventually end up with no net grants, that is, they will find themselves in a situation in which they have to finance their expenditures entirely out of their revenue.

general purpose, there is no mechanism at present to ensure that the minimum national standards are being adhered to. It can, however, be argued that, in Ethiopia's case, even if certain standards were established by the federal government, their monitoring would be extremely difficult in view of its weak administrative capacity.

Options for Improving the Grant System

There are various ways in which many of the above-noted drawbacks of the grant system could be rectified, while ensuring that the grant formula is simple, fair, and transparent. A few options from a range of possibilities are presented below. For illustrative purposes, the impact of different reform options is compared with actual 1995/96 allocations.

Simple Indicators of Inequality and Need

It is easy to replace the present *I*-distance indicator with a more transparent, less discretion-prone indicator of inequality among states. Two possibilities are discussed here. The first is based on two proxies of the relative expenditure need of states, namely the ratio of students to total population and the number of medical personnel to total population. The second possibility uses proxies for economic development or wealth: the density of telephones and electricity consumption in a state. The formulas assign values of over one to states that are below the national average and values of less than one to those that are above.[7] These values are multiplied by population, as in the present formula used in Ethiopia. Table 7 shows a state's allocation and per capita gross and net transfers (that is, after adjusting for own revenues).

---

[7]Each indicator is calculated to measure, for each state, the difference from the national average. That is, for the first variant:
$S_i = Pop_i/Pop - St_i/St$ and $H_i = Pop_i/Pop - He_i/He$,
where
  St_i is the number of students in all schools in state i,
  He_i is the number of medical personnel in state i, and
  Pop_i is total population of state i.
  St and He, and Pop are the corresponding values for the whole country. The two indicators are linked by multiplication.
For the second, the income-related indicator:
$E_i = Pop_i/Pop - El_i/El$ and,
$P_i = Pop_i/Pop - Ph_i/Ph$,
where
  El_i is electricity consumption in state i,
  Ph_i is the number of telephone lines in state i, and
  El and Ph are the corresponding values for the entire country.

Table 7. Ethiopia: Options for Allocating Grants—Simpler Indicators of Inequality and Need[1]

States and Provisional Administrations	Total Existing Allocations (In millions of birr)	Per Capita Transfers (In birr)		Modified Transfer Based on (In millions of birr)		Gross Per Capita Transfer Based on (In birr)		Net Per Capita Transfer Based on (In birr)	
		Gross	Net	Need[2]	Wealth[3]	Need[2]	Wealth[3]	Need[2]	Wealth[3]
Tigray	295.9	91.0	75.0	218.4	219.8	67.2	67.6	51.2	51.6
Afar	128.3	163.4	152.5	49.5	47.0	63.1	59.9	52.2	49.0
Amara	811.8	59.5	50.6	873.4	872.5	64.0	63.9	55.1	55.0
Oromiya	1,076.4	63.1	49.2	1,174.6	1,195.1	68.8	70.0	55.0	56.2
Somali	164.1	93.3	66.1	151.5	146.3	86.2	83.2	59.0	56.0
Benishangul/Gumuz	32.4	65.5	55.7	30.2	28.8	61.0	58.2	51.1	48.3
SEPA[4]	649.0	61.7	52.6	648.2	671.4	61.6	63.8	52.5	54.7
Gambela	9.6	85.8	58.5	9.5	9.2	85.2	82.2	58.0	54.9
Harari	15.0	172.6	82.3	15.0	14.7	172.9	169.5	82.6	79.2
Addis Ababa	480.1	229.4	92.2	491.5	457.6	234.8	218.6	97.6	81.4
Dire Dawa	33.2	241.1	98.0	33.9	33.4	246.4	242.6	103.3	99.6

Sources: Ministry of Economic Development and Cooperation; and authors' estimates.

[1]To include two indicators of need or wealth as defined in the text.
[2]Defined as relative shares of students in population and the number of medical personnel in population, weighted equally.
[3]Defined as the relative shares of telephone use and electricity consumption in population, weighted equally.
[4]Southern Ethiopian People's Administrative region.

Interestingly, the results are broadly similar to those arrived at by applying the existing formula. Amara and Oromiya gain somewhat at the expense of Tigray and Afar. There is no significant difference in the results based on need and wealth proxies. There is some advantage of using the latter, since information for its calculation is readily available from national electric and telephone companies.

Different Weights for the Same Variables

This possibility consists of changing the weights assigned to different variables (and replacing the I-distance indicator with a new proxy for inequality). In this option, the weight assigned to population is increased from the existing 33.3 percent. One of the objectives behind this simulation is to gauge the sensitivity of the grant formula to the weight assigned to the population variable. Using population as the major criterion for grant distribution amounts to assuming that expenditure needs are identical in per capita terms across all areas. Once again, two variants are presented here. In the first one, the population share is increased to 50 percent; in the second, the share is increased to 70 percent.

As expected, transfers to Tigray, Afar, Amara, Oromiya, Benishangul/Gumuz, and SEPA, which are among the poorest states, are higher than in the previous option (Table 8). Per capita gross and net transfers are now negatively correlated with the level of development. The negative correlation increases with the weight assigned to population. Grant allocations for Addis Ababa are clear evidence of this relationship. The gross per capita transfer decreases from Br 182.4 to Br 139.1 when the weight of population increases from 50 percent to 70 percent, compared with Br 234.8 and Br 218.6 in the previous options in Table 7. Similar results hold for Dire Dawa. Such a system—with a high weight of population at the expense of the weight of own revenue effort—would reduce the net per capita transfer amount for states with a strong revenue base such as Addis Ababa. This could, in turn, blunt their incentive to expand their tax collections.

Additional Variables

The additional variables introduced in the simulations are area and a lump-sum grant for each state irrespective of its size or needs. The rationale for using area is that it accounts for differences in the cost of providing services. Public administrations in sparsely populated states face higher production costs than those in more populated areas. Higher costs for building infrastructure and for shipping supplies are some of the examples. Scale economies in the production of services

Table 8. Ethiopia: Options for Allocating Grants—Using Different Weights

States and Provisional Administrations	Total Existing Allocations (In millions of birr)	Per Capita Transfers (In birr)		Greater Weight for Population[1] (In millions of birr)	Per Capita Transfers (In birr)		Greater Weight for Population[2] (In millions of birr)	Per Capita Transfers (In birr)	
		Gross	Net		Gross	Net		Gross	Net
Tigray	295.9	91.0	75.0	225.0	69.2	53.3	231.2	71.1	55.1
Afar	128.3	163.4	152.5	49.8	63.4	52.5	53.1	67.6	56.7
Amara	811.8	59.5	50.6	906.9	66.4	57.5	948.1	69.4	60.6
Oromiya	1,076.4	63.1	49.2	1,211.9	71.0	57.2	1,232.2	72.2	58.4
Somali	164.1	93.3	66.1	142.3	80.9	53.7	137.4	78.1	50.9
Benishangul/Gumuz	32.4	65.5	55.7	30.7	62.1	52.3	33.1	66.9	57.0
SEPA[3]	649.0	61.7	52.6	698.1	66.4	57.2	730.1	69.4	60.3
Gambela	9.6	85.8	58.5	9.0	80.1	52.9	8.7	77.7	50.4
Harari	15.0	172.6	82.3	12.7	145.6	55.3	10.2	117.0	26.6
Addis Ababa	480.1	229.4	92.2	381.9	182.4	45.3	291.1	139.1	1.9
Dire Dawa	33.2	241.1	98.0	27.6	200.5	57.4	20.6	149.9	6.8

Sources: Ministry of Economic Development and Cooperation; and authors' estimates.
[1]Population with a weight of 0.5 and revenue and inequality with a weight of 0.25 each.
[2]Population with a weight of 0.7 and revenue and inequality with a weight of 0.15 each.
[3]Southern Ethiopian People's Administrative region.

such as health care, education, and water provide another justification for using area as an indicator.

The rationale for introducing a lump-sum grant relies on indivisibilities. That is, costs for some activities do not depend on the size of the population served, such as general administration, roads, and airports. It should be noted, however, that area and the lump-sum grant account for different factors. Whereas area is related to density of population, the lump-sum grant benefits states that are very small.

However, the lump-sum grant, when assigned a large weight in the formula, may stimulate formation of new inefficient jurisdictions. Some countries, such as Colombia, are presently confronted with this problem, because they give relatively high weight to lump-sum grants.

Two simulations are reported in Table 9. In the first, the inequality indicator is replaced by an area indicator with a weight of 20 percent. The weight for population is 60 percent, and that of own revenue is also 20 percent. In the second simulation, the weight of population falls to 55 percent, to make room for the lump-sum grant that has a weight of 5 percent. Table 10 reports the results of the simulations with a lower weight given to the own revenue effort variable (10 percent) than in the preceding simulation.[8]

The introduction of two new variables (area and lump-sum grant) allows a better adaptation of the formula to commonly perceived expenditure needs. For example, the Somali state, which is poor, spread out, and sparsely populated, would benefit from the new distribution compared with the baseline allocation for 1995/96. Small and poor states like Benishangul/Gumuz and Gambela are now situated well above the national average. Inclusion of area in the formula appears to give a relatively fairer distribution of grants compared with the baseline. The introduction of a lump-sum grant benefits particularly the smaller states (such as Afar, Benishangul/Gumuz, Gambela, and Harari), as well as the provisional administrations of Addis Ababa and Dire Dawa, compared with the previous option. This benefit disappears when the share of revenue in the formula is decreased.

Conclusions

The existing grant system in Ethiopia plays an important role in financing states and has been modified twice since 1993/94. Transfers to

---

[8]The negative net transfer for Addis Ababa in Table 10 implies that either Addis Ababa will have to transfer part of its resources to other regions or the federal government will have to find additional resources to offset the negative entry.

Table 9. Ethiopia: Options for Allocating Grants—Additional Variables

States and Provisional Administrations	Total Existing Allocations (In millions of birr)	Per Capita Transfers (In birr)		Including Area[1] (In millions of birr)	Per Capita Transfers (In birr)		Including Area and Lump Sum[2] (In millions of birr)	Per Capita Transfers (In birr)	
		Gross	Net		Gross	Net		Gross	Net
Tigray	295.9	91.0	75.0	237.1	72.9	56.9	241.8	74.4	58.4
Afar	128.3	163.4	152.5	105.3	134.1	123.2	119.2	151.8	140.9
Amara	811.8	59.5	50.6	807.8	59.2	50.3	774.1	56.7	47.8
Oromiya	1,076.4	63.1	49.2	1,165.9	68.3	54.5	1,119.6	65.6	51.8
Somali	164.1	93.3	66.1	285.9	162.6	135.4	296.2	168.5	141.3
Benishangul/Gumuz	32.4	65.5	55.7	59.1	119.5	109.7	74.1	149.7	139.9
SEPA[3]	649.0	61.7	52.6	630.7	60.0	50.8	608.6	57.9	48.7
Gambela	9.6	85.8	58.5	25.4	227.2	200.0	41.8	373.7	346.4
Harari	15.0	172.6	82.3	12.4	142.5	52.2	28.9	332.2	241.8
Addis Ababa	480.1	229.4	92.2	333.2	159.2	22.0	342.2	163.5	26.3
Dire Dawa	33.2	241.1	98.0	33.1	240.2	97.2	49.4	358.5	215.5

Sources: Ministry of Economic Development and Cooperation; and authors' estimates.
[1] Population with a weight of 0.60 and revenue and area with a weight of 0.20 each.
[2] Population with a weight of 0.55, area and revenue with a weight of 0.20 each, and lump sum with a weight of 0.05.
[3] Southern Ethiopian People's Administrative region.

Table 10. Ethiopia: Options for Allocating Grants: Using Different Variables

States and Provisional Administrations	Total Existing Allocations (In millions of birr)	Per Capita Transfers (In birr)		Including Area[1] (In millions of birr)	Per Capita Transfers (In birr)		Including Area and Lump Sum[2] (In millions of birr)	Per Capita Transfers (In birr)	
		Gross	Net		Gross	Net		Gross	Net
Tigray	295.9	91.0	75.0	239.4	73.6	57.7	244.2	75.1	59.1
Afar	128.3	163.4	152.5	107.5	136.9	126.1	121.4	154.6	143.8
Amara	811.8	59.5	50.6	858.1	62.9	54.0	824.4	60.4	51.5
Oromiya	1,076.4	63.1	49.2	1,193.5	69.9	56.1	1,147.1	67.2	53.4
Somali	164.1	93.3	66.1	278.9	158.6	131.4	289.2	164.5	137.3
Benshangul/Gumuz	32.4	65.5	55.7	60.7	122.8	112.9	75.7	153.0	143.2
SEPA[3]	649.0	61.7	52.6	668.4	63.5	54.4	646.3	61.4	52.3
Gambela	9.6	85.8	58.5	25.0	223.2	196.0	41.4	369.7	342.4
Harari	15.0	172.6	82.3	9.8	112.2	21.9	26.2	301.8	211.5
Addis Ababa	480.1	229.4	92.2	228.7	109.2	−27.9	237.7	113.6	−23.6
Dire Dawa	33.2	241.1	98.0	25.9	187.9	44.8	42.2	306.2	163.1

Sources: Ministry of Economic Development and Cooperation; and authors' estimates.
[1] Population with a weight of 0.7, area with a weight of 0.2, and revenue with a weight of 0.1.
[2] Population with a weight of 0.65, area with a weight of 0.20, lump sum with a weight of 0.05, and revenue with a weight of 0.1.
[3] Southern Ethiopian People's Adminstrative region.

state governments in Ethiopia have consisted of general purpose block grants only. No specific, conditional grants are presently extended. Given the need to achieve multiple goals and the need to encourage the states to provide at least the minimum standard of services, it may be more appropriate to use a combination of general and specific grants, although in Ethiopia's case the mechanism for monitoring the implementation of these standards may be lacking. General purpose grants, however, are preferred by decentralized units in a federal structure because they do not intrude on their decision-making authority. They also render the distribution of the national resources by the federal government more transparent.

The options for reform presented in this chapter do not consider the introduction of specific grants, assuming a continuing strong preference in Ethiopia for a system of block grants. These options seek to better equip the system to meet its objectives. The initial reform steps could include using more transparent and reliable variables in the present formula, altering the weights assigned to different variables and introducing new variables. The initial reforms could include the following:

- Replacing the present I-distance indicator with a simpler and more transparent alternative.
- Increasing the weight for population.
- Reducing the weight for state revenue.
- Including a state's area.
- Giving a small lump-sum grant, to take into account indivisibilities.
- Applying the grant-determining framework to total resources net of the states' own tax revenues.

The simulations indicate that it is difficult to assign a precise weight for each indicator. To some extent, this would have to be determined by the political process.

The establishment of an independent Grants Commission would also help, by providing the framework and necessary input for strengthening the grant formula. This commission could make recommendations on grant-related matters to the Federal Council, as envisaged under the Constitution.[9]

It should be noted that although the options discussed in the chapter represent improvements over the existing grant formula, they nevertheless amount to "gap filling," that is, they seek to bridge the gap between the state's actual revenues and expenditures rather than to provide transfers on the basis of relative expenditure needs and relative revenue capacities.

---

[9]The Federal Council in Ethiopia is composed of members elected by the State Council.

21

India

RICHARD HEMMING, NEVEN MATES, AND BARRY POTTER

India has a complex system of intergovernmental fiscal relations. This complexity has its roots in a number of factors, including substantial ethnic, social, and economic disparities among regions, as well as the long-standing vertical imbalance between the expenditure and revenue-raising responsibilities of the state governments. This imbalance is in part covered by revenue-sharing arrangements. States also receive a variety of grants from the center, but even then states run deficits. Despite the formal absence of independent borrowing powers, states borrow both from the central government and state-owned commercial banks, with attendant macroeconomic risks. For these reasons, and because of the clear trends toward structural transformation of the economy—away from central planning—and increased claims of the states for fiscal autonomy, a comprehensive reform of center-state fiscal relations is needed.

Structure of Government

Until 1871, government in India was completely centralized, with all provincial spending financed by fixed grants from the central government. In that year, some government departments, together with their sources of revenue, were transferred to provinces, while remaining provincial expenditure continued to be financed by grants from the central government. Revenue sharing for major taxes was introduced in

---

The authors are grateful to Dimitri Tzanninis for his assistance and comments.

1877. The Government of India Act of 1919 formally separated central and provincial revenue sources, which resulted in central government deficits that had to be covered by transfers from provinces.

The current Indian federal structure has its origins in the Government of India Act of 1935 and, following independence, in the Indian Constitution of 1950. India is not a federation but a union state, with a higher degree of centralization than found in most federations. The central (or union) government is empowered to limit the rights of the 25 state governments (and 7 union territories), and even to take over completely their administration in emergencies (including financial emergencies).

Until 1993, the Constitution did not discuss local governments. The authority of local governments—encompassing a variety of urban and rural local bodies—is still determined by the individual states and it can always be revoked. There is wide variation in expenditure and tax assignments, and transfer arrangements across local governments. A 1993 amendment to the Constitution provided for the formation of state finance commissions to review and recommend changes to fiscal relations between the states and local governments.

The Constitution specifies the expenditure responsibilities of different levels of government in three lists defining central powers, state powers, and concurrent powers where both levels of government can exercise authority, although the central government is granted supremacy. It also specifies the taxation powers of the central government and the state governments, and the principles governing the sharing of revenue and certain other resources. A Finance Commission, which is appointed every five years, recommends how the proceeds of taxes should be shared between the central government and states, how the share of states should be divided among them, and how to distribute grants-in-aid to the states. The Planning Commission plays the lead role in deciding the distribution of development grants from the center to the states.

Current Arrangements[1]

Expenditure Assignment

Consolidated government expenditure has been in the range of 27–30 percent of GDP during the 1990s. Table 1 shows that the central government is responsible for a little more than half of the total, and

---

[1]There are many comprehensive descriptions of the Indian federal structure and finance—see, for example, Bagchi and others (1992), Gulati (1987), and Wallich (1982).

Table 1. India: Intergovernmental Fiscal Relations
(In percent of GDP)

	1990/91	1991/92	1992/93	1993/94	1994/95	1995/96[1]	1996/97[2]
Central government							
Gross revenue	13.5	14.5	14.2	12.6	13.2	13.4	14.1
Tax revenue	10.8	10.9	10.6	9.4	9.7	10.1	10.6
Nontax revenue and grants	2.7	3.6	3.6	3.2	3.5	3.3	3.5
States' share of tax revenue (−)	−2.7	−2.8	−2.9	−2.8	−2.6	−2.7	−2.8
Net revenue	10.8	11.7	11.3	9.8	10.6	10.7	11.3
Expenditure	19.1	17.6	17.0	17.3	16.7	16.4	16.3
Of which:							
Grants to states	2.7	2.8	2.6	2.6	2.1	2.0	1.9
Net loans to states	1.9	1.5	1.2	1.3	1.5	1.3	1.4
Deficit	8.3	5.9	5.7	7.4	6.1	5.6	5.0
State governments							
Own tax revenue	5.7	5.8	5.7	5.7	5.8	5.8	5.8
Nontax revenue	1.7	2.1	1.8	1.9	2.3	2.0	1.6
Shared taxes and grants from center	5.4	5.6	5.5	5.4	4.8	4.7	4.7
Expenditure	16.3	16.5	16.0	15.6	15.7	15.5	14.9
Deficit	3.5	3.1	3.0	2.5	2.9	3.1	2.9
Consolidated government							
Revenue	19.7	21.1	20.6	19.1	20.3	19.8	20.1
Expenditure	29.9	28.7	28.0	27.8	27.6	27.3	26.7
Deficit	10.2	7.6	7.4	8.7	7.3	7.6	6.6
Resources transferred to states	7.2	7.1	6.8	6.7	6.3	6.0	6.0

Source: Data provided by the Indian authorities.
[1]Revised estimates.
[2]Budget estimates.

state governments for a little less than half. The Constitution assigns a wide range of government functions to the states. In particular, most spending related to agriculture and social policies is included in the state list. Although the concurrent list admits wider responsibilities for the states in the economic field, most major industries, even if not on the union list, are controlled by the central government. The actual division of expenditure responsibilities is shown in Table 2.

Tax Assignment

One objective of the Constitution is to prevent overlapping tax powers, which translates into a requirement that one type of tax can be levied only by one level of the government. The central government is assigned the most important taxes with economy-wide implications. However, while some taxes are levied by the center for its exclusive use,

Table 2. India: Central and State Government Expenditures and Taxes

Central government expenditures	Central government taxes
Defense	Corporate profit tax
Railways, highways, airways, and shipping	Import duties
Post and telecommunications	Property and wealth taxes (nonagricultural)
Heavy industry	Income tax surcharges
Strategic industries	Stock exchange stamp duties
External affairs	
Foreign trade	
Shared expenditures	*Shared taxes*
Population and family planning	Personal income tax (except agriculture and professional self-employment)
	Excise duties (except on alcohol and narcotics)
	Property and wealth taxes (agriculture)
	Tax on railway tickets
State government expenditures	*State government taxes*
Irrigation	Personal income tax (agriculture and professional self-employment)
Power	Sales tax (including sales tax on interstate sales)
Education	Excise duties on alcohol and narcotics
Health	Urban property tax
Rural development	Mineral taxes
Roads	Stamp and registration duties (except stock exchange)
Public order	
Culture	

Source: Information provided by the Indian authorities.

the revenue from other taxes imposed and collected by the center is shared with the states (see below). The central government levies a personal income tax on all sources of income, except that from agriculture and of self-employed professionals, a corporate profit tax, income tax surcharges, and import duties. State governments are entitled to raise taxes on agricultural income and the income of self-employed professionals, but agricultural income is taxed in only a few states.

The authority to levy taxes on property, wealth, estates, and capital transactions is split between the center and the states according to whether they are related to agricultural or nonagricultural property. This appears to be consistent with the principle that lower-tier governments should be assigned taxes from relatively immobile tax bases. In practice, however, agricultural wealth and property are not taxed in any state. The central government is entitled to raise taxes on nonagricultural estates. However, because all proceeds from these taxes have to be transferred to the states, the central government does not have much incentive to levy such taxes. The states can levy stamp and registration duties, as well as a tax on urban immovable property.

Table 3. India: Structure of Government Tax Revenue, 1995/96
(Percentage shares)

	Central Government		State Governments	
	Before revenue sharing	After revenue sharing	Before revenue sharing	After revenue sharing
Tax revenue	62.1	44.5	37.9	55.5
Income tax	100.0	27.9	...	72.1
Profit tax	100.0	100.0	...	...
Excise duties	100.0	54.1	...	45.9
Sales tax	5.0	5.0	95.0	95.0
Import duties	100.0	100.0	...	...
Other	25.3	25.3	74.7	74.7

Source: Data provided by the Indian authorities.

The central government imposes excise duties at the production stage, except on alcohol and narcotics, which are taxed by the states. A sales tax on a fairly wide range of goods is the states' main source of revenue. A coordinated conversion of state sales taxes into state value-added taxes is just beginning. Only limited services are taxed. States also impose a tax on sales to other states, the ceiling on which is fixed by the center at 4 percent. The states have conceded their right to levy sales tax on certain products (textiles, tobacco, and sugar) to the central government, but the revenue raised by excises on these products is passed on to the states. The distribution of revenue implied by this tax assignment is given in Table 3.

Revenue Sharing

As Table 1 indicates, consolidated government revenue is about 20 percent of GDP, of which two-thirds is collected by the central government and one-third by the states. Given that expenditure is almost evenly divided, there is a large vertical imbalance in state government finances. The gap between states' revenue and expenditure is bridged in part by revenue sharing. The Constitution provides that the sharing of nonagricultural, noncorporate income tax revenue is mandatory, while excise duty revenue may be shared with the states if parliament so decides. The central government retains corporate profit tax, import duty, and income tax surcharge revenue for its exclusive use. Revenue shares are not specified in the Constitution, but are recommended for a five-year period by finance commissions. While the Constitution limits finance commissions to making recommendations, its recommendations have almost always been ratified.

The share of the states in income tax revenue has tended to be increased by past finance commissions, but it was reduced from 85 percent to 77.5 percent by the most recent Tenth Finance Commission (for the period 1995–2000). The distribution of the shared revenue among the states does not follow the derivation principle. Rather, the share of each state is determined by a formula specified by the finance commission. In this sense, revenue shares can be seen as general grants to states. The formula for the five-year period beginning in 1995 attaches a weight of 20 percent to each state's population, 60 percent to per capita income, 5 percent to area, 5 percent to economic and rural infrastructure needs, and 10 percent to tax effort.

Under the new arrangements, 47.5 percent (previously 45 percent) of excise duty revenue is passed on to states. Forty percent is shared among states according to the formula used to share income tax. The remaining 7.5 percent is shared in proportion to nonplan deficits (after revenue sharing), which reflect mainly current transactions. This represents an explicit, if limited, attempt to link shared revenues to the degree of vertical imbalance. Revenues from excises on textiles, tobacco, and sugar are distributed on the basis of estimated local consumption. Shared revenue accounts for about 55 percent of transfers from the central government to state governments. Table 3 also shows the distribution of revenue after revenue sharing.

Grants

Revenue sharing notwithstanding, vertical imbalances remain, which are filled through grants. The central government provides many types of grant to the state governments. Grants-in-aid—which represent only about 7 percent of transfers from the center to the states—are also recommended by finance commissions and are intended to close residual deficits on the state governments' nonplan revenue accounts. Gap filling has in most cases been determined by projecting historical trends in revenue and expenditure. However, the Ninth Finance Commission (1990–95) introduced a controversial normative element into its approach, taking account of the special needs of each state.

The second group of grants is decided by the Planning Commission,[2] which has to approve state development programs as a condition for development grants to be paid by the center. The Planning Commission

---

[2]In contrast to finance commissions, which are appointed every five years, the Planning Commission is a permanent body, which has primary authority over government capital spending. The role of the Planning Commission may decline over time as the Indian economy evolves into a more fully market-oriented one.

used to plan comprehensively all development expenditure by the states, and grants were given for specific projects. Subsequently, plan grants have been given as block grants determined by the "Gadgil" formula, which currently reflects weights of 60 percent for population, 25 percent for per capita income, 7.5 percent for a combined index of tax effort, literacy, and completion of foreign aid projects, and 7.5 percent for special problems. Plan loans to states are distributed according to the same formula. Of the total funds distributed, loans make up 70 percent and grants make up 30 percent. Planning Commission transfers account for about 35 percent of the total, half of which supports state plans while the other half goes to centrally sponsored schemes.

In addition to funds allocated on the preceding basis, states can receive specific purpose grants at the discretion of the Planning Commission, such as assistance for hill area development, tribal area development, and matching grants for foreign aid projects. These have accounted for an increasing share of the grants to states in recent years. One implication of specific purpose grants is that although expenditure responsibilities have remained basically unchanged, a growing share of spending is dictated by the central government. Through its various ministries, the central government gives grants to state governments undertaking nationally important development or welfare programs. The central government also provides discretionary grants for a variety of reasons, most notably in the event of emergencies or to improve specific services.

Not only does the grant system still leave vertical imbalances—which necessitate borrowing—but it also does not fully address horizontal imbalances among states. Recognizing that they have weak revenue bases, because of their physical and economic characteristics, certain states have special category status. Both revenue sharing and grant formulas are biased in their favor, although not by enough to compensate for their additional expenditure needs. However, the largest horizontal imbalance remains in respect of poorer "general category" states.

Borrowing

According to the Constitution, only the central government is entitled to borrow abroad. The states are, in principle, entitled to borrow domestically, but they have to get permission from the central government if they have any outstanding liabilities to the center. All state governments have such liabilities. Market borrowing, in practice mainly from banks, used to be a captive market under the control of the central government, since the latter defined a portion of assets that banks had to invest in state securities approved by the central government. At present, the Reserve Bank of India in effect allocates state securities to commercial banks. The central government also on lends shares in funds from small savings at post offices to states; the shares reflect finance commission recommendations.

Since 1985, the states have not been allowed to run overdrafts with the Reserve Bank, and their net credit has to respect prescribed ways and means limits. However, the central government sometimes provides special assistance to clear overdrafts or short-term outstanding debts of individual states. The total indebtedness of the state governments stood at a relatively high level at the end of 1992/93, exceeding 20 percent of GDP, of which nearly two thirds was outstanding liabilities to the central government. Successive finance commissions have decided that part of state government debts should either be rescheduled or written off. The Tenth Finance Commission (1995–2000), for example, has recommended debt relief that is linked to fiscal performance, as an incentive, and to fiscal stress, out of necessity.

Administrative Structure

Tax Administration

Tax assignment is based in significant measure on the relative efficiency of the central government and state governments in collecting taxes. Thus, all central taxes are collected by the central tax authority and all local taxes are collected by state tax authorities. This arrangement, while sound in principle, raises some problems, particularly in the context of revenue sharing. The fact that the center retains different percentages of different taxes—with the rest being passed on to the states—may provide an incentive to concentrate the collection effort and resources of the central tax administration on those taxes (such as the corporate income tax and import duties) it retains in full, or in a higher percentage. The fact that separate agencies are responsible for income taxation based on the origin of income (agricultural versus nonagricultural) may create difficulties for the reform of the personal income tax. Similarly, the fact that the central government is primarily responsible for taxing production, while the states are responsible for taxing retail sales, may make it more difficult to reform domestic consumption taxes.

Budget Formulation and Implementation

The Indian fiscal year runs from April to March. The central government budget is formulated beginning in October. It is presented to parliament by the end of February and approved shortly thereafter. State budgets are formulated in tandem with the central budget and approved at the state level usually in March. There are linked, yet separate, budget formulation procedures for plan and nonplan spending. Even though an integrated budget is presented to each state parliament, separation of budget-setting procedures causes problems. In particular, the plan embodies an attempt to reconcile central spending priorities with the attraction to states of securing central resources to support local projects. In discussions with the Planning Commission, states overestimate own revenues and underestimate nonplan expenditure, thus presenting a larger-than-justified absorptive capacity for new capital projects. Discussions with finance commissions, by contrast, lay more emphasis on the prospect of rising deficits to attract larger grants (Wallich, 1982).[3]

A further problem in budget formulation is the rigidity of grant formulas determined for five years, combined with uncertainty about the amounts that will actually be received from revenue sharing. Thus, if shared revenue is higher (or lower) than budgeted by the center, there is no mechanism for adjusting transfers, and this is normally reflected in additional spending if revenue is higher and larger deficits if it is lower. While there have generally been three supplementary central budgets a year (in August, December, and March), these have tended to provide mainly for increased grants and loans to states, linked to additional spending at the state level. There is no systematic attempt to fine-tune transfers in response to more general developments in state finances.

Implications

Macroeconomic Management

At first glance, it might appear that the present federal system should not create serious difficulties for the short-term macroeconomic management of India's economy, since the central government can, in principle, control the borrowing and thus also the deficits of states. However, since the mid-1970s, state government deficits have shown an increasing trend, which significantly contributed to growth in the overall public sector deficit. The main factor leading to increased deficits was expansion of states' spending; this in part reflects the misguided in-

---

[3]An additional consequence of the plan/nonplan distinction is that it encourages a segmented approach to public expenditure management and has led to inadequate medium-term planning of nonplan spending.

centives noted above for the states to expand their current and capital expenditure. During the recent stabilization program, the consolidated government deficit was reduced from over 10 percent in 1990/91 to 7.4 percent in 1992/93, of which the largest part was realized at the central government level. This indicates that, regardless of its formal authority, the central government has practical difficulties in imposing financial discipline on states.

The present system also raises questions regarding the incentive structure that it creates for states. The extensive use of revenue sharing and grants to fill budget gaps has had an adverse effect on states' efforts to increase their own revenue and to control expenditure (Rao and Aggarwal, 1990). State finances have weakened mainly as a result of rising current expenditure, most of it on wages and subsidies to loss-making state electricity boards. In the process, expenditure on much-needed infrastructure and maintenance has suffered. At the same time, the link between expenditure and revenue-raising decisions has diminished (Chelliah, 1991). Although, in determining the level of grants, finance commissions have made an attempt to take into account not only the actual level of revenue but also the tax capacity of individual states, it has proved difficult at a technical level to measure tax capacity (Chelliah and others, 1992). Past debt relief has also had adverse effects on the states' financial discipline.

The present fiscal arrangements are coming under further strain as India liberalizes its financial system, which is increasing the burden of interest expenditure and could make borrowing by states more difficult. At present, more than one-half of state financing comes from the central government and the rest from market and other borrowing. But banks do not hold state securities voluntarily, and states might have difficulty undertaking additional borrowing and even refinancing in a more liberal environment, especially if their relatively low level of own revenue and high level of debt are taken into account. This would probably increase pressure on the central government to write off a larger share of its claims on states.

A number of other developments are also changing the present relationship between central and state finances. The opening up of the Indian economy, which is supported by a lowering of tariff protection, is reducing the relative importance of import duty collections. In the past, the central government has tended to reduce its own budget deficit by raising import duties or corporate income tax, since the revenue from these taxes is not shared with the states. Rates of import duty and corporate income tax remain too high, and reducing them will further limit the central government's room for maneuver in this regard.

While the implication is that states will automatically benefit as the center attempts to raise discretionary revenue through increasing personal income tax and excise duty collections, expenditure responsibilities are also shifting in their direction. There is a pressing need to develop economic and social infrastructure, which is largely the preserve of states. Thus, state budgets will tend to expand. At the same time, the political power of states is growing—as demonstrated by the results of the 1996 elections—and greater fiscal devolution is being called for. With the center's ability to control state finances being diminished, greater macroeconomic risk is entailed.

Structural Reform

Besides the impact on macroeconomic management, the present form of fiscal federalism also has implications for structural reform in India. One issue is whether it is possible within this system to establish a modern and efficient tax system. As regards direct taxes, a significant problem is the separation of tax powers on the basis of agricultural versus nonagricultural income. This separation clearly provides opportunities for tax evasion by sheltering nonagricultural income, and in practice results in most agricultural income going untaxed. It also prevents the establishment of a global personal income tax with reasonable progression.

As for domestic taxes on goods and services, assigning excise duties to the central government and sales taxes to the states has created serious distortions. Since the central government is not entitled to impose a sales tax, this has induced broad use of excise taxes. At the same time, administrative difficulties with collecting sales taxes have prompted states to shift this tax increasingly from final sales to the production stage, creating a nontransparent net of cascading transactions taxes. The resulting adverse supply effects are compounded by the taxation of interstate trade. Consequently, Indian exports bear a significant indirect tax element, and states are also able to transfer their tax burden to residents of other states.

In this context, it will not be easy under the present constitutional distribution of tax authority to introduce a modern consumption tax, such as a value-added tax (VAT). The central government has introduced some elements of the VAT principle in excise duties—the so-called MODVAT—while state sales taxes are gradually being converted into state VATs. But the constitutional restriction that final sales can be taxed only by states will necessitate considerable coordination if a dual system of central and state VATs is to function like a nationwide VAT on sales. One solution could be a central VAT with revenue sharing, but this would eliminate the only major tax from which states derive tax autonomy. Anyway, the move from state sales taxes to state VATs almost certainly rules out this option.

Another issue is how to improve on the present approach to grant determination and distribution. A high degree of fiscal dependence is inherent in the tax and expenditure assignments laid out in the Constitution. The criteria adopted by finance commissions for allocating revenue shares are a combination of tax capacity and needs intended to encourage tax collection, promote horizontal equity (that is, ensure that needs are met), and reduce vertical imbalances. However, the distribution of grants-in-aid gives only a small weight to improving vertical balances. The distribution of much larger plan grants also pays little attention to vertical imbalances. A less fragmented and better targeted approach is needed.

Part of the solution lies in ending the separation between plan and nonplan assistance to states. Indeed, the plan and nonplan distinction appears to be an outdated approach to budget formulation more generally. While setting revenue shares for five years imparts useful stability and administrative simplicity to tax collection, the allocation of grants has to be more flexible if vertical and horizontal imbalances are to be more fully addressed. To avoid sharp cyclical fluctuations in states' revenue, smoothing mechanisms could be devised. To make revenue shares more stable and predictable, and to avoid distortionary incentives, the Tenth Finance Commission recommended that the base for sharing should be shifted to total tax revenue. This recommendation has been accepted by the government, and it has been proposed that states receive 29 percent of total tax revenue from 1997/98.

While changing the details of the financial links between the central and state governments would address many of the problems with current intergovernmental fiscal relations, it would not address the more fundamental problem of how to impose effective financial discipline on states. There would appear to be three main elements to a medium-term strategy aimed at this objective: central government transfers that are more closely linked to states' assigned expenditure responsibilities, economic capacity, social needs, and good fiscal performance; increased reliance on market borrowing, supported by the collection and wide dissemination of information on the state finances; and a firm and sustained no-bailout policy. Such arrangements should aim to give states discretion to spend only insofar as they can raise resources through taxation, cost recovery, expenditure cuts, or borrowing. Since access to market borrowing should reflect the sustainability of state finances, it can provide a disciplining mechanism that induces states to undertake reforms that strengthen their finances.

Conclusions

The present structure of fiscal federalism in India was formed at the time when its economy was much less market oriented than today, with the central government having a large role in regulation, administration, and planning of the economy. The allocation of tax powers also reflected a lower level of development in which taxes on international trade and the profits of state monopolies, which were later replaced by the extensive use of excises, were the main source of revenue. In these circumstances, the autonomy of states in expenditure functions was combined with a complicated system of planning arrangements complemented by large transfers of grants and loans from the central government to the states, as well as by state borrowing quotas prescribed by the center. This system is much less efficient in the present circumstances when efforts are being made to open the economy, liberalize the financial system, and increase the role of the private sector. Future economic reform must therefore include substantial changes in the system of intergovernmental fiscal relations, with the ultimate objective of substituting market discipline of state finances for existing central government controls. However, in this connection, a no-bailout policy is critical. If such a policy lacks credibility, and as a consequence states prove reluctant to push ahead with reforms, there would appear to be no alternative but to rely on tight borrowing restrictions combined with cuts in central government transfers as a disciplining mechanism.

References

Bagchi, Amaresh, J.L. Bajaj, and William A. Byrd, 1992, *State Finances in India* (New Delhi: National Institute of Public Finance and Policy).

Chelliah, R.J., 1991, "Intergovernmental Fiscal Relations and Macroeconomic Management in India," Senior Policy Seminar on Intergovernmental Fiscal Relations and Macroeconomic Management in Large Countries (February).

———, M.G. Rao, and T.K. Sen, 1992, "Issues Before the Tenth Finance Commission," *Economic and Political Weekly*, Vol. 27 (November), pp. 2539–50.

Gulati, Iqbal S., 1987, *Centre-State Budgetary Transfers* (Oxford: Oxford Univeristy Press, 1987).

Rao, M.G., and Vandana Aggarwal, 1990, "Intergovernmental Fiscal Transfers in India: Some Issues of Design and Measurement," Working Paper 5/90 (New Delhi: National Institute of Public Finance and Policy).

Wallich, Christine, R.J. Chelliah, and Narain Sinha, 1982, "State Finances in India," World Bank Staff Working Paper 523 (Washington: World Bank).

22

Korea

KE-YOUNG CHU AND JOHN NORREGAARD

Korea broke away from a long tradition of a highly centralized system of government and embarked on a new system of political devolution following the nationwide subnational government elections in 1994. Until that time, the subnational governments were purely administrative arms of the national (central) government and their heads were appointed by the President. Korea's long tradition of a centralized political system had been interrupted only briefly in the early 1960s. The introduction of the new political arrangement gives rise to an entirely new public finance question in Korea: what would be the intergovernmental fiscal arrangement most appropriate for the new political arrangement?

The old framework of highly centralized intergovernmental fiscal relations helped the government pursue centrally formulated policies. The centralized system supported the government's design and implementation of a series of national economic development programs. It enabled the government to maintain the central control of public investment and the provision of services, including some often delivered by local governments in other countries (such as local public safety and justice and primary and secondary education).

The centralized fiscal system, however, leads to various inefficiencies. It is not suitable for subnational governments, now politically autonomous, to meet the demands for locally differentiated public ser-

---

The authors would like to acknowledge Giorgio Brosio's input into the analysis, as well as into the formulation of many ideas in this chapter. They also thank Teresa Ter-Minassian for valuable suggestions.

vices; nor does it promote competition among subnational governments for providing efficient services. As the Korean economy grows and becomes more complex, it becomes increasingly difficult for the central government to control subnational expenditures. Moreover, the political devolution is leading to demands for greater subnational fiscal autonomy.

Korea, therefore, has embarked upon a transition from fiscal centralization toward increased subnational fiscal autonomy. The steps taken by the government so far, however, have increased administrative, rather than fiscal, decentralization. Subnational governments still remain the central government's administrative arms and continue to have only limited autonomy to formulate their own fiscal programs. Their budgetary resources come to a considerable extent from national tax revenues. Subnational governments' fiscal capacities vary substantially throughout the country, given the regional variation in the local tax base, which reflects, inter alia, the cumulative effects of the past regional allocation of public and private investments.

The limited degree of fiscal decentralization to date implies that more fundamental and wide-ranging issues will need to be addressed in Korea than in other countries, which in general have longer-established systems of intergovernmental fiscal relations.

For Korea, the issues to be considered include the following:
- What is the appropriate level of decentralization and local fiscal autonomy and how can the present vertical fiscal imbalance be reduced?
- Which expenditures should be assigned to subnational governments and which should remain under central control?
- What is the appropriate tax assignment?
- How should the transfer system be improved and how should the required degree of equalization be achieved without undermining efficiency?
- What kind of access should subnational governments have to financial markets?
- What are the institutional implications?

A successful transition requires that both macroeconomic stability be preserved and that the right balance be found between an increase in efficiency through better and more varied public services, a reduction in the existing vertical fiscal imbalances, and a reduction of inequalities in the distribution of fiscal capacities across different regions. The transition is taking place against a difficult background of growing demands for central government investments and services (such as increased public infrastructure, social security, and higher-quality health and education services), the economy's structural changes, substantial population migration from rural to urban and from urban to suburban areas, and wide disparities in regional fiscal capacities and needs, given the concentration of wealth, income, and public services in urban areas and certain high-growth regions.

The transition will require substantial preparatory work and political negotiations aimed at achieving the necessary political consensus at all levels of government. The process will take time and has to proceed through cooperation between the national and subnational governments, as the latter strengthen their administrative capacities, while establishing secure roots for local democracy.

This chapter focuses on the key options facing policymakers. The following section briefly outlines the main features of the present system.

Present System of Intergovernmental Fiscal Relations

Structure of Government and Vertical and Horizontal Fiscal Imbalances

The present structure of government has the features of a unitary system with a degree of administrative decentralization. A three-tiered structure of government comprises the national government and two tiers of subnational governments—regional governments and local governments. The national government is referred to as the central government (or government), and the subnational governments as local autonomous bodies. Regional governments comprise the Seoul metropolitan government, 5 direct jurisdictional cities (large cities), and 9 provincial governments; local governments comprise (1) 22 autonomous city districts and 33 self-governing wards under the direct jurisdictional cities and (2) 67 cities (small cities) and 137 counties under the provincial governments.[1] As in other administratively decentralized unitary systems, each tier has its own responsibilities and some own sources of financing, but the higher tier provides transfers to the lower tier. Seoul and the five large cities have been assigned provincial functions and taxes and also receive transfers from the central government.

---

[1] Korea's Constitution has only two articles dealing with local autonomy. Article 117 defines briefly the functions (providing services relating to residents' welfare and managing properties) and authority (establishing ordinances within the framework of relevant laws) of local autonomous bodies. Article 118 states that the local autonomous bodies should have their own legislative bodies. The Constitution does not provide criteria for the distribution of responsibilities either among provinces, small cities, and counties or between the large cities and their autonomous districts. The basic legislation for the establishment and operations of local autonomous bodies is provided in the Law on Local Autonomy and the Ordinance for the Implementation of the Law on Local Autonomy.

Table 1. Korea: Consolidated General Government Fiscal Operations, 1995

	Amount (In trillions of won)	Ratio to GDP (In percent)
General government		
Revenue	90.7	26.0
Tax revenue	72.6	20.8
Other revenue	18.1	5.2
Expenditure and net lending	91.9	26.4
Capital expenditure and net lending	36.0	10.3
Other expenditure	55.9	16.0
Deficit	1.2	0.3
Of which:		
Local autonomous bodies		
Tax revenue	13.3	3.8
Expenditure and net lending	44.9	12.9
Of which: capital spending	19.9	5.7
Deficit	9.2	2.6
Memorandum items:		
Central government transfers to		
local autonomous bodies	22.6	6.5
Current transfers	17.8	5.1
Capital transfers	4.8	1.4
GDP	348.3	

Source: Bank of Korea, *Economic Statistics Yearbook*, 1996; based on the 1995 budget figures.

Note: There are some discrepancies between various estimates of government revenue, expenditure, and deficit. For example, in another set of estimates, the budgeted local government deficit is W 4 trillion rather than W 9 trillion, and general government revenue nd expenditure were somewhat higher than reported in Tables 4 and 6.

A main feature of the system is substantial vertical and horizontal fiscal imbalances.[2] Subnational governments, while accounting for over half of the general government expenditure, raise only some 20 percent of their revenue through taxation, financing the rest mainly through central government transfers (Table 1). There is a wide variation in regional incomes and subnational government capacities to mobilize revenues. For example, in 1994, per capita gross regional product (GRP) ranged between W 4.6 million ($5,750) for Taegu and W 8 million ($10,000) for South Kyungsang. With central government transfers, per capita subnational government expenditures varied considerably, ranging between W 0.5 million for Pusan, Inchon, and Kwangju and W 1.2 million for Kangwon (Table 2).[3]

---
[2]See Lee (1992) for a discussion of local public finance in Korea before the political devolution.
[3]See Jun (1992) for a description of the evolution of the Korean intergovernmental fiscal relations between 1960 and 1992.

Table 2. Korea: Regional Distribution of Incomes and Budgetary Resources

	Population (In millions) 1995	Expenditure (In trillions of won) 1996	Expenditure (In millions of won) 1996	Per Capita Gross regional product (In millions of won) 1993	Transfers (In thousands of won) 1993
Large cities					
Seoul	10.5	8.7	0.8	6.5	21
Pusan	3.9	3.3	0.9	4.9	44
Taegu	2.5	2.4	1.0	4.6	63
Inchon	2.4	2.1	0.9	6.5	29
Kwangju	1.3	1.2	0.9	5.1	130
Taejon	1.3	1.0	0.8	5.7	67
Provinces					
Kyungki	7.8	7.7	1.0	6.2	96
Kangwon	1.5	2.2	1.4	4.9	511
North Chungchong	1.4	1.7	1.2	6.1	356
South Chungchong	1.9	2.6	1.4	5.4	425
North Cholla	2.0	2.9	1.4	4.9	415
South Cholla	2.2	3.1	1.4	6.1	510
North Kyungsang	2.8	3.3	1.2	6.3	422
South Kyungsang	4.0	4.3	1.1	8.0	249
Cheju	0.5	0.8	1.5	5.0	390

Sources: Ministry of Home Affairs (1994); and Seoul Metropolitan Government (1996).

Expenditure Assignment

Principles Underlying Korean Expenditure Assignment

The Law on Local Autonomy provides a broad system of expenditure assignment in line with the new devolved intergovernmental political arrangement. The principles underlying the distinction made between purely national and purely local policies is broadly in accordance with the theory of intergovernmental fiscal relations. According to the law, functions of the local autonomous bodies are limited to the provision of local public services:[4]

- Local public administration (such as local legislation, collection of local taxes, civil defense administration, and firefighting).
- Support for local economies (for example, promotion of farming, small-scale animal husbandry, and consumer protection) and regional development (for example, urban planning and local roads).
- Promotion of social services for local residents and local education, sports, culture, and arts (such as the establishment of local kindergartens and primary and secondary schools).

---

[4]Article 9, Law on Local Autonomy.

The law prohibits local autonomous bodies from engaging in the provision of pure national public goods or those with strong nationwide externalities:[5]
- National security, public order and safety, and foreign relations.
- National economic policy, including such areas as monetary policy, fiscal policy (including national taxation), pricing policy, management of grain stocks, and external trade policies; economic development programs; industrial standards; postal and rail transportation services; and public services requiring high technology.

Main Features of the Expenditure Assignment

Several features of the expenditure assignment deserve attention:.

The practice of expenditure assignment often deviates from enunciated principles. The legislation provides an expenditure assignment in line with the basic theory of intergovernmental fiscal relations. In practice, however, the system still reflects the old centralized regime. Local autonomous bodies are engaged extensively in the provision of central government functions as its agents.

The central government has considerable influence over the fiscal operations of local autonomous bodies. Because of this influence, the local autonomous bodies' relatively high share in general government expenditure does not reflect their relative fiscal autonomy. For example, at present, local autonomous bodies account for some 50 percent of general government expenditure if education board expenditures are consolidated into their expenditures. The central government exercises its influence through at least two channels: (1) its largely conditional transfers and subsidies, which account for some 30 percent of general government expenditure if central government transfers to education boards are considered local autonomous bodies' expenditures,[6] and (2) considerable regulatory authority over local autonomous bodies' operations. Local autonomous bodies have limited authority to introduce new taxes. Moreover, the Ministry of Home Affairs and other central government ministries exert considerable influence on local autonomous bodies' policy formulation and implementation through a combination of mandates and administrative instructions. The central government imposes price controls on certain locally provided public services or privately provided local services, such as intracity transportation.

---

[5]Article 11.

[6]While most of the education board expenditures are provided by the central government, Seoul and Pusan contribute partly to the operations of the education boards in their respective areas.

Table 3. Korea: Distribution of and Budgetary Resources for Cities, Provinces, Counties, and Districts, 1996
(In trillions of won)

	Total Expenditure	Large Cities and Provinces	Small Cities, Counties, and Districts
Large cities			
Seoul	8.7	7.0	1.7
Pusan	3.3	2.9	0.5
Taegu	2.4	2.1	0.3
Inchon	2.1	1.8	0.3
Kwangju	1.2	1.1	0.1
Taejon	1.0	0.9	0.1
Provinces			
Kyungki	7.7	2.7	4.9
Kangwon	2.2	0.9	1.3
North Chungchong	1.7	0.8	1.0
South Chungchong	2.6	1.3	1.3
North Cholla	2.9	1.3	1.7
South Cholla	3.1	1.4	1.8
North Kyungsang	3.3	1.3	2.0
South Kyungsang	4.3	1.6	2.7
Cheju	0.8	0.4	0.4

Sources: Ministry of Home Affairs (1994); Seoul Metropolitan Government (1996); and Government of North Kyungsang Province (1996).

Moreover, the law is not specific regarding many national or subnational government functions. There are many mixed national and subnational government functions that are carried out mostly by local autonomous bodies with central government financial support. There is an extensive overlapping of functions between the various levels of government in many areas (Table 3). These features can result in either underprovision or overprovision of public services.

A large share of the expenditures of local autonomous bodies, presently more than one-third of general government expenditure, is devoted to capital projects, constraining the amount of resources available for the delivery of current services to the population. The demand for current services is rising, as witnessed by popular pressures on the newly elected local autonomous bodies.

Tax Assignment

Basic Structure of Tax Assignment

The tax system consists of nonoverlapping national and subnational (or local) taxes (Tables 4 and 5).[7] The national tax system comprises

---

[7]See Oh (1992) for a discussion of the local tax system.

Table 4. Korea: Functional Composition of General Government Expenditure, 1995
(In trillions of won)

	General Government	Of Which: Local Autonomous Bodies
Total expenditure	91.9	44.9
Public administration	15.9	8.9
General administration	10.0	8.0
Public order and safety	5.9	0.9
National defense	11.0	—
Education	15.1	12.3
Primary and secondary education	12.3	11.3
Tertiary education	2.8	1.0
Health	2.0	1.4
Social welfare	7.9	2.1
Housing and community development	9.8	5.2
Economic services	28.9	14.4
Agriculture and fishery	9.6	4.0
Mining and manufacturing	3.9	1.2
Roads	6.8	3.5
Transportation and communication	4.0	3.4
Other	1.3	0.6

Source: Bank of Korea, *Economic Statistics Yearbook,* 1996; based on the 1995 budget figures.

standard central government taxes, such as the VAT, an income tax, and a corporate tax. The structure of local taxes is shown in Table 6.[8] More than two-thirds of the yield from the 15 different local taxes derives from taxes on property, with only 12 percent deriving from taxes on income, largely from the inhabitant tax.

Local tax revenue in 1994 constituted 18.1 percent of total tax revenue, compared with about 10 percent in 1975. Local taxes reached about 4 percent of GDP in 1995, against 1.6 percent in 1975. Despite this strong increase, the level of local taxes is still fairly modest by international standards.[9] During the past two decades, local taxes have

---

[8]See the Ministry of Finance and Economy (1995).

[9]The overall tax-to-GDP ratio of about 21 percent is also considerably below the ratio, even in low-tax member countries of the Organization for Economic Cooperation and Development (OECD) (for example, Australia, Japan, and the United States, where tax ratios are about 30 percent). With unweighted averages of the ratio of central government taxes to total taxes equal to about 43 percent in federal OECD countries and about 63 percent in unitary OECD countries, the large majority of these countries have allocated a significantly larger share of total tax revenues to subnational governments than has Korea.

Table 5. Korea: Tax System

National Taxes	Local Taxes
Internal taxes	Taxes for provinces and metropolitan cities
Direct taxes	Acquisition tax
Income tax	Registration tax
Corporate tax	Horse race tax
Tax on the excess increase in land value	Community facility tax
Inheritance and gift tax	Regional development tax
Assets revaluation tax	Taxes only for provinces
Excess profits tax	License tax
Indirect taxes	
Value-added tax	Taxes only for metropolitan cities
Special excise tax	Inhabitant tax
Liquor tax	Automobile tax
Telephone tax	Farmland tax
Liquor tax	Tobacco consumption tax
Stamp tax	Butchery tax
Securities transaction tax	City planning tax
Transportation tax	Taxes for cities, counties, and districts
Customs duties	Property tax
Education tax	Aggregate land tax
	Workshop tax
Special tax for rural development	Taxes only for cities and counties
	Inhabitant tax
	Automobile tax
	Farmland tax
	Tobacco consumption tax
	Butchery tax
	City planning tax
	Taxes only for districts
	License tax

Source: Ministry of Finance and Economy (1996).

increased in importance, mainly through a series of tax reforms; these reforms improved the local tax base through the introduction of new local tax sources and the assignment of previously central taxes to the local level.

Main Features of Tax Assignment

Tax assignment has several notable features.

First, the buoyant taxes belong to the central government; local taxes lack buoyancy.

Second, seven different taxes are levied on property, and although land and buildings are key elements in most of them, there are significant differences in the way tax bases are measured. Most property taxes

Table 6. Korea: Composition of General Government Revenue, 1995

	Amount (In trillions of won)	Ratio to GDP (In percent)
Total revenue and grants	90.7	26.0
Tax revenue	72.6	20.8
Taxes on income and profits	21.8	6.3
Social security contributions	5.0	1.4
Taxes on property	10.0	2.9
Taxes on goods and services	27.2	7.8
Taxes on international trade	3.5	1.0
Other taxes	5.1	1.5
Nontax revenue	18.1	5.2
Memorandum items:		
Local autonomous bodies		
Tax revenue	13.2	3.8
Of which: property taxes	7.9	2.3
GNP	348.3	

Source: Bank of Korea (1996); based on the 1995 budget figures.

involving land and buildings are progressive ad valorem taxes,[10] presumably because the ownership of property is considered to be closely correlated with income, and thus a good indicator for ability to pay. Although mostly ad valorem–based in principle, there are elements of specific property taxation, particularly in the registration tax, as indicated by fairly infrequent rate adjustments. The present valuation system, based on computerized local cadasters and administered at the city, district, and county levels, is, in principle, based on market values; however, owing to a complex system of coefficients applied to different areas and different uses of land and buildings, current assessed values deviate significantly from market values. According to some estimates, assessed values constitute on average only 30 percent of market values.

Third, the inhabitant tax, a major local income tax, is primarily a source-based tax (that is, its yield accrues to the jurisdiction of the workplace), with little weight on residence-based taxation (the per family element of the tax, which is based on the taxpayer's place of residence, generates only 5 percent of the total revenue, whereas the source element accounts for the remaining 95 percent). Furthermore, if a person has more than one type of income (for instance, wage and interest income), the source-based tax element may be paid to different

---

[10]This holds for the property tax, the automobile tax (only indirectly related to value), the global land tax, and the community facility tax. In contrast, the city planning tax on land and buildings has a flat standard rate. The acquisition tax and the registration tax are mainly flat rate taxes, but with numerous different rates applied to different types of assets.

jurisdictions, depending on the location of the payment place (in the example, the workplace and the location of the bank, respectively).

Fourth, earmarking is extensively used in the present system of local taxation, including for the facility tax, the regional development tax, the city planning tax, and the workplace tax. An excessive use of earmarking tends to reduce budgetary flexibility and efficiency, particularly when the existence of an element of benefit taxation is not obvious (for example, the automobile tax).

And, finally, although the present tax legislation provides local autonomous bodies with substantial flexibility with regard to varying tax rates, all local entities have chosen not to utilize this option, using instead the standard tax rates.[11]

Intergovernmental Transfers

Overview of the Transfer System

Revenues from local taxes presently cover slightly more than one-third of local expenditure, excluding education expenditures. This vertical imbalance is corrected by a system of central government transfers, with specific conditional transfers dominating over general unconditional transfers. Transfers from the central government are a substantial source of revenue for the local autonomous bodies. These transfers, excluding those for education, represent about 70 percent of the estimated total local tax revenue. A parallel system of transfers is used to finance the education boards.

The transfer system is a multipurpose system, which in its design is similar to those used in many developed countries. The formulas for the distribution of the various transfers as well as the provisions for determining their total amount are very detailed. However, the central government retains large discretionary authority with regard to many aspects of the transfer system.

Main Features of the Transfer System

The transfer programs have the following features.

The local shared tax fund is used for the distribution of general purpose transfers to the local governments (Table 7). The global amount

---

[11]Variations in tax rates are permitted for the following taxes, with the allowed range of variation around the standard rate shown in parentheses: inhabitant tax (plus and minus 50 percent); automobile tax (plus 50 percent); livestock tax (minus 1 percent); city planning tax (plus 50 percent); regional development tax (plus and minus 50 percent); and community facilities tax (plus 1 percent).

Table 7. Korea: Structure of Local Government Tax Revenue, 1995

	Amount (In trillions of won)	Share of Total (In percent)
Total	13.3	100.0
Taxes on income	1.6	12.4
Inhabitant tax	1.4	10.5
Farmland tax	—	—
Taxes on property		
Acquisition tax	9.1	68.3
Registration tax	2.2	16.7
Property tax	2.9	21.8
Automobile tax	0.5	4.0
Global land tax	1.1	8.6
City planning tax	0.6	4.7
Community facility tax	0.2	1.5
Taxes on consumption	2.3	17.6
License tax	0.2	1.4
Butchery tax	—	0.2
Horse race tax	0.2	1.4
Tobacco tax	1.9	14.3
Regional development tax	0.1	0.4
Carryover	0.2	1.7
Memorandum items:		
In percent of total revenue	38.9	
In percent of GDP	3.8	

Source: Bank of Korea (1996); based on the 1995 budget figures.

of the fund corresponds to 13.27 percent of total internal tax revenues (earmarked taxes, such as the transportation tax, are not included in these revenues). The fund has two components. The general component (comprising $10/11$ of the total transfer) is distributed according to a complex formula, which takes into account expenditure needs and the revenue capacity of each jurisdiction. The cities of Seoul and Pusan, Kyungki Province, and nine other local governments are excluded from the distribution because their revenue capacities are believed to exceed their expenditure needs. The distribution is made by the Ministry of Home Affairs, which is also responsible for the design of the formula. The special component (comprising $1/11$ of the total transfer) is used for unforeseeable occurrences, such as natural disasters.

The local transfer fund is used for the distribution of specific transfers, basically for road construction programs, water provision, youth support, and the development of rural areas. Its total amount is determined as 50 percent of the revenue of liquor taxes, plus the entire revenue of the phone tax, 50 percent of the tax on real estate capital gains, and $19/150$ of the special tax on agriculture and fisheries. It is a typical

Table 8. Korea: Transfers to Local Autonomous Bodies
and Education Boards, 1996

Types of transfers	Amount (In billions of won)
To local autonomous bodies	12.8
Local shared tax	6.1
General	5.6
Special	0.6
Local transfer funds	2.6
National treasury subsidies	4.1
To education boards	13.0
Education shared tax	8.5
General	7.7
Special	4.1
Education transfer fund	4.1
Education subsidies	0.4

Source: Bank of Korea (1996); based on the 1995 budget figures.

matching grant distributed by the Ministry of Home Affairs. The matching rate, as well as the criteria for the allocation of the fund among various sectors and local governments, is dictated by sectoral laws and other statutes. The transfers from the fund are predominantly allocated to rural areas. Beneficiary governments are free to determine the characteristics of their projects.

National treasury subsidies include a variety of specific transfers distributed by sectoral ministries and are used mainly for financing capital projects. There are no general criteria for the determination of the total amount, which reflects the implementation of sectoral laws and decrees. The laws also determine the criteria for the selection of the projects to be financed and the matching rates. The distribution is made by the relevant sectoral ministries. Beneficiary governments have to comply with strict and detailed criteria regarding the formulation and the implementation of their projects.

Transfers to the education boards are provided for the administration of primary and secondary schools (Table 8). Each education board is composed of 25 individuals, each selected by municipal councils from a list of persons established by the autonomous districts. Their budgets are financed by students' fees and transfers from the central government and from local autonomous bodies. Transfers from the central government to the education boards replicate those paid to local autonomous bodies. There are three types of transfers: (1) a local education shared tax, with the global amount corresponding to 11.8 percent of the revenue from internal taxes, plus total wages and salaries, to be distributed according to a formula that compares expenditure needs and revenues from transfers and fees; (2) local education transfer funds, an earmarked fund financed by the education tax, to be distributed according to total population; and (3) national subsidies for education, distributed by the Ministry of Education for the construction of school buildings.

The law also mandates regional governments (provinces and large cities) to transfer specific percentages of their own tax revenues to the cities, counties, or autonomous city districts included in their jurisdictions. The structure of these transfers is an almost perfect duplicate of those provided by the central government to regional governments. Thus, there are general purpose transfers, distributed according to a formula based on a comparison between needs and revenue capacities, and specific purpose transfers for projects selected by the donor government. All these transfers are strictly regulated by the central government.

Local Borrowing

Basic Principles of Local Borrowing

As in most other developed countries, local autonomous bodies in Korea are permitted to borrow, but subject to an elaborate regulatory framework, detailing the conditions for bond financing and other debt instruments. The overall objectives of this regulatory framework are:
- To limit the aggregate amount of local borrowing.
- To enhance responsibility on the part of the local autonomous bodies, taking into account that the time horizon of elected officials' decision making might be considerably shorter than the economic lives of the projects financed by borrowing.
- To prevent the concentration of economic power in richer areas of the country.

The Ministry of Home Affairs plays a key role in the regulation of local borrowing—except in the case of foreign borrowing, where the Ministry of Finance and Economy is the key player—by issuing detailed regulations and guidelines for local borrowing. Local governments are required to get approval from the Ministry of Home Affairs—as well as approval by the local councils—for all borrowing. Sector ministries also participate in the approval process through an elaborate hearing procedure within their respective areas of interest, and the Ministry of Finance and Economy is also involved in this process. Furthermore, this ministry may itself extend subsidized loans to local governments to support national objectives and projects, although formally, the lending is executed through the relevant sector ministries (such as the Ministry of Transportation or the Ministry of the Environment).

Key Features of the System of Local Borrowing

Two aspects of the system of local borrowing are noteworthy: the implications of central government regulations and compulsory local bond placements.

The regulations concerning borrowing comprise detailed eligibility criteria[12] that determine (1) which local governments are allowed to borrow—only those with a history of sound financial policies (for instance, those with no overdue obligations, a low debt-service ratio, and a low deficit); and (2) which projects are eligible to borrow—capital projects, revenue shortfalls due to natural disasters, and others that are especially useful for improving the welfare of residents.[13] There is no a priori ceiling set on the overall amount of borrowing, either by the Ministry of Finance and Economy or by any other central authority.

A particular feature of the Korean system is the existence of compulsory bond placements. Through a city ordinance, Seoul and other cities have decided that the beneficiaries of services eligible for local borrowing should also contribute to the financing. Compulsory bond placements, introduced in 1979 initially for "water bonds," continue, primarily relating to Urban Railroad Bonds, and take place when automobiles are purchased, when licenses or permits are issued, and when bids are made for local government projects. The terms, which are decided solely by the city council, comprise a five-year grace period and an interest rate of 6 percent (compared with the market rate of about 11 percent). In addition to these compulsory bond placements, local governments issue bonds on the international market (in Japan and the United States) on market terms and, in recent years, at a much lower interest rate than the domestic level (even after taking into account exchange rate movements).

As a consequence of the historically determined close integration of functions and responsibilities of governments at different levels in Korea, the risks associated with borrowing are also shared in the sense that, when central government approval has been granted, a loan is automatically considered covered by an effective—if not statutory—state guarantee.

Main Reform Issues

The reform of Korea's intergovernmental fiscal relations cannot be considered separately from the country's broader economic goal: sus-

---

[12]Less strict criteria apply to public enterprises.
[13]This criterion is not defined clearly.

tained high-quality economic growth. The central government faces a major task of maintaining the soundness of macroeconomic policy in an increasingly open international economic environment and meeting the country's growing demands for high-quality public investment and social programs, while keeping the tax burden at a modest level. The economy's overall productivity and efficiency must increase. To achieve these objectives, Korea needs to increase public sector productivity, and the public sector must aim its policies at promoting efficiency in the economy's overall resource use. An essential step toward this goal is to reduce government regulations and to improve the quality of regulations. In pursuing these objectives, Korea needs to reduce the existing vertical and horizontal fiscal imbalances, while meeting the local autonomous bodies' increasing demand for fiscal autonomy.

It appears inevitable for Korea to decentralize further its intergovernmental fiscal relations. As a matter of fact, the country is already moving in this direction. The present system does not enable Korea to benefit from the potential efficiency gains that can result from a fiscally decentralized system of intergovernmental fiscal relations.[14] The move toward a system of increased fiscal decentralization will pose significant challenges for the decision makers. A large measure of transparency, cooperation, and consultation in intergovernmental fiscal relations is also required. The pace of reform will have to take into account the development of local governments' administrative capacity. During the process of transition to a new system, Korea must address several closely related issues, as a basic prerequisite for the introduction of a well-functioning decentralized system of government, namely:

- Ensuring that all levels of government play proper market-complementing roles and strengthening macroeconomic management.
- Allocating expenditures properly among the different tiers of government, including the appropriate level of local government autonomy over their expenditures.
- Redesigning the system of tax assignment, including the appropriate degree of local taxation autonomy.
- Defining clearly the appropriate local autonomous bodies' access to borrowing.
- Establishing institutional arrangements, in particular, to address externalities and spillover effects and to coordinate intergovernmental fiscal relations.

The rest of this section discusses these key issues.

---

[14]See Tanzi (1996) for a discussion of fiscal decentralization versus administrative decentralization of intergovernmental fiscal relations.

Role of Public Sector, Vertical and Horizontal Imbalances, and Macroeconomic Management

Role of Local Autonomous Bodies as Public Sector Entities

Facing an increasingly competitive external environment, Korea is searching for ways to improve the efficiency of the economy. The central government is looking for ways to reduce its role, including through substantial deregulation. A danger is that, while the central government pursues policies of deregulation and privatization, local autonomous bodies may expand market-replacing activities for short-term gains in their revenues. This would reduce or offset efficiency gains of central government policy. Without a strict and transparent legal framework aimed at defining the roles of local autonomous bodies, such a danger is real. Local autonomous bodies should be strictly prohibited from engaging in market-replacing activities without clear justification.

Vertical and Horizontal Imbalances

Large vertical fiscal imbalances often reflect the desire of the central authorities to control local government fiscal operations. Excessive transfer financing resulting from large vertical imbalances, however, limits local fiscal autonomy, masks the true costs of the services provided locally, and thereby reduces local political accountability. Vertical fiscal imbalances reduce significantly the potential efficiency gains associated with decentralization. On the other hand, given the substantial inequality in the geographical distribution of the tax base, an assignment of a larger tax base to local autonomous bodies would increase the need for a system of intergovernmental equalization transfers. Moreover, it would imply, with a given overall tax burden, a reduction in the base for central government taxation. While a reduction in the present level of vertical imbalances clearly is warranted, the desired level must balance these conflicting considerations.

To give local autonomous bodies equal opportunities to provide their citizens with adequate public service at comparable "tax prices," fiscal capacities and "objective" expenditure needs (that is, expenditure requirements resulting from external factors outside the control of local autonomous bodies) should be equalized. To this end, two important questions must be addressed: what is the appropriate degree of equalization of fiscal capacities of local autonomous bodies and what are the implications of alternative equalization options.

The first question is a political one, which has to be resolved through the political process, but the Korean authorities must pay attention to the implications of the equalization for efficiency. Equalization may aim at reducing disparities in the actual provision of current services, or at filling existing disparities in infrastructure, or even at reducing existing gaps in income and wealth levels among the various areas.

The second question has a number of aspects. If an increase in the degree of equalization is found warranted, the Korean authorities could consider a mix of the following approaches: (1) The central government could increase the total amount of equalization transfers. For a given level and assignment of taxation, this would reduce the resources available for other central government activities (including "other transfers" to subnational governments). (2) The central government and local autonomous bodies could introduce a transfer aimed at requiring "wealthier" jurisdictions to make transfers to "poorer" jurisdictions. This would increase horizontal equity without changing the vertical balance. (3) The central government could finance an increase in equalization transfers by increasing national taxes. This would increase the national tax burden unless the increased transfers were used by local autonomous bodies to reduce their taxes correspondingly. This option would, of course, worsen vertical fiscal inequity. (4) Local autonomous bodies could increase their tax efforts, which—if successful—would reduce the degree of vertical imbalance, enabling the central government to redirect its transfers to achieving greater equalization. This would also increase the overall tax burden, unless matched by a reduction in the national taxation.

Macroeconomic Management

In Korea's present centralized system of government, a lack of macroeconomic control is not an issue. In any "good" system of multilevel government, the central government maintains a significant measure of macroeconomic control based on a variety of tax and expenditure policy instruments. Ideally, however, this policy should be implemented with a minimum of interference in the activities of local autonomous bodies. When interference is necessary, policies should be implemented through general measures such as reductions in either the overall level of borrowing or general grants. Micromanagement through detailed constraints on either tax policies or expenditure policies would run counter to the rationale for decentralization and would seriously hamper local accountability. There are three specific issues:
- The more own sources of taxation local autonomous bodies are assigned, and the larger the autonomy granted them, the less is generally the degree of central government fiscal control (over expenditures, tax rates, and other tax policy variables). In the pre-

sent circumstances, however, such a possibility appears rather remote in Korea.
- The fixed coefficient for dividing the aggregate national tax revenue between the central government and local autonomous bodies might create difficulties for fiscal adjustment at the general government level. For example, the central government's successful effort to increase revenues from national taxes aimed at correcting deterioration in the general government fiscal balance will be frustrated if local autonomous bodies use the increased transfers to pursue expansionary expenditure policies.
- The local autonomous bodies face a growing need to finance major regional infrastructure projects (for instance, subway systems in major cities). With a limited tax base, the pressure for local borrowing will increase. Sound management of local borrowing is essential for macroeconomic stability. One approach to promoting local fiscal sustainability would be to allow full autonomy of local borrowing, but subject to strict market discipline, with no central government financial backup. The conditions for such an approach to be effective (see Chapter 7) do not appear to be fulfilled in Korea at the present time, and therefore should be considered only as a long-term goal. In the short to medium term, the approach of continued central government control of local borrowing would appear to be necessary to ensure adequate macroeconomic discipline.

Expenditure Assignment

In a decentralized system, the central government has a fundamental role as the provider of national public goods. This role includes pursuing sound macroeconomic policies, setting national standards and basic priorities, and monitoring their implementation and financing. Excessively detailed regulations, however, may be counterproductive. The design of expenditure assignment should aim at the efficient provision of public services and a balanced promotion of national and regional economic objectives. A successful reform of the present system of expenditure assignment would need to address the following weaknesses of the system.

Overlapping of Responsibilities

While the overlapping of responsibilities of different levels of government is unavoidable in practice, and the drawing of boundaries between levels of government is difficult, Korea has an overly complex system of overlapping functions (particularly in the areas of transportation, roads, and regional development). Excessive overlapping reduces accountability and responsiveness in the provision of services. To reduce such overlapping, each level of government should be assigned as clearly defined as possible a sphere of autonomy. The key objectives of this assignment should be simplicity, transparency, and administrative efficiency.

Local Autonomous Bodies' Function as Central Government Agents

In many sectors, local autonomous bodies are acting mainly as agents of the central government, such as in the case of economic development and infrastructure investment. As previously mentioned, this situation is typical of highly centralized states. It may ensure uniformity of service provision across the various areas of a country, but excessive constraints and regulations may impede accountability for local governments by giving rise to claims by local autonomous bodies that inappropriate policies are the result of decisions imposed by the central government. Particularly problematic is the practice of mandating local autonomous bodies to carry out central government functions without providing resources. The practice of imposing unfunded mandates on local autonomous bodies reduces accountability, as well as promoting the emergence of fiscal imbalances at the subnational level.

Externalities and Spillover Effects

Expenditure assignment must be designed to address externalities and spillover effects.
- National public goods can have negative regional externalities. For example, the Korean government recently has met strong local opposition to its plan to build a nuclear power plant. Its construction of a train system connecting Seoul and a new international airport has been delayed as a result of the lack of cooperation of some local autonomous bodies.
- Local public goods can have both positive and negative cross-border spillover effects. Regional public goods can also have negative cross-border spillover effects. The growth of urban areas and greater mobility have increased externalities relating to certain basic services such as mass transit, water provision, and environmental protection, especially in large metropolitan areas. For example, Seoul's subway system benefits not only Seoul's residents, but also those who commute to Seoul from adjoining regions.

New mechanisms are needed for the sharing of responsibilities for these services among affected communities.

Earmarking

While earmarking has its merits (for instance, protecting certain programs against arbitrary allocation of resources and instability in the provision of services), its extensive use in Korea—for transportation, road construction, and education—may result in disadvantages, such as nonadaptation of policies to local needs and excessive rigidity in the supply of services. Moreover, earmarking reduces the political accountability of elected assemblies, since the budget they approve may concern only a limited fraction of the services that are provided to their citizens.

Tax Assignment

In principle, the types of tax bases presently allocated to local autonomous bodies are in conformity with the theory, since local autonomous bodies are given autonomy to set the rates of a number of taxes. However, the local taxes are excessive in number, complicated, and inefficient. They are largely based on property, with only little emphasis on income and sales taxation. The basic objective of the reform measures should be to establish a simple and transparent local tax system that provides local autonomous bodies with sufficient and buoyant tax sources, offers the required level of local autonomy, and at the same time enhances efficiency and fairness. Since property taxes will remain the major revenue source for the foreseeable future, reform efforts should focus on this source.

Efficiency and Transparency of Local Taxes

A proliferation of local taxes, each with a relatively modest yield, has created a complex and not adequately transparent system of local taxation. This has adverse effects on the perceptibility of the true tax burden by local taxpayers and voters, and hampers the price signal effect of the taxation system that is—as described earlier—key to the functioning of a decentralized fiscal system. But even in a situation where local governments are intended mainly to carry out agent functions, the present system is unnecessarily complex, with attendant administrative and compliance costs. The fairly low revenue buoyancy results from the extensive use of property taxes, based on property values that have not been fully indexed to market prices. This has led to the proliferation of new taxes, resulting in excessive complexity of the present system. The inadequate transparency has been accentuated by the significant volatility in the revenue structure over time as a result of the frequent changes in the system, although the reforms have been motivated by a desire to improve the system and to provide subnational governments with the necessary means of satisfying growing needs. The present system is characterized by variations in the set of taxes that have been assigned to the different types of local governments (large cities, provinces, small cities and counties, and districts), even for entities at the same "level," such as provinces and large cities. To the extent that local autonomous bodies are carrying out similar tasks, it could be argued that they should also have access to the same sources of taxes,to maximize transparency.

Autonomy

Although the system formally allows for variations in tax rates by local autonomous bodies, the de facto autonomy is very limited owing to the almost complete absence of incentives to deviate from standard rates. Because of strict central control on expenditures, there is very little scope for local autonomous bodies to provide their populations with services at varying levels of "quality" and "quantity" in accordance with local preferences.

Power of Local Autonomous Bodies to Grant Tax Exemptions

Most countries grant exemptions in well-defined cases to, for example, government buildings under the property tax. However, the fairly extensive power of local autonomous bodies in Korea to grant discretionary reductions and exemptions in a large number of specific cases, particularly for property taxation, involves a risk of local governments engaging in tax competition to attract businesses and economic activity, which involves loss of revenue and complicates tax administration.

Complexity of Property Taxes

Additional structural problems of the present system of property taxes include the following:
- There is a relatively high reliance on transaction taxes as opposed to ownership taxes (about 56 percent of property tax revenues derive from transaction taxes), creating locking-in effects that hamper the efficient functioning of property markets.

- To the extent that property taxes are levied on business property, an issue of perceptibility arises since businesses to some extent can shift the tax burden backward to labor and other inputs, or forward to consumers via higher prices; thus, it is uncertain who ultimately bears the burden of this element of the property tax. Furthermore, there is little rationale for using progressive rates for businesses (a "large" corporation may be owned by numerous individuals with large disparities in personal income levels).[15]
- Infrequent valuations necessitate large changes when made, adding to taxpayer resentment.
- Values used for taxation purposes differ significantly from market values. This might not in itself distort taxation, assuming that the ratio between valuation and market value is constant across areas and uses. However, this condition is not likely to be satisfied, in which case the present system introduces a distortion, in addition to resulting in losses of potential revenue.

Basing Income Taxes on Sources

As regards income taxes, the main problem in the present system relates to the source-based nature of the inhabitant tax. This reduces transparency and results in lack of alignment of expenditure responsibilities and tax financing. Possibly accentuating this is the fact that the inhabitant tax is also levied on businesses (including corporations), part of which may be borne by labor and other factor inputs, whereas another part is borne by the consumers of the products, further severing the relation between those who pay and those who benefit from the services.

Transfers

Korea uses a fairly sophisticated formula that takes into account expenditure needs and revenue capacity, similar to the systems in force in most other developed countries.[16] The system can be improved in a number of respects.

---

[15]Furthermore, progressive property taxes on businesses create an incentive for splitting of businesses.

[16]In fact, it can be shown that the technique applied in Korea of calculating transfers by comparing "standard" revenue with "standard" expenditures for individual subnational governments is identical, in principle, to a system that applies separate equalization schemes to tax capacities and to expenditure needs, respectively.

Complexity of the Formula

The formula for allocating equalization transfers should be simpler and should reflect adequately, and in a more transparent manner, major expenditure needs (such as higher unit costs in some regions). Needs in the present system are evaluated by multiplying, for each of selected categories of expenditure, a need indicator by a unit cost estimated for that category. A distinct unit cost is used for each category of local autonomous body (for example, Seoul, other large cities, and provinces), and calculated on the basis of statistical techniques. While conceptually appropriate, a proper understanding of the calculations, however, is frequently beyond the reach of many, especially the small, local autonomous bodies. Such ambiguities eventually will lead to political resentment.

Objectives of Transfers

Another problem is related to the more general one of the inadequacy between goals and instruments. Transfers are currently used in Korea to meet a number of objectives: to correct the vertical fiscal imbalance between the central government and local autonomous bodies; to equalize expenditure needs and revenue capacity between the various local jurisdictions; to foster national and regional development; to constrain subnational governments' decision-making processes according to existing national priorities; and, finally, to increase efficiency in the provision of services and revenue-raising capacity. While most of these goals are similar to those of other countries' transfer systems, the list of objectives seems somewhat overstretched compared with the means, and has contributed to the complexity of the distribution formula.

Use of Indicators

The formula uses a large number of indicators, but two have played a dominant role: total population and the ceiling on the number of civil servants. Total population is widely used around the world, but is a quite generic indicator of expenditure. When used for a large share of the expenditure, as in the present case, it amounts to implying that expenditure needs are nearly equal on a per capita basis across the various areas. The use of the ceiling on civil servants may also pose some problems, even if there is a ceiling on their total number for each local autonomous body. The ceiling on civil servants is largely an indicator of present capacity, rather than a measure of need. Thus, local autonomous bodies may have no incentive to reduce the number of staff to increase efficiency. The same considerations apply to the size of administrative buildings. In general, expenditure needs should be connected with specific characteristics of the targeted beneficiary population.

According to efficiency and equity criteria, expenditure needs should be compared not with effective tax revenues but with *tax capacity*, that is, with the revenue that could be raised by applying standard tax rates to the effective tax bases. This is only partly achieved with the present formula based on estimated tax revenue and a partial adjustment between this estimate and actual tax collections in the following year. In a given year, if a local autonomous body increases its actual tax collections, by improving tax administration or by increasing tax rates, its revenue projections are subsequently increased, thus reducing central government transfers and partly nullifying the revenue effort.

Capital and Current Expenditures

The present system is geared to provide strong incentives to infrastructure investments. Legal mandates operate in the same direction. This reflects the growth orientation of the national policy. However, the building of infrastructure will rapidly increase maintenance expenditure and the provision of related current services. Local governments are presently eager to use the funds provided by the central government for capital projects. They may, however, face shortages of funds for current expenditure in the not-too-distant future.

Use of Transfers

An important issue is the balance of the transfer system between specific and general transfers. Currently more than half of total transfers are specific transfers. Their sectoral allocation is entirely determined by the central government. While the implementation of national priorities is a legitimate goal for a transfer system, excessive constraints on the use of the funds may be counterproductive (see Chapter 4). A change of balance is therefore needed from specific to general purpose transfers, in order to strengthen local autonomy and scale back central intervention in local priorities unless there is a clear element of externalities or merit goods.

Cyclical Nature and Complexity of the Equalization Transfers

The total amount of transfers should be determined in a way that reduces the procyclical effect on local fiscal operations, for example, the total amount might continue to be determined as a fixed share of internal tax revenue, but with a floor and a ceiling. Another mechanism may be devised to smooth cyclical fluctuations in transfers.

Local Borrowing

A market-oriented system of local borrowing (for example, at market interest rates), with simpler eligibility criteria, has to be established, but within an overall ceiling set in accordance with macroeconomic stabilization objectives. The present system of borrowing has generally been successful in achieving its objectives of regulating local borrowing and in directing borrowing toward high-priority areas. There are, however, a number of potential problem areas, discussed below, that have to be addressed in the reform process. In particular, these are related to the allocation mechanism, the overall ceiling, the eligibility criteria, and the system of bond placements.

Market Orientation of Allocation Mechanism

The present system of allocating credit is not market oriented, except that debt ratios are used as one of the eligibility criteria. Increased reliance on market forces, by letting financial markets evaluate the creditworthiness of subnational governments and pricing loans accordingly, may significantly improve the allocation of credit and also impose borrowing discipline on local governments. This would require, however, that financial markets be fairly well developed and timely and reliable information be available to them on the local government finances (see Chapter 7 for a comprehensive discussion of these issues).

Overall Ceiling

Apparently, no a priori decision is made concerning the appropriate level of the overall borrowing volume, consistent with the prevailing macroeconomic targets. If the degree of local autonomy in coming years is gradually increased, the authorities will probably be confronted with stronger demands for increased local borrowing, which may well raise the question of measures to control the global volume of borrowing.

The argument that there is a need for an overall ceiling, in addition to the existing project-oriented regulations, for local borrowing is based on practical considerations. In a world of perfect capital markets where accurate foresight prevails and the externalities of local capital projects are fully taken into account, project-oriented regulations on borrowing would be sufficient to ensure the sustainability of local borrowing. In practice, however, capital market conditions are volatile, financing costs fluctuate, and externalities may not necessarily be fully taken into account. An overall ceiling for local borrowing, based on macroeconomic conditions, would help ensure the consistency between local government operations and a sustainable macroeconomic framework.

Eligibility Criteria

The complexity of the present eligibility criteria is a key issue. Associated with a possible move away from the detailed control prevalent under the agent function and toward more local autonomy, regulations should set out a general and transparent framework within which greater autonomy is provided to the local bodies in the management of their borrowing operations.

Method of Bond Placements and Use of Proceeds

The system of compulsory bond placements involves an implicit fiscal cost on the consumers and firms affected. The fiscal costs take on three forms: the forced saving implied by the system, the grace period involved, and the lower-than-market interest rates offered. Thus, the "cheap" financing is achieved by imposing a nontransparent fiscal burden on the entities purchasing the bonds, a cost that under normal conditions would be covered by explicit taxation to finance credit on market terms. The cheap credit, furthermore, involves the risk of a "money-illusion" on the part of local autonomous bodies, which may induce them to incur excessive borrowing to finance wasteful or unsustainable spending.

Institutional Arrangements for Coordination

To translate the principles discussed in preceding sections into practice, sound legal and other institutional arrangements should be established.

Role of Local Autonomous Bodies as Public Entities

The Law on Local Autonomy prohibits local autonomous bodies from conducting the functions of the central government, but leaves room for bodies to engage in activities that may be carried out more efficiently by private sector enterprises. It would be helpful for the law to state clearly that local autonomous bodies should not engage in commercial activities.

Expenditure Assignment

There is a clear need to initiate a process to establish a more transparent and consistent legal framework for the assignment of functions between the central government and local autonomous bodies, which necessarily will be a prolonged process and will require regular consultations between the central government and local autonomous bodies. The present assignment of responsibilities does not seem to derive from a single and well-defined legal framework, be it the Constitution or an act of legislation. It is rather the result of the accretion over the years of a number of sectoral laws and decrees. In this situation, officials may find it extremely difficult to understand the exact range of their responsibilities. It would be helpful to introduce a comprehensive legal framework for expenditure and tax assignments as a basis for decentralization.

Nationwide Coordinating Mechanisms

Without appropriate and effective coordinating arrangements, adverse regional externalities can result in the underprovision of a national public good. This calls for a coordinating mechanism to ensure that harmonization of national and local spending priorities takes place in a coherent way and is preceded by technical analysis and political discussions. This could be activated through a two-tier approach: (1) a political forum would decide on the framework and set the priorities, for example, through the parliament or through regular meetings between the different levels of government; and (2) a technical forum would provide the means of implementing the required measures. This latter may take the form of a technical committee with representatives from the central government and local autonomous bodies, supplemented by external experts. It may either work under the auspices of the relevant ministry or take the form of a body independent of existing political and administrative structures. While the majority of developed nations have bodies of this nature, countries have chosen very different approaches with regard to the composition and specific objectives of the coordinating bodies.

Regional Coordinating Mechanisms

Cross-border spillover effects of local public goods call for regional cooperation and coordination. A public good may provide benefits to two or three provinces. In these cases, two or more local autonomous bodies can establish supraprovincial authorities such as metropolitan area authorities or regional environmental corporations.

Main Conclusions

Korea's intergovernmental fiscal relations are now in transition. Although the central government continues to play a key role in the fiscal operations of local autonomous bodies through regulations and the allocation of centrally controlled financial resources, politically independent local autonomous bodies are beginning to explore possibilities for increasing the provision of local public services. At this juncture, Korea faces a number of issues:

- The present intergovernmental fiscal relations are based on a number of complex and often overlapping individual laws, regulations, and practices, rather than on a systematic legal framework that establishes a transparent and streamlined assignment of functions between the central government and local autonomous bodies. The excessive overlapping of responsibilities can result in over- or underprovision. There seems to be an inadequate operational arrangement for effective conflict resolution between the central government and local autonomous bodies.
- There are areas where functions, authority, financing arrangements, and accountability are not adequately aligned. The financing arrangements do not suffficiently take into account the spillover effects of public goods provision between different tiers of government. Also, the financing arrangements do not adequately take into account the costs of carrying out central government functions delegated to local autonomous bodies.
- Intergovernmental fiscal relations do not sufficiently distinguish between two objectives—an improvement of horizontal equity and compensation for performing central government functions delegated to local autonomous bodies. These result in efficiency losses. The inadequate distinction between the two objectives diminishes the effectiveness of central government transfers in promoting national policy objectives.
- Central government control and regulations of local autonomous bodies in some areas remain extensive and may be judged excessive, particularly in such areas as budget formulation and taxation. Local autonomous bodies are still, to a large extent, considered agents of the central government. At the same time, local autonomous bodies are not exploiting potential policy flexibility (for example, flexible tax rates), and have excessive power to grant tax exemptions.
- Local taxes are too numerous, complicated in structure, and not sufficiently buoyant with respect to income. There is excessive reliance on property taxation, which, in turn, relies too much on

transaction taxes, rather than on ownership taxes, with the valuation of property outdated.
- The present system of central government transfers to local autonomous bodies is aimed at achieving too many goals, and relies on an excessively complex allocation scheme, while not adequately taking into account some fiscal needs—such as those arising from changing demographic trends. The determination of the total amount of transfers tends to have a procyclical impact on the fiscal operations of local autonomous bodies. The present system of transfers focuses excessively on capital projects. This would later lead to high demands for recurrent expenditures on operations and maintenance.
- Local borrowing, largely based on nonmarket principles, such as complicated administrative allocation and compulsory bond placements, can lead to excessive, poorly timed borrowing, as well as to the inefficient use of borrowed resources. The lack of an overall ceiling on local borrowing could potentially have adverse macroeconomic implications.

References

Bank of Korea, 1995, *Economic Statistics Yearbook* (Seoul).

———, 1996, *Economic Statistics Yearbook* (Seoul).

Government of North Kyungsang Province, 1996, *A Summary of Budget*.

Jun, Sang-Kyung, 1992, "Intergovernmental Fiscal Relations," in *Public Finance in Korea*, ed. by Kwang Choi and others (Seoul: Seoul National University Press).

Lee, Kye-Sik, 1992, "Local Public Finance," in *Public Finance in Korea*, ed. by Kwang Choi and others (Seoul: Seoul National University Press).

Ministry of Finance and Economy, 1995, *Tax Summary* (in Korean) (Seoul).

———, 1996, *A Survey of Taxation* (Seoul).

Ministry of Home Affairs, 1994, *Statistical Yearbook of Local Government Operations* (Seoul).

Oh, Yeon-Cheon, 1992, "The Local Tax System," in *Public Finance in Korea*, ed. by Kwang Choi and others (Seoul: Seoul National University Press).

Republic of Korea, *The Constitution of the Republic of Korea*.

———, *Law on Local Autonomy*.

Seoul Metropolitan Government, 1996, *A Summary of Budget* (Seoul).

Tanzi, Vito, 1996, "Fiscal Federalism and Decentralization: A Review of Some Efficiency and Macroeconomic Aspects," in *Annual World Bank Conference on Development Economics, 1995* (Washington: World Bank).

Ter-Minassian, Teresa, 1996, "Borrowing by Subnational Governments: Issues and Selected International Experiences," Paper on Policy Analysis and Assessment 96/4 (Washington: International Monetary Fund, April).

23

Mexico

JUAN AMIEVA-HUERTA

Mexico has a complex system of intergovernmental fiscal relations, characterized by a relatively high degree of expenditure centralization and by limited revenue-raising powers of state and municipal governments. In 1994, more than 75 percent of general government expenditures were controlled by the federal government, while own revenues of states and municipalities accounted for only 13 percent of general government revenue. The only sources of own revenues of lower levels of government are basically property taxes, fees, and user charges. All other taxes are assigned to the federal government. Local governments are, therefore, heavily dependent on federal revenue sharing. The federal government also relies on specific purpose grants to promote and finance the provision of certain services by lower levels of government. Specific purpose grants have also been used for horizontal fiscal equalization among states.

Overview of Intergovernmental Relations

Against a historical background of high centralization, attempts have been made since the mid-1980s to decentralize some of the federal

---

This paper was written while the author was in the IMF and was presented at the National Tax Association Conference, Boston, November 10, 1996. The author is grateful for helpful comments received from Ehtisham Ahmad, Katherine Baer, G.A. Mackenzie, Carlos Silvani, Teresa Ter-Minassian, and Charles Vehorn, and from the Mexican authorities.

responsibilities, especially for education and health care services. Since decentralization is not yet fully operative, particularly in health care services, the federal government continues to bear those expenditure responsibilities that have not been effectively transferred to the state governments. This ongoing decentralization process in Mexico could have significant implications for fiscal management and macroeconomic stability. A fuller decentralization would require reforms of the government structure and a substantial strengthening of public financial management, especially at the state and municipal levels.

Government Structure

Since independence in 1821, Mexico has embraced a federal system, established in the Constitutions of 1842, 1857, and 1917, the last of which remains in effect. Constitutionally, Mexico is a democratic, representative, federal territorial structure, consisting of free and sovereign states, but united under a federation. Mexico has a Federal District, 31 states, and 2,392 municipal governments.[1] Each state has its own Constitution, which is subordinate to the federal Constitution. Within each state, each municipality is a separate legal entity, but has limited taxing powers. The federal government is divided into autonomous executive, legislative, and judicial branches; this machinery is duplicated at the state level, that is, each state has the same three branches. As municipalities lack a legislative organ and cannot enact laws, municipal laws are established by the state congresses. Municipalities in Mexico have an autonomous executive branch.

The Constitution specifies that the states will share in the revenue from specific taxes and that the share will be determined by the federal government. State governments are required to transfer a portion of shared revenues to municipalities on a monthly basis. The federal Congress has the power, inter alia, to establish the bases upon which the executive branch may arrange loans and take responsibility for public debt.

The bulk of government spending and hence decisions on its allocation, are carried out by the federal government (Table 1). The social security system, external relations, and defense are under the exclusive jurisdiction of the federal government. Other activities are carried out in cooperation with state and municipal governments. These include education, health care services, and other government services (public safety, transportation, and administration).

---

[1]The 1990 population census indicated that there were 649 municipalities that had fewer than 10,000 inhabitants (27 percent of the total) and 324 had fewer than 5,000 inhabitants (14 percent).

Table 1. Mexico: Federal and Local Government Expenditure and Taxes

Federal government taxes	Federal government expenditures
Corporate income tax	Federal administration
Personal income tax	Service of domestic and foreign debt
Tax on assets of enterprises	Defense
Value-added tax (VAT)	Post and telecommunications
Duty on oil extraction (royalties)	External affairs
Oil export tax	Irrigation
Tax on production and services (excises)	Foreign trade
Tax on new cars[1]	Railways, highways, airways, and shipping
Tax on the ownership or use of vehicles	Federal and border police
Real estate transfer tax[2]	
Import duties	
Miscellaneous	
Shared taxes	*Shared expenditures*
Income taxes	Health
Value-added tax	Education
Excises	Specific purpose grant program
Oil export duties[3]	*Solidaridad*
Import duties	Single development agreements, (*Convenios*
Tax on the ownership or use of vehicles	*Unicos de Desarrollo*)
Tax on new cars	Special police
	National parks
State government taxes	*State government expenditures*
State payroll tax	State administration
Real estate transfer tax	State infrastructures
Tax on motor vehicles older than 10 years	State public order and safety
Tax on the use of land	Sanitation and water supply
Education tax	Service of domestic debt
Indirect taxes on industry and commerce	Public libraries
Fees and licenses for some public services	
Municipal government taxes	*Municipal government expenditures*
Local property tax	Local administration
Real estate transfer tax	Local public order and safety
Water fees	Local transportation
Other local fees and licenses	Local infrastructure including
Indirect taxes on agriculture, industry, and commerce	water supply and sanitation
	Local transit
Residential development	Waste disposal and street lighting
	Slaughterhouses, cemeteries, and parks

Source: Information provided by the Mexican authorities.
[1]This tax was suspended for one year on January 1, 1996.
[2]This tax was abolished on January 1, 1996.
[3]Some federal government tax revenues (oil production and export of hydrocarbons) are not included in the computation of the revenue-sharing fund.

Current Intergovernmental Fiscal Arrangements

The current government system in Mexico is highly centralized, compared with many developing countries, as well as with other member countries of the Organization for Economic Cooperation and De-

Table 2. Mexico: Structure of General Government, 1994[1]

	Federal Government	State Governments	Municipal Governments	General Government
	(In millions of new pesos)			
Total revenue	215,301	53,793	14,761	283,855
Taxes	160,317	2,028	3,253	165,598
Nontax revenue[2]	54,984	24,827	3,060	82,871
Net revenue sharing	—	26,938	8,448	35,386
Total expenditure	221,202	49,955	16,233	287,390
Administration	111,006	28,546	10,306	149,858
Transfers	74,792	8,396	1,101	84,289
Investment	30,422	12,508	4,337	47,267
Deferred outlays	4,982	505	489	5,976
Budgetary balance	−5,901	3,838	−1,472	−3,535
Change in third-party account	−4,027	5,847	292	2,112
Overall balance	−9,927	−2,009	−1,764	−13,700
Financing (net)	9,927	2,009	1,764	13,700
External	−6,595	—	—	−6,595
Domestic	16,522	2,009	1,764	20,295
	(In percent of GDP)			
Total revenue	16.9	4.2	1.2	22.3
Taxes	12.6	0.2	0.3	13.0
Nontax revenue[2]	4.3	1.9	0.2	6.5
Net revenue sharing	—	2.1	0.7	2.8
Total expenditure	17.4	3.9	1.2	22.6
Administration	8.7	2.2	0.8	11.8
Transfers	5.9	0.7	0.1	6.6
Investment	2.4	1.0	0.3	3.7
Deferred outlays	0.4	—	—	0.5
Budgetary balance	0.5	−0.3	−0.1	−0.3
Change in third-party account	−0.3	0.5	—	0.2
Overall balance	0.8	−0.2	−0.1	−1.1
Financing (net)	−0.8	0.2	0.1	1.1
External	−0.5	—	—	−0.5
Domestic	1.3	0.2	0.1	1.6

Sources: Secretariat of Finance and Public Credit (Hacienda); and Instituto Nacional de Estadística, Geografía e Informática (1996c).
[1] Excludes operations of the social security funds.
[2] Includes hydrocarbon royalties.

velopment (OECD). In 1994, only about 3 percent of the general government tax revenue and nearly 34 percent of total nontax revenue were collected by state and municipal governments (Table 2). By comparison, in the United States, these ratios amounted to 18 percent and 53 percent (1993), while in Canada, they accounted for about 43 percent and 57 percent (1992), respectively (International Monetary Fund, 1995). As explained below, state and municipal governments in Mexico rely on transfers from the federal government, mainly through revenue-sharing arrangements. In 1994, these transfers financed more than half of the states' expenditures and about half of those of municipalities. The relative weight of local government expenditures is somewhat greater than that of taxes. In 1994, about 23 percent of the general government outlays were carried out by state and municipal governments.

Revenue Assignment

According to the Constitution, the federal Congress is empowered to levy the taxes necessary to cover federal expenditures. The Congress has powers to levy taxes on public utilities, credit institutions, insurance companies, the use and exploitation of the nation's natural resources, foreign trade, electricity, gasoline, other oil products, and special taxes (see Table 1). Shared taxes with local governments include income taxes, the value-added tax (VAT), excises, oil export and import duties, and the tax on the ownership or use of vehicles.

The fundamental taxation principles—legality, equality, and revenue assignment—are also enshrined in the Constitution. Taxes may be enacted only by the Congress. Taxation must be based on ability to pay—all taxpayers in similar circumstances must be treated equally. Most taxes must be channeled into the federal budget and used for general public expenditures, not earmarked. Some earmarking, however, is allowed, notably for social security contributions. In April 1983, Mexico enacted a federal tax code, which covers tax administration, control, penalties, and procedures.

The most important tax revenue sources for the states are the real estate transfer tax,[2] the tax on older motor vehicles,[3] a state payroll tax,[4] and some indirect taxes on industry and commerce. In addition to these taxes, states can also charge fees for some public services (shows, enter-

---

[2]The sale of immovable property was subject to a federal tax—the real estate transfer tax—and to a similar tax levied by the states. The tax base was the sale price. The rate of the federal tax was 2 percent, and state tax rates could not be higher than the federal rate. The federal tax was abolished on January 1, 1996.

[3]The states operate a tax on motor vehicles older than ten years, based on the residual value of the vehicle, that is, the purchase price adjusted for inflation and depreciation.

[4]The Federal District and some states levy a tax on payrolls to be withheld by employers. State payroll taxes fluctuate between 0.65 percent in the state of Hidalgo to 4 percent in South Baja California.

tainment, and urban public transportation). As noted above, the state legislatures, in turn, establish the percentage of revenue assigned to the municipalities. States are allowed to keep the proceeds of the federal tax on the use of vehicles, which in 1994 amounted to 9 percent of their basic revenue-sharing entitlement. States are also allowed to appropriate 100 percent of the additional VAT collected from joint—federal and state—audits on VAT payers in their jurisdictions. This has created an incentive to audit by state authorities, although, as noted below, the results have not been substantial so far. The most important source of own revenue for the states is the state payroll tax; in 1994, it accounted for 74 percent of the states' total tax revenue, followed by the real estate transfer tax at 10 percent. In 1994, own tax and nontax revenue of the states accounted for only 11 percent of total general government revenue. In the same year, tax revenue of state governments amounted to only about 3.8 percent of their total revenue. Net revenue sharing amounted to about 50 percent of state revenues or 2.1 percent of GDP (see Table 2).

Certain tax revenue is reserved for municipalities, namely, those from the property tax, the real estate transfer tax (partially), and some indirect taxes on agriculture, industry, and commerce, which have very low yields; and duties and legal fees on public services rendered by municipalities. Tax and nontax revenues play a larger role at the municipal than at the state level (excluding hydrocarbon royalties). In 1994, municipal governments collected about 52 percent of their own revenue—excluding revenue sharing—from tax sources.

The most important tax revenue source for the municipalities is the property tax, which accounted for about 29 percent of municipal own revenue in 1994. This share is low compared with other OECD countries. In the United States and Canada, for example, over 50 percent and 61 percent of total local revenue, respectively, is from property taxes (see International Monetary Fund, 1995).

The property tax in Mexico is an ad valorem tax applied to the cadastral value of land or building. The rates are determined by each state and are relatively low by international standard; for example, in the Federal District, the rate ranges between 0.026 percent and 0.483 percent (Departamento del Distrito Federal, 1996). By comparison, in the United States, in 1993, the average effective tax rate in the entire country was 1.67 percent; in Massachusetts, it was 3.5 percent, while in Louisiana it was 0.61 percent, which is lower than the highest rate in Mexico's Federal District.[5] Actual collections from this tax are, in gen-

---

[5]Rural land is normally taxed at half of the rate. In most municipalities, these tax rates are grossly inadequate, but the local authorities prefer to avoid the political problems associated with modifying such rates.

eral, low because some municipalities, particularly the economically weakest, have neither an official register of the quantity, value, and ownership of properties in their territory nor efficient tax administration procedures. In others, the valuation of the properties for tax purposes remains well below their market value. Property values in the cadastre are indexed for inflation in most states. Some municipalities give property tax and water fees relief to certain categories of pensioners.

Given the low level of property tax collection, a comprehensive review of existing cadastral value is necessary to restore the tax base. The revenue potential of this tax could also be enhanced by raising tax rates,[6] eliminating deductions, strengthening its administration, and training local tax officials. Valuation rules on the cadastre and exemptions related to local tax bases could be made uniform throughout the states (as in Canada), to eliminate regional inequities and distortions. Again, this would require coordination among the states on the definition of the tax base. The effective administration of a property tax requires a reliable land cadastre, which may take years to prepare, but the cost of this process will be recouped quickly, provided the property values are updated regularly, in line with market trends.

On balance, there appears to be a need to strengthen revenue-raising capabilities at the state and municipal levels. Local governments could try to develop other more reliable and easier-to-collect tax sources, for example, selective consumption taxes, such as surcharges on utilities including household consumption of gas, electricity, water, and telephone services.[7] Moreover, the experience of other countries suggests that Mexican municipalities could also levy cost recovery charges, such as tolls for use of local roads and other user charges. More substantial presumptive taxes on itinerant fairs and markets, or a business license tax based on presumed or actual turnover, could also be considered.

Revenue Sharing

Federal revenue sharing has changed considerably since 1980, with a clear trend toward equalization. For example, total revenue sharing as a

---

[6] In Mexico, the decision to increase property tax rates must be made by state congresses.

[7] Water and electricity charges for households in Mexico are quite low by international standards.

Table 3. Mexico: Revenue Sharing

	In Percent of GDP	In Percent of Federal Government Revenue
1980	2.30	14.91
1981	2.50	16.28
1982	2.20	14.18
1983	2.80	15.73
1984	2.86	16.88
1985	2.69	15.99
1986	2.57	16.08
1987	2.65	15.64
1988	2.83	16.97
1989	2.85	15.92
1990	3.10	18.08
1991	3.10	18.32
1992	3.20	18.30
1993	3.30	19.35
1994	3.30	19.19
1995	3.10	17.32
1996[1]	3.20	18.93

Source: Secretariat of Finance and Public Credit (Hacienda).
[1]Projected.

proportion of GDP increased from 2.3 percent in 1980 to 3.3 percent in 1994. Similarly, shared revenues increased from about 16 percent of federal government revenue during the mid-1980s to around 19 percent in 1994 (see Table 3). This is the result of continuous revisions to the revenue-sharing formula—particularly since 1990—aimed at increasing the proportion of revenue allocated to state governments. These revisions have raised the weight of shared revenues in total revenues of the states from an average of 45 percent in 1978 to nearly 50 percent in 1994. States receive the bulk of these revenues from the general revenue-sharing fund (Fondo General de Participaciones (GRSF)) and the municipal development fund (Fondo de Fomento Municipal (MDF)). The GRSF encompasses about 18.51 percent of the federal revenue eligible for revenue sharing;[8] of this, 45.17 percent is distributed in direct proportion to the population of each state every fiscal year. This implies a redistribution in favor of the states with lower per capita collections. An additional 45.17 percent is distributed according to a revenue-sharing coefficient that reflects the taxable capacity of a state as well as its

---

[8]This is defined as total tax revenue plus oil levies (except surtaxes and special taxes). Some federal government tax revenues from oil extraction and exports are not included in the computation of the GRSF amounts.

revenue-raising efforts.[9] The remaining 9.66 percent is allocated to the states in inverse proportion to revenue sharing per capita in each entity (equalization component).[10] The Ministry of Finance calculates each month the amount to be distributed to the state governments. A similar procedure is used for the MDF.

Municipal governments obtain revenue-sharing funds from the federal government through three sources. The first source applies to all municipal governments: a 1 percent share of eligible federal revenue through the MDF, 56 percent of which is distributed according to a formula based on the revenue-sharing coefficient of each state government. The formula reflects municipal efforts to collect the property tax and the water fees;[11] therefore, the greater the effort the higher the federal revenue distributed to the municipality. The remaining 44 percent is distributed according to a restructuring program for urban commercial areas. States are obliged to transfer these funds to municipalities.

The second source is for municipalities that are involved in the extraction, sale, and export of oil. The municipalities receive 3.17 percent of the duty on oil extraction collected by the federal government (ex-

---

[9]The GRSF revenue-sharing coefficient is given by

$$B^i = \frac{(CP^i_{t-1})(IA^i_{t-1})}{IA^i_{t-2}}; \quad CP^i_t = \frac{B^i}{TB};$$

where
IA^i_{t-1} = assignable taxes collected in state i in year $t-1$,
$TB = \Sigma B^i$ = total entitlements,
CP^i_{t-1} = revenue-sharing coefficient for state i in year $t-1$, and
B^i = entitlement to state i.

The formula, therefore, takes into account: (1) the fiscal effort indicator, which includes assignable taxes collected in state i (taxes on new automobiles, taxes on motor vehicles, and taxes on production and services); and (2) the state's share in total entitlements of the preceding year. The former is derived by dividing the assignable taxes collected the preceding year by those collected the year before. This formula generates a pie that must be divided so that one state's loss is another's gain.

[10]Poorer states, whose per capita entitlements according to the first two shares fall below the average, receive more out of the 9.66 percent of the pool than those whose per capita entitlements lie above the average.

[11]The MDF revenue-sharing coefficient is given by:

$$CE^i = \frac{A^i}{TA}; \quad A^i = \frac{(CE^i_{t-1})(IPDA^i_{t-1})}{IPDA^i_{t-2}};$$

where
A^i = revenue sharing to state i,
$TA = \Sigma A^i$,
CE^i_{t-1} = revenue-sharing coefficient for state i in year $t-1$, and
$IPDA^i_{t-1}$ = total property tax and water fee collections of state i.

cluding the extraordinary duty). These funds compensate municipalities for environmental damage caused by extraction and sale of oil.

Until 1996, there was a third source for municipalities involved in international trade. They received 0.136 percent of total eligible federal revenues. This mechanism was intended to provide an incentive to control smuggling and control Mexico's fiscal borders, but was discontinued in 1996.

Tax Administration

The Undersecretariat of Revenue in the Ministry of Finance ("Hacienda") is responsible for tax policy and tax administration. International trade taxes are administered by the General Customs Administration, a directorate of the Undersecretariat of Revenue. Among the latter's other functions is intergovernmental fiscal coordination. The National System of Fiscal Coordination is responsible for coordinating the federal tax system with the state and municipal tax systems, and for determining the corresponding share of federal revenue.

In Mexico, federal government revenue is collected by the Undersecretariat of Revenue through the banking system. Revenue collected by the latter is remitted to the federal government (Treasury) for subsequent sharing with the states according to the formulas discussed above.[12] The states and municipalities' own revenues are collected by their respective tax offices. Collection costs and efficiency vary substantially from state to state (the richest states have modern computerized systems and better trained personnel), but this reflects more administrative and institutional factors than the tax structure.

The Undersecretariat of Revenue is organized by functions and in two levels. At the first level there are, inter alia, four general directorates that carry out the main operational functions of tax administration, namely collection, auditing, legal affairs, and customs administration. At the second level of the organization are eight regional tax offices in charge of overseeing the implementation in their territory of the four major tax administration functions noted above. The four aforementioned general directorates provide specific guidelines to the eight regional offices as described below. These eight offices supervise the operations of 65 (previously 261) local tax offices (*administraciones locales*), which are responsible for administering the major federal taxes throughout the country and the local custom offices (*aduanas*) located

---

[12]Since 1992, the VAT is administered exclusively by the federal government.

along the border, and at ports and international airports.[13] At the state level, there are 32 state tax offices (*entidades federativas*) responsible for administering state taxes.[14]

The Directorate for collection determines policies, systems, and procedures for tax collection and enforcement, including control of delinquent taxpayers, recovery of arrears, and application of penalties and sanctions. It formulates computer policies and programs, and administers and updates the national taxpayer register. It also designs the revenue collection systems to be used by local and state tax offices. This Directorate works jointly with a special unit (Unidad de Coordinación con Entidades Federativas), which is responsible for coordinating all tax administration functions with state tax offices.

The Directorate for audit administration formulates the annual audit plan and provides the local tax offices with guidelines on policies and programs for audit, inspection, verification, and compliance with federal tax obligations (including customs). While federal tax audits are the main responsibility of federal auditors, state auditors only participate in VAT audits.

The Directorate for legal affairs regulates collection enforcement and other tax matters involving litigation. It also provides guidelines and assistance to the legal departments of the 65 local tax offices in the exercise of their duties.

The General Customs Administration regulates international trade taxes, free economic zones, cross-border trade, and temporary import exemptions, and also regulates import quotas. It is responsible for customs clearance and for policies dealing with customs agents and representatives.

To modernize the tax administration and improve its effectiveness, in December 1995, the Mexican Government enacted a law creating the Tax Administration Service (Servicio de Administración Tributaria (SAT)), a semiautonomous entity that will operate under the guidance and supervision of a revenue board (presided by the Minister of Finance). The Undersecretariat for Revenue will continue to be in charge of tax policy functions, with advice from the SAT. The latter is

---

[13]The main taxes administered by local tax offices are the income taxes, the VAT, the excise taxes, and the tax on new automobiles. In some states, local offices also administer the tax on motor vehicles and the real estate transfer tax (see Table 1). Since 1993, several important tax administration reforms have been introduced to simplify the existing system (Gil-Díaz, 1995).

[14]The state tax offices administer the following major taxes: the state payroll tax, the tax on use of land, the real estate transfer tax, the property tax, and the business license.

Table 4. Mexico: Public Sector GDP

	1986	1987	1988	1989	1990	1991	1992	1993
Public sector	20.6	21.7	18.8	18.4	20.2	17.2	16.0	15.7
General government	6.6	6.2	5.8	5.9	6.3	6.8	7.6	8.4
Federal government	4.1	3.8	3.6	3.7	4.1	4.3	4.9	3.5
Local governments[1]	1.4	1.2	1.1	1.1	1.1	1.1	1.2	3.3
Social security	1.1	1.2	1.1	1.1	1.2	1.4	1.5	1.6
Public enterprises	14.0	15.5	13.0	12.5	13.9	10.4	8.4	7.3
Private sector	79.4	78.3	81.2	81.6	79.8	82.8	84.0	84.3

Source: Instituto Nacional de Estadística, Geografía e Informática (1994b).
[1]Includes state and municipal governments.

scheduled to become operational on July 1, 1997 (see Secretaría de Hacienda y Crédito Público, 1996).

This new agency will have the authority to collect all federal taxes and will carry out all tax administration functions, including auditing and taxpayer assistance. It will also incorporate customs administration as well as the federal tax police.

Expenditure Assignment

According to the National Institute of Statistics (Instituto Nacional de Estadística, Geografía e Informática, 1994a), in 1993, Mexico's public sector GDP amounted to about 16 percent of total GDP, down from nearly 22 percent in 1987 (Table 4). In the same year, 54 percent of public sector GDP was accounted for by the general government. Of this total, 22 percentage points corresponded to the federal government, 10 percentage points to the social security institutions, and the rest to local governments (state and municipal governments). This implies that the size of local governments in Mexico's economy is relatively small. State enterprises generated about 46 percent of public sector GDP, down from 69 percent in 1990. The relative importance of public enterprises began to decline after 1989—particularly in 1992 and 1993 as a result of privatization[15] (see also Figure 1).

---

[15]During 1983–96, the government divested from most areas of economic activity—hotels, sugar mills, telecommunications, airlines, the banking sector, and the steel industries. Of the 1,155 public enterprises in 1982, 960 firms had been divested by May 1996. During 1989–94, about 300 enterprises were privatized, with total proceeds of about MexN$75 billion (US$25 billion). The Mexican privatization plan has been one of the most extensive in the world, with total dollar proceeds surpassed only by New Zealand and the United Kingdom. Privatization was followed by government deregulation in several sectors and the decentralization of education.

Figure 1. Mexico: Public Sector GDP
(In percent of GDP)

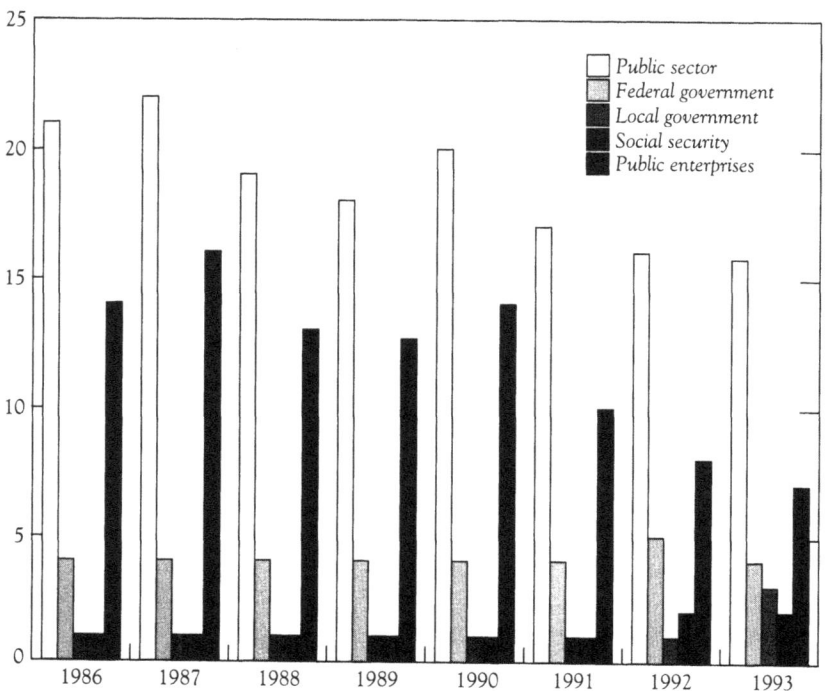

The public sector workforce remained fairly stable from 1986 to 1989 (Figure 2), at 4.3 million remunerated positions or about 15 percent of the labor force. From 1989 to 1993, the overall public workforce declined by about 6 percent because of the impact of privatization of public companies, partly offset by an 8 percent increase in the size of the civil service. The composition of the latter was substantially affected by the decentralization process (see Table 5). In 1993, decentralization in the education sector transferred the administrative apparatus—including personnel—from the federal to state governments. Accordingly, the share of workers employed by the federal government in total general government employment decreased from 71 percent in 1992 to 41 percent in 1993. In the same year, state and local governments accounted for 49 percent of the total and the social security institutions for 10 percent.

In Mexico, the expenditure functions for different levels of government are not clearly determined in the Constitution. The federal gov-

Figure 2. Mexico: Work Force Employed by the Public Sector, 1986–93
(In thousands of workers)

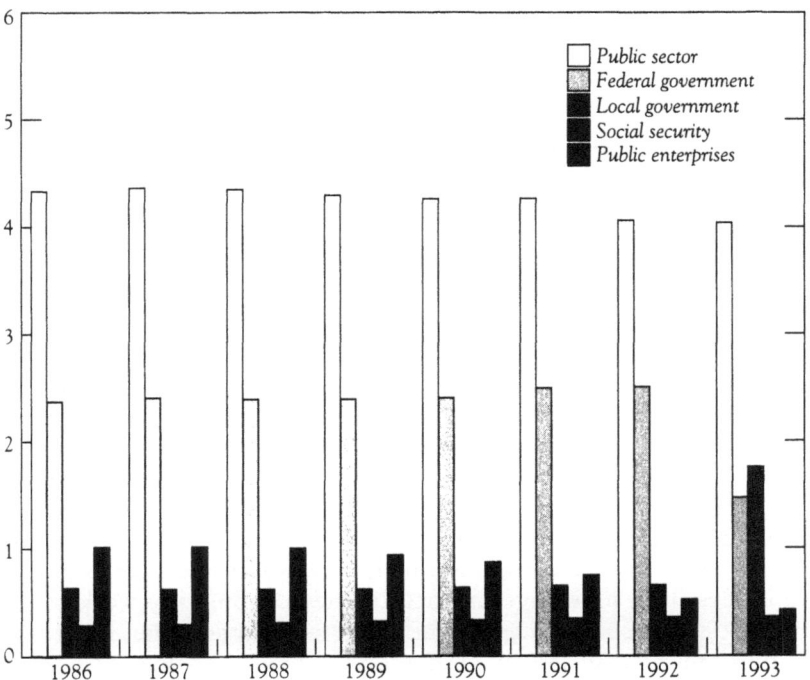

ernment assigns most expenditure functions. In 1994, federal government expenditures on administration amounted to 8.7 percent of GDP, while capital expenditures and transfers represented 2.4 percent and 5.9 percent of GDP, respectively.[16]

The bulk of state government expenditure is concentrated on public order and safety, transportation, health, education, and sanitation. In 1994, states' expenditures on public order, transportation, and administration represented on average about 57 percent of total net state government expenditure (excluding debt amortizations). State expenditure on infrastructure and public works accounted for about 25 percent of total net expenditure. State expenditure on transfers (excluding rev-

---

[16]In Mexico, state and municipal governments do not provide data on the economic classification of their expenditures.

Table 5. Mexico: Workforce Employed by the Public Sector
(In thousands of workers)

	1986	1987	1988	1989	1990	1991	1992	1993
Public sector	4,345	4,377	4,364	4,308	4,273	4,278	4,071	4,049
General government	3,317	3,346	3,348	3,358	3,391	3,518	3,541	3,612
Federal government	2,380	2,412	2,400	2,398	2,408	2,500	2,509	1,473
Local governments[1]	646	633	632	631	643	661	665	1,768
Social security	291	301	316	329	340	357	367	371
Public enterprises	1,028	1,031	1,016	950	883	760	531	437

Source: Instituto Nacional de Esadística, Geografía e Informática (1994b).
[1] Includes state and municipal governments.

enue sharing with municipalities) exceeded 17 percent, reflecting mainly the distribution of subsidies and grants (see Table 2).

As regards municipal government expenditure, in 1994, expenditures on administration, including public order and local transportation, represented about 63 percent of total net spending. Municipal expenditures on infrastructure amounted to 27 percent of total net expenditures, while the remaining 17 percent was allocated to transfers and subsidies to local private and public institutions (Instituto Nacional de Estadística, Geografía e Informática, 1996c). Municipalities spend a larger proportion of their budget on wages and salaries of local employees than state governments. In the economically weakest municipalities, the share of capital outlays in total expenditures is very low. In these municipalities, maintenance for roads and local schools is often carried out by the private sector, mainly through extensive community participation coordinated by the local authorities. Some municipalities have developed infrastructure projects with the assistance of the state or the federation, mainly through the general purpose grant programs described below. Contributions of citizens in the form of work have also been used to match the funding.

In Mexico, the state and municipal governments may spend their revenue-sharing allotments for any purpose. In practice, however, most municipal governments—particularly the economically weakest—use most of their allocations to pay wages to government employees. High administrative expenditure reflects in part inefficiencies in the delivery of goods and services provided by the municipalities.

As discussed above, the federal government has control of major tax sources, as in many countries, particularly in Latin America. This leads to the problems of vertical imbalances because municipal governments' own tax revenue is only a fraction of municipal expenditures. The same vertical imbalance is present at the state governments' level, while in recent years federal government tax revenue has been higher than federal government expenditures. Therefore, an imbalance between own revenues and expenditures net of transfers for each aggregate level of government is present. This implies that the federal government faces an imbalance in its favor, and the balance between own revenues and expenditures is redistributed to local governments to correct their imbalances. In most countries, a substantial vertical imbalance also leads to horizontal imbalances. These imbalances are often redressed through a system of general purpose grants, along with specific purpose transfers (see below).

The Decentralization Process

Decentralization can contribute to the more efficient provision of local public services, because local governments are likely to have better information on social needs, especially in education and health care. Accordingly, a number of countries, particularly in Latin America, have moved to decentralize the provision of education and health care to the state governments. The central governments retain responsibility for defining the main lines of education and health care policies.

Over the short to medium term, Mexico is expected to continue decentralizing authority over a number of functions, including education and health care. While this may increase allocative efficiency, it carries significant risks for macromanagement and distributional equity. This is especially the case when lower levels of government have limited revenue-raising and financial management capacities.

In general, a successful decentralization effort requires a major reform of the government structure and a strengthening of public financial management. Decentralization also requires that there be institutional arrangements for intergovernmental coordination, budgeting, planning, and implementation, as well as strong local institutional capacities. Intergovernmental coordination—through regularly scheduled meetings of relevant officials at the different levels of government—is critical to improve public sector management. For decentralized institutions to succeed, there must be effective monitoring and auditing systems for lower level performance. The federal government must provide technical assistance and training on management issues to local officials.

It is too early to assess the outcome of the decentralization process in Mexico. Since decentralization is not yet complete, the federal government continues to bear expenditure responsibilities that have not been effectively transferred to state governments, particularly in the case of health care expenditures. On balance, it appears that education expenditures are distributed equitably (Shah, 1994; Amieva, 1993), but the health sector lacks comprehensive coverage, and service quality is poor (Amieva, 1993).

Education

Based on the principle that educational development should be propelled by the federation, the Public Education Secretariat (SEP) was created in 1921. The concentration of decision-making power in the central government, however, did not prove conducive to the development of education. A beginning toward decentralization in education was made in 1973 with the creation of nine regional units and subunits for administrative services. Deconcentration,[17] however, was not initiated until 1976, with the creation of 31 state offices of the SEP. The goals were to involve the states in the educational development process, to increase the efficiency of education, and, more generally, to increase participation by the community in the education process.

From 1976 to 1982, the SEP successfully completed the deconcentration process (Pescador-Osuna, 1993). The process of decentralization resumed in 1982 with the creation of advisory committees. The work of these committees consisted of gathering the necessary information related to basic education and extending teacher training to each state. To consolidate these efforts, the federal government created the public education state councils and transformed the educational service units of the states into general departments of coordinated public education services. However, pressure from the powerful national education workers' union during the 1980s slowed the transfer of human and financial resources needed to initiate the decentralization process.

The administration of President Salinas (1988–94) announced its intention to modernize the education sector. This process had two elements: the decentralization of education and the strengthening of society's participation in education. For its implementation, the federation transferred the school institutions in 1993 (basic and postbasic education) to the state governments with all the components being utilized at that point by the Public Education Secretariat (Solís-Cámara, 1993).

---

[17]Deconcentration is a limited form of decentralization, that is, the delegation of executive power from federal to regional agencies. Decentralization means empowering regional agencies to make their own decisions rather than following those made by a regulatory agency.

The National Agreement on Public Education Modernization (1992) stipulates the sequencing of the decentralization. This agreement formally transferred the administrative apparatus and the schools, their assets, and staff from the federal government to the state administrations. The agreement also redefined the Public Education Secretariat's normative functions, and the secretariat was restructured accordingly. The General Education Law (1993) redistributed the educational responsibilities between the federal and state governments; however, the SEP's internal regulations are still being revised to conform with this law.

Mexico is currently consolidating the education decentralization program. The country's 31 state governments are now responsible for managing the publicly financed basic and postbasic education services, which were previously administered by the federal government. This explains the sharp increase in remunerated positions in the local governments (see Figure 2). The SEP, in turn, is focusing more on policy issues, allocation of nonrecurrent resources to regions or municipalities, and evaluation.

Health Care

Mexico's public health programs include the social security system and the Secretariat of Health (SSA). In 1993, the Social Security Institute for private sector employees (IMSS) covered 37.5 million beneficiaries, while the Social Security Institute for public sector employees (ISSSTE) covered about 8.5 million.[18] Together, the two institutions covered only about half of the total Mexican population. Private sector coverage for that year—excluding IMSS—is estimated at about 4.3 million, or 5 percent of the total population. The uninsured population is the responsibility of the SSA. The SSA is in charge of the main specialized hospitals, finances most of the states' health services, and runs the National Institutes of Health.

Historically, health service management in Mexico has been overcentralized. Management staff at the federal level are often unaware of local needs or are limited in their ability to act, owing to bureaucratic requirements. Geographic distances and several levels of administration delay the implementation of remedial actions at the local level (Amieva, 1991). Moreover, the SSA's procedures are inefficient in many respects, and characterized by duplication. As a result, the health

---

[18]In addition, there are special social security institutes for employees of some state governments, PEMEX (the petroleum company), and the social security institute of the armed forces. In 1990, these institutions together covered 1.25 million people, or about 1.5 percent of the total population.

care system is not comprehensive in coverage and suffers from poor quality of services. The system remains inordinately centralized, unable to allocate resources efficiently, and excessively bureaucratic.

A plan to decentralize health care was formulated in the early 1980s. During the De la Madrid administration (1982–88), health care was decentralized in 14 of the 32 states; this transferred some, but not all, decision-making power (including planning, budgeting, and personnel) from the federal to the state level. Decentralization, however, came to a halt during the Salinas administration (1988–94). The present (Zedillo) administration intends to complete and deepen decentralization in all states. A program to delegate the tasks of decentralizing management, budgeting, and planning is under way. This decentralization has been slow, because the states' lack of appropriate managerial and professional skills and information systems has inhibited their effective use of resources. Another obstacle to the decentralization of health care services is the division of responsibility for public health care service between the social security institutes (for public and private sector employees) and the SSA.

Budget Formulation and Implementation

The Constitution does not specify in detail the budget responsibilities of the executive branch. It does state, however, that the executive branch must send to the Congress for approval an annual budget, as well as the tax revenue measures necessary to cover expenditures. The Congress approves (before the beginning of the fiscal year, which coincides with the calendar year) the general outlines of the budget and the details of revenues and loans. The Ministry of Finance prepares quarterly reports to the Congress on the evolution of the main macroeconomic indicators and public finance statistics. Reports are also submitted to the Congress on the execution of the National Development Plan, the evolution of the external and domestic debt, and the general framework of economic policy. The latter document is presented jointly with the budget proposal, and defines the main fiscal policy actions as well as the annual macroeconomic targets.

In Mexico, the Secretariat of Finance and Public Credit is in charge of the federal budget process, and it acts in consultation with the spending departments to establish budget priorities. Mexico's fiscal year involves three distinct processes: formulation, implementation, and audit.[19] In

---

[19]For example, as the 1995 budget went into effect, the audit of 1994 began, with the report due on June 15, 1995; the formulation of the 1997 budget usually begins in April 1996, to be completed for presentation to Congress by November 15, 1996.

practice, there are some important delays in completing these phases, so that the formulation is not begun on time, audit is late, and the implementation of the current budget lags behind schedule. Local budgets follow the same programming-planning-budgeting process. Some states, however, experience considerable delays in some of these phases, particularly in budget formulation and execution. These delays result in a heavy round of activities from September to December as federal and local authorities rush to allocate funds for the current fiscal year at the same time as formulating the budget for the following year. However, over the years, these delays have been reduced in many states as a result of computerization and administrative reforms.

The lack of multiyear budgets and forward expenditure plans is a shortcoming of the Mexican budgetary system. It may affect adversely private investment, both domestic and foreign, and, more importantly lead to the approval of multiyear investment projects without congressional scrutiny of outlays beyond the first year, thus imparting excessive rigidities to future spending decisions.

In Mexico, the Ministry of Finance holds the main budgetary powers and responsibilities, including revenue, expenditure, and public debt. It defines the framework for fiscal policy and prepares the macroeconomic forecasts. The Central Bank also plays a major role in financial programming. The Secretariat of Finance and Public Credit is responsible for paying the civil service wages, coordinating the expenditure programs, and monitoring the revenue and expenditure flows. Its debt management unit manages the government's external and internal debt. The Treasury prepares the monthly cash spending plans and executes budgetary payments to other levels of government and to private sector contractors.

Grants

In Mexico, information on general and specific purpose grants is scanty and not suited to detailed analysis. In the 1980s, Mexico made use of annual federal matching general purpose grants on current and capital investment programs. The federal government prepared the so-called single development agreements (*convenios únicos de desarrollo*) with each state government.[20] With these agreements, fiscal coordination extends to the expenditure budget exercise. At the same time, general agreements are concurrently reached each year on municipal government expenditure policy through the Government Supervision and

---

[20]These agreements must follow the guidelines of the National Development Plan.

Evaluation System, which is used to control the programs and resources agreed upon between the federation, states, and municipalities (Baqueiro, 1992).

Under the single development agreements, each municipal government must verify the execution of programs financed through federal grants. Municipal governments are required to provide quarterly spending plans and financial information, as well as any explanation and record that the federal government requests on the programs. Currently, the federal government develops its public investment program in coordination with local governments. The municipal governments must also verify physical and financial progress and report on them to the Secretariat of the Comptroller General. These programs, however, have lost importance in the 1990s and have been virtually replaced by the national solidarity program (*Solidaridad*).

In addition to funds allocated through the revenue-sharing formula and general purpose grants, this federal government policy instrument, *Solidaridad*, has gained importance in recent years. It allocates federal resources to municipal governments for specific programs.[21] In 1994, *Solidaridad* comprised 32 programs and its expenditures amounted to about 0.8 percent of GDP. *Solidaridad* is, in essence, a specific purpose grants program targeted to the poorest regions of the country. It is coordinated by the executive branch (the Ministry of Social Development) and provides discretionary grants to states and municipalities that are used to finance regional projects. These grants are defined in the context of the so-called social development agreements. Introduced in 1989, these agreements constitute an instrument designed by the federation and the states to define priorities and programs of mutual interest; they represent the channel for support of the decentralization of important functions to the states and municipalities. They strengthen the states' and municipal governments' capacity to make decisions. *Solidaridad* sets policies and strategies, and each state selects the social and productive projects and establishes priorities. Thus, in addition to financing community-based development efforts, *Solidaridad* is also used as a vehicle for combining federal, state, and municipal resources and grants to finance large infrastructure projects.[22] This implies that *Soli-*

---

[21]*Solidaridad* embodies several individual programs: municipal funds, neighborhood urban development programs, water supply and sanitation, rural roads, income-generating projects, agricultural production loans, health, solid waste management, employment training, rural electrification, and special regional development programs.

[22]These works often involve grater participation of responsible federal line agencies and a national development bank (BANOBRAS), which provides additional financing to the investment programs.

daridad is a mechanism allowing the federal government to work with the states and municipal governments and to influence their spending decisions, thereby improving the overall quality of state and municipal investments.

Solidaridad also entails commitments of municipal government resources. For example, *Solidaridad* distributed US$2,248 million in 1992 and US$2,409 million in 1993. Municipal government resources amounted to 48 percent and 50 percent, respectively, of the total amount invested in *Solidaridad*'s projects (Secretaría de Desarrollo Social, 1993). In a context of high centralization, these grants have been a significant tool for improving the physical infrastructure of the states and municipalities. *Solidaridad* grants are also designed in principle to promote horizontal fiscal equalization between states, that is, to reduce differences in income or taxable capacities. Data limitations, however, have so far hindered an analysis of the effectiveness of this program in reducing regional imbalances.

Critics of *Solidaridad* point to several shortcomings of the program. They note that there is neither a clear set of criteria for distributing these grants nor an effective evaluation of the projects financed. The poverty alleviation component of the program has also been questioned, on the grounds that it is not well targeted to the poorest population groups. Clearly, the proliferation of specific purpose grants may become unwieldy and inefficient. The lack of transparent criteria for the allocation of those grants makes them relatively unpredictable.

Borrowing

Since 1988 most state government deficits have been increasing. Their total deficit reached MexN$0.2 billion or about 0.6 percent of GDP in 1994 (see Table 2), while municipalities have shown small deficits. These deficits have been reflected in the growth of their outstanding debt, which has increased by about 62 percent in real terms since 1988 (Gamboa-Gonzalez, 1996). It would appear that the main factors leading to increased deficits were the expansion of states' current and capital expenditure and access to domestic financing by the banking system, as noted below. This suggests that the federal government has had difficulty in imposing financial discipline on the states.

States and municipalities do have the authority to issue securities in the domestic capital market, but only the federal government is entitled to borrow abroad. State debt instruments are generally issued through government-owned national development banks (Baqueiro,

1992). This is a fairly recent development, and has been used by the most developed states to finance toll roads and other infrastructure projects. The rate of return offered by these instruments is market determined and there is no subsidy involved. Also, state governments frequently use their revenue-sharing funds to guarantee loans they receive from the banking system.[23]

States are allowed to borrow domestically, if they have the authorization of their local congress, with most of the states' loans coming from private banks and about 40 percent from government development banks—for specific infrastructure projects. The use of commercial bank borrowing has probably had an adverse effect on the states' efforts to increase own revenue and to control expenditure. On December 31, 1995 total state and municipal government debt to commercial and development banks had reached about MexN$29 billion, or about 1.8 percent of GDP—mostly from state governments.[24] This growth of the state debt is a cause of concern because, if continued, it may eventually have an adverse impact on the federal budget, if the states become unable to service their debt, particularly in view of the current high level of real interest rates and tight credit conditions. Local governments can also accumulate expenditure arrears with the private sector, which in December 1995 amounted to MexN$3 billion or 0.2 percent of GDP.

Municipalities can also borrow from commercial banks, but rarely do so. In recent years, the Central Bank has not provided loans or funds to municipalities. Municipal governments may contract loans intended to finance productive public investment, including those carried out by their decentralized agencies or public enterprises, in accordance with the principles set forth in state legislation. Municipal governments often use their federal revenue-sharing funds to guarantee the loans they receive. To finance local projects that meet federal government requirements, loans can be obtained from the national development banks—a source of considerable financing. State and municipal governments' requests to use their revenue-sharing funds to guarantee their loans are recorded in a special register (Baqueiro, 1992). Lower levels of government can also borrow from the higher levels. All state governments and municipalities have such liabilities.

---

[23]These loans have relatively long maturities (less than seven years).

[24]Local government debt is concentrated in the richest states, which have the largest tax bases. The federal government has introduced some measures recently to prevent excessive borrowing. Furthermore, these states have started to restructure certain debt to both commercial and development banks. The restructuring of states' debts, however, should be accompanied by a decisive adjustment of their finances.

Summary and Conclusions

Since 1980, Mexico has begun various reforms of its intergovernmental fiscal relations. These reforms seek to improve government efficiency and redefine the role of the lower levels of government. A substantial share of state and municipal revenue in Mexico is derived from the revenue-sharing mechanism, federal general purpose grants, and specific purpose grants. Although the redistribution formula has led to some strengthening of the states' tax collection efforts, the results have been limited to date. In 1990, Mexico introduced modifications to the revenue-sharing arrangements, which have improved them in some respects. Currently, the main criteria for distributing tax sharing are population, fiscal capacity, fiscal effort, and an equalization component. There is a risk that further changes in the revenue-sharing mechanism (for example, increasing the pool of funds shared by the states) may weaken the federal government's ability to use fiscal policy for macroeconomic management. This calls for caution in revising the arrangements.

The capacity of state and municipal governments to raise revenue remains limited. States' own resources consist basically of fees and a small number of taxes with low yield. The bulk of municipalities' revenue is derived from the revenue-sharing mechanism. Local governments also continue to depend largely on federal grants. Municipal governments currently have limited capacity to raise own tax revenue mainly because of inadequate cadastres, low property tax rates, deductions, and inefficient property tax collection procedures. The potential for increasing property tax revenue for the municipalities is, however, considerable. Giving the states and municipalities more taxing powers should be considered. Local governments could also levy selective consumption taxes, such as surcharges on utilities including household consumption of gas, water, electricity, and telephone service. Such taxes are easier to collect and create less distortions. Moreover, as in other countries, municipalities could also levy cost recovery charges, such as tolls for the use of local roads and user charges. Presumptive taxes on itinerant fairs and markets could also be considered.

Even after revenue sharing, a significant vertical fiscal imbalance persists. The federal government has utilized specific purpose grants through the *Solidaridad* program to reduce this imbalance. *Solidaridad* grants have also been used to correct horizontal imbalances. *Solidaridad* funds have become an increasingly important source of funding for state and municipal expenditures. *Solidaridad* has played a significant role in channeling social expenditure to the poorer and economically weaker states. Indeed, one of its great successes has been its effectiveness in involving the community in local infrastructure projects. It would appear, however, that there is a need to streamline *Solidaridad*, while continuing to use its other funds for matching grants to states and municipal governments. At a minimum, it should be ensured that *Solidaridad* programs are consistent with the sector strategies adopted by the main line secretariats. Likewise, the distribution of matching funds to local governments should be made transparent and based on need criteria.

Mexico remains a highly centralized federation. In 1994, more than three quarters of general government expenditures were controlled by the federal government. The share of administrative expenditures in total municipal governments' spending is rather high, reflecting inefficiencies in the delivery of municipal services.

In recent years, the government has embarked on a decentralization process, particularly in education and health care, aimed at improving the efficiency and quality of public services. While it is difficult to predict the success of such decentralization efforts, the federal government is likely to play a continuing role in coordinating these efforts and in ensuring that the most vulnerable groups receive some minimum level of services. Decentralization offers potential gains in efficiency and improvements in the quality of education and health care. A successful decentralization, however, requires structural reforms in the federal government, as well as an improvement in the collection of performance indicators, the encouragement of community participation, the establishment of additional societal organizations to provide services, and the strengthening of state and local financial management. There are, moreover, significant macroeconomic risks involved. It is vital that decentralization not unduly weaken the federal government's ability to use fiscal policy for macroeconomic management.

It would appear that the use of state bank borrowing to lessen the states' liquidity constraints has had an adverse effect on their efforts to increase own revenue and control expenditure. Although the states' government debt is currently not very large and the federal government has introduced some measures to prevent excessive borrowing, the lack of effective controls over state borrowing could lead to further strain and macroeconomic instability, especially under conditions of tight money and high real interest rates.

One of Mexico's important fiscal problems has been the lack of coordination of tax policy and administration among levels of government. The lack of uniformity across the states in the kind of taxes levied and their rates, particularly on the property tax, results in an uneven geographic distribution of the fiscal burden. Efforts should be made to improve collection efficiency by strengthening the present tax coordination and harmonization agreements between the federal government and the states. Improving tax collection by local governments would require intensive training and additional funding. Finally, future intergovernmental reforms should include the introduction of multiyear budgets, to help integrate multiyear programs and medium-term macroeconomic objectives.

References

Amieva, J., 1991, "Public Social Expenditures, Labor Markets, and the Poor: The Mexican Experience, 1982–90" (unpublished; Washington: International Monetary Fund).

———, 1993, "Gasto Público y Crecimiento Económico: Una Investigación Empírica," in *México: Desarrollo de Recursos Humanos y Tecnología* (Mexico City: Editorial Porrúa).

Arellano, R., 1994, "Necesidades de Cambio en las Relaciones Hacendarias Intergubernamentales en México" (unpublished; Puebla, Mexico: Universidad de las Américas).

Banting, K.G., D.M. Brown, and T.J. Courchene, eds., 1994, *The Future of Fiscal Federalism* (Kingston, Ontario: School of Policy Studies, Queen's University).

Baqueiro, A., 1992, "La Relación entre las Finanzas Públicas Federales y las Estatales: El Caso de México" (unpublished; Mexico City: Banco de México).

Bomfim, A.N., and A. Shah, 1991, *Macroeconomic Management and the Division of Powers in Brazil: Perspectives of the Nineties*, World Bank Working Papers Series 567 (Washington: World Bank).

Chapoy-Bonifaz, D.B., 1973, *El Régimen Financiero del Estado en las Constituciones Latinoamericanas* (Mexico City: Instituto de Investigaciones Jurídicas, UNAM).

Constitución Política de los Estados Unidos Mexicanos (Mexico City: Editorial Porrúa, 1988).

Departamento del Distrito Federal, 1996, *Código Financiero del Distrito Federal, 1996* (Mexico City).

Fundación de Investigaciones Económicas Latinoamericanas, *Hacia una Nueva Organización del Federalismo Fiscal en la Argentina* (Buenos Aires, 1993).

Gamboa-Gonzalez, R., 1996, "Fiscal Federalism in Mexico" (unpublished Ph.D. dissertation; Berkeley, California. University of California).

Gil-Díaz, F., 1995, "Política Fiscal y Administración Tributaria: la Experiencia de México," in *Reforma de la Administración Tributaria en América Latina* (Washington: Inter-American Development Bank).

Gil-Valdivia, G., 1975, "Fiscal Federalism in Mexico" (unpublished, Cambridge, Massachusetts: Harvard University).

Instituto Nacional de Estadística, Geografía e Informática (INEGI), 1990, *Cuentas de Producción del Sector Público 1986–89* (Aguascalientes, México).

———, 1994a, *Cuentas de Producción del Sector Público 1990–1993* (Aguascalientes, México).

———, 1994b, *Niveles de Bienestar en Mexico* (Aguascalientes, México).

———, 1994c, *Finanzas Públicas Estatales y Municipales de México, 1989–1992* (Aguascalientes, México).

International Monetary Fund, *Government Finance Statistics Yearbook*, 1995 (Washington: International Monetary Fund).

Jannetti-Díaz, M.E., 1989, "La Coordinación Fiscal y los Ingresos Estatales" *Comercio Exterior*, Vol. 39 (Mexico City).

Martínez-Vargas, H., 1977, "Intergovernmental Tax Coordination in the Mexican Structure" (unpublished; Cambridge, Massachusetts: Harvard University).

Pescador-Osuna, J.A., 1993, Decentralization and Education, *International Encyclopaedia of Education* (London).

Premchand, A., 1983, *Government Budgeting and Expenditure Controls: Theory and Practice* (Washington: International Monetary Fund).

Secretaría de Finanzas del Gobierno del Estado de México, 1989, *Prontuario de Legislación Fiscal 1989* (Toluca, México).

Secretaría de Hacienda y Crédito Público (Hacienda), 1973, *Informe sobre las Relaciones Fiscales entre la Federación y los Estados,* Report presented at the Reunión Nacional de Tesoreros Estatales y Funcionarios de la Secretaría de Hacienda (Mexico City).

———, 1993a, *Presupuesto de Egresos de la Federación para el Ejercicio Fiscal de 1993* (Mexico City).

———, 1993b, *Ley del Impuesto al Valor Agregado y Ley de Coordinación Fiscal–1993* (Mexico City).

———, 1994, *Antología de la Planeación en México,* Fondo de Cultura Económica (Mexico City).

———, 1995, *Ley de Ingresos de la Federación para el Ejercicio Fiscal de 1995* (Mexico City).

———, 1996, *Ley del Servicio de Administración Tributaria* (Mexico City).

Secretaria de Desarrollo Social (SEDESOL), 1993, *Solidarity in National Development: New Relations Between Society and Government* (Mexico City).

———, 1994, *Fondos de Solidaridad para la Producción* (Mexico City).

Shah, A., 1994, *The Reform of Intergovernmental Fiscal Relations in Developing and Emerging Market Economies,* Policy and Research Series 23 (Washington: World Bank).

Solís-Cámara, F., 1993, "La Educación Como Impulso al Desarrollo: El Caso de México," in *México: Desarrollo de Recursos Humanos y Tecnología* (Mexico City: Editorial Porrúa).

Tanzi, Vito, 1996, "Fiscal Federalism and Decentralization: A Review of Some Efficiency and Macroeconomic Aspects," in *Annual World Bank Conference on Development Economics, 1995* (Washington: World Bank).

United States, Advisory Commission on Intergovernmental Relations, 1991, *Significant Features of Fiscal Federalism* (unpublished; Washington).

Winkler, D.R., 1994, *The Design and Administration of Intergovernmental Transfers*, World Bank Discussion Paper 235 (Washington: World Bank).

24

Nigeria

MICHAEL MERED

Nigeria has a complex system of fiscal federalism that has undergone important changes since the country became independent in 1960. Several factors have played a key role in shaping Nigeria's federal system. Nigeria is a large country both in terms of land area and population with considerable ethnic, religious, linguistic, and climatic diversity, all factors that favor decentralization. Petroleum production (all on or around the Niger delta) took off in the 1970s, and the country has changed from a poor agricultural economy into a relatively rich, oil-dominated one. The oil sector now accounts for some 27 percent of GDP, 98 percent of exports, and 75 percent of government revenue. The management of the geographically concentrated oil resources has always been the responsibility of the central (federal) government. The political system, entailing a delicate balance between diverse regional, ethnic, and religious interests, has undergone considerable changes since independence; Nigeria has witnessed periods of civilian and military rules and of civil war. While expenditure assignments have remained broadly unchanged over time, tax assignments and the revenue-sharing arrangements have always been a contentious issue between the federal government and the lower authorities.

The Structure of Government

Nigeria operates a federal system with three tiers—federal, state, and local governments (Table 1). The government sector consists of (1) the

---

The author is particularly indebted to Christian Schiller for his substantial input and editorial support.

Table 1. Nigeria: Intergovernmental Fiscal Relations[1]
(In percent of GDP)

	1990	1991	1992	1993	1994	1995
Federal government						
Total revenue (retained)	21.5	17.7	17.6	15.1	10.6	11.0
Federation Account revenue	9.1	8.2	6.9	7.4	5.8	5.0
Other oil revenue	7.6	5.5	5.4	4.9	4.1	4.2
Independent revenue[2]	0.9	0.6	1.1	1.2	0.2	1.3
Federal Stabilization Account	3.9	3.3	4.2	1.7	0.3	0.0
VAT	0.0	0.0	0.0	0.0	0.2	0.5
Total expenditure	24.5	24.4	17.2	33.0	19.4	14.7
Recurrent expenditure	15.9	14.4	14.5	17.5	13.3	10.0
Capital expenditure and net lending	4.9	5.1	3.8	4.3	5.7	4.6
Supplementary and extrabudgetary outlays	4.1	5.3	−0.1	11.4	0.6	0.0
Overall balance (deficit −)	−2.9	−6.7	0.4	−17.9	−8.8	−3.7
States, local governments, and special funds						
Total revenue	13.7	12.5	12.4	10.7	8.3	7.2
Federation Account	8.8	8.2	7.1	7.8	6.2	5.3
Federal Stabilization Account	3.8	3.3	4.4	1.8	0.3	0.0
Independent and VAT revenue[3]	1.0	1.0	0.9	1.1	1.8	2.0
Expenditure and net lending	13.1	9.8	11.5	10.0	8.0	7.3
Recurrent	8.9	5.8	6.1	6.5	5.1	5.8
Capital	3.7	3.7	4.4	3.3	2.6	1.5
Net lending to federal government	0.5	0.3	1.1	0.2	0.3	0.0
Balance (deficit −)	0.6	2.7	0.9	0.7	0.3	−0.1
Consolidated government						
Revenue[4]	35.2	30.1	30.0	25.8	18.9	18.2
Federation Account	25.7	23.0	22.6	18.6	12.5	10.3
Other	9.6	7.1	7.4	7.2	6.3	7.9
Federal government	8.5	6.1	6.5	6.1	4.5	6.0
Other petroleum revenue	7.6	5.5	5.4	4.9	4.1	4.2
Independent revenue	0.9	0.6	1.1	1.2	0.4	1.8
State governments	1.0	1.0	0.9	1.1	1.8	2.0
Expenditure	37.6	34.2	28.7	43.0	27.4	21.5
Recurrent	26.8	22.8	20.6	29.7	18.8	15.9
Capital	10.7	11.4	8.1	13.4	8.6	5.6
Overall balance (deficit −)	−2.3	−4.1	1.3	−17.2	−8.5	−3.8

Sources: Data provided by the Nigerian authorities; and IMF staff estimates.
[1] Transactions are shown on a cash basis. Data for state and local governments are highly provisional and are based on limited budgetary information.
[2] Excludes recoveries at source for debt obligations of state governments.
[3] State governments only.
[4] Excludes Nigerian National Petroleum Company's dedicated oil revenues and cash calls.

federal authority; (2) 30 state governments, which include 9 new states created in 1991; and (3) 589 local governments.[1]

---

[1] For a description of the Nigerian federal structure and finance see Ashwe (1986).

Regional fiscal autonomy was increasingly strengthened before independence, when the colonial authorities decided that budgetary surpluses of the central administration should be transferred to regional governments. In response to the size and ethnic diversity of the country, the system evolved from a unitary to a quasi-federal state and then to a full-fledged federal system in 1954. Following independence, while the Constitution vested much of the legislative and executive authority in the center, political power became highly regionalized. This situation resulted in a stalemate, which led to the eventual collapse of the first republic in 1966 and a military takeover. The federal military government de-emphasized regional fiscal autonomy, weakening the power of the states by increasing their numbers from 4 to 30 by 1991. At the same time, the local governments began to play a more significant role in intergovernmental relations. Local fiscal autonomy was particularly strengthened when the federal authority, in 1976, decided to allocate to the local governments 10 percent of the Federation Account revenue,[2] which was further increased to 20 percent in 1992. The state authorities, however, continue to have significant influence on the budgetary decisions of local governments.

Although all levels of government have their own independent sources of revenue, the funding of government expenditure comes to a large extent from federally collected revenues, which are accumulated in the Federation Account at the Central Bank of Nigeria and then distributed among the different branches of government according to statutory shares (statutory transfers).

Current Intergovernmental Fiscal Arrangements

Expenditure Assignment

The assignment of expenditure to the different levels of government has not changed significantly since independence, except for some instances when the federal government took over some state or local function for a variety of reasons. Nevertheless, the existing disparities in natural endowments and in the level of economic development among the states have tended to create cost and quality differentials in the delivery of public services, requiring either a restructuring of expenditure assignments or increased transfers of resources to the states.

---

[2]While revenue distribution from the value-added tax (VAT) is as indicated above, the allocation to the Federation Account does not include the amount corresponding to the value of certain "priority expenditures," as noted in the annual budget.

Table 2. Nigeria: Federal, State, and Local Expenditure Assignments

Assignment	Jurisdiction
Defense	Federal
Foreign affairs	Federal
International trade	Federal
Interstate trade	Federal
Environment	Federal
Air and rail transport	Federal
Agriculture	Federal and state
Education	Federal and state
Health	Federal, state, and local
Police	State
Natural resources	Federal, state, and local
Highways	Federal, state, and local

Source: Presidential Commission on Revenue Allocation (1980), Vol. 1, Main Report.

For example, in 1976 the federal authority, for the purpose of ensuring minimum standards and in an effort to reduce costs, began to finance all education outlays.

At present, the federal government is responsible for economic planning and for policies aimed at redistribution and stabilization. In addition, the maintenance of law and order, foreign affairs, defense, the regulation of international and interstate trade and, as mentioned above, education are the responsibilities of the federal authorities. State governments are charged with the supply of public services in the areas of health, agriculture, and public utilities, while services such as town planning, sanitation, and veterinary care are within the domain of local governments (Table 2).

The structure of government expenditures has changed markedly in recent years. Up to 1993, the share of federal expenditures in total outlays increased, at the expense of the share of the states. At the same time, local government expenditures rose somewhat, but by less than the increase in their revenues. The growth of extrabudgetary expenditures of the federal government, from less than 1 percent of GDP in 1987 to over 11 percent of GDP in 1993, was the primary cause behind the rise of the share of federal expenditures in total spending. This reflected increased outlays for the construction of the new federal capital in Abuja, for elections of state and local governments, for a number of large capital-intensive projects, and for petroleum and fertilizer subsidies. Furthermore, the depreciation of the naira has contributed to a substantial increase in foreign-exchange-denominated expenditures, which are concentrated in the federal budget. Foreign interest payments in the federal budget, for instance, amounted to an annual average of 6.5 percent of GDP for 1990–94. More recently, however, federal expenditures appear to be better controlled, with total outlays declining from some 33 percent of GDP in 1993 to just 14.7 percent of GDP in 1995.

Tax Assignment

The Constitution specifies the distribution of taxation authority between the three levels of government (Table 3). The federal government has the power to legislate (and collect) import and export duties, excises, mining rents and royalties, petroleum profit taxes, and the value-added tax, the proceeds of which, however, are shared by all governments as part of the Federation Account. In addition to its share in the Federation Account, a few other revenues are assigned to the federal government. These include personal income taxes levied on the armed forces, dividends from public enterprises, and sales tax revenue from the federal capital territory.

While the states remain largely dependent on revenues from the Federation Account (deriving nearly 90 percent of their revenues from this source), there has been some effort towards developing revenue sources outside of the revenue-sharing pool, and the personal income tax and the company tax have become major sources of independent revenue for the states. Other independent revenues include the capital gains tax, the purchase tax, stamp duties, the gift tax, and the property tax. While states have the legal jurisdiction for the setting of rates and

Table 3. Nigeria: Federal, State, and Local Tax Jurisdiction and Assignment

Tax	Legal Jurisdiction	Collection	Retention
Import duties	Federal	Federal	Federation Account
Excise duties	Federal	Federal	Federation Account
Export duties	Federal	Federal	Federation Account
Mining rents and royalties	Federal	Federal	Federation Account
Petroleum profits tax	Federal	Federal	Federation Account
Capital gains tax	Federal	State	State
Personal income tax[1]	Federal	State	State
Sales tax	Federal	State	State
Company tax	Federal	State	State
Stamp duties	Federal	State	State
Gift tax	Federal	State	State
Property tax	State	State	State
Licenses and fees	Local	Local	Local
Motor park dues	Local	Local	Local
Motor vehicle tax	State	Local	Local

Source: Presidential Commission on Revenue Allocation (1980), Vol. 1, Main Report.

[1] Personal income taxes of the armed forces, external affairs, and the Federal Capital Territory are federally legislated, collected, and retained.

the power to define the tax base for smaller taxes such as property taxes, motor vehicle taxes, and entertainment taxes, this jurisdiction belongs to the federal authority with respect to all other taxes, even relating to those collected and retained by the states (see Table 3). Local government revenues outside the revenue-sharing arrangement are small—but potentially buoyant—and include market and trading license fees, motor parking dues, and motor vehicle taxes.

Nigeria's excessive reliance on oil revenues over the years has delayed needed improvements in non-oil revenues. As a consequence, revenues of all levels of government have become highly dependent on developments in the oil sector. Federally collected revenues, including from petroleum, showed steady increases during the oil boom years of 1974 to 1980, while there was a steady decline in the first half of the 1980s, as oil prices began to fall. Subsequently, federally collected revenues increased from 22 percent of GDP in 1986 to 28 percent of GDP in 1993, partly reflecting a rise in petroleum tax and nontax proceeds and the devaluation of the naira; however, these revenues declined to an average of 22 percent of GDP during the subsequent two years, again reflecting developments in the oil sector. During this period, revenues from the company income tax and customs and excise taxes remained at their traditional levels, equivalent to about 1.1 and 2.7 percent of GDP, respectively.

In recent years, accounts have been set up under the broad category of the Federal Stabilization Account. These accounts introduced first in 1989 by the military government, primarily to sterilize windfall oil revenues and to act as financial cushions in the event of a decline in oil prices, have been allocated a significant share of the Federation Account.[3] However, while there have been statutory allocations to the lower levels of government, the accounts have largely been used to finance supplementary outlays and extrabudgetary operations of the federal government. Accordingly, they have been ineffective as a stabilization tool. For example, in 1993, the surge in extrabudgetary outlays was instrumental in the sharp acceleration of inflation (from 13 percent in 1991 to over 57 percent in 1993). Subsequently, the decline of this expenditure category, from 11.5 percent in 1993 to an average of 0.3 percent of GDP in 1994–95, helped to reduce the fiscal deficit from almost 18 percent of GDP in 1993 to 3.7 percent of GDP in 1995.

---

[3]In effect, there are two active accounts under the auspices of the Federal Stabilization Account; for the first account, established by the military government in 1989, both withdrawals and allocations were made on an ad hoc basis, while for the second account, set up under the 1989 Constitution, an allocation was made amounting to 0.5 percent of the Federation Account revenue.

Financing Arrangements

There are three main avenues through which federal, state, and local governments in Nigeria finance their expenditure needs. These are an intergovernmental revenue-sharing arrangement, transfers, and borrowing.

Revenue Sharing

Revenue sharing features prominently in the intergovernmental relations in Nigeria. The current basis for revenue sharing of federally collected revenues among the federal government, states, and local authorities is the Revenue Allocation Act of 1981. With effect from June 1992, federally collected revenues that accrue to the Federation Account are shared among the three tiers of government with 48.5 percent to the federal authority, 24 percent to the states, 20 percent to local governments, and 7.5 percent to other extrabudgetary funds. The revenues accruing to the states are allocated by using a formula that takes into account a number of factors. The weights used in allocating the proceeds of the Federation Account across states are 40 percent, shared equally, to meet the minimum responsibilities of state governments; 30 percent, based on the size of the population; 10 percent, based on geographic size; 10 percent, based on social development needs; and 10 percent, based on the state's internal revenue mobilization effort. A similar approach is used to distribute the local governments' share in the Federation Account.

Revenue sharing has been a key factor in the development of fiscal federalism in Nigeria. Its origins date back from the colonial era, when in 1946 regional councils were established for the Northern, Western, and Eastern regions. The regional councils initially played an advisory role and had only limited fiscal responsibility, but they were eventually given the power to raise taxes and to appropriate independently collected revenues for their particular regions. At the same time, federally collected revenues were allocated to the regions based on a principle of derivation, whereby tax receipts are allocated in accordance with the revenue-generating activities of each region. The states' needs, as measured by population and national interest, were given relatively minor weights. Together with ad hoc considerations incorporated in the revenue-sharing formula, this led to controversies and political strife among the regions.

By 1966 the revenue-sharing scheme was expanded to include proceeds from import and export duties, excises, mining rents, and royalties. The regional governments were allocated, based on the derivation principle, all federally collected revenues from these taxes and 50 percent of revenues from mineral royalties and rents. The distributable pool account, the predecessor of the Federation Account, was created during this period, from which allocations were based on population size and equalization criteria. In addition, the regions were allowed to collect and retain the personal income tax, licenses and user fees, and property taxes.

The military government significantly altered the tax levying authority and the revenue-sharing arrangements of the federal and regional governments. The military reduced the importance of the derivation principle in revenue sharing and the associated income disparities that existed among the states by increasing the share of proceeds accruing to the distributable pool account, particularly from import duties and excises on petroleum and tobacco products and export duties. In addition, in an effort to strengthen the financial position of the federal authority, all tax revenues accruing from off-shore oil production, which previously had accrued to the states on the basis of derivation, were reserved for the federal government.

With economic growth and increased oil production, the tax base of the federal government widened during the military era. At the same time, the expenditure requirements of the regional governments increased, relative to their independently collected revenue base. Accordingly, during the 1970s the states became increasingly dependent on federally collected repeated revenues, including a reassignment of some of their taxation functions to the federal authority. In addition, this period witnessed the decline of the derivation principle in determining revenue sharing. Other criteria such as absorptive capacity, the need to achieve and maintain minimum standards for national integration, equality in access to development opportunities, independent revenue effort, and fiscal efficiency became the major determinants.

The past years have seen a change in the structure of revenue sharing. Recent figures indicate that the share of the federal government in the proceeds of the Federation Account has declined from about 75 percent in 1980 to just over 50 percent in 1994.[4] State governments' share of the account has been fluctuating at about 25 percent for the same period. At the same time, local governments have increased their entitlement from close to zero in 1980 to 20 percent by 1994.

Owing to these developments in the revenue-sharing scheme, a restructuring of total revenue has occurred among the three tiers of gov-

---

[4]The calculation here includes the share of the Federal Stabilization Account, while in Table 1 this is shown as a separate item.

ernment. Federal and state government revenues as a percent of total government revenues have declined, while the local governments' share has increased substantially, as a result of the increase in the statutory allocations, and also because of some increase in independent revenues.

Intergovernmental Grants and Transfers

Along with the revenue-sharing arrangement, there is also a system of nonstatutory and discretionary transfers, albeit of lesser importance than the former. There are two kinds of discretionary transfers. Discretionary recurrent transfers from the federal government to lower levels of government are made to meet specific recurrent needs such as the transfers in the context of the universal primary education scheme. Discretionary capital transfers can be either federal grants given for specific purposes in the context of the national development plan to finance investment expenditures, or transfers that represent on-lending of borrowing by the federal government.

There are also transfers from the state and local governments to the federal government. Beginning in 1989, the federal budget was increasingly coming under pressures, while the state and local governments registered surpluses. Accordingly, during this period transfers from the lower levels of government to the federal government have been made through the Federal Stabilization Account. For example, in 1992, these transfers to finance the federal budget amounted to about 4 percent of GDP.

Borrowing

Prior to 1977, the federal government was the only public authority to contract domestic or foreign loans. Federal government long-term bonds and short-term treasury bills were issued, with the proceeds shared between the federal government and the states on a 40 percent and 60 percent basis, respectively. During the 1970s, when the federal government registered surpluses reflecting increases in oil revenues, substantial amounts of such loans were made to the states, which were later mostly written off as grants. Following the reforms of the Nigerian financial system in 1977, bank financing of state budgets was permitted, and state and local governments were allowed to issue securities to financial institutions. Also, foreign borrowing by states under federal guarantee was authorized, while the ban on the sale of debt instruments to the nonbank public by other than the federal government remains in force. More recently, based on ad hoc decisions by the military government, strict limitations have been placed on domestic borrowing by the states and the federal guarantee for external financing is no longer valid.[5]

Tax Administration

The responsibility for tax administration in Nigeria is shared mainly on the basis of the relative efficiency of the federal government and the state and local governments in collecting taxes. Oil taxes, which constitute the major portion of government revenue, are collected by the federal government, as are customs, excise, and export duties.

Oil revenues derive from two sources: the operations of the private oil companies, and the Nigerian National Petroleum Company (NNPC). The private oil companies are permitted to withhold certain amounts from their export proceeds to cover their costs, including profits, and are obliged to deposit the remainder in a U.S.-dollar-denominated Central Bank account from where the proceeds are transferred to the Federation Account. A similar procedure is applied to the NNPC's export proceeds. The surplus from NNPC's domestic operations is transferred to the Federation Account at the end of each month.[6]

Each month at a meeting of the Revenue Allocation Committee, the balance in the Federation Account is allocated according to statutory shares between the federal government, the state and local governments, and the Federal Stabilization Account. As indicated above, the federal government and the state and local governments also collect revenues that do not enter the Federation Account.

While indirect tax administration has improved with the introduction of the VAT (although other difficulties still remain with the rate and threshold of the tax), the administration of direct taxes appears to have weakened. This is primarily due to the fragmented administration and legislative arrangements between federal and state authorities. Tax avoidance and evasion, particularly with respect to personal and com-

---

[5]Debt statistics for state and local governments are not readily available. Nonetheless, with lower levels of government consistently showing a budgetary surplus in recent years (Table 1), and with the monetary accounts for 1995 indicating only 0.2 percent of GDP in outstanding net credit to these governments, the threat to macroeconomic stability appears minimal.

[6]In this connection, the additional revenue accruing from the October 1994 adjustment of petroleum prices was allocated, in part, to the Petroleum Special Trust Fund (PSTF) to be utilized for special capital projects and social services. The PSTF began operations in January 1995 and is directly accountable to the Head of State.

pany income taxes, have become pervasive. A more uniform legislation to provide a transparent legal basis for income taxation across states, improved coordination between state and federal tax authorities, and the expansion of joint training and tax audits would enhance the effectiveness of federal and interstate tax administration.

Budget Formulation and Implementation

The Nigerian fiscal year coincides with the calendar year. The federal government budget is formulated beginning in October and normally is adopted by the end of February.[7] The federal government's expenditures are controlled by a system of quarterly warrant releases[8] to all government ministries for budgetary items. Extrabudgetary expenditures also require a warrant for additional incurred expenditures.

In addition, the federal government has established and controls five special funds that are outside the federal budget: the General Ecology Fund, for addressing ecological problems; the Federal Capital Territory Fund, for the construction of the federal capital at Abuja; the Mineral Derivation Fund, for the specific benefit of mineral-producing states; the Development of Mineral Producing Areas Fund; and the Statutory Stabilization Account, which serves as a form of savings. In total, the special funds received more than 7 percent of the Federation Account revenues. While these funds primarily finance investment expenditure, at times they have generated large surpluses that have been invested in government paper.

The budgetary process of the state governments is similar to the federal system discussed above. State budget estimates are prepared and funds are withdrawn from the State Consolidated Revenue Fund based on appropriation bills authorized by the State Assembly and backed by spending warrants. However, the state government's budgetary flexibility is relatively limited as much of their resources derive from the Federation Account.

At the local level, however, expenditure management is controlled by financial regulations formulated by the relevant state. Elected local government councils submit their budget to a state ministry for approval. Except for the Lagos city council, which has a financially com-

---

[7]Under the present system, without a functioning parliament, the budget is approved by the Provisional Ruling Council and announced by the Head of State.

[8]A warrant authorizes the Accountant-General to issue funds and the accounting officer of the relevant ministry or agency to incur expenditure (see Oshisami and Dean, 1984).

petent expenditure management system, finances of local governments are for the most part regulated by the states, largely as a result of limited capacity.

Macroeconomic Management

There are many arguments in support of the presumption that in a federal system fiscal stabilization policies should be assigned to the center, and the key role of the federal government in macroeconomic management has never been questioned in Nigeria.

Effective macroeconomic management by the federal government requires that taxes are at its disposal that are both relatively flexible and large in size in relation to the national economy. The federal government must be able to take tax measures that affect aggregate demand and the fiscal balance quickly and significantly. In this context, the federal government's authority over the stabilization account and other funds such as the PSTF, its ability to change the distribution of revenues from the Federation Account, and its retention of control over the tax rates for the VAT and the company income tax augurs well for the execution of demand management policies. On the other hand, the federal government's ability to pursue effective fiscal stabilization policies may be constrained, since many of the major taxes it controls are either collected and retained by the states or pass through the Federation Account. The exclusive assignment of broad-based taxes to the federal government may be called for from a macroeconomic point of view in order to enhance the scope for timely and effective fiscal stabilization measures. In this connection, however, it should be noted that the state sales tax was replaced by a central VAT effective January 1, 1994. While a VAT is typically a broad-based tax with considerable revenue potential, the tax introduced in Nigeria applies to less than half of private consumption and has a low tax rate (5 percent). While 80 percent of the revenue collected from the VAT was originally transferred to the states, the 1996 budget changed the allocation to federal, 35 percent, state, 40 percent, and local governments, 25 percent.

As regards expenditures, the federal government is empowered to approve or reject the budget of state authorities, a fact that provides some leverage to the center on state fiscal policies. In addition, nonstatutory transfers from the federal to lower levels of government for purposes of specific recurrent and capital expenditures give the federal government some influence on the spending behavior of subnational governments. Nonstatutory transfers to the subnational governments can play a useful role in macroeconomic management, as their level and timing can be adjusted to some extent to conjunctural requirements.

With regard to its own finances, the federal government's practice of using the Federal Stabilization Account for the financing of off-budget items and the distribution of the statutory shares of the states on an ad hoc basis may not be conducive to fiscal discipline. This account should be used as intended for siphoning windfall oil revenues and encouraging revenue diversification. In general, the proliferation of extrabudgetary funds presents a problem for effective budget management. These funds reduce the transparency of the budgetary process and create loopholes for government operations not approved through the proper (budgetary) channels, undermining the use of the budget as a macroeconomic instrument.[9]

Following the reform of the financial system in 1977, borrowing by state and local governments has become possible. While state and local governments have been registering fiscal surpluses in recent years, relatively easy access of subnational governments to borrowing has nevertheless increased the risk that the federal government's stabilization efforts may be compromised in the future by excessive borrowing of state and local governments.

Structural Issues

As discussed earlier, revenue sharing plays an important role in financing state and local expenditures in Nigeria. Like unconditional grants, revenue sharing is intended to provide subnational governments with the ability to supply public goods and services independently of their taxable capacity. It is particularly important in a country such as Nigeria, with geographically concentrated and large natural resources. Not surprisingly, the question of how revenues should be shared among regions has always been a controversial issue in Nigeria.

To avoid vertical fiscal imbalances, the expenditure responsibilities of the different levels of government have to match their revenue-generating capacities taking into account both shared and other revenues. The recent increase in extrabudgetary expenditures of the federal government would indicate a mismatch of assignments and a need to review the present arrangement. In addition, when the federal govern-

---

[9]During 1988–94, about US$12.4 billion was allocated to a variety of projects and other outlays outside standard budgetary procedures. In 1995, however, budgetary transparency improved when all dedicated accounts were closed and revenues accruing to these accounts became incorporated into the federal budget.

ment delegates a particular function (for example, agricultural development) to a lower level of government, a corresponding revenue source should be assigned taking into account the administrative capacity of the state and local governments. Also, exchange rate movements tend to have different impacts on federal, state, and local finances. A depreciation of the naira, as witnessed over the past years, tends to improve state and local finances, because state and local governments have only few foreign exchange expenditures, while the impact on the federal budget is less clear, given the large amount of foreign exchange expenditures, including debt service.

With Nigeria currently in the process of redefining political and legal authority under a new constitution, a thorough review of the requirements and obligations of all three levels of government is important. This should take into account, inter alia, Nigeria's vulnerability to changes in the world market price of oil, the treatment of extrabudgetary expenditures of the federal government, and the impact of exchange rate movements on federal, state, and local finances. In this context, particular attention should be paid to further enhancing the stabilization function of the federal government.

In view of the dynamic nature of fiscal federalism, the development of institutions to coordinate and oversee intergovernmental relations on a permanent basis is critical. In Nigeria, the advisory body concerned with intergovernmental fiscal relations is the National Economic Council, which was created in 1955. Its membership consists of cabinet ministers and state governors and it is chaired by the Prime Minister; however, the Council meets infrequently, which limits its effectiveness. Accordingly, there is also a need for a permanent fiscal commission that can periodically review the federal system and recommend modifications to the revenue-sharing arrangements based on changing economic conditions.

References

Ashwe, Chiichii, 1986, *Fiscal Federalism in Nigeria*, Research Monograph No. 46 (Canberra: Centre for Research on Federal Financial Relations, Australian National University).

Oshisami, Koleade, and Peter N. Dean, 1984, *Financial Management in the Nigerian Public Sector* (London: Pitman).

Presidential Commission on Revenue Allocation, 1980, *Report* (Apapa: Federal Government Press).

PART IV

Practice:
Economies in Transition

25

Bulgaria

Željko Bogetić

Bulgaria's prereform economy, roughly before 1991, was a highly centralized state, similar to most countries of the former Soviet Union. With the radical liberalization and stabilization program adopted in February 1991 by the government led by the former opposition, the country entered the transition to market in a political and macroeconomic tumult that continues several years later. This coincided with severe external shocks that were largely responsible for large declines in output and foreign trade: the former Council for Mutual Economic Assistance disintegrated, and foreign trade flows with the former Soviet Union, on which much of Bulgaria's industry depended, collapsed. In 1990–93, output declined by over 20 percent and at the end of the period unemployment reached 14 percent (Bogetić, 1996).

The worsening economic situation affected government finances adversely. Total government revenues fell from almost 60 percent of GDP in 1989 to below 40 percent of GDP in 1994, reflecting a severe erosion of the traditional tax bases (such as the profits tax and trade and nontax revenues). As privatization proceeded at a slow pace, largely led by enterprise insiders, the profits tax base eroded as a result of informal profit shifting from state enterprises to managers and insiders, who often bought cheaply and sold dearly to those enterprises (Bogetić and Hillman, 1995). Government expenditures also fell, but budget deficits remained high and, in combination with a lax monetary policy, continued to sustain inflation.

The author wishes to acknowledge detailed, helpful comments from Teresa Ter-Minassian, Janet Stotsky, and Gerd Schwartz.

Politically, Bulgaria's transition has been characterized by numerous changes in governments and frequent changes in cabinet posts. Against this backdrop, early in the transition, the government adopted a Law on Self-Government that grants wide autonomy to local governments, signaling a major decentralization drive. However, several years later, implementing decentralization has proven difficult, and many questions and policy dilemmas remain.

The chapter begins with an overview of the current state of intergovernmental fiscal relations in Bulgaria, focusing on certain issues that are likely to constrain the process of decentralization. It then discusses major issues in the current debate on this process and suggests how their resolution and implied policy choices might affect decentralization. Finally, it attempts to draw some broader lessons from Bulgaria's limited experience with decentralization.

Intergovernmental Fiscal Relations

Bulgaria is a unitary state, with the present vertical structure of government reflecting the system that had been put in place in 1987. There are 9 regions, 255 municipalities, and over 3,900 settlements. The regions are the arms of the central government without autonomous budgets. The districts, indicated in Figure 1, are not operational, and there is uncertainty about their future. This means that, de facto, Bulgaria has only two layers of government: central and local. Municipalities have elected mayors and municipal councils, usually comprise a number of settlements and, since 1992, have their own budgets, although their revenue sources are still mainly shared or transferred from the center. An average municipality of 30,000 has about 20 settlements. Settlements are the smallest unit of government with an elected mayor, but no budget.

Tax Assignment

In Bulgaria, local governments have a limited tradition of, and actual power to, tax. It was only in 1991, with the passage of the Law on Self-Government, that local governments received limited formal autonomy. In practice, local governments were allowed to have their own budgets for the first time only in 1992. There has been growing realization, at the rank-and-file level of the central bureaucracy and in municipalities, that a successful decentralization of expenditure responsibilities and effective management of budgetary resources at the local level requires greater autonomy in raising revenues. But this realization

Željko Bogetić 617

Figure 1. Bulgaria: Executive Power System and Structure

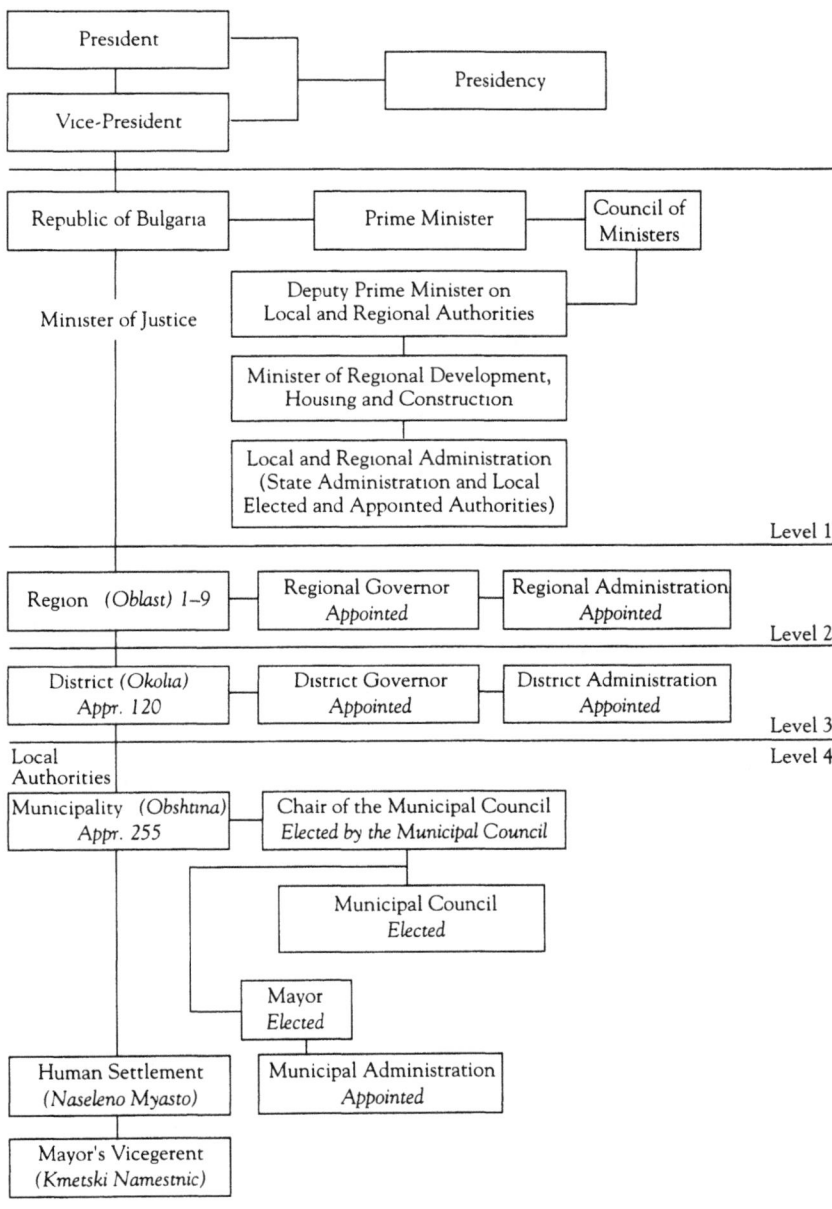

Source: World Bank.

has not gained broader political support, particularly at the central government level, where pressures from local governments for greater budgetary autonomy clash with the inertia of centralized management practices and vested interests. In addition, the need to control the central government deficit under conditions of shrinking tax base and high budgetary interest payments limited the central government's ability to grant more revenue-raising autonomy to local governments. As a result, the tax assignment has remained ambiguous and nontransparent.

Municipalities have three main sources of revenues: (1) local taxes, fees, and charges; (2) shared taxes; and (3) transfers from the central government. The only shared taxes are the profits tax and individual income tax, while indirect taxes accrue to central government. The shares of revenues from different sources fluctuated over time, reflecting the year-to-year instability of local government finances. In 1996–97, the transfers to the municipalities were reduced due to severe budgetary pressures at the central government level.

The proportion of local tax revenues in total revenues of municipalities remains small—between 5 and 12 percent—reflecting the low autonomy with regard to authority to tax. Until 1993, transfers (grants) from the central government were more important: they accounted for close to a half of total revenues of municipalities. But from 1994, transfers were reduced as central government fiscal problems intensified. Municipalities receive over half of their total revenues from the two shared taxes: profits tax and income tax. Until 1993, they also received a share of the turnover and some excises.

Within local revenue sources, a notable feature of the Bulgarian tax system is the relative insignificance of the property tax, which is also indicative of the state of decentralization. This tax is a cornerstone of local taxation in many developed countries. In developing countries, however, this tax is much less dominant among local revenue sources, as it is frequently plagued by problems of outdated and irregular assessments, poor cadastres, and little control of local governments over the rates.

In Bulgaria, local sources of revenues accounted on average for only 12 percent of total revenues of municipalities in 1994. The property tax accounted for only 2.1 percent of those revenues. The reasons are threefold. First, the rates of this tax have been very low, albeit with some variation among cities. Second, the assessments on which this tax is based are not regularly updated, which leads to an erosion of the base in the presence of moderate to high inflation. And third, until very recently, local governments had no control over the rates and assessments, which were decided at the central level; de facto, the property tax was a "central government" tax. Most recently, the rates were raised to more realistic levels (Varga, 1996). The vehicle registration tax, a generally good and equitable local tax, has not represented a significant local revenue source. Various fees and nontax revenues were far more important revenue sources for local governments than the property and vehicle taxes; they accounted for 9.9 percent of total municipal revenues. But many of these fees are often "nuisance charges," controlled from the center, while some major scarce goods continue to be provided at the local level below cost (including water, sanitation, and electricity). Therefore, there is scope for a much wider use and more realistic rates for user charges at the local levels.

A striking conclusion arises from this brief overview of local revenues of municipalities: one may conclude that no tax in Bulgaria fully satisfies the criterion of clarity of tax assignment, whereby local governments should have full control over the rates of local taxes. Indeed, in her comprehensive survey of Bulgaria's taxation, Varga concludes that there are no local taxes, "as regions and municipalities have no taxing powers" (Varga, 1996, p. 83).

Shared Taxes

Shared taxes account for about half of total revenues of municipalities (Table 1). Two key taxes that are shared among the central and local governments are profits tax and individual income tax. Before the introduction of the VAT in 1994, the old turnover tax was also shared. But when the VAT—a central government tax—replaced the turnover tax, its revenue was not shared with the local governments. The profits

Table 1. Bulgaria: Structure of Municipal Budgets
(In percent)

	1990	1991	1992	1993	1994
Revenue	100.0	100.0	100.0	100.0	100.0
Own source revenues	11.1	4.4	5.1	5.0	12.0
Property tax and inheritance tax	3.7	0.7	0.7	1.2	2.1
Fees and other revenues	7.4	3.5	4.4	3.8	9.9
Shared revenues	50.9	72.3	48.7	46.7	63.6
Profit tax	7.4	27.7	21.9	11.6	17.6
Income tax	38.8	32.2	21.5	21.9	46.0
Turnover tax	4.7	8.1	5.2	11.0	1.4
Other shared taxes	—	4.3	—	2.1	—
Transfers	38.0	23.3	46.2	48.0	19.3
Expenditure	100.0	100.0	100.0	100.0	100.0
Current	85.3	88.7	89.2	89.9	90.1
Capital	14.7	11.4	10.8	10.1	8.9

Source: Ministry of Finance.

tax performance has been deteriorating, reflecting pressures on profitability of state enterprises, arising from the competition from the private sector (which has been more difficult to tax), external shocks, but also the appropriation of profits by state managers (Bogetić and Hillman, 1995). Individual income tax, which is essentially a wage and salary tax collected at the source, has remained an important local revenue source.

As regards the profits tax, there is a "municipal tax" (see Varga, 1996), which is levied on all enterprises with state or municipal ownership in excess of 50 percent in a given municipality. The municipal tax is levied on accounting profits (adjusted for tax purposes) at the rate of 6.5 percent. In addition, a standard 36 percent profits tax is levied on all state enterprises under local jurisdiction. Within this standard profits tax rate 2 percentage points are earmarked for the irrigation fund.

As for the individual income tax, the sharing proportion was determined every year in the budget law, leading to much central-local government bargaining. In 1991, this proportion was 70:30 in favor of local governments, but since then, the local proportion of this tax has been declining so that in 1996 the proportion was 50:50. Although this tax remained an important source of revenues for municipalities, the constant bargaining, instability, and unpredictability of shares has constrained the financial autonomy and budget planning of local governments. It has been suggested that a preferable solution for Bulgaria and many transition economies would be a "piggybacked" income tax that the municipalities would be free to impose in their territories, on the same base—incomes—but within specified limits, over and above the standard, "central" income tax rates (Martinez-Vazquez, 1995a). Such a "concurrent" tax would take advantage of this stable, shared income tax base, while providing local authorities with greater autonomy in setting rates, and greater stability revenues over time. Similar piggybacked taxes have been implemented successfully in, among others, Canada and some Northern European countries, and other piggybacked taxes, such as on the corporate income tax, are common in a number of countries (see Chapter 3).

Transfers

Transfers from the central government have been an important source of revenues for municipalities. In the 1990–93 period, their share in total municipal revenues fluctuated between 23 percent and 48 percent, with increases reflecting rising dependence of the municipalities from the center. As the fiscal problems intensified and the local government lost a share of the turnover tax (which was replaced by a

Table 2. Bulgaria: Types of Transfers and Their Relative Importance

Type of Transfer	In Billions of Leva	In Percent of Total
General grants ("subsidy")	30,581	83.6
Specific grants	5,460	14.9
Remittance to the center	515	1.4
Total	36,556	100.0

Source: The 1996 budget, *Sofita* (English translation).

VAT in 1994), the dependance of local governments on central transfers increased. In 1995, the total amount of transfers reached 74 percent of total local revenues (or 3.4 percent of GDP).

There are two types of grants: general purpose grants and specific grants for capital expenditure. General purpose grants, which are the dominant form of transfers (Table 2), are based on a transfer formula determining the level of transfer in each municipality. The specific amounts of transfers to municipalities are determined in annual budgets. Key factors in the transfer formula are the level of transfer in the previous year and an assessment of local needs. In addition, there is a redistributive mechanism built into the formula so that poor municipalities receive higher than average transfers. The transfer formula also incorporates tax effort and a number of other social variables relevant for equalization.[1] While this was a change in the right direction, the current transfer system continues to be adversely affected by the lack of clarity in expenditure assignments.

Specific grants are given for capital expenditure purposes only. Each year, municipalities submit their lists of investment projects to the Minister of Finance, who decides which projects get funded based on specific sector priorities (water supply, health, social welfare, education, and environment).

Expenditure Assignment

Government expenditures have been under pressure from declining government revenues and the need to maintain budget balance for macroeconomic stabilization purposes. Indeed, the decline in revenues in Bulgaria has been rapid and significant, more reminiscent of the situation in former Soviet republics than in other Eastern European countries. It was accompanied by a significant decline in the size of govern-

---

[1]For a detailed review and critique of Bulgaria's system of transfers, see Martinez-Vazquez (1995b).

ment, measured by total expenditure-to-GDP ratio. But expenditure responsibilities of the local governments (health, education, and so on) have not been reduced commensurately. Moreover, under pressure to keep its budget deficit under control, the central government took away some revenue sources, such as the turnover tax, from the local government. Macroeconomic fiscal pressures in many transition countries have pushed the central government deficit down to the local level (Bird, Ebel, and Wallich, 1995). As a result, expenditure pressures on local governments have increased, while adequate revenue-raising instruments have not become available.

In response to budgetary pressures, local governments have been reluctant to reduce employment, particularly in the large sectors such as education and health, which hide considerable inefficiencies and overstaffing (see Bogetić and Chattopadhyay, 1995). This has compounded the budgetary problems of local governments and contributed to continued tensions between the central and local governments under conditions of fiscal stress.

A review of formal expenditure assignments in Bulgaria (Table 3) reveals that many services that, on the basis of the "benefit principle," should be provided locally (such as primary education, primary health, local road maintenance, and, partly, garbage collection) are indeed assigned to local governments. Furthermore, typical central government functions, such as defense and security and foreign economic relations, are assigned to the central government. So, prima facie, there is no gross expenditure assignment mismatch from the point of view of the standard textbook division of central and local government functions. However, a closer examination of this assignment and its functioning reveals at least two issues of concern: the lack of clarity in the assignment of several important expenditure activities and the negative budgetary and efficiency impact of lingering mandates and norms from the central to the local governments.

First, several services (for example, water supply and regional hospitals) that would naturally fall under the category of regional or special district levels of government are, in the absence of such a layer of government, assigned to either the central government (as in the case of water systems) or to specific local municipalities (as in the case of certain hospitals serving several municipalities). This might not pose a problem if such assignments were backed by adequate revenue sources and institutional capacity to implement and monitor programs. In practice, however, there is a danger that such services fall between the cracks of two major levels of government and that their functioning becomes a function of intergovernmental bargaining over the budgets; in that case, functions with the least clear expenditure responsibility are

Table 3. Bulgaria: Expenditure Assignment

	Central Government[1]	Municipalities	Settlements
Defense	• Entire responsibility		
Justice and internal security	• Entire responsibility		
Foreign economic relations	• Entire responsibility		
Education	• All university and research institutions; some technical and vocational schools	• All expenditures (capital and current) of primary and secondary schools) • Some kindergartens • Some technical and vocational schools	• Some kindergartens
Health	• Medical research institutes • Special service hospitals (cardiology, oncology, etc.)	• Tertiary care and psychiatric hospitals • Polyclinics • Some primary care • Drugs	• Some primary health clinics
Roads	• Construction of all roads • Maintenance of state highways and any other roads linking cities and villages	• Maintenance of III and IV class roads and urban streets	• Maintenance of local network road
Public transportation	• Airports • Railway subsidy	• All modes of city transport • Subsidy to inter-village bus service within municipalities	
Fire protection		• Most fire protection services	• Equipment for volunteer services
Libraries	• National Library (Cyril and Methodius)	• Local libraries	
Police services	• National militia and traffic police	• Sofia signed contract with national militia; other municipalities get service free	
Sanitation		• Part of garbage collection and street cleaning	• Part of garbage collection and street cleaning
Water and sewerage	• State enterprises except for Sofia	• Some construction and operation	• Some operation
Public utilities	• Electricity subsidy • Heating subsidy until 1992	• Heating subsidy since 1992 • Water supply infrastructure	

Table 3 (concluded)

	Central Government[1]	Municipalities	Settlements
Housing		• Financing, building, and subsidizing for residential housing	
Price subsidies		• Mass transport • Drugs	
Welfare Payments	• Unemployment • Social assistance	• Homeless; disabled; orphans; subsidies for large families	
Enterprises in productive sector		• Capacity to invest in joint ventures including banks • Keeps a share of the proceeds from privatization of state and local enterprises	
Environment	• Responsible for national environmental issues	• Local environmental issues	
Enterprises	• State enterprises	• Local and municipal enterprises (transport, construction, and other local services)	

Source: World Bank (1994).
[1]There is an intermediate level of government between the central government and the municipalities: the regional government. However, regional governments are just agencies of the central government without discretion and without budgets. For these reasons, regional governments are not shown in the table as separate from the central government.

likely to lose in such bargaining. In fact, there is some evidence that this is happening with regard to hospitals (Normand, 1995).

Second, budgets are still fraught with expenditure norms related to wages paid to municipal employees that, although officially abolished in 1990, continue in practice in a number of municipalities (World Bank, 1994). Originally, the norms were specified either in terms of physical units or costs of specific expenditure items and were mandatory for each municipality and/or relevant line ministry. These norms introduce downward inflexibility in the local budgets, and severely limit within-budget adjustments at the local level that may be necessary. As a result, they also may result in an inefficient pattern of local services, whereby some items are oversupplied (for example, hospital beds and school classrooms), while there may be shortage of others (for example, primary health facilities, teaching materials, and equipment). Indeed, the health sector reflects this pattern of extensive tertiary facilities and has one of the highest ratios of hospital beds per capita in Europe, with relatively modest indicators of health care outcomes.

Furthermore, the lack of clarity of expenditure assignment in some activities and inflexibility in others may cause the central government transfers to be misdirected: a good design of transfers presupposes clear tax and expenditure assignments, from which the need for equalization may be derived through a formula reflecting the precise nature of equalization sought. In this regard, one may argue that as long as the tax and expenditure assignments are not fully clarified, central government transfers will likely continue to change frequently, contributing to the instability of intergovernmental finances.

Capital Budgets

A large share of the capital budget is devoted to sectors and programs with heavy involvement of local governments: health, education and housing, and community services (Table 4). These three sectors account for almost two-thirds of the capital budget.

In health and education, the split between local and central government shares is roughly equal, while local governments spend most of their capital budgets on housing and community services. Given the formal assignment of spending responsibilities, local governments should account for over half of the total capital budget. In practice, however, their role is much more limited: only every third local government project makes it on the final capital budget list (World Bank, 1994). This reflects in part the lack of realistic priorities in the investment budgets of local governments, the lack of institutional capacity to

Table 4. Bulgaria: Shares of Central and Local Governments in the Capital Budget, 1993
(In percent)

Sector	Central Government	Municipalities	Sector Share in Total Budget
Legislative and judicial systems	100.0	—	2.5
Science	100.0	—	0.6
Education	48.9	51.1	18.6
Defense and police	100.0	—	3.7
Health	37.5	62.5	15.3
Social security issues	53.9	46.1	1.0
Housing and community services	15.7	84.3	28.8
Culture	92.2	7.8	1.0
Economic activities	68.6	31.4	28.4
Total	47.2	52.8	100.0

Source: Ministry of Finance.

appraise and rank projects at the local level, and the consequent capital expenditure pressures "from below" on the Ministry of Finance, early in the budget process. Furthermore, the Ministry of Finance exercises considerable discretion in reviewing initial investment proposals from the municipalities. It eventually draws a list of projects included in the capital budget, and, in consultation with the Ministry of Regional Development, the medium-term public investment program.

Another issue is that capital budgets were first to be cut, both at the central and local levels, in response to the decline in revenues and the need to contain the budget deficit. In addition to the real decline in capital budgets of municipalities, its share in the total municipal budget shrank from 14 percent in 1991 to 10 percent in 1993 (see Table 1). This has resulted in a large number of unfinished investment projects, many of which are not likely to be completed (Bogetić, 1996).

Local Government Borrowing

Bulgaria's municipalities follow a simple "golden rule," as in Germany: they are prohibited from borrowing for current expenditures, but may borrow for investment purposes. In practice, however, there has been little or no municipal borrowing from the banks. The only borrowing that has occurred has been from the central government. This reflects a combination of factors, including the fragility of the financial system, high interest rates, and an often forgotten constraint—the lack of adequate legal and institutional mechanisms for borrowing against collateral that prevents most lenders to lend for long-term projects, even local governments, despite the implicit or explicit government guarantees (Bogetić and Fleisig, 1997).

Local Dimension of Expenditure Management

Local governments everywhere have significant spending responsibility. But quality expenditure management framework and practices are, surprisingly, often lacking precisely at the local level, even when expenditure management by the central government is sound. This is even more the case in Bulgaria where local governments in the past were little more than a passive spending agency of the central government, implementing the plan through a variety of mandates and specific expenditure norms. This practice lingers six years after the beginning of economic reforms. One example is the large list of projects that municipalities annually submit to the Ministry of Finance, which often have not been screened or appraised appropriately and bear little direct relation to the budgetary realities of the municipalities or the overall budget. Recently, the Ministry of Finance has commendably started providing guidelines to the municipalities about the likely revenue envelope earlier in the budget process than in the past. But to make the budget process at the local level effective, there is a need for large-scale training in expenditure management, project appraisal, and for improving the overall implementation capacity of local governments.

The proliferation of extrabudgetary funds has also been noted as a general and local fiscal problem, reducing transparency and fiscal accountability (World Bank, 1994). Clear accounting and reporting rules, and the consolidation of many of such accounts is required to enhance fiscal transparency, accountability, and, ultimately, the quality of governance at the local level.

Major Issues

The overall pattern in the evolution of intergovernmental finances in the early transition period (1990-94) has been characterized by three trends: rising expenditure pressures on local governments, continued inadequate and unstable revenue sources, and slow response of local governments to the need for new techniques of expenditure management and project appraisal. These trends gave rise to a situation in which there has been little effective and orderly decentralization, and some key policy issues have been left unresolved. Some of these issues are discussed below.

What Should Be the Next Steps in Decentralization?

This question has been implicitly or explicitly asked by several analysts of Bulgaria's finances (Martinez-Vazquez, 1995b; Chand and Lorie, 1993). The lack of a clear target model of decentralization has hampered the development of a strategy and steps toward that model. While Bulgaria has adopted the European charter for self-government as a model, the new legal framework remains often at odds with the old practice of centralized fiscal management.

While no ready-made prescription is available, a good start in the decentralization strategy would be to focus on expenditure activities that are subject to overlapping or competing jurisdictions and to clarify the appropriate level of responsibility. At the same time, it would be advisable to assign the local governments full responsibility for certain revenue sources (for example, property tax, the motor vehicle tax, and most fees and charges) and to strengthen their institutional capacity to exploit fully these powers (for example, through improvements in their property cadastres).

A special issue arises with respect to the fiscal status of several large cities, including Sofia, Plovdiv, and Varna. It is common even in developing countries for large metropolitan areas to have special fiscal status and a degree of fiscal autonomy beyond the one granted to other local governments (Bahl and Linn, 1993). This allows greater correspondence between local benefits and expenditures in areas of considerable concentration of publicly provided goods and services, which should increase the efficiency in their provision and facilitate their sustainable financing. Bulgaria could consider such special regimes for the largest cities.

Are the Perils of Decentralization Too Great?

The view has been put forward by some (Prud'homme, 1995) that decentralization per se is not a panacea and that it may hamper macroeconomic and fiscal management. Furthermore, the generally strong case for decentralization rests on certain assumptions on the state of local implementation capacity that may be limited in many countries (Tanzi, 1996): the power and ability to tax, effective tax-sharing arrangements, adequate performance of local and national civil service, and sound expenditure management. All of these concerns are certainly relevant to an assessment of the desirable decentralization in Bulgaria. They call for a concerted effort in building local capacity and a local civil service capable of designing, monitoring, and implementing effectively spending programs in the areas of responsibility of the local governments. On the other hand, it may be argued that local implementation capacity is not likely to improve unless and until expenditure responsibilities are effectively devolved to that level of government (McLure, 1995).

Three issues specific to Bulgaria are also likely to influence the choice of decentralization strategy and to constrain the pace of its implementation: the inertia of centralized management and the lack of tradition of local government, the fears of losing macroeconomic control, and the territorial dimension of Bulgaria's politics (the Union of Democratic Forces dominating in major cities, and the Bulgarian Socialist Party in secondary towns and villages). In the past, all three have contributed to the slow and haphazard decentralization. First, the lack of tradition simply reflects the cultural inertia that requires time to overcome. New government institutions and rules of conduct can take root but only after a process of "learning," the length of which depends on a number of cultural and local factors (for example, the strength of local civic associations, the extent of horizontal local social networks, and the education level and skills of the local civil service).

Second, Bulgaria's economy has been under constant fiscal stress since the beginning of the transition. At the outset, the deficit of over 16 percent of GDP had to be drastically reduced in 1991 to prevent hyperinflation. But the high interest payments, which emerged soon thereafter, put further constraints on primary expenditures in the budget. And these developments took place against the backdrop of a severe revenue decline, driven by declines in the bases of the profits tax, trade taxes, and in nontax revenues inherited from the previous regime. The resulting chaotic fiscal and macroeconomic conditions were not a favorable environment for a genuine and carefully thought-out move toward decentralization.

And third, Bulgaria's divided polity, in which the socialist party dominated the politics of the country for most of the transition, while the opposition remained on the sidelines of policymaking (except in 1991 during the radical liberalization and reform program launched by the government led by the Union of Democratic Forces) resulted in much political instability, frequent changes of governments, and government reshuffles. Such a situation did not favor shifting political power to large municipalities where the opposition was strong. Even with the most decentralized-minded government, incentives for central government to embark on significant decentralization would have been minimal in such a setting. More generally, these factors are not dissimilar to what has been happening in other transition economies. To that extent, a broader lesson from Bulgaria's experience may be that instituting and implementing a well-designed decentralization strategy during a prolonged fiscal and macroeconomic crisis is extremely difficult. And when the key political groups in the transition are divided into identifiable territorial units of government, a divided polity will not contribute to decentralization.[2]

---

[2]An extreme example of this situation is the almost complete centralization of fiscal powers in the neighboring Republic of Serbia after the breakup of the former Yugoslavia. The capital city of Belgrade, which had enjoyed considerable fiscal autonomy in the former country, was virtually stripped of most of its fiscal authority, as was the case in other municipalities. As the opposition increasingly gained the upper hand in large cities—their rise culminating in the victory in local elections in October 1996, subsequent mass demonstrations and sharp political divisions—the central republican government has little incentive to return fiscal autonomy to these municipalities. It is likely that genuine decentralization will have to await a more stable political and macroeconomic environment in that country.

Are the Benefits of Decentralization too Elusive?

Theoretically, benefits from decentralization are rooted in the argument for greater efficiency in public goods provision and their closer correspondence to local demand (Musgrave and Musgrave, 1989). Implicitly, this argument assumes existence of effective institutional mechanisms for expressing local preferences for public goods within a local political system, accountable and responsive local governments who also have considerable autonomy, and effective grassroots organizations (Putnam, Leonardi, and Nanetti, 1993). The aforementioned lack of tradition of autonomous local governments in Bulgaria is therefore a constraint on the process of decentralization. But its existence should not make that process less possible or desirable than in any other country. In Italy, for example, regional reforms were introduced in the 1970s and often in communities that had little prior experience with decentralized management. Nevertheless, they had beneficial effects on many such communities. Key to the success of these reforms were building on and a new growth of many civic community associations, which ultimately strengthen the functioning of democratic institutions and help improve the responsiveness of local officials to local demand (Putnam, Leonardi, and Nanetti, 1993; Tullock, 1994).

Should There Be Controls on Local Government Borrowing?

Given considerable pressures on local governments to spend, the current prohibition to borrowing to finance current expenditures is desirable. In principle, a case can be made for allowing a limited amount of borrowing for investment purposes. However, in Bulgaria's current circumstances of severe fiscal and macroeconomic imbalances, weak financial system, and limited own resources of local government, the question arises whether the golden rule should be strengthened to prohibit any local borrowing. There is no simple answer to this question. Perhaps the fiscal authorities should monitor the local fiscal situation closely and be prepared to tighten borrowing limits if signs of rising deficits and indebtedness of local governments emerge. At the same time, the imposition of a no deficit rule must be accompanied by tighter controls on quasi-fiscal activities of local governments, including arrears (see Mihaljek and Hewitt, 1993, for a discussion of a similar case in the former Yugoslavia).

In the medium to long term, as Bulgaria's financial system is consolidated and strengthened, local governments with sound finances and credit rating should be able to tap banks and the capital market for financing quality projects, and the discipline of the financial market should be relied upon to a greater extent as a constraint on local borrowing.

The question of borrowing controls is, logically, part of the larger question of whether there is a need for (and what type of) explicit constraints on the deficits of local governments, including the forms of their financing. Clearly, as decentralization proceeds and local governments gain more financial autonomy, it will be increasingly important for local governments to manage their finances in a fiscally responsible manner. Otherwise, local fiscal deficits would offset sound fiscal management at the center. Furthermore, decentralization poses special challenges to macro-management even in the presence of hard budget constraints on local governments, as changed composition of local spending and revenue sources alone may have expansionary effects on the aggregate demand (see Chapter 1). This means that, as decentralization proceeds, local governments will need to become more involved in the process of fiscal macro-management. In Bulgaria, this raises the question of an appropriate institutional coordinating mechanism beyond the Ministry of Finance, which would serve at least as a forum for reconciling and coordinating local fiscal matters with national spillover effects.[3]

Concluding Remarks

This chapter has attempted to present a brief overview of Bulgaria's intergovernmental finances and to discuss some key policy issues currently facing the authorities. Several conclusions of broader interest may be drawn from the preceding analysis.
- Decentralization may bring important efficiency gains. But it is difficult to design and implement in the tumult of fiscal and macroeconomic crisis that often accompanies the transition to a market economy. Also, heightened political divisions may not bode well for decentralization. This may require postponing a major decentralization drive during the most unstable stages of the transition. Perhaps this is a matter of sequencing: legislative and capacity building effort may proceed first to prepare the ground for the implementation of decentralization under subsequent, more stable conditions.
- Clarifying revenue and expenditure assignments is critical to the design of an effective system of intergovernmental relations. That clarification is also necessary to design an effective and stable sys-

---

[3]One such forum could be the regular meetings of the Ministry of Finance with the association of mayors.

tem of intergovernmental transfers. Uncertainty about tax or expenditure assignments and about the level and timing of transfers hinder effective budgetary management at the central, as well as the local government levels.
- Local borrowing is an issue of special importance owing to its potentially destabilizing impact on the overall finances of the country. Greater reliance on clear and firmly implemented rules of borrowing, perhaps as simple as the rule of "no borrowing for current budget" are likely to be needed in the transition, until the discipline of the market becomes an important supplemental instrument of control of unwise borrowing.
- Strengthening local government's institutional capacity for public expenditure management, accounting and budgeting, local taxation (for example, property tax and vehicle tax), and project appraisal is necessary to make decentralization succeed.

References

Bahl, Roy, and Johannes Linn, 1993, *Local Public Finance in Developing Countries* (Washington: World Bank).

Bird, Richard M., Robert D. Ebel, and Christine I. Wallich, 1995, "Fiscal Decentralization: From Command to Market," in *Decentralization of the Socialist State: Intergovernmental Finance in Transition Economies*, ed. by Richard M. Bird, Robert D. Ebel, and Christine Wallich (Washington: World Bank).

Bogetić, Željko, 1996, "Bulgaria in Transition: An Overview and Some Lessons," in *The Cost of War in Former Yugoslavia* (English Edition), ed. by Željko Bogetić (Paris: Peace and Crisis Management Foundation).

———, and Sajal Chattopadhyay, 1995, "Efficiency in Bulgaria's Schools: A Nonparametric Study," World Bank Policy Research Working Paper No. 1422, Europe and Central Asia, Country Department One, Country Operations Division (Washington: World Bank, February).

Bogetić, Željko, and Arye L. Hillman, 1995, "The Choice of the Tax System," in *Financing Government in the Transition: Bulgaria; The Political Economy of Tax Policies, Tax Bases and Tax Evasion*, ed. by Željko Bogetić and Arye L. Hillman (Washington: Word Bank).

Bogetić, Željko, and Heywood Fleisig, 1997, "Collateral, Access to Credit and Investment in Bulgaria," in *The Bulgarian Economy: Lessons from Reform During Early Transition*, ed. by Jeffrey Miller and Derek Jones (Brookfield, Vermont: Ashgate).

Chand, Sheetal K., and Henrie R. Lorie, 1993, "Bulgaria's Transition to a Market Economy: Fiscal Aspects," in *Transition to Market: Studies in Fiscal Reform*, ed. by Vito Tanzi (Washington: International Monetary Fund).

Martinez-Vazquez, Jorge, 1995a, "Central and Local Government Tax Relations," in *Financing Government in the Transition: Bulgaria; The Political Economy of Tax Policies, Tax Bases and Tax Evasion*, ed. by Željko Bogetić and Arye L. Hillman (Washington: World Bank).

———, 1995b, "Intergovernmental Fiscal Relations in Bulgaria," in *Decentralization of the Socialist State: Intergovernmental Finance in Transition Economies*, ed. by Richard M. Bird, Robert D. Ebel, and Christine I. Wallich (Washington: World Bank).

McLure, Charles, 1995, "Comment on Prud'homme," *World Bank Research Observer*, Vol.10, No.2, pp. 221–26.

Mihaljek, Dubravko, and Daniel Hewitt, 1993, "Intergovernmental Fiscal Relations in Yugoslavia 1972–1990," in *Transition to Market: Studies in Fiscal Reform*, ed. by Vito Tanzi (Washington: International Monetary Fund).

Musgrave, Richard A., and Peggy B. Musgrave, 1989, *Public Finance in Theory and Practice* (New York: McGraw Hill).

Normand, Charles, 1995, "Choosing and Funding a Health Care Program in the Transition," in *Financing Government in the Transition: Bulgaria; The Political Economy of Tax Policies, Tax Bases and Tax Evasion*, ed. by Željko Bogetić and Arye L. Hillman (Washington: World Bank).

Prud'homme, Rémy, 1995, "The Dangers of Decentralization," *World Bank Research Observer*, Vol. 10, No. 2, pp. 201–220.

Putnam, Robert D., Robert Leonardi, and Rafaella S. Nanetti, 1993, *Making Democracy Work: Civic Traditions in Modern Italy* (Princeton, New Jersey: Princeton University Press).

Tanzi, Vito, 1996, "Fiscal Federalism and Decentralization: A Review of Some Efficiency and Macroeconomic Aspects," *Annual Bank Conference on Development Economics, 1995* (Washington: World Bank).

———, and Ludger Schuknecht, 1995, "The Growth of Government and the Reform of the State in Industrial Countries," IMF Working Paper 95/130 (Washington: International Monetary Fund).

Tullock, Gordon, 1994, *The New Federalist* (Vancouver: Fraser Institute).

Varga, Julia, 1996, "Taxation and Investment in Bulgaria," International Bureau of Fiscal Documentation, *Guides to European Taxation*, Vol. 5 (May).

World Bank, 1994, *Bulgaria: Public Finance Reforms in the Transition*, Report No. 12273-BUL (Washington: World Bank).

26

China

EHTISHAM AHMAD

Since 1994, China has undertaken major reforms of its public finances, driven largely by the desire to establish a level playing field to facilitate its entry into the global economy. The authorities have also sought to consolidate the indirect levers of macroeconomic management in the central government, as the economy moves from central planning to greater market orientation. This has involved, inter alia, the establishment of a modern system of tax laws as well as a central government tax collection capability. As a consequence, an overhaul of the fiscal relations between different levels of government has been initiated—replacing the ad hoc contracting arrangements between the central and local governments and between the state and the state-owned enterprise sectors.[1]

Although the changes initiated may give the appearance of greater central control, the decentralization of expenditure responsibilities has continued, a process that China shares with many of the other countries examined in this volume. The net effects on decentralization of the changes in tax policy and administration will depend on the eventual design of the transfer system chosen. This chapter focuses on pol-

---

Comments by Teresa Ter-Minassian, John Norregaard, and Vivek Arora are gratefully acknowledged.

[1]Given that China is a unitary state, some officials prefer the use of the term "intragovernmental" rather than "intergovernmental" in referring to relations between different levels of government in China. However, to be consistent with the usage elsewhere in the volume, this chapter adopts the more standard terminology of "intergovernmental relations."

icy and institutional considerations that will govern the reforms of China's intergovernmental fiscal relations in the immediate future.

The background to the current reforms to the system of intergovernmental fiscal relations in China, covering tax-contracting and expenditure decentralization, is summarized below, followed by a discussion of the macroeconomic constraints facing policymakers in reforming revenue assignments and transfers. The next four sections analyze revenue assignments, tax administration, public expenditure management, and transfer design, respectively. The chapter concludes with an emphasis on the interlinkages between the various policy strands discussed earlier.

Background

Despite a de jure centralized control over revenue bases and rate structures in China (all tax legislation is presently under the jurisdiction of the central government), the reforms during the 1980s led to an increasing de facto decentralization, particularly with respect to expenditures, but also regarding control over revenues. Despite a nominally unified tax collection agency, provinces effectively controlled tax collections, and revenues were effectively shared upward. While this process has been associated with rapid growth, particularly in the township and village enterprise sector,[2] the arrangements meant that there were severe limitations in the central government's ability to conduct macroeconomic management.

The Contract Management System

As market-oriented reforms to the centrally planned economy were initiated during the late 1970s and early 1980s, particularly with the replacement of 100 percent profit taxation (the main source of revenue in the prereform era) by a more standard system of corporate income taxation, China experienced a sharp decline in revenues, which was only partially offset by reductions in public expenditures. In order to provide greater autonomy, the introduction of the contract management system with enterprises was mirrored by contracts between different levels of government during the 1980s and early 1990s.

The Chinese intergovernmental fiscal system in the early 1990s is described in detail in a number of reports.[3] Tax arrangements between

---

[2]See Yusuf (1993).
[3]See, for instance, World Bank (1993); see also Wong, Heady, and Woo (1993).

the central and provincial governments in China were based on a tax or transfer contract system that varied by province. The provinces were distinguished as either remitting revenues to the center or receiving transfers. Contracts remitting revenues to the central government were of three basic types: fixed, incremental, and proportional. Shanghai fell under the first type; Guangdong under the second type with an annual rate of increase of the remittance of 9 percent; and Anhui under the third type with a proportional rate of payment at 22.5 percent of revenues. Most remitting provinces belonged to the second type, with an annual rate of increase of the remittance of 4 percent to 5 percent.

China experimented with a new tax-sharing system for nine provinces during the second half of 1992. The intention was to abandon the contracting mechanisms and move rapidly to a "normally" functioning tax system. A revised tax legislation, creating a level playing field along with new tax assignments, which replaced the previous contracting system, has been in effect since January 1994 (for details see Xu Shanda and Ma Lin, 1995). The establishment of a separate central tax collection capability through the creation of the State Administration of Taxation is a key step in ensuring that central and shared tax bases are not subject to the de facto control and manipulation by local governments.

Grants

During the 1980s and early 1990s, the emphasis in China was more on specific grants than on equalizing or general grants. In 1992, 18 provinces received general grants from the center totaling Y 10 billion (roughly 3 percent of total revenues). There has been a special arrangement for eight of the poorest minority regions including Xinjiang, Inner Mongolia, and Tibet. For these provinces, grants increased by 10 percent annually during 1982–87, and the total amount doubled during this period. For Xinjiang and Nei Mongol the grants covered roughly one third of provincial expenditures in 1992. Since 1988, and the increasing stringency of central resources, these grants were frozen in nominal terms, although local expenditures continued to grow.

In addition, there were transfers to the poorest counties. The transfer criterion, established in 1985, was that eligible counties should have average per capita incomes of less than Y 200 per annum, with less than 200 kilograms per capita of grain available. This criterion remained unchanged in nominal terms. Relatively prosperous provinces, such as Zhejiang, have recognized that this criterion is inadequate, and raised the criterion for transfers from the provincial government to Y 300 per capita to account for price changes. It is not evident that the poorer provinces had the resources to top up the central grant to poor counties within their jurisdictions.

Specific grants amounted to three times the amount spent on general grants and were earmarked for special purposes, such as financing economic and social sector development and natural disaster relief. Information on the distribution of specific grants for 1990 suggests that richer provinces received substantial transfers (for example, Shanghai and Guangdong received Y 171 and Y 57.5 per capita, respectively), whereas poor provinces received less (for example, Guizhou and Guangxi both received Y 28.3 per capita).[4] This pattern is common with specific or earmarked grants, which often have a matching element, in that better-endowed or faster-growing provinces tend to benefit more.

All the central grants were allocated by a baseline adjustment method, using 1979 revenues and expenditures. The baseline year was 1979, and provinces with deficits at that date received grants, while others paid remittances to the center (as described above). This incremental approach was increasingly outdated, given the considerable structural changes that have taken place in China since 1979, in particular the increasing disparity between regions. In addition, the pattern of specific grants would appear to accentuate the differences between regions. Another difficulty with the transfers to poor counties was that it was assumed that the cause and nature of poverty are essentially regional. While this may have been the case in the past, when within-region incomes were fairly equally distributed, there is ample evidence that within-region inequality has increased, and need is apparent even in the better-off regions.[5]

Regional Inequalities

The contract system exacerbated regional fiscal disparities. Richer provinces were better able to meet the devolved expenditure responsibilities than the poorer provinces. For instance, Shanghai and Guangdong had a substantial and growing revenue base, but Tibet's revenues remained limited. Moreover, general grants received by poorer provinces from the central government have had to be restricted in recent years because of the falling revenue base of the center.

In the early 1980s, the central government received more from the surplus provinces than it paid out in transfers and grants. However, with the contract-based system, transfers from the central government in 1989–93 exceeded remittances from the surplus provinces. The center

---

[4]See World Bank (1993).
[5]See Ahmad and Wang (1991).

lacked the resources to narrow the growing regional disparities. Thus, horizontal imbalances increased as a consequence of the contracting arrangements.

Many of the poorer regions in China are fairly well endowed with natural resources. To some extent, the limited development of the resource base in these provinces is a result of administered pricing mechanisms that are being only gradually reformed. While price reform is not addressed in this chapter, it would have major implications for the resource base of the poorer provinces, if accompanied by appropriate resource taxation and sharing of royalties that accrue to the local government (natural resource taxation is discussed further below).

Public Expenditures and Regional Growth

The implication of contracting arrangements for horizontal equity between regions is substantial. A World Bank report suggests that the poorer provinces spend a larger proportion of their budgets on social expenditures, yet their lower revenue base means their per capita spending on such items remains significantly below that of the richer regions (see World Bank, 1993). Meanwhile, there is evidence that the shares of spending on social items and on capital items are inversely related. Richer provinces use their higher revenue capacities to finance more capital spending. Such arrangements have three important implications:
- Lower capital spending may perpetuate slower growth in poorer provinces.
- Lower economic growth means that revenue capacities of poorer provinces will continue to lag behind those of richer provinces.
- In the absence of an adequate system of equalization transfers, lower revenue capacities would doom poorer provinces to inadequate social spending and poor development of human capital, reinforcing the lower growth prospects in the future.

The importance of these horizontal imbalances is magnified by the absence of an effective personal income tax or nationwide social security system, capable of handling inequalities, and by restrictions on the population moving to other regions where they can improve their access to higher standards of government service.

Macroeconomic Constraints

The contract management system generated rigidities that constrained the ability of the central government to conduct macroeconomic policy. Indeed, the fixed, multiyear, fiscal contracts acted as built-in macroeconomic destabilizers. When inflation and growth rates are high, the system permitted enterprises to obtain higher disposable incomes, which proved to be expansionary, and vice versa.[6]

Despite national legislation for the major direct (and some indirect) taxes, the contracting arrangements were based on "negotiations" between the enterprises and the relevant level of government, effectively generating enterprise-specific tax rates that varied across and within regions. This led to distortions, and local authorities engaged in granting all sorts of exemptions (to centrally determined taxes) to attract investment.[7] Moreover, contracts fixed in nominal terms resulted in low tax buoyancy in a period of rapid growth and rising prices.

Declining Revenues

Revenue Trends

As in many other countries that have moved from a centrally planned economy toward a market-based system, in China the tax-to-GDP ratio has fallen sharply since the beginning of the reforms. This partly reflects a changed role for the state, and public expenditure has been reduced to match the fall in the revenue-to-GDP ratio. However, unlike in other former centrally planned economies, where the drop in the revenue-to-GDP ratio has been partly attributed to negative or stagnant growth, China's growth performance since 1978 has been among the best in the world. Table 1 shows the consolidated budgetary revenues of the central and local governments.[8]

As seen in Table 1, the ratio of budgetary revenue to GDP dropped from 31.6 percent in 1978 to under 20 percent in 1987.[9] It declined sharply further to about 13 percent in 1992, following the contract system negotiated with provinces in 1988. Although this phenomenon is common to former centrally planned economies,[10] in China the problem was exacerbated by the contracting arrangements as they applied to enterprise taxes and was reflected in the revenue-sharing arrangements at different levels of government. The decline continued after the implementation of the new revenue-sharing system to 11.9 percent in

---

[6]See Hussain and Stern (1992) and Blejer and Szapary (1989).

[7]Exemptions to central taxes are also given to divert resources into other funds and expenditures over which the local authorities have greater discretion (see below).

[8]Local is taken to denote all lower tiers of government—provinces, municipalities, counties, and townships.

[9]See also Blejer (1993) and World Bank (1990).

[10]See Tanzi (1992). Unlike in China, many transition economies suffered a contraction in their economies, or a period of low growth, associated with the decline in revenues.

Table 1. China: Consolidated Budgetary Revenues of the Central and Local Governments[1]
(In percent)

Year	Share of Revenue in GDP
1978	31.6
1979	28.7
1980	25.9
1981	24.6
1982	23.4
1983	23.6
1984	23.7
1985	23.5
1986	21.9
1987	19.5
1988	16.7
1989	16.7
1990	16.6
1991	14.6
1992	13.1
1993	12.7
1994	11.9
1995	11.2
1996	11.1

Sources: Ministry of Finance; and IMF staff estimates.
[1]Revenues do not include the proceeds of government debt, but include subsidies to state-owned enterprises as negative revenue item.

1994 and to an estimated 11 percent in 1996—during a period of exceptionally high growth.

The 11 percent of GDP in budgetary revenues does not, however, convey a full picture of the true extent of consolidated government revenue. Excluded from the above figure is around 5 percent of GDP collected from fees and contributions for extrabudgetary funds mainly controlled by local governments—such as the Energy, Transportation, and Construction Funds.

In most countries, obligatory social security contributions would be considered part of consolidated revenues. China's social security policy, including provisions for social assistance, is governed by a number of distinct central agencies, with administration and financing at local levels. Since the late 1980s, attempts have been made to unify the system upward, and at present some provinces have unified policies for pensions and unemployment insurance. It is difficult to be specific about the aggregate amounts collected for social security contributions, but the overall figure is roughly estimated to be in the range of 1 percent to 2 percent of GDP.

Thus, a more complete accounting of revenues in China could put the present overall collection in the range of 17 percent to 18 percent of GDP. This figure would not be much out of line with that of other countries and China's level of development. However, a revenue-GDP figure on its own is no more than suggestive; it has to be evaluated in comparison with expenditure outlays. While expenditures have indeed declined in China, reflecting the changing nature of the state as greater market orientation is achieved, pressures on budgets continue to be significant, particularly at the central level. The severe constraints on policymaking at the central government level are largely due to the fact that revenues from relatively buoyant sources accrue mainly to lower levels of government (Gao Qiang, 1995).

Changing Revenue Bases

The main causes for the decline in the revenue-to-GDP ratio are attributed to a structural shift in revenue bases, as well as to policy measures, including tax preferences and exemptions. Prior to the reforms, the state-owned enterprise (SOE) sector generated much of the revenues of the state budget.

Since 1978, the main structural change has been the decline in the role of the SOE sector as a source of budgetary revenues. The share of wages in SOE value added increased from 22 percent in 1979 to 31 percent in 1985 and further to 42 percent by 1993. Partly because of a fall in the profits tax rate, the profits tax as a percentage of value added for SOEs had declined from 27.3 percent in 1985 to 8 percent in 1992.

The ability to collect direct taxes effectively from the growing collective and township and village enterprise sector, and from personal incomes, remains constrained by difficulties in the tax administration. These collection difficulties are compounded by policy shortcomings (such as the assignment of revenues and collection responsibilities for SOEs according to the level of government that owns the enterprise). Similar issues apply to the personal income tax, which is assigned to local governments and collected by the local tax administrations. The personal income tax accounts for less than 1 percent of total revenue collection in China (as opposed to roughly 12 percent in countries at comparable levels of income and 28 percent in industrial countries (Burgess and Stern, 1993)). Thus, a major source of potential revenues in the future has been assigned to a level of government that may have difficulties in fully utilizing the base.

Tax Administration

According to the law, only the central government had legislative powers over taxes, with a unified tax administration. Although in principle a vertical arrangement existed, with the appointments and promotions of directors of local tax bureaus being decided by the center, all taxes were effectively collected by local tax bureaus. Local governments were able to grant exemptions at will to the centrally determined taxes, and exercised considerable suasion over the tax collectors. Ad hoc levies imposed at the lower local levels also proliferated, inter alia, to finance extrabudgetary funds, leading to a clouding of the effects of taxation on revenues, incentives, and equity. Despite the vertical hierarchy, the central government had little effective control over revenue collection.

Exemptions and Preferences

Until recently, revenue contracts between the central and local governments, and between SOEs and various levels of government, were accompanied by an extensive system of exemptions and preferences, particularly by local governments in relation to centrally determined taxes. Since 1993, the central government has made concerted efforts to eliminate such local preferences. Although central regulations may have reduced local exemptions to central taxes, a vast number of centrally approved exemptions and preferences remain—particularly to loss-making SOEs, joint ventures, and imports. Widespread exemptions reduced the average tariff rate on imports from the nominal level of about 35 percent to an effective rate of 7 percent to 8 percent in 1994 and below 5 percent in 1995 and 1996.

Rising Expenditures

A devolution of expenditure authority from central to local governments, down to the township level, led to a rapid increase in local expenditures, particularly administrative costs and health, education, and science expenditures. The increase in local government expenditures was partly financed by the expansion in extrabudgetary funds under the control of the local authorities, agencies, and SOEs. Extrabudgetary funds in China include (1) revenues managed by local finance bureaus—such as surcharges on various taxes, profit remittances from enterprises, and government project income; (2) user charges and income from nonprofit and administrative units; and (3) income received from SOEs and bureaus from depreciation accumulation and renovation funds and management income from other funds.[11] However, the ex-

---

[11]Excluded from the definition of extrabudgetary funds since 1993.

pansion in such funds has been, to some extent, at the expense of regular tax revenues accruing to the formal budgets of provinces and the central government. This, in turn, has put pressures on the budgets of several provincial governments (as the formal expenditure requirements to be met out of the budget have increased). Thus, even governments of relatively prosperous regions, such as Zhejiang, faced deficits in 1992. In general, this results in either reduced transfers to the central government or an increased requirement for support from the center.

Despite a reduction in certain own expenditures of the central government, such as for defense, the increased demand for financing lumpy investments and for meeting the needs of poorer provinces continued to exert an upward pressure on the expenditures of the center. Moreover, with vaguely defined expenditure responsibilities, some local governments have been tempted to "pass the buck upward" to the central government (see Gao Qiang, 1995). The net effect is that reduced central revenues are inadequate to meet the continued expenditure needs of the central government. However, there is little scope for additional central government expenditures (for example, for a greater degree of horizontal redistribution) without a major restructuring of the vertical imbalances.

Overall Deficits

Reported budget deficits in China have been relatively small and have been generally maintained at under 3 percent of GDP (Table 2). However, the inclusion of quasi-fiscal activities of the banking sector suggests a less favorable picture. Thus, "policy lending" by the banking sector to cover the deficits of the SOEs suggests that the actual budget deficit may have been substantially greater than the "reported" deficit. If such quasi-fiscal operations of the banking system, covering the losses of the SOEs, are taken into account, the consolidated deficit would have exceeded 5 percent of GDP in 1991 at a time when the reported deficit was 2.2 percent of GDP. As with the revenue decline, there are formidable data difficulties in establishing the full extent of the deficit in China.

Borrowing by Local Governments

Legally, local governments are not permitted to run deficits,[12] and borrowing from the local branches of the People's Bank of China is not

---

[12]Under the pre-1994 Chinese definition, receipts from borrowing were treated as a revenue item, so the stricture on zero deficits has had a somewhat different connotation than under the classification system in the IMF's *Government Finance Statistics Yearbook*.

Table 2. China: Revenues, Expenditures, and Deficits[1]
(In percent of GDP)

	1990	1991	1992	1993	1994	1995
Total revenue	19.2	17.0	14.7	13.8	12.4	12.1
Tax	16.9	15.3	13.0	11.6	10.3	11.2
Current expenditures	21.1	19.2	17.0	15.8	14.1	13.8
Overall balance	−2.0	−2.2	−2.3	−2.0	−1.6	−1.7

Source: IMF staff estimates.
[1]The data reflect the consolidated budgets of the central government, provinces, municipalities, and counties, and transfers between levels are netted out. Extrabudgetary financial operations are excluded, as is seigniorage revenue of about 2.5 percent of GDP in recent years.

permitted. However, there have been clear examples of expenditure overruns. In general, four avenues are available for financing such overruns: (1) increased transfers from the Ministry of Finance; (2) borrowing from commercial banks; (3) indirect borrowing, including a buildup of arrears; and (4) foreign borrowing. Financing by the Ministry of Finance has been rather limited owing to the tight fiscal situation of the center. However, borrowing from local commercial banks occurs. Local governments undertake "indirect borrowing" mainly by creating dummy financial companies that are able to borrow to provide resources for local government expenditures. Another method of indirect borrowing has been through a buildup of arrears, as well as IOUs on the procurement of agricultural products. The government has been taking steps to prohibit the issue of IOUs to farmers, but the control of arrears is a more complex task. Foreign borrowing is made through joint ventures, the issuance of bonds, bilateral agreements with foreign financial institutions, and international organizations such as the World Bank and Asian Development Bank.

The most important source of financing has been through commercial banks, and local authorities have exercised the discretion to sanction projects below Y 50 million (above this amount, the project needs to be referred to the State Planning Commission) through commercial and indirect borrowing. This is a consequence of the current system of "fuzzy property rights," where the distinction between government functions and the private sector are blurred. During 1991–92, the People's Bank set aside 7 percent of total credit in a stabilization fund in order to supplement and facilitate credit flows to special banks.

The People's Bank has been required to engage in "policy lending" (later taken over by so-called policy banks) at subsidized interest rates to designated enterprises, to support the poorer provinces, and to perform a quasi-fiscal function. Although the Ministry of Finance was to reimburse the interest differential, this form of transfer is opaque at best, is discretionary, and adds to the difficulties with the reform of the financial sector. It is preferable to reform the system of grants to provide support explicitly to deserving regions.

Reforms to Tax Policy and Administration

In the early 1990s, China began to experiment with reforms to tax policies and assignments. A tax-sharing experiment was initiated in 1992, and, after assessing the difficulties faced in the interim period, a new set of tax laws was promulgated in 1994, which affected tax assignments as well as revenue sharing. Tax administration arrangements were also completely overhauled.

Tax-Sharing Experiments

In 1992, a tax-sharing experiment was introduced in three provinces (Zhejiang, Xinjiang, and Liaoning) and six large cities (Tianjin, Chongqing, Wuhan, Qingdao, Shenyang, and Dalian). The basic precept was to replace the contract-based system of revenue sharing by assigning taxes to particular levels of government—that is, the center and the provinces. There was, in addition, a shared tax category, and the revenues generated from five major taxes—the product tax, the VAT, the business tax, the consolidated industrial-commercial tax, and the resource tax—were divided on a 50:50 basis between the central government and the local government. Another five shared sources of income were characterized as "fixed rate shared incomes."

The tax-sharing experiment suffered from a number of drawbacks. Some provincial governments, particularly along the coast, feared that they would lose revenue from the new system. For instance, in two provinces, Zhejiang and Liaoning, the local retention rate decreased from 61.5 percent and 58.5 percent, respectively, under the previous contract system, to 50 percent for shared revenues—which accounted for a major part of total provincial revenues. In addition, local government control over rates and bases for taxes assigned to them had not been introduced. Moreover, local fixed revenues mainly comprised SOE income taxes, and these were limited by the low efficiency of SOEs, the contract system for enterprises, and the wide range of tax deductions. The buoyancy of the main local taxes was low relative to that of shared revenues. However, provinces such as Zhejiang were guaranteed revenues—no less than under the previous contracting arrangement—thus reducing the incentive to improve tax collections.

A number of problems associated with tax policy and administration arose during the experimental period (see, for example, the discussion in Tanzi, 1996). These included, inter alia:
- *Lack of standardization.* While the lines of demarcation used to be reasonably clear, the growth of share ownership vitiated the distinction between foreign and domestic enterprises and between central and locally owned firms. Thus, taxation and assignment of revenues by ownership type became cumbersome.
- *Variations in rate structure.* Varying rates for the same tax (for example, the personal income tax) for different groups or individuals were anomalous and a source of distortions, while complicating administration. Another case in point was the excessive differentiation of the VAT.
- *Variations by region.* The use of differential incentives, such as those for the special enterprise zones, caused distortions and excessive tax competition across regions, leading to an overall loss of revenue.

The 1994 Reforms

In 1994, China undertook a major tax reform with the intention of increasing the central share of revenues (before transfers to lower levels) from around 35 percent of total revenue collection to around 58 percent (see Gao Qiang, 1995). The reform had two main elements: policy changes (for the VAT, enterprise income taxes, and revenue sharing between different levels of government) and the establishment of the State Administration of Taxation, with responsibility for administering the taxes assigned to the central government, as well as the shared taxes, including the VAT. The establishment of a national tax administration was achieved by splitting the existing tax administrations largely under the control of local governments into the national and local components.

Tax Policy Changes

Tax policy changes enacted included the following: (1) unifying the domestic corporation income tax, rationalizing the base and rate structure, and abolishing the tax deductibility of principal repayments; (2) amalgamating the personal income tax and the income adjustment tax and simplifying the resulting tax; (3) reducing the myriad VAT rates to two positive rates and supplementing these by selective product taxes (excises) on final goods; and (4) introducing a natural resource tax. It was expected that these policy reforms would simplify ad-

Table 3. China: Tax Assignments Under the 1994 Revenue-Sharing Arrangement

Central fixed revenues
- Enterprise income taxes on centrally owned enterprises
- Customs duties
- Consumption tax (excises)
- VAT on imports
- Business turnover taxes on railways, banks, nonbank financial institutions, and insurance companies

Local fixed revenues
- Enterprise income taxes on locally owned enterprises, collectives, private enterprises, and joint ventures
- Personal income taxes
- Agricultural income tax
- Business turnover taxes (except on railways, banks, nonbank financial institutions, and insurance companies)
- Urban maintenance and development tax
- City and town land use taxes
- VAT on real estate transactions
- Stamp taxes
- Transactions taxes

Shared revenues
- VAT on domestic transactions, other than real estate (75 percent central government, 25 percent provinces)
- Securities and exchange tax (50:50 sharing)
- Resource taxes

Source: Mihaljek (1997).

ministration and go a long way toward increasing the buoyancy of the tax system.

Tax Assignments

The revenue assignments follow the basic principles set out in the experiments—with central and local taxes and shared revenues. Unlike in the experiments, the VAT is the main major tax to be shared—on a 75:25 basis—with the subnational levels of government. This will reduce the incentives to "play strategic games" that are evident in other countries, such as India, where different sharing ratios apply to various taxes. However, some features of the new tax assignments in China might need to be revisited in the years to come. The 1994 tax assignments are set out in Table 3.

The assignment of the corporate income tax. The corporate income tax on central enterprises is designed to be part of central fixed revenue, under the jurisdiction of the State Administration of Taxation, while that on local enterprises would form part of fixed local revenues and be collected by the local tax administrations. While this assignment is understandable in the light of underdeveloped alternative local tax bases, it creates a number of problems. The assignment could perpetuate the anachronistic division of tax revenues by ownership types and would become impossible to administer as increasing share-ownership blurs the distinctions between different levels of government. It may in the future also inhibit the development of national markets and privatization of enterprises. Furthermore, with local variations in the effective rates of tax, there would be an added tendency to create subsidiary companies in various localities to reduce tax payments. It would also be unnecessarily expensive to duplicate the administrative arrangements for the corporate income tax at different levels of government.

In the future, the corporate income tax should be treated as a unified tax, administered by the central tax administration, in order to minimize tax competition across regions and reduce collection costs. Revenues could be allocated to the central pool for division according to a grants formula or be treated as shared on a derivation basis (that is, a share would accrue to the locality in which the income is generated). But this reform would require a reassignment of revenues or an adequately functioning transfer mechanism to compensate for the loss of own revenues that might be entailed.

The reformed personal income tax. The personal income tax is to be part of local fixed revenue. There may be some merit in allocating 100 percent of the personal income tax revenues to the local level in the medium term in China. The problems associated with the administration of a tax with incomes derived from different regions would be offset in China by the limited mobility of labor and greater information on incomes at the local level. It is important to note, however, that the personal income tax has important stabilization and redistributive properties and should be among the most rapidly increasing taxes in the future.

An alternative assignment would permit collection of the personal income tax by the State Administration of Taxation, with revenues from a central rate structure accruing to the central government. Local governments could be allowed some control over rate structures by a surcharge (within a predetermined range) to be levied on the central tax rates, with collection by the State Administration of Taxation. Another option is to share the personal income tax, with administration by the State Administration of Taxation. However, this variant does not easily permit the setting of marginal tax rates by the subnational level of government, and is thus less attractive than the piggybacking of a local income tax on a central tax base.

The natural resource tax. Given the potential revenues that are likely to be generated, it may be advisable to treat a natural resource tax as a shared tax, with a number of components. First, there could be a charge to pay for the environmental cleanup that is often needed. This should be paid directly to the local government where the resource extraction is based and should be treated as a cost item. Second, there could be an excise, which would provide much of the revenues from natural resources to the central government. Finally, there should be a royalty that would also normally accrue to the region that claims ownership rights and would form the basis of local revenues.

The need for regional transfers would be greatly reduced in China as price reform, particularly for energy products, proceeds apace. Many of the poorest regions of China are rich in natural resources, and appropriate pricing, together with the introduction of resource taxation, would allow the development of natural resources, which could narrow the gap between rich and poor regions considerably.

Payroll contributions. While the move toward a level playing field is a major step, the local setting of payroll contributions for pensions, in particular, presents a significant lacuna. At present there is city-level pooling of payroll contributions for pensions, with considerable variation in exemptions and differences in payroll contribution burdens across enterprises.

In order to avoid tax competition across regions, the payroll contribution for pensions should be set and the revenue pooled on a national basis. This would parallel the efforts to standardize and simplify other taxes. A national pool would encourage solidarity between current workers and those who have already made their contributions to society. Interregional equity issues would be addressed through the grants mechanism (see below). Provincial pools, on the other hand, may be more acceptable to local governments, but could exacerbate more parochial interests.

Other local taxes. These consist of property taxes, a capital gains tax, and a variety of other levies.

Property taxes. In order to establish a proper base for the main local taxes, such as the land tax and property tax, it would be necessary to begin work on a property registry, as well as a valuation mechanism. In the interim, as ownership rights and the registry are being established, appropriate rentals for the use of local state property may constitute an important source of local revenue. The increasing use of land rentals has begun to provide a major source of own revenues for cities such as Shanghai.

Capital gains. While a capital gains tax on property transfers and sale of securities is needed to close an important loophole in the personal income tax, the implementation of such a tax would need to follow the work on the property register and valuation mechanisms.

Other levies. Ad hoc levies imposed by subprovincial governments have proliferated, and the central government has attempted to rescind some of these. Such levies should be subject to legislation by the People's Congress at the appropriate level of government. In order to avoid abuse by administrators, all such measures should be properly announced to the public, explicitly form part of the local budget, and be subject to the normal audit procedures.

While the reforms introduced in 1994 standardize VAT and personal and corporate income tax rates and bases, approximating standard international practices, a number of problems remain particularly relating to the design and assignment of the main taxes. Specific issues to be addressed in the future include the following:

- Revise corporate income tax assignments. The assignment of corporate taxes to the level of government that owns the enterprise is anachronistic and unworkable in the longer term (see Tanzi, 1996; and Shi Yaobin, 1995). It would be important to review the options for a more efficient assignment of the corporate income tax, to facilitate administration and generate revenues.
- Unify the domestic and foreign enterprise income taxes.
- Reduce tax exemptions.
- Examine improvements in the design of the personal income tax, so as to tap a growing tax base. As discussed above, this may involve the State Administration of Taxation in administering the personal income tax and could lead to a reconsideration of the assignment of this tax to subnational levels of government. A surcharge on a centrally administered personal income tax would be a more effective assignment for lower levels of government.
- Assign local government authority for legislative powers, especially over rate structures for locally assigned taxes. This is an issue of great importance if local governments are to achieve a degree of accountability in their budgetary processes (see Brosio, 1995).

Tax Administration

A key feature of the 1994 reform was the establishment of the National Tax Service—a central agency—to collect central and shared revenues. Subnational governments were permitted to establish their own collection agencies—or local tax services—for their assigned taxes.

Concern has been expressed that the overall budgetary revenue has continued to decline. This raises questions as to the effectiveness of the newly established administrative structures, as well as of the perfor-

Table 4. China: Growth of Central Indirect Taxes, 1993/94
(In percent)

Sector	Value-Added Tax (VAT)	VAT/Excise	Business Tax	Buoyancy
Industry	29.8	31.9		>1
Commercial	31.2	31.9		1
Tertiary	28.0		32.8	>1
Construction	38.7		29.9	<1
Transportation	18.2		20.3	>1
Total				−1

mance of taxes under the control of the National Tax Service. The new administrative procedures are still at an early experimental stage; thus, the revenue performance for the central taxes should be viewed as the efforts of the National Tax Service based on traditional collection methods—with all the inefficiencies involved. The main taxes under its control are the VAT and excises on the industrial and commercial sectors and the enterprise income tax on centrally owned SOEs.

Table 4 presents an estimate of gross revenue collections for the indirect taxes for 1993 and 1994. Since 1993 had been declared to be the base year for guaranteed transfers to provinces (see below), there was an extraordinary effort to boost revenues during the fourth quarter of the year. Despite this effort, the 1994 outcomes for the main indirect taxes suggest revenue outcomes that kept pace with the growth of the revenue base, or exceeded it, as with the VAT and business taxes on the tertiary sector and construction.

The 1994 reform reduced the tax burden on enterprises, and direct tax revenues (of which only the enterprise income tax on centrally owned enterprises is the responsibility of the National Tax Service) grew considerably slower than nominal GDP. Together with the disappointing outcome for tariffs—which was mainly policy induced—the overall ratio of tax to GDP declined during 1994. The year 1994 was the first year of the National Tax Service's operations, involving the splitting of the tax administrations. It appears that the taxes under its control performed better than the others, and that there should be room for further improvement as the new tax administration procedures being tested by the National Tax Service at four experimental sites are extended in the future.[13]

---

[13]However, in the years following 1994, local taxes have consistently performed better than central taxes.

The estimations above for the VAT are gross of rebates to exporters. It is believed that these rebates are posing great difficulties because of irregularities and fraud that are difficult to combat with the current procedures. However, the overall net VAT collection in excess of 5 percent of GDP is comparable to that of other countries, given China's existing rate structure. This percentage was achieved during a year of major reform.[14]

The separation of the central and provincial tax administrations has been pursued with relative success by all provinces, except for Shanghai and Zhejiang, where no separation had taken place by mid-1995. However, in the latter two provinces, designated officials collect central taxes, which are directly credited to central treasury accounts with the People's Bank of China. Hainan Province has yet another formulation, with three tax authorities—the central, the local, and the computerized tax collection agency. The central agency only has the right to audit information collected by the computer center, and the formulation is not approved by the State Administration of Taxation. In general, the wealthier provinces had been able to attract the best officials through incentives including promotions and benefits.

The main issues relating to tax administration are as follows:
- Clarification of the roles of the national and local tax services, for example, for the joint ventures and foreign enterprises.
- Joint audits leading to coordination between the National Tax Service and local tax authorities.

A major objective of the tax reform was to create a level playing field, so as not to generate disincentives for labor or capital in different parts of the country. However, the sharp differences in *payroll contributions* for pensions, in particular across provinces (and still in some cases within provinces), vitiate the efforts in this regard. The reform of the social security system would have important implications for revenue assignments, as well as expenditure responsibilities across regions. Thus, a reformed social security system will have a significant impact on public finances, net revenue positions, and the adequacy of benefit levels, and consequently on the need for special purpose transfers from the central to local governments. A payroll tax, with pooling at the central level, for a minimum benefit, would have a major redistributional impact and could provide a mechanism for tapping a growing resource base. One could then consider a supplementary funded system that could be organized locally, if so desired.

---

[14]The basic rate of 17 percent on the producer price (or 14.5 percent on a tax-inclusive basis) is supplemented by two additional rates of 13 percent and 6 percent (11.5 percent and 5.6 percent on a tax-inclusive basis).

Expenditure Assignments and Management

Expenditure Assignments

A distinction could be drawn between the level of government responsible for expenditure policies, the financing agency, and the level at which the expenditure is administered. Under the Constitution there are broad guidelines for expenditure responsibilities. Central responsibilities include defense, foreign affairs, foreign aid, fixed-asset investment for large and key projects, and technological transformation and experiments for SOEs. For education, in particular, primary and secondary education fall under local responsibilities, but responsibilities for higher education are shared between the central and local governments. Extensive social benefits are still provided by enterprises, particularly SOEs, but the scope of the pension and unemployment insurance funds is under review. There is considerable scope for overlapping responsibility at the present juncture.

In China, the administration of expenditures generally follows a sound benefit principle. There is, however, less clarity in the determination of policy—for example, standards for education or health are mandated by higher levels of government but are administered by counties and townships. Financing such expenditures also poses problems, given spatial externalities, as well as crucial implications of the distributional or equity objectives of the central government. In Sichuan and Zhejian, for example, the administrative responsibilities for expenditures[15] appear to be quite sensibly based on the benefit principle, with local governments catering for those expenditures that benefit local residents—and higher level governments becoming involved as the benefits spill over into other jurisdictions.

The trade-offs between central policies and local administrations are brought out clearly in relation to the social safety net. The central government might consider that its responsibility extends to ensuring the establishment of minimum standards. In this regard, national basic standards for pensions and unemployment benefits, financed by a national earmarked fund, are an important element. Local social assistance could be designed to cater for varying provincial standards, subject to the national minimum for transfers to poor areas. Such a minimum has to be established (such as the minimum Y 200 per capita poverty standard established in 1985 to identify poor counties) but

---

[15]In Zhejiang and Sichuan, local responsibilities include fixed-asset investments for local enterprises, technological experiments, support for agricultural products, urban construction and maintenance, education, cultural development, and social relief.

would need to be adjusted for price changes. The pattern of redistribution (for example, across generations—pensions, or to the unemployed) through nationwide institutions may benefit more individuals living in better-off regions, given demographic patterns. Thus, safety nets within a province would be addressed not only through the centrally mandated social security institutions, but more importantly with locally based social assistance (such as with *wu bao*—or five guarantees for basic needs, including inter alia, housing, clothing, and nutrition). However, financing for the latter may be an important constraint.

A major difficulty arises with the financing of local expenditures, particularly as more responsibilities for administration are assigned to lower levels of government. Thus, pleas for financial assistance for some worthy primary education project in various townships are heard in provincial capitals, but requests for assistance are often referred to higher levels of government on an ad hoc basis. Greater problems are observed with the provision of basic facilities in the poorer regions than in the coastal districts. This points to the need for a more effective transfer mechanism to ensure adequate provision of basic public services.

A detailed evaluation of expenditure assignments in China is a major task, one that will take a considerable time given the "fuzzy" nature of property rights and the provision of social benefits by state-owned-enterprises, which will be resolved over time. For this reason, the Chinese authorities focused on reforming revenue assignments, tax policies, and administration before resolving the expenditure assignment problem. The interim arrangements concerning grants have been based on the current rough allocation of expenditure responsibilities. As these expenditure responsibilities develop, with an evolving role of the state, it may be more efficient to vary the transfers rather than to adjust the revenue assignments or administration in tandem. There is some merit in keeping the revenue system stable for a period of time (once the immediate policy reforms have been completed). Nonetheless, clarifying the responsibilities of the state and consequent allocation of expenditure assignments among different levels of government remains a major task that should not be delayed.

Public Expenditure Management

A difficulty in China is that a significant proportion of public expenditures are met through extrabudgetary accounts, particularly at the local levels. It is important that all expenditures of agencies be included as part of the budget at a given level of administration, so that the necessary trade-offs between policy options at that level of government might be assessed. This issue is also inextricably linked with the financing of expenditure responsibilities relative to resource constraints, including transfers from higher levels of government.

China promulgated an organic budget law in 1995. However, further work needs to be instituted to formulate additional rules and regulations. As discussed in Ahmad, Kennedy, and Klering (1995), budgetary mechanisms are needed to achieve fiscal discipline, including effective controls on borrowing by subnational levels of government agencies. Classifications need to be reformed urgently, and while work has been initiated on a refinement of budget classification, along the lines of the IMF's *Government Finance Statistics*, much more needs to be done for implementation at the central and local levels. Also, rules for accounting and auditing, together with the requirements of proper cash management, need to be clarified. A redefined role for the Treasury is also crucial in establishing instruments for effective budget execution, information flows, expenditure control, management of cash, assets and liabilities, and accounting.

Although a new budget law delegates an important role to the Ministry of Finance, the ministry at present lacks the means to induce spending agencies to provide the needed information and to follow the required procedures. Appropriate information flows on budget execution available to the central agencies responsible for audit and control, and to the Ministry of Finance, will be essential to underpin the reformed system of intergovernmental fiscal relations in China, particularly the administration of the new transfer arrangements.

A problem to be addressed with regard to intergovernmental fiscal arrangements is that while those between the center and provinces are moving toward a unified format, those between the province and lower level governments continue to be administered on a piecemeal basis. In Beijing, for instance, four "poor" counties (defined as those where expenditures exceed revenues) retained all their revenues and received grants from the Beijing Municipal Government. Four districts and six urban counties that were defined as rich (revenues exceed expenditures) remitted all their revenues to Beijing Municipal Government, which allocated their expenditures. This divorce between revenue collection and expenditures could promote fiscal irresponsibility.

In Zhejiang province and its 70 counties, four different sharing rates—30, 50, 70, and 100 percent—were applied to four groups of counties that are classified in an indeterminate manner. Further, in Sichuan, four different remittance arrangements obtain based on whether revenues R exceed expenditures E in 1987. Eight cities with $R_{87} > E_{87}$ were required to increase remittances to the provincial government by 6.6 percent annually, whereas five cities and prefectures remitted a fixed nominal amount. Four municipalities received subsidies from the province, equivalent to the gap between 1987 expenditures and revenues, and for three minority prefectures, the 1987 subsidy was increased 5 percent annually.

Ill-defined and variable rules for management of public resources and expenditures at the subnational level can open the way for "creative" accounting by local officials, a process that could facilitate corrupt local practices (see also Tanzi, 1996). Thus, the importance of both national and local public expenditure management procedures cannot be underestimated—but this is an area where there has been relatively little progress in China.

Grants

The vertical and horizontal imbalances associated with China's existing system of resource flows and expenditures have been discussed in the preceding sections. The tax-sharing system on its own would tend to favor the better-endowed provinces. There is thus a redistributive role that should be performed by the central government. Where certain expenditures are mandated by the central government but carried out by local governments, these should be paid for by the central government. Matching grants, which correspond to the current practice, would also favor richer provinces over less well-off regions that may lack the initial resources. There is thus a case for a more analytical and unbiased determination of equalization transfers.

As a result of the changed tax assignments (in particular, the phased assignment of 75 percent of VAT and all of excises to the central government) and a large expansion of the VAT base, the central government's share in total revenues is expected to gradually increase from about 38 percent to about 58 percent (Gao Qiang, 1995). As the present assignment of expenditures is likely to remain unchanged in the medium term (that is, the central government is responsible for about 40 percent of total expenditures), the central government could use the resulting fiscal surplus (about 20 percent of total revenue) to finance a new system of grants to provinces. In the medium term, this amount is likely to remain the maximum that might be achieved, since after the one-time structural shift associated with the new tax assignments, the central government's share of total revenue will increase more slowly, contingent on improvements in tax administration and relative revenue buoyancies.

Given that it will take some time to work out a new grants mechanism, the central government and the provinces have agreed that the increased revenues accruing to the central government will be used to finance a "revenue return" to the provinces to assure them of 1993 levels of expenditure (see Lou Jiwei, 1997). As estimated by Mihaljek (1997), the "guaranteed revenue return" would be phased out by 1999. The central government should no longer have to make such gap-filling transfers because local revenue is expected to grow strongly, and the "basic guaranteed amount of expenditures" would remain fixed in nominal terms.

A "cooperative solution" to the equalization transfers[16] is needed in China, to underpin the new tax assignments and revenue-sharing arrangements. Direct redistribution from the richer provinces to poorer provinces may prove politically difficult and divisive, given the pockets of poor individuals and counties in even the richest provinces. Lou Jiwei argues that, in the medium term, the general transfers need to be determined on the basis of the relative capabilities of the provinces, including both revenue capacities, as well as expenditure needs (given the significant differences between the costs of provision of a "standardized" set of public services across the different regions of China). However, there are significant data and expenditure management difficulties that would complicate the introduction of a full equalization model based on both expenditure needs and revenue capacities (as in Australia).[17]

In the short run, an acceptable mechanism needs to be found to provide transfers in a manner that does not reintroduce "bargaining." The 1993 guarantee was politically expedient. The task is now to establish an approximation to a full equalization process based, for expenditure needs, on a few basic public functions, such as education and primary health care, and to utilize information on readily available factors, such as the characteristics of the population, to determine the relative needs. The use of such factors would be fairly robust, and also would not facilitate bargaining. Another feature that is important in China would be to allow the grant to cover small capital investments, in addition to current expenditures (Lou Jiwei, 1997), given the vast differences in capabilities across provinces to provide basic public services. A modest step toward the introduction of an equalization grant was taken in 1996 with the introduction of the so-called transitional period transfer that embodies elements of expenditure needs and tax capacity equalization across regions. This transfer is, however, of limited size (Y 2 billion in 1996).

---

[16]A cooperative solution is one where all provinces receive transfers out of the resources available to the central government. This may be contrasted with a "Robin Hood" approach, where only the "poorer" provinces receive transfers (see Ahmad, 1997).

[17]See Lou Jiwei (1997).

The design of grants will have incentive effects influencing public finances in a key manner—if the grants are used simply to fill subnational budget gaps, local governments will have little incentive to raise own revenues or control own expenditures. If the grants are not based on objective criteria, the system will remain open to bargaining, and regional disparities are likely to widen.

Concluding Remarks

The Chinese case presents an interesting experiment in the reform of the entire fiscal system in a country with multiple levels of government. It is clear that, in China, the first priority was to reform the tax system and revenue assignments, given the macroeconomic preoccupations of the government in the transition to a market economy. However, the 1994 tax reform is not sustainable without a new system of transfers to compensate losing provinces and strengthen redistribution across provinces. But it is also clear that both special purpose transfers, as well as a new system of equalization transfers, would depend crucially on the information flows generated by a reformed public expenditure management system.

References

Ahmad, Ehtisham, and Yan Wang, 1991, "Inequality and Poverty in China: Institutional Change and Public Policy," *World Bank Economic Review*, Vol. 5 (May), pp. 231–57.

Ahmad, Ehtisham, Maurice Kennedy, and Ingrid Klering, 1995, "Budget Laws, Control, Review, and Management in China," in *Reforming China's Public Finances*, ed. by Ehtisham Ahmad, Gao Qiang, and Vito Tanzi (Washington: International Monetary Fund).

Ahmad, Ehtisham, ed., 1997, *Financing Decentralized Expenditures: An International Comparison of Grants* (Cheltenham, England; Brookfield, Vermont: Edward Elgar).

———, Gao Qiang, and Vito Tanzi, eds., 1995, *Reforming China's Public Finances* (Washington: International Monetary Fund).

Blejer, Mario I., 1993, "Reforms and Fiscal Controls in China," in *Transition to Market*, ed. by Vito Tanzi (Washington: International Monetary Fund).

———, and Gyorgy Szapary, 1989, "The Evolving Role of Fiscal Policy in Centrally Planned Economies Under Reform: The Case of China," IMF Working Paper 89/26 (Washington: International Monetary Fund).

Brosio, Giorgio, 1995, "Local Taxation in an International Perspective," in *Reforming China's Public Finances*, ed. by Ehtisham Ahmad, Gao Qiang, and Vito Tanzi (Washington: International Monetary Fund).

Burgess, Robin, and Nicholas Stern, 1993, "Taxation and Development," *Journal of Economic Literature*, Vol. 31 (June), pp. 762–830.

Gao Qiang, 1995, "Problems in Chinese Intragovernmental Fiscal Relations, Tax-Sharing System, and Future Reform," in *Reforming China's Public Finances*, ed. by Ehtisham Ahmad, Gao Qiang, and Vito Tanzi (Washington: International Monetary Fund).

Hussain, A., and N. Stern, 1992, "Economic Reforms and Public Finance in China," in *Public Finance in a World of Transition*, ed. by P. Pestieu, Supplement to *Public Finances*, Vol. 47, pp. 289–317.

Kojima, R., 1992, "The Growing Fiscal Authority of Provincial Governments in China," *Developing Economies*, December, pp. 315–46.

Levin, Jonathan, 1991, "Measuring the Role of Subnational Governments," in *Public Finance with Several Levels of Government*, ed. by Rémy Prud'homme (The Hague: Foundation Journal Public Finance).

Lou Jiwei, 1997, "Constraints in Reforming the Transfer System in China," in *Financing Decentralized Expenditures: An International Comparison of Grants*, ed. by Ehtisham Ahmad (Cheltenham, England; Brookfield, Vermont: Edward Elgar).

Mihaljek, Dubravko, 1997, "The New Revenue-Sharing Arrangement in China: An Illustrative Example," in *Financing Decentralized Expenditures: An International Comparison of Grants*, ed. by Ehtisham Ahmad (Cheltenham, England; Brookfield, Vermont: Edward Elgar).

Shi Yaobin, 1995, "Unifying the Enterprise Income Tax and Reforming Profit Distribution Between Government and State-Owned Enterprises," in *Reforming China's Public Finances*, ed. by Ehtisham Ahmad, Gao Qiang, and Vito Tanzi (Washington: International Monetary Fund).

Tanzi, Vito, 1996, "Fiscal Federalism and Decentralization: A Review of Some Efficiency and Macroeconomic Aspects," *Annual World Bank Conference on Development Economics, 1995* (Washington: World Bank).

———, ed., 1992, *Fiscal Policies in Economies in Transition* (Washington: International Monetary Fund).

Wong, C., C. Heady, and W.-T. Woo, 1993, "Economic Reform and Fiscal Management in the People's Republic of China" (unpublished; Manila: Asian Development Bank).

World Bank, 1990, *China: Revenue Mobilization and Tax Policy* (unpublished; Washington: World Bank).

———, 1993, *Budgetary Policy and Intergovernmental Fiscal Relations*, Report No. 11094-CHA (Washington: World Bank).

Xu Shanda, and Ma Lin, 1995, "Reform and the Market Economy and Tax in China," in *Reforming China's Public Finances*, ed. by Ehtisham Ahmad, Gao Qiang, and Vito Tanzi (Washington: International Monetary Fund).

Yusuf, Y., 1993, "China's Collective and Private Enterprises: Growth and Financing" (unpublished; Washington: World Bank).

27

Hungary

MARK LUTZ, EDGARDO RUGGIERO, PAUL BERND SPAHN, AND EMIL M. SUNLEY

Prior to 1990, Hungary had a unitary and centralized system of government with lower tiers having little independent revenue or expenditure autonomy. Hungary has since reformed its Constitution and decentralized many public functions in order to render government more responsive to its citizens. Lower tiers of government have been given significant scope for self-rule, but the basic precept assigning to the central government a dominant role has been retained.

In a series of legislative acts and administrative reforms in 1990 and 1991, Hungary established the legal framework for a two-tier system of government under which municipalities are constitutionally independent entities and have responsibility for their jurisdictions.[1] These laws assign expenditure and revenue functions to the lower level of government, and they specify the system of intergovernmental relations, including the system of transfers from the central budget.

Hungary's reform of the government sector is typical for most former communist countries on their way toward a market economy. After a period of centralized planning and decision making, the delivery of public functions in education, health, and social welfare has been devolved to lower levels of government in order to render the provision of public services more responsive to local demand, to strengthen the

---

[1]Law on Local Self-Government (1990), Law on the Capital (1991), Law on Local Taxes (1990), and Property Transfer Act (1991). Moreover, the Law on Public Finances (1992) enumerates the rights and obligations of local governments regarding budget preparation, monitoring, control, and reporting.

accountability of local politicians, to mobilize initiatives at the municipal level, and to enhance general economic welfare. Hungary may serve as an example to illustrate the main thrust of such reforms and the various problems encountered by formerly communist countries on the pace of transition.

Structure of Government

The current structure[2] of Hungarian government is extremely decentralized. At the central government level, there are 29 budgetary chapters, comprising the spending ministries, offices of the President and Prime Minister, parliament, and other agencies. In 1995, attached to these chapters were 1,424 central budgetary institutions, excluding those pertinent to defense and related activities. Of these, 697 had budgetary autonomy. In addition, at the central government level, there were 29 extrabudgetary funds administered by the budgetary chapters,[3] and two self-governed social insurance funds, which were responsible for health care and pensions.

At the municipal level, there were 3,168 governing bodies, which in turn operated, in 1995, 13,627 local budgetary institutions (that is, service providers such as elementary schools, clinics, trash collection services, hospitals, and universities in large municipalities) of which 7,972 had budgetary autonomy.[4] Local governments are now directly responsible for most decentralized functions.

Budapest itself enjoys a special status. The municipality executes functions that affect the whole or a large part of the capital. But, in addition to the municipality, Budapest is divided into 22 autonomous districts directly responsible for providing local services.

General government financial flows are also quite decentralized in Hungary. The consolidated budget and intergovernmental flows of

---

[2]For a further discussion of the structure of government in Hungary see Lutz (1992), Bird and Wallich (1992), and Bird, Péteri, and Wallich (1995). Data in this chapter refer to 1995, unless otherwise stated.

[3]In 1996, there were 30 budgetary chapters and 1,343 central budgetary institutions (of which 659 with budgetary autonomy); the number of extrabudgetary funds was reduced to six.

[4]In 1996, there was almost no change in the number of municipalities (3,169), although the number of budgetary institutions operated by the local governments declined to 13,509, of which 7,801 had budgetary autonomy. Prior to 1986, the budgets of local councils, as they were then referred to, were consolidated with the state budget and, therefore, approved on a gross basis. Beginning in 1989, the activities of the social insurance fund were separated from the state budget, and the fund was separated into the two social insurance funds in 1994.

funds are shown in Table 1. The state budget acts as a partial clearinghouse for the majority of all centrally imposed tax revenues, and finances producer and consumer subsidies, family allowances, centrally decided investments, debt servicing and transfers to other components of the general government. The central budgetary institutions also receive payments and fees for services, some of which are commercial in nature. The extrabudgetary funds receive earmarked tax revenues (such as petrol excises to the road fund), payroll contributions (for example, to the solidarity fund for unemployment compensation), earmarked privatization revenues, and other payments. The social insurance funds collect payroll contributions, and local governments collect fees and revenues from a number of local taxes. The official presentation of budgetary data by the authorities fails to consolidate a large number of intragovernmental fiscal transactions (for example, contributions by budgetary institutions to the social insurance funds), thereby overstating significantly the size of the government relative to the total economy. Even after netting out known intragovernmental transactions, considerable double counting is thought to remain.

The necessity to circulate information between the central government (in particular the Ministry of Finance and the Ministry of Interior) and local and county governments has led to the creation through a government decree of administrative bodies, called TAKISZ, whose basic functions are established by government decrees and parliamentary decisions. The TAKISZ are attached to the general directorate of the Ministry of Interior, and their operation is assured jointly by the Ministry of Finance and the Ministry of Interior. These institutions support local governments in preparing their budgets in line with national framework legislation and provide technical assistance in all daily operations of a financial and economic nature. Furthermore, they collect and consolidate statistical information on the lower tiers of government, as needed for setting national priorities and for intergovernmental fiscal relations. They also provide other types of assistance to local governments—for instance, regarding tax collection, social policy, accounting, and local services, either free of charge or on a fee-for-service basis.

Intergovernmental Arrangements

Expenditure Assignments

As is typical for unitary states, all state functions are discharged by the central government unless explicitly stated otherwise by the Constitution or by law. The Local Self-Government Act of 1990 transferred a number of important public functions to the lower tiers of govern-

Table 1. Hungary: Consolidated General Government Budget, 1995[1]

	Total	Central Government					Local Government
		Total	State budget	Central budgetary institutions	Extra-budgetary funds	Social security	
(In billions of forint)							
Revenues	2,825.3	2,487.6	1,582.5	149.9	144.4	610.8	337.8
Taxes	2,126.4	1,983.9	1,318.0	—	98.0	567.9	142.5
Income taxes	498.6	405.0	405.0	—	—	—	93.6
Payroll taxes	628.5	628.5	—	—	60.6	567.9	—
Taxes on goods and services	999.3	950.4	913.0	—	37.4	—	48.9
Nontax revenues	699.0	503.7	264.5	149.9	46.4	42.9	195.3
Privatization receipts	155.9	150.0	150.0	—	—	—	5.9
Other	543.0	353.7	114.5	149.9	46.4	42.9	189.4
Expenditures	3,007.5	2,312.7	989.8	514.5	119.2	689.1	694.8
Current expenditures	2,714.6	2,137.6	881.6	464.7	105.1	686.2	577.1
Wages and salaries	459.0	210.3	—	208.5	1.8	—	248.7
Other goods and services	521.9	260.9	146.7	62.7	32.3	19.1	261.1
Interest payments	513.6	513.6	502.9	—	10.7	—	—
Subsidies and transfers	1,220.1	1,152.8	231.9	193.5	60.3	667.1	67.3
Capital expenditures	292.8	175.1	108.2	49.8	14.1	2.9	117.8
Fixed capital formation	191.8	102.7	48.4	49.8	1.6	2.9	89.1
Capital transfers	101.0	72.4	59.9	—	12.5	—	28.7
Subbalance	−182.1	174.9	592.7	−364.6	25.2	−78.36	−357.0
Plus: Net transfers to							
State budget	—	−320.2	−818.4	466.5	31.7	—	320.2
Central budgetary institutions	—	−6.0	11.5	−100.9	2.5	80.7	6.0
Extrabudgetary funds	—	−7.1	—	46.6	−69.0	15.2	7.1
Social insurance funds	—	−127.1	—	46.5	—	−173.6	127.1
Local government	—	105.2	1.0	—	—	104.2	−105.2
Balance	−182.1	−180.3	−213.2	94.2	−9.5	−51.7	−1.9
Financing	182.1	180.3	213.2	−94.2	9.5	51.7	1.9
Domestic bank financing	...	...	...	−94.2	9.5	51.7	1.9
Domestic nonbank financing	...	...	...	—	—	—	—
(In percent of GDP)							
Memorandum items:							
Revenue	47.5	41.9	26.6	2.5	2.4	10.3	5.7
Expenditure	50.6	38.9	16.7	8.7	2.0	11.6	11.7
Subbalance	−3.1	−2.9	10.0	−6.1	0.4	−1.3	−6.0
Balance	−3.1	−3.0	−3.6	1.6	−0.2	−0.9	—

Sources: Hungarian authorities; and authors' estimates.
[1] Authors' estimates based on data contained in August 1996 Ministry of Finance submissions to parliament.

ment. Moreover, the new local governments have responsibility for many areas that were previously assigned either to the central government or to companies and cooperatives. However, the welfare system remains highly centralized and offers relatively high levels of social benefits. Generous child support, early retirement schemes (with the result that one quarter of adults are pensioners), and unemployment assistance (that can be taken up immediately by school leavers) put a heavy burden on the central budget. This entails high nonwage labor costs in the form of social security contributions, which rank among the highest in the world (although these were cut somewhat in 1996–97) and represent a significant burden to the economy. The size of the overall public sector is large in Hungary, compared with other European countries. General government expenditures (including social security) were about 51 percent of GDP in 1995. Nevertheless, this is about 10 percentage points of GDP lower than in the early 1990s.

The importance of local spending has been growing since the reforms. In 1995, local governments spent roughly Ft 700 billion[5] (or about one-fourth of total government expenditures), which illustrates the importance of this sector. Main areas of local responsibility are education (28 percent), health (17 percent), and housing (10 percent of total local government outlays), as well as other social and cultural services (Figure 1). A significant part of local spending is devoted to creating and improving local infrastructure through investments (15 percent of total outlays).

The local governments are self-governing organizations, which creates some tensions with the central government, especially for those services (such as health, welfare, and education) whose delivery, financing, and policy functions are assigned to multiple levels of government. For example, in 1995, the central government (which sets general policies in the area of social expenditures) decided to reform the health delivery system and to reduce hospital capacity by around 10,000 beds—as a first step toward rationalization of the supply of curative health services. However, the local governments are the owners of several hospitals (the remaining ones are owned by the central budgetary institutions); therefore, on constitutional grounds, they are the only ones who ultimately have to approve the reduction in the number of beds in their own territory. The local governments have resisted the

---

[5]Included is about Ft 127 billion in expenditures on local health care financed by the health fund. Local expenditures also include social insurance contributions totaling Ft 108 billion and significant value-added tax payments, which are received by other organizations within the general government—the social insurance funds and the state budget, respectively.

Figure 1. Hungary: Local Government Expenditure by Sector of Activity, 1995

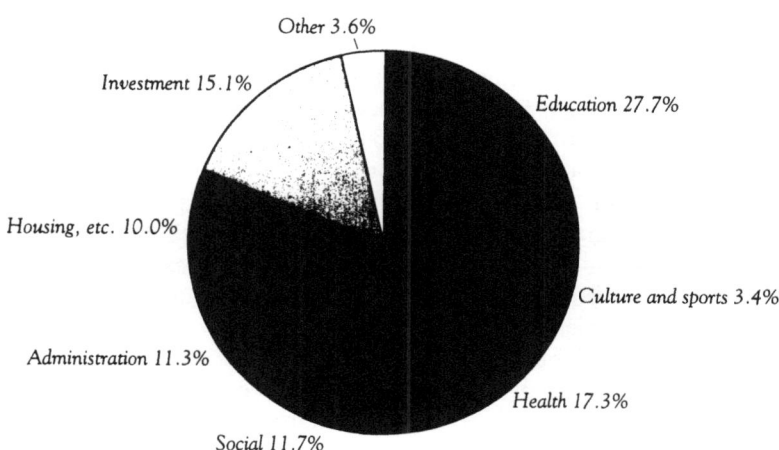

Sources. Hungarian authorities; and authors' estimates.

closure of hospitals beds, leading to a delay in the reduction in hospital capacity.

Tax Assignments

Hungary has introduced, through reforms in 1988 and 1989, a modern tax system consisting of a value-added tax (general turnover tax), a personal income tax, and a business profits tax. Moreover, various excises and fees are associated with specific transactions. All these taxes are national taxes, based on uniform rules, and their proceeds accrue to the central government, with the exceptions of a share in personal income tax collected by the central government, but distributed to municipalities, and a small amount of shared motor vehicle taxes.

Most national taxes are administered by the central government in Hungary under the Tax and Financial Audit Board (APEH), which has regional offices in each county and in Budapest. Within the Ministry of Finance, the Customs and Excise Police (VPOP) administers customs duties, domestic excises, as well as value-added tax and excises payable on imports. In addition, local tax offices and county directorates administer and collect local taxes.

The Act on Local Self-Government defines local tax competence for taxes on local properties, communal taxes, and local business taxes. In 1994, only about half of the Hungarian local governments imposed some, albeit not all, local taxes; the other half imposed no local taxes. Local taxes raised Ft 48.9 billion—or 6.1 percent of total nonconsolidated revenue of local governments in 1995.[6] While the overall tax ratio is high in Hungary, the local tax burden is almost negligible (without fees, 0.8 percent of GDP in 1993).

The tax on property is divided into a tax on buildings and a tax on unimproved land. There is an option between a physical tax base (square meters) and a valuation base, but the latter is rarely used. Generous exemptions—25 square meters a person, for example—exempt most households from these taxes. There is a maximum limit on the annual rate chargeable.[7]

The "communal taxes" include a tax on tourism (based on guest nights and on rented or owned secondary dwellings), and lump-sum taxes levied on local residents (tenancy rights or rental contracts) and on local firms according to their average number of employees. The maximum lump-sum tax is Ft 3,000 per tenancy right (equivalent to US$24), or Ft 2,000 per employee.

The local business tax is now the main own source tax for local governments. In 1995, it raised Ft 37.6 billion (0.7 percent of GDP), with about half of the revenue accruing to the Budapest municipality. This tax attempts to capture local commercial activity and is essentially based on net turnover with certain qualifications. The entrepreneur liable for the tax can be a private person, a legal entity, or an organization (such as churches, state enterprises, and housing cooperatives). In small municipalities (as defined by national rules), retail trade is specifically exempt (except for the sale of liquors).

The tax base is normally "net sales revenue of products sold and services provided, reduced by the purchase value of the goods sold and the value of services provided by subcontractors" (Section 39(1) of the Act). The deduction of the costs for goods purchased is limited to those sold without transformation; in the case of subcontracted services, the deductibility applies only to those services that directly form part of the service provided "as such." If goods are purchased and transformed (as in manufacturing), and if services enter the price of the product sold or the service provided only indirectly (as legal services for a computing

---

[6]Inclusive of vehicle tax (Ft 2.5 billion).

[7]This limit is Ft 300 per square meter or—in the case of an ad valorem base—3 percent of the adjusted market value.

firm), the deductibility of such costs is denied. A fortiori, investment expenditures cannot be deducted.

In the case of financial institutions, the tax base is gross turnover—the total of interest received in the case of banks and the total of the technical revenue in the case of insurance companies. Neither deductions for the banks' interest payments on liabilities nor for the insurers' payments to settle claims are allowed. This puts financial institutions at an unequal footing compared with other commercial enterprises.[8]

The maximum tax rate of the business tax is 0.8 percent (or Ft 5,000 a day in the case of occasional activities).[9] Local governments can vary the rates according to economic activities as long as the rate remains below the ceiling. They can also grant exemptions and deductions from the tax base through local regulations as long as these are general, specified by economic activity, for instance, and not for particular firms. There is no minimum rate for the business tax, and a local government may also choose not to levy the tax at all.

The main issue relating to own local taxes is their limited revenue significance. Own local taxation has to be strengthened in Hungary in order to mobilize fully the potential of this tier of government. This could partly be achieved through the business tax and the introduction of modern property taxation. Also, the business tax base has to be streamlined and standardized, in order to mitigate locational distortions and cascading, in particular with regard to financial operations. In addition, a local income tax as exists in Scandinavian countries, which is collected by the central government, could help to boost local revenue and to foster local accountability at the same time.

Revenue Sharing

Own local tax revenue is now complemented by a share of the personal income tax to local governments, which constitutes essentially a transfer from the central government. In 1995, 35 percent of the personal income tax collected by the central government was returned to local governments;[10] of this, a 29.5 percent share was returned to local

---

[8] In Budapest, for instance, more than half of the revenue of the business tax is obtained from the financial sector.

[9] The ceiling was raised to 1.2 percent in 1996.

[10] Prior to 1995, for the poorer municipalities, there was a minimum per capita guarantee for the personal income tax share. Any shortfall of personal income tax revenue collected with respect to the per-capita minimum was compensated by a separate supplementary grant with regional equalization effects. The supplementary grant was abolished in 1995, with equalization transfers subsumed into previously existing grants to disadvantaged areas.

governments on a derivation basis, and another 5.5 percent share was transferred on an equalization basis.[11] In addition, fees collected by counties are subject to sharing with the central government with some horizontal equalization among counties.[12]

These transfers from the income tax share are effected in 12 monthly installments with, owing to administrative difficulties, a two-year lag that, given inflation, reduces the real value of the transfer and increases the reliance on additional intergovernmental grants. A period of two years is, in fact, needed by TAKISZ to calculate the shares for each municipality on the basis of the income tax data provided by APEH. The two-year lag provides a "buffer" for those municipalities where an important local employer may cease his business operation. A further rationale for the two-year lag is, therefore, that a cashflow-oriented, personal income tax share would be procyclical and would cause an immediate disruption of local services on top of a local unemployment problem.[13]

The government plans to increase the local governments' share to around 40 percent by the year 2000 and to reduce the portion shared on a derivation basis to 20 percent. The derivation-based portion of the personal income tax sharing scheme benefits, of course, Budapest, where the revenue potential of this tax is greater. Any variation in the share must thus have uneven horizontal distribution effects among local jurisdictions, given differences in their economic potential.

The main issue with the shared tax is that it is a grant from the central government (albeit out of an earmarked revenue source) and not a local revenue source. To increase accountability of local governments and to improve local flexibility to meet the demands for services, each local government could be given the right to apply its own tax rate on the national income tax base. A local income tax surcharge would give

---

[11] In 1990, local governments had received 100 percent of 1988 personal income tax collections. The local governments' share was then reduced to 50 percent in 1991 and 1992, and to 30 percent in 1993 and 1994. In 1996, the income tax share was raised to 36 percent; of this, 25 percent was distributed on a derivation basis and 11 percent on an equalization basis.

[12] As a rule, 50 percent of the fee remains at the county level, and 50 percent is transferred to the central government. This applies fully for fees collected on properties located in the county capital. In the case of Budapest, the fee accrues to the metropolitan government, not the districts. The horizontal equalization scheme applies to properties not located in the county capital. In this case, 30 percent of the entitlement is allocated to the county government while the remainder is divided equally among all counties. Budapest does not participate in this equalization mechanism.

[13] One may argue that it has the opposite effect on localities with growing economic activities and related demand for local services, but in this case the municipality may be able to borrow against expected cash flow from the tax.

Figure 2. Hungary: Local Government Revenue by Type, 1995

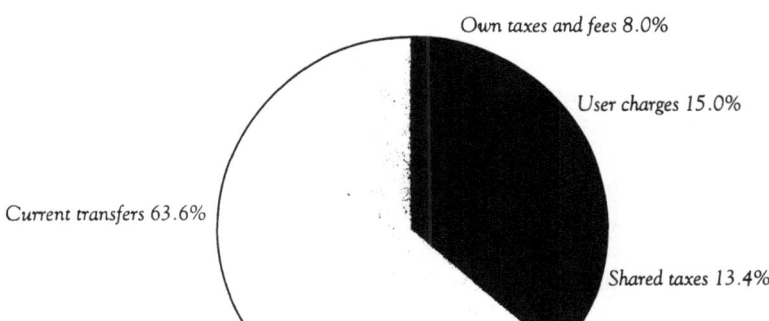

Sources: Hungarian authorities; and authors' estimates.

localities a powerful revenue tool and increase the link, at least at the margin, between local public services and taxes payable. This would not necessarily diminish the importance of any equalizing supplementary grants for poorer municipalities.

Grants

Given the limited significance of own local taxes and personal income sharing in financing local budgets, the dependency of the municipal sector on grants remains high in Hungary. Grants from the central government, extrabudgetary funds, and the social security funds, of which the normative grant is by far the largest, provided about 64 percent of the recurrent finance available to local governments in 1995 (Figure 2).

The normative grant is intended to address the vertical and horizontal imbalances of the present fiscal system and to attenuate the consequences of the fragmented local government structure.[14] It is based on

---

[14]This is not the case for the norm that matches revenue from the tourism tax (Table 2). Budapest, already the municipality with the largest income tax base, is the main beneficiary of this matching component of the normative grant.

simple indicators of expenditure needs such as the number of inhabitants, or indicators of capacity use (such as the number of care days for the elderly, children, the homeless, or the mentally ill). In 1994, the normative grant consisted of 27 norms, as shown in Table 2. For each norm the budget specified a unit cost; for example, Ft 41,000 per elementary school student or Ft 250 per capita for cultural activities. The normative grant for a municipality is obtained by multiplying the number of units for each norm by the unit cost, and then summing up the result for the 27 different norms. The grant can thus be considered to be closed-ended. This puts a lid on local budgets and constitutes an improvement over the prereform negotiated gap-filling approach. Although based on objective parameters for distribution, the normative grant can be used at the discretion of local governments once they fulfill these criteria. The formula is revised each year.[15]

In addition to normative grants, local governments receive targeted grants for investment purposes, and they obtain direct transfers from social security funds. The latter are mainly expenditure related and thus constitute "soft" financing, although cost coverage is below 100 percent. Other small transfers include grants for distressed localities.

While own revenues and the derivation share of personal income tax exhibit no regional redistribution effects among local government (since they are all on a derivation base) the normative grants, as well as the equalization portion of the personal income tax share, exert important equalization effects in favor of poorer municipalities.

Horizontal equalization schemes have to deal with horizontal redistribution in order to equalize (1) standard own taxable capacity and (2) standard expenditure needs reflecting also the effects of population density and agglomeration on local expenditure needs. Some countries have formally adopted this approach by equalizing the difference between standard own fiscal capacity and expenditure needs and correcting it by factors that account for density and agglomeration effects.

In Hungary, where own fiscal capacity of local governments is low, no attempt to standardize local government budgets is made. However, the grants system exhibits similar effects to that under an explicit stan-

---

[15]In terms of the classification of grants presented in Chapter 1, the normative grant can be regarded as being made up of subgrants belonging to different categories. The norms 1 through 3 identify transfers that are essentially general purpose grants, as they are given to—often poor—municipalities to satisfy general funding needs. The norms 4, 46, and 25 through 27 identify block grants, as they are given to municipalities to deliver specific services (such as educational and mental institutions) to cover a portion of the production cost. These are open-ended specific grants, as the amount transferred increases with the number of students enrolled in schools or people housed in institutions or nursing homes. Within the specific grants, norm 5 is an open-ended matching grant.

Table 2. Hungary: The 27 Normatives in 1994, Norm Costs and Actual Costs

Type of Normative	Norm Unit	Receiving Local Authority	Norm Unit Costs, 1994 (In forint)	Average Coverage (In percent)
1. Lump-sum grant to village municipalities	Per village	Residence	2,000,000	—
2. Operational costs	Per capita	Residence	3,820	—
3. Underdeveloped municipalities	Per capita	Residence	2,300	—
Municipalities in underdeveloped areas	Per capita	Residence	1,200	—
4. Public housing	20–30 years old	Residence	4,680	—
5. Matching per forint in tourist tax	—	Residence	2	—
6. Social subsidy	Per capita	Residence	2,500–4,700	—
7. Juveniles and orphans	Per case	Producer	245,000	63.4
8. Social institutions	Per case	Producer	186,400	68.8
9. Day care, social	Per case	Producer	30,850	41.9
10. Hostels for elderly, homeless, etc.	Per case	Producer	87,000	37.3
11. Temporary for homeless	Per case	Producer	78,000	50.0
12. Children, multi-handicapped or mentally ill	Per case	Producer	275,000	71.9
13. Mentally ill adults	Per case	Producer	234,000	86.4
14. Kindergarten	Per case	Producer	27,500	36.1
15. Kindergarten, ethnic	Per case	Producer	5,500	—
16. Elementary school	Per case	Producer	41,000	66.0
17. Art training	Per case	Producer	25,100	83.7
18. Schools for invalids	Per case	Producer	70,700	—
19. Gymnasium	Per case	Producer	62,500	79.3
20. Special secondary school	Per case	Producer	66,000	68.0
21. Vocational schools, theory	Per case	Producer	42,100	93.8
22. Vocational schools, practice	Per case	Producer	40,600	42,2
23. Bilingual schools	Per case	Producer	16,500	—
24. School boarding	Per case	Producer	66,000	
Elementary schools				53.8
Secondary schools				70.6
25. Sports	Per capita	Residence	50	—
26. Cultural activity	Per capita	Residence	250	—
27. County and capital operations, library, theater, etc.	Per capita	Residence	490	—

Sources: Hungarian authorities; and authors' estimates.

dardized budget approach. For instance, the grants to disadvantaged areas and the equalization-based portion of the personal income tax sharing scheme are revenue equalizing, while norms based on general need criteria equalize expenditure needs. The derivation-based portion of the personal income tax sharing scheme, which benefits higher-income agglomerations, in particular Budapest, may be understood as a correction for agglomeration effects. It constitutes a bonus with regard to fiscal capacity, which is correlated with higher income levels.

As illustrated in Figure 3, the overall importance of grants transferred solely for the purpose of fiscal capacity equalization is low in

Figure 3. Hungary: Transfers to Local Government Classified by Equalization Effect, 1995[1]

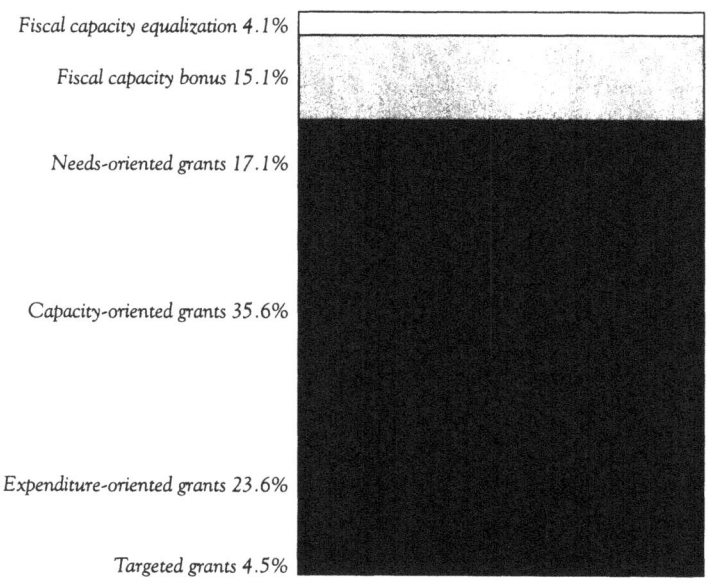

Sources: Hungarian authorities; and authors' estimates.
[1]The classification of transfers is made according to the following principles. Fiscal capacity equalization corresponds to the transfer to disadvantaged areas and the 5.5 percent equalization portion of the income tax share; the fiscal capacity bonus is personal income tax sharing based on the derivation principle. Needs-oriented and capacity-oriented grants together form the normative grant and other grants. Those elements that are based on standard criteria outside the control of local government (essentially the lump-sum and residence-based elements of the normatives) are classified as needs oriented. Normative grants received by producing institutions are all classified as capacity oriented. All social security transfers are classified as expenditure oriented.

Hungary. In 1995, only 4.1 percent of total grant money was distributed according to this element. Also, the general importance of need-oriented grants remains limited, although it is significant for the poorer jurisdictions. The majority of the grant money is disbursed on the basis of capacity-use or expenditure-related criteria. Capacity-use and expenditure-related (gap-filling) grants are appropriate to the extent that lower-tier public services are "mandated" by the central government or the social security funds. However, those types of grants are inappropriate for financing "own policies" of local governments. Such grants tend to relax the budget constraint at the lower level of government. They afford incentives to provide subsidized services, while they fail to exert control on production costs and indeed do not force the local government to evaluate the need for the service against its cost. Needs-oriented grants tend to exert a stronger discipline on local government budgets. As decentralization is intended to strengthen self-rule at the lower tiers of government, while ensuring compliance with macroeconomic constraints, this would call for a reduction of capacity-use and expenditure-related grants in favor of transfers that are based on objective needs criteria.

Borrowing

All governments in Hungary are in principle free to finance their budget deficits through capital markets. The National Bank of Hungary was granted legal independence in December 1991. However, it may provide credits paying market-related interest rates to the central government in an amount not exceeding 3 percent of annual revenues.[16] Moreover, the Act on the Central Bank was amended in 1993 to allow for a short-term liquidity credit facility, which may not exceed an additional 2 percent of projected annual budget revenues and which may not last for more than 15 days.[17]

Although Hungarian municipalities can borrow on the private market without central government interference or control, most local governments are reluctant to incur debt, even for capital outlays where revenue could be generated in the form of user charges. This reflects conservative and prudent behavior, but also the tradition of the former system in which local councils had no discretion in borrowing. Total local sector borrowing (including the issue of municipal bonds) was Ft 19.7 billion (or 2.5 percent of their nonconsolidated expenditures) in 1995. Larger villages and towns and, notably, the Budapest municipality and its districts resort to borrowing more than smaller villages and cities. Only the capital city is able to mobilize significant funds through issuing bonds. This also reflects the fact that local governments face varying obstacles when entering this market.

At present, there seem to be no significant risks in excessive borrowing and indebtedness by lower tiers. Nevertheless, Hungary may

---

[16]This amount was applied in 1995 and 1996, with higher but declining amounts (unlimited in 1992, 5 percent in 1993, and 4 percent in 1994) available in earlier years. However, in 1994 the National Bank was obliged through the Annual Budget Law to purchase government securities in an amount equivalent to 7.1 percent of budgeted revenues.

[17]The Central Bank Act was amended in 1996 to enhance independence of the National Bank. The new legislation, inter alia, eliminates direct credit to the government—with the exception of the liquidity facility.

want to limit long-term borrowing by local governments to nonoperational purposes and primarily to capital formation that can be financed by user charges.[18] In the medium term, more attention must be given to financing capital expenditures of local governments. For instance, local governments, at this stage, seem not to realize fully the relationship between local capital formation and its financing. There is no capital budgeting that would allow them to take a longer-term perspective extending beyond the annual budget period.

Budget Formulation and Implementation

The present system of budget preparation, execution, and cash management is the result of reforms—beginning as early as the New Economic Mechanism introduced in 1968—that permitted increasingly decentralized decision making on the part of budgetary institutions' managers, and of recent requirements included in the Law on Public Finances, which took effect in July 1992. This increasing decentralization has led to a proliferation of central and local budgetary institutions. The central authorities, both in the Ministry of Finance and in the spending ministries, have little timely information and limited effective control on the operations of these decentralized budgetary institutions. The separation of the central government budget into subsystems and the related pervasive earmarking of revenues has tended to promote fiscal rigidity, both in the preparation of annual budgets and in their execution during the year. Moreover, the budgetary institutions have been allowed to engage in activities of a commercial nature to supplement transfers from the state budget (for example, note the large share of local government revenues from user charges in Figure 2). These commercial activities are largely inconsistent with the role of government in a market economy and can in some circumstances be regarded as inhibiting the growth of the private sector.

---

[18]In 1996, a law specifying a ceiling on the amount of bank borrowing of local governments, expressed as a percentage of own revenue, was adopted. However, it is not certain how binding this ceiling is. Local budgets violating the ceiling can be approved; it is then up to the prefect (the representative of the central government at the local level and an employee of the Ministry of Interior) to ask in writing to the concerned local government to change its budget or borrowing plans. If such suasion does not work, the prefect can then cite the local government in an administrative court, whose verdict may arrive well after the end of the fiscal year.

Conclusions and Policy Implications

Macroeconomic Management

Despite the substantial reduction in recent years of Hungary's revenue and expenditure shares in GDP, they remain above the average of member countries of the Organization for Economic Cooperation and Development. Although these are likely to be substantially overstated by nonconsolidated activities among government agencies, these ratios easily exceed those recorded in Western European economies when they were at Hungary's present level of development. This remains a legacy of the old central planning system. Therefore, in addition to maintaining the sustainability of its external and fiscal imbalances, Hungary must continue to reduce the scale and scope of its governmental activities, increasingly relying on the market economy to provide, generally more efficiently, goods and services presently provided by the state. This will allow for an eventual reduction in tax rates, especially social insurance contribution rates that retard growth in legitimate economic activity.

It is essential that policies at the local government level support the general effort to contain the consolidated budget deficit and that budget constraints are enforced at all levels of government. The relationship between the central government budget and the local government sector and its development bears on macroeconomic stabilization in many ways.

First, transfers to local governments and their implicit incentive effects are crucial for macroeconomic management. Although the central government has abandoned the negotiated "gap-filling" approach of the previous system and emphasizes local self-government through own taxation and the provision of needs-related general revenue grants, the importance of capacity- and expenditure-related normative grants remains high. The open ended character of many elements of the grant system may still create risks for fiscal policy, in so far as it establishes incentives for excessive demand for local services and, therefore, for aggregate demand. For example, schools and institutions have an incentive to attract—and self-generate—local demand, given that the average cost coverage of the grants to these recipients is quite large (Table 2, last column). Moreover, the system lends itself to corruption, as attendance records to schools and institutions (which represent the bulk of the specific norms within the normative grant) could be artificially inflated by the recipient, in order to qualify for larger grants. Grants for social, health, and educational services are still perceived as "entitlements" by local government officials.

Second, an efficient provision of local public services calls for a higher proportion of local taxation to strengthen accountability, efficiency, and flexibility at this level. This is the essence of decentralization of the public sector. The central government may have to make room for local taxation, particularly as the total tax burden is high in Hungary. However, if local governments—unaccustomed to revenue-raising responsibilities under the previous system—make insufficient use of their scope for own taxes, pressures on the central government could result that could exacerbate the fiscal position of the consolidated government. Though the recently introduced limits on bank borrowing by local governments are effectively nonenforceable (see section on Intergovernmental Arrangements), the risk of local governments incurring excessive debt is not large, because of traditional reluctance in incurring debt. However, the risk of excessive debt creation lies not so much with the municipalities themselves, but with the local budgetary institutions with budgetary autonomy.[19] For example, hospitals (many of which are owned by the municipalities) have accumulated large debts with suppliers. At the end of 1996, these debts were cleared through loans by the health fund (which is part of the central government) to the hospitals. Though formally the hospitals have to repay these loans, it is unclear where they will find the resources to do so. Through this clearing operation the central government has bailed out the institutions delivering public services at the lower level of government, and effectively sent the message that there is no hard budget constraint on these institutions. It is therefore important to create adequate incentives (in particular through a hard budget constraint and the establishment of a "no bailout clause") for the local authorities and institutions to exercise their revenue-raising capacities, including through wider recourse to user fees.

Structural Reform

Hungary has made significant progress in adapting its structure of government to the challenges of a market economy and to democracy. It was indeed the first country of formerly communist rule to decentralize government and to adopt a system based on the Local Government Charter of the Council of Europe. Hungary is still in the process of consolidating and furthering these achievements, and the benefits will only be reaped in the longer run. Apart from the need to improve

---

[19]This problem has arisen also in Italy, where the overspending at the subnational level has been generated by the local institutions delivering health and transportation services, rather than by the regions or the municipalities themselves (see Chapter 11).

the political and administrative machinery of the public sector, the structural economic reforms should focus on the following areas.

Local taxation. Local tax potential is poorly exploited in Hungary. In order to improve the efficiency of local government, local taxation has to be strengthened. A main contribution could come from an own local income tax, which could be collected as a piggyback tax in conjunction with the national income tax. In order to keep the global tax ratio unaffected by this structural policy, the central government would have to make room for such a tax. Also, the local business tax could be exploited more fully, although there are limits imposed by the need to contain distortions of remaining cascading effects and to keep Hungarian companies competitive on international markets. In the longer run, a local property tax and the greater use of user charges could also contribute to improving local finance.

Budgetary procedures. Although expenditure assignment among Hungarian government institutions follows international practice and is based on the principles of federalism, difficulties remain. These are clearly related to the proliferation of autonomous budgetary entities and the resulting complexity of budgetary procedures. At present, it is difficult to obtain a clear picture of government operations owing to double counting of intergovernmental flows of funds and the absence of economic and functional classifications of government expenditures. The complexity of budgetary procedures also affects accountability, as it is difficult to identify clear responsibilities despite explicit definitions in the Constitution. This is particularly important for revenue responsibilities as intergovernmental grants are still widely perceived as "entitlements." As to the expenditure side of budgets, a clearer separation of investment from operational outlays, and medium-term costing of investment projects would help improve choices in this important area.

Privatization and local entrepreneurship. Related to budgetary reform of the public sector is the fact that many Hungarian municipalities engage in entrepreneurial activities by administering state assets of the previous regime that had been handed over to them for privatization. This is a temporary problem and may even be appropriate for some state assets (like housing); it clearly implies severe risks for local budgets where municipal activities extend to production and commerce. Business activities of local government also run counter to national privatization policies, and they impede the development of a private sector, as public entities (which could benefit from implicit bailout) compete with firms without such guarantees. There is also a conflict of interest in that local business activity may be subject to tax. It is essential that business activities of local government should be restricted to basic utilities (water, sewerage, waste disposal), and that these activities be formally separated from public service delivery and administration.

Grants system. The Hungarian grants system is still characterized by a significant reliance on capacity- and expenditure-related transfers that resemble the previous gap-filling approach, although cost coverage is now only partial. A reformed system of intergovernmental grants should take into account both expenditure needs and tax capacity in order to equalize the resources of municipalities. Needs-oriented grants for local government are typically more efficient as they can be designed independent from local decision making and strategies. Their amount should also be positively related to the full utilization of the local tax capacity, in order to establish disincentives for municipalities to engage in tax competition. Whether Hungary should reinforce the equalization effect of the present grants system or foster the higher-income municipalities (such as Budapest) as centers of growth is essentially a political question related to value judgments on horizontal regional equity and to development strategies.

Coordination. The proliferation of local governments and autonomous budgetary units makes coordination of policies necessary. TAKISZ was set up to respond to certain information and coordination needs, yet it has no clear mandate for fostering cooperation and coordination of local policies. The counties are not able to respond to these needs, and municipalities strongly resent interference in their newly won self-rule by the Ministry of Interior. Partly for these reasons, the TAKISZ network has not fully developed an information system capable of providing up-to-date information on the budgetary and financial position of the local governments. The first entities that would stand to benefit from a more efficient network would be the municipalities themselves. In fact, the two-year lag currently needed by TAKISZ to compute the personal income tax shares for each municipality could be considerably reduced if cooperation between TAKISZ and the local governments and the tax authorities were enhanced.

Coordination of local policy can be achieved in various ways. One form is the regional consolidation of municipal jurisdictions, which is always possible on a voluntary basis. Municipalities could be encouraged through specific purpose grants to establish collaborative forms of supply through special purpose administrative units with clearly defined functions. It is indeed more efficient to consolidate the supply of certain local functions with spillovers outside the boundaries of the municipality where they are located (such as curative health care and nonelementary education). The establishment of these entities would not result in an increase in local government employment; rather, it may yield to its reduction, as the rationalization of supply may involve a consolidation of existing manpower. These entities could be financed through user charges, and through the sharing of costs by those local governments whose residents benefit from their services.

References

Bird, Richard, and Christine Wallich, 1992, "Financing Local Government in Hungary," Policy Research Working Papers, Public Economics, WPS 869 (Washington: World Bank, March).

Bird, Richard M., Gábor Péteri, and Christine I. Wallich, 1995, "Financing Local Government in Hungary," in *Decentralization of the Socialist State*, ed. by Richard M. Bird, Robert D. Ebel, and Christine I. Wallich (Washington: World Bank).

Ebel, Robert D., and Peter Simon, 1995, "Financing a Large Municipality: Budapest," in *Decentralization of the Socialist State*, ed. by Richard M. Bird, Robert D. Ebel, and Christine I. Wallich (Washington: World Bank).

Lutz, Mark, 1992, "Fiscal Structure and Development in Hungary," Volume II, Annex 2 in *Hungary: Reform of the Public Sector* (Washington: World Bank).

Ministry of Finance, 1996, *Törvényjavaslat A Magyar Köztársaság 1995. Évi Költségvetésének Végrehajtásáról* (Budapest).

O'Toole, Laurence J., Jr., 1994, "Local Public Administrative Challenges in Post-Socialist Hungary," *International Review of Administrative Sciences*, Vol. 60, pp. 291–304.

28

Russian Federation

JON CRAIG, JOHN NORREGAARD, AND GEORGE TSIBOURIS

The Russian Federation has a system of fiscal federalism that has been undergoing rapid and substantial changes since it became a sovereign country at the end of 1991. Centrifugal forces have played an important role in easing the grip of centralized control that marked the former communist system. These forces have in some cases been driven by ethnic and historic regional differences, but significant discrepancies in the fiscal capacities between different regions, as well as regional resource concentration, have also been important.

Overall, the reforms of intergovernmental fiscal relations carried out so far have not been governed by a clear strategy, but have been introduced in a trial and error manner, reflecting in part the ongoing political struggles between the federal government and the regions.[1] While legislation has been put in place that assigns revenue powers to different levels of government, such a system has not taken into account sufficiently the revenue-raising capacity and expenditure assignments of the regions. Furthermore, several regions have entered into special fiscal regimes with the federal government. At the same time, there has been a shift of expenditure assignments, relating mainly to social and capital outlays, toward subnational levels of government. Given the limited ability of subnational governments to borrow, the system of equalization transfers was to play a crucial role in addressing the mismatch between assigned revenues and expenditures. However, there are still significant technical shortcomings in the equalization formula, and the redistribu-

---
[1]See Le Houerou (1994).

tion of resources it affords remains insufficient when judged against the goal of greater equalization of per capita outlays for the social safety net, education, health, infrastructure, and administration.

Intergovernmental fiscal relations are still in a state of flux in Russia. Issues discussed in the following sections may quickly be superseded by ongoing developments. However, it is evident that continuing reform of the system of fiscal federalism in Russia is an important priority.

Structure of Government

Russia is a three-tiered federal state. The central government forms the first tier. The second tier comprises 89 geographic administrative units that carry varying descriptions, largely reflecting differences in the relative degree of autonomy from the center and in the ethnic mix of the population of the region concerned. The status of these units has been changing substantially as pressures for greater independence have emerged. In early 1993, there were 20 ethnic republics, 2 soviet republics, 2 soviet socialist republics, 1 autonomous soviet republic, 49 oblasts, 3 autonomous oblasts, 4 autonomous okrugs, 6 krays, and 2 metropolitan cities with oblast status (Moscow and Leningrad, now called St. Petersburg). There is also a third tier of administration covering, within the urban areas, the major municipalities (except Moscow and St. Petersburg, which have oblast status), and their cities and urban districts and, within the nonurban areas, the rayons.

The basis for distinction between the various 89 second-tier administrative units (see Table 1 for a full listing) came originally from the former constitution adopted in 1977 that adopted a nationality-based logic for distinguishing between units. Thus, ethnic republics were seen as having the greatest autonomy from the center in terms of, inter alia, trade and foreign policy and, importantly for fiscal policy, control over the land and resources within their boundaries. One step below in terms of autonomy were the other forms of republics, oblasts, the metropolitan cities, autonomous oblasts, and autonomous okrugs. The nonethnic republics did not have a sufficiently large proportion of a non-Russian nationality group to be called an ethnic republic, but nevertheless had boundaries that recognized some nationality groups. They also shared the privilege of having their own governments (supreme soviets) with at least some autonomy. An oblast is an administrative unit that contains no significant non-Russian group. A kray, like an oblast, has purely administrative boundaries, but contains within its borders autonomous oblasts or autonomous okrugs that themselves are based on nationality groups.

Table 1. Russia: Regional Budgets, 1992

Region	Population (In thousands)	Own Revenue Total (In thousands of rubles)	Own Revenue Per Capita (In rubles)	Own Expenditure (In thousands of rubles)	Expenditure Per Capita (In rubles)
North	6,136	108,940	17,754	114,965	18,736
Arkhangel Oblast	1,517	18,789	12,386	19,359	12,761
Nenets Aut.Rep.	54	642	11,884	2,656	49,188
Vologda Oblast	1,362	20,620	15,140	20,464	15,025
Murmansk Oblast	1,148	26,359	22,961	24,933	21,719
Karelian Republic	800	15,286	19,108	21,150	26,438
Komi SSR	1,255	27,244	21,708	26,403	21,038
Northwest	8,270	99,364	12,015	106,415	12,868
St.Petersburg City	5,004	62,068	12,404	62,953	12,581
Leningrad Oblast	1,673	20,997	12,551	19,934	11,915
Novgorod Oblast	752	8,909	11,848	11,560	15,372
Pskov Oblast	841	7,389	8,786	11,967	14,230
Central	30,383	436,797	14,376	401,277	13,207
Bryansk Oblast	1,464	12,496	8,535	13,529	9,241
Vladimir Oblast	1,656	22,289	13,460	17,933	10,829
Ivanovo Oblast	1,312	14,716	11,217	14,131	10,771
Tverskaya Oblast	1,668	16,691	10,007	15,185	9,104
Kaluga Oblast	1,081	9,142	8,457	9,905	9,163
Kostroma Oblast	812	9,091	11,195	10,339	12,732
Moscow City	8,957	187,464	20,929	178,165	19,891
Moscow Oblast	6,707	76,464	11,401	61,206	9,126
Orel Oblast	903	9,577	10,605	11,349	12,568
Ryazan Oblast	1,344	16,002	11,906	14,393	10,709
Smolensk Oblast	1,163	13,436	11,553	12,694	10,914
Tula Oblast	1,844	22,444	12,171	19,050	10,331
Yaroslavl Oblast	1,472	26,986	18,333	23,398	15,895
Volga-Vyatka	8,483	101,002	11,906	107,847	12,713
Nizhegorod Oblast	3,704	57,714	15,582	49,339	13,321
Kirov Oblast	1,700	19,224	11,309	19,088	11,228
Mari Republic	762	5,191	6,812	10,250	13,452
Mordovian Sov. Soc. Rep	964	7,808	8,100	13,280	13,776
Chuvash Oblast	1,353	11,065	8,178	15,889	11,743
Central Chernozem	7762	93603	12059	88867	11449
Belgorod Oblast	1408	21499	15269	20675	14684
Voroneszh Oblast	2475	23536	9509	23046	9311
Kursk Oblast	1335	17993	13478	15225	11405
Lipetsk Oblast	1234	18669	15129	16403	13293
Tambov Oblast	1310	11905	9088	13518	10319
Volga	16,641	280,720	16,869	247,739	14,887
Astrakhan Oblast	1,010	8,127	8,046	10,762	10,655
Volgograd Oblast	2,643	36,830	13,935	33,099	12,523
Samara Oblast	3,296	70,310	21,332	58,668	17,800
Penza Oblast	1,514	11,727	7,746	12,902	8,522
Saratov Oblast	2,711	28,509	10,516	26,564	9,799
Ulyanovsk Oblast	1,444	18,590	12,874	17,938	12,423
Kalmyk Oblast	327	1,968	6,018	5,619	17,184
Tatar Republic	3,696	104,659	28,317	82,187	22,237

Table 1 (continued)

Region	Population (In thousands)	Own Revenue Total (In thousands of rubles)	Own Revenue Per Capita (In rubles)	Own Expenditure (In thousands of rubles)	Expenditure Per Capita (In rubles)
North Caucasus	17,246	142,391	8,256	162,377	9,415
Krasnodar Kray	4,797	48,506	10,112	45,626	9,511
Adygey Republic	442	3,599	8,142	4,828	10,924
Stavropol Kray	2,536	19,379	7,642	18,468	7,282
Karachay-Cherkess SSR	431	2,973	6,897	4,217	9,785
Rostov Oblast	4,363	48,372	11,087	43,878	10,057
Daghestan Oblast	1,890	4,801	2,540	21,239	11,238
Karardino-Balkar SSR	784	4,617	5,889	7,790	9,936
North Ossetin SSR	695	5,160	7,425	9,690	13,942
Ingush-Checken Republic	1,308	4,984	3,810	6,640	5,077
Urals	20,430	393,866	19,279	331,653	16,234
Kurgan Region	1,115	10,914	9,788	12,759	11,443
Orenburg Oblast	2,204	29,128	13,216	25,885	11,745
Perm Oblast	2,949	47,007	15,940	43,691	14,816
Komi-Perm Aut. Okrug	160	814	5,088	1,907	11,919
Ekatermburg Okrug	4,719	80,475	17,053	73,911	15,662
Chelyabinsk Oblast	3,638	61,525	16,912	66,561	18,296
Bashkortıstan Republic	4,008	142,764	35,620	86,178	21,502
Udmurt Republic	1,637	21,239	12,975	20,762	12,683
Western Siberia	15,167	304,163	20,054	296,076	19,521
Altai Kray	2,666	24,134	9,053	30,607	11,481
Altai Republic	198	1,022	5,160	3,055	15,431
Kemerov Oblast	3,181	62,728	19,720	63,719	20,031
Novosibirsk Oblast	2,803	27,259	9,725	28,950	10,328
Omsk Oblast	2,170	29,411	13,553	31,529	14,529
Tomsk Oblast	1,012	14,114	13,947	13,970	13,804
Tyumen Oblast	1,353	24,324	17,978	27,761	20,518
Khantı-Mansi Aut. Okrug	1,305	88,206	67,591	66,788	51,179
Yamal-Nenets Republic	479	32,965	68,821	29,697	61,998
Eastern Siberia	9,260	143,728	15,521	156,520	16,903
Kransnoyarsk Kray	2,973	59,998	20,181	53,000	17,827
Khakasia Aut. Okrug	581	7,997	13,764	7,460	12,841
Taymır Okrug Aut. Oblast	53	1,175	22,173	1,971	37,186
Evenk Autonomous Oblast	25	361	14,426	1,018	40,738
Irkustsk Oblast	2,732	50,820	18,602	50,418	18,455
Ust-Orda Buryat Aut. Okrug	140	513	3,663	2,029	14,494
Chita Oblast	1,312	12,432	9,475	16,169	12,324
Aga-Buryat Aut. Oblast	79	213	2,699	1,680	21,264
Buryatt SSR	1,059	9,123	8,615	16,199	15,296
Tuva SSR	306	1,097	3,586	6,575	21,487
Far east	8,032	209,241	26,051	229,517	28,575
Primoskiv Kray	2,309	30,907	13,385	31,790	13,768
Kabarovsk Oblast	1,634	2,905	17,780	30,296	18,541
Jewish Aut. Okrug	221	1,897	8,586	3,300	14,931
Amur Oblast	1,075	12,759	11,869	14,471	13,462
Kamchatka Oblast	433	6,798	15,700	11,566	26,711
Koriak Oblast	39	439	11,254	3,157	80,948

Table 1 (concluded)

Region	Population (In thousands)	Own Revenue Total (In thousands of rubles)	Own Revenue Per Capita (In rubles)	Own Expenditure (In thousands of rubles)	Expenditure Per Capita (In rubles)
Far east (continued)					
Magadan Okrug	363	12,997	35,805	14,378	39,609
Chukchi SAR	146	4,473	30,636	9,955	68,182
Sakhalin Oblast	719	13,183	18,335	19,157	26,644
Sakha Republic (Yakutiya)	1,093	96,735	88,504	91,446	83,665
Kaliningrad Oblast	894	9,901	11,075	10,130	11,331
Total all regions	148,704	2,323,717	185,217	2,253,382	185,840

The territory of administrative units created on the basis of nationality groups (namely all republics, autonomous oblasts, and autonomous okrugs) covers 53 percent of the territorial area of Russia and includes 20 percent of the total population. Forty-nine oblasts, 2 metropolitan cities, and 6 krays (excluding the territory and population of the administrative units within their borders) constitute the remaining 47 percent of the territory and 80 percent of the population. The territory and population of the three resource-rich republics—Yakutia, Tatarstan, Bashkorostan—that have demonstrated a strong desire for greater autonomy, and particularly control over revenue from their own resources, account for about 20 percent of the territory and 6 percent of the population.

Over time, however, administrative units without nationality-based distinctions have also been seeking greater autonomy. This is evidenced by the number of oblasts and krays—including St. Petersburg City, Rostov Oblast, Krasnodar Kray, and Stavropol Kray—that have demanded republic status, as well as by the demands of lower-level administrative units, such as okrugs, to gain a higher status.

Expenditure Assignment

Although the expenditure assignments to different levels of governments inherited by Russia after the breakdown of the U.S.S.R. had a sound conceptual base, subsequent developments have been marked by discretionary changes that do not appear to fit into a consistent long-term strategy.

The theoretical assignment of recurrent expenditure responsibilities under the U.S.S.R. was broadly consistent with that which might have been expected from application of the "subsidiarity principle" (see

Chapter 2). The central budget included activities and enterprises that were considered to be of national importance (such as transport, heavy industry, and defense) including, importantly, subsidies to large state-owned enterprises. The center was also responsible for foreign affairs, national law enforcement, debt servicing, university education, technical and vocational education, medical and pure research, national parks, and cultural services. Subnational administrative units were responsible for small and light industry (including consumer goods), public services, and regional roads. Rayons and cities had responsibility for housing, utilities, trade, and public services such as health care and pre-university education.

However, in practice, subnational governments never had the autonomy to determine either the level or the composition of their services. All substantive decisions were taken at the central level of government, and only the execution was left to the subnational governments. The decision-making process with regard to capital expenditures was highly centralized both in form and practice. All investments were financed and implemented by the former Gosplan with the exception of those funded directly by the Ministry of Finance or by specific public enterprises.

Since the breakdown of the U.S.S.R., expenditure responsibilities have become more blurred, with particular responsibilities and projects often being assigned on a case-by-case basis. As a result, while the basic structure of assignments (Table 2) still follows the logic of the former U.S.S.R. system, there is now greater variance of subnational responsibilities across regions.

Despite the greater diversity in subnational responsibilities, it is possible to delineate some important trends since 1991. First, the central government shifted responsibility to subnational governments for funding and administration of most price subsidies (milk, bread, baby food, and so on), and some cash subsidies for vulnerable groups, some welfare programs for pensioners, family allowances and child compensation, and support for the homeless. These outlays were quite substantial at the outset; for example, aggregate price subsidies accounted for about 4 percent of GDP when they were transferred in the first quarter of 1992. However, over time these expenditures have declined in magnitude, particularly as the majority of price subsidies were phased out. It should be noted that most subnational governments received only partial compensation for the tasks they took over.[2]

---

[2]Although a recent presidential decree mandates full cost recovery in the housing sector to be achieved by 1998.

Table 2. Russian Federation: Expenditure Assignment in the Russian Federation

Expenditure	Federal	Oblasts	Rayons	Village Soviets
Defense	100 percent except military housing	Military housing		
Justice and internal security	100 percent			
Foreign economic relations	100 percent			
Education[1]	All university and research institute expenditures. All technical and vocational school expenditures	Several special vocational schools	Wages, operations construction, and maintenance of all primary and secondary schools	
Culture and parks[2]	National museums. National theater	Some museums with oblast significance	Some museums. All recurrent expenditures of all sport and park facilities and all other cultural facilities	
Health[3]	Medical research institutes	Tertiary hospitals, psychiatric hospitals, veteran hospitals, diagnostic centers, and special service hospitals (cardiology, etc.)	Secondary hospitals. Primary health clinics. Medicines	Paramedics
Roads[4]	Construction of all roads. Maintenance of federal roads	Maintenance of oblast roads	Maintenance of rayon and city roads	Maintenance of commercial roads
Public transportation	(Previously interjurisdictional highways, air, and rail)	Most public transportation facilities (earlier assigned to federal government)	Some transportation facilities including subway systems	
Fire protection		Most fire protection services	Voluntary, military and enterprise services possible at this level	
Libraries	Special libraries, e.g., Lenin Library	Special library services	Most local library services	
Police services	National militia	Road (traffic) police	Local security policy (since 1991)	
Sanitation[6] (garbage collection)			Part of garbage collection	Part of garbage collection

Sewerage[7]	Infrastructure capital investment	Most of the operational expenditures
Public utilities (gas, electricity, and water)		Some operational expenditures
Housing[8]	Building and development	Maintenance and small-scale building
Price subsidies		Subsidies to households (not enterprises) Fuels Mass transport Food: bread, milk Medicines
Welfare compensation	Part central government responsibility	Part oblast government responsibility Managing programs funded by upper level governments
Public enterprises (productive sectors)	"Group A" enterprises, e.g., transport and heavy industry	Capacity to invest in joint ventures (keeps 50 percent of privatization proceeds if rayon subordination) Capacity to invest in joint ventures (keeps 50 percent of privatization proceeds if rayon subordination and 10 percent of any other subordination)
Environment	Responsible for national environmental issues	Responsible for local environmental problems, e.g., preservation of forests If transferred to local level
Enterprises	"Group A" enterprises, e.g., transport and heavy industry "Group B" enterprises, e.g., light industry, transport, and agriculture	"Group C" enterprises, e.g., local light industry, housing construction, and food industry

[1]Public enterprises also build schools but typically do not operate them. They frequently operate kindergarten services.
[2]Some enterprises build sport facilities.
[3]Some enterprises build hospitals and in some cases also operate them. Social insurance mostly financed by enterprises pays for health services of those covered.
[4]There is a "special extrabudgetary fund" financed by an excise tax on oil consumption.
[5]There are special fire protection services provided by enterprises, but on the decrease.
[6]Usually there are no separate user charges for garbage collection.
[7]There are separate user charges for sewerage.
[8]Enterprises have been important builders of housing and own close to half of the housing stock in Russia. The central government has transferred housing to local governments; maintenance is the responsibility of the level of government or enterprises owning it. Capital expenditures are included unless otherwise noted.

Second, regional and local governments have been taking over the social safety net provisions previously carried out and financed by state-owned enterprises. The total social spending by enterprises has been estimated to constitute more then 3 percent of GDP in 1993, equal to 14 percent of the wage bill, or about a quarter of total budget spending on social purposes. About 40 percent of these expenditures are used for housing maintenance. Although enterprises' social spending has declined in real terms during the last couple of years, this burden is still a key constraint on enterprise restructuring and privatization, and a successful completion of this transition is important for the establishment of a well-functioning private sector.

It is an unresolved empirical question whether such divestiture of social assets imposes a net burden on local governments. A part of the increase in budgetary expenditures would be compensated by higher profit taxes because the costs for the enterprises have been deductible for tax purposes, and the federal government partly compensates local governments for the increased expenditure burden through increased specific transfers. In addition, a local government turnover tax of 1.5 percent was introduced in 1993 to help finance the extra expenditures. The increased local expenditures would be partly neutralized by reductions in subsidies previously extended to enterprises maintaining large stocks of social assets.

Third, responsibility for funding many capital projects was also shifted to subnational governments. The projects in question appear to include some that might be considered national projects usually undertaken by central governments, such as airports, inter-oblast highways, and housing for military personnel.

Revenue Assignment

Russia took over the revenue and expenditure responsibilities for its regions from the former Soviet Union at the end of 1991 and began to pursue "sovereign" tax policies. Many of the tax-sharing arrangements between the central and subnational governments initially remained in place. This situation began to change in late 1991, however, as new market-oriented taxes were introduced to replace the former system of state financing, which relied heavily on profit remittances from state enterprises.

Russia introduced its own budget toward the end of 1991 and, by mid-1992, a wide range of new tax laws were in place, including those for the value-added tax (VAT), the corporate income tax, excise taxes, and a revised personal income tax. This reform package was spelled out in the Law on the Basic Principles of Taxation and a series of laws on particular taxes. The Law on the Basic Principles of Taxation set down a unified structure together with accompanying rules, penalties, tax administration powers, and maximum rates for some taxes.

Under the law, the following taxes accrued fully to the federal level, with the central government having control over the rate and the tax base: VAT, export taxes (abolished in 1996), excises on motor vehicles and alcohol, taxes on bank and insurance profits, taxes on "exchange activities" and securities operations, and customs duties. Natural resource taxes are to be shared with subnational governments.

The revenues assigned to subnational governments, where the central government would retain control over the base and the rates of tax, include revenues from personal income tax, corporate income tax, and all excises except motor vehicle excise and alcohol. In addition, the subnational governments were to set their own rates on taxes imposed on the following tax bases to be defined by the central government: property and asset taxes on enterprises, forestry taxes, and payment for water use. The subnational governments were also to receive all revenues, at rates established by them, from road fund taxes, stamp duty, estate duty, gift tax, and inheritance taxes.

Rayons were to be permitted to set both the rate and base on 21 taxes and fees: property tax on natural persons including the land tax; business registration fees; construction in resort areas; resort fees; tax on the right to trade; special purpose taxes for maintenance of militia; taxes on advertising, resale of cars, computers, and ownership of dogs; license fees for sale of wine and liquor; conduct of auctions; occupancy of apartments; car parking; trademarks; participation in horse racing, winnings at horse races, and totalizer games at races; commodity exchange transactions; and cinema and television film production.

The Law on the Basic Principles of Taxation, however, has never been fully implemented. In practice, the corporate income tax has been shared between the federal and oblast levels, and personal income tax revenues have flowed to the subnational levels, including some allocation by oblasts to rayons (up to 1996, the personal income tax was a shared tax). In 1994, the corporate income tax (including the excess wage tax) was shared in accordance with tax rates of 13 percent for the federal government and a maximum of 25 percent in each of the regions. This system continued through 1996, but with a maximum for the regional rate of 22 percent. The personal income tax, which previously had accrued solely to the local level, was shared in 1995–96, with 10 percent of total revenues accruing to the federal level, but apparently was earmarked to finance special local expenditure programs. The 1997 budget envisages a return to this tax accruing exclusively to the local level.

Initially, the VAT was shared with oblasts according to a formula that varied the share across regions, in line with some unspecific assessment of revenue capacity (for example, oblasts with large VAT collections often retained a smaller portion of collections in that region than oblasts that had relatively lower collections). However, starting in April 1994, the federal VAT statutory share has been a uniform 75 percent. The main reason why the recorded federal share of the domestic VAT revenues in 1994–96 has been well below the statutory 75 percent was a set of negotiated settlements with individual regions according to which the regions were allowed to keep part of the federal VAT proceeds against offsetting reductions in the federal transfers to the regions in question. This system was allegedly implemented to simplify the flow of funds between the two levels of government. In addition, there are indications that some regions did not fully comply with their legal obligations to remit a share of VAT revenues (and other tax revenues) to the federal government, albeit little is known about the precise nature and magnitude of this phenomenon.

In common with duties and other taxes on foreign trade, the VAT on imports, which was gradually introduced during 1993, accrues solely to the federal government. The special 3 percent VAT surcharge, in force in 1994, was maintained through March 1996, but with a lower rate of 1½ percent. Proceeds were earmarked for special sectors, in particular agriculture. The special surcharge was eliminated after March 1, 1996. The excise on vodka was shared equally with the oblasts.

Table 3 shows the outcome of the tax-assignment and tax-sharing systems (all of which are based on the derivation principle) that occurred during 1992–95.

To alleviate uncertainties at a time of presidential, regional, and local elections, the Law on the 1996 Federal Budget committed the government to maintain existing revenue-sharing proportions for three years. This feature has been maintained in large part in the 1997 budget. The tax code, which is in the process of being drafted and could be approved by the parliament in 1997, aims to consolidate existing legal tax provisions into a comprehensive, consistent, and transparent legal basis for the future tax system, including arrangements for tax assignment and tax sharing.

Regional Expenditure and Revenue Budgets

Table 1 shows the considerable disparities between administrative regions in per capita revenues and expenditures in 1992. These regional disparities largely reflect differences in economic wealth and activity

Table 3. Russia: Revenue-Sharing Arrangements
(In percent of total)

	Initial Plan in 1992: Basic Principles		1992 Actual		1993 Actual		1994 Actual		1995 Actual	
	Federal	Local	Federal	Local	Federal	Local	Federal	Local	Federal	Local
Value-added tax (VAT)	100	0	75	25	64	36	73	27	74	26
Of which:										
Domestic VAT	...	...	...	...	...	...	...	...	71	29
Import VAT	...	...	...	...	...	...	...	...	100	0
3% (1.5%) VAT	...	...	...	...	...	...	...	...	67	33
Profit tax	0	100	41	59	33	67	35	65	35	65
Personal income tax	0	100	0	100	0	100	0	100	10	90
Excise on alcohol	100	0	50	50	50	50	50	50	50	50
License fee on alcohol	...	...	...	...	...	...	...	...	100	0
Other nonenergy excises	...	...	40	60	42	58	...	...	...	...
Energy excises	...	...	100	0	100	0	100	0	100	0
Natural resource taxes	...	...	52	48	48	52	22	78	35	65
Property tax	0	100	0	100	0	100	0	100	0	100
Land tax	0	100	0	100	0	100	0	100	0	100
Foreign trade taxes	100	0	98	2	98	2	100	0	100	0
Total revenue, excluding transfers	...	...	57	43	48	52	46	54	49	51
(In percent of GDP)	...	...	16.4	12.6	13.7	14.8	11.8	13.9	10.6	11.1

Sources: Ministry of Finance; World Bank; and IMF staff estimates.

between regions. As the main regional tax revenues come from the profit tax, the VAT, and the personal income tax in regional budgets, regions with strong industries or natural resources, particularly oil and precious metals, tend to have higher per capita revenues. Regions with large rural communities generally fare poorly, and this situation is exacerbated by the tax exemptions available to agriculture, which erode the tax bases.

Since few regions have the capacity to finance substantial ongoing deficits, per capita expenditures are governed by available own account revenues, loans, and subventions from the center. Almost 80 percent of expenditure is made in two functional areas, the national economy (including, in particular, subsidies to housing, enterprises, and agriculture) and sociocultural activities (mainly health and education outlays). Sociocultural expenditures have tended to be more equal across regions, while national economy outlays and other more discretionary expenditures are considerably higher in the richer regions.

Despite the inability of most regions to run substantial deficits on a sustained basis, the aggregate position of regional budgets has deteriorated over the years. While subnational governments had a fiscal surplus of 1.5 percent of GDP in 1992, this position weakened to a surplus of 0.5 percent in 1994 and estimated deficits of 0.2–0.3 percent in 1995 and 1996 (Table 4). These deficits were largely financed by the issuance of local debt instruments, such as *veksels*, and privatization proceeds.

New System of Transfers

The Law on Basic Principles and other relevant legislation established no explicit arrangements for transfers and grants to lower-level governments. This situation appears to reflect experience in the U.S.S.R., where transfers and grants were supplanted by the complex tax-sharing arrangements, which largely negated the need for such payments. Where such payments were made—usually to fill temporary gaps—they tended to be negotiated on an ad hoc basis with no explicit rules or formula for their determination. Thus, there was no concerted attempt to "equalize" the fiscal capacities of the various regions to sustain the provision of public services of similar standard.

Intergovernmental fiscal relations during the 1991–93 period of transition were based on three main pillars: (1) a quasi-equalizing tax (VAT), with local shares differentiated according to the supplementary revenue needs of local budgets in relatively weaker financial positions; (2) transfers from the federal government to the regions, which took

Table 4. Russia: Summary Operations of the Enlarged Government
(In percent of GDP unless otherwise indicated)

	1992	1993	1994	1995	Est. 1996
Enlarged government balance (deficit –)	–18.4	–7.4	–10.4	–5.1	–6.6
Revenues	39.3	36.2	34.6	27.9	24.5
Expenditures	57.7	43.6	45.0	33.0	31.1
Federal government balance[1]	–10.4	–6.5	–11.4	–4.8	–6.3
Revenues	16.6	13.7	11.8	10.6	9.5
Expenditures	27.0	20.2	23.2	15.4	15.8
Interest	0.7	2.0	2.0	2.9	4.5
Transfers to local government	1.7	2.6	4.1	1.3	2.1
Local government balance[1]	1.5	0.6	0.5	–0.3	–0.2
Revenues	13.5	16.7	18.0	12.4	11.6
Of which: federal transfers	1.7	2.6	4.1	1.3	2.1
Expenditures	12.0	16.1	17.5	12.7	11.8
Extrabudgetary funds balance[1]	2.5	0.6	0.5	0.0	–0.1
Revenues	10.9	8.6	9.0	6.6	5.6
Of which: federal transfers	...	0.2	0.1	0.4	0.0
Expenditures	8.4	8.0	8.6	6.6	5.7
Unbudgeted import subsidies	11.9	2.1	...	0.0	0.0
GDP (in trillions of rubles)	19.2	171.5	611.0	1,862.1	2,823

Sources: Ministry of Finance; Central Bank of Russia; Goskomstat; and IMF staff calculations.
[1]Unconsolidated revenues and expenditures (inclusive of intragovernmental transfers).

the form of grants or budget loans;[3] and (3) special treatment granted to selected regions on a case-by-case basis, often involving exemptions from paying export taxes or import duties, as well as exemptions from transferring federal taxes to Moscow.

Although several attempts were made to place the system on a transparent and permanent basis, bargaining remained the centerpiece of intergovernmental fiscal relations in the first two years of reform. Recognition of these shortcomings led to a redesigned system of fiscal relations, which came into effect in April 1994.

Under the new system, the Fund for Regional Support was instituted and was financed by 22 percent (27 percent since 1995) of total VAT receipts out of the federal government's 75 percent share (see above). These resources, determined on the basis of formulas, were intended to serve as the sole source of federal transfers to local governments and largely replace subventions, but shortfalls in actual VAT collections relative to budget projections resulted in the continuation of other types of discretionary transfers (that is, regions being allowed to withhold a larger proportion of VAT, discretionary lending, and other ad hoc transfers with an important subsidy element).

---

[3]These were short-term, interest-free loans from the federal budget, which, in theory, were to be repaid within the fiscal year, although typically they were not repaid.

Federal transfers were provided from the Fund for Regional Support according to two formulas, depending upon whether a region was deemed "in need of support" or "very much in need of support." For each subsequent year, while the size of the fund was set by that year's VAT revenues, each region's share in the fund[4] was determined on the basis of 1993 data.

Regions were classified as in need of support if their per capita revenues fell below a threshold equal to the average for Russia.[5] This determined the unadjusted size of a region's notional transfer. In order to scale the transfer up or down to reflect different cost structures in different sections of the country, the unadjusted transfers were adjusted according to average expenditure patterns in each of Russia's 12 economic districts.[6] To determine the adjustment, average per capita expenditures (net of investment) were multiplied by 0.95,[7] yielding a per capita expenditure norm for each region, denominated in 1993 rubles.

Regions were considered very much in need of support if their own revenues plus the adjusted notional transfer would not have been sufficient to cover their current expenditures. In this case, an additional transfer would be required.

A large and increasing number of regions have been classified as both "needy" and "very needy." The number of needy regions increased from 59 (of the 89) in 1993 to 64 and 78 in 1994 and 1995, respectively. Very needy regions increased from 23 in 1993 to 53 in 1995. For the most part, the very needy regions are located in the southern part of European Russia (such as the Republics of Dagestan and Kalmykia), Western Siberia (such as Kemerova and Omsk oblasts), Eastern Siberia (such as the Buriat and Tuvinian Republics), and the Far East (such as Kamchatka and Sakhalin oblasts). Regions that are not needy at all tend to be either large cities (such as Moscow, Moscow oblast, St. Petersburg, and Nizhnyi Novgorod oblast) or located in the northern or central part of European Russia, the Urals, or—in the case of energy-producing regions like Tuymen oblast—Western Siberia.

---

[4]This relates to the last nine months of 1994 only, as the old system was still in operation during the first quarter.

[5]The average per capita local government revenue for Russia as a whole, multiplied by 0.95, which serves to leave some regions (in 1994, three in European Russia) otherwise eligible out of the transfer system. Certain regions, notably those administered by the Ministry of Defense and the city of Sochi, will be excluded from this scheme and will be subject to a special financial regime.

[6]Including Kaliningrad oblast. There is some evidence that the average for Russia as a whole has been used so far, instead of that for each economic district.

[7]According to the authorities, the intent of this step is to stimulate additional own revenue generation by the regions.

Despite a move toward greater transparency and reliance on rules rather than discretion with this system of transfers, a series of problems have arisen. First, the transfer mechanism is based on actual expenditure and revenue data for each region rather than underlying objective measures of revenue capacity and expenditure needs. This implies that, to some extent, regions may be able to manipulate the formula to their advantage. For instance, regions will continue to have a strong incentive to place resources in local extrabudgetary funds, whose revenues and expenditures are not included in the formula. The hoarding of resources in such extrabudgetary funds would alter the amount of transfers due to them. Such strategic budgetary accounting explains in part the significant increase in eligible regions. With regard to transfers to the very needy regions, the mechanism provides incentives for regions to overspend with the transfer being relegated to gap filling rather than equalization of needs and fiscal capacity. Finally, the degree of equalization that is possible to achieve in the present system is constrained by the financing limit of 22 percent (27 percent since 1995) of the total VAT revenues. In other words, the degree of equalization, which in any case is fairly modest owing to the limited size of the transfers relative to total regional budget expenditures, will vary over time in accordance with the revenue buoyancy of the VAT.

The Russian authorities are currently discussing ways of further improving the system of transfers, and parliamentary hearings on this issue have been initiated. Already for 1997, it is intended that the criteria for eligibility to the Fund for Regional Support be tightened so as to include only remote regions, regions with an extended heating season, and regions with a limited period in the year in which they can receive commodity supplies (mainly in the far North). Further work in modifying the transfer arrangements is planned in 1997, including the possible introduction of conditional transfers that reward regions that implement local policies in accordance with federal guidelines.

Natural Resource Taxation

The uncertainties created by political and economic events in Russia suggest that further changes to revenue assignments will evolve over time, particularly in natural resource taxation. Russia has vast untapped natural resources, many of which are located in ethnic regions. At present, the natural resource taxes are directed mainly at oil and gas extraction where a combination of royalties, export taxes, and fees are imposed. Under the present system, certain of these taxes are assigned to the center and some are shared according to either negotiated or fixed sharing systems.

Recent events have indicated that this situation could change. The Law on Ethnic Minorities has given indigenous populations an effective veto power over the development of natural resources in their traditional lands. The native peoples of Khanti Manisk already have such veto power under a presidential decree. Contracts formed between development enterprises and the tribe will define compensation and govern the resource exploitation process. Similar arrangements now apply in other republics. For example, the Republic of Sakha has secured significant concessions to sell directly substantial portions of the mineral resources in the republic, including 20 percent of diamonds produced there.

These pressures for local control are accentuated by past experience that has seen regional poverty and environmental problems coexist with considerable natural resource wealth. Although the pressures now emerging run the risk of going to the other extreme—preserving huge amounts of wealth for a very small proportion of the total population— some populations in oil-rich areas see their claims as a form of indemnification for past neglect under the Soviet system.

Special Treaties

In the absence of clear assignments for each level of government, the central government has found itself agreeing to a number of de facto relationships with various regional governments under which it has negotiated some share of overall regional revenues in return for the provision of a range of services such as defense and foreign affairs. Under these special treaties, the regional governments concerned seek to become largely independent, taking responsibility for the bulk of their own affairs in return for a single payment to the central government. The region of Bashkiria is one such case. The oblast government has established a "single channel" agreement with the federal government, retaining all revenue from all taxes collected in its territory and transferring a fixed amount each month to the federal budget.

Borrowing

Laws passed in 1992[8] give oblasts, cities, and rayons the right, in principle unlimited, to borrow. However, in practice, different factors, including the building up of substantial payment arrears, have pre-

---

[8]Law on the Rights of Local Self-Government and Law on Budgetary Rights of Local Self-Governments.

vented a surge in subnational borrowing. Although some subnational governments may be able to borrow against natural resource developments and other assets, most have limited assets or income that could be used as collateral for loans. Moreover, institutional factors, such as lack of commercial bank facilities and financial markets capable of absorbing market-style debt instruments, inhibit subnational borrowing. Nevertheless, there are indications that these obstacles are slowly being overcome, and that some subnational governments have issued or are in the process of preparing issues of securities (there is even some talk of regions borrowing abroad). This is a worrisome trend in a still underdeveloped and nontransparent capital market, in the absence of clearly specified and firmly enforced rules limiting such borrowing to levels that can be serviced in the future, and due to the fact that such borrowing could carry an implicit guarantee that the federal government would bail out the subnational government in case of default.

Administration of Subnational Governments

Tax Administration

Until 1990, the tax administration was highly decentralized. Regional and local offices were supervised by their respective Offices of Finance. However, in November 1991, the State Tax Service was separated from the Ministry of Finance and made an autonomous agency with ministerial ranking. It is now in charge of administering all taxes in Russia, including taxes imposed by the regional and local governments. Tax policy remains the responsibility of the Ministry of Finance. These arrangements were endorsed by the Law on the Basic Principles of Taxation.

The new arrangements have substantially reduced the dual leadership problems of the former decentralized administration, which raised potential conflicts in setting priority in collection of national versus local taxes. This issue has not been entirely overcome, however, since local administrations are still responsible for allocating and providing housing to State Tax Service staff and for paying their fringe benefits (only their wages are paid from the central budget). Furthermore, the increased frequency of payments of shared taxes to local tax offices in the form of local debt instruments or in kind has further complicated the relationship between the center and the local tax administrations.

Budget Formulation and Implementation

If the planned devolution of fiscal policy is to have its maximum impact, it is important that local officials be responsive to local needs.

That, in turn, requires local officials to have more discretion to decide on the planning and implementation of local expenditure. As noted earlier, the recently passed Laws on the Rights of Local Self-Government and Basic Principles of the Budget System and Budgetary Process purport to grant full autonomy to subnational governments in the formulation and implementation of their budgets.

In practice, this autonomy appears heavily constrained. For example, the central government still determines the salary levels of all employees and sets ceilings on public enterprise prices and rents. Most important, the central government still determines the tax-sharing arrangements vital to subnational budget financing. Local governments are also constrained by the process of norm setting by the central government, which prescribes the level of specific services that local governments are expected to provide. These features render the system of local governance nontransparent and question the degree of accountability of regional and local governments.

The technical basis for subnational governments' ability to perform the tasks of budget execution, expenditure control, and revenue collection also needs to be improved, and ought to be developed in parallel with the ongoing program for setting up a new federal treasury system with regional and local offices. In addition to serving as a model of financial management by the subnational governments, that project could also have positive spillover effects for local governments, to the extent that it achieves the expected improvements in revenue collections for taxes, including shared taxes.

Policy Implications

It is only quite recently that Russia has made significant inroads toward financial stabilization. The general government deficit amounted to about 4.8 percent of GDP in 1995, compared with about 20.5 percent in 1992, and is provisionally estimated to have reached 6.3 percent of GDP in 1996. The combination of further efforts aimed at consolidating stabilization, the fundamental structural changes in the economy, and strong centrifugal forces and regional conflicts have created an extremely complex setting for the reform of intergovernmental fiscal relations.

Faced with intense pressure on the state budget, the central government has reacted in two ways during the transition. First, it has sought to divest a substantial portion of its social and new capital spending to subnational levels of government. Second, it has sought in different ways to boost its revenues by increased taxation and other charges, although these attempts so far have not been sufficient to reverse a major decline in revenue collections. More seriously, while these short-term reactions may be understandable, they do not necessarily present longer-term solutions for two reasons.

First, notwithstanding recent progress in reducing the fiscal deficit, the central budget appears vulnerable. Unlike a number of other federations reviewed in this book, the central government in Russia has financed an overwhelming majority of the national fiscal deficit. Further devolution of revenue powers to the subnational governments, therefore, threatens to leave the central government (and to some extent also the social funds) without sufficient revenue resources to meet the many national expenditure needs, including the maintenance and further development of a social safety net, clean-up expenditures for the environment, and basic infrastructure development. This situation could be exacerbated if the emergence of special treaties with regional governments leaves the federal government unable to tax prospective resource developments effectively, or to benefit fully from the movement of oil and other resource prices to world levels.

Second, while the attempt to push expenditure responsibilities down the line to subnational governments may be a natural reaction in current circumstances, not all these governments will have the capacity to fund such added responsibilities. One of four choices will therefore face these governments: (1) important expenditures will not be made, (2) new and possibly less efficient revenue sources will have to be tapped, (3) some regional governments will try to exploit their borrowing powers and capacities, or (4) the regional government can seek to become independent via the creation of a special treaty with the central government. The choice will largely be determined by the revenue sources available to the regions concerned. Those regions with access to natural resource revenues will face a strong temptation to tap these resources, either directly or indirectly through the added borrowing capacity that such revenue bases may generate, and to establish special treaties with the central government. As noted earlier, however, widespread implementation of special treaties would weaken the revenue capacity of the central government.

In some sense, the mounting fiscal pressure may force local governments to implement policies supportive of a transition to a market economy, including speeding up privatization of municipal property, which may constitute a drain on local budgets, issuing local government securities (municipal bonds), which may assist in developing regional capital markets, and decontrolling prices and improving cost-recovery for utilities and local service provision, which will improve economic efficiency as well as the local budget position.

A potentially detrimental side effect of the above-mentioned budget devolution is the scope for further divergence in the already wide regional disparities in the provision of public services. Such regional disparities may ultimately set in train added strains on the federation, including demands on the central government to make equalizing grants to regions that find themselves incapable of meeting acceptable nationwide standards in the provision of public services. Added pressure may fall on the central government to maintain and improve social safety net mechanisms in the poorer provinces.

Against this background, an intergovernmental fiscal program with a medium-term time perspective is urgently called for. Such a program should encompass the following elements.

- Clarification of, and adjustments to, present expenditure assignments. Ultimately, the goal must be implementation of a comprehensive, transparent, and stable system of expenditure assignments, which allocates clear responsibilities for the different tasks to each level of government, including the social responsibilities now borne by enterprises. The system must leave room for subnational governments to vary service levels in accordance with local needs, but must also set strict limits for local government price regulation powers and for the possibility of providing subsidies to local enterprises and households.
- A comprehensive, consistent, and transparent legal basis for the tax system, including arrangements for tax assignment and tax sharing. Over the medium term, regional and local governments should be assigned at least one major source of revenue, for which they could determine the rate, to enhance their accountability and responsibility. The sharing of other sources of revenue should be adequate to cover the gap between revenue powers and expenditure responsibilities. Revenue sharing based on derivation principles should be complemented by vertical or horizontal transfers designed to achieve a desired degree of equalization of revenue capacities and expenditure needs across regions.
- To the extent that borrowing by subnational governments is allowed, it should be limited in accordance with clear and transparent principles that take into account the debt-servicing capacity of each government.

Finally, concerning most of the areas referred to above, there is a clear need to improve the scope and quality of statistical reporting covering the operations of the subnational levels of government in Russia, with the aim of enhancing the transparency of these operations and thereby improving the basis of economic analysis and future policymaking.

References

Le Houerou, P., 1994, "Decentralization and Fiscal Disparities among Regions in the Russian Federation," World Bank Discussion Paper (Washington: World Bank).

World Bank, 1994, *Russia and the Challenge of Fiscal Federalism* (Washington: World Bank).

Lightning Source UK Ltd.
Milton Keynes UK
UKHW012250170320
360526UK00001B/9